WILEY

Guide to Fair Value under IFRS

WILEY

Guide to Fair Value under IFRS

International Financial Reporting Standards

James P. Catty
General Editor

Dita Vadron
Text Editor

Andrea R. Isom
Copy Editor

WILEY

JOHN WILEY & SONS, INC.

Library of Congress Cataloging-in-Publication Data

IFRS fair value guide / [edited by] James P. Catty.
    p. cm.
  Includes bibliographical references and index.
  ISBN 978-0-470-47708-3 (pbk.)
  1. International financial reporting standards. 2. Financial statements--Standards. 3. International business enterprises--Accounting--Standards. 4. Fair value--Accounting. I. Catty, James P.
HF5681.V3I47 2010
657'.3--dc22
                                                                        2009037067

Egibi & Co., Babylonian Bankers (c. 600 BC–435 BC)
The First Client
and
Sir Tim Berners-Lee (1955–)
Founder of the World Wide Web
That makes modern business possible

CONTENTS

FOREWORD

Relationships, Dependency, and Reliability[1]

LIU PING

CHINA

Today's expanding global business environment demands that all professionals responsible for financial information have to work together and rely on each other. Accountants, auditors and appraisers (valuators) must ensure that stakeholders in an entity—management, shareholders, creditors, and regulators—receive reliable, up-to-date financial information, enabling them to make the right decisions in fulfilling their duties and responsibilities. Errors in incorrectly recording, valuing, and auditing data at any stage will lead to wrong, possibly even damaging results. With the expansion of International Financial Reporting Standards (IFRS) throughout the world, the roles of the accountants and auditors are becoming harmonized, with appraisers supplying the basis for many conclusions. Now is the era of the appraiser; this book is a start.

To generate profits and run efficiently, management has to know in detail the costs involved in producing, selling, and distributing the entity's various goods and services. In addition, it has to ascertain that there is enough cash available for capital expenditures, for working funds, and to pay shareholders the dividends that ensure continuing investment. Finally, such information, both financial and operational, allows management to demonstrate to regulators that the entity is in full compliance with all laws and regulations.

Shareholders need such material to decide whether to buy or sell securities, to establish trading prices and, in particular, as a measure for portfolio performance and stability. Today investors have many choices; to make wise and advantageous decisions, they need reliable financial information.

Lenders and creditors, including banks and suppliers, use such know-how when deciding to make new loans, extend existing ones, or enhance lines of credit, and also to gauge a firm's ability to pay its bills and properly service both its short- and long-term debt. It is also of importance to vendors, who rely on it to grant trade credit and enter into long-term contracts.

Last, but not least, regulators insist on reliable financial information as part of their duty to protect the public trust. To supply this accurately requires the combined talents of the three separate sets of interrelated professionals: accountants, auditors, and valuators, each of whom relies on data from both the others. Their interaction is illustrated by Exhibit F.1.

---

[1] *Based on a speech in Beijing to the International Network of Auditors & Accountants (INAA) in May 2007.*

Exhibit F.1

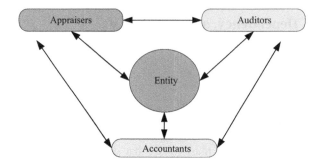

Accountants deal mostly with the present, recording on a daily basis the activities of every entity involved. Auditors, who are also accountants, deal with the past, confirming that the accounts they had been given present "fairly" the results of preceding activities, while appraisers, among whom I have the honor to serve, look to the future, calculating what someone will pay now for benefits that are yet to come.

Based on information and data from the entity's accountant and advice from its auditors, we perform our services and reach our conclusions. Those may encompass numerous steps, including determining: the fair value of the whole firm; an individual division, subsidiary, or department; specific financial, physical, or intangible assets; or a potential acquisition target.

Valuing individual assets, especially intellectual property, is essential to the impairment tests, which since 2003 have been required by IFRS at least once a year. To conduct such an engagement properly, valuators must be able to rely on accurate financial information, continuously and freely provided as required by management through its accounting staff. The quality of any valuation is adversely affected by inaccurate or inadequate inputs. Valuators then deliver to the accountant and management their conclusions to be incorporated into the entity's records for confirmation by the auditors. Similarly, the auditors have to rely on the professional efforts of both the accountant and the valuator.

The close business ties between eastern and western economies and global financial interaction over the past decades have led Africa, Asia, and Australia to adopt IFRS and its related fair value accounting. This in turn caused all valuators to become much more aware of approaches, methods, and techniques developed in North America and Europe. With contributors from six continents, this book offers a thorough grounding in all of those approaches.

PREFACE

JAMES P. CATTY

UNITED KINGDOM

For some years, the world has experienced accelerating globalization that has exceeded any commercial interchanges of previous centuries by an order of magnitude. Common sense dictates that such networks require an equally universal approach to accurately valuing inter-related holdings, following the same worldwide accounting principles; this is under way, as, by 2011, approximately 150 countries will have adopted International Financial Reporting Standards (IFRS). This book offers thorough assistance in such an undertaking, creating a unified language and giving advice concerning relevant methodologies.

While there are many national valuation textbooks, mainly in the United States, there are no international ones. To fill this void, our book is a collaboration of over 30 participants from 14 countries; it was written during an unprecedented downturn in the world economy and sets out best practices in many segments of valuation, for good times and bad. The concept is also to assist readers to react quickly to the *new normal* when it arrives.

When, as chairman of the International Association of Consultants, Valuators and Analysts (IACVA), I signed the contract with John Wiley & Sons, Inc., in October 2008, the world stock markets had been in virtual free fall for a month; I thank Wiley for its courage in taking on this project. After that, values continued to decline, in the United States a further 33%, before, in early March 2009, staging a remarkable resurrection. Now most indexes are back to or above their October levels, as massive, stimulative government policies are taking effect.

This has been the greatest turmoil in the markets since I first became involved in valuations more than 50 years ago. During the long period of Goldilocks economies, which lasted until 2007, risk premiums for virtually every feasible asset were low, reflecting comparatively limited recent losses. In 2008, a combination of repricing of risk, and fears that the financial world, as we knew it, was coming to an end changed everything and gave rise to the continuing worldwide crisis.

Recent Bubbles

Most investors profited from 1995 to 2007; that was a period of asset bubbles in many stock markets, most commodities (oil, copper, nickel, iron ore) and real estate; unfortunately, nearly everyone lost in the subsequent multiple collapses. Worldwide share and commodity value declined, following the huge decreases in home prices in many countries, principally: Australia, Britain, Spain, and the United States. The result was the greatest destruction of fortunes since the Dirty Thirties. According to some commentators, over one-third of world-wide wealth vanished in the last 12 months. Each bubble had four phases.

Stealth. "Smart funds" get in quickly, quietly, and cautiously; asset prices gradually increase, but the general population remains unaware.

Awareness. Price increases get attention; there is some profit taking, but selling is short-lived, as investors treat the dips as opportunities to buy more.

Mania. Masses peg relevant investments, first Internet shares, then real estate, as "the opportunity of a lifetime"; phrases like "prices can only go up" are passed around as indisputable facts but turn out later to be nasty viruses. More unsophisticated money pours in, as "smart funds" begin to unwind their position.

Blow-off. The absence of fresh capital lowers prices, but many late-to-the-party players insist that the wreck can be salvaged. They get evermore adamant about their "buy" recommendations as prices drop. That stubbornness creates a brief pause before the final nosedive.

The New Normal

It has become increasingly clear that the current situation is fundamentally different from all other recessions since World War II. Virtually every country is experiencing not merely another manifestation of the business cycle but a profound restructuring of its economic order. For some organizations, near-term survival is their only possible motivation, resulting in not merely cutting fat but also flesh. Others are peering through the fog of uncertainty, thinking about how to position themselves once things return to normal.

What is the *new normal* going to look like? It is unlikely that it will resemble any of the "before" situations; rather it will be shaped by several powerful forces, of which two—less borrowing and more government impact—will be dominant. A return to tighter regulation and the inclusion of activities such as derivatives that were under consideration long before the downturn began can also be expected.

It is important to realize that past avalanches of borrowings for virtually any purpose and the related underpricing of risks had two sources. The first was financial innovations that apparently reduced risks and added value to the economy. The second was a credit bubble, led by U.S. borrowers, fueled by misaligned incentives, irresponsible risk taking, lax oversight, and fraud. Where the former ends and the latter begins is hard to discern, but it is clear that the future will involve significantly lower leverage and higher prices for risks than we had all come to expect during the years of euphoria. Only entities that boost returns on equity the old-fashioned way, namely through productivity gains, will be rewarded.

Another feature will be expanded government activities. In the 1930s, during the Great Depression, participants in various economic sectors of most countries redefined their roles in the financial system; in the 1980s and 1990s, many such restructurings were unwound in the name of deregulation.

All signs point to an equally significant regulatory restructuring, with governments around the world laying down the ground rules in all financial sectors, including those that were once only lightly, if at all, regulated. They and other bodies, such as the International Accounting Standards Board (IASB), will demand new levels of transparency and disclosure and get involved in decisions that were once the sole prerogative of corporate boards, including executive compensation.

Some forces arise directly from the financial crisis, but others, which already existed, have been strengthened. For example, it was clear before the crisis began that U.S. consumption, which depends on income gains, could not continue to be the locomotive for global growth. For over 40 years, U.S. disposable income has been boosted by a series of one-time factors, such as the expanded entry of women into the workforce, increases in college graduates, the ability to refinance homes, and easy credit for all sorts of purposes; those have now played themselves out.

Peak spending of the baby boomers helped boost consumption in the 1980s and 1990s. Now aging, they are beginning to live on retirement savings that were insufficient in the first place, even before a great deal of housing and stock market wealth evaporated. As a result, the world's economic center of gravity will continue its westward movement toward Asia. Fortunately, likely ongoing technological innovation and increasing human knowledge will tend to offset the declining value of aging auto plants.

Valuators who want to succeed in the *new normal* must focus on that which is changing and what remains basically the same for their clients, businesses, and industry. The resulting environment, while very different from the past, will give major opportunities to those who are prepared.

Scope

This publication is divided into two sections written by a combination of academics and practitioners. The first 13 chapters deal with subjects that have to be considered by all valuators on every assignment. The remaining chapters deal with particular areas that may or may not be of immediate significance but which, at some time or other, will become important.

As shown by their biographies, our contributors are all highly qualified, with most practitioners having taught professional development classes, many in several countries. They all realize that readers need comprehensible material that gets to the bottom of things and eliminates extraneous information.

The potential audience is everyone—managers, accountants, investors, bankers, teachers, and students—who is involved professionally with finance. Principle-based standards cannot, by their nature, give detailed guidance about how fair value is to be determined. This book fills numerous gaps so that all involved have greater understandings of value conclusions.

Theme

Accountants deal with activities in the past; managements deal with the reality of the present; valuators deal with expectations of the future. Value reflects the recognition and pricing of all the risks involved. Neither accountants nor managers are trained to quantify those; valuators are.

The world is drowning in data; by some estimates, corporate digital material in 2010 will amount to one zettabyte (21 zeros). To put values on the entities involved, such data will have to be compressed and summarized into useful information and the nuggets of actionable gold extracted from the mounds of informational ore. In addition, gold must be separated from any pyrite. Our objective is to help all readers in identifying and extracting that gold.

Fortunately, none of the contributors found it necessary to follow Raymond Chandler's perfect literary advice:

> *When in doubt have a man come through the door with a gun in his hand.*

May that never happen to any of us.

Good reading.

Jim Catty
Klosterneuburg, Lower Austria and Toronto, Canada,
August 2009

ACKNOWLEDGMENTS

To write a book is a complicated endeavor. Having gone that route before, I know the importance of partners, contributors, and associates

Therefore, I would first like to thank my partners in IACVA—Bob Brackett, Richard Claywell, Bill Hanlin, and Terry Isom of the United States; Susan Yi of China; and Lionel Newton of Canada—for their continued support and encouragement.

Second, I would like to thank the contributors, who, especially in view of language differences, did so much illuminating work.

Third, I thank my clients for being understanding about delays in delivering reports.

Fourth, I thank the leaders of the IACVA charters throughout the world for their confidence and backing of the project: Zhou Yi and Samuel Chen, China; Wolfgang Kniest and Elke Stetter, Germany; Fafa Amable and Bennet Kpentley, Ghana; Sung-yeol Cho and Sung-Soo Seol, South Korea; Assem Safieddine and Zeina Barakat, Lebanon (Middle East); Jennifer Chen and Joseph Hsieh, Taiwan; and Parnell Black, United States.

Last, but not least, I thank my wife, Dita Vadron, who edited the final texts in her third language, English, and our assistant, Hellen Cumber, who kept me on schedule and applied strict control over numerous versions of individual chapters.

ABOUT THE CONTRIBUTORS

Ms. LIU PING, PH.D., CPA

SECRETARY GENERAL, CHINA APPRAISAL SOCIETY, CHINA

Ms. Liu holds a Ph.D. in economics. She is a senior accountant serving as a member of the China Accounting Standards Committee. She is also a member of Chinese Oversight Committee for Acquisition and Restructure of Listed Companies. She was involved in practical accounting work for many years and is knowledgeable in accounting, business finance, state-owned assets regulation, auditing, and appraising profession. She has published a number of academic works, including *Research on the Practice Environment of Appraisal Profession* and *The Management and Practice of Assets Valuation Business,* as well as more than 100 articles in professional journals. Ms. Liu is currently vice president and secretary general of the China Appraisal Society, board member of the International Valuation Standards Council and of the World Association of Valuation Organizations, and the head of China Valuation Standards Team.

JAMES P. CATTY, MA, CPA/ABV (U.S.), CA•CBV (CANADA), CVA, CFA, CFE

CHAIRMAN, IACVA, CANADA

Jim holds BA and MA degrees from Oxford. He has been engaged in business valuations around the world for more than 50 years. He has undertaken speaking engagements in Canada, China, France, Germany, Romania, Taiwan, Turkey, the United Kingdom, and the United States. He is chairman and CEO of the International Association of Consultants, Valuators and Analysts with members in 12 countries; president of Corporate Valuation Services Limited, Toronto, and of counsel to Hanlin Moss, PS, Seattle, Washington, and X'ian, China.

ALFRED M. KING, MBA, CMA

VICE CHAIRMAN AND DIRECTOR, MARSHALL & STEVENS, UNITED STATES OF AMERICA

A native of Boston, Alfred graduated magna cum laude in economics from Harvard and received an MBA from Harvard Business School (1959). His expertise includes litigation support, valuation of intangible/intellectual assets, business valuations, solvency and reasonable equivalent value issues, valuation issues relating to domestic and international taxes and financial reporting, and complex allocation-of-purchase-cost assignments, including retrospective studies. He has personally appraised over $100 billion of assets.

A specialist in cost management systems, Alfred has lectured on the subject and has consulted with profit and not-for-profit organizations as well as several federal government departments on activity-based costing. He has also taught classes in cost management at Fordham University and is currently teaching at University of Mary Washington. He has written more than 80 articles for professional journals, receiving eight certificates of merit as well as a silver and a bronze medal. In addition, he is the author of *Valuation: What Assets Are Really Worth, Fair Value for Financial Reporting,* and *Executive's Guide to Fair Value* (all published by John Wiley & Sons) and *Total Cash Management* (McGraw-Hill). He has been an instructor in valuation for professional valuation organizations.

YEA-MOW CHEN, PH.D., AVA

PROFESSOR OF FINANCE, SAN FRANCISCO STATE UNIVERSITY, UNITED STATES OF AMERICA

From 1991 to 2000, Yea-Mow was director of the U.S.-China Business Institution at San Francisco State University. Over the last six years, he has moved into the practical area of business valuation. Currently he is chairman of China Intangible Asset Appraisal Corp. Inc., which has undertaken more than 500 engagements and is one of the leading valuation firms in Taiwan. He serves as a board member of the China Intangible Assets and Business Valuation Association, also in Taiwan. Yea-Mow was an advisor to the Taiwan Securities Industry Association (2008–2009) and to the Taiwan Gretai Securities Exchange (OTC market) (2007–2008). He received his Ph.D. in economics from Ohio State University, United States.

STEPHEN L. BARRECA, BSEE, ASA, CDP, PE

FOUNDER AND PRESIDENT, BCRI VALUATION SERVICES, UNITED STATES OF AMERICA

Stephen specializes in the valuation of high-tech industries and utilities. He is president of the Alabama Chapter of the ASA, past president of the Society of Depreciation Professionals, and a member of International Association of Assessing Officers and the Institute of Electrical and Electronic Engineers. Stephen has published numerous articles on valuation and is a regular speaker and trainer in the subject. He received his BS degree in electrical engineering from the University of New Orleans (1978).

WILLIAM A. HANLIN, JR., BA, CPA, CFE, CVA, CFD

PRESIDENT, IACVA, UNITED STATES OF AMERICA

Bill received his BA from the University of Washington. He entered public accounting in 1969; since then he has obtained vast experience in tax matters. He is cofounder and managing partner of Hanlin Moss, P.S. of Seattle, Washington, and X'ian, China, which is a member of the International Network of Accountants and Auditors. As a Certified Fraud Examiner and Certified Fraud Deterrence Analyst, he is frequently engaged to detect, investigate, and deter fraud. Bill also provides litigation support as an expert witness in all kinds of cases, including contract disputes, divorce, bankruptcy cases, loss-of-income cases, and partnership disputes. Since 1994, Bill has been a CVA and has concentrated his practice in valuation. As president of IACVA, he has been involved in training in Brazil, China, Germany, Korea, Taiwan, Thailand, Turkey, the United Kingdom, and the United States.

J. RICHARD CLAYWELL, BA, CPA/ABV, CVA, CM&AA, CFFA, CFD

VICE PRESIDENT, IACVA, UNITED STATES OF AMERICA

Richard has worked in accounting since 1974; since 1985, he has practiced business valuation and has prepared almost 1,000 valuation reports. Richard's practice is limited to valuing closely held businesses, litigation support, and exit planning. He has assisted clients with exit planning and prepared business valuation reports for estate and gift tax purposes, buy/sell agreements, sale and purchase of a business, adequacy of life insurance, reorganization, charitable contributions, divorce, economic loss analysis, partner disputes, dissenting shareholder actions, and disruption of a business. Richard has served on the Executive Advisory Board of NACVA and as chair of the Government Valuation Analyst Board, which oversees the Internal Revenue Service on business valuations. He is the chief architect of the computer-based valuation programs Business Valuation Manager Pro (BVM Pro), its report writer, and Business Valuation Quality Control Editor (BVQ). Richard was the only financial expert to present at the fifteenth Annual National Expert Witness Conference (2006). He presented at a National Exit Planning Conference in Denver on valuing deferred compensation plans (August 2007), on business valuations in Frankfurt, Germany (September 2008), and copresented in China for a weeklong business valuation training course.

BENNET KPENTEY, MA, CVA, CPC

FOUNDER AND CEO, SYNC CONSULT LIMITED, GHANA

Bennet has 15 years professional experience and has consulted for clients in the private and public sectors as well as international agencies, including the World Bank, Department for International Development, United Nations Development Programme, and the Danish International Development Agency. He is currently a part-time lecturer in strategic management in the executive MBA program at the University of Ghana. He holds an MA in international relations (economics major) from the International University of Japan (1994) and a BA in economics and geography from the University of Science and Technology in Ghana (1992). Before establishing Sync Consult, Bennet worked with Deloitte Touché Tohmatsu (1995–2000) and as a principal consultant in setting up Deloitte & Touché Management Solutions Practice in Ghana. At PricewaterhouseCoopers Africa Central (2000–2002), he had responsibility for corporate finance in Ghana. His research interests are in strategy and business valuation.

WOLFGANG KNIEST, DIPL.-KFM., CVA

FOUNDER AND MANAGING DIRECTOR, IACVA-GERMANY GMBH

PRINCIPAL, KCVC, GERMANY

Wolfgang has 10 years of experience in business valuation; his areas of expertise include valuation of intangible assets, midsize businesses, and global enterprises for domestic and international clients with a special focus on financial modeling. Wolfgang is a coauthor of the third edition of *Unternehmensbewertung: Praxisfälle und Lösungen* with K. Henselmann and W. Kniest. Wolfgang holds a Diplom-Kaufmann from the University of Bayreuth (1997) and is on the editorial board of the business valuation journal *Bewertungs Praktiker*. Previously, Wolfgang was an assistant professor in the Tax and Auditing Department at Chemitz University of Technology and worked for KPMG, Frankfurt. Wolfgang received his CVA accreditation in 2005.

BRANDI L. RUFFALO, MBA, AVA

FOUNDER AND PRESIDENT, THE BUSINESS DEVELOPMENT COMPANY

COFOUNDER, VALUATION AND FORENSIC PARTNERS, LLC, UNITED STATES OF AMERICA,

Brandi offers comprehensive business valuation, forensic accounting, fraud investigation, and litigation support services for shareholder disputes, damages, lost profit calculations, marital dissolution, financial record reconstruction, financial reporting, business transactions, and tax purposes. She holds the designation of Accredited Valuation Analyst and is active in the NACVA and the Institute of Business Appraisers. Her publications and teaching include materials for the CVA credentials. Brandi was named a NACVA Instructor of Exceptional Distinction for 2006, 2007, and 2008, and she has spoken at the most recent three NACVA national conferences.

ROBERT C. BRACKETT, BSIE, MBA, CPA, CVA

PRESIDENT, CRANDALL & BRACKETT, LTD., UNITED STATES OF AMERICA

Bob has served as president of Crandall & Brackett, Ltd., a Chicago-area valuation firm, since 1991. He is active in many of the world's professional organizations that provide training or standards setting for accountants and other professionals performing business valuation services. He is a founding member of IACVA, where he serves as corporate secretary, and he has served on NACVA's Executive Advisory Board. Bob teaches courses for the AICPA, the Illinois CPA Society, NACVA, and the Thai Appraisal Foundation, among others. He continues to serve on the Standards Committees of IACVA and NACVA. He received his BS in industrial engineering from Iowa State University (1975) and his MBA from Northwestern University (1952).

WARREN D. MILLER, MBA, CFA, ASA, CMA, CPA

PRESIDENT, BECKMILL RESEARCH, LLC, UNITED STATES OF AMERICA

Warren cofounded Beckmill Research with Dorothy Beckert, CPS, in 1991. Wherever possible, the firm's perspective is to help clients learn and understand ways to increase the value of their businesses. In addition to disciplined growth, a key component in enhancing value is reducing unsystematic risk. An expert on Austrian economics, industrial organization, and evolutionary economics, Warren has written many articles for valuation publications and contributed to several books. He also teaches extensively on a variety of financial subjects. His MBA is from Oklahoma State University (1991) and his BBA is from the University of Oklahoma (1975), United States. Warren is a member of the Financial Reporting Committee, Institute of Management Accountants, and the Editorial Review Board of the IBA's publication *Business Appraisal Practice*.

WILLIAM C. QUACKENBUSH, MBA, ASA, CBA

MANAGING DIRECTOR, ADVENT VALUATION ADVISORS, UNITED STATES OF AMERICA

Bill has taught accounting and finance at several universities at both the graduate and undergraduate levels. He has been providing business valuation services since 1991. Previously he was in the banking industry in New York, having last served as president and CEO of a community bank. Bill has taught for both the IBA and the ASA in the United States, Europe, and Asia and has written professional development courses, articles, spoken at conferences, and lectures regularly to various groups on valuation issues. He currently is the editor of the ASA's BV E-Letter and the vice chair of its Business Valuation Committee.

WOLFGANG BALLWIESER, PH.D.

FULL PROFESSOR, MUNICH UNIVERSITY, GERMANY

Wolfgang teaches accounting and business valuation. He graduated from Goethe University at Frankfurt/Main. His Ph.D. dissertation was about cash management, with a second dissertation on business valuation. He has an honorary doctorate from the University of Wuppertal, Germany, and is a fellow of the Bavarian Academy of Sciences and Humanities. He has written nine books and many articles on financial reporting, auditing, and business valuation.

JOERG WIESE, PH.D.

ASSISTANT PROFESSOR, INSTITUTE FOR ACCOUNTING AND AUDITING, LUDWIG-MAXIMILIANS UNIVERSITY, GERMANY

Joerg was born in Germany and is a graduate in business administration from the Ludwig-Maximilians University. After earning his doctorate in cost of capital and business valuation, he worked for the mergers and acquisitions department of Munich Re Group for one year. His research interests include valuation theory and financial statement analysis. He has published in several academic journals.

MARTIN COSTA, MBA, CPA, CVA

STEUERBERATER OF COUNSEL, R P RICHTER, GMBH, GERMANY

After a banking traineeship at Deutsche Bank AG, Munich, Martin studied business administration at Ludwig-Maximilians University, Munich. He practiced at C&L Deutsche Revision AG, Munich (today: PWC) until 1995, had his own accountancy firm until February 2006, and since then has worked at RP Richter GmbH accountancy firm as counsel. Martin's main practice areas are auditing, with a focus on private equity and venture capital, forensic reports, business appraisals, financial due diligence, consolidated accounting according to German commercial law (HGB) and IFRS. Martin is a member of the German Institute of Certified Public Accountants, German Chamber of Certified Public Accountants, German Chamber of Tax Advisors, German Association of Tax Advisors, and International Association of Consultants, Valuators and Analysts—Germany e.V. Martin was a coauthor of "Hinzurechnungen und Kürzungen" in *Gewerbesteuer—Gestaltungsberatung in der Praxis* (Wiesbaden, 2008) and is the author of several articles in professional journals.

KLAUS HENSELMANN, PH.D, CVA

UNIVERSITY ERLANGEN-NUREMBERG, GERMANY

Klaus is head of the Institute for Finance Auditing Controlling Taxation at the University of Erlangen-Nuremberg. He is the author of 6 books and over 70 articles. In addition to his academic career, since 1997 he has had a professional consulting and valuation practice that focuses on financial planning, implementation of discounting and valuation models, due diligence, analyzing historical data, industry analysis, premiums and discounts, mergers and acquisitions, and litigation advice. Klaus obtained his Ph.D. in business administration from the University of Bayreuth, Germany (1992).

FRANK BOLLMANN, MBA, CVA

DIRECTOR, DUFF & PHELPS, GERMANY

Frank leads Duff & Phelps valuation advisory services practice for Germany, focused on financial reporting (IFRS), tax, intellectual property, fairness opinions, and other capital measures. Before returning to Germany, Frank gained experience in international corporate finance and valuations during many years working in the Silicon Valley, California, as well as Amsterdam, the Netherlands. He has taught valuation classes at the University of Cologne as well as the European Business School. Furthermore, he serves as a member of the International Valuation Standards Board of the IVSC.

ANDREAS JOEST, MBA, PH.D.

SENIOR ASSOCIATE, DUFF & PHELPS, GERMANY

Andreas focuses on finance consulting and valuation services for IFRS, tax, intellectual property, value-based management, and transaction opinions. Previously, Andreas was an adjunct professor of accounting at the University of Augsburg, Germany, and the University of Dayton, Ohio, United States. Among other subjects, he taught financial and managerial accounting as well as corporate valuation.

ANDREAS BERTSCH, PH.D.

PROFESSOR, HOCHSCHULE KONSTANZ, UNIVERSITY OF APPLIED SCIENCES, GERMANY

Andreas is a professor of accounting and controllership. He was previously team leader of currency and derivatives accounting at Landesbank Baden-Württemberg. He received his Ph.D. from the University of Bayreuth, Germany.

FERNANDO TORRES, MSC.

SENIOR ECONOMIST, CONSOR®, UNITED STATES OF AMERICA

Fernando has over 25 years of experience in economics, financial analysis, and business management in the United States and Mexico. He holds a B.A. in economics from the Metropolitan University in Mexico City (1980), a graduate diploma from the University of East Anglia (UK, 1981), and a master's of science in econometrics from the University of London (UK, 1982). From then until 1990, Fernando was a professor of economics at Metropolitan University. He regularly presents on topics related to intangible asset valuation in a variety of venues, many of which qualify for CLE credit. During the past two years, Fernando has been an instructor for the course "Valuing Intangible Assets for Litigation," which is part of the requirements of the Certified Forensic Financial Analyst designation issued by NACVA.

SAMUEL YAT CHIU CHAN, MBA, CVA, CM&AA, CEPA

DIRECTOR, GREATER CHINA APPRAISAL LIMITED, CHINA

Samuel is a director and the head of the Business and Intangible Asset Valuation Department of Greater China Appraisal, a national valuation firm with offices in Hong Kong, Beijing, Shanghai, Guangzhou, and Fuzhou, specializing in valuations of businesses, intangible assets, financial instruments, and fixed assets. He has provided valuation and advisory services to closely held businesses, public companies, and state-owned companies in China for merger and acquisition, initial public offerings, financial reporting compliance (GAAP and IFRS), ligation support, and exit planning purposes. He is vice president of education of IACVA China, teaching business valuation courses in universities, accounting firms, government authorities, and accounting associations.

LISA CHENG, MSC.

ASSOCIATE, GREATER CHINA APPRAISAL LIMITED, CHINA

Lisa is the chief financial engineer of the Greater China Appraisal. She specializes in valuation of derivatives and financial instruments including convertible bonds, bank loans, convertible preference shares, derivatives, forward contracts, currency swaps, accumulators, real options, share appreciation rights, and employee share options. She has written articles on enterprise risk management and taught various financial instrument valuation courses in universities.

WESTON ANSON, MBA

CHAIRMAN, CONSOR®, UNITED STATES OF AMERICA

Weston is an international authority on trademark, patent and copyright licensing, valuation, and litigation support through Consor, an intellectual assets consulting firm. After receiving his MBA (honors) from Harvard, he served with the management consulting firm of Booz-Allen & Hamilton in the United States. Subsequently, he was the youngest vice president and corporate officer at Playboy Enterprises, Inc., where he launched many of its licensing programs. He was also senior vice president of Hang Ten International, which grew to nearly 100 licensees in 30 countries under his direction. For the last 20 years, he has led the way in developing and establishing accepted methods to value brands, technologies, and other intellectual property for companies. He is an expert in establishing licensing strategies for brands as well as developing and managing licensing programs for a number of clients. Weston is a lecturer and author of over 150 articles on the subjects of licensing, valuation, reorganization in bankruptcy, technology and brand values, and the impact of licensing on value. His most recent book is *The Attorney's Guide to the Business Mind.*

RICHARD PEDDE, MBA

PRESIDENT, PEDDE FARM LTD., CANADA

From 1987 to 2001, Richard held management positions in major dealers in derivatives. They include director, global head of Emerging Markets Fixed Income Trading, ABN AMRO Incorporated; managing director, Equity Trading, Nomura Securities International; principal, Fixed Income Derivative Products, Morgan Stanley Dean Witter; and managing director, vice president, Derivative Products, Bankers Trust Company, United States. Richard obtained his MBA at Columbia University, United States (1986), and has published articles including "Canadian Wheat Board Performance Benchmarking" and "Reform of the Canadian Wheat Board: A 'Made in Canada' Approach to Marketing Grain" (Western Centre for Economic Research, University of Alberta, 2007 and 2008), and "A Bushel Half Full: Reforming the Canadian Wheat Board" (C.D. Howe Institute, 2008).

JEONG BYEONGIL, PH.D, LL.M., M.ENG.

PROFESSOR, INHA UNIVERSITY, SOUTH KOREA

Byeongil is a specialist in intellectual property rights (IPR) including its related law. He spent 27 years teaching the law of patents, utility models, design patents, copyrights, and trademarks at INHA Law School in Korea. The subjects include IP information, IP valuation, patent strategy, IP transfer, and industrial security. He is combining studies in science/technology and law. He has been an engineer, jurist, IP valuer, IP transferor, and security expert. He is a vice president of the Korea Valuation Association and has published several books, including *IP Law* and *Science/Technology and Law* and 20 papers on IPR. Byeongil received his Ph.D. in intellectual property law (2005) from INHA University, South Korea; his LLM in intellectual property law (1999) from Franklin Pierce Law Center, United States, and his master's of management information system engineering (1994) from Korea Advanced Institute of Science and Technology.

STAN SORIN, PH.D.

SENIOR RESEARCHER, IROVAL

RESEARCH IN VALUATION, ROMANIA

Stan is a member of the National Association of Romanian Valuers and a lecturer in business valuation. He has authored and coauthored several books on business and intangible assets valuation. Stan received his Ph.D. from Academia de Studii Economice, Bucharest, Romania.

ANDREA R. ISOM, MBA, MSJ, CVA

ASSISTANT EXECUTIVE MANAGER, IACVA, UNITED STATES OF AMERICA

As managing editor for *International Treasurer* and FAS133.com, publications of The NeuGroup in New York City, Andrea specialized in breaking news and enterprise stories on the subjects of derivatives, foreign exchange markets, derivative accountings and issues surrounding the landmark implementation issues of Financial Accounting Standard 133. During her tenure at The NeuGroup, she worked closely with the editorial advisory board, which included senior executives at General Electric, Intel and PWC. As a reporter and editor, she has covered presidential press conferences and interviewed senators and governors.

TERRY A. ISOM, MBA, CPA, CVA

SENIOR VICE PRESIDENT, SENTRY FINANCIAL CORPORATION, UNITED STATES OF AMERICA

Terry is the team leader at Sentry, in charge of accounting and tax issues, and is integrally involved in program and transaction structuring. In December 1994, Terry authored *Asset Financing Strategies,* which addressed the issues of lease versus buy and sale lease-backs. He has been the primary author of four books on leasing: *The Handbook of Equipment Leasing* (Amembal & Isom, 1988), *Leasing for Profit* (American Management Association, 1980), *Handbook of Leasing: Techniques and Analysis* (Petrocelli Books, 1982), and *Guide to Captive Finance Company Equipment Leasing* (Amembal American Association of Equipment Lessors, 1984); he recently coauthored the two-volume *Operating Leases—The Complete Guide* (Amembal & Associates). Before his current activities, Terry was a member of the University of Utah's accounting faculty, during which time he consistently ranked among the top three instructors based on student evaluations. He taught both undergraduate courses in finance and accounting and graduate courses in managerial accounting. He currently serves as chairman of the board of NACVA and as a director of IACVA.

KARRILYN WILCOX, B.COMM

RESEARCHER, CANADA

Karrilyn has experience researching and valuing companies and has worked in equity research and business valuation. She has received numerous awards in business, finance, and research, including the Canadian Institute of Business Valuators First Place Research Award and the Chartered Financial Analyst First Place Research Award. She has also published several research articles and received a number of scholarships and research grants in accounting and finance. Her B. Comm. in finance and entrepreneurship is from Saint Mary's University, Halifax.

EMRE BURCKIN, PH.D., CPA

CHAIRMAN, CONSULTANT CERTIFIED PUBLIC ACCOUNTANCY AND AUDITING COMPANY, TURKEY

FULL PROFESSOR, MARMARA UNIVERSITY, ISTANBUL

Emre currently is a full professor at Marmara University, Istanbul. His doctoral dissertation was titled *Determination of Going Concern Value in Merger Operation.* He has published many articles and books on the subjects of accounting, valuation, and audit and has presented numerous papers at national and international conferences.

AYSE PAMUKCU, PH.D.

LECTURER, MARMARA UNIVERSITY, TURKEY

Ayse completed her doctorate at the Marmara University in 2005; her dissertation was titled *Audit Organization Supported by Computers in Accounting.*

ZEYNEP BURCKIN EROGLU, MA

RESEARCH ASSISTANT, MARMARA UNIVERSITY, TURKEY

Zeynep completed her M.A. in 2003 at Marmara University in the Faculty of Economic and Administrative Sciences. She now works in the Economy branch while studying toward her doctorate.

MICHAEL J. LAWRENCE, BSC., FAUS AMM, FIMM, FAIG, MIA, MX, C.ENG, CPG

MANAGING DIRECTOR AND CHIEF VALUER, MINVAL, AUSTRALIA

Michael is a geologist who has spent most of his professional career (spanning 43 years) as a mining and geological consultant with major international resource consultancies and as managing director of their regional operations: from 1970 to mid-1982 for the French government's BRGM/SEREM; and from mid-1988 to 1990 for the Robertson Group plc (UK). In 1991, he founded Sydney-based Minval Associates Pty Limited (MINVAL), which specializes in mineral property audits/due diligence and valuation, and minerals industry dispute resolution solutions. While at the NSW Department of Mineral Resources and Energy (mid-1982–mid-1987), he completed his studies for his graduate diploma in public sector management and participated in corporate planning, internal management strategy reviews, and organization analysis and redesign projects. He also developed skills in dealing with government administration (at local, state, and federal levels) and the political process as well as how public interest/civil society groups use their influence. His consultancy work (1970–1982 and 1988 to date), including the time he spent as a mining analyst with stockbroker Lancaster Securities (mid-1987 to mid-1988), involved him in mineral economics, financial analysis, and resource asset/company valuation. He has published 94 technical papers and made major contributions to AusIMM's VALMIN Code since 1991 (chair, VALMIN Committee, 2000–2002); and development of AusIMM/MICA Alternate Dispute Resolution Scheme (chair, Interim Board, 2000–2003).

LAURA JANE TINDALL, PH.D., CPA, BVAL, CVA, MCBA

LAURA J. TINDALL COMPANY, UNITED STATES OF AMERICA

Laura has been valuing businesses and business damages since 1981. She has held several leadership positions in organizations, including serving on the boards of the Associate of

Eminent Domain Professionals, AICPA, IBA, and NACVA. In addition to being a frequent lecturer at local, regional, national, and international conferences on the topics of valuation, expert testimony, and ethics, she has authored many articles and coauthored two AICPA guides, including AICPA Consulting Services Special Report 03-1, "Litigation Services and Applicable Professional Standards," and AICPA Practice Aid 05-1, "A CPA's Guide to Family Law Services." Laura is the author of *Ethics Reference Guide for Expert Witnesses*.

JOHN L. CASALENA, LIB, CPA/ABV/PFS/CFF, BVAL, CFE, CDFA

JOHN L. CASALENA COMPANY, UNITED STATES OF AMERICA

John has a varied background, including COO and CFO positions and a traditional CPA tax practice. Currently his sole-practitioner practice is limited to M&A, family and business dispute resolution, income tax controversy, and litigation support. He is an author of published articles on Med/Val™ and personal goodwill and covenants not to compete. He presents on the subjects of mediation, collaborative divorce, taxation in divorce, personal goodwill, and covenants not to compete, for national conferences of AICPA, IBA, and NLSS as well as for the State Bar of Arizona, PESI, NBI, and many other organizations.

HEINZ GODDAR, PH.D.

PARTNER, BOEHMERT & BOEHMERT; PARTNER, FORRESTER & BOEHMERT, MUNICH, GERMANY

Heinz is a German patent attorney and a European patent and trademark attorney with a background in physics. He teaches patent and licensing law as an honorary professor at the University of Bremen, Germany, as a lecturer at the Munich Intellectual Property Law Center, at the University of Washington, Seattle, U.S., at the National ChengChi University, Taipei, at Tokai University, Tokyo, as a Consultant Professor at the University of Huazhong, Wuhan, China, and as a member of the Professors Committee at the Institute for International Intellectual Property at Peking University, Beijing. He is an associate judge at the Senate for Patent Attorneys Matters at the German Federal Court of Justice and a senior advisor to Investment in Germany GmbH, Berlin, with a specific responsibility for life sciences and chemicals and a consultant to the Global Institute of Intellectual Property, Delhi. Heinz is past president of LES International and of LES Germany.

ULRICH MOSER, PH.D., WIRTSCHAFTSPRÜFER, STEUERBERATER, CVA

PROFESSOR, ACCOUNTING AND FINANCE, ERFURT UNIVERSITY OF APPLIED SCIENCES, GERMANY

Ulrich obtained his Ph.D. from the University of Stuttgart (1989). He acts as a management consultant in the field of intellectual property and business valuation. He has over 15 years of experience in the field with a strong focus on valuing intellectual property rights, portfolios of them, early-stage technologies, and purchase price allocations (FAS 141/142, IFRS 3). Recent projects include valuing a portfolio of more than 100 trademarks as well as the product pipeline of a biotech company. He spends considerable time supporting strategic business decisions of clients based on advanced valuation techniques. He also assists in developing and implementing intangible asset management systems. Ulrich often speaks at national and international business valuation and intellectual property conferences. He regularly publishes articles on corporate finance and valuation topics and is editor of *Praxis der Unternehmensbewertung* (practitioner's guide to valuation).

SUNG-SOO SEOL, PH.D.

PROFESSOR, DEPARTMENT OF ECONOMICS, HANNAM UNIVERSITY, SOUTH KOREA

Sung-Soo is also director, Hi-tech Business Research Institute, Hannam University (2000–); honorary president, Korea Technology Innovation Society (2007–); honorary president, Korea Valuation Association (for technology and business) (2007–); and visiting professor, Department of International Business and Marketing, California State Polytechnic University. His professional history includes credit analyst, Chase Manhattan Bank, Seoul; senior fellow, Daeduck Society for Science & Technology Policy; visiting fellow, Science Policy Research Unit, Sussex University, U.K.; cofounder, president, Korea Valuation Association (for technology and technology business); editor in chief, *Technology Innovation Society Journal* (Korea); member, National R&D Program Coordination Committee, National Science & Technology Council; president, Korea Technology Innovation Society; and member, Advisory Committee, Minister of Education, S&T. He has given many lectures and authored several books and papers.

EVŽEN KÖRNER, MSC., MBA

DIRECTOR, AMERICAN APPRAISAL, FIXED ASSET MANAGEMENT GROUP, CENTRAL EUROPE

In his professional capacity, Evžen provides consulting services relating to valuation of plant and equipment for diverse range of corporate clients in numerous countries. He has experience of a diverse range of industries including aerospace, automotive, biotechnology, chemical, telecommunication, computer services, electronic, semiconductor, power generation, steel and metal, public utilities, commercial banks, food and beverage, health care, insurance, consumer packaging, pulp and paper, and pharmaceuticals. Prior to joining American Appraisal, Evžen was employed by various manufacturing companies, responsible for specification and coordination of production processes and as a head of the engineering development division, in charge of development and restructuring program of a manufacturing company. His MSc. is from the Czech Technical University and his MBA is from the Open University Business School.

LAN YUAN LIM, MBA, MSC., BSC., LLM, LLB, PH.D.

CHAIR, SINGAPORE INSTITUTE OF SURVEYORS AND VALUERS

CHAIR, WORLD ASSOCIATION OF VALUATION ORGANISATIONS

Lan Yuan has over 40 years of extensive experience in property business concerning property development and management, valuation, training and consultancy; he is a licensed appraiser. He is also a senior master mediator and an accredited arbitrator who sits as a tribunal member on the Valuation Review Board, Strata Titles Board, and the Appeals (Acquisition) Board in Singapore. Lan Yuan has been a consultant to UN agencies and is currently chairman of the World Association of Valuation Organisations. His MSc. is in construction management and his BSc. is in economics.

SHARI OVERSTREET, CPA/ABV, CVA, CM&AA

MANAGING DIRECTOR, THE MCLEAN GROUP, UNITED STATES OF AMERICA

Shari has more than 25 years of financial, accounting, business valuation, and M&A experience. Shari began her career in public accounting, working for a regional and then a national firm in both audit and tax divisions. She then held financial and operational leadership roles in various Austin-based companies. She has performed business valuations for many companies in the Austin area, a good many of which are technology based. Shari received her bachelor of business administration with a concentration in finance from the University of Texas, United States.

ANDY SMITH, CPA/ABV, ASA, CVA, CMA

PARTNER AND SENIOR MANAGING DIRECTOR, THE MCLEAN GROUP, UNITED STATES OF AMERICA

Andy manages the company's business valuation practice. He has a broad background of experience, including public accounting, investment banking, and financial operations management. He is a National Association of Securities Dealers registered representative and financial and operations principal and has also been an instructor with NACVA.

SUSAN M. SAIDENS, BA, CPA, ABV, ASA, CVA, CFE, CFF

PRESIDENT, SMS VALUATION & FORENSIC SERVICES, LLC, UNITED STATES OF AMERICA

Susan's firm is a niche business valuation and forensic accounting Certified Public Accounting Practice with big firm experience and expertise. She is a former member of NACVA's Executive Advisory Board, former chair of NACVA's Valuation Credentialing Board, and has received NACVA's "Outstanding Member" award. She has lectured extensively on business valuation topics for organizations such as the Pennsylvania Institute of Certified Public Accountants, the Institute of Management Accountants, and state and local bar associations. Susan is a member of the team that annually authors and teaches the "Current Update in Valuation" course around the country for NACVA. She was an original member of the Appraisal Issues Task Force working with the Financial Accounting Standards Board and the Public Company Accounting Oversight Board on goodwill, intangible assets, stock options, and other fair value measurement issues for U.S. financial reporting purposes.

ANKE NESTLER, MBA, PH.D., CFA

PARTNER, VALNES CORPORATE FINANCE GMBH, GERMANY

Anke's previous experience includes working for the corporate finance team of PricewaterhouseCoopers; for six years she was managing director of O&R Corporate Finance GmbH, a company associated with Linklaters LLP. Anke is a Certified Public Appraiser for Valuation of Companies and Intellectual Property (CCI Frankfurt/M.) and a member of the expert panel in the field of business valuation of the IHK Frankfurt/M. (Chamber of Commerce and Industry, Frankfurt/M.). She specializes in business valuation as well as the valuation of intangible assets, valuation in the field of restructuring, consultation in M&A transactions, financial due diligence, and financial statement analysis.

ROGER SINCLAIR, PH.D.

PROFESSOR EMERITUS, UNIVERSITY OF THE WITWATERSRAND, JOHANNESBURG, SOUTH AFRICA

Roger has taught for many years at Witwatersrand, where he was previously professor of marketing and head of the department. In the 1990s he led a team from the university in developing BrandMetrics, a brand valuation methodology. In 2009, this was bought by Prophet, a strategic consultancy with expertise in branding, marketing, design, and innovation. Roger obtained his Ph.D. at University of the Witwatersrand, South Africa.

LIONEL W. NEWTON, BA, FCA, TEP, CVA, CFFA

PARTNER, RUBINOVICH NEWTON LL, CANADA

Lionel obtained his CA designation in Ontario in 1972 and has been in public practice in Toronto since 1974. He was elected a fellow of the Ontario Institute of Chartered Accountants in June 2003. From 2001 to 2005, he was chairman of the board, International Network of Accountants and Auditors. Lionel has published various articles, participated in panels dealing with small business and income tax matters, including United States and Canada cross-border taxation. He has also provided testimony to the Finance Committee (Canadian House of Commons) and the Ontario Superior Court of Justice, with respect to valuation, economic damages, inappropriate investment advice, family law, estate matters, claims of constructive and/or resultant trusts, and income tax issues.

CHRISTOPHER J. STEEVES, BA, LL.B.

PARTNER, FRASER MILNER CASGRAIN LLP, BARRISTERS & SOLICITORS, CANADA

Christopher was ranked in the *2006 Chambers Global Guide* as one of Canada's leading tax lawyers. His practice focuses on corporate restructurings and acquisitions. He provides advice on the taxation of complex domestic and international financings, securities issuances and investment funds, and has specialized expertise with respect to cross-border tax planning. Christopher is coeditor for the *Corporate Tax Planning* feature of the *Canadian Tax Journal*, a member of the Editorial Board for the *Canadian Tax Reporter* (CCH Canadian Limited) and for *Corporate Structures and Groups* (Federated Press). He was also coeditor for *Canadian Transfer Pricing* (CCH Canadian Limited), 2002.

1 FAIR VALUE CONCEPTS

ALFRED M. KING

UNITED STATES

INTRODUCTION

Being asked to write about fair value concepts for a book with numerous chapters, each dealing with an aspect of fair value for International Financial Reporting Standards (IFRS), by an expert in the field implies that the general editor believes the author has some specialized knowledge of the subject, based on 40 years of active experience. The author will do his best not to disappoint. In this chapter, the terms "fair value" and "fair market value" are capitalized when they refer to the latest definition in the United States.

HISTORIC EXPERIENCE

The concepts underlying fair value for financial reporting draw on the more than 100 years of valuators' experiences. In that context, our activities today bear only a passing relationship to the work performed by our predecessors. Within the past 10 years, major changes have occurred in our firms, as the International Accounting Standards Board (IASB) and the Financial Accounting Standards Board (FASB) have incorporated their ideas of fair value into financial reporting. At the outset, it should be understood that those concepts, as used in both IFRS and generally accepted accounting principles (GAAP), are merely a subset of the more generalized experience developed in the derivation and application of (fair) market value in tax practice in many countries; while the names are confusingly similar, the concepts are very different.

Taxes

The definitions and underlying concepts of the traditional "standard of value," fair market value, cover applications designed to provide useful information for a range of disparate purposes—from insurable values at the high end, through tax amounts, to bankruptcy realizations at the low end. Until quite recently, most valuations pertained, in one way or another, to business transactions.

In fact, there have been three distinct waves of interest in valuation. The original use was not for financial reporting but to determine tax liabilities. In the ancient world, Egypt, Babylon, Greece, Rome, Persia, and China all taxed an individual's or a partnership's assets, which needed a valuator. In those eras, a valuator, serving as a tax assessor, could be a very important individual. Often, after a king died, his ministers were killed and buried with him; in many cases, the tax valuator was the only one spared, as the heir needed that person's knowledge. Later, in the year 10 A.D., China introduced an income tax; fortunately, it soon vanished, until the British reintroduced it in 1798 to pay for their fight against Napoleon; after that, it again disappeared for nearly a century. In the United States, the income tax started in 1861 to finance the North in the Civil War; again, after the conflict, it was dropped until 1913. During the past five decades, taxation of capital gains has become almost universal, leading to intensification in the use of tax valuations.

Business Transactions

The second use, which soon followed, was to obtain neutral and unbiased conclusions relating to actual or proposed business transactions. Since, by definition, the valuator had no financial interest in the transaction or its outcome, his initial role was that of "honest broker." In 1821, the Hudson's Bay Company, incorporated in 1670, acquired the North West Company, its principal competitor in the Canadian fur trade. As part of the transaction, all the assets of the two entities, in Canada, London, and at sea, had to be valued.

The assistance of a valuator allowed:

- Insurable values to be determined based on professional judgment.
- Buy and sell agreements settled by a neutral observer.
- Purchasers of securities assurance that they were not overpriced.
- Prospective sellers to know the amount at which one asset could be sold, or another item bought, without informing the market about a possible deal.

While there are almost always parties with differing interests in business, when it comes to taxes, appraisers have to be particularly careful not to become advocates. Clients want low figures for property taxes and either high or low, depending on the circumstances, for income taxes. Within the bounds of professional practice, valuators always try to help their clients. By the second half of the twentieth century, the profession in much of the world had split into three branches: real-estate appraisers, business valuators, and security analysts. The contributors to this book include all of them.

Financial Reporting

After centuries, a recent, third step in the use of valuations has arrived: the push by accounting regulators to incorporate fair values into financial statements. Businesses have long been perceived by investors as always looking for the most favorable accounting and financial reporting treatments so as to convey as optimistic an outlook as possible. The increasing use of fair value information is perceived by regulators, analysts, and investors as a more objective approach to financial reporting, a tool that may help or hurt the entity. In turn, this belief has placed great pressure on valuators to arrive at "correct" answers that enhance the objectives of financial reporting.

IASB and FASB have agreed to move toward a convergence of financial reporting standards, with the ultimate objective of GAAP users completely converting to IFRS standards. At the time of writing (March 2009), it appears that the push for rapid convergence, followed by conversion, has slowed down. Nonetheless, it is inevitable that GAAP and IFRS will come together, particularly with respect to fair value information. This chapter deals with the subject as it is currently conceived and used.

IASB, however, has announced that an exposure draft for a new IFRS standard on fair value measurement will be issued in the second quarter of 2009. This is anticipated to follow closely Statement of Financial Accounting Standards (SFAS) 157 with some variations; the expected differences are set out in the appendix to this chapter.

Fair Value

The entire push to fair value accounting and disclosure seems to be predicated on the fundamental assumption that a true estimate of fair value can be developed and disclosed and that the world will be a superior place because of this "better" financial reporting. Unfortunately, that fundamental premise is deeply flawed; massive efforts by many professionals have failed to communicate that valuation involves a vast amount of judgment. Therefore, any fair value conclusions are far from precise and perhaps not even totally reliable.

Analysts, accountants, and standard setters have trouble with the idea that the same asset can have different values for different owners or for different purposes. Accountants consider their activities, though many involve assumptions, estimates, and judgments, to be precise and expect that valuation should have equal "precision." Of course, as those who actually perform valuations know, the very concepts of Fair Value or Fair Market Value are difficult to pin down.

IMPORTANCE OF JUDGMENT

This section discusses the role of judgment in the determination of each of the two separate concepts, which have many critical differences. After the profession had spent over 100 years developing Fair Market Value, in June 2001, FASB introduced fair value with SFAS 141, followed in September 2006 with a new definition in SFAS 157, which totally changed the fundamental concept and instituted a brand-new approach to value, as discussed subsequently. In general, IASB has been an acquiescent follower.

Professional judgment is always involved in a valuation, even if only with respect to knowledge of the asset or business; no one would hire a real estate specialist to determine the fair market value of antique furniture, nor a financial expert for insurable values of machinery or equipment. However, these distinctions, while well known and understood, deal only with training and experience. A different, also important, kind of judgment, which users of valuation information often disregard, is that normally there is really not a single answer but a *range* of correct answers in any specific valuation situation, whether for real estate financing, placement of insurance, or an allocation of the purchase price in a business combination.

Valuators have created the regrettable situation where clients receiving an appraisal report feel that the indicated amount is in fact "the" value. Most end up with a single-point estimate, a number that is sometimes carried to five significant figures; such deterministic answers actually promote confidence because of their seeming precision. However, in our view, this aura of precision is the cause of much of the discussion regarding weaknesses in fair value, its determination, and its use in financial reporting.

In the course of an assignment, every skilled appraiser inevitably has to make many individual decisions. These choices—and they are choices—rarely show up in the narrative reports and certainly are invisible to those reading them. If two equally skilled valuators were given the same assignment but did their work entirely independently, it should not surprise anyone that their conclusions may differ. Yet many ordinary nonprofessional recipients *are* surprised when two seemingly equal valuators come up with conflicting amounts; in this author's view, they should be within 10 percent of each other, but not necessarily any closer.

The target audiences for the realities of valuation have to be (1) setters of accounting standards; (2) auditors who try to make sure that complex accounting rules are being faithfully followed; and (3) preparers of financial statements. Those groups, however, still generally believe that there is a single "true" fair value, which should be determined and then disclosed. That the same asset can have far differing values to various people for diverse purposes is not yet fully accepted. When preparers of financial statements complain about the difficulty and cost of obtaining fair value information, or protest about its relevance, some security analysts and academics often assert that "the company does not want to disclose Fair Value because they have something to hide."

There are at least three different premises of value: value in use, value in exchange, and value in liquidation. This fact has not prevented FASB from putting unwarranted emphasis on value in exchange in "active markets." Fortunately, IASB has not yet followed suit and also includes in its impairment testing "value in use"; this is normally "entity specific" yet often most relevant to actual market participants.

FAIR VALUE VERSUS FAIR MARKET VALUE

For many years, there has been a standard definition of Fair Market Value (slightly different between Canada and the United States) developed for the International Glossary of Business Valuation Terms by a group of North American valuation organizations, including the National Association of Certified Valuation Analysts, IACVA's U.S. charter and the American Institute of Certified Public Accountants (AICPA). It is:

> *The price, expressed in terms of cash equivalents, at which property would change hands between a hypothetical willing and able buyer and a hypothetical willing and able seller, acting at arm's length in an open and unrestricted market, when neither is under compulsion to buy or sell and when both have reasonable knowledge of the relevant facts. (NOTE: In Canada, the term price should be replaced with the term highest price.)*

The International Valuation Standards Council (IVSC) has a definition of Market Value used in much of the rest of the world; this is similar in that it deals with an arm's-length transaction between a willing buyer and a willing seller:

> *The estimated amount for which a property should exchange on the date of valuation between a willing buyer and a willing seller in an arm's-length transaction after proper marketing wherein the parties had each acted knowledgeably, prudently, and without compulsion.*

The first definition, or one conceptually very close to it, served the valuation profession and clients in the United States and Canada without controversy for over 100 years; in it, "fair" qualifies "market," not "value." The very similar concept, called just "market value," dates back centuries in Europe. These definitions acknowledge that different premises of value can coexist depending on the purpose of the assignment and the interests of the parties while insisting that the perspectives of both buyer and seller had to be explicitly recognized. Therefore, various views about the future outlook still could result in diverse conclusions of value.

Business Combinations

In a business combination, valuators should deal with the actual economics of the specific transaction. "What did the buyer acquire?" "Why did he pay that particular price?" Different buyers for the same business potentially would have distinctive allocations of the same purchase price. That seems both realistic and in accord with the actual decisions implemented by a real exchange of funds; initially FASB and IASB seemed to agree. In 2001, on FASB's introduction of the term "fair value," its definition in SFAS 141, *Business Combinations*, did not mention arm's length but dealt with willing parties:

> *The amount at which an asset (or liability) could be bought (or incurred) or sold (or settled) in a current transaction between willing parties, that is, other than in a forced or liquidation sale.*

A number of IFRSs, which at the time of writing are still in force, use the next definition. It is closer than SFAS 141 to Fair Market Value and market value as it includes both the arm's-length principle (see "Transfer Pricing") and willing parties; also, it does not confuse readers with references to liabilities:

The amount for which an asset could be exchanged between knowledgeable, willing parties in an arm's-length transaction.

SFAS 157

In September 2006, FASB radically changed established valuation practices in the United States with the issuance of SFAS 157, *Fair Value Measurements*, which amended the definition of Fair Value to make it an "exit" price:

The price that would be received to sell an asset or paid to transfer a liability in an orderly transaction between market participants at the measurement date.

All references to "arm's length" and "willing parties" are totally gone, and the application to liabilities is no longer only in brackets. However, between this definition of Fair Value and that of Fair Market Value, there are two key differences; they are equally important in the way the terms are defined and used and they cause severe dislocations to the usual concepts of valuation. Subsequent interpretations based on this new definition have created additional problems, both in valuation and in financial reporting.

At the time of writing, IASB has not yet adopted the SFAS 157 definition of fair value but appears to be moving in that direction. The balance of this chapter assumes IFRS will, in the name of convergence, adopt a very similar definition. Many commentators wish the convergence would go the other way. While the discussion is primarily based on U.S. experience, there is no reason to believe that IFRS will take a different direction. It should be pointed out, however, that FASB did not apply the SFAS 157 definition to fair value with respect to SFAS 123R, *Share-Based Payments*.

Exit price. The main distinction in the differing concepts of value is that for Fair Value, the premise is solely from the viewpoint of the seller, i.e., what it would receive on the sale of the asset, while Fair Market Value, with its "willing buyer" and "willing seller" components, takes both perspectives into account. In practice, fair value may lead to results that are hard to understand and even harder to explain. As an example, assume at a Christie's art auction the last two buyers are competing for a Rembrandt with bids going up in increments of $1 million. At $29 million, one drops out, and the remaining bidder wins the picture at $30 million.

Most observers would think the Fair Market Value of the painting had just been established at $30 million, as there was a willing buyer (successful bidder) and a willing seller (consignee), neither being under compulsion, and it can reasonably be assumed that both had equal knowledge that the picture was genuine. However, under SFAS 157, the Fair Value is only $29 million, as it has to be appraised at what it could be sold for to another "market participant." There is a willing buyer at $29 million (the bidder who dropped out) and no one else will pay $30 million because the winner was the last man standing.

This is the first major problem with the FASB concept of Fair Value. The definition creates an anomalous situation in that the winner bought the painting for $30 million and its "Fair Value" is only $29 million, an apparent instant loss of $1 million, which actually would be reflected in goodwill as an "overpayment." This is referred to as the "Day 2" problem, when a buyer acquires an asset and is forced to value it at what *someone else* might pay for it. This was pointed out to FASB during its deliberations; it heard and understood the implications but declined to change the definition.

In addition, there is the problem of "transaction costs." Under conventional accounting, for over a century, the costs of purchasing and installing an asset have been capitalized together with the purchase price; IFRS 3 and SFAS 141 both treated them as part of the "cost of the acquisition" and allocated them to the assets acquired, including goodwill and liabilities assumed. This is no longer true for business combinations as they do not form part of fair value; therefore, IFRS 3R, following SFAS 141R, requires acquisition costs to be charged to earnings. In the case of the Rembrandt just discussed, Christie's 10 percent "buyer's premium" might have to be charged to earnings.

Market participants. The second unique twist to the FASB definition of Fair Value is that it is not measured by what the actual buyer really paid. Instead, valuators have to try to determine what some *other* hypothetical market participant *might* pay. This moves "values" from real prices in actual transactions to a notional world of hypothetical market participants paying theoretical prices.

Throughout SFAS 157 and in many other communications, FASB has clearly stated that it does not like, or trust, values developed or based on "entity-specific" assumptions. In other words, not only is what the firm actually did not important, but the reasons for the amount paid are dismissed as potentially misleading. It is disconcerting to management when a valuator tries to explain why he or she cannot, in good faith, use the actual transaction price. Fortunately, IFRS considers "value in use," established by discounting cash flows, using entity-specific assumptions as well as "fair value less costs to sell" in determining impairment losses.

Trying to arrive at values based on what some market participant *might* do is difficult, as there is not always a clear understanding of just who those market participants are. SFAS 157 defines "market participants" as "buyers and sellers in the principal or most advantageous market for the asset or liability." They are also supposed to be:

- Independent of the reporting entity
- Knowledgeable (having all relevant information, including results of usual and customary due diligence)
- Able to deal and willing (motivated but not compelled) to transact

This is very unsatisfactory; despite thousands of deals every year, there is no organized "market for corporate control," much less for most intangible assets. Therefore, market participants would appear to be every potential purchaser, starting with all competitors and going on to include any trade or financial buyer who, based on past activities, might be interested.

Purchase Price Allocations

Purchase price allocations are supposed to be performed using the assumptions that a market participant would make. For example, Exclusive Auto buys Super Body, both auto parts suppliers, as a strategic acquisition. Should the seller's customer relationships be ascribed a high or low value? From the perspective of the actual buyer who is dealing with the same customers, they have little value. If all market participants were deemed to be trade buyers, then the valuator would be justified in assigning them a low figure, with more of the purchase price as nonamortizable goodwill.

If, however, the "market participants" were deemed to be "financial buyers," the answer would be very different. Such purchasers have few contacts in the industry, and therefore, the seller's customer relationships would be critical and have a higher value. As intangible assets must be amortized over their useful lives, the larger the amounts assigned to them, the greater the negative effect on reported earnings. How does a valuator determine who the *appropriate* market participants are? Are they strategic or financial buyers? Obviously, the choice affects not only the purchase price allocation but also the subsequent reported earnings of Exclusive Auto, the purchaser.

The second problem with the SFAS 157 definition of fair value is now apparent. Suppose management says, "We think all the other buyers would be competitors at present in this industry, so let us assume that for the valuation." At that point, the auditor, or later a regulator, can challenge the assumption and say, "Well, no, in *our* opinion, the only realistic market participants are financial buyers; therefore, you must assign a high value to the customer relationships." All too often the auditor, who must sign off on the values in the financial statements, digs in his heels and insists on following his inclination, even though there may be no more support for that view than the client has for its view; meanwhile the valuator is caught in the middle.

HOW DID WE GET HERE?

Why would FASB, in full consultation with IASB, throw out over 100 years of experience with Fair Market Value and substitute its own new and unique definition of Fair Value? The answer is straightforward and understandable, but a result of the law of unintended consequences. The reasoning can be traced back directly to the Sarbanes-Oxley Act (SOX), enacted by the United States Congress in 2002, following a series of financial reporting scandals in which managements distorted GAAP. The objective of SOX was to preclude any future such disasters. A key element is the requirement that senior management personally sign a report confirming that the entity had an effective system of internal controls; this, in turn, has to be attested to by their independent auditor.

Congress then ordered the Securities and Exchange Commission (SEC) to develop standards for reporting value information by its registrants. In the United States, the SEC has the power to determine auditing and accounting standards; for accounting, this is delegated to FASB. Many of the FASB staff had experience with a number of standards that are concerned, in one way or another, with current values of financial instruments. Over the years, numerous problems in such matters had been dealt with by FASB staff and board members. As a result, they had become experts with regard to the fair value of financial instruments. After deliberation, FASB reached the conclusion that a new definition of fair value, one suitable for financial instruments, would be equally valid for all assets, including intangibles. Unfortunately, the characteristics of many assets like intangibles and some machinery and equipment simply do not fit that mold.

MARKET APPROACH FOR FAIR VALUE OF FINANCIAL INSTRUMENTS

Many accounting problems surfaced after the Enron debacle; a major enterprise with 22,000 employees that claimed revenues of $101 billion in 2000, it collapsed into bankruptcy in 2001 as a result of major frauds, including numerous misuses of fair value. Put simply, Enron created its own financial derivatives, for example, selling a contract to provide electricity to various entities at agreed-upon prices for 20 years. It owned an electric generating plant and was confident that it could produce power at an assumed rate of $0.08 per kilowatt-hour (k-Wh). Meanwhile the customer agreed to pay an assumed rate of $0.10 per k-Wh. This contract seemingly assured Enron a guaranteed profit of $0.02 per k-Wh on all the electricity it covered. A very large number was developed for the present value of this contract, and the total anticipated 20-year profit stream was taken into income during a single quarter!

This was too good to be true, and it was, if the new FASB definition of Fair Value had been applied. Enron had developed and valued the contract on its own. It did not test the conclusion by going to market participants—in this case, investment banks like Goldman Sachs or Morgan Stanley—and asking them what they would pay to purchase the contract. The new FASB definition, had it been in effect, would have precluded Enron from generating its own earnings through its internally generated instruments. With no outside test of the true economic reality, Enron was able to comply with the then-current rules, and the auditors had no basis to question their values. SFAS 157 was a real step forward for financial instruments; the exit value/market participant combination was both necessary and sufficient to shut down those kinds of games.

Unfortunately, FASB, when asked by the SEC to tackle the difficulties of the previous definition of fair value, had no experience with, or knowledge of, valuation practices for physical or intangible assets. Therefore, it assumed that what worked for financial instruments should be equally valid for all other assets and liabilities.

RELEGATION OF COST AND INCOME APPROACHES

This is the reason behind SFAS 157's definition and why it places primary emphasis on the Market Approach and downgrades the Cost and Income Approaches. If an active market exists, the Market Approach should be used for financial instruments. For other assets, the situation is more complex. Commercial and industrial real estate, of course, often has many buyers and sellers; in the markets, plant, machinery, and equipment have a number of participants, mostly specialist dealers and numerous auctioneers, but they all tend to be limited in scope. Intangibles, due to their unique characteristics, have virtually no market participants. Valuators therefore have consistently used the Cost and Income Approaches for these asset categories.

Under Uniform Standards of Professional Appraisal Practice (USPAP), which covers real estate valuations in the United States, appraisers must consider all three approaches. If one or more is not used, an explanation is required in the report. In a desire for a one-size-fits-all approach to Fair Value, FASB turned this fundamental principle of valuation upside down. It knew the Market Approach was best for financial instruments and once again assumed the same rules should apply to all.

FASB's discomfort with entity-specific amounts, such as value in use based on the owner's intentions, which IASB accepts in part, can also be traced back to the financial scandals of 2000 to 2002. Entities played games with financial reporting, claiming to be within GAAP, even though the final results were positively misleading.

SFAS 157 is explicit that only market data are considered as "Level 1" or "Level 2" inputs in evaluating the strength and relevance of the valuation information being disclosed. Whenever a valuator uses the Cost Approach or Income Approach, then SFAS 157 automatically places the inputs and resulting conclusions of value in Level 3. Further compounding the problem is that many security analysts believe that Level 1 and Level 2 values can be trusted while organizations descending to Level 3 must have something to hide.

AUDITING FAIR VALUE

As mentioned earlier, professional judgment is inherent in the valuation process. If, as previously stated, two equally competent appraisers should come within 10 percent of each other, this still leaves substantial leeway, particularly for auditors who aim at precision. Put another way, despite the seeming precision of many valuations—where the answer is carried out to four or more significant digits—in practice the "true" answer is nearly always within a range of 5 percent more or less.

The essential element of valuation is that it looks to the future to estimate the cash flows anticipated to be derived from the asset(s); those are then discounted back to a present value. Future developments are always uncertain, and best estimates of them are generally wrong. Hindsight is less likely to support previous assumptions than to show up flaws in earlier judgments. Valuations are audited after the fact, when it is easy to poke holes in the original beliefs. Even if the audit is contemporaneous, it is all too easy to ask "Why did you assume this?" or "Why did you not consider that?" Since valuation involves significant professional judgment, it is easy to see how even highly experienced auditors can and will make different decisions in good faith.

Auditors like to validate what they examine (the purchase of a lathe is confirmed by reviewing the invoice); they find it frustrating when they cannot put "proof" of a valuation into their working papers. In some countries, such as the United States, this problem is even more serious, because regulators periodically review the working papers of the auditors of publicly traded entities. A year or so later, it is easy for a regulator to ask "How did you accept this valuation report prepared for the client? Why did you not verify the assumptions used by the appraiser?" One or two cases like this will make all the auditors in a particular office question every valuation report. This is extremely annoying, because, at the end of the day, it is not possible to audit professional judgment. An auditor can, and should, question the appraiser's assumptions or suggest that another methodology would produce a different answer. However, the auditor can no more prove his or her (different) answer is correct, and the valuator's original conclusion wrong, than vice versa; this fact frustrates auditors and valuators.

MARK-TO-MARKET ACCOUNTING AND FAIR VALUE

In late 2008 and early 2009, questions about the proper valuation of financial instruments hit the headlines. The application of SFAS 157—exit price and market participants—to the wide range of subprime mortgages and financial derivatives threatened to bring down the banking systems in many countries. Calls were heard to repeal mark-to-market reporting because, it was asserted, the system had created a death spiral. Some institutions had to sell certain assets at distressed prices; in turn, those were taken to be the "market," and auditors pressured other banks to write down their holdings to such lower amounts. The required impairment charges then reduced bank capital, forcing additional sales, which drove prices even lower, with no end in sight.

Some frustrated bankers wanted to abolish mark-to-market accounting altogether. In its place, financial instruments would be valued by "models" to account for anticipated future cash flows; in other words, they would disregard actual prices and substitute theoretical values. Needless to say, FASB, IASB, and the SEC fought this proposal tenaciously.

What most observers failed to realize was that the SFAS 157 rules on "market" transactions should not be applied to forced or liquidating sales, which are those made by an unwilling seller and do not represent Fair Value. Local assessors base the value of your house neither on a foreclosure sale next door nor on an estate sale across the street, because they know that neither is Fair Market Value. Only transactions between truly willing buyers and sellers should establish fair value. Regrettably, the definition in SFAS 157 uses the word "sell"; auditors, reluctant to have their clients apply judgment, found it all too easy to force them to mark their securities to the last reported sale, even though it totally failed the test of true Fair Value.

The real flaw of mark-to-market accounting is in determining what the market was or is. Using an inappropriate transaction as indicative of a Fair Value transaction, which some auditors demanded in fear of being second-guessed, is what really drove the so-called death spiral. It was not bad accounting, merely bad valuation. At the time of writing, FASB and IASB have come up with staff positions regarding inactive and not orderly markets suggesting why recent reported transactions may or may not be indicative of Fair Value. They are encouraging companies to apply judgment. Now it will be seen how comfortable auditors are in trying to audit that.

PROBLEMS WITH FAIR VALUE—AND POLITICAL SOLUTIONS

The issuance of certain IFRS has caused individual governments to "exempt" their national firms from the full rigor of those accounting requirements. In such situations—and admittedly they are relatively infrequent—political decisions are made about technical issues. In the United States, certain members of Congress have threatened the independence of FASB "unless they straighten out the situation." Although it would be comforting to think that accounting and valuation issues can be determined by professionals in an unbiased manner, in the real world, this is unlikely. Whenever such rules are perceived to have actual economic consequences—producing winners and losers—there is a rush to the ramparts by politicians trying to save their constituents from unpleasant and potentially damaging situations.

That FASB developed its own new definition of Fair Value, which IASB seems likely to adopt, is an indication that arbitrary changes to well established traditions can be undertaken with the best motives in the world. Unintended consequences then cause an equally arbitrary reaction. Depending on the political strength of the parties, the standard setters usually will be upheld, but sometimes they are overturned. Once an arbitrary definition of Fair Value was adopted, no one should have been surprised that there were real-world consequences. Some may have welcomed the changes; others viewed them with alarm. The one thing that is certain is that within the next few years, there will be major changes in financial reporting and the development and use of value information in financial reporting. No one can predict the specific outcomes, but for the valuation profession, these will be, as the Chinese say, "interesting times."

IMPLEMENTING FAIR VALUE

The next exhibits are a series of flow charts on implementing Fair Value under SFAS 157, whose definition is likely to be accepted by IASB. They are reprinted with permission from *Business Combinations with SFAS 141R, 157 and 160—A Guide to Financial Reporting* by Michael J. Mard, Steven D. Hyden, and Edward W. Trott (Hoboken, NJ: John Wiley & Sons, 2009).

The first flowchart summarizes the various steps whose details are on the next five charts.

Exhibit 1.1 Subjects of the Charts

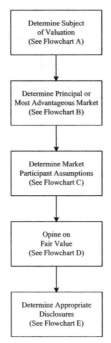

Exhibit 1.2 Flowchart A: Subject of Valuation (Asset or Liability and Unit of Account)

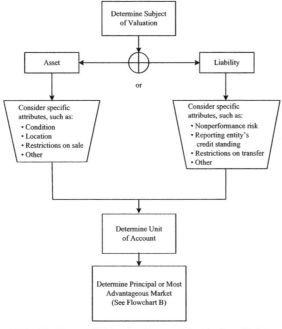

Exhibit 1.3 Flowchart B: Principal or Most Advantageous Market

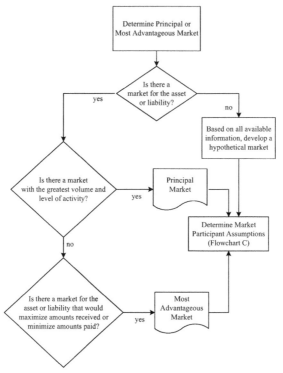

Exhibit 1.4 Flowchart C: Market Participant Assumptions

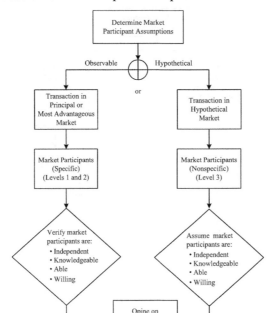

Exhibit 1.5 Flowchart D: Fair Value Measurement

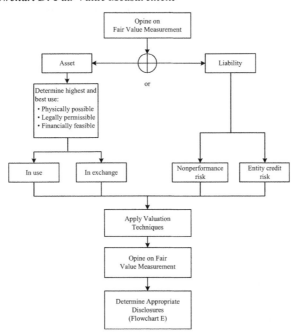

Exhibit 1.6 Flowchart E: Appropriate Disclosures

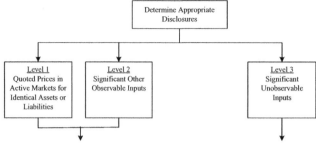

Determine Appropriate Disclosures

| Level 1 Quoted Prices in Active Markets for Identical Assets or Liabilities | Level 2 Significant Other Observable Inputs | | Level 3 Significant Unobservable Inputs |

- Fair value measurements at the reporting date
- The level within the fair value hierarchy in which the fair value measurements in their entirety fall
- The amount of the total gains or losses for the period included in earnings (or changes in net assets) that are attributable to the change in unrealized gains or losses relating to those assets and liabilities still held at the reporting date and a description of where those unrealized gains or losses are reported in the statement of income (or activities)
- In annual periods only, the valuation technique(s) used to measure fair value and a discussion of changes in valuation techniques, if any, during the period

- The fair value measurements at the reporting date
- The level within the fair value hierarchy in which the fair value measurements in their entirety fall
- A reconciliation of the beginning and ending balances, separately presenting changes during the period attributable to the following:

  (1) Total gains or losses for the period (realized and unrealized), segregating those gains or losses included in earnings (or changes in net assets), and a description of where those gains or losses included in earnings (or changes in net assets) are reported in the statement of income (or activities)
  (2) Purchases, sales, issuances, and settlements (net)
  (3) Transfers in and/or out of Level 3 (for example, transfers due to changes in the observability of significant inputs)

- The amount of the total gains or losses for the period included in earnings (or changes in net assets) that are attributable to the change in unrealized gains or losses relating to those assets and liabilities still held at the reporting date and a description of where those unrealized gains or losses are reported in the statement of income (or activities)
- In annual periods only, the valuation technique(s) used to measure fair value and a discussion of changes in valuation techniques, if any, during the period

POSTSCRIPT

This chapter was written in the spring of 2009. By late January 2010, a number of significant developments, described in this postscript, had occurred. As expected, IASB, in May 2009, issued an Exposure Draft (ED), *"Fair Value Measurement"* on which it received 156 comment letters, including one from the General Editor. This ED reflected FASB's view, set out in SFAS 157, *Fair Value Measurement*, that Fair Value was an exit price, while continuing to reflect the exchange notion previously adopted by IASB. The proposed new definition is

> *the price that would be received to sell an asset or paid to transfer a liability in an orderly transaction between market participants at the measurement date.*

Responses to the ED

Nearly all the responses to the ED were in favor of the document's concept and the resulting likelihood of full worldwide convergence as to valuation guidance. Most think the proposed definition as an exit price, is acceptable because it retains the exchange notion in the current definition and sets out a clear measurement objective.

Other significant comments were:

- The exit price concept is not relevant for an asset which an entity does not intend to sell as (a) it is being used in the operations of the business or (b) it is a financial asset that is not held for trading
- Fair value is an appropriate measurement basis only for assets and liabilities that are initially and subsequently measured using it
- The proposed guidance is most appropriate for financial instruments and not as much for physical and intangible assets or liabilities
- A liability should reflect a settlement rather than a transfer price if it cannot legally be transferred or if the entity does not intend to do so
- There may be major problems in applying the concept in emerging and transition economies where there are limited markets and few valuators

January 2010 Joint Meeting with FASB

At an IASB/FASB joint meeting in January 2010, the following topics related to fair value measurement were discussed at length:

1. Definition of fair value
2. Measuring fair value when markets become less active
3. Fair value at initial recognition
4. Recognition of day one gains or losses
5. Measuring liabilities at fair value
6. Nonperformance risk
7. Restrictions on the transfer of a liability
8. Measuring own equity instruments at fair value
9. Market participant view
10. Reference market

The tentative decisions then taken, which are summarized below, are expected to be reflected in a new converged standard to be issued in 2010Q3; this is not likely to be effective before 2012.

1. *Definition of fair value*

   To retain the term *fair value* and to continue to define it as an exit price. The Boards will discuss in a future meeting where that definition should be used, when they address the scope of a converged fair value measurement standard.

2. *Measuring fair value when markets become less active*

   The guidance for measuring fair value in markets that have become less active pertains to when there has been a significant decline in the volume and level of trading in the asset or liability. It should focus on whether an observed transaction price is orderly, not on the level of activity in a market. An entity should consider any observable transaction prices unless there is evidence that the deal is not orderly. If there is not sufficient information to determine whether a transaction is orderly, further analyses should be undertaken to measure fair value.

3. *Fair value at initial recognition*

   The transaction price may not represent the fair value of an asset or liability at initial recognition if, for example, any of the following conditions exist:

   a.   The transaction is between related parties
   b.   It takes place under duress or the seller is forced to accept a price
   c.   The unit of account represented by the transaction is different from the unit of account for the asset or liability measured at fair value
   d.   The market in which the transaction takes place is different from that in which the entity would sell the asset or transfer the liability

4. *Recognition of day one gains or losses*

   The Boards will discuss this at a future meeting.

5. *Measuring liabilities at fair value*

   In the absence of a quoted price in an active market representing the transfer of a liability, an entity should measure the fair value of a liability as follows:

   a.   Using the quoted price of the identical liability when traded as a corresponding asset (a Level 1 measurement)
   b.   If that price is not available, adjusting quoted prices for similar liabilities or similar liabilities, when traded as assets (a Level 2 measurement)
   c.   If observable inputs are not available, using another valuation technique such as:

      (1) An income approach (for example, Discounted Cash Flows method, including the compensation a market participant would demand for taking on such an obligation)
      (2) A market approach (for example, the amount that a market participant would pay to transfer the identical liability or receive to enter into it).

   d.   An entity must determine if the fair value of a liability when traded, whether or not on an exchange, as a corresponding asset represents its fair value. When an entity determines that the fair value of the corresponding asset does not represent the fair value of the liability, it must make adjustments to the fair value of the asset to offset the extent that its fair value does not represent that of the liability, in particular:

(1) The fair value of the corresponding asset should be measured using a method market participants would apply

(2) A quoted price for a corresponding asset in an active market is a Level 1 measurement for the liability when no adjustments are required

(3) The transfer of a liability assumes that a market participant transferee has the knowledge and ability to fulfill the identical obligation

6. *Nonperformance risk*

The fair value of a liability includes the effect of nonperformance risk; the Boards agreed to clarify what, in addition to credit risk, nonperformance risk represents.

7. *Restrictions on the transfer of a liability*

The fair value of a liability should not be adjusted further for the effect of a restriction on its transfer if that factor is already included in the other inputs to the measurement.

8. *Measuring own equity instruments at fair value*

Further guidance for measuring the fair value of an entity's own equity instruments will be provided.

9. *Market participant view*

Fair value is market based and reflects the assumptions that market participants would use in pricing the asset or liability. In particular:

a. Market participants should be assumed to have a reasonable understanding about the asset or liability and the transaction based on all available information, including that which might be obtained through usual and customary due diligence efforts

b. "Independence" of market participants means that they are unrelated to each other as well as the entity

c. A price in a related-party transaction may be used as an input to a fair value measurement if the transaction was entered into on market terms

d. The unobservable inputs derived from an entity's own data, adjusted for any reasonably available information that market participants would take into account, are considered market participant assumptions and meet the objective of a fair value measurement

10. *Reference market*

The reference market for a fair value measurement is the principal (or most advantageous) market provided that the entity has access to it. The principal market is that with the greatest volume and level of activity for the asset or liability; it is presumed to be that in which the entity normally transacts; there is no need to perform an exhaustive search for markets that might have more activity than that one. The determination of the most advantageous market should consider both transaction and transportation costs.

There undoubtedly will be more developments in 2010.

2 THE COST APPROACH

YEA-MOW CHEN

TAIWAN

STEPHEN L. BARRECA

UNITED STATES

INTRODUCTION

The Cost Approach to value is one of the three generally accepted approaches to estimate the fair value of an asset or physical property; its theoretical basis is reproduction cost. The sales comparison method of the market approach holds that, if an exact duplicate (reproduction) of the subject, in regard to age, condition, and utility, is available in the open market, then the purchase price of the duplicate property represents both the reproduction cost and the fair value of the subject. In other words, the reproduction cost of a property on the valuation date provides a measure against which prices for similar properties may be judged.[1]

The underlying concept is the *principle of substitution*, which holds that a prudent buyer would not pay more for an asset than the cost to acquire a similar item of equivalent desirability and utility without undue delay. Thus, the reproduction cost of a similar property constitutes an upper bound (or maximum) of the market value of the subject asset or property.[2]

Unlike the sales comparison method, which seeks an exact replica in the market, the Cost Approach develops an indication of value by comparing the subject to the costs to acquire a similar *new* substitute property. The estimate of expenditures to construct such an item on the valuation date constitutes the current cost basis of the approach. The valuator then depreciates (reduces) this amount to reflect any and all differences in the age, condition, and utility between the subject and the newly created substitute. In summary, in applying the Cost Approach, the valuator attempts to estimate the differences in worth to a buyer between the subject and a newly constructed property with optimal utility; this difference in worth (i.e., value) is, by definition, depreciation.

PRACTICAL APPLICATIONS

The Cost Approach is especially suited for recently constructed properties because they suffer only minor depreciation and the reproduction cost is likely to be similar to the actual incurred expenditures. It is also applicable to older properties when reliable data are available to measure depreciation and estimate reproduction costs.

It is often the preferred approach when estimating the fair value of tangible personal property independently from the going-concern value of the entity. Such valuations are often

---

[1] *See* **The Appraisal of Real Estate**, *11th ed. (Appraisal Institute, 1996), pp. 336, 340.*

[2] **Valuing Machinery and Equipment: The Fundamentals of Appraising Machinery and Technical Assets**, *2nd ed. (American Society of Appraisers, 2005), p. 582.*

performed for property taxes, insurance, charitable gifts, purchase price allocations, and other situations where the influences of the intangible assets of the business on the value are excluded.

When there is no viable market, recent transactions are insufficient to support a sales comparison method, or the subject does not directly generate cash flows, the Cost Approach is recommended. Some examples are:

- Intangible assets that contribute to but do not produce accountable cash flows
- Telecommunication networks where the income directly attributable to the various assets cannot be reliably determined
- Estimating rates of return on intangible assets that are cost based, such as for transfer pricing or royalty rate analyses
- Determining damages suffered by the owner of an intangible asset in infringement, expropriation, breach of contract, or similar type of litigation

In practice, the most frequent applications of the Cost Approach are to value assets such as software, machinery and equipment, and real estate. It is not frequently applied in valuing businesses because measures of the component costs for some assets are not well formulated or documented. This approach is not desirable when:

- The subject is unique.
- Estimates of costs and depreciation are unreliable.
- The asset benefits from legal protection such as a trademark or copyright.
- Market values have little relationship to current costs new.

CURRENT COST NEW

The basis used normally in the Cost Approach is *current cost new* (CCN). While theoretically this should be reproduction costs, in practice, it may be either duplicate (reproduction) or replacement costs. Although the two are related, they represent different concepts and may be significantly different amounts. Yet in many instances they are reasonably equivalent. The cost basis chosen will have a significant impact on the nature and scope of the amount of depreciation to be deducted for a reliable estimate of the fair value of the subject. It is therefore imperative that a valuator understand the differences. The following definitions are important:

Duplication (reproduction) cost new (DCN): The estimated costs to construct a duplicate or replica of the subject at the valuation date; as such, the DCN typically would embody all of its functional deficiencies and obsolescence.

Replacement cost new (RCN): The estimated costs to construct the most economically prudent substitute property with equivalent utility and functionality at the valuation date; as such, the RCN typically would have cured all functional deficiencies and many forms of obsolescence. The RCN of a substitute property with greater utility than the subject may be utilized when equivalent utility is no longer available.

Excess capital (EC): The difference between the DCN and RCN, representing a form of inherent depreciation of the subject.

Functionality: An engineering concept concerning the ability of an asset to perform the task for which it was designed (effectiveness).

Utility: An economic concept referring to providing benefits to the owner equivalent to that of the original, such as generation of cash flows (efficiency).

Distinction Between Methods

To appreciate the distinction from a valuation perspective, consider a subject property that, due to external factors, operates at 60% of rated capacity with no increase in utilization anticipated in the foreseeable future. In this case, the 40% underutilization represents external obsolescence, sometimes referred to as inutility.

The DCN reflects the cost to replace the property at its current size; hence, a reduction due to inutility would be necessary to determine fair value. Conversely, the RCN reflects the cost to build a substitute with 40% less capacity; hence, no inutility adjustment is necessary because the cost basis has already been reduced specifically to reflect this form of external obsolescence.

Both DCN and RCN represent new property without any physical deterioration. Therefore, an amount for this deterioration commensurate with the effective age (physical condition) of the subject has to be deducted from either to determine fair value. Generally the choice of which current cost new to adopt is based in the availability of reliable data on which the cost and depreciation estimates will be made.

Composition of Current Cost New

Regardless of whether it is a replacement or duplication cost, the figure for current cost new must include all expenditures necessary to construct the substitute property and render it ready for use. Construction costs are typically classified into two broad categories: *direct* and *indirect.*

Direct costs. Also called hard costs, direct costs represent material, labor, and related expenses normally and directly associated with the construction and installation of the property; they include but are not limited to:

- Material and suppliers
- Construction and installation labor
- Sales and use taxes
- Shipping, handling, and storage
- Supervision and direct overhead

Indirect costs. Also called soft costs, indirect costs represent other costs of involved with but not normally directly associated with the purchase and installation of the property; they include but are not limited to:

- Engineering, architecture, and other professional services
- Administration, accounting, and general
- Insurance and interest during construction
- Licenses, permits, and related fees

In a Cost Approach valuation, only current direct and indirect expenditures that are normal and customary should be included; atypical or extraordinary items generally are excluded.

Entrepreneurial reward. There are two forms of entrepreneurial rewards. *Entrepreneurial incentive* is a market-derived figure that represents the amount an entrepreneur expects to receive as compensation for assuming the risk associated with the development of a property; this is the entrepreneur's motivation. *Entrepreneurial profit* is the amount the entrepreneur actually achieves by the end of the development.[3]

Without the anticipation of a reasonable financial reward, no entrepreneur would invest time, money, or expertise in creating a profitable property. Therefore, in determining fair

---

[3] *The Appraisal of Real Estate*, p. 347.

value by a cost-based method, the valuator should consider inclusion of entrepreneurial profit in addition to all direct and indirect costs. A theoretical technique to measure entrepreneurial profit is to apply an appropriate rate of return to the opportunity costs incurred by the entrepreneur for time, money, and experience.

Estimating Current Cost New

Various techniques are available for valuators to estimate current costs new. A few of the more popular and commonly accepted methods are described briefly in this section; entrepreneurial profit is excluded because it is generally calculated independently.

Direct unit pricing method. The *direct unit pricing method,* often referred to as the *detail method,* the *summation method,* and the *engineering method,* estimates the current cost new for each component necessary to replace or re-create the subject asset. The property is itemized, or *detailed,* such that the sum of the cost of each component yields the current cost new.

The cost components are generally classified into five categories: material, labor, overhead, developers' profit, and entrepreneurial incentive.[4]

The direct method is commonly used to estimate RCN. While also appropriate for DCN, other more suitable techniques are available to the valuator, such as trended historic cost.

Example: Floating Fish Hatchery (A)

The next table gives data on a floating hatchery built in South Korea for a fish-farming business in Chile.

	Notes	DCN $'000		RCN $'000		Change $'000
Direct Costs						
Material & Supplies	A	1,545		1,335		210
Construction & Installation Labor	B	958	62%	860	64%	98
Sales & Use Taxes		77	5%	67	5%	11
Supervision & Direct Overhead		751	30%	659	30%	92
Shipping, Handling & Storage		655		590		65
		3,986		3,510		476
Indirect Costs						
Engineering, Architecture & Services		279	7%	246	7%	33
Administration, Accounting & General		319	8%	281	8%	38
Insurance & Interest		598	15%	527	15%	71
Licenses & Fees		119	3%	106	3%	12
		1,314		1,159		155
Total Construction		5,300		4,670		631
Profit		530	10%	467	10%	63
Entrepreneurial Incentive		265	5%	233	5%	32
Creation Costs		6,095		5,370		725
Transportation & Site		1,075		1,075		--
Total Costs		7,170		6,445		725
Component Analysis						
Material		1,622	26.6%	1,402	26.1%	
Labor		958	15.7%	860	16.0%	
Overhead		2,720	44.6%	2,408	44.8%	
Developer's Profit		530	8.7%	467	8.7%	
Entrepreneurial Incentive		265	4.3%	233	4.3%	
Creation Costs		6,095	100.0%	5,370	100.0%	

Notes
A: New design reduces tonnage by 20%
B: Most jobs are unchanged

---

[4] *Reilly and Schweihs,* **Valuing Intangible Assets** *(New York: McGraw-Hill, 1999), chap. 8.*

Use of samples. While the depreciated current cost method is the most desirable, it is often impractical to implement reliably for large and complex properties, such as telecommunication networks or regional shopping centers. For these types and other intricate assets, statistical sampling may be used. The first step in this variation of the detailed method is to establish as the sample, say, the network in a medium sized city. The second is to develop the RCN for the sample by this technique and the DCN by another technique. The EC is calculated as a percentage of DCN. The DCN for the complete project is then determined, and the total RCN is estimated by using the EC percentage.

Example: Telecom Network

Sample:

$$DCN = \$1,035,000 \ (8.2\%) \ RCN = \$982,000$$

$$EC = DCN - RCN = \$1,035,000 - \$982,000 = \$53,000$$

$$EC \ \% = EC \ / \ DCN \ \$53,000 \ / \ \$1,035,000 = 5.12\%$$

Subject:

$$DCN = \$12,640,000 \ RCN = DCN \times (1 - EC\%)$$

$$= \$12,640,000 \times (1 - 5.12\%) = \$11,993,000 = \$12,000,000 \ (rounded)$$

This variation of the direct method is applicable only if (a) the sample property is representative of the whole, and (b) both the sample's RCN and DCN can be estimated reliably.

Trended historic costs method. Another common method of estimating the DCN is by trending the original installed costs (historic costs) of each property from its commencement to the valuation date. This is accomplished by using indices that reflect changes in installed costs over time. For example, if the installed cost has increased 10.8% in the last year, then the DCN of an asset installed 12 months ago for $100 would be $100 \times (1 + 0.108)$ today.

Mathematically, if the valuation date is time 0 and x is the date of placement of the subject property, then DCN can be estimated as:

$$DCN_{T=0} = (Index_{T=0} / Index_{T=x}) \times DCN_{T=x}$$

It should be noted that RCN and DCN may be, and often are, equal. If the replacement equipment is substantially the same as the subject property (e.g., a newer model of the same type) or the installed costs of replacing the functionally with different equipment are substantially the same, than $RCN \approx DCN$. In other words, EC is zero, or at least immaterial.

Besides its ease of use, a major advantage of this method is that reliable public price data are available in many countries from government agencies and industry associations; they include indices for commodities, labor, manufacturing, and construction costs. Additionally, for many sectors, industry-specific construction cost trend indices are readily available from private research firms. In mathematical terms, the adjustment is:

$$DCN_{T=0} = \frac{Index_{T=0}}{Index_{T=x}}$$

The valuator has to be cautious that in trending historic costs, as the changes over time in an index are for an average asset. If the historic construction costs of the subject property were unusual, the resulting estimated current cost could be proportionally abnormal. Additionally, statistically, trending becomes less reliable the longer it is projected into the future.

For building and other structures, the current costs are usually calculated by construction estimating software that fairly accurately assesses materials and costs involved. Many such software packages have programmed tiebacks to databases such as those published monthly for United States cities by *Engineering News Record*.

Example: Floating Fish Hatchery (B)

The next table gives data regarding a floating hatchery built in South Korea during 2002 for a fish-farming business in Chile.

	Trended DCN 2002 $'000 Actual	Historic Index Ratio	Costs Method DCN 2009 $'000	Direct Method DCN 2009 $'000
Direct Costs				
Material & Supplies	1,264	1.2165	1,538	1,545
Construction & Installation Labor	737	1.2462	918	958
Sales & Use Taxes	63	--	77	77
Supervision & Direct Overhead	598	1.2462	745	751
Shipping, Handling & Storage	575	1.1497	661	655
	3,237		3,939	3,986
Indirect Costs				
Engineering, Architecture & Services	227	1.2532	284	279
Administration, Accounting & General	239	1.2462	298	319
Insurance & Interest	456		591	598
Licenses & Fees	88		118	119
	1,010		1,291	1,314
Total Construction	4,248		5,231	5,300
Profit	765		523	530
Entrepreneurial Incentive	--		262	265
Creation Costs	5,013		6,015	6,095
Transportation & Site	987	1.1352	1,120	1,075
Total Costs	6,000		7,135	7,170
Component Analysis				
Material	1,327	26.5%	1,615	26.8%
Labor	737	14.7%	918	15.3%
Overhead	2,183	43.6%	2,698	44.8%
Developer's Profit	765	15.3%	523	8.7%
Entrepreneurial Incentive	--	0.0%	262	4.3%
Creation Costs	5,013	100.0%	6,015	100.0%

Unit of production method. As described by Smith and Parr,[5] the construction of certain types of assets has been uniform enough that valuators have developed rules of thumb. For assets, a unit of production method can be used for current cost measurements. For example, building construction may be calculated as dollars per square foot, fast food outlets as dollars per seat, highways as dollars per mile, and so on.

For producing certain types of machinery and equipment, component costs as a percentage of total unit cost are often fairly uniform. Once a total unit cost is known, then each component, either a direct or an indirect cost, can be calculated as a fixed percentage. For example, the various percentages for direct and indirect costs for each component of a mineral processing plant are estimated as shown in the next table.

Assumptions		$'000
Cost per '000 tonnes per day		1,230
Planned Output (tonnes-per-day)	2,500	
RCN		3,075

---

[5] *Gordon V. Smith and Russell L. Parr,* **Intellectual Property: Valuation, Exploitation, and Infringement Damages** *(Hoboken, NJ: John Wiley & Sons, 2005).*

| | Range of Percentages | | | |
	Low	High	Chosen	
Direct Costs				
Piping	10%	30%	25%	769
Instrumentation & Controls	5%	25%	15%	461
Electrical	10%	15%	13%	400
Installation + Materials	10%	12%	12%	370
			65%	2,000
Indirect Costs				
Design, Engineering & Supervision	10%	12%	10%	308
Construction Expense + Materials	10%	12%	10%	308
Contractors Fee + Materials	5%	6%	5%	153
Contingency	10%	10%	10%	308
			35%	1,075
			100%	3,075

Alternatively, if the actual amounts are known for the major component costs, then a figure can be established for the total unit cost.

DEPRECIATION

Depreciation is the loss in value of a property over time; the accumulated depreciation of a property is the difference between its original value and the current value. Depreciation manuals define depreciation as "the loss in service value incurred in connection with the consumption or prospective retirement of a property."[6] For valuations it may be summarized as "the difference between the initial value of a property and its current value."[7] These two concepts essentially have the same meaning; however, it should be noted that valuators are not concerned with changes in cost over time nor are they typically interested in losses in value due to economic obsolescence that does not directly impact the utilization or useful life of the assets.

The previous section developed the concept of the current cost new; in the Cost Approach, *depreciation* is the difference between the CCN and the price to acquire an exact replica of the subject in a free and open market. More simply, depreciation is the difference between the valuator's estimate of CCN and the fair value (FV) of the property.

Fair Value = CCN – Depreciation

Curable and Incurable Depreciation

The difference between DCN and RCN is the EC. This is generally equal to the *curable depreciation*; that is, the change that is economically feasible to cure because the resulting increase in value is greater than the costs involved. In contrast, *incurable depreciation* is that which is not economically feasible to cure because the resulting increase in value is less than the cost to cure.[8]

The nature and scope of the depreciation to be deducted in the Cost Approach is driven in large part by the appraiser's choice of either the RCN or the DCN. However, there is no set rule that all curable depreciation is included in the replacement costs; some forms are dealt with more readily by adjusting the economic life. A prime example is obsolescence resulting from a technological substitution; in this, a new technology causes a decline in utilization and/or premature replacement of equipment with an older process. This is especially important when the valuator obtains economic lives or depreciation factors from published sources; in such cases, the valuator needs to know what depreciation has been included in the

---

[6] *Public Utility Depreciation Practices,* National Association of Regulatory Utility Commissioners, 1996, p. 318.

[7] *Ibid.*

[8] *Valuing Machinery and Equipment,* pp. 562, 571.

lives before the RCN or DCN can be estimated. Otherwise, some forms may be double counted.

Forms of Depreciation

There are many causes of depreciation; however, typically they are classified into three broad categories: physical deterioration, functional obsolescence and economic decline. We describe each cause next and explain how to model their impacts on value.

Mansfield and Pinder[9] provide an in-depth review of depreciation and obsolescence for real property and highlight the practical difficulties in pricing them. The various causes can and do overlap. Accidental destruction, for example, is generally considered and included with physical depreciation, yet it better meets the definition of external obsolescence. In modeling depreciation and estimating value, *it is not critical how the appraiser classifies each cause of depreciation. What is important is that the appraiser accounts for all forms depreciation impacting the subject property, and does so only once.*[10] For example: If the valuator reduces the useful life to less than the physical life based on the owner's modernization plans, and then also applies a functional obsolescence adjustment due to rapid technology change, it is very likely that some obsolescence will be double counted. This point also applies to other tangible and intangible assets.

Physical deterioration. *Physical deterioration* is the loss in value of an asset due to exposure to the elements; causes include: wear and tear, usage (fatigue), deterioration with age and exposure, accidental or chance destruction, and/or lack of maintenance. This definition is similar to that of Baum.[11] Physical depreciation is best modeled using traditional physical mortality techniques discussed later.

The *physical life* of a property is the period that the asset can remain in service, reflecting *only* the impact of physical deterioration. Such a life could never be achieved, because ordinary external obsolescence is always present in any business. It is common practice, however, to reflect both physical deterioration and ordinary obsolescence in the physical life. Take furniture, for example: most chairs, desks, and the like can easily remain in service for over 20 years; however, studies indicate that, on average, furniture remains in service in a firm between 14 and 15 years. In other words, while the *physical life* is likely greater than 20 years, the *average service life (economic useful life)* is 14.5 years. This difference is the result of the ordinary obsolescence present in all commercial environments. Thus, in contrast to the accepted definition, it is a common practice to cite the average service life as the physical life.

Functional obsolescence. *Functional obsolescence* is the loss in value resulting from a flaw or deficiency in the property that inhibits its ability to function for its intended purpose, relative to current market expectations. Functional requirements of equipment alter over time due to changing expectations. For example, additional consumer requirements may need new functionality that older equipment cannot accommodate, thus resulting in its functional obsolescence and causing additional depreciation (loss in value) of the asset. Similarly, technological enhancements in newer models may offer increased economic efficiency, thereby decreasing the relative productivity of the older item and reducing its value.

Functional obsolescence has been defined as "the obsolescence that arises where the design or specification of the asset no longer fulfils the function for which it was originally

[9] John R. Mansfield and James A. Pinder, "'Economic' and 'Functional' Obsolescence: Their Characteristics and Impacts on Valuation Practice," *Property Management 26*, No. 3 (2008): 191–206.
[10] Stephen L. Barreca, BCRI Inc., Birmingham, AL, United States.
[11] Andrew Baum, *Investment, Depreciation and Obsolescence* (London: Routledge, 1991).

designed (or intended)."[12] Changes in technology, economic conditions, and/or regulations can make an asset less efficient, resulting in excess capacity or requiring increased operating and maintenance expenses; the new replacement asset may have also added functionality.

The factors that might cause functional obsolescence have been summarized by Barreca.[13] These include:

- Regulatory and legislative changes
- Increased competition
- Changes in market demand and expectations
- Improved efficiency of new equipment
- Lower prices for new equipment
- Increased functionality of replacement
- Greater capacity of new products
- Other technical changes

Functional obsolescence relative to newer similar equipment may result in the subject asset having a lower value due to: offering excess capacity, lacking some desirable functionality, or requiring higher operating or maintenance expenses. It should be noted, however, that when the replacement asset has more advanced technology, layout, materials, and/or production process, its price and the RCN may already reflect an "optimized" asset; a further deduction of an amount for functional obsolescence may therefore not be necessary.

Economic decline. *Economic decline* is the loss in value resulting from causes not inherent to the subject and generally outside the control of its owner. The classic example is the construction of a major new expressway that diverts traffic away from a service station on the old parallel highway. The station's profitability is reduced, resulting in an overall loss in value of the business due to economic decline.

Ordinary and abnormal obsolescence. Because some forms of obsolescence exhibit patterns that vary from those of other causes of depreciation, for analytical purposes, it is helpful to differentiate between *ordinary* (normal) and *abnormal* (excessive) obsolescence.

Ordinary Obsolescence

Ordinary obsolescence may be defined as "ongoing obsolescence that has achieved a state of equilibrium such that anticipated future patterns of depreciation are generally consistent with recently observed experience." In other words, past depreciation patterns are a reliable indicator of the future. Typically, the depreciation impact of ordinary obsolescence is captured in mortality/actuarial and analyses of historic experience.

Abnormal obsolescence. *Abnormal obsolescence* is defined "as obsolescence that is expected to result in significantly different levels of depreciation over recently observed experience." Therefore, it cannot be predicted reliably from historic experience. When abnormal obsolescence is present, the valuator may have to model it separately and add it to the other forms.

Abnormal obsolescence is often associated with the substitution of one technology for another, such as glass fiber for copper cables. During the first roughly 50% to 70% of a technology substitution period, the rate of change steadily rises. While traditional mortality models capture recently experienced obsolescence, they may not adequately reflect future levels

---

[12] *Royal Institution of Chartered Surveyors "The DRC Method of Valuation for Financial Reporting," Valuation Information Paper No. 10.*

[13] *Stephen Barreca, **Assessing Functional Obsolescence in a Rapidly Changing Marketplace**, BCRI Inc. (August 1999), www.bcri.com/Downloads/Technology%20Obsolescence/pdf.*

if the expected increase is significant. Specialized technology substitution models have proven to depict reliably future depreciation from abnormal obsolescence.

Differences

The history of telecommunication cable provides a good illustration of the difference between ordinary and abnormal obsolescence.

Throughout the 1960s and 1970s, drastically improved new generations of buried metallic cable technology were introduced. During this period, five major generations of metallic cables were introduced:

1. Air core, paper insulated, lead sheath
2. Air core, plastic insulated, plastic sheath
3. Air core polypropylene insulated conductors and sheath (PIC)
4. Dual-expanded PIC (DPIC)
5. Petroleum-jelly-filled DPIC, the current standard for today's buried metallic cables

Each generation represented a significant improvement over the previous generation.

While the impact on depreciation was significant, it did not cause the wholesale replacement of prior generations of metallic cable. Rather, the remaining life of older cables fell gradually and slightly as the economics of replacing them incrementally improved. The increased depreciation resulting from this technological substitution was readily captured in traditional mortality studies and models. Hence, the introduction of successive generations of metallic technology resulted in *ordinary* functional obsolescence.

In stark contrast, the introduction of fiber optic cables in the late 1970s resulted in abnormal functional obsolescence of metallic cable. Unlike successive generations of metallic cable, fiber cable resulted in the wholesale replacement of metallic cable. While this situation has been ongoing for over 30 years and is still under way, it significantly increased the depreciation of most metallic cable.

Today, all long-distance and nearly all interoffice metallic cable has been replaced with fiber; and roughly 50% of all feeder networks have been replaced. The substitution of fiber for metallic cable in the distribution network (the last mile) has begun; however, here fiber penetration is still low. Fiber resulted in *abnormal* functional obsolescence of metallic cable.

Documenting Obsolescence

Industry seems constantly to find additional uses for computers, such as Enterprise Resource Planning (ERP) systems, and to develop new technologies and processes. The value of the firm is enhanced by such activities, which require a constant turnover of capital assets. Some entities face capacity constraints or cannot afford such additional investments. They are forced to maintain their existing equipment, although it clearly shows the effects of technological substitution and keep it in service for longer than is technically or economically appropriate.

To document this situation, we recommend:

*   Comparing the cost, speed, and efficiency of all technology-oriented assets with those of the newest, most efficient alternatives available
*   Compiling market data, such as list prices, useful lives, and current trade-in amounts for such alternatives
*   Following economic trends, gathering market reports on the industry and on the practices of competitors
*   Collecting plant-level cost amounts to identify the effect on profitability of retaining existing assets

- Estimating what it would cost to refurbish and debottleneck plants that are not functioning at capacity
- Asking plant engineers and equipment operators for information on the need to replace particular items

Modeling Depreciation

There are many methods for measuring depreciation; the most common is physical inspection and appraisal judgment. This technique is applicable only to physical personal assets, and its accuracy is tied to the skill and experience of the valuator. Other more objective methods are:

- Applying the age-life concept. This is applicable to all forms of depreciation and obsolescence and is discussed later.
- Measuring the physical deterioration by a variant of age-life concept through the ratio of accumulated to total potential use. This method, expressed in either physical (cubic meter of material) or time (operating hours), is commonly employed for heavy construction machine, aircraft engines, and much industrial equipment such as bulldozers, fork-lifts turbines, and other mechanical devices.
- Identifying deficiencies in the asset and estimating the cost to cure them.

Valuators apply two fundamental techniques to quantify the depreciation of a firm's assets. The first is to directly estimate the figure for each asset, property, or groups of identical properties, and reduce the cost bases accordingly; this is commonly referred to as the fee appraisal method. The second is to utilize average economic lives and depreciation factors and apply them to broader homogeneous (each having similar life and depreciation characteristics) groups of assets, usually segmented by age. This method is generally referred as the mass appraisal cost method.

Mass appraisal cost method. The term "mass appraisal cost method" implies the application of average economic lives, average depreciation factors, and/or average cost indexes to combinations of similar assets (i.e., mass property groups) under the cost approach. Note that *mass appraisal* in this context should not be confused with the same term used in analyzing market prices of real estate, such as sales ratio studies and the like.

Mass appraisal techniques and parameters are quite common under the cost and income approaches. For instance, estimates of the economic lives are typically the result of statistical analyses of observed life and obsolescence indications for large populations of homogeneous properties. The resulting lives therefore reflect the average or mean of the population; then the related depreciation factors are derived by the *age-life* concept.

Age-life concept. The *age-life* concept simply states that the accumulated depreciation can be measured reliably by the ratio of the effective age of an asset to its life. In practice, the age is more aptly the effective age, and the life is the anticipated economic life.

$$\text{Accumulated Depreciation} = \frac{\text{Effective Age}}{\text{Economic Life}}$$

For large industrial properties and many intangibles, the age-life ratio is applied to the entire asset in a single step. The economic life represents the expected period the property is likely to be productive and contribute to the ongoing cash flows of the business; in this form, the age-life ratio is applied in the fee appraisal method.

For large groups of homogeneous properties of various ages, a more exact form of the age-life ratio should be used.

$$\text{Accumulated Depreciation} = \frac{\text{Effective Age}}{\text{Effective Age} + \text{Remaining Economic Life}}$$

Countless empirical studies dating back to the mid-1800s have documented that as a property ages, in all probability, its anticipated economic life tends to increase. This can be seen from the furniture example. Although the economic life of newly installed furniture is 14.5 years, the economic life of a specific item that has been in use for 10 years is, in all probability, much greater than a further 4.5 years.

Prior to the late 1970s, the application of the age-life concept was, for the most part, limited to physical deterioration. However, it is equally useful for other forms of depreciation, especially abnormal obsolescence.

Example: Age-Life Concept

One often-observed effect of technological substitution is a decline in utilization of older technology. Suppose that as a result of technological obsolescence, the utilization of the subject property, a 10-year-old machine tool in an aerospace supplier, is anticipated to decline uniformly to zero over its remaining useful life. In this case, the valuator would reduce the remaining economic life by 50%; the resulting application of the age-life formula (shown next) would yield 80% as a reasonable estimate of the accumulated depreciation of the subject reflecting technological obsolescence.

$$\text{Accumulated Depreciation} = \frac{\text{Effective Age}}{\text{Effective Age} + \text{Remaining Economic Life}}$$

$$= \frac{10}{10 + 2.5} = \frac{10}{12.5} = 80\%$$

Depreciation Factors

Depreciation is often presented as a form of remaining value/life *percent good factors*. When applied to the current cost basis of a property, percent good factors yield an estimate of the current value.

Age-life ratio. Depreciation factors may be determined as the percentage of the economic life of the property remaining. Consider an asset that has been in service for 3 years and is expected to contribute for another 2 years. The asset has an estimated total service life of 5 years (3 + 2); as shown in Exhibit 2.1, it has consumed 60% of its productive life (3 years) and has 40% life remaining (2 years).

Exhibit 2.1

The value of the subject property is dependent on the remaining productive life expectancy. This is the second fundamental premise of the Cost Approach. Normally in applying this formula, the *effective age* is known while the *remaining life* is not. To assist valuators, depreciation analysts in the United States have developed tables of depreciation factors for many types and ages of property.

Mathematically, depreciation factors are computed using the age-life ratio. As discussed, it gives the relative accumulated depreciation for the subject; 1 minus the age-life ratio yields the remaining (nondepreciated) value.

$$\text{Depreciation Factor} = \frac{\text{Remaining Life}}{\text{Effective Age} + \text{Remaining Life}}$$

Modeling Physical Deterioration and Ordinary Obsolescence

Physical deterioration and ordinary obsolescence are modeled commonly using mortality analysis actuarial techniques. This involves the statistical analyses of observed market data—primarily retirements by age of plant. The result is a survivor curve and useful service life. Together they reflect the ongoing depreciation of the subject *resulting from both physical deterioration and ordinary obsolescence.*

Mortality analysis was first introduced in the mid-1800s and is the basis for actuarial analyses used by life insurance companies. Around 1910, the American Telephone and Telegraph Company (AT&T) analyzed over 1,000 homogeneous groups of fixed assets involving hundreds of thousands of observed life indications. These empirical studies proved conclusively that actuarial theory was directly applicable to physical property. In the 1920s, Iowa State University undertook various studies of mortality characteristics of industrial property, which resulted in the development of the popular Iowa Survivor Curves.

Mortality analysis uses observed retirement history to establish a survivor curve that reflects past and anticipated physical deterioration patterns. A number of *standard* families of survivor curves have been published, including Iowa curves, Bell curves, H-curves, and others. Wolf and Fitch present a comprehensive and respected reference on this topic that presents data on all the Iowa curves.[14]

Modeling Abnormal Obsolescence

Survivor curves reflect physical depreciation, ordinary functional obsolescence, and economic decline. To the extent that *abnormal* obsolescence is expected to be significant in the future, it must be quantified and added to the normal depreciation.

One method to quantify the impact of abnormal obsolescence using and extension of the technology substitute model was proposed by Barreca.[15] He illustrates this concept with the previously discussed example of replacing copper with fiber optic cables. Some of the drivers causing copper cables to be functionally obsolete include the deregulation of long distance and the telephone industry, increasing competition, lower customer charges, changing user expectations, increased demand for high-speed Internet access, and the technical superiority of fiber optics. The total functional obsolescence from all the drivers is reflected in the decline in relative usage of copper cables, as shown in the figure presented later; this shift is called *technology substitution.*

The analysis of this phenomenon measures and projects the market takeover (substitution) of a new technology for an older one. When the relative market penetration of the newer technology is plotted over time, the result is an S-shaped curve. This pattern has been known for some time; however, it was not until 1971 when two General Electric researchers defined the Fisher-Pry model for the curve. This model has proven to be very accurate in predicting the pace of technology substitution and the resulting obsolescence. Based on the diffusion of innovation theory as developed by Everett Rogers,[16] technology adoption also occurs in an S curve: innovators (2.5%), early adopters (12.5%), early majority (34%), late majority (35%), and laggards (16%).

Documentation of technology substitution in terms of the relative usage of old versus newer equipment provides an indicator of the functional obsolescence of the older technology. This indicator may then be used to directly determine the accumulated depreciation. In

---

[14] *Frank Wolf and Chester Fitch,* **Depreciation Systems** *(Iowa State University Press, 1992).*

[15] *Stephen L. Barreca, "Technological Obsolescence—Assessing the Loss in Value of Utility Property,"* **Journal of the Society of Depreciation Professional 8** *(1998).*

[16] *Everett Rogers (1983).*

Exhibit 2.2, the curve labeled "Obsolescence" relates to older technology. Once the obsolescence pattern is established, the impact can be calculated in terms of an annual rate that reflects the probability of depreciation directly resulting from technological obsolescence. In any given year, the net annual probability of depreciation, FO(t), is equal to the market share, OB(t), at the beginning of year less the market share at the end of year, divided by the beginning of year value.

$$FO(t) \quad = \quad \frac{OB(t) - OB(t+1)}{OB(t)}$$

Technological obsolescence.

Exhibit 2.2

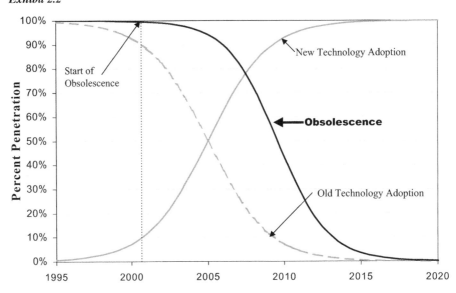

In terms of market penetration, Exhibit 2.2 shows the adoption of a new technology, the corresponding loss in market share of the older technology, and its resulting obsolescence. While the obsolescence curve is similar in appearance to a survivor curve, it is conceptually quite different as it represents a *life-cycle* plot showing the decline in value surviving by *year*. In contrast, a survivor curve plots the percent surviving by *age* of plant. However, physical survivor curves are typically converted and combined with others to yield a composite life cycle, from which the net economic lives and composite depreciation can be determined. This method allows the valuator to quantify *objectively* abnormal obsolescence.

Modeling Economic Decline

Economic decline may be caused by items such as a reduced demand for the product, increased competition, changes in raw material supplies, increased costs of raw materials and labor, inflation, changes in the labor supply, market accessibility, governmental regulations, or a reduction in the contributed earning power to the business. For real estate, economic (decline) can be divided into locational and external obsolescence. A typical example is a permanent shift in demand or supply that adds excess capacity to a particular industry and therefore reduces the value of an asset regardless of how modern or efficient it may be.

Comparing the actual utilization of an asset to the originally designed capacity gives an indication of economic decline. This form of economic decline is called *inutility;* it exists when equipment is underutilized and capacity usage is not expected in the near term, generally over its useful service life. The appropriate adjustment for inutility is the difference between the RCN of the subject and that of the most economically prudent (i.e., optimally sized) substitute; this should have sufficient capacity to accommodate current use expected, future demand, an allowance for adequate downtime capacity, and the use of standard size equipment.

This is a well-known methodology for the inutility adjustment based on the classic *cost-to-capacity* concept:

$$\text{Inutility Penality (\%)} = \left[1 - \left(\frac{\text{Optimal Capacity}}{\text{Current Capacity}} \right)^n \right] \times 100$$

Where
  n = cost-to-capacity factor

Typically, the inutility adjustment is expressed as a percent good factor of 100% minus the penalty. The relationship just shown is based on the notion that because of economies of scale, the cost of plant or equipment is related to its size exponentially. Such exponential factors vary depending on the type of equipment and labor/material ratios, but typically they are between 0.4 and 1.03, with 0.6 being the most common.[17] The *n* factor, often called the six-tenths factor, can also be used to measure economic decline assuming that this expense is exponentially related to underutilization of an asset.

Example: Economic Decline

A canning line has a maximum capacity of 1,000 tonnes a day but currently is processing only 700 tonnes per day. The excess capacity is due to changing consumer demand, which is not expected to be reversed in the foreseen future; the line has excess capacity due to economic decline. Bethel[18] provides a clear example of the calculation of economic decline:

$$\text{Economic Decline} = [1 - (\text{actual utilization/intended utilization})^n] \times 100$$

$$= [1 - (700/1{,}000)^{0.7}] \times 100 = 22.1\%$$

Modeling inutility from technology substitutions. Technological substitution often gives rise to inutility in the older property; the model presented earlier fully captures the resulting effect. The annual displacement in utilization is quantified, and the remaining economic life is reduced accordingly; it is not uncommon for the reduction to the economic remaining life to be very significant.

Some valuators apply a different technique by adjusting the current cost new to reflect the excess capacity. This is acceptable; however, care must be taken not to double count the inutility penalty. For instance, if the valuator reduces economic life from substitution analyses and also utilizes an RCN based on a reduced size substitute, the inutility/obsolescence would be double counted. In this situation, the higher average service or physical life excluding the influence of the technology substitution should be chosen as the economic life in any calculation of the remaining depreciation.

Modeling other economic decline. Abnormal external obsolescence may take a variety of forms. The form of the loss dictates the approach to take when assessing its contribution to depreciation. The life cycle approach used for technological substitution is often applicable to other forms of abnormal depreciation and obsolescence.

---

[17] *Details are found in **Machinery and Equipment: The Fundamentals of Appraising Machinery and Technical Assets**, 2nd ed. (American Society of Appraisers, 2005).*

[18] *Stephen Bethel, **The Business Valuation Resource Guide**, 2nd ed. (Mattatall Press, 2006), chap. 9.*

COMBINING TYPES OF DEPRECIATION

The loss in value of an asset due to physical deterioration, functional obsolescence, and economic decline generally take place simultaneously. When the total amount of each form is determined, the amounts can simply be added together. However, when they are expressed in terms of a percentage or probability of loss, adding them together will overstate the total. The obvious solution is to convert them into currency and then add them. Although it is not relevant to the magnitude of the total depreciation, the order in which the depreciation percents are applied to the current cost bases is relevant to the specific dollar amounts attributed to each form of depreciation.

By convention, depreciation is applied on a first-come, first-serve basis:

1. Excess capital
2. Inutility
3. Physical deterioration
4. Functional obsolescence
5. Economic decline

Example: Floating Fish Hatchery

The next table presents data for a floating hatchery built in South Korea during 2002 for a fish-farming business in Chile.

Depreciation Rankings
Excess Capital
Inutility
Physical Deterioration
Functional Obsolescence
Economic Decline

Excess Capital	**$'000**	*Inutility*	
DCN–Direct Method	7,170	Planned Utilization–million hatchings	325.0
RCN–Direct Method	6,445	Actual 2008 Utilization–million hatchings	326.1
Excess Capital	725		
Conclusion	10.0%	Conclusion	0.0%

Physical Deterioration		*Functional Obsolescence*		
Effective Age–years	7.25	Cost per '000 hatchlings	$	6.27
Total Physical Life–years	50.00	Industry Average	$	5.98
Conclusion	14.5%	Conclusion		4.8%

Economic Decline	
Industry Capacity–thousand tonnes	260.6
Current Production–thousand tonnes	238.5
Conclusion	8.5%

		$'000
Duplicate Cost New		7,170
Excess Capital	10.1%	(725)
		6,445
Inutility	0.0%	--
		6,445
Physical Deterioration	14.5%	(935)
		5,510

Functional Obsolescence	4.8%	(267)
		5,243
Economic Decline	8.5%	(445)
Fair Value		4,798
Fair Value–Rounded		4,800
Total Depreciation		2,370
		33.1%
Effective Age–years		7.25
Remaining Economic Life		21.93

COST APPROACH CONSIDERATIONS

Each of the three traditional valuation approaches designed to yield fair value has strengths and weaknesses. One is not inherently better than any other, but in any given situation, one may be more suitable. Each valuation assignment is different, with a specific premise of value, an indicated purpose, and limited quantity of reliable data.

In any assignment, the valuator should consider methods under each approach for which reliable data are available. It is essential that the valuator exercise professional judgment and reconcile the results of the chosen methods.

3 THE MARKET APPROACH

WILLIAM A. HANLIN JR. AND J. RICHARD CLAYWELL

UNITED STATES

INTRODUCTION

In many countries, mainly in the English tradition, including Australia, Britain, Canada, Ghana, Hong Kong, India, Malaysia, Singapore, South Africa, South Korea, Taiwan, and the United States, a great deal of corporate financing is arranged through stock exchanges. In addition, some of those nations have developed transparent markets for many types of assets (art, equipment, real estate, etc.) as well as commodities and other securities. Therefore, these countries are biased to the position that the best measures of value are prices in active markets. Other countries, such as France and Germany, while operating long-established, well-developed bourses (stock exchanges), take a more nuanced view.

The authors strongly believe that where active markets exist in appropriate assets (commodities, equipment, real estate, or securities), their prices should be taken into account through applying various methods under the Market Approach. This chapter provides an understanding of how such techniques can improve the quality of valuation conclusions.

In particular, the narrative relating to the Market Approach in a valuation report should:

- Discuss its applicability
- Present the reasons for selecting particular transactions or databases
- Summarize the chosen deals and supply enough detail about the publicly traded guidelines so that a reader can understand their comparability to the subject
- Present the relevant data in an easily followed form
- Explain how the values were developed

There is no right or wrong approach to valuation, there are only supportable conclusions; any amount obtained by the Market Approach should be confirmed by other methods.

OVERVIEW OF THE MARKET APPROACH

When applied to an entity, the Market Approach utilizes information relating to transactions in either public or private firms similar to the subject; its uses for individual assets are discussed in other chapters. The approach is based on the principle of substitution and the assumption that comparable opportunities, in fact, do yield appropriate values; the various methods apply multiples from such data to the subject's financial information in order to obtain comparable measures of value. Historically, the use of the Market Approach in business valuation is rooted in the concepts developed by real estate appraisers for whom sales of similar properties are a strong indicator of the value of a building.

In the United States, due to the influence of the Internal Revenue Service's fair market value standard, Revenue Ruling 59-60, the Market Approach has to be considered in almost every business valuation. The amounts determined by it will vary, based on the financial condition of the entity, the industry in which it operates, and the impact of external factors such as investor enthusiasm as well as its year-to-year profitability.

The burden of proof is on the valuator to demonstrate that the Market Approach is suitable for the subject. In many valuation engagements, it is often overlooked when it might support the value conclusion; however, suitable data may be difficult to find for small to medium enterprises (SMEs).

STANDARD AND PREMISE OF VALUE

It is generally accepted that the Market Approach directly provides fair value, since it is based on transactions that are normally consummated between willing buyers and willing sellers in an open market; that certainty, however, is open for debate. The Guideline Company Method (discussed in detail later) clearly provides a standard of value with willing buyers and willing sellers; it is more doubtful that the Completed Transaction Method always involves fair values. It relies on large numbers of deals reported in databases; it is highly likely that a significant portion of them are at fair value, but it is also quite possible that many are synergistic and represent investment value, which is defined by the International Glossary as "the value to a particular investor based on individual investment requirements and expectations."

This problem is aggravated by the business brokers, who provide selling prices and other information after transactions take place. Many of them admit that they handle numerous transactions in SMEs because the owner is ill, has died, the business is in trouble or can no longer compete, as well as other such situations. In other words, there may be compelling reasons to deal without a willing seller.

USE OF THE MARKET APPROACH

The foremost reason to use the Market Approach is that, when suitable data are available, it provides a verifiable and objective measure of value. Actual sales, in a public market at arm's length of similar interests, are compelling evidence. Revenue Ruling 59-60, Section 3.03, requires the use of the Market Approach:

> *Valuation of securities is, in essence, a prophecy as to the future and must be based on facts available at the required date of appraisal. As a generalization, the prices of stocks [ordinary shares] that are traded in volume in a free and active market by informed persons best reflect the consensus of the investing public as to what the future holds for the corporations and industries represented. When a stock is closely held, traded infrequently, or is traded in an erratic market, some other measure of value must be used. In many instances, the next best measure may be found in the prices at which the stocks of companies engaged in the same or similar line of business are selling in a free and open market.*

Section 4.02(h) of Revenue Ruling 59-60 goes on to say:

> *Section 2031 (b) of the [U.S. Tax] Code states, in effect, that in valuing unlisted securities the value of stock or securities of corporations engaged in the same or similar line of business which are listed on an exchange should be taken into consideration along with all other factors. An important consideration is that the corporations to be used for comparisons have capital stocks, which are actively traded by the public. In accordance with section 2031(b) of the Code, stocks listed on an exchange are to be considered first. However, if sufficient comparable companies whose stocks are listed on an exchange cannot be found, other comparable companies that have stocks actively traded on the over-the-counter market also may be used. The essential factor is that whether the stocks are sold on an exchange or over-the-counter there is evidence of an active, free public market for the stock as of the valuation date. In selecting corporations for comparative purposes, care should be taken to use only comparable companies. Although the only restrictive requirement as to comparable corporations specified in the statute is that their lines of business be the same or similar, yet it is ob-*

vious that consideration must be given to other relevant factors in order that the most valid comparison possible will be obtained. For illustration, a corporation having one or more issues of preferred stock, bonds or debentures in addition to its common stock should not be considered to be directly comparable to one having only common stock outstanding. In like manner, a company with a declining business and decreasing markets is not comparable to one with a record of current progress and market expansion.

CHOICE OF METHOD

There are two primary methods to be considered when utilizing the Market Approach:

1. Completed transaction method (CTM)
2. Guideline company method (GCM)

Although there are inherent differences, the underlying theory of both is the same; transactions used as evidence come from the market, where willing buyers and willing sellers meet, each looking out for his or her own interests, to negotiate the best deal. There are some distinct differences: GCM relies on the best-fits whereas CTM is based on the total market. That is, GCM requires selecting those entities that are deemed most comparable as guidelines, while CTM applies parameters from the overall market, using as many suitable transactions as can be found.

COMPLETED TRANSACTION METHODS

CTM is based on the principle of substitution, which states that the economic value of any asset or "thing" tends to be determined by the cost of acquiring an equally desirable item, with similar utility and functionality; therefore, no reasonable person would pay more than the amount required for such a reasonable alternative. This principle does not require that the substitute be identical, only that it is equivalent in desirability and so on. To be a "qualified substitute," the comparable businesses or items need only to be substantially qualitatively and quantitatively similar.

Thus, CTM looks at completed sales transactions in the subject's industry; that is most frequently the purchase or sale of an entire business, which may result from:

- Publicly traded firms acquired by similar entities
- Private companies bought by publicly traded firms
- Publicly traded entities taken private

In the United States, the Securities and Exchange Commission (SEC) requires that any publicly traded entity acquiring more than 5 percent of a private company has to disclose the target's financial data, typically in an 8-K filing. Nothing is required for the purchase of private companies by similar firms, but, as mentioned previously, there are a number of databases (discussed next) of such transactions.

The best use of CTM is in valuing controlling interests, since the sales reported are nearly always for entire companies and not partial interests; obviously, it gives a control level of value. Whether a discount for lack of marketability (DLOM) should be taken is debated among professionals, but, if deducted, it is typically small.

U.S. Transaction Databases

Transaction databases exist in many countries; the most common in the United States are:

- *BizComps®;* Mostly comprised of SMEs, with approximately 11,200 transactions in total
- *IBA Database:* mostly comprised of SMEs, with over 19,000 transactions

- *Pratt's Stats:* mostly comprised of SMEs, with approximately 14,000 transactions
- *DoneDeals*: range from $1 to $100 million, with approximately 8,600 transactions
- *Mergerstat:* comprised entirely of transactions valued at not less than $1 million reported by publicly traded entities

Using Transaction Information

While GCM may be suitable for larger private firms or cash-generating units (CGUs), it is not as useful for SMEs or smaller GCUs; for them, CTM is more important. Sources of data range from local land registries through national business sales reports to complex multinational licensing and royalty records. Some of the most helpful for sales of businesses in the United States are mentioned in the list of transaction databases.

Coverage. There are substantial differences between the sizes and industries of the businesses covered by U.S. databases. In early 2008, a sample of them included information on the following numbers of transactions in three industries:

	Restaurants	Auto Dealers	Computer Programming
BizComps ®	839	10	14
Pratt's Stats	235	55	141
DoneDeals	60	26	277

There are many situations where an entity falls into a size or profitability range that does not neatly conform to any of the transaction databases or the guidelines. To deal with this, Hans Schroeder of Business Equity Appraisal Reports Inc. recommends an integrative technique.[1] By this, various sources of data can be combined so as to reinforce each other and narrow the gaps. Schroeder concludes that expressing market data in graphic form using regression analysis:

- Simplifies choosing appropriate valuation multiples.
- Provides strong evidence to support the amounts adopted.
- Eliminates the possible misleading use of medians and quartiles in selecting valuation multiples.
- Reduces the effects of differences in size and varying levels of profitability as well as helping place the entity in its proper context.
- Offers a more cohesive view of the market; transactions that appear to be outriders in one database sometimes fall neatly into line with deals from another.
- Indicates significant differences in the specific pricing mechanisms of various industries.[2]

Problems with Transaction Data

Utilizing information from transaction databases concerning entities similar to the subject is more complicated than applying valuation multiples from guidelines. Because few transactions are truly comparable, it is hard to determine the actual multiples and what adjustments may be needed. While stock markets are generally quite efficient in handling high-volume trading between investors, diffusing information among them is slow and leads to a range of reactions; the same report may cause some to buy and others to sell. With a touch of herd instinct when it comes to following trends, the conclusion is that people are not always totally rational in the way they invest. The situation is completely different when the deal involves a change of control, which is a negotiated, one-time event. Each buyer and seller has his

[1] Hans Schroeder, "Graphic Analysis of Market Data," *Business Valuation Review* (March 2003).
[2] See also Toby Tatum "Transaction Patterns: Gaining Market Knowledge from the BizComps Database," RDS Associates, 2000.

or her own individual reasons for acting, some of which have little to do with the business; synergies may enter the picture, as will available financing, and whether it is a share or an asset purchase.

Even if a number of homogenous transactions by businesses similar to the subject have taken place, it is often difficult to assess exactly what was paid and how the proceeds were allocated. Was any real estate omitted? Were all operating assets included? Was any significant amount paid for a non-competition agreement or personal goodwill? If the deal included public company shares, was the buyer's multiple on the announcement more meaningful than at closing? Was the selling price reduced for the seller to receive above-market compensation for a certain period? The comparisons must differentiate between apples and bananas; if the deal implies a high multiple because current industry profits are believed to be temporarily depressed, the valuator has to be careful not to apply it directly to the normalized earnings of the subject.

Implementation

The procedure for using transaction data to estimate the value of a business includes these four steps:

1. Analyze the available transaction databases to determine which valuation multiple (discussed later) can be calculated.
2. Chose the multiples that best describe the subject's business as a whole.
3. Multiply the selected ratio by the relevant revenue or earnings of the subject as if the assets and liabilities included were identical with those of typical sales in the database.
4. Adjust the amount (from step 3) to compensate for differences between the elements of a typical sale and those of the subject.

Rules of thumb are considered a market method because they are based on multiples determined over time from sales in certain industries. They should never be used as a primary technique but may provide a reality check on values determined otherwise.

Total Enterprise Value

When applying the Market Approach to an entity, value multiples can be calculated for either the ordinary share equity or the total enterprise value (TEV). This is the market capitalization, adjusted for the value of outstanding options and convertible securities, plus the fair values, not book values, of any preference shares and debt. There are two schools of thought regarding the appropriate debt: the first includes only amounts shown on the balance sheet as long-term liabilities. The other combines all interest-bearing obligations of any kind, as rolling over short-term borrowings has often been seen as an alternative to long-term loans. Although the first method is theoretically correct, the second is preferable, as it relates to how businesses are actually financed.

Whichever method is chosen, it is essential that the amounts for the entity, guidelines, or databases use the same definition and that, for example, dividends on preference shares (whether paid or not) are deducted in calculating any ordinary equity value multiple, also that the interest added back for certain TEV multiples is, when appropriate, adjusted for income taxes so that all figures are either before or after tax and not mixed. In calculating the fair values of preference shares and debt, the techniques for valuing liabilities that reflect the firm's credit standing should be applied. As the amount of cash held by the entity may be very different from that of the guidelines or databases, it is better to deduct it from either the market capitalization or the TEV and apply the valuation multiples to the net equity or net enterprise values.

GUIDELINE COMPANY METHOD

The GCM uses prices for ordinary shares of comparable quoted firms to establish valuation multiples that may be applied to the subject.

Do Stock Market Prices Represent Fair Value?

The International Accounting Standards Board (IASB) presumes that stock markets are efficient and that prices of publicly traded shares at all times represent fair value. Recent studies on the various forms of the efficient-market theory suggest that it is no longer a useful concept. In the authors' experience, security prices are not only a matter of buyers being gullible, emotional, or perhaps a little greedy, but also depend on the entity's growth stage, intensity of the competition, market penetration, and the market cycle at the time, as shown in Exhibit 3.1.

Exhibit 3.1 Emotions Depend on the Stage of the Market Cycle

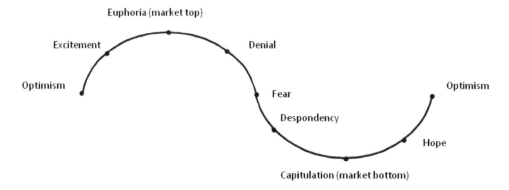

Most of those stages recur in every cycle; being aware of them helps a valuator to keep a historic perspective. Under IASB's definition, "fair value" is an amount established by a market, although at any particular time, such prices may be higher or lower than those considered "fair" by most buyers, based on their required rates of return.

Stock market volatility. Computers altered the nature of trading on stock markets in the mid-1990s, and those changes are continuing. In the United States, securities have been swinging up and down more frequently and more violently than at any time since the Great Depression. In a number of cases, the shares of nearly every member of an industrial group decreased or increased by over 30 percent in a single quarter; on several occasions, daily price gains or losses exceeded 25 percent. It is questionable whether fair values really changed that quickly and by that much.

Most valuators use closing share prices as of the valuation date for the numerator of various value multiples; that number is normally available the next day. However, many practitioners believe that day-to-day price fluctuations reflect psychological factors that are not relevant to fair value. To avoid this, they prefer to rely on the mean of daily prices for a period of up to the past 30 days; prices after the valuation date should not be included. In view of recent events, it is questionable if even such an average is appropriate.

The view that quoted prices of securities on a stock exchange do not necessarily reflect fair value goes back to Baron James de Rothschild's 1871 Paris Commune quote: "Buy when there is blood in the streets." It was more eloquently put by Benjamin Graham of Columbia University, coauthor of the first great book on securities analysis in 1934.

In the short term, the stock market is a voting machine, with its prices based on the continually changing opinions of emotional, fickle investors, but in the long haul, the market is like a weighing machine, measuring the value of stocks' underlying businesses.[3]

This, he wrote, offers investors "an opportunity to buy wisely when prices fall sharply and to sell wisely when they advance a great deal." He considered that the most important principle of investment was a "margin of safety," still a core concept for mutual fund managers. This is the gap between the trading price of a security and its intrinsic underlying value.

U.S. Experience

Revenue Ruling 59-60 embraces this method when valuing closely held companies. As a result, valuators spend considerable time and effort searching for potential guidelines and establishing if, in fact, they are significantly similar to their subject. The GCM relies on selecting those firms that are deemed most comparable. Conversely but equally important is determining whether the subject, often an SME, has the attributes necessary to make a comparison to public companies relevant.

Generally, it is believed that the GCM provides a minority, marketable value. This is because the multiples that are applied to the subject come from shares not owned by controlling interests that are freely traded on open markets.

Dilution

The basis for all guideline value multiples is the quoted price of the related shares times the number outstanding, which gives the market capitalization. How to determine that price was discussed earlier in this chapter. For the resulting amount to be meaningful, it must be adjusted for any securities (debt or preference shares) that can immediately and profitably be converted into ordinary shares (described as in-the-money), including share purchase warrants and employee stock options.

Traditionally, the treasury stock method has been used to establish the number of shares considered outstanding. This method assumes that all cash from the exercise of warrants or options is used to repurchase existing shares at market prices; however, it does not reflect what usually happens. For valuation purposes, it is therefore preferable to assume full conversion of all applicable debt and preference shares, together with complete exercise of the stock options and warrants. The total is the number of shares that might be issued. In order to properly calculate the earnings per share (EPS), the profit has to be adjusted by first eliminating the interest and dividends previously payable on those securities and then assuming that the excess cash is used to repay the debt bearing the highest interest rate, thus reducing the pro forma interest charges.

Employee stock options. Employee stock options are the most complex source of dilution; they are a specialized form of compensation accounted for under IFRS 2. (See Chapter 32.) For valuation purposes, not only exercisable options but also those likely to be granted in the future under existing, approved plans should be taken into account using current market prices for the notional exercise.

SELECTING VALUE MULTIPLES

When using guidelines, valuators usually establish various value multiples for each and use them to determine a value for the subject. Their numerator is either adjusted market capitalization or TEV, while the denominator is nearly always a measure of operating performance, such as sales for a certain period.

---

[3] *Benjamin Graham, **Intelligent Investor**.*

Economic Levels of a Business

The next table depicts the various economic levels of a business.

	Revenues (REV)
Less	Cost of Sales (Direct Costs)
=	Gross Profit (GRP)
Less	SG&A (Sales General & Administrative) Expenses
=	Operating Cash Flow (EBITRAD)
Less	Research & Development & Major Marketing Expenditures
=	Business Cash Flow (EBITDA)
Less	Depreciation & Amortization
=	Operating Profit (EBIT)
Less	Interest
=	Pretax Profit (EBT)
Less	Income Taxes
=	Net Income (NINC)
Less	Preferred Dividends
=	Earnings for Ordinary Shares (ERN)
Less	Common Dividends (DIV)
=	Retained Earnings

Any of the economic levels named may be used as a measure of operating results; other value multiples have been developed from several forms of cash flows (gross cash flow, net cash flow, free cash flow, discretionary earnings) as well as from measures of shareholders' equity (net book value, tangible book value, net asset value).

Measurement Period

Once the measure of operating results has been chosen, the period for which it is to be calculated must be determined; the most common are:

- Trailing 12 months (TTM, last four quarters)
- Latest reported fiscal year (LFY)
- Average of complete business cycle (two to five years)
- Projected results for current or next fiscal year
- Various averages of past and projected years, usually weighted toward the most recent periods

Such a selection requires judgment and experience. Conceptually, fair value is based on the future; however, the use of expected results is dependent on having both credible projections for the entity and reliable estimates for the guidelines. For many publicly traded businesses, EPS forecasts are available from analysts' reports; in some cases, management has supplied guidance by various means, such as conference calls or press releases. If reliable figures are available for the guidelines, the use of a weighted average, based on the last four completed fiscal years and a projection for the current year, is recommended; otherwise, the TTM is the most useful.

Nonfinancial Metrics

Some nonfinancial metrics that are used in industry comparisons, particularly as rules of thumb, may also be helpful:

- Revenues per square foot of selling space (retailers, real estate)
- Revenues per employee (technology)
- Volume changes from previous year
- Tons of ore mined (or milled) a day (mineral properties)
- Barrels of oil (or oil equivalent) produced (or refined) a day (oil and gas)
- TEV to next year's estimated revenues
- TEV to number of employees
- Advertising linage (or minutes) sold
- TEV to replacement cost of the property, plant, and equipment ("Tobin's Q"
- TEV per daily ton of capacity (mines, steel or forest entities)

These metrics are normally industry specific and should be applied only if they are generally accepted within the field. With many valuations, such as for early-stage enterprises, some traditional methods cannot be used, because the entity has not matured enough to generate profits. In such cases, nonfinancial metrics may be suitable in conjunction with available financial information; an example is the trend in sales per square feet for retailers.

MOST COMMON VALUE MULTIPLES

Although the price earnings ratio (PER) market capitalization divided by net income less preferred dividends, whether paid or not, is the most often applied valuation multiple, there are three potential pitfalls in relying on the mean or median of the guidelines' PER.

1. It will likely include firms with very different degrees of operational gearing and financial leverage as well as some with high cyclicality.
2. There is an unexpressed premise that PERs will continue at current levels rather than be influenced by future interest rates and economic conditions.
3. There is an implicit assumption by the buyer that the entity can be resold at the same PER; this is often not the case, especially if the expected growth is not achieved.

As with book value, despite its limitations, PER is a widely used benchmark, but it is not necessarily the best. Erik Lie and Heidi J. Lie concluded that earnings before interest, taxes, depreciation and amortization (EBITDA) multiples are among the most satisfactory.[4]

Market Capitalization/Cash Flow

Cash flow is often defined as adjusted net income plus noncash charges, such as depreciation, impairment losses, amortization, and deferred taxes, less maintenance capital expenditure and the extra working capital necessary to support projected growth.

A value multiple based on cash flows is normally applied when:

- It is an industry standard, such as for oil and gas producers.
- Some guidelines or the entity has negative or marginal net incomes.
- The economic life for the property, plant, and equipment exceeds the amortization period in the financial statements, as for instance in real estate.

---

[4] *Erik Lie and Heidi J. Lie,* **Financial Analysts Journal** *(March/April 2003).*

Market Capitalization/Revenue

The financial data for all guidelines and the entity usually must be adjusted to ensure comparability, although such alterations may lead to subjectivity. As a result, many valuators rely on multiples that do not require any adjustment. Because sales are totally unaffected by differences in operational gearing, financial leverage, and accounting practices, the most common choice is market capitalization divided by revenue, usually known as the price/sales ratio (PSR). Some consider the net enterprise value divided by sales, more suitable than the PSR.

Generally, there is a relationship between a firm's PSR and its pretax return on sales (ROS); the higher a firm's ROS, the higher its PER. However, if a valuator has sufficient data to calculate the ROS for all entities involved, he or she can easily arrive at the PERs, which are preferable. The PSR is a measure that managements often take into account when making acquisitions. Many analysts use it together with the PER and the price/earnings growth factor (PEG: the PER divided by the expected growth rate in EPS) to determine relative stock market values. For example, in certain industries, such as automotive, there are times when none of the major manufacturers or their principal suppliers reports any profits. Utilizing the cyclical swings in their PSRs to establish fair value may result in wrong amounts.

The PSR normally is employed when:

- A sanity check is needed for an equity value determined by another method, particularly for service industries or firms with low variable costs.
- Erratic earnings or temporary losses make other value multiples inappropriate.
- A new owner might achieve a significantly different return from the same activities.
- The adjustments required to the financial data of the entity and the guidelines are significant.
- The business is in an industry with a relatively standard cost structure.

The valuator should confirm if the value obtained by this technique takes into account all assets.

Applying the PSR. If the mean or median of the multiples from the guidelines is applied to the entity's current revenues, the result may be misleading. It is preferable to calculate both the PSR and the ROS for each guideline and plot them against each other on a graph. As there are rarely more than 10, fitting a trend line is not difficult. As the entity's ROS is known, the trend line establishes an appropriate PSR. This process is illustrated in the next table, using the guidelines from the strategic assessment section later in this chapter.

	ROS %	*PSR*
Guideline 2	10.1	0.40
Guideline 9	9.0	0.35
Guideline 1	7.5	0.25
Guideline 3	6.0	0.30
Guideline 6	5.3	0.20

Linear regression calculates a PSR of 0.31 for the subject based on its ROS of 8.1%, with a coefficient of determination (R^2) of 76.7%, as shown in Exhibit 3.2.

Exhibit 3.2 Return on Sales/Price to Sales Ratio

Return on Sales/Price to Sales Ratio

$$Y = 3.82E - 02 + 3.45E - 02X$$
$$R - Sq = 76.7\%$$

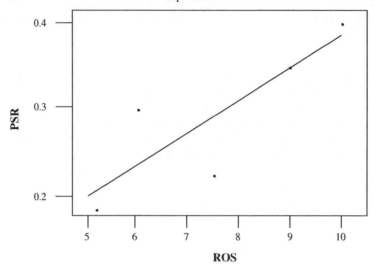

As is to be expected, the PSR increases in line with the ROS, because fair value is considered to be more dependent on earnings than on sales. In general, the slope of the trend line will be below 1; in other words, doubling ROS does not double the value of the business, as opportunities for margin improvements decline at a higher ROS.

Total Enterprise Value/EBITDA

Valuators commonly deal with situations where some guidelines have high financial leverage and some have low financial leverage. To balance out these effects, they move from net income to other levels, such as: sales, Earnings Before Interest, Taxes, Research & Development, Amortization and Depreciation (EBITRAD), EBITDA, and Earnings Before Interest and Tax (EBIT). Of those, the most widely used is EBITDA, which effectively relates to TEV or net enterprise value. The advantage of the TEV/EBITDA ratio over the PER is demonstrated in the next table, which compares, for the year 2000, two publicly traded Canadian firms, Rogers Cablevision, a cable TV multiple systems operator, and Inco, a mining company. The table also shows that, when compared to this value multiple, exaggerated PERs can be detected.

$'000

	Rogers	*Inco*
Net Income	(100)	50
Depreciation	500	200
Interest	400	1500
Tax	-	20
EBITDA	800	420
Debt at Book Value	5,000	2,000
Market Capitalization	4,000	5,000
Total Enterprise Value	9,000	7,000
EPS $	−0.55	0.33
PER	n/a	100
TEV/EBITDA	11.3	16.7

For technology-oriented firms, the preferred value multiple is TEV/EBITRAD; this combines research and development and major marketing expenditures, such as new product launches, with EBITDA. Both additions are written off as incurred but normally result in the creation of continuing value. TEV/EBITDA generally rises with revenues, suggesting risks decline with increasing size. In the same manner, the ratio tends to fall as the EBITDA/Sales ratio goes down. This reflects the fact that a high rate of EBITDA in relation to sales is riskier than a lower one.

Price/OCF

Discretionary earnings, often referred to as owners' cash flow (OCF), give rise to the multiple most widely used by business brokers for pricing and valuing SMEs. It is defined as pretax income plus interest, noncash charges, and all compensation and benefits to the owners/managers—in other words, EBITDA plus the owners' total compensation, benefits, and optional expenses. The price/OCF, which is included in many acquisition databases, can be converted into a TEV/EBITDA ratio by these four steps:

1. Deduct the fixed assets from the "selling price" to establish notional goodwill.
2. Calculate net worth/sales and debt/sales ratios for the industry, using, in the United States, data from Risk Management Associates.
3. Use these ratios to calculate normalized net worth and debt for a given level of sales; their sum is the TEV.
4. Gather information from www.salary.com or another source to obtain a normal compensation/sales ratio, in the industry, for the owners. Deducting this from the OCF generates EBITDA.

From these amounts, calculate TEV/EBITDA, price/book value, and PSR.

Price/Book Value

The value multiples previously discussed relate to the operating statement; the final one, Price/Book Value (P/BV) which is obtained from the balance sheet, uses some version of ordinary shareholders' equity as the denominator. The multiple most often chosen is book value adjusted only for accounting differences; another is tangible book value; and a third, adjusted net asset value. The last restates financial, physical, and intangible assets to fair values, generally using the cost approach, taking into account the going concern component, which represent the costs to create certain unrecorded intangibles essential to the operation of the business.

This multiple is applied using regression in a similar manner as PSR, except that it is plotted against Return On Equity (ROE) rather than ROS. The guidelines used in the PSR example lead to these results:

	ROE %	*PBV*
Guideline 2	20.1	4.6
Guideline 9	17.9	4.2
Guideline 1	14.2	2.0
Guideline 3	13.1	3.6
Guideline 6	11.8	1.1

If the entity's ROE is 17.0 percent, linear regression results in a PBV of 3.7 times, with an R^2 of 67.8 percent as shown in Exhibit 3.3.

Exhibit 3.3 Return on Equity/Price to Book Value

Return on Equity/Price to Book Value

$$Y = 2.41398 + 0.358051X$$
$$R - Sq = 67.8\%$$

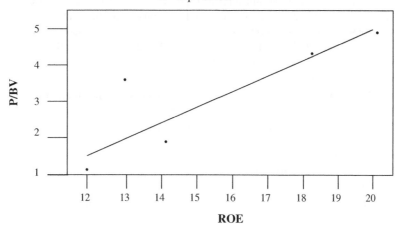

GUIDELINE SELECTION PROCESS

The results of the GCM are only as good as the selected guidelines; in choosing them, these four steps are suggested:

1. Even if you are on another continent, determine the North American Industrial Classification (NAIC) code(s) for the entity; the principal NAIC code is the single most important criterion, as valuation multiples nearly everywhere tend to be industry specific. For example, the average PSR in the United States during 2008 of computer processing firms (NAIC 54151) was 1.52, or 4.6 times the 0.33 for auto dealers (NAIC 44111).
2. List as candidates:

    a. Significant existing or potential competitors.
    b. All public companies with the same four-digit NAIC code.
    c. Entities in the NAIC group that have merged in the last year.

    The basic concept is to select publicly traded entities in the same or a comparable industry that have similar relevant investment characteristics, are financially solvent, and whose shares are not subject to speculative activity; because exact matching is not required, firms with equivalent business and financial risks are also appropriate. If the sample is too small (fewer than 10), the range may be expanded to add firms in related industries with similar underlying characteristics: markets, products, growth, or cyclical similarities.

    Locating candidates is normally not difficult, as numerous companies have sold shares to the public over the past 200 years; of them, more than 30,000 are still active. Of those, over 16,000 file reports with the SEC in the United States, which are accessible through the Internet at no cost. Nearly 12,000 are operating entities; the remaining are mutual funds, limited partnerships, and real estate investment trusts. Thousands more trade in the United States through the Over-the-Counter Bulletin Board or the Pink Sheets. Those do not have to but may file with the SEC, and their financial data are generally not as readily available.

When an entity is so unusual that it is difficult to find suitable comparables, the valuator may identify a group sufficiently similar to suggest a value multiple. Under such rare circumstances, the data for the whole group should be examined, giving extra weight to the most similar firm.

3. Obtain the latest annual and interim reports for each candidate as well as any analysts' reports; it is essential to use actual amounts rather than relying on databases.

4. Use these documents to compare the candidates with the subject; in determining if a particular one qualifies as a comparable, this external and internal criteria from United States tax cases may be helpful:

External	*Internal*
Products	**Depth/Experience of Management**
Markets	Capital structure
Nature of competition	Stage of development (maturity)
Credit status	Dividend-paying capacity
Position in industry	Earnings growth
Customer relationships	
Industries served	

Although this list is fairly comprehensive, the valuator may need to consider additional entity or industry factors, such as revenue, product mixes, location, or customer profiles; the criteria must be tailored to the specific facts and circumstances.

Comparative Analyses

Products, services, and markets	Guidelines should not deviate greatly and be reasonably similar.
Revenues	Preferably, guidelines should not have revenues of more than five times or less than 20% of the entity.
Position in industry	Do not use the dominant producer as a guideline for a low-ranked firm.
Earnings	If the candidate has a pattern of losses and profits, it is not likely a guideline for one with strongly growing earnings, or vice versa; trends and standard deviation of margins are important.
Maturity of the business	The numbers of years operating and where it stands in the product life cycle; a start-up is not a guideline for a well-established firm.
Customer relationships	Firms using distributors are not necessarily guidelines for one in direct sales.

Adjustments are normally required for:

- Size
- Capital structure (level of debt and equity)
- Credit rating
- Experience of management
- Financial, physical, and intangible assets on and off the balance sheet
- Asset utilization
- Margin stability and investment volatility

- Debt structure
- Growth potential

Based on the similarities and differences between the candidates and the subject established, the valuator will choose various guidelines.

Strategic Assessment

One important point often overlooked in selecting guidelines is a strategic assessment of the various product and services sold by the entity and the candidates. Plotting "market attractiveness" against "competitive position" for each candidate and the entity makes this relatively easy. Exhibit 3.4 illustrates nine candidates in alphabetical order, and the subject, a manufacturer, marked *. On this basis, candidates 4, 5, and 8 are not compatible.

Exhibit 3.4 Strategic Assessment

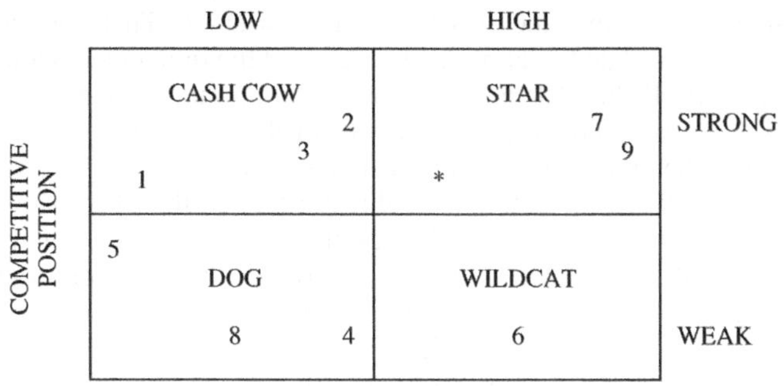

	LOW	HIGH	
	CASH COW 2 3 1	STAR 7 9 *	STRONG
COMPETITIVE POSITION	5 DOG 8 4	WILDCAT 6	WEAK

Lack of Comparability

Even applying the most careful selection process will not prevent differences in comparability, but they should never be resolved through these solutions:

- Ignore strategic assessments.
- Choose the lowest multiple of the guidelines.
- Apply the same discount to all public market multiples.
- Use a weighting scheme for market multiples based on judgment.
- Adopt a size discount reflecting lack of marketability studies.

The More the Merrier

Having more guidelines has these advantages:

- May eliminate impact of disparities in valuation multiples.
- Provides an industry benchmark as a starting point.
- Reduces reliance on firms experiencing recent changes in risks that are not reflected in their beta, usually 60 months of history.

And disadvantages:

- May sacrifice the degree of comparability.
- Requires more comparative analyses.

IMPLEMENTING THE GUIDELINE COMPANY METHOD

The GCM is most appropriate when pricing an initial public offering. It also has obvious application when valuing securities owned by an employee share ownership plan. The process has nine steps:

1. Select the guidelines as previously discussed.
2. Adopt an appropriate measurement period; as mentioned, if reliable figures are available for the guidelines, a weighted average based on the last four completed fiscal years and a projection for the current year is recommended; otherwise, the TTM is the most useful.
3. Determine any major differences between the guidelines and the subject. This requires the analyses of all financial statements. Of special importance is consideration of their relative growth and size. As Z. Christopher Mercer, a prominent valuator in the United States, stated a few years ago: "Bold adjustments (downward) of public P/E's frequently must be made before applying them to private companies. Some of the reasons for this that we all know are size, financial strength, management depth, product and geographic diversification, access to financing, etc."[5]

   By definition, the PER is the reciprocal of the capitalization rate, which is equal to the discount rate minus the growth rate, or $C = D - g$. Therefore, a portion of the PER reflects risks related to current earnings, and the remainder is attributable to the expected growth. If the PER is 9.5 (a capitalization rate of 10.5%, represented by a 15.0% discount rate and long-term growth of 4.5%), then 30% (4.5/15ths) of the PER relates to the expected annual growth in earnings.

   Size on its own appears to have a direct effect on the PER; a study by Jerry O. Peters of Mergerstat data clearly indicates that "small privately-held companies tend to sell at a significantly lower multiple of earnings than publicly-traded companies and the magnitude of the difference is directly related to the relative difference in total market value between companies."[6]

4. Calculate appropriate valuation multiples for the guidelines. As indicated, these should relate to the most comparative aspect of the subject. There are two types of multiples: those attributable to common equity and those attributable to all the entity's funds. Generally, invested capital multiples should be used to value a controlling interest, since only that kind of shareholder can modify the capital structure; the most common is TEV/EBITDA.
5. Adjust the ranges of multiples from the guidelines and apply appropriate ones to the subject.
6. Consider whether discounts or premiums are necessary.
7. Prepare valuations for all the subject's nonoperating assets.
8. Establish a range of fair values for a conclusion.
9. Undertake reality checks by alternative methodologies.

WEAKNESSES OF THE MARKET APPROACH

Completed Transaction Method

- Sufficient transactions may not be available.
- Available information may be dated.
- Many transactions may be for entities of a significantly different size.
- Data is sometimes missing or incomplete.
- Some details of actual transaction are unknown.
- Limited information to develop ratios.
- Purposes of transactions are unknown.
- Deals may or may not be at arm's length.

---

[5] *Z. Christopher Mercer*
[6] *Jerry O. Peters*

- Purchases may be synergistic in nature.
- Histories of entities sold are unknown.
- Management structures of firms sold is unspecified.
- Available sales are diverse, and no consistent figures are obtainable.

Guideline Company Method

- Not sufficient number of similar entities by NAICS code.
- Guidelines are significantly larger than subject.
- Guidelines are diversified in operations.
- Geographically the entities are more diverse.
- Firms may have complex equity structure.
- Normalization between subject and guidelines may be difficult.
- Detailed financial information may not be available.
- Management depth may be different.

Discounts

There is a distinct dichotomy among practitioners as to whether a value determined by GCM is for a minority or a controlling interest. Some believe it to be minority interest because the public market is made up of minority interests; others consider the benefit stream to be the deciding factor of control or minority. Fortunately, there is a consensus that a discount for lack of marketability is needed when valuing a minority interest. A discount for lack of control is another area of debate. Some believe none is warranted while others apply only a small figure relating to liquidity.

Weaknesses

Almost all of the data, methods, and theory for applying the Market Approach are based on perfect markets. They are then adjusted for differences in risks, comparability, and marketability to arrive at values for SMEs. The application of those subjective factors is highly dependent on accurate information. It also may be difficult to assess whether an acquisition by a public or private entity provides a buyer with synergistic efficiencies, causing the acquisition price to reflect elements of investment as opposed to fair value.

CONCLUSION

When the information is available, methods under the market approach are useful means of estimating fair values, especially when calculating fair value less costs to sell for impairment tests under International Accounting Standard 36, *Impairment of Assets*. The use of these techniques is strongly recommended as a reality check, if not as the primary method.

APPENDIX

Information on the Internet

Search for guidelines can be undertaken on the Internet, where a great deal of information, both financial and operational, concerning publicly traded entities is available. The first step is to determine the ticker symbol (see Yahoo Finance, Ticker Symbol Look-up); with this, material can be obtained at these sites:

- *One Source*: A comprehensive subscription service that can be searched by NAIC code to identify competitors, www.onesource.com
- www.reuters.com: A source of financial information on over 10,000 public companies, www.sec.gov/edgar/searchedgar/webusers.htm: The "next generation" Edgar search engine.
- Damodaran Online, http://pages.stern.nyu.edu/~adamodar: An excellent Internet source
- Hoover's Online: A respected service providing timely and detailed information on over 50,000 public and private companies
- Yahoo Market Guide: Provides summary information on companies, including financial and valuation ratios
- Corporate Information, www.corporateinformation.com: Offers worldwide company data, including profiles, research studies, reports and earnings information
- Business.com: News, research and contacts for 10,000 public and 44,000 private companies
- Industry Watch: High-level information similar to Hoover's Online but organized differently

Financial portals, which contain timely financial data, product details, and marketing trends, are found at these sites:

- Yahoo! Finance: Comprehensive data on public companies from Reuters, PR Newswire, Businesswire, and Market Guide
- Daily Stocks: Extensive company information, including quotes, profiles, charts, news, SEC filings and articles
- Wall Street Research Net: A variety of data with an excellent assortment of graphs and charts on financial performance

Industry Background

An important part of selecting guidelines is learning about the industry. Questions to consider are:

- What are the revenue trends and areas of growth?
- How do companies rank by market share?
- Which products and services are in greatest demand?
- When will new technologies have any effect?

Answers to such questions can often be found at one of these sites:

- Hoover's Industry Snapshots: Overviews of a variety of industries with links to relevant sites
- Hoover's Sector Analyses: Detailed surveys of and news articles on 28 sectors
- Yahoo! Industry News: Industry press releases and current information
- Fuld & Company, and Industry Research Desk: Links to U.S. and international industry home pages in over 30 areas

- http://valuationresources.com/: Provides a number of resources for the valuator.
- Corporate Information: Links to industry resources in more than 30 sectors
- FindArticles.com and MagPortal.com: Allow searches of over 300 periodicals, journals, and newswires
- www.ibbotson.com: Information regarding cost of capital for each industry.

4 INCOME APPROACH: CAPITALIZATION METHODS

BENNET KPENTEY

GHANA

INTRODUCTION

Capitalization of sustainable earnings is one of the most frequently adopted methods under the Income Approaches to value an asset or business; its underlying concept is that the amount a potential buyer is willing to pay for a business is directly linked to the expected rate of return, taking into consideration the associated risks.

The concept behind the method is Shakespeare's quotation "what's past is prologue," which assumes that the future benefits from ownership of the asset or business will be substantially the same as those that have previously been received. It therefore uses some average of annual historic results as a proxy for the future performance. In applying this method, all the assets of the entity, financial, physical and intangible, together contribute to generating economic benefits and as a result do not need to be separated. The basic assumption, therefore, is that the critical component to the value of the business is its current earnings.

APPLICATION

Under this method, the value of an asset or business is determined by dividing its expected economic benefits by a capitalization rate that represents the risks involved. Before using the capitalization of earnings method, a valuator has to determine two critical variables: the total economic benefits being generated and as accurate an estimate as possible of the risks associated with the economic benefits. Those and the risk-free rate are the elements that make up the applicable discount rate; the capitalization rate is obtained by deducting the expected growth.

The capitalization of earnings method can be summarized as:

$$\text{Value} = \text{Benefits in coming year } (d-g)$$

Where:

d = Discount rate
g = Growth rate

It is important to note that this formula is forward looking, as the coming year's benefits are divided by a capitalization rate which includes a growth factor. As a result, if it is to be applied to the current/latest year's figure, the capitalization rate has to be adjusted to take out the growth rate component (g); otherwise, the results will be distorted. The adjustment retroactive to the current year is to multiply the capitalization rate by the:

$$\text{Adjustment for assumed growth rate} = \frac{1}{(1+g)}$$

This formula suggests that the value of an asset or business is a function of three key variables:

1. Measure of the economic benefits (net earnings)
2. Discount rate
3. Growth rate

ECONOMIC BENEFITS

The economic benefits of a business can be defined in several ways depending on which measure is most appropriate under the given circumstances. Valuators use a wide range of earning indicators to gauge the economic benefits generated by an asset or business. To a large extent, they depend on the purpose of the assignment and are influenced by the method selected (see Chapter 11). The most common are:

- Earnings before interest, taxes, depreciation, and amortization (EBITDA)
- Earnings before interest and taxes (EBIT)
- Earnings before taxes (EBT)
- Net earnings
- Earnings available to ordinary shareholders (after preferred dividends)
- Activity earnings (EBITDA less taxes actually paid)

When valuators are confronted with such a wide range of choices, it is important to stress that, whichever particular definition they select, the figure adopted should be complemented by adjustments appropriate to the specific item being valued.

ANALYSES OF HISTORIC PERFORMANCE

Adjustments to historic financial statements, after extensive analyses, are essential to determining the level of maintainable earnings of an entity. The reason is that the reported financial statements may not reflect true earnings power; as a result, they cannot necessarily be taken at face value. This may be due to several factors, including underlying differences between cost- and cash-based accounting systems; for example, the depreciation method adopted may distort profits by altering the timing of their realization.

The valuator therefore has a responsibility to review and analyze past financial statements and make the necessary adjustments required to normalize the reported amounts. Doing this will provide a more precise overview of the entity's past economic benefits.

Detailed year-on-year analyses of the entity's historic financial statements will provide the valuator with adequate information to understand fully issues such as:

- Variances between projected gross margins and those actually realized
- Alternative for financing growth in the absence of the ability to borrow
- The effect of budgeted capital expenditures on returns on total assets
- How historic loss positions may be transformed into future profits
- Changes in depreciation policies
- Sustainability of future stable growth

It is essential that the analyses of the historic financial performance of a business are backed by a good grasp of the external environment within which the entity operates, as this may have an impact on earnings. A good understanding of this context will strengthen the valuator's appreciation of the sustainability of the relevant earnings.

WHICH EARNINGS TO CAPITALIZE?

Some valuators use the earning of a single period (normally the last full fiscal year) as a proxy for the figure to be capitalized. Others take some representation of historic performance, such as, for instance, the mean or median of the past three to five years. A common technique is a weighted average with more emphasis on the most recent results. The most important consideration is to ensure that the review period is long enough to cover cyclical fluctuations and takes into account factors such as the length of the business cycle, which varies across industries. Good professional judgment with respect to the period of review is an important consideration in establishing earnings that are truly representative of the firm's future operations.

Even when the appropriate basis has been established, a number of conventions indicate which level of earnings to capitalize. Examples of the range of possible earnings that can be capitalized are set out next.

Gloria Plantation Limited $'000

		2004	2005	2006	2007	2008	2009 *Projection*	*Possible Figure*
Entity Data								
Normalized Net Earnings		1,790	1,650	1,905	2,100	2,436	2,300	2,030
Growth			−7.8%	15.5%	10.2%	16.0%	−5.6%	
Inflation Rate		6.0%	8.0%	10.0%	12.0%	6.0%	3.0%	
Inflation Factor		1.000	1.040	1.134	1.213	1.308	1.305	
Real Net Earnings 2004 $		1,790	1,587	1,680	1,732	1,862	1,763	1,736
Real Growth			−11.4%	5.9%	3.1%	7.5%	−5.3%	
Real Net Earnings 2008 $		2,342	2,075	2,198	2,265	2,436	2,306	2,270
Real Weighted Averages								
2004–2008	Weights	1	2	3	4	5		
	Product	2,342	4,151	6,593	9,062	12,180		2,288
2006–2009	Weights			1	2	4	3	
	Product			2,198	4,531	9,744	6,919	2,339
Real Means								
2004–2009		2,342	2,075	2,198	2,265	2,436	2,306	2,270
2004–2008		2,342	2,075	2,198	2,265	2,436		2,263
2006–2009				2,198	2,265	2,436	2,306	2,301
Real Medians								
2004–2008		2,342	2,075	2,198	2,265	2,436		2,265
2006–2009				2,198	2,265	2,436	2,306	2,280
Average of 7 Choices								2,287

This partial list, which omits trend line and other projections for 2009, shows that, in a country with significant inflation, a valuator should restate past earnings to current dollars before applying any conventions. Seven of the most common methods (2 real weighted average, 3 real means, and 2 real medians) are illustrated in the table. Adding the last completed year (2008) and the projection for the next (2009) gives a valuator nine possible measures with significant variances. Care is required in selecting the most appropriate measure, given the potential distortion that may occur if the wrong selection is made. Generally, an arithmetic mean of the last three to five years is recommended.

NORMALIZATION ADJUSTMENTS

Reported earnings often do not truly reflect an entity's normal capacity to generate economic benefits. This is because earnings are a residual, calculated as revenues less costs; small variations in either revenues or expenses may have a significant bearing on net earnings. Consequently, the valuator should look behind financial statements, ascertain, and adjust for items which are not representative of the entity's ongoing earning capacity (see Chapter 11). For example, the accounting of private companies is often tax driven. It is therefore not uncommon for them to show a history of poor profitability but to accumulate a relatively large asset base. An understanding of the entity's operations and the motivations of the owners is paramount, as entrepreneurs typically are concerned with cash flow and wealth creation, not paying income tax.

Through the normalization of the financial statements, relevant adjustments may be made for understatement of revenues, overstatement of costs, and inclusion of personal items, so that the bottom line is not representative of the firm's ongoing earning capacity. Among the potential adjustments are:

- Standardization of accounting policies to International Financial Reporting Standards consistently applied
- Elimination of unusual transactions
- Correction of excessive or inadequate owners' remuneration
- Financing costs when an alternative funding structure is anticipated or where borrowing is at a fixed rate and interest rates have moved significantly
- Nonrecurring items
- Income and expenses from non–arm's-length transactions
- Personal ownership of assets used in the business
- Whether depreciation policy correctly reflects asset consumption

The objective in adjusting historic results is to arrive at a representative level of maintainable earnings for the entity. Significant care is required when assuming that past growth rates for profit or revenue will continue into the future and when using them as value drivers for projections.

Once unusual transactions have been identified and the necessary adjustments have been made, the valuator should have arrived at a reasonable estimate of the earnings to be capitalized that truly reflects the entity's situation.

Core Earnings

An important concept is core earnings, that are described by Thomsett.[1] This is similar to sustainable net income and has gained ground among valuators attempting to define accurately the earnings to be capitalized.

Core earnings is a measure of the recurring operating income derived from an entity's "core" business and excludes revenues and expenses from unrelated activities. Underlying the notion is the general belief that accounting statements often contain amounts not directly associated with the operations or that they do not report some that are associated with the operations; possible adjustments are:

- Employee share options: the fair value of current year options is expensed
- Impairment or amortization of goodwill is added back
- Capital gains and losses are removed as nonrecurring items
- Pension gains are excluded, as such income relies on projected rates of return
- Litigation and insurance settlements are excluded as nonrecurring items

Once these and other adjustments, which may become necessary after thorough analyses of the financial statements and related notes, have been made, the resulting earnings are expected to represent truly only the core business of the entity.

---

[1]   *Michael Thomsett, **Stock Profits: Getting to the Core: New Fundamentals for a New Age** (Financial Times Prentice Hall, 2004).*

CAPITALIZATION RATE

A capitalization rate is a risk-weighted yield used to convert a single payment or measure of economic benefits from an asset or entity into a present value while a discount rate converts all expected future payments or benefits to a present value. The capitalization rate represents only the current rate of return that is received in a single period, as opposed to the related discount rate, which represents the total rate of return.[2]

Relation with Discount Rate

It is not uncommon to find a capitalization rate incorrectly used as if it were interchangeable with a discount rate. Even though the two names are similar and one is calculated from the other, they are essentially different; therefore, the maintenance of their distinction is imperative if estimates of values are not to be distorted.

In a typical valuation, the discounted cash flow method, where expected cash flows are projected into the future and then discounted back to the present, can readily be applied to estimate the value of an entity. Mathematically, experience has shown that, if the growth rate is fairly stable, it may not be necessary to undertake a painstaking projection of cash flows. The same amount will be obtained if the historic earnings are divided by the capitalization rate in what is referred to as a single-period method; the capitalization rate is the discount rate less the growth rate.

Calculation of Discount Rate

While the growth rate is normally established from historic financial performance, the discount rate is calculated through an elaborate process. The two main techniques used in estimating the cost of equity for discount rates are the Capital Asset Pricing Model (CAPM) and the build-up model; this chapter focuses on the build-up model. For CAPM, see Chapter 9.

The build-up model defines the discount rate in terms of a composite of multiple risk elements, including the risk-free rate of return (normally the yield on government bonds with an appropriate term) plus the extra return expected by investors for investing in equity securities (equity risk premium), as well as expected additional returns to compensate for specific risks related to the industry and firm. The greater the risks of any entity, the higher the discount rate necessary to compensate investors; the components of the build-up model are:

- Risk-free rate
- Equity risk premium
- Industry premium
- Specific entity premium
- Assessment of risks

Risk-free rate. Since any investment should return at least as much as a riskless asset, the risk-free rate is the starting point of the model. Typically, it is the yield to maturity, as of the valuation date, on government bonds with a term that matches the expected hold period of the asset or entity.

Equity risk premium. The equity risk premium (EPR) is the extra return an investor expects as compensation for the additional risks associated with investing in equities rather than government bonds. It is estimated by subtracting the long-term average income return on riskless assets from the average stock market return over the same period. The EPR normally is estimated from historic trends and other factors. Obviously it changes over time and

---

[2] *See Shannon P. Pratt, **Cost of Capital: Estimation and Applications** (Hoboken, NJ: John Wiley & Sons, 2002).*

between countries. A survey by Pablo Fernandez, of IESS Business School in Pamplona, Spain (IEES Research Paper D/796), determined that, at business schools, in 2008 before the crash, ERP was higher than in 2007 by 0.3% in both the United States and the euro area, 0.6% in Britain and 0.2% in Canada; in Australia, driven by a mining boom, and in the rest of the world, ERP was lower by 0.1% and 0.2% respectively. The next table sets out the survey's 2008 figures for 18 countries.

	Mean	Standard Deviation	Median		Mean	Standard Deviation	Median
Australia	5.9%	1.4%	6.0%	Isreal	7.3%	3.1%	7.5%
Belgium	4.1%	0.8%	3.9%	Italy	4.9%	1.5%	5.0%
Britain	5.5%	1.9%	5.0%	Netherlands	5.3%	1.5%	5.5%
Canada	5.4%	1.3%	5.1%	Norway	5.6%	1.6%	5.0%
China	6.3%	1.9%	5.5%	Portugal	5.9%	1.0%	5.8%
Finland	5.3%	1.9%	4.5%	Singapore	6.6%	1.7%	6.5%
France	5.9%	2.0%	5.8%	Spain	5.4%	1.5%	5.0%
Germany	4.8%	1.3%	4.9%	Switzerland	5.6%	1.4%	5.5%
India	10.5%	4.4%	8.0%	United States	6.3%	2.2%	6.0%

Industry premium. An industry risk premium is needed in the build-up model to quantify the entity's industry-related risks or benefits; the distinction between risks and benefits results mainly from industries falling into and out of favor with investors. To quantify accurately such risks, a full information beta, reflecting pure-play securities within the industry, generally is preferred. That premium offers a better measure of systematic risk than the risk differential between large and small company shares.

Specific entity premium. The specific entity premium is added in the build-up model to reflect risks specific to the entity which may not have been captured by the preceding elements. It covers factors such as cyclicality, competitive encroachment, size, operating concentrations, key-executive dependency, and customer concentration.

Assessment of risks. To determine accurately the risks involved, a valuator should undertake thorough analyses of the entity, taking into account both internal and external factors. Even though the risks and the relevant issues vary across sectors and individual entities, the areas that should be covered include:

- Management (strength and weaknesses, technical capacity, retention, etc.)
- Products/marketing (stage in life cycle, brand strength, distribution system, research and development, etc.)
- Customers (concentration versus diversification, nature of long-term relationships, contracts, financial strength of major customers, loyalty to brand, etc.)
- Suppliers (single or multiple sources, bargaining power, long-term contracts on favorable [unfavorable] terms/prices, difficulty or ease of accessing raw materials, etc.)
- External and competitive context (economic outlook, government regulations, relative strengths and weaknesses of competitors, barriers to entry, market shares of players, etc.)
- Intangible assets (patents, trademark, copyrights, proprietary technology, etc.)

This list covers a sample of possible issues to be addressed to establish the risk parameters adequately; substantial time and effort are required to quantify the potential risks for a valuation properly.

Example: Capitalization of Earnings

Pongo Palm Limited
Valuation of Business

Calculation of Sustainable Net Earnings			$'000
Normalized EBIT	Growth	5,351	
2006	11.6%	5,971	
2007	9.8%	6,556	
2008	10.7%	17,878	
3-year Average Normalized EBIT			5,959
Current Year's Interest			(1,352)
Interest Coverage			4.4
Sustainable Earnings Before Taxes			4,607
Income Tax		30%	(1,382)
Sustainable Net Earnings			3,225
Normalized Net Earnings 2008			3,643
Reported Net Earnings 2008			2,735
Normalization Increase			33%
Calculation of Adjusted Capitalization Rate			
Risk-Free Rate			6.0%
Equity Risk Premium			7.5%
Industry Premium			3.0%
Entity-Specific Premium			5.0%
Discount Rate ("d")			21.50%
Expected Annual Income Growth Rate ("G")			10.00%
Implied Capitalization Rate			11.50%
Growth Adjustment (1/1+g)			0.91
Adjusted Capitalization Rate			10.45%
Calculation of Fair Value			**$'000**
Sustainable Net Earnings			3,225
Adjusted Capitalization Rate			10.45%
Calculated Fair Value			30,849
Rounded Fair Value			31,000

Sensitivity of Capitalization Rate

It is essential that estimating the capitalization rate is undertaken with care; as shown in the next table, minor variations can have enormous impact on the final value.

Pongo Palm Limited
Sensitivity of Valuation

Sustainable Net Earnings		$'000	3,225	
Calculated Values at Various Capitalization Rates				
Rate	10.00%	10.45%	11.00%	11.50%
$'000	32,251	30,849	29,319	28,045
Change	4.55%	0.00%	–4.96%	–9.09%

An earnings multiple or price earnings ratio (PER) is the inverse of a capitalization rate. In the example just given, the 10.45% rate is equivalent to a multiple of 9.57(100/10.45) times. This is useful information for the valuator, as it allows benchmarking against publicly traded comparables whose PER is available daily; it also may give an indication as to whether the estimated value is too high or low.

Problems with Earnings Measures

The use of net earnings as a measure of economic benefits presents problems to some valuators who hold the view that management can manipulate earnings by modifying accruals. This group has a strong preference for cash flows, which it considers to be more reliable. However, cash flows may be influenced by changes in timings. Therefore, notwithstanding management's ability to affect net earnings, it is a generally accepted starting point to determine the present and future cash results of the entity's activities, regardless of when items are received or paid.

When Is the Method Suitable?

The capitalization of earnings method can be applied to value most ongoing businesses; however, it is most valid where the:

- Current growth rate is stable, with expected changes being predictable and moderate enough for the relationships to hold.
- Business has recently undertaken necessary major capital expenditures (apart from ongoing maintenance).

Businesses that are heavily indebted and have significant ongoing capital requirements should use the capitalization of earnings method. However, it should be used with caution. When used in such situations, the calculated value should be cross-checked against one from methods under the cost approach.

5 INCOME APPROACH: DISCOUNTING METHOD

WOLFGANG KNIEST

GERMANY

INTRODUCTION

According to International Financial Reporting Standards (IFRS) 3 (Revised), *Impact on Earnings*, the three fundamental valuation approaches, income, market, and cost, are generally employed in measuring the fair value of:

- An entity
- Individual assets or liabilities
- Noncontrolling interests
- Previously held equity interests

The nature and characteristics of the entity, assets or liabilities, or equity interest being measured will influence which techniques are appropriate.

The Income Approach applies several methods to convert estimated future amounts to a single capital sum. Those methods may involve either capitalization of some form of earnings or discounting future benefits. The most common is capitalization of earnings, while the most satisfactory is the discounted cash flow (DCF) method, which requires:

- Estimating future after-tax economic income for a projected period
- Projecting a terminal amount (if appropriate)
- Discounting those amounts to a present value at a rate of return that accounts for the time value of money and the relative risks, whether the expected benefits materialize or not

Common variations of the Income Approach for the valuation of intangible assets include the relief from royalty, incremental income, and excess earnings methods.

International Accounting Standard (IAS) 36 has a one-step impairment test that differs significantly from the two-step methods of Statement of Financial Accounting Standards (SFAS) 142 and SFAS 144; it will yield different results based on the same facts and circumstances. In this test, an asset or cash-generating unit (CGU) is impaired when its carrying amount exceeds its "recoverable amount." According to IAS 36.18, the latter is the higher of "fair value less cost to sell" or "value in use." The value in-use is specified in detail in IAS 36.30 to IAS 36.57 and involves discounting the future pretax economic income as defined at an appropriate pretax discount rate (IAS 36.55 and IAS 36.BCZ85).

DISCOUNTING PROCEDURES

All discounting methods start with these expressions:

$$V_0 = \frac{I_1}{(1+k)^1} + \frac{I_2}{(1+k)^2} + \frac{I_3}{(1+k)^3} + \ldots + \frac{I_{T-1}}{(1+k)^{T-1}} + \frac{TV_{T-1}}{(1+k)^{T-1}} \qquad (5.1)$$

Where:

V_0	=	(Present) value
I_i	=	expected economic income generated in the period i
TV_{T-1}	=	Terminal value
$T-1$	=	last year of the discrete planning period
k	=	appropriate discount rate for the risk of the income and time value of money

Terminal Value

If appropriate, a terminal value (TV) is included at the end of the projected period (Y_{T-1}) to reflect the value of the benefits expected to be generated thereafter. For business entities, this is usually assumed to be in perpetuity, because they generally have indefinite lives. For a relatively new firm, an assumption may have to be made as to its expected life after the end of the projection period (e.g., future liquidation value). The terminal value in year T is discounted by the same present value factor as the economic income of the final year ($T-1$) of the projection period.

Often the terminal value is calculated using the Gordon growth model, which is equivalent to a capitalization technique.[1]

$$TV_{T-1} = \frac{I_T}{k - g_I}$$

Where:

I_T	=	expected sustainable economic income
g_I	=	expected long-term sustainable growth rate in the economic income

Two-Stage Model

Equation 5.1 describes the second, capitalization, stage of a typical two-stage discounting model (see Chapter 4). This is applicable if the assumptions at the end of the projection period (year $T-1$) relating to operations, net working capital, fixed asset investments and debt policy are expected to remain more or less unchanged in the future.

Example: Two-Stage Model, Infinite Life

Assumptions

Discount Rate	12.0%	Long-Term Growth	2.0%	Valuation Date:	31 December 2008
Capitalization Rate	10.0%	Transition Period	None		

---

[1] *See J. B. Williams, "Theory of Investment Value" (1938) and M. J. Gordon and E. Shapiro, "Capital Investment Analysis: The Required Rate of Profit," **Management Science** (1956): 102–110.*

	2008	2009	2010	2011	2012	$'000 2013	Terminal Amount
	Actual			Projected			
Cash Flow	113.1	100.0	104.6	110.2	113.1	110.1	112.3
Growth		-11.6%	4.6%	5.4%	2.6%	-2.7%	2.0%
Terminal Amount							1,123.00
PV Factors							
Year-End		0.8929	0.7972	0.7118	0.6355	0.5674	0.5674
Midyear		0.9434	0.8423	0.7521	0.6715	0.5995	0.5995
Last Quarter		0.9050	0.8080	0.7214	0.6441	0.5751	0.5751
Present Values							
Year-End		$ 89.3	$ 83.4	$ 78.4	$ 71.9	$ 62.5	$ 637.2
Midyear		$ 94.3	$ 88.1	$ 82.9	$ 75.9	$ 66.0	$ 673.3
Last Quarter		$ 90.5	$ 84.5	$ 79.5	$ 72.9	$ 63.3	$ 645.9
DCF Value	Year-End	$1,023	Midyear	$1,081	Last Quarter	$1,037	

Three-Stage Model

If the value-driver assumptions for income margins, growth rates, capital turnover, and net investments (capital expenditure [CAPEX] less depreciation) for the last projected year differ significantly from those expected for the terminal period, a convergence period should be added between the projected period (normally years 1 to 5) and the terminal period (say year 10 onward). The resulting three-stage (or multistage) discounting model provides the possibility to adjust the value driver assumptions to reflect steady state conditions at the beginning of the terminal year.[2]

Discounting Conventions

The discounting procedure for the three stage model will be the same as in equation 5.1, which assumes that the expected income is received at the end of each year. However, if it is normally fairly realistic to assume that the benefit streams are more or less evenly distributed throughout the year, the discounting procedure should be modified for the so-called midyear convention:

$$V_0 = \frac{1_1}{(1+k)^{0.5}} + \frac{1_2}{(1+k)^{1.5}} + \frac{1_3}{(1+k)^{2.5}} + ... + \frac{1_{T-1}}{(1+k)^{T-15}} + \frac{TV_{T-1}}{(1+k)^{T-15}} \quad (5.2)$$

If the annual projected income streams are identical in equations 5.1 and 5.2, the midyear convention will produce a higher value because it assumes the investor receives the benefit streams half a year earlier.

The general relationship is:

$$V_0^{midyear} = V_0^{end\ of\ year} \times (1+k)^{0.5} \quad (5.3)$$

For retailers, whose profits are usually earned in the fourth quarter of the fiscal year generally ending January 31 of the next calendar year, a last-quarter convention $(1+k)^{0.875}$ is used. The previous and next examples display the results for the end of year, midyear, and last quarter conventions.

---

[2] See J. Levin, *Essays in Company Valuation* (Stockholm: Stockholm School of Economics, 1998), p. 45.

Example: Three-Stage Model, Infinite Life

Assumptions

Discount Rate	12.0%	Long-Term Growth	2.0%	Valuation Date: 31 December 2008	
Capitalization Rate	10.0%	Transition Period	4 years		

	2008	2009	2010	2011	2012	$'000 2013
	Actual	------	------	----Projected----	------	------
Cash Flow	113.1	100.0	116.0	129.9	142.9	154.3
Growth		–11.6%	16.0%	12.0%	10.0%	8.0%
PV Factors						
Year-End		0.8929	0.7972	0.7118	0.6355	0.5674
Midyear		0.9434	0.8423	0.7521	0.6715	0.5995
Last Quarter		0.9050	0.8080	0.7214	0.6441	0.5751
Present Values						
Year-End		$ 89.3	$ 83.4	$ 78.4	$ 71.9	$ 62.5
Midyear		$ 94.3	$ 88.1	$ 82.9	$ 75.9	$ 66.0
Last Quarter		$ 90.5	$ 84.5	$ 79.5	$ 72.9	$ 63.3

	2014	2015	2016	2017	Terminal Amount
	------	------	----Projected----	------	------
Cash Flow	163.6	171.8	178.7	184.0	187.7
Growth	6.0%	5.0%	4.0%	3.0%	2.0%
Terminal Amount					1,877.00
PV Factors					
Year-End	0.5066	0.4523	0.4039	0.3606	0.3606
Midyear	0.5353	0.4780	0.4267	0.3810	0.3810
Last Quarter	0.5135	0.4585	0.4094	0.3655	0.3655
Present Values					
Year-End	$ 82.9	$ 77.7	$ 72.2	$ 66.4	$ 676.9
Midyear	$ 87.6	$ 82.1	$ 76.2	$ 70.1	$ 715.2
Last Quarter	$ 84.0	$ 78.8	$ 73.1	$ 67.3	$ 686.1
DCF Value Year-End	$ 1,361	Midyear	$ 1,439	Last Quarter	$ 1,380

Finite Lives

Assets with finite useful lives are valued by discounting their anticipated future income year by year over them.

Example: One-Stage Model, Finite Life

Assumptions

Discount Rate	12.0%	Long-Term Growth	2.0%	Valuation Date: 31 December 2008	
Capitalization Rate	10.0%	Remaining Life	9 years		

	2008	2009	2010	2011	2012	$'000 2013
	Actual	------	------	----Projected----	------	------
Cash Flow	$113.10	$ 100.0	$104.60	110.20	$113.10	$ 110.10
Growth		–11.6%	4.6%	5.4%	2.6%	–2.7%
PV Factors						
Year-End		0.5066	0.4523	0.4039	0.3606	0.3606
Midyear		0.5353	0.4780	0.4267	0.3810	0.3810
Last Quarter		0.5135	0.4585	0.4094	0.3655	0.3655
Present Values						
Year-End		$ 50.7	$ 47.3	$ 44.5	$ 40.8	$ 39.7
Midyear		$ 53.5	$ 50.0	$ 47.0	$ 43.1	$ 42.0
Last Quarter		$ 51.4	$ 48.0	$ 45.1	$ 41.3	$ 40.2

	2014	2015	2016	2017
	----------------------------Projected--------------------			
Cash Flow	$112.3	$ 114.5	$116.8	$ 119.2
Growth	2.0%	2.0%	2.0%	2.0%
Terminal Amount				
PV Factors				
Year-End	0.5066	0.4523	0.4039	0.3606
Mid-Year	0.5353	0.4780	0.4267	0.3810
Last Quarter	0.5135	0.4585	0.4094	0.3655
Present Values				
Year-End	$ 82.9	$ 77.7	$ 72.2	$ 66.4
Mid-Year	$ 87.6	$ 82.1	$ 76.2	$ 70.1
Last Quarter	$ 84.0	$ 78.8	$ 73.1	$ 67.3

DCF Value	Year-End	$ 522.1	Midyear	$ 551.6	Last Quarter	$ 529.2

Partial-Year Adjustments

If the valuation date is not the entity's fiscal year-end, partial-year adjustments should be made. The next example has a valuation date of August 31, 2009. The income projections are first assumed to be realized at the end of each future year (end-of-year discounting). Assuming an equal distribution of income over the months, from the perspective of the valuation date, the partial period represents four of the 12 months of the first calendar year (33.4%).

Exhibit 5.1 Timeline for Valuation Date August 31, 2009 (End-of-Year Discounting)

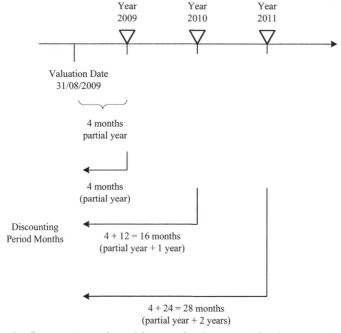

Therefore, the first year's projected income is discounted for four-month partial period; each subsequent projected year is discounted for the partial period plus one year. The next example displays those discounting procedures.

Example: Two-Stage Model, Infinite Life, Partial-Year, Year-End Discounting

Assumptions

Discount Rate	12.0%	Long-Term Growth	2.0%	Valuation Date: 31 August 2009	
Capitalization Rate	10.0%	Transition Period	None		

	2008	2009	2010	2011	2012	$'000 2013	Terminal Amount
	Actual	Projected					
Cash Flow	$ 113.1	$ 100.0	$ 104.6	$ 110.2	$113.1	$ 110.1	$ 112.3
Growth		–11.6%	4.6%	5.4%	2.6%	–2.7%	2.0%
Terminal Amount							1,123.00
Partial-Year Adjustment		33.4%					
PV Factors							
Discounting Period Years		0.3342	1.3342	2.3342	3.3342	4.3342	4.3342
Year-End		0.9614	0.8584	0.7665	0.6843	0.6110	0.6110
Present Values							
Year-End		$ 32.1	$ 89.8	$ 84.5	$ 77.4	$ 67.3	$ 686.2
DCF Value	Year-End	$1,037					

Midyear Discounting

Assuming midyear discounting, the first income is expected to be realized two months after the valuation date, which is half of the partial period. The first full year's income following the partial period is then anticipated to occur 10 months after the valuation date, as shown in Exhibit 5.2.

Exhibit 5.2 Timeline for Valuation Date August 31, 2009 (Midyear Discounting)

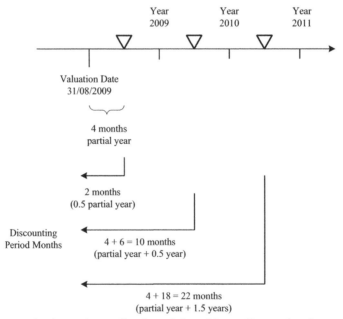

The next example shows the application of the midyear discounting for a valuation date of August 31, 2009.

Example: Two-Stage Model, Infinite Life, Partial-Year, Midyear Discounting

Assumptions

Discount Rate	12.0%	Long-Term Growth	2.0%	Valuation Date: 31 August 2009		
Capitalization Rate	10.0%	Transition Period	None			

	2008	2009	2010	2011	2012	$'000 2013	Terminal Amount
	Actual----	-------------	--------------	--Projected--	------------	----------	
Cash Flow	$ 113.1	$ 100.0	$ 104.6	$110.2	$113.1	$110.1	$ 112.3
Growth		–11.6%	4.6%	5.4%	2.6%	–2.7%	2.0%
Terminal Amount							1,123.00
Partial-Year Adjustment		33.4%					
PV Factors							
Discounting Period Years		0.167	0.834	1.834	2.834	3.834	3.834
Midyear		0.9804	0.9090	0.8116	0.7247	0.6470	0.6470
Present Values							
Midyear		$ 32.8	$ 95.1	$ 89.4	$ 82.0	$ 71.2	$ 726.6
DCF Value		Midyear	$1,097				

SELECTING INCOME STREAMS

The income stream is defined differently, depending on which discounting method is selected. Equity can be valued directly using some version of cash flow, normally flow to equity (FTE), or indirectly, by first calculating the value of the invested capital. This is the total of the fair values of interest-bearing debt, preferred shares, and ordinary share equity. It is known as total enterprise value (TEV) using the free cash flows (FCFs) and then subtracting the value of the net debt.

Free cash flow is that available to the entity's suppliers of capital (both debt and equity) after all operating expenses and corporate taxes have been paid, and necessary investments in fixed assets and net working capital have been made (see Chapter 11).

FTE is that portion of the FCF that accrues to the equity holder after all transactions with respect to the debt (interest, principal repayments, new debt issued) have been made. In addition, the FTE includes the benefits of tax deductibility of interest payments (tax shields). Therefore, the firm's choice of capital structure has an impact on it.

Calculation of Flow to Equity and Free Cash Flow

Equity Application		**Entity Application**	
EBIT		EBIT	
Less	Interest expenses		
=	EBT less taxes	Less	Related taxes on EBIT
=	Net earnings	=	Net operating profit after tax (NOPAT)
Plus/Less	Noncash expenses/income	Plus/Less	Noncash expenses/income
Plus/Less	Change in noncash net working capital	Plus/Less	Change in noncash net working capital
Less	Capital expenditures	Less	Capital expenditures
Plus	New debt raised		
Less	Debt repayments		
=	Flow to equity	=	Free cash flow

In other words, FCF is the operating cash flow after taxes of a (hypothetically) debt-free entity; FTE is the operating cash flow after taxes paid by the firm and all payments to and from the debt holders (see Chapter 12).

When the entity is neither growing nor shrinking (and therefore net working capital remains constant), spends on fixed assets an amount identical to its depreciation charges, keeps debt constant, and only writes off or sells assets which are fully depreciated, the FCF equals the NOPAT and the FTE equals the net earnings.

Example: Relationship between FCF and FTE

Assumptions

Tax Rate	30.0%	Long-Term Growth	3.5%	Valuation Date: 31 December 2008	
Capitalization Rate	10.0%	Transition Period	None		

Income Statement

	2008	2009	2010	2011	2012	$'000 2013
	Actual	------	------	--Projected--	------	------
Sales	3,700	3,000	3,500	3,200	3,312	3,428
Growth		–18.9%	16.7%	–8.6%	3.5%	3.5%
Cost of Sales	(1,400)	(1,000)	(1,300)	(1,200)	(1,242)	(1,278)
Gross Profit	2,300	2,000	2,200	2,000	2,070	2,150
Margin	62.2%	66.7%	62.9%	62.5%	62.5%	62.7%
Expenses						
Operating	(700)	(600)	(650)	(700)	(700)	(700)
Depreciating	(260)	(230)	(200)	(170)	(170)	(170)
EBIT	1,340	1,170	1,350	1,130	1,200	1,280
Interest–net	(200)	(200)	(250)	(140)	(140)	(140)
EBIT	1,140	970	1,100	990	1,060	1,140
Income Taxes	(342)	(291)	(330)	(297)	(318)	(342)
Net Earnings	798	679	770	693	742	798
Margin	21.6%	22.6%	22.0%	21.7%	22.4%	23.3%

Example: Two Stage Model Infinite Life

Assumptions

Discount Rate	12.0%	Long-Term Growth	2.0%	Valuation Date: 31 December 200?	
Capitalization Rate	10.0%	Transition Period	None		

	2008	2009	2010	2011	2012	2013
	Actual	------	------	--Projected--	------	------
Cash Flow	113.1	100.0	104.60	110.2	113.1	110.10
Growth		–11.6%	4.6%	5.4%	2.6%	–2.7%
Terminal Amount						
PV Factors						
Year-End		0.8929	0.7972	0.7118	0.6355	0.5674
Midyear		0.9434	0.8423	0.7521	0.6715	0.5995
Last Quarter		0.9050	0.8080	0.7214	0.6441	0.5751
Present Values						
Year-End		$ 89.3	$ 83.4	$ 78.4	$ 71.9	$ 62.5
Midyear		$ 94.3	$ 88.1	$ 82.9	$ 75.9	$ 66.0

	Actual		--Projected--		
Business Value		15,123	15,620	15,967	16,247
Tax Shield		1,658	1,598	1,567	1,566
Total Enterprise Value		16,781	17,218	17,534	17,813
Debt Beginning		(10,000)	(9,000)	(8,000)	(7,000)
Equity Value		6,781	8,218	9,534	10,813
D/E Ratio at Market		147.5%	109.5%	83.9%	64.7%
E/(D+E) Ratio at Market		40.4%	47.7%	54.4%	60.7%
D/)E+D) Ratio at Market		59.6%	52.3%	45.6%	39.3%

Equity Application

The next tables show the calculation of both the FCF and the FTE and the conversion of one to the other.

Free Cash Flow $'000

	2008	2009	2010	2011	2012	2013
	Actual	------------------------Projected------------------------				
EBIT	1,340	1,170	1,350	1,130	1,200	1,280
Related Tax	(402)	(351)	(405)	(339)	(360)	(384)
NOPAT	938	819	945	791	840	896
Depreciation	260	230	200	170	170	170
CAPEX	(200)	(100)	(200)	(300)	(50)	(50)
Inventory/Rec	(60)	(50)	(30)	(20)	(20)	(10)
Payables	20	20	10	10	10	50
Provisions	--	--	--	300	--	--
Free Cash Flow	958	919	925	951	950	1,056

Flow to Equity $'000

	2008	2009	2010	2011	2012	2013
	Actual	------------------------Projected------------------------				
Net Earnings	798	679	770	693	742	798
Depreciation	260	230	200	170	170	170
CAPEX	(200)	(100)	(200)	(300)	(50)	(50)
Inventory/Rec	(60)	(50)	(30)	(20)	(20)	(10)
Payables	20	20	10	10	10	50
Provisions	0	0	0	300	0	0
Repayments	(100)	(150)	(500)	(100)	(50)	(50)
Borrowings	--	100	100	50	--	--
Flow to Equity	718	729	350	803	802	908

Flow to Equity from Free Cash Flow $'000

	2008	2009	2010	2011	2012	2013
	Actual	------------------------Projected------------------------				
Free Cash Flow	958	919	925	951	950	1,056
Repayments	(100)	(150)	(500)	(100)	(50)	(50)
Borrowings	0	100	100	50	0	0
Interest—net	(200)	(200)	(250)	(140)	(140)	(140)
Tax Shield	60	60	75	42	42	42
Flow to Equity	718	729	350	803	802	908

Because of its dependency on the capital structure, the FTE has a higher exposure to the effects of future changes in leverage than the FCF. Assuming a constant cost of equity, if, using market values, future debt to equity ratios are expected to change, mistakes in projecting FTE are to be expected. However, the FTE model is especially suitable for valuing financial institutions (e.g., banks and insurance companies).

Entity Application

Using the entity application to calculate the equity value of a business requires the net debt to be deducted from the TEV. Net debt is defined as the market values of the interest-bearing debt less financial assets. The earnings/cost of those financial liabilities/assets included in the net-debt should not be reflected in the EBIT. As most such financial items are short term, their face amounts are often acceptable as proxies for market values.

SELECTING APPROPRIATE DISCOUNT RATES

Depending on which method is selected, the appropriate discount rate will differ.

Equity Application

For the equity application (FTE), the discount rate is the cost of equity. This is often estimated based on the Capital Asset Pricing Model (CAPM), modified CAPM, or a build-up method. (See Chapters 9 and 10.)

$$k_E^l = i_{rf} + \left(r_M - i_{rf}\right) \times \beta^l \qquad (5.4)$$

Where:

k_E^l = cost of equity (levered)

i_{rf} = risk free rate

$r_M - i_{rf}$ = market risk premium

β^l = Levered beta

Discounting the FTE by the cost of equity results directly in an equity value. A CAPM cost of equity is commonly developed using levered equity betas derived from past data for publicly traded shares via regression analyses. Normally the calculations are based on monthly return data for the last five years or weekly for the last two or three years. It assumes that this historic measured beta is the best estimate of the relevant future beta.

Sometimes adjusted betas are used to incorporate a forward-looking perspective. For example, Morningstar, in its Beta Book, includes adjusted betas to reflect the position that, in the long run, an entity's beta tends to revert to its industry's average.[3] Another view is that, over time, an entity's beta tends to revert to the market's beta of 1.0. The latter assumption is used by Bloomberg, whose adjusted betas are a weighted average of two-thirds entity beta, and one-third market beta.

Betas for publicly traded entities reflect their actual capital structures and incorporate two factors that have a bearing on systematic risks: operating risk and financial leverage. Once comparable publicly traded guidelines have been identified, their betas must be adjusted for differences in capital structure; this involves three steps:

Step 1: Unlevering: Elimination of financial leverage effects. A popular formula for unlevering a beta is:

$$\beta^a = \cfrac{\beta^l}{\left[1 + (1-t)\dfrac{D}{E}\right]} \qquad (5.5)$$

Where:

β^a = unlevered beta (Asset beta)
β^l = levered beta
D = market value of debt of the peer group company
E = market value of equity of the peer group company
t = corporate tax rate

During the measurement period of the levered beta calculation, that of the peer group may change significantly. If this is so, it is recommended to use an average leverage for that period. Calculating the CAPM cost of equity, with an unlevered beta, leads to a similar result.

---

[3] *For details, see S. Pratt and R. Grabowski, **Cost of Capital** (2008), p. 353.*

Step 2: Select an appropriate beta for the entity. Normally the mean or a median of the peer group betas is chosen as a proxy for that of the subject.

Step 3: Relevering: Replacing the financial leverage effect. The popular formula for re-levering the beta is:

$$\beta^l = \beta^a \left[1 + (1 - t) \frac{D}{E} \right] \qquad (5.6)$$

Where:

β^l	=	levered beta
β^a	=	unlevered beta (Asset beta)
D	=	market value of debt of the peer group company
E	=	market value of equity of the peer group company
t	=	corporate tax rate

Example: Unlevering Beta

Assumptions

Risk Free Rate	4%	Market Risk Premium	5%		Tax Rate	30%

Peer Group	Levered βeta	Debt/Equity at Market	Cost of Debt	Cost of Equity	Debt βeta	Asset βeta
Alpha	1.2	25%	5.7%	9.0%	0.34	1.03
Gamma	1.4	30%	6.3%	9.0%	0.46	1.18
Omega	1.6	40%	7.0%	9.0%	0.60	<u>1.31</u>
Subject				<u>9.9%</u>	**Median**	<u>1.18</u>

Entity Application

Generally, the appropriate discount rate for an entity application is the weighted average cost of capital (WACC).

$$\text{WACC} = k_E^l \frac{E}{E + D} + k_D \times (1 - t) \frac{D}{E + D} \qquad (5.7)$$

Where:

k_E^l	=	cost of equity (levered)
k_D	=	cost of debt (pretax)
D	=	market value of debt
E	=	market value of equity
t	=	corporate tax rate

The cost of debt can be derived based on credit and rating information (see Chapter 23). The factor $(1-t)$, in which t denotes the corporate tax rate, reflects the tax deductibility of interest payments (tax shield) in most jurisdictions. The value of the tax shield is included in the standard formula for WACC. Discounting the FCF by WACC results in the TEV. To obtain the ordinary share value from this, the fair values of all interest-bearing debt and preferred shares must be deducted.

Adjusted Present Value

A second version of the entity application is the adjusted present value (APV) method. This starts with the same free cash flow stream as the WACC model. The major difference is the fact that the value of the expected tax deduction on interest payments for the debt financing (tax shield [TS]) is calculated separately. Discounting the FCF with the unlevered cost of equity (k_E^a) results in determining the value of the operating business. The tax shields are discounted separately at an appropriate rate, reflecting the assumption concerning the riskiness of the expected tax shields. The sum of the values of the operating business and the tax shields is the TEV.

For the constant growth model, the relationship between the different methods is:

Exhibit 5.4 DCF Methods

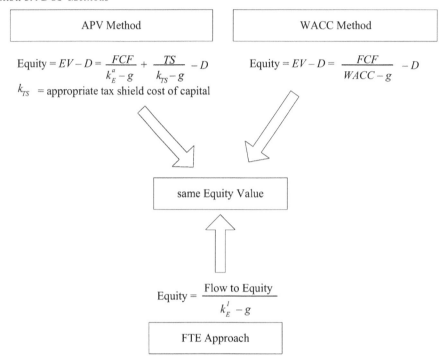

Choice of Technique

The choice of the DCF version should not have an impact on calculated TEV. For practical purposes, the WACC technique is recommended if the assumed debt to equity ratio at market values during the projected period is constant. If so, the WACC will be uniform, because the levered beta leads to a fixed cost of equity. If the debt is expected to change over time independently of the development of the market value of equity, the WACC technique will deliver inappropriate results. For example, this might be the case in highly levered transactions, such as in the private equity industry, where most of the future FCF is used for debt repayments. Capturing the changes in capital structure (as in market values) requires calculating a WACC for every future year.

In that case, the cost of equity will also vary, because the changing debt/equity ratio alters the weights for the costs of debt and equity within the WACC formula. A market value capital structure that varies over time creates an inherent circularity problem. Practitioners solve this by using an iteration process, starting with the terminal year and calculating backward during the projected periods up to the valuation date (the so-called rollback approach).

The APV technique is better equipped to deal with changing leverage. The first term of the formula, the value of the business, $\dfrac{FCF}{k_E^a - g}$ is independent of the capital structure, so that there are no circularity problems when it changes. The value of the tax shields, the second term of the APV method $\dfrac{TS}{k_{TS} - g}$ can be calculated easily as the present value of the tax shields (Interest payments × Corporate tax rate) at the appropriate discount rate. Conversely, with an assumed constant capital structure at market values, the future debt, interest payments, and tax shields will depend on the future value of the entity. These time problems arise when applying the APV method with that assumption.

Debt Beta, Riskiness of Tax Shields, and Growth

The so-called Hamada formulas for un- and releveraging betas (equations 5.4 and 5.5) are based on the concept of Modigliani and Miller.[4] The formulas make these assumptions:

- No debt beta is taken into account.
- The tax shields are as risky as debt.
- The entity will generate a perpetual fixed free cash flow and its debt will be constant.

Debt beta. Debt beta is relevant if the debt holder will absorb parts of the operating risks of the firm. For absorbing parts of those risks, the debt holders require a spread over the riskless rate for their loan. Debt beta is then calculated as:

$$\beta^D = \frac{k_D - i_{rf}}{MRP} \qquad (5.8)$$

Where:

β^D	=	debt beta
k_D	=	cost of debt (pretax)
i_{rf}	=	risk-free rate
MRP	=	market risk premium

Both equations 5.4 and 5.5 assume that the tax shields have the same risks as the debt itself. Underlying that is the further assumption that all future amounts of debt have been determined at the valuation date and that the entity is following a fixed repayment plan.

Riskiness of tax shields. The assessment of the riskiness of the expected tax shields is further influenced by possible changes in future corporate tax rates, future losses of the entity, or tax-loss carryforwards. For example, if a firm is losing money, the tax savings from current interest payments will not be realized immediately but deferred to the future. Therefore, it may be more realistic to assume that the expected tax shields are riskier than the debt; many practitioners assume that they are as risky as the operating business.[5]

Finally, equations 5.4 and 5.5 are consistently derived using a perpetual annuity without growth while the typical model for calculating the terminal amount is based on constant growth. Taking all this into account and realistically assuming debt has some risks, with a

---

[4] *Modigliani and Miller's formulas are set out in R. S. Hamada's "The Effect of the Firm's Capital Structure on the Systematic Risk of Common Stocks," **Journal of Finance** (1972): 435–452.*

[5] *See R. S. Harris and J. J. Pringle, "Risk-Adjusted Discount Rates—Extensions from the Average Risk Case," **Journal of Financial Research** (1985): 237–244.*

debt beta >0 the next formulas have been developed from the basic concept that all DCF methods should lead to the same equity value.[6]

Case 1: Zero-Growth Perpetual Annuity

	Risk of Tax Shield = Debt Risk	**Risk of Tax Shield = Operating Risk**
Unlevered Beta	$\beta^a = \dfrac{\beta^l + \beta^D\,(1-t)\,\dfrac{D}{E}}{\left[1+(1-t)\dfrac{D}{E}\right]}$	$\beta^a = \dfrac{\beta^l + \beta^D\,\dfrac{D}{E}}{\left[1+\dfrac{D}{E}\right]}$
Levered Beta	$\beta^l = \beta^a + (\beta^a - \beta^D)\,(1-t)\dfrac{D}{E}$	$\beta^l = \beta^a + (\beta^a - \beta^D)\dfrac{D}{E}$

Case 2: Constant-Growth Perpetuity Annuity

	Risk of Tax Shields = Debt Risk	**Risk of Tax Shields = Operating Risk**
Unlevered Beta	$\beta^a = \dfrac{\beta^l + \beta^D\left(1-\dfrac{t \times k_D}{k_D - g}\right)\dfrac{D}{E}}{\left[1+\left(1-\dfrac{t \times k_D}{k_D - g}\right)\dfrac{D}{E}\right]}$	$\beta^a = \dfrac{\beta^l + \beta^D\,\dfrac{D}{E}}{\left[1+\dfrac{D}{E}\right]}$
Levered Beta	$\beta^l = \beta^a + (\beta^a - \beta^D)\left(1-\dfrac{t \times k_D}{k_D - g}\right)\dfrac{D}{E}$	$\beta^l = \beta^a + (\beta^a - \beta^D)\dfrac{D}{E}$

The procedures for unlevering and relevering beta should both be based on the same assumptions regarding the risk profile of tax shields and consider the debt beta. As shown in cases 1 and 2, the assumption that the tax shields have the same risk profile as the operating business makes the formulas identical; this assists in avoiding application errors.

APV version. The next example shows an application of DCF assuming a changing capital structure in market values during the projected period. It further assumes that debt is risky (debt beta > 0) and the risks of the tax shields are the same as the operating risks of the entity; end-of-year discounting is used. The risk-free rate is presumed to be 4%, and the equity risk premium (ERP) 5%. The cost of debt will decrease from 7.5% in 2009 to 6.0% in 2012 due to an improved credit rating because of debt repayments in the years 2009 to 2011. The corporate tax rate is 30% and the long-term growth is expected to be 2%; it is also assumed that the market value of the debt always equals its face amount.

To calculate the debt beta, equation 5.9 is used. The asset beta is calculated as:

$$\beta^a = \frac{\beta^l + \beta^D\,\dfrac{D}{E}}{\left[1+\dfrac{D}{E}\right]} \qquad (5.9)$$

The median of the peer group asset betas (1.18) is assumed to be a good proxy for the operating (systematic) risk of the entity.

---

[6] *See T. Koller, M. Goedhart, and D. Wessel,* **Valuation** *(2005), Appendix D, pp. 707–713.*

The unlevered cost of equity is:

$$k\frac{a}{\beta} = 4\% + 5\% \times 1.18 = 9.9\%$$

Because of the changing capital structure during the projection period, APV is the most appropriate DCF version.

Step A: Calculate the value of the operating business by discounting the FCF with the unlevered cost of equity.

Example: APV Method, Total Enterprise Value, Year End Discounting

Assumptions

Discount Rate	9.9%	Long-Term Growth	2.0%	Valuation Date: 31 December 2008	
Capitalization Rate	7.9%	Tax Rate	30%		

Step A					$'000	Terminal
	2008	**2009**	**2010**	**2011**	**2012**	**Amount**
	Actual------	----------------------------------Projected------------------------------				
Free Cash Flow	$ 1,250	$ 1,000	$ 1,200	$1,300	$1,400	$1,300
Growth		–20.0%	20.0%	8.3%	7.7%	–7.1%
Terminal Amount						16,424
Business Value Beginning		15,123	15,620	15,967	16,247	16,456

Step B: Calculate the value of the tax shields. Based on the assumption that they have the same risks as the operating business, the unlevered cost of equity is the appropriate discount rate.

Step B					$'000	Terminal
	2008	**2009**	**2010**	**2011**	**2012**	**Amount**
	Actual------	--------------------------------Projected-----------------------------				
Debt Beginning	11,000	10,000	9,000	8,000	7,000	7,000
Repayments	(1,000)	(1,000)	(1,000)	(1,000)	--	--
Debt End	10,000	9,000	8,000	7,000	7,000	7,000
Borrowing Rate	7.5%	7.5%	7.0%	6.5%	6.0%	6.0%
Interest		750	630	520	420	420
Tax Shield		225	189	156	126	1,592
Tax Shield Value		1,658	1,598	1,567	1,566	1,595

Step C: Details the TEV of the entity, combining the business value and that of the tax shields. The equity value is obtained by deducting the debt.

Step C					$'000	Terminal
	2008	**2009**	**2010**	**2011**	**2012**	**Amount**
	Actual------	--------------------------------Projected-----------------------------				
Business Value		15,123	15,620	15,967	16,247	16,456
Tax Shield		1,658	1,598	1,567	1,566	1,595
Total Enterprise Value		16,781	17,218	17,534	17,813	18,051
Debt Beginning		(10,000)	(9,000)	(8,000)	(7,000)	(7,000)
Equity Value		6,781	8,218	9,534	10,813	11,051
D/E Ratio at Market		147.5%	109.5%	83.9%	64.7%	63.3%
E/(D+E) Ratio at Market		40.4%	47.7%	54.4%	60.7%	61.2%
D/(E+D) Ratio at Market		59.6%	52.3%	45.6%	39.3%	38.8%

WACC Version

Using the WACC method with equation 5.7 first requires calculation of the levered beta with equation 5.10:

$$\beta^l = \beta^a + (\beta^a - \beta^D)\frac{D}{E} \qquad (5.10)$$

and the equivalent cost of capital with equation 5.4. Due to the changing capital structure in market values and the declining cost of debt, the levered beta, cost of equity, and all WACC vary during the projected period.

Example: DCF Method, Varying WACC, Year-End Discounting

Assumptions

Discount Rate	WACC	Long-Term Growth	2.0%	Valuation Date: 31 December 2008	
Capitalization Rate	7.2%	Tax Rate	30%		

Calculation of WACC	2009	2010	2011	$'000 2012	Terminal Amount
			----Projected----		
Asset βeta	1.18	1.18	1.18	1.18	1.18
Risk Free Rate	4.0%	4.0%	4.0%	4.0%	4.0%
Market Risk Premium	5.0%	5.0%	5.0%	5.0%	5.0%
Cost of Debt	7.5%	7.0%	6.5%	6.0%	6.0%
Debt βeta	0.70	0.60	0.50	0.40	0.40
Debt/Equity	147.5%	109.5%	83.9%	64.7%	64.7%
Levered βeta	1.89	1.82	1.75	1.68	1.67
Cost of Equity	13.4%	13.1%	12.8%	12.4%	12.4%
E/(D+E) Ratio at Market	40.4%	47.7%	54.4%	60.7%	60.7%
D/(D+E) Ratio at Market	59.6%	52.3%	45.6%	39.3%	39.3%
WACC	8.6%	8.8%	9.0%	9.2%	9.2%

Discounting the free cash flows with the time-varying WACC will result in the same enterprise value for the entity.

	2008	2009	2010	2011	$'000 2012	Terminal Amount
	Actual--			--Projected--		
Free Cash Flow	$1,250	$ 1,000	$ 1,200	$1,300	$1,400	$1,300
Growth		−20.0%	20.0%	8.3%	7.7%	−7.1%
Terminal Amount						18,158
WACC		8.6%	8.8%	9.0%	9.2%	9.2%
Enterprise Value Beginning		16,781	17,218	17,533	17,813	18,051
Debt Beginning		(10,000)	(9,000)	(8,000)	(7,000)	(7,000)
Equity Value		6,781	17,218	17,533	17,813	11,051

Calculating Value in Use

As mentioned earlier, value in use is specifically detailed in IAS 36:30 to IAS 36:57. One requirement according to IAS 36.55, IAS 36:BCZ85, and IAS 36:BC94 is that all calculations be pretax.

IAS 36:BC94 states:

> *[T]he Board observed that, conceptually, discounting post-tax cash flows at a post-tax discount rate and discounting pre-tax cash flows at a pre-tax discount rate should give the same result, as long as the pre-tax discount rate is the post-tax discount rate adjusted to reflect the specific amount and timing of the future tax cash flows. The pre-tax discount rate is generally not the post-tax discount rate grossed up by a standard rate of tax.*

Because of the statement that a posttax Income Approach should give the same result as a pretax Income Approach, practitioners normally use these three steps to calculate the value-in use for a cash-generating unit (CGU):

1. Discount the FCF of the CGU at an appropriate after-tax cost of capital using equation 5.6 to calculate WACC.
2. Rebuild the same model on a pretax basis by eliminating corporate taxes from the FCF.

3. Use a goal-seeking function to obtain the pretax cost of capital, which gives the same result as in Step 1.

The next example illustrates the procedure.

Example: Value in Use, Year-End Discounting

Assumptions

WACC	12.0%	Long-Term Growth	2.0%	Valuation Date: 31 December 2008	
Capitalization Rate	10.0%	Tax Rate	30%		

Step A after Tax Calculations

	2009	2010	2011	$'000 2012	Terminal Amount
			--Projected--		
Free Cash Flow (after tax)	100	105	110	113	110
Terminal Amount					1,100
PV Factor	0.8929	0.7972	0.7118	0.6355	0.6355
Present Value	89.29	83.71	78.30	71.81	699.07
Value in Use	31 December 2008	$ 1,022.17			

Step B Pretax Calculations

	2009	2010	2011	$'000 2012	Terminal Amount
			--Projected--		
Free Cash Flow (pre-tax)	143	150	157	161	157
Pretax Discount Rate	16.2948%	16.2948%	16.2948%	16.2948%	16.2948%
Terminal Amount					1,098
PV Factor	0.8599	0.7394	0.6358	0.5467	0.5467
Present Value	122.96	110.91	99.82	88.02	600.45
Value in Use	31 December 2008	$ 1,022.17			

The appropriate pretax WACC in the example is 16.2948% (rounded to 16.3%), which gives the identical value in use compared to the (normal) after-tax discounting procedure in step 1.

CONCLUSION

The selection of the most suitable DCF technique has to be made individually for each valuation; it depends on a variety of factors, such as:

*   *Credit rating of the entity.* An investment grade (BBB or better) probably will lead to ignoring the debt beta.
*   *Capital structure.* WACC is best suited if it is reasonably constant, while APV is preferable if it is expected to change
*   *Risk of tax shields.* The Hamada formulas (equations 5.4 and 5.5 for un- and relevering betas imply that tax shields have the same risk as the debt and that the market values of equity and debt are constant. Assuming the tax shields have the same risk as the business results in different, easier formulas.
*   *Industry.* Financial institutions are evaluated by the FCF.
*   *Country.* Common procedures differ more or less around the world and between valuators in their various disciplines: real estate, business, machinery and equipment.
*   *Accounting rules.* Rules affect the choice and the application of the discounting technique; an example is the specific framework for calculating value in use according to IAS 36.

6 EXCELLENT VALUATION REPORTS

BRANDI L. RUFFALO AND ROBERT C. BRACKETT

UNITED STATES

INTRODUCTION

Preparing a valuation the report is probably the most difficult, yet the most underanalyzed, element of the appraisal process. Most valuators use it to record which boxes on the checklist they have filled in and to vaguely describe what was done. Real standards for reports are much higher than that. The purpose of a valuation report—whether for a purchase price allocation under International Financial Reporting Standard (IFRS) 3, an impairment test required by International Accounting Standard (IAS) 36, taxes, or a divorce (subject to local laws)—is to tell a story. The story begins with the entity and its owners, explains any complex concepts involved, dodges industry jargon, and ultimately compels the reader to believe that the assumptions and ultimate conclusion of the valuator are reasonable. A report that achieves those objectives will assist in early dispute resolution, reduce the risk of serious challenges to the final value, and increase the likelihood that it is read and understood.

> *The objective is to resolve the issues as early in the examination as possible . . . we could not agree more. A well-documented appraisal that is complete, factual and easy to understand is at the cornerstone of resolving these kinds of disputes. Early resolution is in the best interest of all of the parties.*
>
> —*IRS Proposed Business Valuation Guideline,* quoted in Mercer Capital's BizVal.com 13, No. 2 (2001)

> *Valuation is both an art and a science. A good valuator approaches the subject from a well-rounded business perspective, is able to see deeper than the numbers and formulas, and clearly communicates the foundations upon which the opinion of value is built. A well-researched, soundly reasoned report can be instrumental in generating a settlement agreement in a dispute."*
>
> —*Common Mistakes in Valuation Reports,* Michael Goldman & Associates, LLC, www.michael.goldman.com/valuation_mistakes.htm

DIFFICULTIES

Valuations and their associated reports are difficult for a number of reasons. Some arise from a specific client and subject; others are the result of the nature of the analyses.

Each Assignment Is Unique

Although there are some consistent components to nearly every business valuation, each assignment has unique characteristics. Differences are driven by:

- Purpose
- Type of report
- Features specific to the entity being valued

- Circumstances surrounding the underlying need
- Client expectations

As these factors change, the complexity varies, and so do the unique requirements and presentation. The nature of most projects forces valuators to write much of the report from scratch, each and every time. This is the only way to ensure that all specifics of the particular engagement are addressed and dealt with.

Clients Are Anxious

The reasons for valuations vary greatly and often include emotional components such as death, litigation, retirement, or divorce. Clients are especially anxious about the process when it comes to such personal matters.

Valuations May Be Subjective

All analyses and the accompanying report are replete with the valuator's personal assumptions concerning the industry, local/national economic issues and timing, as well as the global situation. To that the valuator's views on management capabilities, supply constraints, employment conditions, and variable costing has to be added. Many of the assumptions and views are influenced by the engagement's parameters, such as its purpose and use.

There Is No Style Guide

Numerous professional associations provide lists of things to be included in a valuation report, but detail only the most widely applicable minimum requirements. None offers any guidance as to how to actually write it. Formats for satisfactory reports vary dramatically depending on their purposes.

COMMON MISTAKES

The potential errors and flaws in valuation reports are limitless. The details of the analyses necessary to generate supportable conclusions are difficult to explain; they are outside the scope of this chapter and contain a number of subjective components.

Advocacy

Attorneys and accountants often act as advocates for their clients. The job of the valuator is to offer an independent, objective conclusion of value. Regrettably, reports that focus exclusively on the client's position, suppressing unfavorable material, exaggerating the importance of positive factors, and presenting only information that supports the resulting opinion are not uncommon. Numerous commentators consider advocacy as the most significant valuation failure and suggest that it quite often invalidates the conclusions.

> *The most significant failure on the part of any valuator is to lose his or her independence and advance the client's perspective instead.*

> —Marc A. Keirstead, *CA Magazine.com*

> *Valuators will employ independent and objective judgment in reaching conclusions and will decide all matters on their merits, free from bias, advocacy and conflicts of interest. This is good advice to all.*

> —*Mercer Capital* 13, No. 2 (2001)

The appraiser must be unbiased and independent and not act in any way as an advocate for the client or any other party in arriving at an opinion of value. If independence and ethics are sacrificed, users cannot place any reliance on an appraiser's opinion of value.

—George B. Hawkins and Michael A. Paschall, *Valuation Report Content Is Key in Jointly-Retained Valuation Assignments,* Banister Financial, Inc., Fair Value 2001

Failure to Define the Engagement

The second common flaw in valuation reports is failure to clearly define the purpose, objective, standard of value, and effective valuation date. These four assumptions set the tenor for almost everything the valuator has to do to reach a reasonable conclusion.

This short section defining the engagement sets the stage for all the remaining report content. Failure to include it early in the report leaves the reader distracted as they attempt to identify these basic tenets. The International Glossary does not currently contain a definition of "purpose" or "objective." We are defining them as is commonly referred to: state the purpose of the report (and analysis) and your objectives. For fair market value analysis, these statements may be clear and straightforward. For related projects such as business loss or interruption studies, these answers may be harder to present. Standard of value is a specifically defined term within business valuations: "the identification of the type of value being utilized in a specific engagement; e.g. fair market value, fair value, investment value."

—Robert C. Brackett, *Current Update in Valuations,* NACVA (2006), Chapter 2

The valuator should ensure that the standard of value is defined at the beginning of the engagement and again at the beginning of the valuation report. Most problems seem to arise from failure to specify correctly and completely the standard of value at the start of the engagement. This issue is extremely important in controversial situations, where the standard of value is mandated by statute, judicial, or other binding requirements such as family law cases, dissent or dissolution cases, and valuation performed pursuant to covenants in buy-sell or arbitration agreements. Failure to use the applicable standard of value will result in an inappropriate value."

—BDO Dunwoody, *Common Valuation Mistakes,* The Complete Picture (November 2001)

Lack of Supporting Information

Supporting information provides the who, what, when, where, why, and how of the valuation report; it sets the stage for the analyses and is a critical input to the conclusions. The important areas for which it is required are:

- *Unique facts and circumstances.* This is perhaps the single most useful section of any valuation report since it frames the context of the analyses as well as substantiating the conclusions.
- *Background.* This part provides critical supporting information with respect to an entity's ability to capitalize on future opportunities. This is an important input in estimating growth rates and the ability of historic financial performance to represent expected future activities.
- *Industry.* The specific industry must be discussed because its outlook may affect future financial performance. Ensure that the indicated industry trends are directly linked to the value calculation and conclusions.
- *Market.* The market defines the overall potential for an entity. The ability of the entity to exploit its market should be factored into valuation calculations and conclusions.
- *Competition.* Competition has a direct bearing on both the ability of an entity to grow and the pricing of its products. The report should outline competitive impacts on future growth, volumes, pricing and costs, and be linked directly to the value conclusion.

- *Economic outlook.* This area identifies the investment climate as of the valuation date. This analysis identifies the current market returns for similar investments and historic returns generated by comparable assets. The valuation calculations and conclusions should reflect directly the economic outlook.

Understanding how a business started and has evolved over time to the present tells a great deal about the risks and opportunities that impact the company and its value. Additionally, it is important to consider the management of the business, its strengths and weaknesses, products and services offered, customers, supply relationships, sales and marketing, competition, credit relationships, contractual arrangements, facilities and location of the company's activities, and a variety of other factors that impact the business.

　　—George B. Hawkins and Michael A. Paschall, *Valuation Report Content Is Key in Jointly-Retained Valuation Assignments,* Banister Financial, Inc., Fair Value 2001

Inadequate Financial Analysis

Most valuators have no problems performing financial analyses; many reports present pages of such material, which, however, is never linked to the conclusion. The key to avoiding this deviation is to ensure that the report explains the importance of each factor and how it is used in the valuation calculations and conclusions. The valuator should explain the whys of the assumptions chosen, the valuation methods selected, and the adjustments made to the financial statements. The analyses should show how the entity has been performing, the quality of its management, its risks and opportunities, as well as its investment attributes.

For example, trend, ratio, and comparative analyses provide indications of risks for the entity (its ability to continue at present, expected changes, etc.). The financial analyses should include historic trends and identify key factors that affected past results as well as comparisons of the entity's financial performance and ratios with similar industry measures. Any ratios considered important, such as gross margins, should be supported by an explanation of how they were calculated, what they represent, and their implications. Those trends and ratios not looked on as important or not directly used by the valuator should be explained in summary form, along with reasons why they were not applicable.

Mathematical Errors

Mathematical errors are going to occur in any analyses or presentation. The essential issue is to minimize their size, quantity, and impact on the conclusions.

- *Hand calculate all included totals.* Do not rely on a computer spreadsheet, such as Microsoft Excel, to be completely error free. Spreadsheets only complete identified tasks; hidden cells, changes to the model, and incorrect formulas often result in placing mathematical errors front and center in the report. The final proofing should include checking all calculations.
- *Confirm data flows between spreadsheets.* Relying on the spreadsheet to use the right sources through the constant and relentless changes in models, inputs, and analyses is dangerous. Manually going to each source and ensuring that it really provides the input represented is part of final proofing.
- *Verify inputs to models.* When a valuation report is finished, a valuator should consider providing a prerelease draft to the referring attorney, accountant, or manager for an external review of significant input and outputs. It is very difficult to catch all errors, even with the use of run totals and other input checks. Once the source numbers stop moving and the final parts of the model begin to settle, verify again the original inputs; this is likely not a job for an intern.

Leaps of Faith

The most grievous error committed by report writers is when they ask the reader to take a leap of faith. What do we mean by leap of faith? It means leaving out parts of a report that should not be left out.

— L. Deane Wilson, "Directions on Report Writing," *Shannon Pratt's Business Valuation Update* 6, No. 6 (June 2000): 2

With only the report in hand and without supporting working papers, the reader should be able to see and understand how and why the valuator made particular decisions and choices, which should be supportable, reasonable, and unbiased. Most potential readers do not know anything about valuation. The report must educate them about the concepts, the subject, appropriate valuation methods, and how they were applied.

Valuation reports should contain all the information necessary to ensure a clear understanding of the valuation analyses and demonstrate how the conclusions were reached. The primary objective of a valuation report is to provide convincing and compelling support for the conclusions reached.

—Internal Revenue Service, *Business Valuation Guidelines,* Sections 4.1.1–4.1.2

Common leaps of faith.

* *Using only one method.* Practitioners typically employ only those methods with which they are familiar, often failing to indicate why they chose a particular one and why they did not use another. Multiple methods enhance the credibility of the conclusion, particularly when the results of the various techniques are compared and reconciled. It is important to recognize that valuators may encounter large variances in the results obtained from different methods. If there is no logical explanation for the variances, the practitioner should perform additional research and analyses to understand and reconcile the differences. It is desirable for the various results to fall within a relatively tight (±10%) range; when they do not, the reader will expect a detailed explanation of why that leads to the final value conclusion.
* *No discussions of methods, variables, and calculations in the report.* It is important to define and fully discuss the major steps, significant variables, principal inputs (including data sources), and complete calculations for each method. Based on this information, a client should be able to replicate the results, from source data to conclusions.
* *Focusing on one aspect of the business and not exploring the overall potential.* Every business has weaknesses as well as strengths. Entities with less than $5 million in sales often have a single key employee. Larger firms may have a dominant customer or a limited geographic focus. The valuator should look for strengths as well as weaknesses and ensure the analyses do not rest on key assumptions that are unsupported in the report yet have a significant impact on the conclusions.
* *Relying on calculations.* A value is not developed by numerical analysis alone. Every report should demonstrate the qualitative aspects of the business. The underlying assumptions and application of the selected methods have to be supported with entity and industry background information.
* *Unsubstantiated discount or capitalization rates.* In most engagements, it is desirable to develop within the report the appropriate discount and capitalization rates using multiple techniques (e.g., Capital Asset Pricing Model, build-up models, etc.). Such presentations not only support the rate employed but also ensure the valuator took into account the many different factors that are combined to develop such rates.

- *Unsupported discounts and premiums.* Many discounts and premiums (control premium, discount for lack of marketability, etc.) are applied as part of a conclusion of value. Practitioners should enhance their reports by citing (even briefly) the empirical support (e.g., articles, studies, etc.) that persuaded them that the selection and application of specific discounts and premiums were appropriate for the subject equity interest.

  > *A report may spend 40–60 pages or more analyzing a company to arrive at a sound and supported preliminary value. Then with no supporting rationale, the valuator arbitrarily, and without any stated basis or support, reduces the value by a discount for lack of marketability, often in the 30% to 40% range. This is of no help to the reader. Readers must have a clear indication of adjustments, their basis, and their rationale.*

  > —George B. Hawkins and Michael A. Paschall, *Valuation Report Content Is Key in Jointly-Retained Valuation Assignments,* Banister Financial, Inc., Fair Value 2001

- *Guideline companies.* Many valuators do not clearly outline why the identified guideline companies are or are not comparable with the subject. Applying a mean, median, or some other average valuation multiple from such observations without substantiating the rationale will never persuade a reader of their applicability.
- *Conclusions.* Practitioners should discuss how they arrived at their final conclusion of value. If more than one method was employed and considered, the individual indications of value were part of the process of selecting the final amount. It is essential to provide the reader with a picture window into the final consideration and analyses.

  > *Valuation reports should be well written, communicate the results and identify the information relied upon in the valuation process. The wording used in the report should effectively communicate important thought, methods and reasoning, as well as identify the supporting documentation in a simple and concise manner, so that the user of the report can replicate the process followed by the valuator.*

  > —Internal Revenue Service, *Business Valuation Guidelines,* Section 4.2.2.

Inadequate Disclosure

Preferably, information sources are listed in a distinct section but may be footnoted throughout the report. Regardless, they must be included to allow the reader to replicate the analyses. Citing and using published resources (books, articles, conference papers, etc.) also strengthens the conclusions and helps when decisions may be controversial (e.g., litigation, regulatory filings, minority discounts, pass-through entities premiums, sales projections, capitalization rates, etc.). An opposing expert reviewing the analyses will have greater difficulty challenging the conclusions when critical elements of the analyses rely on third-party sources rather than merely the valuator's personal opinions.

WRITING

When writing a valuation report, it should be remembered that it is not intended for another valuator to read and critique but for a client to read, understand, and use, often as an input in managing the entity.

Common Mistakes

Every effort should be made to avoid the next common mistakes.

- *Addressing the wrong audience for the wrong purpose.* The letter of engagement and the opening of the report should identify its purpose and users. Make sure that the report achieves that objective. More time should be spent explaining and supporting those decisions in the process that were important to that end; thus, a report written to assist two shareholders in transferring the business to a third shareholder might spend more time on owners' functions and capabilities than a similar document that was prepared to assist the owners sell the business to an unrelated purchaser.

- *Information and analyses that result in an illogical conclusion.* It is not uncommon to read reports that assume sudden increases in growth rates when the summary of the industry and economic outlook indicate limited short-term prospects for growth.
- *Failure to communicate believable conclusions.* Many valuation reports omit supporting material necessary for a reader to be convinced of the veracity of the final amounts.

Readability

Ensure that the report is prepared in a manner that enhances its readability.

- *Tie everything together.* When all assumptions, relationships, background and analyses are linked together, the resulting report encourages the reader to believe in the choices and resulting conclusions.
- *Do not assume that following standards guarantees a convincing report.* Remember that readers generally are not well versed in valuation standards, nor do they care if the report addresses each and every item identified in the valuator's professional standards.
- *Technically correct valuations lose their effect when presented poorly.* A well-written and readable report will generally be more effective than a technically correct analysis and commentary that is hard to read.
- *A well-written report.* Such a report often will result in shortened depositions and minimal need for verbal clarifications.

> *...you are persuading the reader that what you wrote is correct. If they disagree, you have controlled what they must argue. You will have framed the discussion. If they do not like your rate then they must give their rate and even more consequential, they must support their choice. If they do not like your reasons then they must give theirs. The key is their reasons must be better, stronger, and more applicable than yours, for their argument to supersede yours. Qualifying your position is just as good as quantifying it. Just ask any attorney."*
>
> —L. Deane Wilson, "Directions on Report Writing," *Shannon Pratt's Business Valuation Update* 6, No. 6 (June 2000): 3

Plain Language

What follows are some quick writing tips from Bryan A. Garner.[1]

- *Order your material.* Put your material in order in a logical sequence; use chronology when presenting facts; keep related items together.
- *Format the report using sections and subtitles.* Divide the document into sections and then the sections into smaller parts as needed; use informative heading for each section and subsection.
- *Choose your words.* Omit needless words; this is important when writing to a global reader; adjectives have different meanings in different societies.
- *Parallel structure.* Use parallel phrasing for parallel ideas.
- *Simplify but do not stupefy.* Teach yourself to detest jargon that could be simplified.

---

[1] Bryan A. Garner, *Legal Writing in Plain English: A Text with Exercises* (Chicago: Chicago Guides to Writing, Editing and Publishing, 2001).

- *Carefully select your verbs.* Use strong, precise verbs; minimize use of: *is, are, was,* and *were.*
- *Write as you would speak.* Make everything you write speakable.
- *Connect your thoughts.* Write a sentence linking paragraphs in sections; introduce each section with a summary sentence.
- *Keep your paragraphs short.* Vary the length of your paragraphs but strive to keep them short.
- *Use quotations.* Weave quotations deftly into your narrative.
- *Write to your reader.* Write to an ordinary reader, not a mythical judge who might someday review the document.
- *Highlight the important points.* Highlight ideas with attention-getters, such as bullets.
- *Use proofreaders and peer reviewers.* Embrace constructive criticism and edit yourself systematically.

Jargon

Each profession has certain words with very specific meanings; equally, some abbreviations have different meanings in other professions. In addition to the client, business valuations are read by accountants, regulators, attorneys, and judges, each with their own specific professional vocabulary. A valuator needs to be aware of as many of these specific phrases and words as possible so as to either avoid using them or preface them with the applicable definition pertinent to the report. The North American business valuation professional associations have a directory of approximately 110 frequently used terms, which are included in the glossary of this book.

Types of Reports

There are many types of valuation reports; this chapter mainly deals with formal (traditional or comprehensive) written reports, which are the most common type requested by regulators, auditors, and clients. These reports may be full or summary, are typically quite long—up to 200 pages—and are used most often in litigation and tax valuations. The time to produce each type varies substantially; thus, it is important that the valuator knows what the client needs so that the budget is sufficient. As all reports follow from similar analyses and research efforts, consider the next points before starting the engagement in order to identify the type of report necessary.

- *Purpose.* The client's situation with respect to intended purpose and use of the report.
- *Regulatory requirements.* These often dictate or strongly suggest acceptable report types and styles.
- *Statutory authority.* Pertinent statutory authorities may dictate or suggest appropriate report types and styles.
- *Court rules.* Relevant courts often have written and unwritten rules of evidence, which may include acceptable report types and styles.
- *Interest valued.* The type of interest being valued may have an impact on the allowable report type or style.
- *Problem to be solved.* The nature of the problem that requires a valuation may provide input to the selection of the preferred report type as well as the style.

Presentation

A few easy-to-implement presentation ideas will improve the readability of a report; when preparing the written portion of the report:

- *Create an outline.* Map out a strong structure before starting to write.

- *Organize the report logically.* Choose a numbering system that provides a logical order and helps the reader follow the presentation.
- *Table of contents.* Place a table of contents near the front to allow a reader to identify specific sections easily.
- *Be consistent with formatting.* Use consistent formatting and justification throughout. Readers tend to rely on those attributes for clarification and visual clues indicating where they are within the report.
- *Use of color.* Summarize written presentations and highlight key points through appropriate choices of color graphics. Be careful as overuse can be distracting and confusing.

Charts

The type of chart used should be appropriate for the point to be made. Valuators often prepare several different charts in order to find the one with the most impact. Poorly chosen or prepared graphs will be hard to understand because of missing labels, poor color choices, or incorrect data selected. Types of charts commonly used in valuation reports include:

- *Column.* Columnar charts generally are chosen to present large quantities of source data, such as historic financial statements.
- *Line.* Line graphs often are inserted to demonstrate changes over time, such as revenues or earnings.
- *Bar charts.* Bar charts frequently are selected to show the significant components of an item, such as sales or gross profits. To indicate changes over time, some valuators prefer line charts, others bar charts.
- *Pie charts.* They often are used to show the relative sizes of individual components of a total at a given moment in time, such as details of customers or expenses.
- *Scatter graph.* Scatter graphs, often with a regression line, show changes in a specific performance factor over time, such as sales, earnings, or free cash flows.

Appearance

Some readers judge a report's validity based on its appearance. In *Understanding Business Valuation*, Gary Trugman[2] makes two interesting points:

- If it is cosmetically attractive, the reader will believe that a great deal of time went into the work product.
- We have found that many judges will not read the report but will comment on the fact that it appears to be a well-constructed document.

Documentation

The report should document all important and material items, issues, assumptions and limiting conditions embedded in the valuator's conclusions; examples include:

The indication of value included in this report assumes the company will maintain its character and integrity through any reorganization or reduction of existing owners/managers' participation in the existing activities of the company.

> —Timothy W. York, *Start a BV Engagement the Right Way,* Journal of Accountancy, Vol. 196, 2003 p. 1

If a summary analysis of the economic outlook is included in a valuation report to document the overall economic conditions of the industry, the nation, or the world, the valuator

---

[2] *Gary Trugman, **Understanding Business Valuation, Second Edition** p. 429. AICPA 2002*

should not only indicate the sources of the data but also provide a short synopsis of the key points that are used for the calculations and conclusion of value.

Certificate

In the United States, various professional bodies require that each written valuation report contain a signed statement similar to that set out below. The International Association of Consultants, Valuators and Analysts recommends that all valuators comply with the concepts in their disclosure, even if they do not include such a document in their reports the format is:

> I am the person who has primary responsibility for the opinion of value contained in this report and attest that, to be best of my knowledge and belief:

> The reported analyses, opinions and conclusions are limited only by the reported assumptions and limiting conditions, and are my personal, impartial, unbiased professional analyses, opinions and conclusions.

> I have no present or prospective interest in the property that is the subject of this report, and I have no personal interest with respect to the parties involved.

> I have no bias with respect to the property that is the subject of this report or to the parties involved with this assignment.

> My compensation is not contingent on an action or event resulting from the analyses, opinions or conclusions in, or the use of, this report.

> My analyses, opinions and conclusions were developed, and this report has been prepared in conformity with the applicable valuation standards.

> *[Date]*

> *[Signature]*

Technology

Use all the technology at your disposal. In 2009, word processing, spreadsheet, and packaged valuation programs are universally available; the first two are essential, and the third is desirable to valuators.

Word processing tools:

- Allow use of predefined headers to create tables of contents
- Provide spell and grammar checking routines
- Offer ways to track changes
- Include find-and-replace capabilities

Valuators are cautioned against relying completely on the last feature as it will generate more errors in reports than are fixed if employed document-wide. The global find-and-replace command will not only change every "animal" to "animals" but may (if not properly used) make changes inside words, turning "animalization" into "animalsization."

Available business valuation software has many advantages in that it provides:

- Automated calculation of entity values using all commonly accepted methodologies
- Automatic calculation of firm ratios
- Preformatted presentations of industry and company financial information and performance characteristics
- Prebuilt graphs and tables for insertion into reports
- The ability to update a valuation by inputting the new data and then pressing a button
- Templates that establish standard report components
- Link spreadsheets with word processing to reduce potential errors in both calculations and presentations

All business valuation software provides validated calculations, but the valuator still must double-check all inputs.

CONCLUSION

A valuation report is a demonstration of expertise and a permanent record for the client of the valuator's efforts. Anything not included bears the risk of becoming lost in time. It has been only about 500 years since the voyages of the great western European explorers Christopher Columbus (1451–1524) of Spain and Vasco da Gama (1469–1524) of Portugal. Yet, many of the great civilizations they discovered along with the ruins of the magnificent cities visited during their travels have vanished; only recently rediscovered, they are now slowly being opened to tourism. So too will the efforts documented only in an appraiser's working papers go unknown in history.

The report is a chance to show off as well as justify the final fees. Therefore, as the report is completed, be sure to do these things:

- When a concept or method is used, explain it, as well as why it was selected.
- Find and present the key factors that drove the value determination; focus on them.
- If a matter discussed in a report draft is not a key factor, move it to an appendix.
- Tie each analysis back to the source, whether qualitative or quantitative.
- Focus on appearance; the appearance of the report is almost if not as important as the analyses; many valuation reports are issued as hardbound books.
- Make sure that all of the report is comprehensible; this is especially critical when employees prepare financial analyses or draft the report.
- Explain everything, including theory, underlying assumptions, and formulas; when appropriate, some of this may be in the appendixes.
- Undergo a review process, be willing to accept that you may be wrong; the authors often hand a report to a peer for a final read and check for continuity; occasionally, such a reviewer challenges an application of multiples from industry, economic assessments, projections of free cash flows, or risk analyses.
- When assumptions of relationships do not convince a reviewer, make adjustments.
- Always recalculate critical numbers outside the spreadsheet; if it seems too complicated to do so, the spreadsheet usually has an error or the presentation needs improvement.

7 ASSESSING EXTERNAL RISKS[1]

WARREN D. MILLER

UNITED STATES

INTRODUCTION

Unsystematic, entity-specific risk is the bane of small and midsize enterprises (SMEs) for their owners as well as the valuation community. Academics have rendered the issue moot by assuming that rational investors hold fully diversified portfolios. This is not true for an SME owner who typically has at least 95 percent of his or her net worth tied up in the illiquid equity of a closely held business. To this owner, paraphrasing a statement about winning, widely attributed to the legendary U.S. football coach Vince Lombardi, "Unsystematic risk isn't everything. It's the only thing."

SUITABLE FRAMEWORK

Having assumed away the problem, scholars leave us not only with no data but, alas, without even a framework, which must come first. Nobody knows what data are needed without it. The details of unsystematic risk are nearly infinite; a questionnaire to cover all of them would take an 18-wheeler to cart it around. The author has struggled with this problem for over a decade; a number of different ideas from several sources (Porter, McKinsey, Galbraith, etc.) were tried out without success.

Finally, he looked to the literature of other disciplines and came up with a framework that is simple, intuitive, and easy to remember. Organization theory (the macroenvironment) and industrial organization (domain) supplied the first two levels of the trilevel framework. For nearly a decade, he struggled with the entity level; finally, in 2005, he came up with SPARC (*s*trategy, *p*eople, *a*rchitecture, *r*outines, *c*ulture).

The objective is to determine the alignment of an entity's internal strengths and weaknesses (the "SW" of a SWOT analysis) with the external opportunities and threats in its domain and macroenvironment. Such an alignment, if it exists, should give the firm one or more distinct advantages that enable it to outperform its rivals over some period.[2] The challenge for the valuator is to apply the trilevel framework, do the analyses, and then ask management appropriate questions.

Firms and industries are constantly evolving; therefore, the assumptions of traditional microeconomics, insistence on equilibrium, homogeneity among competitors, and static analyses are a hindrance to valuators. The most successful entities are the toughest to value because they are the ones that have been able to keep hitting moving targets; management matters!

---

[1] This chapter is adapted from Warren D. Miller, **Value Maps: Valuation Tools That Unlock Business Wealth**, Copyright © 2010, John Wiley & Sons, Inc.; used with permission.

[2] See Warren D. Miller, Value Maps: Valuation Tools that Unlock Business Wealth (Hoboken, NJ: John Wiley & Sons, 2010), chapters 11 and 12, for extensive discussions.

Because each level of risk has a different proximity to the entity, it has a potentially different range of impacts on total risks. The macroenvironment has the narrowest, the entity itself the widest, because it has the greatest effect, for better or worse, on its own performance. Published research affirms this and even begins the job of quantifying the range of risk premiums.[3]

DEFINING THE DOMAIN

The first step in an external risk assessment is to define the domain (industry or segment) in which the entity competes. This is necessary because the unit of analysis is not the entity but the domain. The fact that few smaller companies compete industry-wide has given rise to the analysis of industry subgroups. Such segments are called strategic groups, a term that originated with Michael S. Hunt.[4]

Here is an excerpt from a valuation report:

In this engagement, we define the domain as a strategic group. Such a group is a subset of competitors that do not compete industry-wide. The seven pharmacies and their retail customers in and around Rockbridge County, Virginia, comprise the relevant strategic group in this engagement.

Beginning with a detailed definition, the research must be precise and productive. In the United States, this is greatly helped by material from sources such as Factiva or LexisNexis; elsewhere in the world it is more difficult but the concept is the same. Even if a given article is not about, say, pharmacies in Rockbridge County, Virginia, USA, it still can supply information on economic conditions in that area, the local unemployment rate and economic trends, past natural disasters, demographics, lifestyles and values, and so on—in fact, a complete picture of what is and probably will be happening in the region. Demographic trends, in particular—population growth and age cohorts—will have a major impact on future demand for a pharmacy's goods and services, as will political activity.

Examples of Strategic Groups

A group's members compete head to head with one another but tend not to compete with firms in other groups. One example is the cadre of nonnational certified public accountant firms offering traditional services in a county or metropolitan statistical area. Yes, the "Big Four" might also be there, but these behemoths do not encroach on the turf of the SMEs because their scale is such that they price themselves out of that market; smaller firms in many countries make a good living picking up the crumbs of the Big Four.

The lodging industry is loaded with strategic groups: resorts; luxury; full service/expensive; full service/moderate; extended stay; budget; bed-and-breakfasts. Each has its own target market; within a group, the business models tend to be similar.

A final example is new cars: again, groups within this broad domain run the gamut: luxury; subluxury; sports cars; moderate-price sedans; low-price sedans; convertibles; SUVs (large); SUVS (small); crossovers. If, instead of "new cars," we said "new vehicles," then the strategic groups would also include several different types of pickup trucks.

Importance of Strategic Groups

Within an industry, the underlying economic structures of most strategic groups tend to differ from those of industry-wide competitors. For example, the Big Four is an oligopoly

---

[3] See Warren D. Miller, "Using SPARC to Enhance Value for Clients," **Value Examiner** (March–April 2008): 25–27.

[4] Michael S. Hunt, **Competition in the Major Home Appliance Industry**, 1960–1970, PhD diss., Harvard University, 1972.

that dominates the U.S. market for auditing publicly traded entities; it evaporates when the universe is expanded to include closely held firms. The (U.S.) Federal Trade Commission found major differences in the structures of these groups. In particular, the incidence of oligopoly is higher in some local and regional domains than nationally.

Just as barriers to entry are a key parameter of industry definition, mobility barriers separate one strategic group from others. This construct came to the fore in 1977.[5] Those mobility barriers discourage members of one group from competing with members of others. The primary criterion for a strategic group is its target market; if a particular entity aims at only local or regional customers, then its "industry" is a strategic group defined by that particular geography. Because a strategic group is basically a mini-industry, its structure is analyzed in that same way.

Structures within Industries

The structure of an industry derives, in part, from its degree of concentration. The following summary of concentration in the United States by major Standard Industrial Classification (SIC) groups is Scherer and Ross.[6]

- Agriculture/Forestry/Fishing (SICs 01–08): not concentrated
- Mining (SICs 10–14): "loose oligopolies"

  - Limestone/Sand/Gravel: low nationally: high locally and regionally
  - Copper/Iron Ore/Uranium/Lead, etc.: moderate to high nationally
  - Chromium/Molybdenum/Nickel/Diamonds: high
  - Crude oil refining: moderate to high nationally

- Construction (SICs 15–17): low nationally, some locally
- Manufacturing (SICs 20–39): varies greatly[7]
- Transportation (SICs 40–47): fragmented, except locally
- Communications (SIC 48): generally high, except in radio broadcasting
- Public Utilities (SIC 49): generally high but with pockets of local competition
- Wholesale/Retail (SICs 50–59): generally low concentration nationally and in larger local markets; smaller (less than 100,000 population) markets are concentrated
- Food Retailing: has been locally concentrated, is becoming less so
- Financial Services (SICs 60–67): vary

  - Banking: high locally, increasing nationally
  - Health/Life Insurance: concentrated at state level (because of regulation)
  - Other Insurance: low
  - Securities Brokerage: high, but changing due to policy
  - Real Estate Brokerage: low, except in very small towns

- Service Industries (SICs 70–89): vary

  - Hotels/Motels: low
  - Laundry/Dry Cleaning/Barber-Beauty Shops: low
  - Accounting: low except in very small towns
  - Law: low except in very small towns

---

[5] *See Richard E. Caves and Michael E. Porter, "From Entry Barriers to Mobility Barriers: Conjectural Decisions and Contrived Deterrence to New Competition,"* **Quarterly Journal of Economics** *91 (1977): 241–261.*

[6] *F. M. Scherer and D. Ross,* **Industrial Market Structure and Economic Performance***, 3rd ed. (Boston: Houghton Mifflin, 1990), pp. 79–81.*

[7] *Ibid., pp. 82–85, shows that 199 of 448 four-digit manufacturing SIC codes have 4-firm concentration ratios (4CR) greater than or equal to 40, which policy makers see as a threshold for oligopoly.*

- Medicine: moderate; regulation/entry barriers combine to keep prices high
- Repair Services: low
- Amusement/Recreation Services: high except in large cities

In the United States, the general incidence of national oligopoly is low, but in many local and regional markets, it occurs frequently. It has implications for valuators because well-functioning oligopolies have lower risks due to tacit collusion—in essence, all the players know the rules but competitors do not talk about them (illegal price-rigging).

UNIT OF ANALYSES

In analyzing external risk factors, the unit of analyses is the domain, not the firm. For most SMEs, the domain is the strategic group, although, depending on the firm and its scope, it may be the industry itself. All firms within a given competitive domain face the same set of external factors and, in turn, have the same external risk premiums. It is how each competitor responds to those forces that matters. Therefore, the first order of business in an assignment is to define the domain. Different companies respond in various ways, so significant distinctions are not surprising.

There are two rules for the research phase of a valuation engagement:

1. Define the domain by determining the key parameters that explain the strategic group
2. Do the research top down: Start with the macroenvironment, then the domain, and finally the entity itself. By then, the valuator should have many clues about what to look for in the analyses subjects.

Example

The strategic group in this engagement consisted of the eight biggest janitorial supply companies competing in the five counties south and a little west of Harrisburg, Pennsylvania, with an estimated population of 830,000, about 6 percent of that state.

SOURCES OF VARIANCES IN RATES OF RETURN

Many appraisal professionals give short shrift to industry analyses, believing that, within an industry, a domain is a domain is a domain. That is a mistake.

Each of the papers cited in Exhibit 7.1 measures some variation in rate of return (ROR); they use different data sets, different time frames, and different statistical methodologies but reach similar conclusions. Most have their roots in analysis of variance (ANOVA); with multiple regressions as the primary. ANOVA uses a dependent variable (rate of return) and several independent ones, both domain and company related, to infer how the dependent one is affected by changes in the independent ones. The greater the change in the dependent variable, as a result of fluctuations in an independent one, the greater the percentage of the variance that is accounted for by it. A higher percentage means that variable has greater predictive power.

As the analyses show, the median effect of industry factors in these papers accounted for over 15% of the variance in rate of return for individual firms. Therefore, a 20% to 30% equity cost of capital can include 300 to 450 basis points (100 basis points equals 1 percentage point) of industry risk for a typical small firm. That is not every such entity, of course. Domain risk factors may be disproportionately large (or small) in some arenas. No matter how it is sliced, though, industry factors matter. Among other things, they help explain how competition happens and also whether a given domain structure suggests how to compete...or how not to.

Exhibit 7.1 Industry Analysis

Date	Citation[1] (pub/vol/pp)	Title of Paper (Author[s])	Cohort	Sources of Variation in Rates of Return (ROR)[2]								
				Domain (DOM)					Company (CO)			
				IND	SG	Year	IND × Year	Total	Corporate	Firm	Firm × Year	Total
1991	*SMJ*, 12, 167-185.	How Much Does Industry Matter? (*Rumelt*)	A	8.3%	NI	0.0%	7.8%	16.1%	0.8%	46.4%	36.7%	83.9%
			B	4.0%	NI	0.0%		4.0%	1.6%	44.2%	NI	45.8%
1996	*SMJ*, 17, 653-664.	Markets vs. Management: What Drives Profitability? (*Roquebert, et al.*)		10.1%	NI	0.4%	2.3%	12.8%	17.9%	37.1%	NI	55.0%
1997	*SMJ*, 18 (Summer Spec. Issue), 15-30.	How Much Does Industry Matter, Really? (*McGahan & Porter*)		8.1%	NI	NI	NI	8.1%	10.5%	35.0%	NI	45.5%
				18.7%	NI	NI	NI	18.7%	4.3%	31.7%	NI	36.0%
1999	*JIE*, 47, 373-398.	The Performance of U.S. Corporations: 1981-1994 (*McGahan*)		27.9%	NI	NI	NI	27.9%	-0.1%	37.1%	NI	37.0%
				10.7%	NI	NI	NI	10.7%	-0.2%	23.7%	NI	23.5%
				14.0%	NI	NI	NI	14.0%	-0.2%	27.0%	NI	26.8%
2000	*SMJ*, 21, 739-752.	Corporate and Industry Effects on Business Unit Competitive Position (*Chang & Singh*)	A	19.4%	NI	0.9%	0.9%	21.1%	4.3%	52.7%	NI	57.0%
			B	25.4%	NI	0.3%	1.8%	27.5%	8.5%	46.8%	NI	55.3%
2002	*MS*, 48, 834-851.	What Do We Know About Variance in Acct'g Prof.? (*McGahan & Porter*)	Hi	16.3%	NI	1.1%	NI	17.4%	23.7%	59.1%	NI	82.8%
			Lo	6.9%	NI	0.2%	NI	7.1%	8.8%	32.5%	NI	41.3%
2003	*SMJ*, 24, 1-16.	Is Performance Driven by Industry- or Firm-Specific Factors? (*Hawawini, et al.*)		6.5%	NI	1.9%	4.2%	12.6%	NI	27.1%	NI	27.1%
				11.4%	NI	1.3%	2.9%	15.6%	NI	32.5%	NI	32.5%
				8.1%	NI	1.0%	3.1%	12.2%	NI	35.8%	NI	35.8%
2003	*SO*, 1, 79-108.	The Emergence and Sustainability of Abnormal Profits (*McGahan & Porter*)		29.6%	NI	1.7%	NI	31.3%	30.0%	38.7%	NI	68.7%
				22.5%	NI	0.4%	NI	22.9%	22.8%	54.3%	NI	77.1%
2007	*SMJ*, 28, 147-167.	Firm, Strategic Group, and Industry Influences on Performance (*Short, et al.*)		14.7%	6.4%	NI	NI	21.0%	NI	79.0%	NI	79.0%
				19.2%	15.0%	NI	NI	34.2%	NI	65.8%	NI	65.8%

MEANS

DOM 17.7%
CO 51.4%

Standard deviation — DOM 8.3% — CO 20.0%

Mean R² of Company effects	51.4%	
Mean R² of Domain effects	17.7%	
Company R² ÷ Domain R²	**2.9**	

[1] AER = American Economic Review
JIE = Journal of Industrial Economics
MS = Management Science
SMJ = Strategic Management Journal
SO = Strategic Organization

[2] *Average R² if in a narrow range; presented separately if range isn't narrow*

NI = Not Included in research

In the table, the 2.9 figure in the box at the bottom indicates that, overall, variations in ROR caused by company-level factors (CO) are 2.9 times those arising from the domain (CON). In other words, changes in entities' rates of return are greater from *intra*industry sources than from *inter*industry differences. Therefore, the dominant characteristic of markets tends to be heterogeneity, not homogeneity.[8]

The implications of this research for valuation professionals are far-reaching:

- Variation is one key to survival of any species, including economic entities.
- Domain definition is essential because it provides the constraints that enable the facts and circumstances of a given valuation to be analyzed.
- Published industry risk premiums are useless in most valuation contexts. Competitors' different performances suggest major disparities among them over how, and even which, long-lived assets should be deployed.
- Those disparities point up significant variances in companies' assumptions about their rates of return.
- Different ROR means divergent views about prices of long-lived assets in general and in particular about what "market participants" would pay for a given item.

COST OF CAPITAL MODEL

Virtually every valuation of SME uses the build-up method. The author is no keener on published industry betas than on such industry risk premiums. Therefore, he tends to avoid the cost of capital model, unless dealing with a bigger enterprise that has plenty of guideline public companies.

$$E(R_a) = R_f + (R_m - R_f) + U_a \quad (7.1)$$

Where:

$E(R_a)$	=	Required rate of return on security a
R_f	=	Risk-free rate of return (typically the yield to maturity on a Treasury security, short, medium, or long term, depending on facts and circumstances)
R_m	=	Market rate of return for large-cap stocks
U_a	=	Unsystematic risk associated with security a

Unsystematic Risk

Data from Morningstar and Duff & Phelps confirm that in the United States, size, however measured, and the rate of return are negatively correlated. However, there are more components of unsystematic risk, macroenvironment (six forces), industry/strategic group (six forces), and company (risk is a function of alignment and the durability of value-creating mechanisms).

Mathematically unsystematic risk is:

$$U_a = RP_{size} + RP_{mac} + RP_{dom} + RP_{co} \quad (7.2)$$

Where:

U_a	=	total unsystematic risk for firm a
RP_{size}	=	Risk premium for size
RP_{mac}	=	Macroenvironmental risk in the industry/strategic group
RP_{dom}	=	Risk in the domain (industry or strategic group)

---

[8] See D. G. Hoopes and T. L. Madsen, "A Capability-Based View of Competitive Heterogeneity." ***Industrial and Corporate Change*** *17, No. 3 (2009): 393–426.*

RP$_{co}$ = Company-specific risk

ERP = Equity risk premium

This simplifies to:

$$E(R_a) = R_f + ERP + RP_{size} + RP_{mac} + RP_{dom} + RP_{co} \quad (7.3)$$

Solid data are available to quantify the first three terms but not for the others, which complicates the valuation of smaller companies. An analytical framework is essential as, lacking reliable data, there is no choice except to make subjective assessments to estimate macroenvironmental, industry, and company-specific risks; the objective is qualitative rigor. This process supplies insights and a comprehensive understanding of the business(es). Understanding a smaller firm's business requires an in-depth grasp of its unsystematic risks.

There is a mathematical constraint on quantifying non-size-related unsystematic risk at the low end, which will vary over time. ERP changes, and so do size premiums. And there is more than one figure for each—Aswath Damodaran's "implied" (i.e., forward-looking) ERP jumped from 4.37% at year-end 2007 to 6.43% at the end of 2008. The ERP by Duff & Phelps is pegged at 3.84%, while the "supply-side" is at 5.73%, and Morningstar's (formerly Ibbotson) is 6.47%.[9]

Like the ERP, the size premium varies depending on: (10, 10a, 10b, microcap), index (Standard & Poor's 500 or New York Stock Exchange Composite); on measurement frequency (annual or monthly); and on beta method (sum versus nonsum). Done one way, the constraint could be about –9 percentage points (5% ERP, 4% size); applied another, it could approach 17 percentage points (7% ERP, 10% size). It all depends on the valuator's viewpoint.

Industry Risk Premiums

The 2008 edition of *Stocks, Bonds, Bills, and Inflation* (*SBBI*) covered 477 SIC codes at the 2-digit (68 companies), 3-digit (192), and 4-digit (217) levels.

High end. At the 3-digit level, 5 SICs comprising 79 business segments had industry risk premiums (IRP) equal to or greater than 10 percentage points; their weighted average was 11.42%; at the 4-digit level. The 7 SICs with 63 segments had IRPs $\geq$ 10% for a weighted average of 11.35%. Rounding down the mean (11.39%) for the 142 segments might make the ceiling too low. Therefore, a robust upper limit for total *external* unsystematic risks is 12%. Subtracting 3% for the macroenvironment leaves a maximum domain risk premium of 9%.

Low end. At the 3-digit level, there were 4 SIC codes, 73 segments, with IRPs $\leq$ –5%; the weighted average was –6.02%. At the 4-digit level, 12 SIC codes, 114 segments, had a weighted average IRP of –5.90%. Those two means are near –6%, so the lower bound for total external unsystematic risk is –6%. Subtracting a –3% lower limit for macroenvironmental risk leaves –3% from the domain. Therefore, the IRP ranges are –3% to 3% for the macroenvironment and –3% to 9% for the domain. The choice of figures within the ranges should be based on qualitative analyses.

Company factor. Under normal market conditions the low-end constraint is –900 basis points (bp), reflecting 500 bp for the ERP and 400 for size. That is the maximum negative premium that can come from nonsize unsystematic risk: Σ RP$_{mac}$ + RP$_{dom}$ + RP$_{co}$ $\geq$ –900 bp. To keep what is already plenty complicated from becoming more so, we make a simplifying assumption for a maximum possible negative risk premium of –300 bp at each of the three

---

[9] *See www.stern.nyu.edu/adamodar/pc/datawets/histimpl.xls; 2009 Duff & Phelps, LLC, Risk Premium Report (p. 9); and* **Stocks, Bonds, Bills, and Inflation (SBBI)—2009 Yearbook**, *Valuation Edition (Chicago: Morningstar, 2009), Table 5.6 on p. 69, respectively.*

levels: macroenvironment, domain, entity. The upper bound is for the entity itself; that is obtained by multiplying the external upper bound (12%) by the 2.9 factor from sources of variances in rates of return earlier in this chapter; this gives 34.8%, which, rounded, makes the range for the firm itself from –3% to 35%.

To put this into context, consider an early-stage, venture capital–funded company in the first quarter of 2009; at that time, its maximum cost of equity would have been:

Risk-free rate	3.0%
ERP	7.0% (special economic conditions)
Size premium	4.0%
RP_{mac}	3.0%
RP_{dom}	9.0%
RP_{co}	35.0%
Total	61.0%

TRILEVEL UNSYSTEMATIC RISK MODEL

The framework shown in Exhibit 7.2 has six macroenvironmental forces, six more in the domain, and a large number for the entity itself. These three levels comprise the foundation of the well-known SWOT analysis; "Opportunities" and "Threats" are external (macroenvironment and domain) while "Strengths" and "Weaknesses" are internal (the firm).

Exhibit 7.2 Trilevel Unsystematic Risk Framework

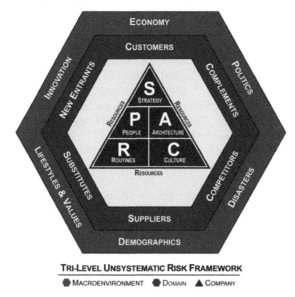

MACROENVIRONMENT

This graphic began its life at the General Electric Company in the 1950s as a four-force model; expanded and refined, it now reflects not only PEST (politics, economy, sociocultural, and technological) but also lifestyle and values.[10]

---

[10] See Michael A. Hitt, R. D. Ireland, and R. E. Hoskisson, **Strategic Management: Competitiveness and Globalization**, 8th ed. (Cincinnati: South-Western Publishing, 2009).

How Remote?

An entity can affect only two facets of its domain's macroenvironment. The first is innovation, which often has far more to do with management processes than with technology or intellectual property rights. It covers new ways of doing things, organizing things, seeing things as well as defining a domain and the firms comprising it. The second is political, which is accessible to, if not wholly controllable by, industries, coalitions of firms, and individual companies. Of course, in nearly every country, "all politics is local": The closer politicians are to an industry, the more likely they may be affected by it or even a particular firm. This happens most often through lobbying by trade associations, campaign contributions by individuals, and fundraising efforts by parties.

Why Does the Macroenvironment Matter?

From one perspective, the macroenvironment—which is not synonymous with the macro economy (gross domestic product [GDP], monetary and fiscal policy, business cycles, and growth), nor with macroeconomics (the study of whole economies)—matters because it affects risks. Logically, overall risk rises as more factors are assessed; however, macroenvironmental forces actually may decrease risk in a domain. An example: While high interest rates are the bane of most economic activities, they are precursors of higher profits in the pawnshop and outplacement sectors.

Beyond risk, awareness of the macroenvironment helps one understand a business. If valuators do not know how and why a firm works the way it does, how can they defend their conclusions? Stowe et al. put it this way:

> *[Understanding the business] involves evaluating industry prospects, competitive position, and corporate strategies. Analysts use this information together with financial analysis to forecast performance.*

This is the first of five steps the authors say "that an analyst undertakes" in a valuation. Subsequent aspects include: "insight into the structure of its domain," "overall supply and demand balance," "competitive analyses," and the "ability of the firm's people to execute its strategy successfully."[11]

FORCES

Investment-specific risks at the macroenvironmental level influence the domain's risk profile and its performance. As they are remote, it is difficult to manipulate them in favor of any given firm. Even during an economic crisis like the one occurring at the time of writing in spring 2009, the very remoteness of the macroenvironment results in a range of risk premiums that is narrow compared to those of the domain and the entity. Individual firms can, with investment, time, and luck, at the domain level, directly influence its structure in their favor; at the macroenvironmental level, the influence is more subtle.

As previously illustrated, the six dimensions of the macroenvironment are economy, innovation, lifestyles and values, demographics, disasters, and politics. To their detriment, managements of smaller companies everywhere in the world fail to think through how they should respond to changes in these forces. Small business owners seem to believe that they cannot do anything about them, so why bother? Many do not even join trade associations.

In contrast, valuators must analyze, interpret, and quantify them. The impact will vary across domains because not one is the same as another. Moreover, the effect of free markets guarantees that such analyses, like conclusions of value, are only snapshots at a particular

---

[11] *John D. Stowe, Thomas R. Robinson, Jerald E. Pinto, and Dennis W. McLeavey,* **Equity Asset Valuation** *(Charlottesville, VA: CFA Institute, 2007).*

time—the valuation date. Like markets generally, macroenvironmental forces change, albeit more slowly.

Economy

In most domains, the economy is the most important macroenvironmental factor. For business owners and managers, it is usually the most frustrating, as it involves interest rates, inflation, unemployment, GDP, and fiscal and monetary policy—all factors completely beyond their control. Except for unemployment, in the United States each is measured nationally. It is important for the valuator to comprehend how changes in these forces affect the domain's risk profile.

Some practitioners, especially in the United States, cut and paste into their valuation reports summaries from well-regarded sources under the heading "Economic Outlook." Besides failing to include any attribution, they are apt not to make explicit the connection between economic factors and the domain(s) in which the entity competes; readers are supposed to figure it out for themselves. Section 4 of Revenue Ruling 59-60, the Bible of tax fair market value in the United States, sets out eight "factors to consider"; the second is: "The economic outlook in general and the condition and outlook of the specific industry in particular." Throughout the world, valuators should accept that concept, substitute "domain" for "industry," and connect the dots.

Innovation

As pointed out earlier, most innovation relates to management: that is, new perspectives, new understanding, new measurements, new reports, and new ways to bundle resources. In contrast to patents, copyrights, and breakthrough products and services, management innovation operates below the radar; it is a major contributor to the heterogeneity across competitors in a given domain.

However, research and development (R&D) activities are intended to result in innovations; they tend to occur in larger firms, especially in industries with short shelf lives for new products or services. In less volatile domains, especially so-called low-tech industries, firms do not engage in much R&D. For valuators, the problem with R&D-related innovation is that it is virtually never disclosed in advance. Besides making it hard to understand and harder to forecast, proclaiming a breakthrough, like the announcement of an engagement to be married, may create expectations that do not materialize; they may also have an effect on sales using existing technology. For a longer-term perspective, *Technology Review magazine* (*www.technologyreview.com*) and the World Future Society (www.wfs.org) are useful sources.

Black swans. Valuators should also consult www.asaecenter.org/directories/association search.cfm for a searchable database of over 51,000 trade associations; their libraries can be incredible and invaluable resources. In their absence, the valuator must consider remote possibilities, so-called black swans. For waste disposal firms, revenues are based on volume handled, frequency of pickups, and tip fees paid to operators of refuse dumps. A valuator need not know about a U.S. firm, Liftpak, L.C., of Oklahoma City, which holds patents on compacting technology that can reduce the volume of waste by as much as 90 percent, to envisage the potential impact of such an innovation on the industry. Even without knowing about it, a savvy appraiser should include in analyses, a caveat about what could happen if a breakthrough black-box contraption came to market.

More important, such a caveat should be followed, at the entity level of risk assessment, as a discussion about what the firm is doing to protect itself from such an eventuality. Does it even recognize the possibility? What is the mix of commercial and residential customers?

Has it given its salespeople incentives to try to increase the number of residential customers because they are less likely to invest in a compactor? Has it tried to offer more attractive pricing to such customers? Has it attempted to create switching costs for residential customers?

Lifestyles and Values

Trends in values and lifestyles can affect demand for a firm's products or services. Divorce rates can matter, as may trends in food, clothing, housing, education, and entertainment. That is true even in a business-to-business (B2B) industry; on the surface, a distributor serving appliance stores and homebuilders might seem impervious to divorce rates and single parents. Nevertheless, a mother and father living apart will need two refrigerators, even if they are each smaller than the single unit needed if they had continued as one household; the inventories of savvy distributors should reflect that. Perhaps because they are inculcated early, in most countries, values change more slowly than lifestyles. For instance, mothers who never marry are good news for the daycare industry, even if kids growing up without fathers in the home are often bad news for society as a whole.

Demographics

Both consumer and industrial demography subsume the characteristics of a population. For consumers, for instance, age, education, family size, rate of household formation, disposable income, and birth and mortality rates affect not only demand but also the design and delivery of products and services; think about those single-adult appliances. At a minimum, the valuator needs to investigate the domain's demographics: how many firms, how fast they are growing, their mortality, the rate of new entrants, and how growth in demand for the industry output compares with that of GDP.

If either the target market or the end users are consumers, then both the valuator and management should be aware of such metrics as disposable income, rate of household creation, the primary age cohorts of that target market, the growth rate in those cohorts, and how much they have to spend. In the United States, data on consumers are relatively easy to come by through the Department of Commerce and its Bureau of Economic Analysis; many countries in Europe and some in Asia have similar organizations.

Business demographics data, in contrast, are harder to come by and, may not be free. The first choice, nearly everywhere, is always a relevant trade association; however, the quality and depth of these vary widely. Investment research reports can be extraordinarily helpful, as can the various business censuses taken in a number of countries; in the United States, they are compiled every five years. ZapData (www.zapdata.com) offers a searchable database of 14 million U.S. businesses; the cost of the material varies according to the number of firms and data elements involved.

Disasters

Originally, this factor was labeled "International," but global competition has obviated the need for that; in the wake of the September 11, 2001, terrorist attacks, it was relabeled "Disasters." Those come in many forms, some not as visible as others. In Europe, for instance, low birth rates are causing shrinkage in many countries' populations, which leads to increased immigration, even though a significant number may be Muslims. Basic pensions in Europe, similar to Social Security in the United States, tend to be funded by governments, unlike the private plans for individual common in North America. The combination of falling birth rates and limited private pensions means that Europeans are likely to hit the entitlement wall long before much of the rest of the world.

Politics

The politics factor covers four essential facets: (1) legislative initiatives, (2) regulatory policies, (3) judicial decisions, and (4) electoral trends. As shown by the new (2009) administration in Washington, winning politicians are apt to push for legislative, regulatory, and judicial changes. In the summer of 2008, anyone could confidently predict that the legislative agenda, regulatory policies, and judicial nominees of President Obama would differ significantly from those of President McCain. It is possible that the United States midterm (2010) elections may mean "change we can believe in" in the opposite direction. Those differences affect the performance of domains, and valuators must anticipate and explain potential changes based on different electoral outcomes.

In most countries, local politics are more susceptible than national governments to pressure from business groups and large employers. That influence is seen in political contributions and lobbying activities. If a corporate officer is a major supporter of an influential political figure, it can mean a less restrictive political environment for the industry and maybe for his firm.

SUMMING UP THE MACROENVIRONMENT

The configuration of factors in the macroenvironment can help or hurt a domain. Its effect depends on the "facts and circumstances" of the situation at hand. Revenue Ruling 59-60 states: "No formula can be devised that will be generally applicable to the multitude of different valuation issues arising in estate and gift cases"— or any other situations either. However, it is essential to define the domain before any analyses. More than any other single action, this improves the valuator's efficiency, increases effectiveness, and reduces mistakes. The author considers it the sine qua non (without which, nothing) of business valuation. If we do not get that right, we are unlikely to get anything else right, either.

The data involved in analyzing macroenvironmental risks other than the economy and demographics is "soft." Whatever the material, though, the analyses must be comprehensive, thorough, and rigorous. According to Revenue Ruling 59-60, they must also reflect "the elements of common sense, informed judgment, and reasonableness." Even if a valuator believes that the aggregate impact of the macroenvironment in a given scenario is neutral, such analyses are essential because they enhance an understanding of how the business works.

A valuation report should contain a single summary paragraph, focusing on the two or three most important macroenvironmental findings and explaining why they matter. Whatever approach adopted—cost, market, or income—a sound, done-from-scratch macroenvironmental analysis will help the reader to better comprehend the domain of which the entity is a member and the external risk factors it faces. That understanding allows a better and more accurate estimate of value, along with increased credibility for the conclusion.

Example: Microenvironment

Commonwealth Industrial Supply Company (CISC) is a $12 million sales firm that distributes janitorial supplies to small and medium-size enterprises in the five counties south and west of Harrisburg, Pennsylvania. Founded in 1959, CISC grew steadily until the mid-1990s, when it hit a revenue plateau. After that, due to Internet competition and increased deployment of information technology throughout the industry, gross margins declined. By the valuation date, December 31, 2007, the gross margin had fallen over the preceding 15 years from 39% to 22%.

The next summary of the macroenvironmental analyses would have been preceded by six paragraphs discussing each of the relative forces:

Summing up, the U.S. economy was struggling at the valuation date. Nationally, interest rates were down slightly, but for the year, unemployment had jumped to 4.9% from 4.4% in the spring. Nominal GDP growth during the last quarter of 2007 was an anemic 2.3%, down by two-thirds from the preceding quarter. While a recession had not "officially" been declared, fear was in the air. That was especially true in southern Pennsylvania, where population and jobs have been declining for 30 years.

The eight larger janitorial supply companies in the five-county area were facing stiff resistance to the needed higher prices in the face of skyrocketing commodities costs. Their customers were laying off employees, and some firms had even taken to going to Wal-Mart for cleaning supplies.

Innovation in this sector was low, except for increasing deployment of information technology in all phases by most competitors. The minimum wage was expected to rise in 2008, which would further retard economic growth in arenas where unskilled labor was the norm. The war in Iraq raged on, though there were signs that the tide was turning in favor of the Iraq government.

There was great uncertainty about the overall economy, as the country and the domain moved into another presidential election cycle with nearly 20 potential candidates. Janitorial supply is a cyclical business that depends on rising employment and economic growth for its sustenance. Because of this, and the increasing margin pressure from rising costs, including huge increases in gasoline prices, the outlook for this strategic group is poor. Accordingly, on a scale of –3% (most benign) to +3% (most hostile), a macroenvironmental risk premium of +2% is considered appropriate for this domain.

DOMAIN

This section discusses how to apply the middle level of the trilevel framework to establish unsystematic risk. The level of analyses is not difficult based on a precise definition of the competitive domain. Industry analysis came to the fore in the late 1970s through the influence of Michael Porter of Harvard Business School, a specialist in industrial organization (IO), which concerns itself with two major topics: (1) antitrust and regulatory issues, and (2) the structure, conduct, and performance (SCP) of industries; this level uses IO in the latter sense.

Tenets

In a firm, the domain structure drives the domain competitors' conduct (behavior, strategy), which drives the domain's performance. The related feedback loops, shown in Exhibit 7.3, reflect the dynamic nature of markets, which are always evolving, quickly, slowly, or irregularly.

Exhibit 7.3 Domain Structure

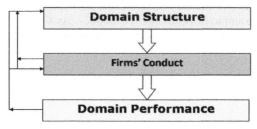

Any sports coach will attest that it is a lot easier to become number one than to remain there. Assume that an entity has become phenomenally successful; money is raining on the firm and its employees, especially the senior executives. The last thing anyone in that situation wants to do is change anything; it is human nature to want to keep still and let the cornucopia continue to flow. That is why most hugely successful companies, and nearly everyone in them, resist any change; they want to continue to delude themselves that they really are the smartest people on the planet.

That is not reality in free markets; competition will not permit it. What worked yesterday may not work today, and certainly will not tomorrow. Joseph Schumpeter, the Austrian economist, described capitalism as a system of "creative destruction." It simultaneously renews itself as it kills off declining parts; it can be a not-fun system, too—at the time of writing, stock markets are melting down nearly everywhere, and home prices in Britain, Spain and the United States, to name a few, are still in free fall. It is an unforgiving system, no matter how much politicians and policy makers try to hide reality from angry voters. For every company that changes, evolves, and remains on top, there are thousands that do not. To use American examples; for every P&G (Procter & Gamble), there are myriads like AIG (American International Group); for every GE, there are scads of GTE (General Telephone & Electronics Corporation merged with Bell Atlantic in 2000 to form Verizon) ; for every Southwest Airlines, there is a pile of Braniffs, PanAms, and Easterns (all now defunct). The exceptions really do prove the rule. Those that do survive, adjust, and continue to succeed have the capacity to change with their domain and sometimes even to influence that change to play to their own strengths; ask Microsoft about Google.

Industrial Organization Analyses

Individuals are apt to have different perspectives on this branch of IO, depending on the lens through which they are looking.

- *Economists*: "Does the structure of this industry lead to efficient outcomes?"
- *Regulators*: "Does the structure mean that firms can engage in anticompetitive behavior at the customers' expense?"
- *Executives*: "How does the structure of this domain affect our ability to create distinctive advantages?"
- *Valuators*: "What is the risk profile of this domain's underlying structure?"

A key tenet of IO is "equilibrium" analysis, but there is not much use for such situations in valuations. The problem is that equilibrium is an unstable end state. Most firms want to be in a domain and earn "normal profits" at a slightly better rate than their rivals. How can a mechanism as complex and multifaceted as the multitrillion-dollar economies of many advanced industrial nations ever be "in balance" in the first place? Equilibrium-related research produces elegant mathematics, but it is not much use to business owners and their advisors. However, although the SCP paradigm comes from an equilibrium context, it is a useful launching pad for thinking about domain dynamics.

A second IO tenet is that industry structure has an impact on the conduct (strategy) of individual entities: an example of behavioral economics. As shown in Exhibit 7.4, there are four basic states of domain structure along the continuum of competitive intensity.

Exhibit 7.4 Levels of Competition

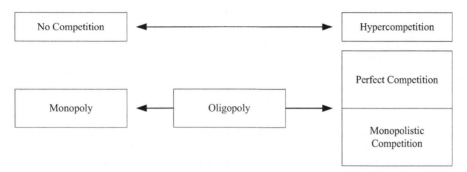

Monopolists do not have to ponder competitors, but they must, except in "natural" situations, consider regulators and politicians (think public utilities and cable television). At the other end of the spectrum, participants in hypercompetition do not worry much about regulators but are constantly looking over their shoulders. The really interesting structure that occurs often in local and regional contexts is the oligopoly.

The key to those situations is to understand that domain structure affects conduct, which influences performance. This branch of IO is the study of market structures and the behavior of firms within markets; it deals with the economics of imperfect competition, where the most money is made.

Concentration Ratios

In the United States, every five years, the Census Bureau collects and publishes volumes of industry data showing levels of concentration by SIC code; from those it calculates "concentration ratios" for the largest 4, 8, 20, and 50 firms in an industry at the 2-, 3-, and 4-digit level. However, they tell us nothing about how market share is distributed among the firms involved. So CR4 = 100 could mean market shares of: 25%–25%–25%–25%; 40%–30%–20%–10%, or even 97%–1%–1%–1%. In the latter case, of course, the smaller firms are all "price takers."

Beginning in the 1980s, the Herfindahl-Hirschmann Index (HHI) became the measuring stick for whether a U.S. merger would be challenged under antitrust law.[12] The HHI carries more information than any CR, because, by squaring the share of *every* competitor, disparities among them become evident. The hypothetical maximum HHI is 10,000 (100^2) for a monopoly where market share = 100%.

In the first example two paragraphs back, the HHI = 2,500 ($25^2+25^2+25^2+25^2$); in the second, the HHI = 3,000 ($40^2+30^2+20^2+10^2$); and in the last, the HHI = 9,412 ($97^2+1^2+1^2+1^2$). This shows that HHI takes a quantum leap when the share of the largest firm increases or when the number of firms involved declines. Domains in which the HHI is greater than 1,800 are considered to be concentrated while those between 1,000 and 1,800 are moderately concentrated. While the HHI is clearly the better of the two measures, the CRs work just fine for most situations involving SME. Regardless of the metric, the underlying economic structures of most strategic groups are apt to differ from those of their corresponding industries.

---

[12] *For a short but clear discussion of HHI, see www.usdoj.gov/atr/public/testimony/hhi.htm.*

Oligopolies

The combination of deregulation, new technologies, rising imports, and antitrust action has eliminated many of the oligopolies that existed in the United States in the 1970s; at that time: three television networks, ABC, CBS, and NBC, served over 90% of TV viewers, and the "Big 3" had about 70% of automobile sales. Some American oligopolies remain—ready-to-eat breakfast cereal, for example; anyone who doubts an oligopoly is power need only visit the dry-cereal aisle of the nearest grocery store, pick up a box that weighs only marginally more than a feather, half empty to boot, and then ask why customers will pay $3.99 for it.

Like anything else in valuations, though, the question of oligopoly "depends"; in most cases, the key is the definition of the domain. Unlike many countries, in the United States, competition and antitrust actions have knocked down many national oligopolies, but regionally and locally, they are alive and well. When there are indications of an oligopoly, the valuator must always ask: "On what basis do y'all compete?" If the answer is "We kill 'em on price," the unsystematic risk at the entity level is high.

Implicit in the concept of oligopoly is the notion of interdependence among the participants; their fortunes are intertwined, so they sink or swim together. That is especially true if a black sheep decides to compete on price. It can be a domain wrecker if the errant firm cannot be punished quickly and severely. Rivals may try to accomplish that by dropping their prices further, faster than the originator; however, this only leads to lower profits and more risks all round.

New Entrants

The threat of new entrants creates risks for incumbents. The extent of those risks depends on a myriad of factors, the most important of which are growth and profitability in the domain. New players typically face significant barriers to entry that they must clear in order to compete. Whether they are entry or mobility barriers, the analyses must deal with these five categories of which the first two are "natural barriers":

1. *Economies of scale.* This refers to falling cost per unit of output within a given time frame. Traditionally, economies of scale are thought of in terms of manufacturing; however, larger companies can reap them in other fields such as advertising and purchasing; market leaders typically enjoy them.
2. *Differentiation.* This refers to buyers' perceived uniqueness of either a product or service; differentiation is the source of "brand awareness." It is why such companies as Lexus, Chanel, Budweiser, Ralph Lauren, Bose, St. John, and Ritz-Carlton advertise in carefully chosen media.
3. *Cost disadvantages independent of scale.* These include inefficiencies caused by uncontrollable factors, such as problems with proprietary technology, favorable access to raw materials, geographic locations, and the learning curve.
4. *Contrived deterrence.* investments that firms make to deter entry by others have the following three characteristics; they: (a) lead to a fight if a new player enters; (b) are highly specific; and (c) are proclaimed loudly and publicly. A common example is highly specialized production or warehouse facilities.
5. *Government policy.* This is less important than in the past but still a factor. Examples include sanctioned monopolies (electric, gas, cable TV); prohibited entry (foreign airlines inside the United States); tariffs/import quotas (sugar); nontariff trade barriers (slot machines in Japan).

Customers

Certain aspects of customer groups can reduce or increase a domain's risk by reducing/increasing its revenues and margins. Factors that increase customers' bargaining power include:

- *Undifferentiated industry output.* It makes customers' decision making easier by focusing their attention on price.
- *Industry output is a significant portion of customers' cost structure.* It induces customers to bargain hard and shop for alternatives.
- *Customers' bottom lines are low.* This increases their sensitivity to price and encourages them to haggle when, if the customers were highly profitable, they would not.
- *The threat of backward integration.* It depends on entry/mobility barriers.
- *Switching costs are low.* This means that changing suppliers will not extract much pain from the user. Gasoline is a prime example, word-processing software is not.
- *Access to full information.* Buying airline tickets on the Internet has put downward pressure on prices, despite the industry, stopping the payment of commissions to travel agents, which for "only" 80% of revenues.

If the domain's output (goods or services) has low to no impact on the quality of customers' products or services, this increases their sensitivity to price; increases can induce them to seek alternatives.

Complements

First popularized by the book *Co-Opetition* by Brandenburger and Nalebuff, this sixth force has come to the fore in advanced industrial economies.[13] Complements do not behave the same as substitutes. When demand for a complement goes up, demand for the related product or service also rises. Today firms are looking for complements to their products and services. Besides contributing to the expansion of networking, complements are a force in the domain framework. Their popularity has also increased the frequency with which strategic alliances are formed; a few complements:

- Golf clubs, golf balls, golf tees, golf lessons, rounds of golf
- Airline transportation, lodging, car rentals
- Broadway shows and New York restaurants
- Computers, software, information technology services
- TV programming, TV networks/cable TV
- Baseball games, hot dogs, popcorn, peanuts, beer
- Razors, razor blades, shaving cream, after-shave lotion
- Cell phones, cellular minutes
- Men's suits, dress shirts, neckties
- Swimming pools, diving boards, bathing suits, sunscreen, beach towels
- Automobiles, gasoline, car insurance, tires

Competitors

How intense is margin pressure among players in a given domain? How is market share distributed among them? Price reductions induced by slackening demand in high-fixed-cost sectors (e.g., airlines), frequent innovation, quick actions/reactions, protracted advertising campaigns—all reduce margins. Structural factors that increase competition are:

---

[13] *Adam M. Brandenburger and Barry J. Nalebuff,* **Co-Opetition: A Revolutionary Mindset That Combines Competition and Cooperation** *(New York: Currency Publishing, 1996).*

- Numerous players that are about the same size (no advantages)
- Slow growth in demand (according to Warren Buffett: "It's not until the tide goes out that you can tell who's been swimming naked.")
- Undifferentiated output (Audit firms have this problem.)
- High fixed costs/perishability (fresh produce; airlines; hotels/motels)
- Capacity must be added in large increments (new planes)
- Exit barriers (These keep players that should retire from doing so.)
- Diverse competitive strategies (No firm can be all things to all comers.)

Suppliers

Like customers, supplier groups may increase or decrease a domain's costs; conditions that increase suppliers' power include:

- Supplier group is highly concentrated (few suppliers, many buyers).
- No substitutes are available for suppliers' output (and so no price ceiling).
- Domain is not a significant purchaser of suppliers' output.
- Suppliers' output is highly differentiated.
- Suppliers could benefit by buying customers.

Substitutes

A substitute uses different technologies to satisfy the same needs as the entity's products or services; thus, it tends to put a ceiling on the price that can be charged. When demand for a substitute goes *up*, that for the subject tends to go *down*; examples of substitutes include:

- Driving versus flying
- Cell phones versus cameras
- Beer versus wine versus distilled spirits
- Oil versus coal versus electricity versus natural gas versus nuclear plants versus "green" power
- Dining out versus carry-out versus grilling steaks at home
- Movie tickets versus movies-on-demand via cable/satellite versus DVD rentals
- Compact discs versus long-playing records versus mp3 downloads
- Mediation/arbitration versus lawyers
- TV news versus online sources of information versus newspapers
- E-mail versus national postal services

SUMMING UP THE DOMAIN

After analyzing the domain, the positive and negative influences should be summarized in a single paragraph, just as for the macroenvironment. This is the lead-in to the major challenge in analyzing unsystematic risk: quantifying it. As set out earlier, the range of the domain's risk premium is greater than that of the macroenvironment but not as wide as the entity's. The key points about domain analyses are:

- Define the domain precisely.
- Strategic groups are common in domain analysis for SMEs.
- Always have SCP (structure, conduct, performance) in mind.
- Avoid boilerplate, except in the first paragraph or two.
- Except for competitive analyses, avoid discussing individual firms.
- Explain, do not assert.
- Oligopoly is alive and well in many regional and local domains.

- Individual forces in the six-force framework do not exert equal influence on domain risk.
- Government regulation often reduces risk. (Check the rates of return that "regulated" electric utilities enjoy.)
- A price-cutting oligopolist is the economic equivalent of a cheating spouse.

Example: Domain

This summary paragraph would have been preceded by six other paragraphs, devoted to the relevant forces.

The janitorial-supply sector in southern Pennsylvania is in serious trouble. Growth is slow, price competition is ferocious, some customers are replacing their suppliers of cleaning solvents and the like, complements are hard to come by, and barriers to entry are extremely low because some suppliers will sell to anyone whose check or credit card will clear. Because products sold tend to be generic (to keep costs down), there are few discernible switching costs. Customers have high bargaining power, and so do suppliers; the firm and its competitors are caught in the crossfire. Accordingly, on a scale of –3% to +9%, our analyses lead us to the conclusion that the domain risk premium is +7%. It would be higher, but substitutes are few, and most customers are loyal to their longtime suppliers, at least until they decide they can no longer afford loyalty.

CONCLUSION

The techniques discussed in this chapter should help valuators assess the impact of external risks on the cost of capital. At the time of writing (May 2009), such factors were still having an adverse effect on values nearly everywhere in the world.

RECOMMENDED READING

Brock, James. *The Structure of American Industry,* 12th ed. Upper Saddle River, New Jersey: Prentice Hall, 2008.

Cabral, Luís M. B. *Introduction to Industrial Organization.* Cambridge, MA: MIT Press, 2000.

Carlton, Dennis W., and Jeffrey M. Perloff. *Modern Industrial Organization*, 4th ed. Boston: Addison-Wesley, 2004.

Child, John, David Faulkner, and Stephen Tallman. *Cooperative Strategy: Managing Alliances, Networks, and Joint Ventures*, 2nd ed. New York: Oxford University Press, 2005.

Carroll, Glenn R., and Michael T. Hannan. *Organizations in Industry.* New York: Oxford University Press, 1995.

Ferguson, Paul R., and Glenys J. Ferguson. *Industrial Economics: Issues and Perspectives,* 2nd ed. New York: New York University Press, 1994.

Fahey, Liam, and V. K. Narayanan. *Macroenvironmental Analysis for Strategic Management.* St. Paul: West Publishing, 1986.

Hitt, Michael A., R. Duane Ireland, and Robert E. Hoskisson. *Strategic Management: Competitiveness and Globalization—Concepts and Cases*, 8th ed. Cincinnati: South-Western College Publications, 2009.

McGahan, Anita M. *How Industries Evolve: Principles for Achieving and Sustaining Superior Performance.* Boston: Harvard University Press, 2004.

Miller, Warren D. "Three Peas in the Business Valuation Pod: The Resource-Based View of the Firm, Value Creation, and Strategy." In R. F. Reilly and R. P. Schweihs, *The Handbook of Business Valuation and Intellectual Property Analysis*, pp. 305–327. New York: McGraw-Hill, 2004.

Oster, Sharon M. *Modern Competitive Analysis*, 3rd ed. New York: Oxford University Press, 1999.

Porter, Michael E. *Competitive Strategy: Techniques for Analyzing Industries and Competitors*, updated ed. New York: The Free Press, 1998.

Shepherd, William G., and Joanna M. Shepherd. *The Economics of Industrial Organization*, 5th ed. Long Grove, IL: Waveland Press, 2004.

Tirole, Jean. *The Theory of Industrial Organization*. Cambridge, MA: MIT Press, 1988.

www.beckmill.com/libraryRegister507.asp. Free registration will give you access to the graphics in this chapter and to various papers and articles.

8 STRATEGY AND BENCHMARKING

WILLIAM C. QUACKENBUSH

UNITED STATES

INTRODUCTION

Other chapters describe in detail approaches, methods, and procedures available to measure the value of business interests as well as the sources of market evidence for deriving estimates of the metrics used in valuation formulas. Simply summarized, three key factors must be determined to estimate values: B (benefits), R (risks), and G (growth).

Regardless of the approach applied, appraisers must support their selection with market evidence to the extent it is available in the particular country. However, even carefully selected and fully analyzed empirical evidence may indicate valuation metrics that may not reflect the economic benefits, growth, or risks associated with the subject business. Selected guideline public companies for the Market Approach may be materially larger and the source of their revenues significantly more diverse than the subject; those differences in size or diversity may have a significant impact on the comparative risks, growth, and/or expected benefits.

As a result, one of the more difficult processes in valuing businesses is the adjustment of market evidence for the differences between those firms from which it is derived and the subject. Most valuators would appreciate procedures for easy conversion of such analyses to quantifiable adjustments; however, the process is usually neither empirically obvious nor formulaic, particularly when adjusting for risks.

Rather, valuators must use significant professional judgment based on research and analyses to quantify the factors that cause those differences. For example, a company-specific risk premium (CSRP) is part of developing an appropriate discount or capitalization rate; similarly, a fundamental adjustment is made to the market multiples from guideline public companies when applying the Market Approach.

Understanding the firm allows a valuator to contextualize the market's perspective on its economic benefits, growth, and risks. Traditionally, this is done by some form of historic financial analyses as well as qualitative assessments of the business, its operations and management. An effective application of those analyses is to use them to understand how well management aligns its actions with the entity's strategic objectives. Is there a strategy that considers the current and expected environmental issues in which the entity must operate? Does management have the resources necessary to implement its strategy successfully? Is management's responsibility to create value for the owners? Does management have an appropriate strategy? Have resources been acquired and deployed effectively to implement the strategy successfully? To what extent has value been enhanced?

Valuators' answers to those types of questions, as well as their understanding of the value implications of those answers, will help in both assessing risks and estimating expected future economic benefits. Analyzing the internal perspectives of a business either qualitatively or quantitatively is not an isolated, checklist-type procedure. In determining valuation metrics, measuring alignment, such as identifying appropriate strategies and management's effectiveness in acquiring/utilizing the entity's assets, people, and systems in implementing them, is critical.

This chapter discusses traditional entity analyses, both quantitative and qualitative, and then suggests a more holistic concept on the internal perspectives affecting value; this may provide a clearer picture and more supportable conclusions.

TRADITIONAL ANALYTICS

Traditionally, appraisers have attempted to measure entity-specific value metrics with both quantitative analyses of operational and financial performance and qualitative assessments of the internal factors that differentiate the subject from the empirical market guidelines, including quality of management and nature of the assets. Those types of analyses play an important role, for example, in a valuator's assessment of CSRP.

Modeling

One of the primary purposes of internal analyses is to estimate entity-specific risks. The accounting background of many valuators and the context of most assignments continue to drive the profession to seek quantifiable models supported by empirical evidence. Much progress has been made in this area over the past 30 years. In markets where there is sufficient evidence, these models can be immensely helpful in assessing risks.

For example, for several years, Roger Grabowski and David King, of Duff & Phelps, LLC, have analyzed market data for U.S. public companies to develop equity risk premium (ERP) data based on size; it is published as *Risk Premia Report*. If one accepts the argument that most entity-specific risk is related to size—that small firms have higher required rates of returns because of their nature—these studies capture both the ERP and much of the CSRP.

Using these data, valuators can estimate discount and capitalization rates as well as adjustments to market-derived value multiples. The next table illustrates a size-adjusted ERP of approximately 12% for an entity with the indicated characteristics. When used in conjunction with the study's identified long-term historic market ERP of 4.85%, the difference of approximately 7% is attributable to the additional risks associated with size.

Risk Premiums (Market plus Size) over Risk-free Rate: Using Regression Equations

	Company Size ($ million)	Constant Term %	Slope Term %	Log (Size)	Premium over Risk-free %
Market Value of Equity	120	20.591	-3.515	2.079	13.3
Book Value of Equity	100	17.397	-2.949	2.000	11.5
5-year Average Net Income	10	14.216	-2.715	1.000	11.5
Market Value of Invested Capital	180	20.182	-3.303	2.255	12.7
Total Assets	300	18.036	-2.725	2.477	11.3
5-year Average EBITDA	30	15.583	-2.709	1.477	11.6
Sales	250	16.420	-2.192	2.398	11.2
Number of Employees	200	17.675	-2.210	2.301	12.6
Mean premium over risk-free rate					12.0
Medium premium over risk-free rate					11.9

*Source: **Risk Premia Report**, 2008.*

Butler and Pinkerton[1] proposed measuring entity-specific risks of similar publicly traded companies by analyzing and breaking down total beta; they consider this useful in determining the specific risks of the subject.

---

[1] Peter Butler and Keith Pinkerton, *"Quantifying Company-Specific Risk: Empirical Framework with Practical Applications,"* **Business Appraisal Review** *(Spring 2006).*

Each of those models and several others attempt to measure at least a material portion of the entity-specific risks; however, they suffer from two limiting conditions. First, any model is only as good as the data; the Duff & Phelps study is supported by decades of detailed data from U.S. Treasury and equity markets. This is sufficient to generate supportable size-adjusted ERPs for a U.S. valuation. However, many non-U.S. markets have neither a sufficient quantity nor quality of available data to use such a model effectively.

Second, quantitative models look to empirical data from other, usually publicly traded entities and conclude, from analyses, that there is a direct application to the subject. In fact, that is often the case; however, if the analyses ignore risks unique to the subject, valuators may not have fully considered all factors in developing the valuation variables. Appraisers can analyze empirical evidence from many other sources while not identifying, let alone quantifying, the fact that the subject's plant is sitting atop a toxic waste site or that the chief financial officer is about to be indicted for embezzlement.

Modeling can provide valuators with insights on risks as identified in the market and may assist in assessing entity-specific risks. However, alone they do not provide a complete picture. The balance of this chapter discusses methods that identify the internal factors that affect entity-specific risk.

QUANTITATIVE ANALYTICS

Traditional quantitative tools concentrate on the analyses of historic, and sometimes projected, financial performance. By such an undertaking, valuators can identify operational, turnover, financial, and liquidity entity-specific risks. Once their levels are identified and measured, the information may be used to support valuation metric assumptions. Such analyses can be divided into three categories: financial ratios, performance trends, and peer comparisons; each is discussed in detail.

Financial Ratios

Financial ratio analyses consist of identifying and measuring performance relationships from data in financial statements. The purpose is not to provide a primer on how to calculate such ratios—there are many good texts and courses—but, rather, on how to apply them in risk assessment; they are generally divided into five groups:

1. *Growth* ratios measure changes over time. They are generally used to measure growth in income measures (revenues, incomes, cash flows) and balance sheet categories (working capital, operating assets, debt, and equity). A risk assessment should focus on both growth rates and their volatility.
2. *Leverage* ratios measure financial risk by assessing the relative amount of debt, as opposed to equity, in the entity's invested capital. The risks in highly leveraged companies are generally greater, as, over time, the fixed costs of interest may increase the volatility of earnings and cash flows. Conversely, minimally leveraged companies limit their growth to that which can be funded internally.
3. *Profitability* ratios measure how effectively expenses and profits are managed. They may be measured at different levels of income or as returns on sales, assets, invested capital, or equity. Similar to growth ratios, their levels and volatility are both important.
4. *Utilization* ratios, also referred to as efficiency or turnover ratios, measure how effectively a company employs its assets in generating returns to its ownership interests. While superficially easy to calculate, there may be widely varying reasons for the actual level. If an entity has a very high capital asset utilization rate, is it be-

cause management is extremely competent in deploying its assets, or because the physical plant is very old and suffering from deferred maintenance?

5. *Liquidity* ratios measure the ability of an entity to meet its short-term financial obligations as they become due. Liquidity drains caused by a mismatched balance sheet and/or insufficient earnings have the most dramatic impact on risk of any measure. An entity can tolerate lack of profitability, inefficient use of assets, and high leverage for a considerable period; insufficient liquidity for even a short time may lead to insolvency.

Financial ratio analyses are essentially the measurement of management's success in implementing the entity's strategy. The next table illustrates an abbreviated ratio analysis for an entity.

Growth		**Profitability**	
Sales Growth	3.0%	Gross Margin	24.2%
Operating Earnings Growth	7.1%	Pretax Profit Margin	2.9%
Net Earnings Growth	-23.3%	Net Profit Margin	1.8%
		Return on Total Assets	10.6%
Leverage		Return on Equity	25.2%
Total Debt/Total Assets	62.4%		
Interest-Bearing Debt/Equity	83.3%	**Turnover**	
Times Interest Earned (X)	4.2	Inventory Turnover (X)	15.2
Fixed Charges (X)	4.8	Receivable Turnover (X)	16.2
Total Assets/Equity (X)	2.7	Average Collection Period (days)	22.3
		Fixed Asset Turnover (X)	15.2
Liquidity		Working Capital Turnover (X)	15.9
Current Ratio (X)	1.3	Total Asset Turnover (X)	5.3
Quick Ratio (X)	0.7		

Performance Trends

Performance trend analysis is a review of financial performance over time and may include both common size and financial ratio reviews. Comparing an entity against itself over time reveals risks associated with volatility of performance and the progress management makes in implementing its strategies. Common size analysis consists of assessing changes over time in financial statement data, restated as a percentage. Balance sheets are expressed in relation to total assets and income statements to revenues. Those analyses allow for an understanding of trends associated with balance sheet allocations or profitability/returns that might not be revealed when reviewing trends in the reported currency amounts.

Suppose an entity's reported revenues and net earnings have been growing over the past several years in terms of currency. In isolation, this is good and bodes well; however, if, as a percentage of sales, net earnings are falling every year, a different perspective emerges. Why are revenues growing by X%? What causes expenses to grow more quickly? Is the incremental value of the additional profits decreasing? If so, why? The answers will help evaluate the risks in the stated and expected benefits. Similarly, financial ratios may be analyzed over time to measure volatility in performance trends. Is the growth financed with increasing leverage? Is asset utilization improving or declining? Is liquidity deteriorating because of buying sales through relaxed credit standards?

The next table illustrates an abbreviated trend analysis for an entity.

	Year 1	*Year 2*	*Year 3*
Growth			
Sales Growth	3.0%	8.5%	13.3%
Operating Earnings Growth	7.1%	11.8%	13.0%
Net Earnings Growth	-23.3%	16.4%	32.7%
Leverage			
Total Debt/Total Assets	62.4%	53.7%	44.8%
Interest-Bearing Debt/Equity	83.3%	53.8%	34.2%
Times Interest Earned (X)	4.2	6.4	10.7
Fixed Charges (X)	4.8	7.7	10.9
Total Assets/Equity (X)	2.7	2.2	1.8
Profitability			
Gross Margin	24.2%	25.4%	25.3%
Operating Expenses/Sales	19.5%	20.8%	20.2%
Operating Margin	2.9%	3.2%	3.8%
Pretax Profit Margin	2.9%	3.2%	3.8%
Net Profit Margin	1.8%	1.9%	2.3%
Return on Total Assets	10.6%	10.9%	12.5%
Return on Equity	25.2%	22.5%	22.5%
Turnover			
Inventory Turnover (X)	15.2	13.8	14.4
Receivable Turnover (X)	16.2	17.4	18.4
Average Collection Period (days)	22.3	20.7	19.6
Fixed Asset Turnover (X)	15.2	14.9	14.3
Working Capital Turnover (X)	15.9	14.7	14.5
Total Asset Turnover (X)	5.3	5.4	5.5
Liquidity			
Current Ratio (X)	1.3	1.5	1.7
Quick Ratio (X)	0.7	0.8	0.9

Peer Comparisons

In addition to evaluating the entity's financial condition and performance, currently and over time, these ratios may be compared and contrasted to various benchmarks. This topic is discussed further later in this chapter; here it is important to note that comparing an entity to itself, even over time, reveals risks only somewhat. Are the profitability ratios "good" or "bad"? This is unknown unless compared to some level of peer group or industry data.

In applying the guideline public company method to value an entity, the initial step is to identify some suitable guidelines; the next is to obtain market multiples associated with benefits that appear to be statistically significant. If these benefits of the guidelines are growing at twice the rate of the subject entity, and its similarly measured benefit is half that of the guidelines, some adjustments to the market multiples are warranted; without this analysis, valuators might not even raise the question.

The valuation methods selected and the availability of data drive the type and extent of peer comparisons. In some cases, there is a preponderance of data, which allows valuators to delve deeply into the subject's relative performance and develop a qualitative risk assessment based on empirical data. At other times, there is very little peer data; nonetheless, a quantitative analysis of whatever is available aids in assessing the subject's relative risks. Considered in isolation, weaker performance and greater volatility, however measured, generally indicate higher risks; similarly, stronger performance and lower volatility suggest lower risks.

The next table illustrates an abbreviated combination of financial, trend, and peer analyses for an entity. What financial and operational risks does the financial analysis reveal? How does that compare to its peers? The answers help support a specific risk adjustment as well as a basis for supportable estimates of future economic benefits and their potential growth.

	Year 1			Year 2			Year 3		
	Subject	Peers	Var	Subject	Peers	Var	Subject	Peers	Var
Growth									
Sales Growth	3.0%	3.9%	-0.9%	8.5%	8.9%	-0.4%	13.3%	13.5%	-0.2%
Gross Profit Growth	7.1%	5.7%	1.4%	11.8%	7.6%	4.2%	13.0%	8.9%	4.1%
Net Earnings Growth	-23.3%	68.8%	-92.1%	16.4%	10.6%	5.8%	32.7%	7.5%	25.2%
Leverage									
Total Debt/Total Assets	62.4%	65.9%	-3.5%	53.7%	61.7%	-7.9%	44.8%	59.2%	-14.5%
Interest-Bearing Debt/Equity	83.3%	56.0%	27.2%	53.8%	41.9%	11.9%	34.2%	39.1%	-5.0%
Times Interest Earned (X)	4.2	6.2	(2.0)	6.4	8.5	(2.1)	10.7	13.3	(2.7)
Fixed Charges (X)	4.8	9.0	(4.2)	7.7	9.0	(1.3)	10.9	9.0	1.9
Total Assets/ Equity (X)	2.7	2.9	(0.3)	2.2	2.6	(0.4)	1.8	2.5	(0.6)
Profitability									
Gross Margin	24.2%	25.4%	-1.2%	25.4%	25.9%	-0.5%	25.3%	26.2%	-0.9%
Operating Expenses/Sales	19.5%	22.0%	-2.5%	20.8%	22.2%	-1.4%	20.2%	22.0%	-1.8%
Operating Margin	2.9%	2.4%	0.5%	3.2%	2.8%	0.4%	3.8%	3.4%	0.4%
Pretax Profit Margin	2.9%	2.6%	0.3%	3.2%	3.0%	0.2%	3.8%	3.7%	0.1%
Net Profit Margin	1.8%	1.7%	0.1%	1.9%	2.0%	-0.1%	2.3%	2.2%	0.1%
Return on Total Assets	10.6%	6.7%	4.0%	10.9%	7.6%	3.3%	12.5%	8.2%	4.3%
Return on Equity	25.2%	18.7%	6.5%	22.5%	19.0%	3.5%	22.5%	19.1%	3.4%
Turnover									
Inventory Turnover (X)	15.2	7.7	7.5	13.8	7.4	6.3	14.4	7.2	7.1
Receivable Turnover (X)	16.2	11.5	4.7	17.4	11.6	5.7	18.4	11.4	7.0
Average Collection Period (days)	22.3	31.3	(9.1)	20.7	31.0	(10.2)	19.6	31.7	(12.1)
Fixed Asset Turnover (X)	15.2	17.2	(2.0)	14.9	16.7	(1.8)	14.3	16.1	(1.9)
Working Capital Turnover (X)	15.9	11.9	4.0	14.7	11.2	3.5	14.5	10.2	4.3
Total Asset Turnover (X)	5.3	3.7	1.6	5.4	3.6	1.8	5.5	3.5	2.0
Liquidity									
Current Ratio (X)	1.3	1.5	(0.2)	1.5	1.5	(0.1)	1.7	1.6	0.1
Quick Ratio (X)	0.7	0.8	(0.1)	0.8	0.8	(0.0)	0.9	0.9	(0.0)

OPERATING METRICS

Most industries use nonfinancial metrics to measure performance. For example, the restaurant industry looks at revenue per seat and the seat turnover rate as important productivity measures; similarly, retailers consider sales per employee and per square foot, for stores open more than one year, as significant. Depending on the size and nature of the industry, certain metrics may be widely disseminated and accepted. To the extent they are available, valuators' understanding of the subject and its relative performance will be enhanced.

The next table illustrates some operating metrics for the restaurant industry.

	Fast Food	*Full Service*
Sales per Seat	$ 10,169	$ 9,412
Sales per Square Foot	$ 759	$ 332
Seat Turnover Rate	5.10	1.25
Employee Turnover Rate	83%	117%

QUALITATIVE ANALYTICS

In addition to quantitative analyses of an entity at one specific time, over a period, and compared to industry peers, a qualitative analysis of the subject should also be performed. While valuators often feel more comfortable with quantitative analyses because it is easier to justify a conclusion with empirical data, a qualitative assessment of company-specific risks is recommended, as it may supply additional, helpful, and, many times, revealing information.

A valuator has performed a detailed financial analysis which revealed that, over time, compared to its peers, the subject consistently outperformed in terms of growth, profitability, and asset utilization, and is debt free. Earnings have evidenced minimal volatility, and management provided projections evidence more of the same. This appears to be a very healthy entity with little, if any, additional risk compared to industry or guideline data.

However, suppose the firm is managed fairly autocratically by the 87-year-old certified public accountant (CPA) founder who recently developed severe health problems. There is a disputed succession plan between the 64-year-old son, the president, and a 57-year-old CPA as chief financial officer; the second-tier management does not have the same skill set. This new information gives a completely different perspective on entity-specific risks, one that could not have been developed solely by a quantitative analysis of historic and prospective financial data. Traditionally, qualitative risk assessments are either a review of management's skills or an assessment of unique entity-specific characteristics.

Management Skills Review

Through a review of financial and operational reporting, management interviews and site inspections, experienced valuators may be able to assess the quality and depth of management. Often they will categorize and document this analysis with a checklist of items deemed important to the assessment process. They may be short, intuitively driven schedules of management issues, such as succession, depth, and specific skills. Alternatively, some firms have detailed checklists, treated like a scorecard, identifying 50 to 100 items. Whichever technique is adopted, an assessment of management's ability to bring about the expected benefits and growth is an integral part of risk assessment. A sample checklist is presented next.

Competition

Proprietary Content	Medium
Relative Size of Company	High
Market Strength	High
Ease of Market Entry	Medium
Patent/Copyright Protection	n/a
Competition Risk Index Factor:	*Medium/High*

Financial

Total Debt to Assets	High
Long-Term Debt to Equity	High
Current Ratio	High
Quick Ratio	High
Interest Coverage	Medium
Financial Risk Index Factor:	*High*

Management

Operating Asset Management	Medium
Working Capital Management	High
Management Depth/Succession	Medium
Internal Controls	Low
Planning/Strategy	Medium
Contracts	Low
Management Risk Index Factor:	*Medium*

Stability

Years in Business	High
Industry Risk relative to Economic Conditions	Medium
Industry Life Cycle	High
Stability Risk Index Factor:	*High*

Entity-Specific Characteristics

In addition to risks associated with management, often,there areitems unique to the subject that may not be reflected on the financial statements but nonetheless affect the value of the business. These are likely to be diverse; examples are:

- Identifiable, unrecorded intangible assets, such as patents, trademarks, secret recipes, or issues relating to location
- A unique source of supply
- Unaddressed property environmental issues

Such nonfinancial issues can be either risk enhancing or risk inhibiting.

Care must be taken not to include them twice in developing valuation variables. An entity may hold key patents that give it a real and measurable competitive advantage; generally, that would be reflected in gross profit margins that surpass industry performance. If a valuator applies an income method using these patent-enhanced margins and also reduces entity-specific risks based primarily on the patents, the valuator may very well be double counting the economic benefits and generating an overstated value.

There may be risks associated with the operations of any particular entity that cannot be identified through detailed financial analyses, though such activity may often lead to hints of these issues. The answer to the question "Why are gross margins so high?" may reveal the existence of patents. Or it may simply be that the entity's accounting policies differ from industry practice. Similarly, marketing costs well below industry norms may suggest the existence of key customer dependencies or a very strong brand franchise.

Quality of Management

A more holistic approach brings together both quantitative and qualitative assessments and focuses on entity-specific risks. According to FASB, "a business is an integrated set of activities and assets conducted and managed for the purpose of providing (a) a return to investors, or (b) lower costs or other economic benefits directly and proportionately to owners, members, or participants." *Minutes of the February 4, 2004 Board Meeting.* This definition links the firm's financial and operational resources with management's competency. This bond occurs not only in assembling the income producing assets but also in doing it in such a way that internal strengths are leveraged, internal weaknesses are mitigated, external opportunities are capitalized on, and external threats are thwarted.

*S*trength, *w*eakness, *o*pportunity, and *t*hreat (SWOT) analysis is a tool often used by management for strategy development; for more information, see the work by Mard et al.[2] Valuators can use it as a framework to identify the environmental and situational risks associated with management's strategy and its deployment. The next lists suggest the types of questions to ask.

---

[2] *Michael J. Mard, Robert R Dunne, Edi Osborne, and, James S. Rigby Jr.,* **Driving Your Company's Value: Strategic Benchmarking for Value** *(Hoboken, NJ: John Wiley & Sons, 2004).*

Strengths	Weaknesses
• What does the entity do well? • What is its market position or share? • Does the entity have a clear communicable vision or direction? • Does the entity have a positive corporate culture that makes for a work environment that will attract the employees desired? • What are the entity's definable resources (tangible and intangible)? • Does the entity have a history of meeting its operational and performance goals?	• What systems could be improved at the entity? • What does the competition do better? • What does the entity do poorly? • Does the entity have the financial resources to purchase needed equipment, technology, or facilities? • Does the entity have the financial resources to withstand a downturn or unforeseen negative circumstances? • Can the entity support its expected growth rate?
Opportunities	**Threats**
• What changes are taking place in the market that open up opportunities? Is the entity positioned to take advantage of the opportunities? • Is the entity entering new markets? • Can the entity upgrade its technology to lower costs or expand capacity and/or improve service? • Can the entity expand its geographic coverage? • Can the entity improve its use of the Internet for marketing or customer relations?	• What obstacles/challenges is the entity facing? • What are the entity's competitors doing that might affect future performance? • Are regulatory requirements or customer demands forcing a change in the entity's products or services? • Is technology threatening the entity's market position? • Is there pressure on profit margins? If so, what is its source?

STRATEGY: MANAGEMENT'S RESPONSE TO THE EXTERNAL CONTEXT

Every company has a strategy. It may be formally developed and articulated, or it may be unspoken and ad hoc; it may be proactive or reactive, but there is one. Generally, a strategy is, at least in part, a response to the external context in which the entity operates. This chapter deals with internal perspectives; external issues are addressed in Chapter 7, Assessing External Risks, because they are important to the valuator's assessment of strategic alignment. For example, the current and expected economic situation drives management decisions from both short-term (tactical) and long-term (strategic) perspectives. The cost and access to capital is driven to a significant degree by the economic outlook, as are growth expectations.

Certainly, the 2009 economic outlook steers management's strategic decisions in a radically different direction from those of 2004. The regulatory background and the amount of existing and expected government intervention in the activities of the entity are important; the trends in the industry and markets in which it operates also have a dramatic impact on the appropriate action. Management will not only attempt to forecast future trends and develop its strategy accordingly but may also attempt to influence them to the extent that it can.

Finally, the competitive surroundings affect the strategy. For example, considered in isolation, it is hard to accept as reasonable a forecast of both growth and margins at twice industry averages in a mature and highly competitive sector. However, in such a milieu, an entity like General Electric can experience above-average growth and profitability for a long time if it develops and implements an effective strategy. Successful managements develop plans in the context of the competitive settings in which they operate.

Identifying Strategy: The Porter Model

Before assessing management's ability to align strategy with resources, it is essential to recognize the strategy. Michael Porter proffered a powerful framework for classifying strategies.[3] He suggests that five fundamental competitive forces affect a business as well as three "generic" responses; the five forces are:

1. Threats of new competitors into the marketplace
2. Relative bargaining power of customers
3. Relative bargaining power of suppliers
4. Threat of substitute products or services
5. The relative rivalry among existing firms in the marketplace

How they play out in a particular market and the position of a specific entity relative to other competitors affect that firm's ability to compete effectively and has direct implications on its profitability and growth.

The three strategic responses often implemented by successful competitors are: (1) cost leadership, (2) differentiation from competitors, and (3) focus on market segments and/or core competencies. The next table correlates the five forces and three responses.

	Cost Leadership	**Differentiation**	**Focus**
Threats of New Entrants	Ability to cut price in retaliation deters potential entrants	Customer loyalty can discourage potential entrants	Focusing develops core competencies that can act as an entry barrier
Customer Power	Ability to offer lower price to powerful buyers	Large customers have less power to negotiate because of few close alternatives	Large customers have less power to negotiate because of few alternatives
Supplier Power	Better insulated from powerful suppliers	Better able to pass on supplier price increases to customers	Suppliers have power because of low volumes, but a differentiation-focused firm is better able to pass on supplier price increases
Threat of Substitutes	Can use low price to defend against substitutes	Customers become attached to differentiating attributes, reducing threat of substitutes	Specialized products and core competency protect against substitutes
Competitive Rivalry	Better able to compete on price	Brand loyalty to keep customers from rivals	Rivals cannot meet differentiation-focused customer needs

This framework provides valuators with a context for measuring and evaluating strategic alignment. Management has to identify the firm's competitive situations and develop effective strategies to improve the returns, and hence increase a value to the owners. After this, managers' effectiveness can be measured by how well they align the available resources with the strategy.

---

[3] *In Michael Porter, **Competitive Strategy: Techniques for Analyzing Industries and Competitors** (The Free Press, New York, 1980), **Competitive Advantage: Creating and Sustaining Superior Performance** (The Free Press, New York, 1985), **On Competition** (Harvard Business School Publishing Corporation, Cambridge MA 2008)*

Illustration

Consider Wal-Mart Stores, Inc.'s strategy in the highly competitive retail industry. Reporting nearly $400 billion in revenues in its fiscal year ending January 2008, by that measure the company is one of the world's largest single businesses, yet it still represents only a small percentage of overall global retail sales. However, historically Wal-Mart has dominated nearly all the markets in which it participates. As of 2008, it operated nearly 7,100 units, of which 42% were outside the United States. A 2004 documentary describes Wal-Mart in this way:

> *As the dominant discount retailer...Wal-Mart has transformed the standard retail marketplace, making it more difficult for traditional retail businesses to compete against the Wal-Mart superstore model. While there are other "big box" mass retailers, Wal-Mart's success has forced other retailers to change the way they do business if they want to survive. That makes Wal-Mart incredibly unique....It has trail-blazed the discount business, brought down prices for the average consumer, making it very hard for others to compete against. Because it is an extremely effective company at delivering low prices consistently, Wal-Mart has consequently forced other retailers to lower their prices as well.*[4]

The documentary went on to state that Wal-Mart's size allows it to operate distribution and inventory systems that give it greater operating efficiencies and productivity than their competitors. Clearly, Wal-Mart's strategy has been one of cost leadership. In its 2008 annual report, the company states: "Management believes return on investment ('ROI') is a meaningful metric to share with investors because it helps investors assess how efficiently Wal-Mart is employing its assets."[5]

High asset utilization, then, is a key driver of effective cost leadership. To support analyses of economic benefits, growth, and risks, valuators should measure the asset utilization for an entity with such a strategy, then compare that asset utilization with that of the industry as a whole, the entity's peers, or itself over time. This gives insight as to management's ability to create alignment between resources and its plans. Similarly, the drivers of effective strategies may be identified and measured through various analytics, including benchmarking.

BENCHMARKING STRATEGY IMPLEMENTATION

Benchmarking is the process of comparing an entity's condition and performance using objective and/or subjective criteria, whether historic or in relation to some standard or group. As used by management, it is generally an alignment improvement process; looking at performance relative to "best practices," the objective is to gain insights as to management's effectiveness and find ways to improve its processes and practices.

Valuators typically utilize benchmarking to frame more directly the discussion. Has management successfully implemented its business strategy? What are the expectations regarding future growth, earnings, efficiency, and leverage associated with the strategy? How do these expectations compare to the industry at large or to entities from which value metrics are to be derived?

Linking Operations and Financial Performance

One well-established analytical tool available to valuators is the DuPont formula. This is an analysis of return on equity (ROE) that shows the relative contributions of profitability, utilization, and leverage; the traditional version is:

---

[4] *Public Broadcasting Service, "Wal-Mart: Impact of a Retail Giant," August 20, 2004, MacNeil/Lehrer Productions, www.pbs.org/newshour/bb/business/wal-mart/unique.html.*

[5] *Wal-Mart, 2008 Annual Report, p. 14, http://walmartstores.com/sites/AnnualReport/2008/.*

$$\text{ROE} = \frac{\text{Net Income}}{\text{Equity}} = \frac{\text{Net Income}}{\text{Sales}} \times \frac{\text{Sales}}{\text{Assets}} \times \frac{\text{Assets}}{\text{Equity}}$$

Those components can be broken down by financial statement categories to further understand their contributions, both good and bad, to ROE. Exhibit 8.1 illustrates how the various financial components of profitability, asset utilization, and leverage relate directly to ROE.

Exhibit 8.1 Expanded DuPont Formula

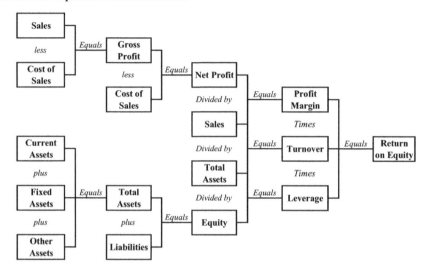

There are three direct benefits to using the DuPont Formula in developing valuation metrics:

1.   Compare the contributing factors to ROE for the subject to either industry peers or guidelines; how similar are they?

The next table sets out the breakdown of the ROE using the DuPont formula for Company 1 (the subject) and Company 2 (a peer).

$$\text{ROE} = \frac{\text{Net Income}}{\text{Equity}} = \frac{\text{Net Income}}{\text{Sales}} \times \frac{\text{Sales}}{\text{Assets}} \times \frac{\text{Assets}}{\text{Equity}}$$

Company 1:

$$\text{ROE} = \frac{4{,}200}{16{,}000} = \frac{4{,}200}{175{,}600} \times \frac{175{,}600}{25{,}200} \times \frac{25{,}200}{16{,}000}$$

$$26.3\% = 2.4\% \times 6.97 \times 1.58$$

Company 2:

$$\text{ROE} = \frac{1{,}750}{6{,}650} = \frac{1{,}750}{175{,}600} \times \frac{175{,}600}{43{,}200} \times \frac{43{,}200}{6{,}650}$$

$$26.3\% = 1.0\% \times 4.06 \times 6.50$$

What do these analyses show? A traditional ratio analysis indicates that the two are very similar, with an identical ROE of 26.3%. However, a look at the components of the ROE—profitability, utilization, and leverage—reveals two very different entities. Company 1 relies on efficient use of its assets (whatever they may be) to help drive profitability, with both utilization and profitability driving ROE. Company 2, however, is focused on leveraging its equity to drive returns, with nearly twice as much debt in its invested capital than Company 1, even though it has little more than a third of its equity.

2. *Identify either underutilization (low economic benefits) or capacity constraints (high risks).*

Particularly when comparing an entity to itself over time or to peers, the DuPont formula can highlight potential extremes in profitability, efficiency, and/or leverage. Extremes at either end of the spectrum generally do not contribute to value. Identifying such extremes should lead to important "why" questions.

Gildersleeve's comments are informative:

> [T]he more income a company earns from an equity investment, the better. Shareholders like to see very large ROEs. High ROEs typically drive up share prices since the company is efficiently earning money with its equity capital. The relationship between ROE and net income is apparent from the first formula [above]; however, that formula does not appreciably help management decide what to change to improve ROE.
>
> Although the second formula [above] yields the identical result for ROE, it helps the manager more than the first. In the second formula, ROE is equivalent to profitability multiplied by asset turnover multiplied by financial leverage. By increasing any of these factors, management can enhance ROE.
>
> High ROE values generally indicate good performance although it is important for you to understand the reasons for a higher or lower trending ROE. Higher ROEs may not be desirable if the company must assume too high a risk in its product offering or degree of debt leverage. Higher ROEs indicate that net profit, and/or asset turnover, and/or financial leverage are increasing. Increases in net profit are good to the extent that a company does not sacrifice growth potential, sales levels, and quality. Increases in asset turnover are good to the extent that a company retains sufficient assets to optimize operations efficiencies. Increases in financial leverage can be positive to the extent that the company has not acquired so much debt for the purchase of assets that the company is at risk of default.[6]

3. *Measure management's ability to align resources with strategies—what is driving ROE? Is that consistent with the entity's strategies? How well is the strategy being implemented?*

With these questions the chapter comes full circle; its purpose is to offer a framework for developing valuation metrics from an analysis of the subject—an internal perspective—whether considering entity-specific risk, the selection of appropriate market data, or expected future economic benefits, including long-term sustainable growth.

All experienced valuators are aware of the importance of aligning resources with strategies; in fact, a substantial portion of the analyses performed and reports prepared by appraisers address this subject. This chapter has provided a simple outline of some of the basic techniques typically applied, as well as suggesting a holistic approach, bringing together various processes to provide a context for the analyses and help answer the "whys" as well as the "whats." The DuPont Formula is merely one gadget in a valuator's toolbox. The illustration of Wal-Mart highlighted that firm's focus on asset utilization. In no other way would this be as clearly evident as in a comparative DuPont analysis. Combining qualitative and quantitative analyses of the subject, the economy, and the industry should allow valuators to derive suitable value metrics and provide empirical support for their conclusions.

---

[6] Rich Gildersleeve, **Winning Business: How to Use Financial Analysis and Benchmarks to Outscore Your Competition** (Houston: Cashman Dudley, 1999), as quoted in Mard et al., **Driving Your Company's Value**, pp. 6–7.

9 COST OF CAPITAL[1]

WOLFGANG BALLWIESER AND JÖRG WIESE

GERMANY

INTRODUCTION

The cost of capital comprises both debt and equity. Among other things, it is needed for investment and financing decisions, business valuations, capital budgeting, and determining "recoverable amounts" for impairment testing. Normally, while the cost of debt is determined by contracts (except for items such as defined benefit pension plans), the cost of equity, the expected risk-adjusted rate of return required by (often anonymous investors) is usually unobservable and has to be estimated by financial models. The most important of such models are the Capital Asset Pricing Model (CAPM), the arbitrage pricing theory (APT), the Fama-French three-factor model, numerous build-up models and ex ante or implied cost-of-capital (ICC) models.

They differ mainly with respect to their assumptions. CAPM is an equilibrium model with a large set of restrictions (perfect capital markets, risk-averse investors, and a one-period planning horizon), whereas APT only requires the absence of arbitrage possibilities and is independent from equilibrium conditions. They also vary in their time perspective when implemented. Although CAPM is ex ante in theory (meaning that it uses expectations of capital market participants to explain expected returns of financial assets in market equilibrium), in practice, it is used through statistical analyses to estimate the past betas and market risk premiums, which are then extrapolated into the future. In that respect, past results determine, or at least influence, future expectations. This is totally different from ICC models, which use market prices of shares at the valuation date and forecasts of future profits and dividends as inputs to estimate the cost of equity.

The next section discusses theoretical factors which determine the cost of equity and that of debt. It is followed by short descriptions of the most important models to determine the cost of equity. Both components contribute to the weighted average cost of capital (WACC), which is employed in discounting free cash flows and also to determine fair value (International Accounting Standard [IAS] 39 and International Financial Reporting Standard [IFRS] 3) and value in use (IAS 36). Empirical data and examples are included; additionally, there is a discussion of the weaknesses of all models and a warning against drawing false conclusions.

DRIVERS OF COSTS OF CAPITAL

This section deals first with the cost of debt, followed by the cost of equity.

---

[1] *Portions of this chapter covering application of CAPM and build-up models use, with permission, material from Chapter 5, "Capitalization/Discount Rates," of the course "Business Valuations: Universal and Fundamental Applications," © 2007 International Association of Consultants, Valuators and Analysts (IACVA), Toronto, Canada.*

Cost of Debt

Lenders expect payments of their loans on the due date and for the contracted amount. They face the risk that payments are made late and for a lesser amount, including the possible total loss of capital. To protect themselves against such events, lenders restrict their loans to certain amounts, require security, and adjust their interest rates to compensate for the known risks; these are usually spreads over the risk-free rate of return reflecting the creditworthiness of the borrowers.

The risk-free rate is that which an asset would yield without any possibility of default, timing, or exchange rate; as such, it is a nonobservable theoretical construct that is measured usually by the rates of return on government securities in any particular currency. To derive it, two questions need to be answered:

1. Which market data should be chosen?
2. Since returns are time dependent, which maturity is appropriate?

Concerning the first question, the obvious answer would be an average of historical yields on government loans. However, that is not appropriate, since investment and financing decisions or business valuations are based on future cash flows. Therefore, they should be related to expected rates of return, as there is no reason to assume historic rates can be reasonably extrapolated; the capital market environment at a valuation date will surely differ from past circumstances.

Another possibility is the use of yields to maturity or internal rates of return on government bonds at the valuation date. The problem is that their use implies, contrary to reality, a flat (time-independent) yield curve. Therefore, spot rates, which explicitly reflect the term structure of interest rates, should be applied in discounting future cash flows; those are the yields to maturity of government zero-coupon bonds. In other words, they are defined by only two cash flows, one at the valuation date, and the other at a later time; thus they are time dependent, as is the yield curve. The latter shows the relationship between market interest rates and the time to maturity of zero-coupon bonds. In some markets, where so-called stripped government bonds are traded, the relationship is directly observable.

Stripping a bond means separating the coupons from the principal; a 10-year coupon bond generates 10 interest strips, with maturities of 1 to 10 years and a single 10-year principal strip; each strip consists of only two cash flows and thus represents a spot rate. However, the trading volume of government strips is normally much lower than that of equivalent bonds; hence, the majority of the European central banks apply the Svensson method[2] to estimate the yield curve from implied zero-coupon returns of a series of government coupon bonds with different maturities. In valuing businesses, German auditors are required to apply this method. In it, the relationship between the continuous spot rate is at the valuation date t and time to maturity T is assumed to be estimated by the equation

$$i_c(t, t+T, b) = \beta_0 + \beta_1 \frac{1-e^{(-T/\tau_1)}}{T/\tau_1} + \beta_2 \left(\frac{1-e^{(-T/\tau_1)}}{T/\tau_1} - e^{(-T/\tau_1)} \right) + \beta_3 \left(\frac{1-e^{(-T/\tau_2)}}{T/\tau_2} - e^{(-T/\tau_2)} \right) \qquad (9.1)$$

Where

$b = (\beta_0, \beta_1, \beta_2, \beta_3, \tau_1, \tau_2)$ = parameter vector to be estimated

e = Eulerian number (2,718...)

---

[2] *Lars E. O. Svensson, "Estimating and Interpreting Forward Interest Rates: Sweden 1992-1994," NBER Working Paper No. 4871, Cambridge, MA, September 1994.*

This equation allows spot rates to be estimated at any time.

Exhibit 9.1 shows the yield curve as estimated by the European Central Bank (ECB) as at December 1, 2008.

Exhibit 9.1 Yield Curve as at December 1, 2008

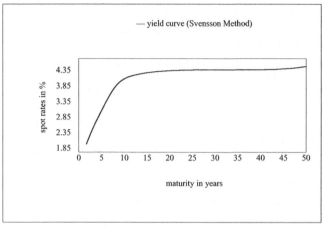

Source: Authors' calculations, using parameters estimated by ECB (discrete spot rates).

To use bonds with sufficient market depth, the ECB covers maturities ranging from three months to 30 years; beyond that, an assumption on the shape of the curve has to be made; in Exhibit 9.1, as is common, the extended curve is treated as flat. The resulting spot risk-free rates may be applied to develop individual discount rates for periodic future cash flows. Alternatively, the estimated yield curve can be aggregated to a single flat rate of return that is consistent with the Svensson method but not time dependent. For this, a simplified discounted cash flow model is used; this assumes cash flows increase at a constant rate (g) over an infinite time horizon.[3] This model is described by the next equation.

$$V_0 = \sum_{t=1}^{\infty} \frac{CF_0(1+g)^t}{(1+i_{d,t})^t} = \frac{CF_0(1+g)}{i-g} \quad i > g \qquad (9.2)$$

Where

V_0 = business value
CF_0 = cash flow in t = 0
$i_{d,t}$ = discrete spot rate for period t
i = flat risk-free rate of return
g = constant growth rate of cash flows

The first present value in equation 9.2 is calculated with period specific spot rates and represents the correct business value. Equating this amount with the simplified formula in the right-hand side of equation 9.2 and solving the equation yields the flat rate (i). The value of CF_0 can be chosen arbitrarily, because the cash flows in equation 9.2 cancel out.

On December 1, 2008, the method yields the flat rates for certain selected cash flow growth rates shown Exhibit 9.2.

---

[3] *Martin Jonas, Heike Wieland-Blöse, and Stefanie Schiffarth, "Basiszinssatz in der Unternehmensbewertung," Finanz Betrieb 7 (2005): 647–653.*

Exhibit 9.2 Risk-free Rates of Return as at December 1, 2008

Growth Rate (g)	Flat Rate (i)
0.00%	4.17%
1.00%	4.21%
2.00%	4.25%

Source: Authors' calculations.

This method also answers the second question concerning the maturity of bonds to be chosen: Market data should be used when it is available for government bonds with sufficient trading activity in most countries; those with a maturity of less than 30 years meet this requirement.

The premium added to the risk-free rate of return depends on the risks of which the lender is aware. An indicator of the required spread is given by the grade given to a borrower by a rating agency; they differentiate between many categories of risk, which are summarized as an investment or speculative grade. The most important rating agencies, Moody's, Standard & Poor's (S&P), and Fitch, use the categories shown in Exhibit 9.3.

Exhibit 9.3 Rating Categories of Established Rating Agencies

	Moody's	S&P	Fitch	Debt is
investment grade	Aaa	AAA	AAA	**of highest credit quality.** Assigned only in case of exceptionally strong capacity for payment of financial commitments.
	Aa	AA	AA	**of very high credit quality.** AA indicates very strong capacity for payment of financial commitments.
	A	A	A	**of high credit quality.** A denotes expectations of low credit risk. The capacity to meet its financial commitments is still strong. However, this may be more vulnerable to changes in circumstances or economic conditions than obligations in higher rated categories.
	Baa	BBB	BBB	**of good credit quality.** The lowest investment grade indicates expectations of low credit risk. The capacity for payment of financial commitments is considered adequate, but adverse changes in circumstances and economic conditions are more likely to impair this capacity.
speculative grade	Ba	BB	BB	**of speculative credit quality.** There is a possibility of credit risk developing; however, business or financial alternatives may be available to allow financial commitments to be met.
	B	B	B	**of highly speculative credit quality.** The borrower currently has the capacity to meet its financial commitments. Adverse conditions probably will impair its capacity or willingness to meet its commitments.
	Caa	CCC	CCC	**vulnerable to nonpayment within one year** and depends on favorable conditions to meet financial commitment.
	Ca	CC	CC	**currently highly vulnerable to nonpayment.**
	C	C	C	**extremely vulnerable to nonpayment.** Rating may be used to cover a situation where a bankruptcy petition has been filed or similar action has been taken but payments on this obligation are being continued.
		D	RD	**defaulted.** This rating is not prospective; rather, a default has actually occurred.
	1, 2, 3 in the areas of Aa to Caa	+/- in the areas of AA to CCC	+/- in the areas of AA to CCC	Modifiers may be appended to a rating to denote relative status within the major rating categories.

Exhibit 9.4 shows credit spreads of 5-year government bonds denominated in euros (€) and U.S. dollars ($) comparing German Bundswith U.S. Treasuries as of February 27, 2009. {Bund=ferederation}

Exhibit 9.4 Credit Spreads of Government Bonds from Several Countries Compared to German Bunds (€) and U.S. Treasury Bonds ($)

Rating (S&P)	Currency	Credit Default Spreads (basis points)	Countries
AAA		0	Germany
AAA		(3)–273	France, Netherlands, Austria, Ireland
AA+, AA		51–133	Spain, Belgium, Slovenia
A+, A, A–	€	46–282	Portugal, Italy, Czech Republic, Greece, Poland
BBB, BBB–		238–713	Morocco, Lithuania
BB+		701–1.000	Latvia, Romania
AAA		0	USA
AA+, AA		92–277	New Zealand, Abu Dhabi
A+, A, A–	$	160-350	China, Chile, Malaysia, Korea
BBB+, BBB, BBB–		210–673	Thailand, Mexico, South Africa, Russia, Bulgaria, Peru, Colombia, Brazil
BB+, BB–		399–569	Turkey, Egypt, Indonesia
B–		427	Lebanon

Source: Bloomberg

In early 2003, S&P modified its treatment of pension obligations in the rating process. Previously it did not include them in its financial ratios; now, S&P regards any part of a firm's pension obligation not covered by related assets as debt. This had a significant impact on many firms. "Most prominently, German industrial conglomerate ThyssenKrupp AG experienced a two-notch downgrade, resulting in the assignment of non-investment grade status to its bonds."[4] According to management, interest increased by €20 million per year; two years later investment grade was restored.

Although ratings help in determining the interest spread, it has to be kept in mind that rating agencies concentrate their activities on big, very often global firms. Therefore, many borrowers in which (potential) lenders are interested are not covered. In recent times, because of the financial market crisis, there has been great doubt about the reliability of the conclusions of rating agencies with respect to so-called structured products. Rational lenders consider opportunity costs; they make a loan only if the expected rate of return is at least as high as it could be gained in the best alternative.

Cost of Equity

Equity investors receive any income remaining after all contractual and noncontractual claims. This residual is not stable with respect to time or amount and reflects numerous risks.

Equity Risks

The most significant risks incorporated into the cost of equity are:

- Operational (or investment)
- Financial (or capital structure)
- Systematic (in contrast to idiosyncratic)

---

[4] *Bernhard Pellens and Nils Crasselt, "Funding Strategies for Defined Benefit Plans and the Measurement of Leverage Risk," p. 5, in: Wolfgang Ballwieser, ed.,* **Current Issues in Financial Reporting and Financial Statement Analysis,** *Special Issue of* **Schmalenbach Business Review** *2, No. 5 (2005): 3–33.*

- Currency
- Location (or country)

Operational risks result from the firm's business model, independent of its financing. They are influenced to some extent by the sector in which it operates, such as airlines or computer chips. However, this classification, on its own, is too varied to be effective because different members of the same sector face different risks. One only has to compare Lufthansa and Alitalia, or Intel and Infineon.

Financial risks result from the capital structure, especially the rates and repayment terms of the debt that in most cases has to be serviced regardless of the state of product or service demand, competition, or regulation.

Systematic risk is defined in CAPM; one of its basic assumptions is that every investor constructs an efficient portfolio which has either (a) the minimum risk for a specific expected return, or (b) the maximum return for a certain level of risk. Therefore, at equilibrium, a premium is paid only for those risks that are not diversifiable through portfolio composition. The nondiversifiable portion is systematic risk; the diversifiable portion, attributed to individual securities, is idiosyncratic risk.

Operational and financial risks are both idiosyncratic because the entity is considered on its own rather than in a portfolio context. According to CAPM, this is not relevant for determining the cost of equity. Instead, the possibility of reducing risk by means of developing a portfolio has to be used in order to lower the overall risk; the remaining component is systematic risk.

Currency risk results from positions denominated in foreign currencies. Any investor in the United States with holdings in euro-based entities has a foreign currency risk, as the exchange rate between the U.S. dollar and the euro is not stable. The same is true for British firms with sales in the United States: during 2008, the amount for £1.00 declined 26% from $1.98 to $1.46. As CAPM cannot consider currency risk, a multicurrency version has been developed, but it is too complex to apply in practice.

It is almost impossible to combine all risk elements in a meaningful way. While idiosyncratic risks can be measured by standard deviations or variances of probability distributions of cash flows, other measures, such as correlation coefficients, are needed to gauge systematic risk; those may also be used for currency risks, but none of them can be combined easily with measures of country risks, since the latter are ordinal scores, which combine numerous, very different factors.

Size-dependent risks[5] are not part of those factors. This is important since practitioners sometimes use small stock risk premiums (SSRP), which depend on the size of a listed company.[6] SSRP are not part of CAPM and go back to multifactor models; that point is discussed later.

COST OF EQUITY METHODS

There are five generally accepted methods to establish the cost of equity for an entity:

1. Capital Asset Pricing Model
2. Arbitrage pricing theory
3. Fama-French three-factor model

---

[5] *Rolf W. Banz, "The Relationship between Return and Market Value of Common Stocks,"* **Journal of Financial Economics** *9 (1981): 3–18.*

[6] *See Shannon P. Pratt and Roger J. Grabowski,* **Cost of Capital—Applications and Examples** *(Hoboken, NJ: John Wiley & Sons, 2008).*

4. Build-up models
5. Implied cost of capital models

Capital Asset Pricing Model

The Capital Asset Pricing Model, known by its acronym, "CAPM," is the most often used method, but, as it depends on the efficient-market hypothesis, which has been called into question by the 2008 stock market collapse, it is not necessarily the most effective model to establish the cost of equity capital. Its past dominance might be explained by the fact that it is easy to understand. Equation 9.3 determines the expected rate of return of a security $\mu(\tilde{r}_j)$ in capital market equilibrium:

$$\mu(\tilde{r}_j) = r_f + \beta_j [\mu(\tilde{r}_M) - r_f] \beta = \sigma_{jM} / \sigma^2_M \qquad (9.3)$$

Where

rf	=	riskless interest rate
$\mu(\tilde{r}_M)$	=	expected rate of return of the market portfolio M
β_j	=	beta; risk factor of a share of company j
σ_{jM}	=	covariance between returns of security j and returns of the market portfolio
σ^2_M	=	variance of return on market portfolio.

The term $\left[\mu(\tilde{r}_M) - r_f\right]$ is the market risk premium. Beta is intended to measure the systematic risk of a share and shows how sensitive its expected return is to changes in that of the market portfolio $\mu(\tilde{r}_M)$. CAPM is theoretically an ex ante model, but its application is usually based on ex post data, since its parameters are not observable.

For empirical application, equation 9.3 is written as a regression line with beta as its slope:

$$r_{j,t} = r_{f,t} - \beta_{j,t} i_t + \beta_{j,t} r_{m,t} + e_{j,t} = a_{j,t} + b_{j,t} r_{M,t} + e_{j,t} \qquad (9.4)$$

Where

t = a moment in time
a = intercept of the regression line
e = a random error term with (by assumption) an expected value of zero and a variance $\sigma^2_{e_j}$

As illustrated in Exhibit 9.5, parameters a and b are estimated by regression analyses from a sample of historic returns on the particular asset and the market portfolio.

Exhibit 9.5 Characteristic Line of Security j

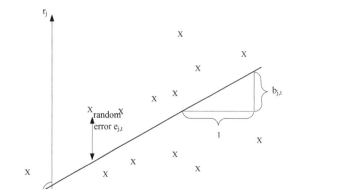

To assess the statistical accuracy of the estimates, standard errors of the coefficients a and b as well as the R^2 of the trend line have to be considered; furthermore, estimated coefficients should be tested for significance.

In determining market risk premium and beta, several critical decisions need to be made concerning the:

- Risk-free rate of return
- Stock index proxy for the market
- Intervals for measuring returns
- Estimation period (including the base year and the length)
- Calculating the average market risk premium
- Historic or adjusted betas

The factors determining appropriate choices are discussed next.

Risk-free rate of return. Since CAPM is a single-period model, the use of long-term bond yields is not appropriate to obtain the market-risk premium. Multiperiod applications require a single-point rate, as the yield curve is usually not flat. To determine the risk-free rate, spot rates from the Svensson method should be converted into implied forward rates, to be used consistently in calculating expected returns as well as the market risk premium.

Another problem arises from unanticipated interest rate changes. While stocks usually benefit from rate cuts in terms of capital gains, this process does not necessarily apply to bonds, as those with a short remaining maturity do not necessarily benefit. Thus, the market risk premium—the difference between stock and bond returns—may be overestimated if a short-term bond index is used for the risk-free interest rate.[7]

Stock index proxy for the market. The stock index chosen should be as broad as possible to offer a good proxy for the market, which theoretically contains all risky assets worldwide. For an index to be representative of the market, it must be value weighted. Normally the choices are: in the United States, the S&P 500 or the New York Stock Exchange (NYSE) Composite; internationally, the Morgan Stanley Capital International (MSCI), Barra

---

[7] Ekkehard Wenger, *"Verzinsungsparameter in der Unternehmensbewertung—Betrachtungen aus theoretischer und empirischer Sicht,"* **Die Aktiengesellschaft, Sonderheft** (2005): 9–22.

World, which covers 23 countries. The problems of a United States–based index are that its capital market conditions may not be relevant for other countries or for other currencies.

Intervals for measuring returns. Estimates of beta are affected by the intervals for measuring returns and their frequency. Data are available and may be collected daily, weekly, monthly, quarterly or annually. While preferable for actively traded issues, daily data are not appropriate for illiquid shares, since the estimate may be biased downward;[8] in those cases, weekly or monthly intervals should be chosen. For short periods, there may be problems stemming from a systematic relationship between the frequency and the resulting beta; the longer the interval, the smaller the problem. Even in such circumstances, estimated betas for illiquid shares are often biased; figures of less than 0.5 are normally observed only for this group.[9] However, for a given estimation period, longer intervals imply higher standard errors. Thus, the estimation period and the measurement interval have to be determined simultaneously. For short intervals, a lesser estimation period is enough to obtain sufficient data for a valid beta. Since beta varies over time, separate figures should be calculated for varying periods (e.g., 250 days, 52 weeks, 60 months) and numbers of observations.

Estimation period. There is no theoretical base for selecting a particular historic estimation period. To obtain a large sample, it is desirable for it to be as far ranging as possible, say, from 1900 to 2008; however, there is a trade-off between the estimation period and possible biases from structural breaks in the time series, such as the Great Depression and two world wars. Therefore, it seems appropriate to start shortly after 1950, when Europe was at peace and the Treasury-Fed Accord (1951) had terminated the wartime fixed interest rate policy in the United States. Stehle, who did one of the most comprehensive studies on German market risk premiums, adopted 1955 to 2003.[10]

Tied to the estimation period is the choice of base year. Excluding a short period or even a single year can easily change the reported premium by 1.0% or 1.5%. Dimson, Marsh, and Staunton (2006), for example, chose 1900 to 2005.[11] Exhibit 9.6 summarizes their results.

Exhibit 9.6 Annualized Equity Premiums for 17 Countries, 1900–2005

% p.a.	Historical Equity Premium Relative to Bills				Historical Equity Premium Relative to Bonds			
Country	Geometric Mean	Arithmetic Mean	Standard Error	Standard Deviation	Geometric Mean	Arithmetic Mean	Standard Error	Standard Deviation
Australia	7.08	8.49	1.65	17.00	6.22	7.81	1.83	18.80
Belgium	2.80	4.99	2.24	23.06	2.57	4.37	1.95	20.10
Canada	4.54	5.88	1.62	16.71	4.15	5.67	1.74	17.95
Denmark	2.87	4.51	1.93	19.85	2.07	3.27	1.57	16.18
France	6.79	9.27	2.35	24.19	3.86	6.03	2.16	22.29
Germany*	3.83	9.07	3.28	33.49	5.28	8.35	2.69	27.41
Ireland	4.09	5.98	1.97	20.33	3.62	5.18	1.78	18.37
Italy	6.55	10.46	3.12	32.09	4.30	7.68	2.89	29.73
Japan	6.67	9.84	2.70	27.82	5.91	9.98	3.21	33.06
Netherlands	4.55	6.61	2.17	22.36	3.86	5.95	2.10	21.63
Norway	3.07	5.70	2.52	25.90	2.55	5.26	2.66	27.43
South Africa	6.20	8.25	2.15	22.09	5.35	7.03	1.88	19.32
Spain	3.40	5.46	2.08	21.45	2.32	4.21	1.96	20.20
Sweden	5.73	7.98	2.15	22.09	5.21	7.51	2.17	22.34
Switzerland	3.63	5.29	1.82	18.79	1.80	3.28	1.70	17.52
U.K.	4.43	6.14	1.93	19.84	4.06	5.29	1.61	16.60
U.S.	5.51	7.41	1.91	19.64	4.52	6.49	1.96	20.16

---

[8] *Peter Zimmermann, Schätzung und Prognose von Betawerten, Eine Untersuchung am deutschen Aktienmarkt (Bad Soden/Ts.: Uhlenbruch, 1997).*

[9] *Ibid.*

[10] *Richard Stehle, "Die Festlegung der Risikoprämie von Aktien im Rahmen der Schätzung des Wertes von börsennotierten Kapitalgesellschaften," Die Wirtschaftsprüfung 57 (2004): 906–927.*

[11] *Elroy Dimson, Paul Marsh, and Mike Staunton, "The Worldwide Equity Premium: A Smaller Puzzle," Working Paper, London Business School, April 7, 2006.*

% p.a.	Historical Equity Premium Relative to Bills				Historical Equity Premium Relative to Bonds			
Country	Geometric Mean	Arithmetic Mean	Standard Error	Standard Deviation	Geometric Mean	Arithmetic Mean	Standard Error	Standard Deviation
Average	4.81	7.14	2.21	22.75	3.98	6.08	2.11	21.71
World-ex U.S.	4.23	5.93	1.88	19.33	4.10	5.18	1.48	15.19
World	4.74	6.07	1.62	16.65	4.04	5.15	1.45	14.96
* Germany omits 1922-23								

Source: Elroy Dimson, Paul Marsh, and Mike Staunton, "The Worldwide Equity Premium: A Smaller Puzzle," Working Paper, London Business School, April 7, 2006, p. 18.

Another frequently used database of historic returns (1926–2008) is from Ibbotson Associates. However, many practitioners choose shorter periods, as they provide a more up-to-date figure, even though the estimate will suffer from greater volatility. Damodaran concludes: "The cost of using shorter time periods seems...to overwhelm any advantages associated with getting a more updated premium."[12]

Calculating the average market risk premium. Choosing the appropriate average is subject to controversy.[13] Practitioners disagree as to which is superior: the (higher) arithmetic mean, the (lower) geometric mean, or a mixture of both. The differences are not negligible, as shown in Exhibit 9.6 and in the German data, calculated by Stehle set out in Exhibit 9.7; this uses two different measures of the market: DAX (Deutsche Aktien Index, German 30 share index) and Composite DAX (CDAX 320 shows):

Exhibit 9.7 Estimated Market Risk Premium in Germany

1955–2003	Market Risk Premium Arithmetic Mean	Market Risk Premium Geometric Mean
CDAX	5.46 % = 12.40 % – 6.94 %	2.66 % = 9.50 % – 6.84 %
DAX	6.02 % = 12.96 % – 6.94 %	2.76 % = 9.60 % – 6.84 %

*Source: Richard Stehle, "Die Festlegung der Risikoprämie von Aktien im Rahmen der Schätzung des Wertes von börsennotierten Kapitalgesellschaften," **Die Wirtschaftsprüfung** 57 (2004): 921.*

To answer the question of which is preferable for estimating the market risk premium, one must investigate the stochastic process which stock returns follow. The arithmetic mean is correct if returns are stochastically independent and identically distributed over time, and their expected value must be known. Empirical evidence[14] suggests that returns are negatively correlated or stochastically dependent; therefore, the correct amount is somewhere between the arithmetic and geometric means. Since assumptions concerning the stochastic process cannot be verified, a pragmatic deduction from the arithmetic mean is recommended. However, stochastically dependent returns are incompatible with CAPM. While stochastically independent, identically distributed returns are consistent with CAPM, in the long run, they imply extremely right-skewed distributions of the cash flows from investment projects.[15]

PUBLISHED BETAS

In the United States, valuators can obtain public company betas from a number of sources, such as Bloomberg, Ibbotson, and CompuServe. There is no uniformity regarding the market proxy, adjustments, and/or period and frequency of data used by those organizations. Accordingly, for the same entity, they will vary, sometimes substantially.

---

[12] Aswath Damodaran, *Investment Valuation*, 2nd ed. (Hoboken, NJ: John Wiley & Sons, 2002), p. 161.

[13] Marshall E. Blume, "Unbiased Estimators of Long-Run Expected Rates of Return," *Journal of Business Finance and Accounting* 69 (1974): 634–638. Ian Cooper, "Arithmetic versus Geometric Mean Estimators: Setting Discount Rates for Capital Budgeting," *European Financial Management* 2 (1996): 157–167.

[14] Eugene F. Fama and Kenneth R. French, "Permanent and Temporary Components of Stock Prices," *Journal of Political Economy* 81 (1988): 246–273.

[15] Eugene F. Fama, "Discounting Under Uncertainty," *Journal of Business* 69 (1996): 415–428.

Historic or Adjusted Beta

Raw betas, estimated by regression analyses, are often adjusted, as empirical evidence suggests that they tend to revert over time to a mean.[16] This might be the industry average or that of the market (1.0); Bloomberg, therefore, reports an adjusted beta that assumes convergence toward the market by modifying, somewhat arbitrarily, the "raw" figure, as shown in equation 9.5.

$$\text{adjusted Beta} = 2/3 \times \text{raw Beta} + 1/3 \times 1 \qquad (9.5)$$

Another adjustment is necessary for a beta derived from a peer group. Although, in theory, the only relevant figure is that for the entity, that of a peer group is often used for privately owned firms. An appropriate peer group should have the same systematic risk as the entity to be valued. However, the individual betas reflect their different capital structures. Those levered betas (β^L) have to be adjusted to remove the effect of the firm's leverage; therefore, so-called Hamada betas are calculated.[17]

The first step is to convert β^L into a beta of a notionally unlevered company (β^U) by equation 9.6:

$$\beta^U = \beta^L \Big/ \left[1 + (1-T) \times \frac{D}{E}\right] \qquad (9.6)$$

Where

T   =   peer's (compound, effective) tax rate, which reflects the benefits of a (partial) deductibility of interest
D   =   peer's market value of debt
E   =   peer's market value of equity

The second step is to adjust the unlevered beta to reflect the capital structure of the subject entity by the formula shown in equation 9.7:

$$\beta^U = \beta^L \times 1 + (1-T) \times \frac{D}{E}\bigg] \qquad (9.7)$$

Example

Assume the following published data for guideline company Ascendo SA:

Published levered βeta: 2.1; tax rate: 24%; capital structure: 60% debt, 40 % equity

$\beta^u = 2.1/[1 + (1-.24)(.60/.40)] = 2.1/[1 + 1.14] = 2.1/2.14 = 0.98$

Assuming the subject has a capital structure of 35% debt at market value and a 30% tax rate

$\beta^L = 0.98 - [1 + (1-0.30) \times .35/.65] = 0.98 \times [1 + 0.70 \times 0.5385] = 0.98 \times 1.3769 = 1.35$

In practice, book values of debt and market capitalizations are often used as approximations.

APPLICATION OF CAPM

CAPM is the most often used model to determine the cost of equity. Its advantages lie in its sound theoretical basis and the ability to use market data. There are, however, serious disadvantages, including restrictive assumptions, unanswered empirical validity, and the subjective assumptions needed to apply the model. These criticisms should not lead to a complete rejection, as the alternatives, to be discussed, also have serious shortcomings.

---

[16] Roger Buckland and Patricia Fraser, "Political and Regulatory Risk: Beta Sensitivity in U.K. Electricity Distribution," *Journal of Regulatory Economics* 19 (2001): 5–25.

[17] Robert S. Hamada, "The Effect of the Firm's Capital Structure on the Systematic Risk of Common Stocks," *Journal of Finance* 27 (1972): 435–452.

To fully comprehend beta, a valuator must understand:

- Variance is a squared measure of the deviation of the actual return on a security from its expected return.
- Covariance is a statistical measure of the relationship between two variables; in this case, it is between returns on securities.

When the price of the entity's shares is not known, some valuators modify CAPM to allow the calculation of a synthetic beta. This is done by using intermediate term (5- to 10-year) government bond yields for the risk-free rate (R_f), assuming that the systematic risk is captured and represented by the covariance of the pretax return on equity (ROE) of the entity, with that of other guideline companies or industry averages, divided by the variance of the industry average ROE. The expected return on a market portfolio [$E (R_m)$] is replaced by the average pretax ROE of the guidelines or the industry.

Exhibit 9.8 Calculation of Synthetic Beta

	A Subject Company ROE	B (1) Industry ROE	(A – C) x (B – D) Covariance	(B – D)2 Variance
1982	9.9	7.6 (1)	346.920 (2)	426.4225 (3)
1983	7.8	8.1	374.790	406.0225
1984	18.9	19.7	66.690	73.1025
1985	24.4	24.0	9.775	18.0625
1986	33.9	34.3	43.560	36.6025
1987	36.7	37.8	95.500	91.2025
1988	36.5	44.6	160.230	267.3225
1989	41.9	42.5	216.600	203.0625
1990	30.3	35.7	26.820	55.5025
TOTAL	240.30	254.30	1,340.8850	1577.2825
	C	D	E	F
AVERAGE	26.70	28.25	148.99 (4)	175.25 (5)

$$\text{BETA} = \frac{\text{COVARIANCE} \quad (E)}{\text{VARIANCE} \quad (F)}$$

$$\text{BETA} = \frac{148.99}{175.25}$$

$$\text{BETA} = .8501$$

(1)   Upper quartile, pretax ROE from RMA Annual Statement Studies for year indicated. The upper quartile was selected based on companies operating at a similar level as the subject.
(2)   Covariance calculation for year indicated (9.9 – 26.70) × (7.6 – 28.25) = 346.920.
(3)   Variance calculation for year indicated (7.6 – 28.25)² = 426.4225.
(4)   Covariance = Average of covariances.
(5)   Variance = Average of variances.

This synthetic beta of 0.85 indicates that the subject is less volatile than the industry and appears to have fewer risks. Thus, a total risk premium less than that of the industry would seem appropriate. Based on this analysis, the expected rate of return for a security is positively related to its beta.

Beta is a measure of market volatility, generated by share transactions. Generally in valuing a closely held entity, a beta is developed from publicly traded guidelines or a synthetic beta using the pretax ROE (for equity) or return on investment (ROI; for investment) of the specific company. ROI, as used to develop "β," is:

Ending Share Price – Beginning Share Price + Dividends Beginning Share Price

This generates an after-tax rate, as the capacity to pay dividends (a key element) is based on after-tax earnings. When CAPM is used to generate a capitalization rate, the risk rate for the general public market is an after-tax rate; therefore, it is an after-tax method. Ibbotson considers its build-up method, loosely based on CAPM, to be after tax. However, RMA's ROE is pretax. When quantifying a capitalization or discount rate, it is essential to identify the variables and conclusions as pretax or after tax.

ARBITRAGE PRICING THEORY

CAPM states that security rates of return are linearly related to a single factor, the expected rate of return on the market. The arbitrage pricing theory (APT) formulated by Ross[18] is based on a similar concept but assumes that several common risk factors generate rates of return.

$$\mu(\tilde{r}_j) = \lambda_0 + \beta_{j1} \times [\mu(\tilde{\delta}_1) - \lambda_0] + \beta_{j2} \times [\mu(\tilde{\delta}_2) - \lambda_0] + \bullet \bullet \bullet + \beta_{jN} \times [\mu(\tilde{\delta}_N) - \lambda_0] \qquad (9.8)$$

Where

$\mu(\tilde{r}_j)$	=	expected rate of return of security j
λ_0	=	constant
$\mu(\tilde{\delta}_k)$	=	expected return on a portfolio with unit sensitivity to factor k (k = 1,…,N) and zero sensitivity to all other factors,
$[\mu(\tilde{\delta}_k) - \lambda_0]$	=	risk premium associated with factor k
β_{jk}	=	sensitivity of security j to factor k (factor loading)

APT is built on two key concepts: (1) the no-arbitrage principle and (2) a multifactor risk model[19] with the constant λ_0 equal to the riskless rate of return.[20] Although APT assumes several risk factors, it is not a generalization of CAPM as the two models are based on different sets of assumptions.[21] While CAPM is applied by means of a single regression, APT utilizes multiple regressions. Since the factors are undefined, they are mostly specified by macroeconomic or industry specific items, such as the term spread, growth in industrial production, unexpected inflation, or the credit spread (the yield difference between corporate and government bonds). The number of factors is arbitrary but must be small.

Compared to CAPM, the assumptions underlying APT are less restrictive. Furthermore, APT allows the expected rates of return to depend on more than one factor and the market portfolio does not necessarily play a role; unlike CAPM, it can also be easily extended to a multiperiod framework. The central shortcoming is not specifying the risk factors; there is no consensus about the most suitable. Since tests of APT, like those of CAPM, are always joint tests of the theory, methodology, and quality of the data, unambiguous empirical evidence for or against APT is difficult to find.[22]

---

[18] Stephen A. Ross, "The Arbitrage Theory of Capital Asset Pricing," *Journal of Economic Theory* 13 (1976): 341–360; Stephen A. Ross, (1977). "Risk, Return, and Arbitrage," pp. 189–218, in Irwin Friend and James L. Bicksler, eds. **Risk and Return in Finance** (Cambridge: 1977).

[19] Haim Levy and Thierry Post, **Investments** (Harlow et al.: Prentice Hall, 2005).

[20] Ross, "Arbitrage Theory of Capital Asset Pricing."

[21] Levy and Post, **Investments.**

[22] Ibid.

FAMA-FRENCH THREE-FACTOR MODEL

APT is a multifactor risk model using historical returns and factors. Thus, factor loadings can be estimated by multiple regressions. Another multifactor risk model that has gained great attention is the Fama-French Three-Factor Model developed by Eugene Fama and Kenneth French, which is represented:[23]

$$\mu(\tilde{r}_j) - r_f = b_j \left[\mu(\tilde{r}_M) - r_f \right] + s_j \ \times \ \mu(S\tilde{M}B) + h_j \ \times \ \mu(H\tilde{M}L) \qquad (9.9)$$

This assumes that the excess return of the security j over the risk-free interest $\left[\mu(\tilde{r}_j) - r_f \right]$ rate is a linear function of three factors:

1. The excess return of a broad market index (as a proxy of the market portfolio) over the risk-free rate $\left[\mu(\tilde{r}_M) - i \right]$

2. The difference between the expected returns on a portfolio of small and large stocks $\mu(S\tilde{M}B)$ ("small minus big")

3. The difference between the expected returns on a portfolio of high and low book-to-market stocks $\mu(H\tilde{M}L)$ ("high minus low")

Parameters b_j, s_j, and h_j are factor sensitivities estimated by a time-series regression. While the first is CAPM's risk premium, the other two are motivated by empirical findings. As a consequence, their economic interpretations remain unclear. The discussion of this model is combined with that of the small stock risk premium mentioned earlier. It must be borne in mind that a SSRP is not compatible with the CAPM, and SSRPs are not reliably measurable.

As investors are presumed to be diversified, in CAPM, conceptually, a single risk factor (beta) captures all relevant systematic risks of the business. Consequently, there is no premium for any additional unsystematic risks, which might be associated with smaller entities. This is confirmed by Stehle,[24] who states that CAPM has to be rejected when size effects are found in practice. Fama and French[25] report evidence of a size effect using their three-factor model instead of CAPM; consequently, SSRP is not associated with CAPM.

The reported size effect has not been proven empirically, as it "could simply be a coincidence."[26] A recent paper by van Dijk states:

> Although many of the early empirical studies identify a significant and consistent size premium in U.S. equity returns, the overall evidence of a size effect in the U.S. is not overwhelming and several papers report that the effect has disappeared after 1980....the instability of the size effect reinforces the concern that data snooping biases may have played a role in the discovery of the effect....Concluding, we assess the empirical evidence for the size effect to be consistent at first sight, but

---

[23] *Eugene Fama and Kenneth R. French, "The Cross-Section of Expected Stock Returns,"* **Journal of Finance** *47 (1992): 472–465; Eugene Fama and Kenneth R. French, "Common Risk Factors in the Returns on Stocks and Bonds,"* **Journal of Financial Economics** *33 (1993): 3–56; and Eugene Fama and Kenneth R. French, "Multifactor Explanations of Asset Pricing Anomalies,"* **Journal of Finance** *51 (1996): 55–84.*

[24] *Richard Stehle, "Der Size-Effekt am deutschen Aktienmarkt,"* **Zeitschrift für Bankrecht und Bankwirtschaft** *9 (1997): 237–260. See also Banz, "Relationship between Return and Market Value of Common Stocks."*

[25] *Fama and French, "Cross-Section of Expected Stock Returns" and "Common Risk Factors in the Returns on Stocks and Bonds."*

[26] *Richard A. Brealey, Stewart C. Myers, and Franklin Allen,* **Principles of Corporate Finance**, *8th ed. (New York: McGraw-Hill, 2006), p. 203.*

> *frail at closer inspection. More empirical research is needed to establish the robustness of the size effect in international equity markets.*[27]

For these reasons, the German Institute of Certified Public Accountants (IDW), declines to add an SSRP to the discount rate.[28]

BUILD-UP MODELS

For small and medium-size companies, which are often not publicly traded, valuators in practice often use build-up models.

Ibbotson's Build-Up Method

The most common in the United States is Ibbotson's Build-Up method, which derives a cost of equity by adding together a market-based rate of return (systematic risk) and premiums for unsystematic risks associated with the subject company; the basic formula is:

$$\mu(\tilde{r}_j) = r_f \ + \ \mu(\text{ERP}) \ + \ \mu(\text{SSRP}_j) \ + \ \mu(\text{SCR}_j) \tag{9.10}$$

Where

ERP = expected equity risk premium for market
SSRP = small stock risk premium (size premium)
SCR = entity-specific risk

ERP is the long-term premium over the risk-free rate an investor would expect to receive from investing in a portfolio of large equity securities, such as the S&P 500. The SSRP is adjusted for CAPM's β, so that excess returns of small companies that can be explained by their higher betas are not included; however, risks specific to the entity are, as well as the size premium. The SCR premium measures the risk arising from specific factors, such as characteristics of the industry or the firm. These may include high volatility (measured by the standard deviation) of returns, poor management, key person and supplier dependence, pending lawsuits, regulatory situations, or lack of access to capital. As the CAPM assumes those unsystematic risks can be eliminated through diversification, the build-up method is not consistent with CAPM.

RISK RATE COMPONENT MODEL

A similar method, less widely used in the United States except for valuing small companies, is the Risk Rate Component Model (RRCM); however, it is generally accepted in countries where there is little or only unreliable information about the rates of return of publicly traded entities. The RRCM begins with a local risk-free rate of return and adds a weighted average risk premium, covering these four general categories of risks: competition, financial strength, management ability and depth, and profitability and stability of earnings.

---

[27] *Mathijs A. van Dijk, "Is Size Dead? A Review of the Size Effect in Equity Returns," Working Paper, RSM Erasmus University, February 2007, pp. 29, 31.*

[28] *Institut der Wirtschaftsprüfer (ed.), **WP Handbuch 2008—Wirtschaftsprüfung, Rechnungslegung, Beratung**, vol. 2, 13th ed., (Düsseldorf: IDW Verlag), p. 155, par. 434*

Competition		Financial Strength	
	Proprietary content (including patents and copyrights)		Current ratio
	Relative size of company		Quick ratio
	Relative product or service quality		Sales to working capital ratio
	Product or service differentiation		Accounts receivable to working capital ratio
	Covenant not to compete		Inventory to working capital ratio
	Market strength—competition		Net sales to inventory turnover
	Market size and share		Total assets to sales
	Pricing competition		Net fixed assets to net worth
	Ease of market entry		Miscellaneous assets to net worth
	Other pertinent factors specific to the subject company		Total debt to net worth
			Total assets to total equity
Management Ability and Depth			Total debt to assets
	Accounts receivable turnover		Long-term debt to equity
	Accounts payable turnover		Interest coverage
	Inventory turnover		Other pertinent factors specific to the subject company
	Fixed asset turnover		
	Total asset turnover	**Profitability and Stability of Earnings**	
	Employee turnover		Years in business
	Management depth		Industry life cycle
	Facilities condition		Return on sales (before taxes)
	Family involvement		Return on assets
	Books and records—quality and history		Return on equity
	Contracts for sales		Operating earnings growth rate
	Contracts for purchases		Sales growth rate
	Contracts for management		Trading ratio (sales to net worth)
	Contracts—other		Other pertinent factors specific to the subject company
	Gross margin		
	Operating margin		
	Operating cycle		
	Other pertinent factors specific to the subject company		

The RRCM risk premiums and risk-free rate are on a pretax basis; therefore, they generate a pretax capitalization rate. The suggested ranges of percentage risk factors, by degree of risk, are shown in Exhibit 9.9.

Exhibit 9.9 Range or RRCM Factos

General Categories of Risk Factors	High	Medium High	(Average) Medium	Medium Low	Low
Competition	9–10	7–8	5–6	3–4	1–2
Financial strength	9–10	7–8	5–6	3–4	1–2
Management ability and depth	9–10	7–8	5–6	3–4	1–2
Profitability and stability of earnings	9–10	7–8	5–6	3–4	1–2

Economic Conditions	Weak	No Effect	Strong
National	+1	0	−1
Local	+2	0	−2

Risk Factors	(1) Risk Indicator	(2) Weight	(3) Weighted Risk Indicator
Competition			
Proprietary Content	6.0	1.00	6.0
Relative Size of Company	7.0	1.00	7.0
Relative Product/Service Quality	4.0	1.00	4.0
Product/Service Differentiation	4.0	1.00	4.0
Covenant Not to Compete	2.0	1.00	2.0
Market Strength—Competition	7.0	1.00	7.0
Market Size and Share	6.0	1.00	6.0
Pricing Competition	7.0	1.00	7.0
Ease of Market Entry	5.0	1.00	5.0
Total Weight Factors		**9.00**	**48.0**
Weighted Average			**5.3%**
Financial Strength			
Current Ratio	4.0	1.00	4.0
Quick Ratio	4.0	1.00	4.0
Sales to Working Capital	6.0	1.00	6.0
Accounts Receivable to Working Capital Ratio	6.0	1.00	6.0
Inventory to Working Capital	6.0	1.00	6.0
Net Fixed Assets to Net Worth	4.0	1.00	4.0
Miscellaneous Assets to Net Worth	4.0	1.00	4.0
Total Debt to Assets	4.0	1.00	4.0
Long-term Debt to Equity	4.0	1.00	4.0
Interest Coverage	2.0	1.00	2.0
Total Weight Factors		**10.00**	**44.0**
Weighted Average			**4.4%**
Management Ability and Depth			
Accounts Receivable Turnover	5.0	1.00	5.0
Accounts Payable Turnover	5.0	1.00	5.0
Inventory Turnover	5.0	1.00	5.0
Fixed Asset Turnover	5.0	1.00	5.0
Total Asset Turnover	5.0	1.00	5.0
Employee Turnover	8.0	1.00	8.0
Management Depth	8.0	1.00	8.0
Facilities Condition	6.0	1.00	6.0
Family Involvement	8.0	1.00	8.0
Books and Records Quality and History	6.0	1.00	6.0
Contracts	8.0	1.00	8.0
Gross Margin	4.0	1.00	4.0
Operating Margin	6.0	1.00	6.0
Total Weight Factors		**13.00**	**79.0**
Weighted Average			**6.1%**
Profitability and Stability of Earnings			
Years in Business	2.0	1.00	2.0
Industry Life Cycle	4.0	1.00	4.0
Return on Sales (before taxes)	8.0	1.00	8.0
Return on Assets	8.0	1.00	8.0
Return on Equity	8.0	1.00	8.0
Operating Earnings Growth Rate	8.0	1.00	8.0
Sales Growth Rate	8.0	1.00	8.0
Trading Ratio (sales to net worth)	6.0	1.00	6.0
Total Weight Factors		**8.00**	**52.0**
Weighted Average			**6.5%**
Total Risk Premium Factor			**22.3%**
Risk-Free Rate			**3.7%**
			26.0%

IMPLIED COST-OF-CAPITAL MODELS

While applications of CAPM or APT are based on ex post data, the ICCM determines the cost of equity by a forward-looking approach. It uses current share prices and forecasts of future profits or dividends by financial analysts to obtain a discount rate that equates the present value of the future cash flows to the current share price. The method is not new[29] but is experiencing a revival through a variety of models based on dividends, residual income or earnings.

Used as inputs are:

- (Consensus) Forecasts of earnings per share (eps) provided by financial analysts
- Forecasts of dividends per share (dps)
- Expected growth rates of earnings, dividends, or residual income for the time beyond the explicit forecast period
- Current share prices

All of these potential inputs have in common the long-established dividend discount model as their theoretical basis; this determines the value of a share P as the present value of future dps:

$$P_{j0} = \sum_{t=1}^{\infty} \frac{dps_{jt}}{(1+r_j)^t} \qquad (9.11)$$

The cost of equity implied by the share price and the projected dividends is obtained by solving equation 9.11 for r_j or by iteration. The equity risk premium is r_j less the riskless rate. Since DPS projections are available only for three to five years, an assumption about their subsequent growth has to be made. Assuming constant growth at rate g from the valuation date, equation 9.11 becomes equation 9.12.[30]

$$P_{j0} = \frac{dps_{j1}}{r_j - g} \qquad r_j > g \qquad (9.12)$$

so that cost of equity is

$$r_j = \frac{dps_{j1}}{P_{j0}} + g \qquad (9.13)$$

Alternatively, models based on residual income EPS are used; for example:

$$P_{j0} = bps_{j0} + \sum_{t=1}^{\infty} \frac{eps_{jt} - r_j \cdot bps_{jt-1}}{(1+r_j)^t} = bps_{j0} + \sum_{t=1}^{\infty} \frac{rps_{jt}}{(1+r_j)^t} \qquad (9.14)$$

Where

bps = book value per share
eps = projected earnings per share

Equation 9.14 is theoretically equivalent to the dividend discount model (equation 9.11) if the so-called clean-surplus relation is fulfilled:

$$bps_t = bps_{t-1} + eps_t - dps_t \qquad (9.15)$$

---

[29] *Myron J. Gordon and Eli Shapiro, "Capital Equipment Analysis: The Required Rate of Profit,"* **Management Science** *3(1956): 102–110.*

[30] *Ibid.*

Unfortunately, this is not in conformity with IFRS. Equations 9.11 and 9.14 assume that residual income or dividends can be forecast indefinitely, which is not true in practice. Hence, two- or three-stage models are used; in those, residual earnings are forecast explicitly for some period and subsequently extrapolated at a fixed growth rate. Sometimes an intermediate stage is inserted to reflect a reversion of the growth rate to the industry mean. Claus and Thomas,[31] for example, employ the next two-stage residual income model:

$$P_{j0} = bps_{j0} + \sum_{t=1}^{5} \frac{eps_{jt} - r_j \cdot bps_{jt-1}}{(1+r_j)^t} + \frac{(eps_{j5} - r_j bps_{j4})(1+g)}{(r_j - g)(1+r_j)^5} \quad r_j > g \qquad (9.16)$$

Where

g is assumed to be the long-term growth rate

Exhibit 9.10 shows how the implied market risk premium varies over the years.

Exhibit 9.10 German Implied Market Risk Premiums

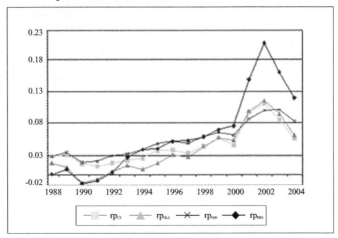

NOTE: *According to the models of Claus and Thomas (CT); Gebhardt, Lee, and Swaminathan (GLS); Ohlson and Jüttner-Nauroth (OJN); and price-earnings-growth model (PEG).*

Source: *Raimo Reese,* **Schätzung von Eigenkapitalkosten für die Unternehmensbewertung** *(Frankfurt am Main: Peter Lang, 2007), p. 102.*

The advantages of such models are that they are forward-looking, with both cash flows and discount rates based on market expectations. Their disadvantages are circularity, sensitivity to the particular factor selected, and dependency on consensus forecasts. The circularity results from the fact that this cost of equity capital can only be calculated if new investments have the same risks as the current business (also applies to CAPM); that is not always the case. The sensitivity to the particular model is shown in Exhibit 9.10. The reason is that the assumed growth rate of g leads to different results when applied to dividends, EPS, or residual income. The use of market capitalization ignores the difference between this and the value of a business. In practice, control premiums, which are often considerable, are paid for acquisitions; furthermore, there is evidence that financial analysts' forecasts tend to be systematically optimistic.[32]

[31] *See James Claus and Jacob Thomas, "Equity Premia as Low as Three Percent? Evidence from Analysts' Earnings Forecasts for Domestic and International Stock Markets,"* **Journal of Finance** *56 (2001): 1629–1666.*
[32] *See ibid.*

WEIGHTED AVERAGE COST OF CAPITAL

IAS 36.90 requires that a cash-generating unit to which goodwill has been allocated shall be tested for impairment at least annually, and also whenever there is an indication that the unit may be impaired. This is done by comparing its carrying amount, including good-will, with the recoverable amount. For a cash-generating unit, the recoverable amount is the higher of its fair value less costs to sell and its value in use.

Value in Use

IAS 36.30 states:

The following elements shall be reflected in the calculation of an asset's value in use:

(a)   An estimate of the future cash flows the entity expects to derive from the asset;
(b)   Expectations about possible variations in the amount or timing of those future cash flows;
(c)   The time value of money, represented by the current market risk-free rate of interest;
(d)   The price for bearing the uncertainty inherent in the asset; and
(e)   Other factors, such as illiquidity, that market participants would reflect in pricing the future cash flows the entity expects to derive from the asset.

According to IAS 36.55, the discount rate should be pretax, reflecting both current market assessments of the time value of money and the risks specific to the asset for which the future cash flow estimates have not been adjusted. IAS 36.A17 states as a starting point

[The] entity might take into account:

(a)   The entity's weighted average cost of capital determined using techniques such as the Capital Asset Pricing Model;
(b)   The entity's incremental borrowing rate; and
(c)   Other market borrowing rates.

It goes on in IAS 36.A18:

Consideration should be given to risks such as country risk, currency risk and price risk.

The rate to be chosen under the so-called free cash flows method is the WACC:

$$\text{WACC} = r_E^L \frac{E}{D+E} + r_D (1-T) \frac{D}{D+E} \qquad (9.17)$$

Where

r_D is the cost of debt

The suggestion to use WACC is astonishing, since it is influenced by both capital structure and taxes, whereas, according to IAS 36, financing and taxes are to be ignored in determining the value in use.

Neglecting taxes, assuming the entity's cost of debt equal to the risk-free rate ($r_D = r_f$) and applying the Modigliani/Miller concept,[33] the cost of equity of an unlevered firm is the same as its WACC. In practice, a firm's cost of debt will exceed the risk-free rate. However, this assumption follows from the Modigliani/Miller model, where no bankruptcy risk is accepted.

---

[33]   Franco Modigliani and Merton H. Miller, "Corporate Income Taxes and the Cost of Capital: A Correction," *American Economic Review 53 (1963): 433–443.*

$$WACC = r_E^L \frac{E}{D+E} + r_D \frac{D}{D+E} = \left[r_E^U + \left(r_E^U - r_D \right) \frac{D}{E} \right] \frac{E}{D+E} + r_D \frac{D}{D+E} \qquad (9.18)$$

$$= r_E^U \frac{E}{D+E} + r_E^U \frac{D}{D+E} - r_D \frac{D}{D+E} + r_D \frac{D}{D+E}$$

In practice, WACC is usually calculated on an after-tax basis (most costs of equity are after tax) as shown in equation 9.19:

$$WACC \quad = \quad \frac{r_E^L}{(1-T)} \quad \frac{E}{D+E} \quad + \quad r_D \quad \frac{D}{D+E} \quad (1-T) \qquad (9.19)$$

Normally the WACC of equation 9.17 is grossed up for taxes at the firm's marginal rate, usually around 40%, using either (A) a target capital structure of say 50% debt is used, or (B) the actual capital structure; this is approximated by the book value of the debt and the market capitalization. In the example, the debt is $56,117,000, at an average cost of 4.8%, while the market capitalization is $42,840,000, at a PER of 8.2 times. In those circumstances, the results of equations 9.18 and 9.19 are identical only by chance, whereas equation 9.18 follows consistently from the Modigliani/Miller model.

The different assumptions yield varying results:

Net Cost of Debt	=	4.8(1–.40)		=	2.88%	
Net Cost of Equity	=	(100/8.2)		=	12.31%	
Case A Debt	=	50% Equity		=	50%	
Case B Debt	=	56,117/98,957		=	56.7% Equity	= 43.3%
Case A WACC	=	2.88% × 50% + 12.31% × 50%		=	7.60%	
Case B WACC	=	2.88% × 56.7% + 12.31% × 43.3%	=	6.96%		

At the valuation date, the actual capital structure will differ from management's target. Neither can it be assumed that the cost of equity is determined correctly, since equation 9.11 requires an assumption perpetuity that normally does not occur. Generally, the amounts of the errors cannot be established, as they depend on many factors.

IAS 36 recommends determining value in use through discounting free cash flows by WACC, but defines both measures very differently from standard valuation theory. Its free cash flows are not affected by taxes, while the WACC will be higher than the conventional figure. How the capital structure, essential for determining WACC, can reflect a calculation before financing is not discussed in the standard.

Establishing the cost of capital is one of the most important issues in a valuation. There are nevertheless numerous difficulties, especially on a conceptual level, in satisfactorily combining the various components. For example, a size premium is not consistent with the assumptions underlying CAPM, which however, may not capture all relevant risks.

Since the cost of capital cannot be observed directly, it must be estimated indirectly. There is a joint hypothesis problem, because tests and applications of CAPM, APT, and ICCM are always combined tests of the respective model and market efficiency. Even if a model, such as CAPM, is assumed to be true, it cannot be applied mechanically, as several critical decisions concerning the selection of the underlying empirical data need to be made. Thus, the process of deriving the cost of capital should not result in a point estimate but in a range based on reasoned judgment of financial and other data as well as the experience of the practitioner.

REFERENCES

Gebhardt, William R., Charles M. C. Lee, and Bhaskaran Swaminathan. "Toward an Implied Cost of Capital." *Journal of Accounting Research* 39 (2001): 135–176.

Inselbag, Isik, and Howard Kaufold. "Two DCF Approaches for Valuing Companies Under Alternative Financing Strategies (and How to Choose between Them)." *Journal of Applied Corporate Finance* 10 (1997): 114–122.

Ohlson, James A., and Beate Jüttner-Nauroth. "Expected EPS and EPS Growth as Determinants of Value." *Review of Accounting Studies* 10 (2005): 349–365.

Vasicek, Oldrich A. "A Note on Using Cross-Sectional Information in Bayesian Estimation of Security Betas." *Journal of Finance* 28 (1973): 1233–1239.

10 RISKS AND REWARDS

WILLIAM A. HANLIN, JR., AND J. RICHARD CLAYWELL

UNITED STATES

INTRODUCTION

One important element is present in all valuation engagements: the valuator must consider the risks associated with the subject entity, division, subsidiary, or affiliate. Modern valuation theory accepts that high risks to investors require a larger discount or capitalization rate than when the rewards of ownership are more certain. This concept defines risk broadly as the rate of return required to attract investors to the entity. Functionally, it is the cost of equity used in calculating discount or capitalization rates, which differ only by the anticipated growth.

Although the efficient market hypothesis has been shown to be no longer valid, many valuators, especially in the United States, continue to use the Capital Asset Pricing Model (CAPM), or a modification of it, such as Ibbotson's build-up model, to assist in arriving at a reasonable cost of equity. Those techniques are most useful when the entity is of substantial size, similar to those firms whose statistics are included in the various databases that have, over many years, collated and analyzed the earnings and returns of numerous publicly traded entities.

Relevant Data

The challenge faced by every valuator when utilizing such models is finding information relevant to the subject. The conundrum is that all data used in both CAPM and build-up models are from public companies. These data usually are voluminous and can be accessed in many instances on a day-to-day basis. Globally, valuators have available material from national or regional stock exchanges, major banks, or organizations that provide stock performance analyses, such as Bloomberg, Duff & Phelps, and Dow Jones.

Small and Medium Enterprises

However, the vast majority of all valuation engagements involve small to medium enterprises (SMEs) entities, which have much smaller revenues and even fewer assets than their publicly traded counterparts. Most SMEs also differ fundamentally in management capabilities. Most SMEs have only one or two people who by themselves manage and control the overall operations, making the day-to-day decisions about everything: sales, marketing, ordering supplies, supervising personnel, and paying bills. This arrangement is in stark contrast to the multilayered management found in public companies, which often have more than one location and several lines of businesses operated with hundreds, sometimes thousands of employees.

Most SMEs do not look or behave like public companies. Yet many valuators assign them discount rates that are more appropriate to public companies. According to Alan S. Zip, CPA, JD:

> *The small company stocks measured by Ibbotson Associates [a modified CAPM database] are publicly traded and enjoy substantially less risk of failure than a small closely-held business. Even the large size of these "small" companies allows them to spread business risk among several lines of products, employ teams of qualified managers, hire outside consultants as needed, and engage in large-scale marketing and advertising campaigns.*[1]

IBBOTSON BUILD-UP MODEL

A full description of CAPM is found in Chapter 9, which also discusses build-up models in general. Typically, the Ibbotson build-up model will have five elements:

1. Risk-free rate (normally government bond yields)
2. Equity risk premium (ERP)
3. Company size premium (CSP)
4. Industry risk factor (IRF)
5. Company-specific risk premium (CSRP)

The first two, which are also part of CAPM, approximate the measured rate of return of publicly traded shares. As shown in the appendix to this chapter, such returns have varied widely since 1927, when Ibbotson's data starts. On a statistical basis, the figures are:

	Risk-free Rate	*Equity Risk Premium*	*Cap-Weighted Market Return*
1927–2008 (82 years)	%	%	%
Mean	3.76	7.64	11.39
Standard Deviation	3.10	21.01	20.75
T(mn)	10.99	3.29	4.97
1927–1962 (36 years)			
Mean	1.31	10.65	11.96
Standard Deviation	1.23	24.35	24.14
T(mn)	6.41	2.62	2.57
1963–2008 (46 years)			
Mean	5.67	5.28	10.95
Standard Deviation	2.57	17.91	17.92
T(mn)	13.97	2.00	2.00

T(mn): a measure of probability; the ratio of the mean to the standard deviation divided by the square root of the number of years.

The very large standard deviations of the ERP relation to its mean—2.75 times, 2.9 times, and 3.39 times respectively for the periods—support the view that there are problems in drawing conclusions for SMEs from public company data.

Other Premiums

As the size and industry premiums are obtained from the same public company data as the ERP, similar problems arise. Difficulties with the CSRP are even greater; various authors have attempted to devise consistent means/models for determining CSRPs, but no model has become generally accepted. Since the data do not disclose or describe the specific risks of the underlying public companies that are being measured by the ERP, CSP, or IRF, it is impossible to know what risks are, or are not, included in their rates of return. Therefore, the only way to establish a CSRP for an SME is to guess or otherwise make use of "professional judgment," probably through some form of index numbers. This is very unsatisfactory to

---

[1] Alan S. Zip, *"Divorce: Valuation, Tax and Financial Strategies,"* Title 30 of the RIA Tax Advisors, Planning System, Research Institute of America (RIA), Thomson-Reuters, Fort Worth, TX, 1995.

both the valuator and the reader of a valuation report, as such a figure is difficult, if not impossible, to support.

From many points of view, a discount or capitalization rate devised from CAPM is irrelevant to the value of an SME. Yet a valuator has a professional responsibility to adopt an appropriate discount or capitalization rate for each engagement.

Rate of Return versus Risks of the Entity

CAPM was originally designed to assess the hypothetical behavior of investors in public companies; the addition of size and industry premiums plus a CSRP is generally accepted to be necessary to obtain the required rate of return for an SME, because calculating a synthetic beta for private companies is problematic. The resulting cost of equity is used by valuators to represent the inherent risks of the business; however, that is not exactly correct. Public company rates of return are considered by the profession as the minimum required for an investor to be interested in the entity; yet they are not a measure of the associated risk.

Consider Moloch Inc., an entity that was valued at December 31 of both 2007 and 2008, with a cost of equity determined by the Ibbotson model; between the valuation dates the worldwide economy experienced a huge downward shift. Historically, such changes see risk-free rates drop, and the actual and implied risks of businesses rise substantially.

For the 2007 valuation, the analyses of available information showed that Moloch was well established, with an excellent history of management, operations, and earnings. Therefore, the valuator decided that the appropriate CSRP was 6.0%. By the 2008 valuation, very little had changed with respect to management, operations, or earnings, although pretax profit before a 2007 capital gain of $8,575,000 on a move to a new location rose 1.2% to $2,683,000, which was higher than any year before in the amount of $2,651,000.

The next table illustrates the cost of equity calculated from the Ibbotson data in its 2008 and 2009 *Valuation Yearbooks*.

	2007	2008
Risk-free Rate	4.5%	3.0%
Equity Risk Premium	7.1%	6.5%
Size Premium—10th Decile	5.8%	5.8%
Minimum Required Rate of Return	17.4%	15.3%
CSRP	6.0%	6.0%
Cost of Equity—Discount Rate	23.4%	21.3%

In spite of the economic crisis, the apparent cost of equity dropped by 210 basis points, or 9%, from 2007 to 2008; this would give an apparent 10% increase in value, while, in reality, stock markets, using the United States as a proxy, declined by 40%. The only explanation is the overall drop in the apparent rate of return for public companies from 2007 to 2008. However, the risks to investors in Moloch had not changed significantly, except with respect to the economic outlook. In this instance, the rate of return obtained through CAPM using Ibbotson data cannot be considered a true measure of the related risks for investor in Moloch at the end of 2008.

AN ALTERNATIVE: RRCM

As an alternative to a CAPM-based technique, since 1991, many valuators have used the Risk Rate Component Model (RRCM), which focuses on the inherent risks of a business. This model is not based or premised on rates of return for public companies; rather, it uses a system of ratio and other comparative analyses to assist the valuator in discovering both the risks and the rewards of the individual SME and thus to arrive at a reasonable cost of equity.

RRCM, like CAPM, begins with a so-called risk-free rate, typically the yield on 10- or 20-year government bonds. To this, it adds four separate premiums, covering the risks associated with competition, financial strength, management ability and depth, and profitability and stability of earnings. It allows further adjustments when there is an impact on the subject from national or local economic circumstances. The categories represent material and significant aspects of a business, with each being ranked on a scale of 0 (none) to 10 (high).

Categories and Levels of Risks

Category	High	Medium High	Average	Medium Low	Low	No Risk
Competition	10	7.5	5.0	2.5	1.0	0.0
Financial Strength	10	7.5	5.0	2.5	1.0	0.0
Management Ability and Depth	10	7.5	5.0	2.5	1.0	0.0
Profitability and Stability of Earnings	10	7.5	5.0	2.5	1.0	0.0

Economic Conditions	Weak	Medium Weak	Neutral	Medium Strong	Strong
National	Add 2	Add 1	0	Less 1	Less 2
Local or Regional	Add 2	Add 1	0	Less 1	Less 2

Assuming the risk-free rate in Xanadu is 5%, the RRCM will develop a cost of equity from a low of 5% to a high of 47% (5% + 10% + 10% + 10% + 10% + 2%).

Risks and Discount Rates

The range of discount rates given by RRCM is consistent with the conclusions set out next.[2]

Class	Level of Risk	Discount Rate
I	Very low	10–11.99%
II	Low	12–14.99%
III	Medium	15–19.99%
IV	High	20–24.99%
V	Very high	25–50.00%
VI	Key man business	50.00% +

Under the RRCM, a well-run and properly financed SME would have a cost of equity of around 25%, which would rise to about 47% if the firm were undercapitalized, were only marginally profitable, and the economy was deteriorating. The model assumes that every entity has at least an average risk for each category. When the analyses show that, for a particular component, a business is less or more risky than average, then it is assigned a lower or higher amount; this makes RRCM an efficient model to quantify both the risks and rewards of a specific business.

[2] *Johannes R. Krahmer,* **Tax Management Portfolio—Valuation of Shares of Closely Held Corporations**, *2nd ed. (Bureau of National Affairs, Arlington, VA, 1985), pp. 1–24.*

Implementation: Competition

The next table shows how Moloch might be graded for the competition category in 2008.

Indicator	Risk Level	Weight	Weighted Risk Factor
Proprietary Content (including Patents and Copyrights)	1.5	2.0	3.0
Relative Size of Company	7.5	2.0	15.0
Relative Product or Service Quality	5.0	2.0	10.0
Product/Service Differentiation	2.5	2.0	5.0
Covenant Not to Compete	1.0	2.0	2.0
Market Strength—Competition	6.0	2.0	12.0
Market Size/Share	8.0	2.0	16.0
Price Competition	3.5	2.0	7.0
Ease of Entry	5.0	2.0	10.0
Other	0.0	0.0	0.0
Total Weight Factors		18.0	80.0
Weighted Average Premium			4.4

Proprietary content. Risks associated with proprietary content are assessed by reviewing the relevant documents, the time remaining in the protection period, and the importance placed by management on its contribution to the success of the business. In this case, a more efficient process gives the firm significant advantages by lowering the cost of sales.

Relative size. compares the subject's revenue to that of the entire relevant market and gives an indication of the comparative risk. For instance, a local hardware store may operate in a single location; its size (and therefore risk) is measured against the revenues, asset size, and number of employees for all such stores in the appropriate geographic and demographic areas. Conclusion: Small is bad!

Relative product or service quality. Relative product or service quality is analyzed by comparing the entity's products or services to those offered by its competitors. How do they differ from others in the industry? If they are the same, then a figure of 5.0 would be assigned for an average risk; if better, a lower figure would be used.

Product or service differentiation. Assessing product or service differentiation involves many considerations: How many competitors are there? What factors affect customer buying patterns (timing, seasonal, etc.)? Are substitute products or services available? How important are pricing, name recognition, use of technical knowhow, customer loyalty, and licensing restrictions?

Covenants not to compete. All key personnel should have employment agreements containing nondisclosure provisions and a covenant not to compete for a reasonable period after employment ceases. If such agreements exist, the valuator should review their terms with management, including expiry date, territory covered, and likelihood of competition.

Market strength. Market strength is a measure of risks associated with longevity, reputation, and customer care and depends on which portion of a market the firm serves. There is usually only average risk in a business with a lot of small competitors, such as auto repair. However, high risks may occur in an industry with only a few large competitors, if one dominates due to technology, size, or innovation.

Price competition. Customer price sensitivity is a major factor in higher or lower risks. It may be measured by comparable profit margins subject to pressure from competitors able to offer products or provide services at significantly lower prices.

Ease of entry. This factor measures the ability of a new competitor to enter the market. For example, an established dentist in any community will surely see new competitors from time to time, but the newcomers have significant costs to enter the business, including education, equipment, premises, and marketing.

Implementation: Financial

The next table shows how Moloch might be graded for the financial strength category in 2008.

Indicator	Risk Level	Weight	Weighted Risk Factor
Level of Liquidity			
Current Ratio	2.0	3.0	6.0
Quick Ratio	5.0	2.0	10.0
Sales to Working Capital Ratio	3.5	2.0	7.0
Quality of Liquidity			
Receivables to Working Capital	5.0	2.0	10.0
Inventory to Working Capital	6.0	2.0	12.0
Asset Utilization			
Net Sales to Inventory Turnover	7.5	2.0	15.0
Total Assets to Sales	5.0	2.0	10.0
Net Fixed Assets to Equity	7.5	2.0	15.0
Miscellaneous Assets to Equity	2.5	1.0	2.5
Leverage Ratios			
Total Debt to Equity	5.0	2.0	10.0
Equity Multiplier (Total Assets Equity)	6.0	2.0	12.0
Total Debt to Assets	5.0	3.0	15.0
Long-term Debt to Equity	5.0	3.0	15.0
Interest Coverage	5.0	2.0	10.0
Total Weight Factors		30.0	149.5
Weighted Average Premium			5.0

The subject's normal financial ratios are the bases for most of those risk factors; some also require a comparison to the "industry." In most developed economies, such data are available; in the United States, the major sources are Risk Management Associates (RMA), which draws its data from banks, and Integra.

Ideally, the valuator will compare the financial ratios of the firm with those of comparable entities in their local economies. If, because of lack of data, this is impractical, the easily available United States databases, although they are not specifically relevant, allow a benchmark comparison between the subject and businesses in an established economy, which can be modified on a global basis.

Implementation: Management

The next table shows how Moloch might be graded in the management ability and depth category.

Indicator	Risk Level	Weight	Weighted Risk Factor
Accounts Receivable Turnover—Days	7.0	2.0	14.0
Accounts Payable Turnover—Days	7.0	2.0	14.0
Inventory Turnover—Days	5.0	2.0	10.0
Fixed Asset Turnover	5.0	2.0	10.0
Employee Turnover	2.0	2.0	4.0
Management Depth	5.0	2.0	10.0
Facilities Involvement	5.0	2.0	10.0
Family Involvement	0.0	0.0	0.0
Books and Records—Quality and History	5.0	2.0	10.0
Contracts	5.0	2.0	10.0
Gross Margin	5.0	2.0	10.0
Operating Margin	5.0	2.0	10.0
Operating Cycle	5.0	2.0	10.0
Other	0.0	0.0	0.0
Total Weight Factors		24.0	122.0
Weighted Average Premium			5.1

Ability Measures

The first five indicators, which can be calculated from the financial records, assess management's abilities. When the data are available, the indicators should be compared to industry averages, as the intention is to determine the relative risks of the subject through comparisons with other participants. A manufacturer turns over its inventory 4.1 times a year; is this high or low? The answer lies in the answer to whether this turnover is similar to, slower, or faster than the industry norm.

Depth Measures

A good way of assessing management depth is by investigating the entity's structure. In situations where the owner is dominant, with no one else allowed to make any important commitments, the risks are much higher than for one with several staff trained and accustomed to making decisions.

Facilities. Facilities can increase risks above average if they are unsuitable for the business. This could be if there is too little, too much, or badly laid out space. Similarly, an entity that is in older facilities that need to be updated (wiring, loading docks, etc.) could be at a significant disadvantage and thus be assigned a higher than average risk.

Family involvement. Family involvement can mean lower risks if the members work together in harmony or higher risks if some collect paychecks but perform no meaningful work, or are not capable of contributing sufficiently to the business.

Books and records. The books and records should be reviewed for adequacy; those that generate appropriate information are useful to management; a business with few or inadequate records beyond a ledger and a checkbook has higher risk due to the lack of current information that might help management plan for the future or avoid downturns.

Contracts. Contracts can be an advantage or a detriment. A contract that guarantees delivery of scarce materials is a benefit; similarly, one that currently requires payment of higher-than-spot market prices may be a disadvantage. Examples of adverse contracts include: leases at above current market rates, commitments to purchase material not immediately required, and restrictive union agreements.

Margins. The gross and operating margins are efficiency ratios. When compared to those of the industry, they may reveal different overhead structures and administrative costs. Some will be static in nature (rent, utilities), and the mix of fixed and variable costs should be investigated to address what discretion management has over such expenses.

Operating Cycle. *Operating cycle* is the term used to describe the peaks and valleys of any business; the peak is the busiest time, and the valley is that before the next cycle starts. For many firms, this is seasonal; for others, each phase may last a full year or more; some extend for a full presidential term (four years in the United States). A few do not have measurable operating cycles at all because of constant high demand for their products or services.

Implementation: Profitability

The next table shows how Moloch might be graded in the profitability and stability of earnings category in 2008.

Indicator	Risk Level	Weight	Weighted Risk Factor
Time in Business	7.0	2.0	14.0
Industry Life Cycle	5.0	2.0	10.0
Return on Sales (before taxes)	2.5	2.0	5.0
Return on Equity	8.5	3.0	25.5
Return on Assets	2.5	3.0	7.5
Trading Ratio	5.0	2.0	10.0
Operating Earnings Growth Rate	5.0	2.0	10.0
Sales Growth Rate	5.0	2.0	10.0
Standard Deviation of Earnings	8.5	2.0	17.0
Altman Z-Score	2.0	2.0	4.0
Other	0.0	0.0	0.0
Total Weight Factors		22.0	113.0
Weighted Average Premium			5.1

Time in business. The number of years a business has existed can be an important measure of risk; statistically, most SMEs fail in their first five years of existence. This is due to many factors, such as lack of adequate capital, sufficient knowledge to be an effective competitor, and time to reach business maturity. Many consider new businesses to be the most risky since they lack a sufficient period of operations to prove that they can continue to exist. A rule of thumb is: under one year a risk of 10.0, declining by 1.0 percentage points for each profitable year until reaching 5.0; this should not drop until at least 10 consecutive profitable years have been achieved.

Industry life cycle. Every industry is introduced, becomes successful, and eventually declines. A firm at an early stage of its industry's life cycle may be less risky than average because of a longer expected period of profitability, while a business nearing that end could have higher risks. Consider a printer where equipment has an expected life of some 60 years; when it was new, the firm was considered low risk. As technological advances changed the industry's processes and the equipment's useful life became shorter, the plant could be considered higher risk if the cost of replacing it has not been planned.

Return on sales. Pretax profit is one of the most important items on a financial statement to the owner of a business. For Moloch, pretax profit increased from $1,620,496 in 2004 to $2,683,085 in 2008, and its pretax margin has exceeded its industry average for the past five years. This is an indication that Moloch is earning more profit from each dollar of sales and thus is better able to compete.

The next table shows Moloch's operating profit percentage compared to the industry.

Return on Sales (before taxes)	2004	2005	2006	2007	2008
Moloch	2.1%	1.8%	2.5%	10.3%	2.5%
Industry	–0.5%	–0.6%	–0.6%	–0.5%	0.5%

Moloch's ratio is well above the industry and therefore a lower risk at 2.5.

Return on equity. The key ratio for determining profitability is return on equity (ROE), which is calculated by dividing net income by total shareholders' equity. With all else being constant, it is generally preferable for this ratio to be high. Profits are directly affected by a firm's ability to control costs, generate sales and use debt effectively. The next formula shows not only the rate of profit but also its causes: profit margin, asset turnover, and the equity multiplier.

$$\text{Return on Equity} = \frac{\text{Net Income}}{\text{Total Equity}} = \underbrace{\frac{\text{Net Income}}{\text{Sales}}}_{\text{(Profit Margin)}} \times \underbrace{\frac{\text{Sales}}{\text{Total Assets}}}_{\text{(Assets Turnover)}} \times \underbrace{\frac{\text{Total Assets}}{\text{Total Equity}}}_{\text{(Equity Multiplier)}}$$

As shown next, Moloch's return on equity increased from 9.9% in 2003 to 11.4% in 2007.

Return on Equity	2003	2004	2005	2006	2007
Moloch	9.9%	8.5%	12.1%	46.8%	11.4%
Upper Quartile	50.7%	49.3%	51.7%	50.2%	44.1%
Median	27.9%	26.9%	26.2%	25.5%	22.4%
Lower Quartile	12.0%	10.9%	8.8%	7.8%	7.7%

As Moloch falls between the median and the lower quartile, it ranks as an above-average risk at 8.5.

Return on assets. The return on assets (ROA) divides the net income with total assets; it may be interpreted in two ways:

1. As a measure of management's ability and efficiency in using the firm's assets to generate operating profits
2. As the total return accruing to all providers of capital, both debt and equity, irrespective of the source

The return is measured by net operating profit after tax (NOPAT), which is calculated by adding after-tax interest expenses to net income. Return on assets (ROA) also can be determined on a pretax basis using earnings before interest and taxes (EBIT) as the measure of return. This results in a figure that is unaffected by differences in the entity's tax position or financing policy.

The previous analyses have used RMA information as the industry benchmark. Between 2003 and 2007, as shown next, the ROA for Moloch increased from 5.8% to 6.5%, exceeding the industry median for each of the five years. Therefore, it has provided its shareholders with a better return than most of its competitors.

Return on Assets	2003	2004	2005	2006	2007
Moloch	5.8%	5.1%	7.5%	28.6%	6.5%
Upper Quartile	9.0%	8.3%	8.2%	8.7%	8.1%
Median	4.8%	4.2%	3.7%	3.8%	3.6%
Lower Quartile	1.6%	1.4%	0.8%	0.6%	0.6%

Therefore, Moloch is considered a medium-low risk at 2.5.

Trading ratio. The trading ratio (net sales divided by net worth) is a measure of how well a firm has financed its growth. If the sales rise and the net worth does not increase proportionally, then it is experiencing "unrestrained" growth. If not financed at least in part by net worth, growth must result in declining liquidity (working capital) and/or increased leverage. The trading ratio for Moloch has decreased over the period as shown:

Trading Ratio	2004	2005	2006	2007	2008
Sales ($'000)	77,383	87,633	93,733	105,519	106,068
Net Worth	16,437	18,832	19,089	23,290	23,568
Trading Ratio	4.7	4.7	4.9	4.5	4.5

RMA does not supply figures for this factor, but other data suggest that the firm is average.

Operating earnings growth rate. The next table depicts the annual year-to-year percentage change in Moloch's operating earnings; its growth rate has fluctuated during the years, being negative in 2005, with a return to excellent performance during 2006. Such an erratic pattern would be of concern to creditors and investors, as it means there is less predictability for Moloch's earnings and increasing risk.

	2005	2006	2007	2008
Moloch	–27.7%	100.7%	6.8%	14.7%
Industry	20.0%	0.0%	–16.7%	0.0%

Although Moloch has performed significantly better than the industry in the past, it is not likely to continue to do so; therefore, an average risk has been assumed.

Standard deviation of earnings. The standard deviation, defined as the square root of the variance, is a measure of the spread between two numbers.[3] It is a statistical measure of the tendency of data to be spread out as well as of the dispersion of a probability distribution. The smaller the deviation, the tighter the distribution and, thus, the lower the riskiness of the investment.[4]

Calculations of standard deviations of the pretax profits for the industry are based on data from RMA. The next table shows the industry and Moloch's historic standard deviations of pretax profits.

Standard Deviation	2005	2006	2007	2008
Moloch	0.1%	0.3%	3.6%	3.5%
Industry	0.2%	0.2%	0.1%	0.1%

Moloch exceeded that of the industry each year, except 2005. This means its earnings are less predictable than the industry's and a greater risk to a prospective investor. This, in turn, means less value would be assigned in the marketplace; it has been therefore ranked at 8.5.

Altman Z-Score. The Altman Z-score is a common method of estimating the likelihood of a firm becoming bankrupt that has been found to be accurate over 70% of the time. It is important to understand that all changes to the Z-score as well as its level must be monitored; a business whose score drops from 2.80 to 1.95 in a single year would be of greater concern than one that had remained between 1.70 and 1.85 for five years. The Z-score may be regarded as an early warning system that balances and puts into perspective five financial indicators; the calculation is:

$$Z = .012X(1) + .014X(2) + .033X(3) + .006X(4) + .999X(5)$$

---

[3] *See David F. Groebner and Patrick W. Shannon, **Business Statistics: A Decision-Making Approach**, 2nd ed, Charles Merrill, 1981.*

[4] *See Joel G. Siegel, Jae K. Shim, and Stephen W. Hartman, **The McGraw-Hill Pocket Guide to Business Finance—201 Decision Making Tools for Managers** (New York: McGraw-Hill, 1992), p. 119.*

Where

X(1) = Working Capital/Total Assets
X(2) = Retained Earnings/Total Assets
X(3) = Earnings before Interest and Taxes/Total Assets
X(4) = Total Equity/Total Debt

NOTE: Variables X(1) to X(4) are percentages, not decimals, while X(5) is a decimal.

If X(1) = 15%, it is recorded as 15.0, not 0.15.
Moloch has these ratios:

X(1) = –20.3%, X(2) = –15%, X(3) = –9.4%, X(4) = –5.2%, X(5) = 118%

Z = (.012)(–20.3), + (.014)(–15), + (.033)(–9.4), + (.006)(–5.2), +(.999)(1.18)

= –0.2436 –.02100 –0.3102 –.0312 +1.1788 = 0.03838 or 3.84%

Z-Score significance

Range	*Chance of Failure*
1.8% or less	Very high
1.81% – 2.7%	High
2.71% – 2.9%	Possible

Other Risks

Other items to be considered when using the RRCM are the effects of regional and national economic outlooks.

Regional outlook

- Average annual employment growth
- Business services employment average growth
- Health services employment average growth
- Local, state/province, and federal/central government growth
- Changing economic diversity
- New business creation
- High-tech employment
- Export potential
- Population trends
- Employment in transportation, communications and utilities
- State/province outlook
- Personal income
- Per capita income
- Production and consumption rates
- Economy, past and present
- Gross state/province product annual percentage change
- Personal income annual percentage change
- Nonfarm employment annual percentage change
- Unemployment rate

National Outlook

- Gross domestic product annual percentage change
- Consumer price index annual change
- Nonfarm employment—past and present
- Sales outlook for the industry
- Patents issued

To utilize the RRCM successfully, valuators must have a working knowledge of ratio analyses. The model allows using entity-specific qualitative and quantitative factors to estimate a reasonable cost of equity for a specific SME.[5]

CONCLUSION

The impact of the RRCM is best shown by returning to Moloch Inc., which was discussed in detail. In Xanadu, the risk-free rate at December 31, 2007, was 4.5% and at December 31, 2008, 3%. This gave Moloch a cost of equity of 22.7% in 2007 and 26.3% in 2008:

	2007	*2008*
	%	%
Risk-free Rate	4.5	3.0
Competition	4.5	4.4
Financial	4.4	5.0
Management	4.8	5.1
Profitability	4.5	5.1
Local/National	0.0	4.0
Cost of Equity	22.7	26.3

Those percentages are 3.0% lower than those of Ibbotson for 2007 but 23.5% higher in 2008. As a result, even though net earnings were up 1.2%, the value would have decreased by 12.6% from $11,675,000 in 2007 to $10,200,000 in 2008, a not-unreasonable conclusion.

---

[5] *For a more comprehensive explanation of risk ratios and factors, see Hanlin and Claywell,* **The Value of Risk** *(NACVA, Salt Lake City, UT, -2002).*

APPENDIX

Market returns for 1927 to 1963 cover only the New York Stock Exchange; the American Stock Exchange was added in 1964, and NASDAQ from 1973 on. The risk-free rate is the cumulative return from rolling over one-month Treasury bills during a year.

Year	Equity Return Market	Market Risk Premium	Risk-free Rate	Year	Equity Return Market	Market Risk Premium	Risk-free Rate
1927	33.40	30.27	3.13	1968	14.16	8.94	5.22
1928	39.07	35.53	3.54	1969	-10.85	-17.42	6.57
1929	-15.02	-19.76	4.74	1970	0.06	-6.45	6.52
1930	-28.83	-31.25	2.43	1971	16.19	11.80	4.39
1931	-44.36	-45.44	1.09	1972	17.33	13.50	3.84
1932	-8.47	-9.42	0.95	1973	-18.77	-25.70	6.93
1933	57.52	57.22	0.30	1974	-27.95	-35.96	8.01
1934	4.29	4.11	0.18	1975	37.35	31.55	5.80
1935	44.85	44.71	0.14	1976	26.77	21.68	5.08
1936	32.15	31.97	0.18	1977	-2.97	-8.10	5.13
1937	-34.61	-34.90	0.29	1978	8.53	1.34	7.19
1938	28.17	28.21	-0.04	1979	24.39	14.01	10.38
1939	2.12	2.11	0.01	1980	33.24	21.98	11.26
1940	-7.44	-7.42	-0.02	1981	-3.98	-18.70	14.72
1941	-9.63	-9.67	0.04	1982	20.43	9.90	10.53
1942	16.31	16.03	0.28	1983	22.66	13.87	8.80
1943	28.06	27.70	0.36	1984	3.17	-6.67	9.84
1944	21.36	21.03	0.33	1985	31.41	23.69	7.72
1945	38.45	38.13	0.32	1986	15.55	9.40	6.16
1946	-5.91	-6.27	0.36	1987	1.81	-3.66	5.47
1947	3.37	2.87	0.50	1988	17.56	11.20	6.36
1948	2.36	1.55	0.81	1989	28.42	20.04	8.38
1949	20.08	18.96	1.12	1990	-6.09	-13.93	7.84
1950	30.03	28.81	1.22	1991	33.63	28.03	5.60
1951	20.83	19.34	1.49	1992	9.06	5.56	3.50
1952	13.29	11.64	1.65	1993	11.58	8.68	2.90
1953	0.36	-1.47	1.83	1994	-0.75	-4.66	3.91
1954	50.22	49.36	0.86	1995	35.67	30.07	5.60
1955	25.33	23.76	1.57	1996	21.15	15.95	5.20
1956	8.48	6.01	2.47	1997	30.33	25.08	5.25
1957	-10.36	-13.52	3.15	1998	22.28	17.42	4.85
1958	44.84	43.31	1.53	1999	25.27	20.58	4.69
1959	12.61	9.63	2.98	2000	-11.09	-16.97	5.88
1960	1.17	-1.50	2.67	2001	-11.27	-15.13	3.86
1961	26.95	24.83	2.12	2002	-20.83	-22.46	1.63
1962	-10.33	-13.06	2.73	2003	33.13	32.10	1.02
1963	20.89	17.78	3.11	2004	13.01	11.82	1.19
1964	16.30	12.78	3.53	2005	7.32	4.34	2.98
1965	14.39	10.47	3.92	2006	16.24	11.42	4.81
1966	-8.69	-13.44	4.75	2007	7.27	2.61	4.67
1967	28.56	24.35	4.21	2008	-38.31	-39.96	1.64

Source: Eugene F. Fama and Kenneth R. French, "How Unusual Was the Stock Market of 2008?" (May 2009).

ADDITIONAL RESOURCES

Bruno, Sam J. *Entrepreneurship—Small Business Consulting: A Handbook*. Houston: School of Business and Public Administration, University of Houston, Clear Lake, revised 1993.

Claywell, J. Richard. "Black/Green Build-Up Method." NACVA Course Materials (December 1999).

Walsh, Ciaran. *Key Management Ratios*. New York: Financial Times/Prentice Hall, 1996.

Zukin, James H. *Financial Valuation: Business and Business Interests*. Boston: Warren, Gorham & Lamont , 1998.

11 FINANCIAL STATEMENT ANALYSES

MARTIN COSTA

GERMANY

INTRODUCTION

There are two primary objectives of financial statement analysis:

1. Evaluate the past performance of an entity in order to prepare informative and pertinent data for comparisons with the results of other entities in the same industry (benchmarking).
2. Develop value drivers for reliable projections of future financial statements.

The process involves:

- Considering business cycles and trends as well as the firm's strengths and weaknesses, opportunities and threats.
- Adjusting numbers and eliminating extraordinary earnings and costs.

The analyses influence the preparation of the integrated financial plan, which in turn is the basis for the value drivers.

INTEGRATED FINANCIAL PLAN

The integrated financial plan is developed from an entity's financial history. Many changes in the economic and natural environment can have a bearing on a firm's development; moreover, strategic plans may change or, over the years, be altered by management, again influencing the process. All those circumstances have to be considered when analyzing historical financial statements; otherwise, the numbers are not comparable to those of other entities.

RELIABLE RESULTS

An important objective of financial statement analysis is to obtain reliable results for the future in terms of judging an entity's long-term, sustainable ability to generate cash. Nonrecurring items are not part of this; they only affect individual years and do not have an impact the sustainable profits. For example: a firm sells its city center office building and moves its head office to a converted suburban plant; the gains from this transaction may be substantial, but they have no bearing on the entity's long-term profitability. For the same reason, items that recur randomly or after very long periods also have to be eliminated.

Forecasts cannot be generated simply by extending the trends in past financial figures. Business cycles, such as general economic conditions, technical innovations, and actions by the competition have to be taken into consideration. In many cases, specific patterns exist that need to be analyzed. Those could be constant growth over a certain period, ups and downs following the general economic development, trade cycles, product life cycles, or seasonal patterns. Periods used for analyses may vary from short term (one year) to long term (five years). Unusual events, such as the present financial market crisis, can change cycles and even break up historical patterns.

COMPARATIVE ANALYSES

As a basic rule, all items, both quantitative and qualitative, relating to an entity's operations have to be analyzed. Qualitative items are soft facts, such as internal resources, market share, and strategic opportunities, which are discussed later. Quantitative items, mainly financial but sometimes operational, are normally analyzed by ratios for rates of return, capital availability, age structure of assets, operational gearing, the financing structure, and leverage effects based on past financial statements. Trends in the following measures are used frequently in comparing financial statements:

- Size: Revenues, locations, assets, staff
- Growth: Revenues, various levels of earnings (gross profit; earnings before interest, taxes, depreciation, and amortization [EBITDA], earnings before interest and taxes [EBIT], etc.)
- Liquidity: Free cash, working capital, current ratio, quick ratio
- Profitability: Margins at various levels of earnings, return on assets (ROA), return on investment (ROI)
- Turnover: Sales/assets, benchmarking
- Leverage: Assets/equity, debt structure

VALUE DRIVERS

Various techniques are used in order to determine value drivers, which are needed for plausible and reliable forecasts, from historic financial information; analyses of the financial statements for several years, at least five, preferably 10, to ensure a full business cycle is covered, give essential information to establish:

- Adjusted growth rates
- Adjusted earnings and costs
- Adjusted profits
- Additional capital necessary for the business development

These key figures depend on the business strategy as well as on the economic and natural environment. An entity's ability to create cash earnings in the past is the basis for judging the plausibility of sustainable profits in the future. To generate those requires both investment in assets and staff to maintain the existing productive capacity and a reinvestment strategy for future expansion.

Valuation methods using multiples are mainly based on:

- Adjusted profits at an appropriate level
- Adjusted revenues

The necessary adjustments include elimination of special arrangements, coincidences or nonrecurring events to allow satisfactory comparisons within peer groups.

Profit Defined

In this context, *profit* is defined as the total of:

1. Operating profit from regular business activities
2. Gains from financial and investment transactions, including interest received less interest paid, as well as profits and losses from unconsolidated subsidiaries and affiliates

3. Extraordinary items from unusual transactions, discontinued operations and incidents (strikes, natural disasters, moves, etc.) which are nonrecurring
4. Other benefits from transactions in nonessential business assets, such as results from properties that are not used for business activities

DATA SOURCES

Financial statement analyses are complex as they cover assessments of the general economic environment; the industry, including competitors and markets; as well as internal and external accounting.

General economic data can be obtained from national agencies, banks, or information services. To get a reasonable understanding of business developments over the period, data should cover at least the past five years but, preferably, for the same time span as the financial statements. Forecasts from outside sources, such as stockbrokers, for future years should be analyzed based on the historic pattern.

Material about an industry is available either directly or through the Internet; from unions, organizations, trade publications, and documents such as annual reports published by competitors. In particular, the changes in the entity's market position during the last five years should be compared with those of the main competitors. Facts about future trends and forecasts for specific industries or sectors should also be collected. Additional information can be derived from the firm's own publications, such as annual or quarterly reports, announcements, articles in newspapers or magazines, analysts' reports, or pronouncements of rating agencies.

Internal data includes information and documents about the firm's structure and legal form, taxation, strategic decisions, shareholder resolutions, important agreements, and internal accounting (cost) records. One of the essential components of a satisfactory valuation is an understanding of the business model and the related strategies; those include planned new products and services, anticipated technological changes, management structure, and sales and marketing programs. Their past performance must be reviewed with management and key decision makers; in addition, any problems anticipated when executing the plans and strategies should be discussed.

As previously mentioned, the external accounting information should cover at least five years, preferably longer, to identify business and product cycles and nonrecurring events as well as the sustainable business development in the past. The main sources of information are:

- Financial statements, audited, reviewed, or management prepared
- Segment reports
- Cash-flow statements
- Tax statements, returns, or declarations
- Information about the accounting standards applied (local, generally accepted accounting principles, or International Financial Reporting Standards [IFRS]). As many of those as possible combined with additional data (payables, receivables, inventories, fixed asset schedules) are necessary for a complete analysis.

In particular, transactions with related parties should be analyzed carefully to ensure arm's-length pricing (see Chapter 36). Related-party transactions include contracts, loans, leases, or business arrangements with a parent, subsidiaries, affiliates, management members, shareholders and their families. This important subject is dealt with in more detail later.

The analyses should emphasize significant investments, especially in intangible assets (research and development [R&D], licenses, training, marketing), specific growth drivers (locations, regions, new products, new customers), structural changes (management, shareholders, key personnel), and financing (additional capital, bank relationships, external lenders) and state the reasons underlying any changes in these factors.

ADJUSTMENTS

The main objective of adjustments on financial statements is to determine the true earning power of the entity in the past. Doing this requires elimination of all nonrecurring items and those that have no permanent influence on the future earning power. As a result, past earnings are made comparable with projected earnings, and the forecasts can be corroborated by the use of plausibility checks. The final result is a reliable basis for the entity's valuation.

Applicable Items

With respect to adjustments, there are two questions:

1. Is the item nonrecurring?
2. Is it related to discontinued operations or assets not essential to operations?

Unless the answer to either question is yes, adjustments are necessary; otherwise, the respective amount needs to be eliminated in the same way assets, liabilities, revenues, and expenses have to be separated into those that are essential and nonessential. Items that are immaterial do not have to be analyzed, eliminated, or adjusted; the normal materiality limit is about 1% of net income after tax.

Examples of nonrecurring items are presented next.

Valuation Changes

- Profits and losses resulting from changes in asset values related to mergers
- Impairment losses related to goodwill, fixed or intangible assets
- Payments that have been made on receivables and other items previously written off
- Unrealized profits and losses from changes in fair values of financial instruments and hedging transactions
- Actuarial gains and losses related to pension plans
- Earnings from the reversal of a provision
- Reversal of an asset impairment loss
- Profits and losses stemming from changes in deferred taxes due to modifications in tax laws, regulations, rates, or losses carried forward

Other Nonrecurring Items

- Sales and profits caused by extraordinary events at other companies (a strike at a competitor)
- Proceeds from government grants
- Profits and losses resulting from asset disposals
- Nonrecurring earnings from subsidiaries (tax recoveries, distribution of reserves)
- Profits and losses related to mergers or acquisitions
- Extraordinary losses from defective products and warranties (only material amounts)
- Gains or losses from litigation, strikes, settlements of claims

Systematic Adjustments

From time to time, entities make basic changes to their financial reporting, such as adopting IFRS. In such cases, to ensure comparability, adjustments have to be made, although allocating such amounts to different past years, normally based on sales or EBIT, may be somewhat arbitrary.

Changes in accounting principles. There can be fundamental variations between many national accounting standards and IFRS. When analyzing financial statements, one of the basic questions is: Which accounting standards were applied? Differences can arise from recognition of realized or unrealized profits, use of fair value, items that result in profits or losses, or changes in equity. Some national accounting standards prescribe that no retrospective adjustments are to be made; IFRS, however, requires them.

Changes in valuation practices. Changes in valuation practices include profits and losses caused by changes in methods of:

- Cost calculations (cost of goods)
- Inventory measurement (average cost, including overhead and depreciation elements, which may be zero)
- Depreciation techniques (straight line, declining balance, sinking fund)
- Impairment testing (fair value less costs to sell, value in use)

Generally, this information is found in the notes to the financial statements.

Changes in accounting policies. Dealing with this item is one of the most difficult parts of financial statement analyses, as there is a wide range of possible, acceptable changes in accounting policies. Information comes primarily from interviews with management and notes to the financial statements. Changes in accounting policies fall into three categories:

1. *Estimates.* The probability of an event or contingency, the result of litigation or an uncertain liability, the useful life of an asset
2. *Valuation methods.* Amortized historic cost, fair values, value in use
3. *Alternative treatments of controlled entities.* Full consolidation, pro rata inclusion

Any of those items and procedures can result in an increase or decrease in profit, which will vary in amounts and materiality. Likely triggers are:

- Replacement of key personnel (chief executive or financial officer, management in general)
- Contemplated initial public offering
- Intended sale of the entity
- Reorganization of an operation

Regular modifications of basic business strategy should be treated as ordinary items with no elimination being required. However, their effects must be taken into account in the analyses of sustainable profits.

Singular events. Singular events cover the losses (occasionally gains) caused by:

- Strikes
- Fires
- Office or plant moves
- Natural disasters (floods, avalanches etc.)
- Asset disposals
- Property sales
- Recalls due to product defects
- Extraordinary warranties

Usually, their effects are seen directly in the financial statements since some of the costs (net of any insurance proceeds) will be charged to normal expenses (rent, advertising, interest), with the balances generally being posted to "other income" or "other operating expenses."

Unless the notes to the financial statements or some internal report contains the pertinent information, only questioning senior management followed by fundamental analyses of income or expense accounts will indicate their existence. Indicators are unexpected increases in certain expenses or individual postings of unusual amounts. Frequently both are offset by claimed extraordinary increases in earnings.

Related parties. The profits of small and medium-size businesses may be strongly influenced by related-party transactions; therefore, they have to be very critically analyzed. Areas of concern are:

- Employment arrangements
- Dual-purpose assets
- Loans
- Personal benefits
- Leases

In many cases, family members are employed whose remuneration may be too high (very common) or too low (not unusual) in relation to the services they provide. Some entities even "employ" family members who get paid little or nothing for their activities. When such a firm is sold, those unpaid functions have to be evaluated and an imputed cost deducted.

It is common for family firms to have dual-purpose assets that may be used for business or private purposes (e.g., cars, real estate, investments). Contracts covering employment or related to the use of such assets may contain conditions that are not at arm's length. In that situation, full adjustment has to be made to assets, liabilities, revenues, and expenses.

Interest payments on loans due to or by family members may not be in accordance with market rates. A common situation is to withdraw bonuses, pay the personal tax, and lend the balance back to the entity without interest; in all cases, the agreed-on interest rate needs to be adjusted to market.

Certain types of expenses give opportunities for personal benefits; they include travel, entertainment, legal, and tax advisory services. It is always essential to separate business from private use; the latter has to be eliminated completely.

Another frequent practice, on purchasing a business, is to strip out any real estate and lease it back at a fixed rental, which may be above the market rate for similar properties. Also, leases covering other assets, such as equipment, may contain unusual conditions that could affect their useful lives or values.

Minority shareholders. Minority shareholders in general merely have a minor influence on business activities. Unlike a controlling interest, they can affect business strategy and policy only within a very narrow range. Therefore, when valuing a minority position, no adjustment should be made to profits for transactions with related parties; the relative positions of the shareholders may have an impact on the value conclusion; therefore, the structure needs to be assessed as part of the process.

Group relationships. Several levels of effects from group entities have to be taken into account. Transfer prices in particular should be analyzed very carefully to ensure they are in line with the market; these issues can refer to a wide range of goods, services, loans, leases, license agreements, and the like. Benefits from group synergies (more advantageous purchasing, lower borrowing costs), which may no longer exist once an entity is sold, are rarely considered; their absence may adversely affect profits once the firm becomes a stand-alone entity.

Firms forming part of a controlled group are usually part of a complex logistic and financial system. There are investments, sale-leaseback agreements, and other contracts that often are not at market rates. Odd effects, such as unexpected goodwill, and major changes in the structure may sometimes result from a first-time consolidation, inclusion of formerly nonconsolidated subsidiaries (particularly those financing customer purchases), or changes in consolidation procedures.

Discontinued operations. As defined in IFRS 5, *Noncurrent Assets Held for Sale and Discontinued Operations,* a discontinued operation is a component of an entity that represents a separate major line of business or geographical area of operations, and either

(a) has been disposed of, or (b) is classified as held for sale. To qualify for this status, the sale must be part of a single coordinated plan to dispose of the separate major line of business or geographical area of operations. The category also includes any subsidiary acquired exclusively for future disposal. Profits and losses from such operations may be treated as part of the regular results or as nonrecurring items, depending on the individual situation.

Taxes. The results of special tax-driven items or transactions generally have to be analyzed critically; all tax-based values should be adjusted.

Presentation of facts. Differences in timing can affect many items; for example, announced increases in tax rates may lead to bringing forward investments. Critical economic situations often result in postponing required repairs or replacement of machines and lead to reducing expenses for marketing, research, and training. Such events directly affect liquidity, balance sheet structure, and profit of the entity not only at the time of the decision but also in following years. Therefore, adjustments should be looked at in the context of at least a five-year analysis to discover these long-term effects.

OTHER MEASURES

NOTE: The sections of this chapter covering EBITDA and standardized free cash flow draw from **Improved Communication with Non-GAAP Financial Measures: General Principles and Guidance for Reporting EBITDA and Free Cash Flow,** *issued in 2008 by the Canadian Performance Reporting Board, a unit of the Canadian Institute of Chartered Accountants.*

EBITDA

Earnings before interest, taxes, depreciation, and amortization is the most commonly used non-IFRS financial measure. It is conventionally calculated as earnings (net income) before discontinued operations plus interest expenses, taxes, depreciation, depletion, and amortization with all elements being at the amounts reported in the IFRS financial statements. The objective is to quantify an entity's operating performance without the effects of its financing or the recovery of the carrying amounts of its physical and intangible assets.

There are many applications beyond financial reporting for EBITDA; it is frequently used in valuations, often forming a part of debt covenants and executive compensation plans. EBITDA is also the basis for the total enterprise value (TEV) of an entity, which covers all interest-bearing debt, preferred shares, and ordinary shareholders' equity.

Proxy for Cash Flow

Occasionally, EBITDA is described as a proxy for cash flows from operations. This is not correct. Even ignoring the cash costs of financing and taxes, it totally ignores the effects of changes in working capital, which may have significant effects when an entity is growing quickly or is in a seasonal business involving variations in inventories.

By design, EBITDA does not recognize any expense for the usage of capital assets. Most managers and investors do not consider the amortization of the historic costs of physical and intangible assets to be indicative of the future cash expenditures needed to maintain existing productive capacity. Once an investment has been made in a plant, its historic cost is usually no longer relevant. This is particularly true because of the different accounting treatment given to internally developed (expensed) and acquired (capitalized) intangible assets; in general, TEV/EBITDA ratios are likely to be more comparable within an industry than the often-used price earnings ratio.

Standardized Definition

EBITDA is only loosely defined, which complicates comparisons between entities. Therefore, International Association of Consultants, Valuators and Analysts (IACVA) has followed the Canadian Performance Reporting Board (CPRB) by recommending that valuators and entities both prepare EBITDA in accordance with this definition:

Net income or net loss before discontinued operations as reported in the IFRS financial statements, including that net income or net loss related to any non-controlling interest, excluding amounts included in net income or net loss for: (a) income taxes; (b) interest expense; and (c) depreciation, depletion, amortization and impairment charges for capital assets.

Standardized EBITDA should be reconciled to net income or loss for the period as determined in accordance with IFRS. In the CPRB's view:

Standardized EBITDA ("SEBITDA") represents an indication of the entity's continuing capacity to generate income from operations before taking into account management's financing decisions and costs of consuming physical and intangible assets, which vary according to their vintage, technological currency, and management's estimate of their useful life.

Variants of EBITDA

Often a valuator may wish to reflect entity-specific items not addressed in SEBITDA (such as removing mark-to-market gains or losses). In that event, a supplemental figure should be presented. In addition, there are two commonly accepted variants, OPEBITDA (*oper*ating EBITDA) and OPEBITRAD (*ope*rating earnings before interest, taxes, R&D, amortization, and depreciation); the latter is used mainly for software and other technology entities where R&D is the major form of capital expenditures (CAPEX).

Example: Calculation of Valuation Measures

The relationships between the concepts of the variants of EBITDA and other valuation measures are best illustrated by the example of HiTech Company PLC, shown in the next table. It is based on a real firm. For simplicity, mark-to-market gains and other comprehensive income have been omitted. As the valuator progresses from net income, margins increase noticeably.

The starting point is profit attributable to ordinary shares (margin 3.9%), the basis for the traditional earnings per share. This is followed by:

Net Income	(4.6%)
Net Earnings (before discontinued operations)	(6.4%)
EBT Earnings Before Taxes	(9.4%)
EBIT Earnings Before Interest and Taxes	(9.5%)
SEBITDA Standardized Earnings Before Interest, Taxes, Depreciation and Amortization	(15.2%)
OPEBITDA Operating Earnings Before Interest, Taxes, Depreciation and Amortization	(19.1%)
OPEBITRAD Operating Earnings Before Interest, Taxes, R&D, Amortization and Depreciation	(30.2%)
Gross Profit	(67.4%)

The table demonstrates the significance of SEBITDA and its two variants that are generally accepted non-IFRS measures.

HiTech Co. PLC

	Market Indicator	*$'000*	
Sales	Yes	182,056	100.0%
Profit Attributable to Ordinary Share	Yes	7,104	3.9%
Dividends on Preferred Shares	No	1,260	0.7%
Net Income	No	8,364	4.6%
Discontinued Operations	No	3,208	1.8%
Net Earnings	Yes	11,572	6.4%
Income Taxes	No	5,615	3.1%
Earnings Before Taxes	Yes	17,187	9.4%
Interest Expense	No	174	0.1%
Earnings Before Interest & Taxes	Yes	17,361	9.5%
Depreciation	No	2,488	1.4%
Depletion of PP&E	No	64	0.0%
Amortization of Intangibles	No	6,830	3.8%
Impairment of Assets	No	857	0.5%
SEBITDA	Yes	27,600	15.2%
Non-Operating Items			
Interest Income	No	(3,579)	–2.0%
Gains on Asset Sales	No	(145)	–0.1%
Other (Income) Expense	No	(246)	–0.1%
Share-Based Compensation	No	7,398	4.1%
Foreign Exchange Losses	No	1,274	0.7%
In Process R&D	No	1,674	0.9%
Restructuring Charge	No	757	0.4%
Total Non-Operating Items		7,133	3.9%
OPEBITDA	Yes	34,733	19.1%
R&D	No	20,282	11.1%
OPEBITRAD	Yes	55,015	30.2%
SG&A	No	67,652	37.2%
Gross Profit	No	122,667	67.4%
Cost of Sales	No	59,389	32.6%
Sales	Yes	182,056	100.0%

FREE CASH FLOW

An entity's cash flows can be analyzed in a variety of ways; an IFRS cash flow statement classifies them as operating, financing, and investing. Other aggregations are used for analyzing the periodic amounts of cash generated and consumed by an entity; all combine operating activities with elements of financing and investing to measure the internally generated cash flows available for debt repayment, internal growth, acquisitions, or distributions. One such measure, free cash flow (cash from operations net of CAPEX), is considered an indicator of financial strength and performance; its primary objective is to assist in projecting future cash flows for valuations.

Standardized Definition

As there is no generally accepted definition for free cash flow, many different calculations are used. The CPRB in 2008 developed this standardized definition:

Cash flows from operating activities as reported in the IFRS financial statements, including operating cash flows provided from or used in discontinued operations; less: (a) total capital expenditures as reported in the financial statements; and (b) dividends, when stipulated [such as on cumulative preferred shares], unless deducted in arriving at cash flows from operating activities.

Standardized free cash flow should be reconciled to cash flows from operating activities for the period, determined in accordance with IFRS.

Entity-Specific Versions

IACVA recommends the definition in the last section unless special circumstances require adjustments be made to cash flows from operations. An example might be when they are cyclical or periodic; in certain industries, inventory is built up (consuming cash) in the summer and is sold (producing cash) in the winter; another might be removing the effects of discontinued operations or mark-to-market gains and losses.

In several industries, such as forest products, noncapitalized major repairs and maintenance costs occur cyclically; a number of firms have multiyear cycles of capital expenditures on compressors or capacity rebuilds that may require some plants to be shut down for lengthy periods. The relative predictability of free cash flows may suggest describing them not in terms of actual historic patterns but after adjusting for the cyclical or seasonal elements.

This is undesirable; such items are part of the explanation of the variances in periodic standardized free cash flow (SFCF). Cyclical events such as these also may be addressed by reporting entity-specific free cash flows that adjust for such known patterns. In that case, any significant assumptions should be justified. For example, an adjustment to eliminate the seasonal fluctuations of working capital changes may involve decisions about future selling prices.

Adjusted Free Cash Flow

Similarly, management or the valuator may wish to adjust free cash flows for the special or nonrecurring nature of certain transactions, which in their view, will not be part of future free cash flows, such as restructuring charges, which are frequently considered nonrecurring. Other entity-specific adjustments may include significant commitments for future capital expenditures to be funded from operations.

The term "free cash flow" suggests that the measure should reflect cash that is generated in a particular period which is available to be spent at management's discretion; this is not necessarily the case if it is restricted by a financial covenant or held in a subsidiary. Circumstances such as those should be reflected through an entity-specific adjustment or set out by the valuator as part of the entity's financing strategy.

When a valuator calculates adjusted free cash flow for an entity, the purpose of each adjustment should be discussed; for example, when working capital is modified, the accompanying disclosure should identify the specific elements that have been changed, together with an explanation of each element, such as seasonality or growth.

The valuation report should complement SFCF with information about its relationship to the firm's investing and financing activities, the entity's capital expenditures and its productive capacity strategy, and financing activities included in operations.

Relationship of SFCF to Investing and Financing Activities

The relationship of an entity's SFCF to its investing and financing activities may best be explained by an analysis of how those activities complement or compete with it. In addition, disclosure of the entity's financing strategy will assist readers to understand this relationship. This disclosure could include:

- The entity's target debt to equity or leverage ratio
- The degree to which it has fixed but uncapitalized obligations, such as operating leases and long-term purchase commitments
- The likelihood of noncompliance with loan covenants

Productive Capacity Strategy

Assessing the likelihood of an entity's free cash flows being sustainable requires an understanding of its strategy for maintaining and growing productive capacity. This needs, in the valuator's working papers, discussions about the entity's productive capacity, changes in that capacity, and the factors that affect capacity—for example, capital expenditures, acquisitions, intellectual property, and information systems. Productive capacity strategies may range from the simple maintenance of a basic service to a business plan intended to enable the entity to grow cash flows through the deployment of the latest technologies.

Such a strategy may be opportunistic: Capacity is maintained when it is affordable and expected to yield positive returns and permitted to decline when market conditions indicate that it would not be profitable to maintain. In some circumstances, the intent may be not to replace capacity at all but to permit it to run down.

Any of these strategies may be appropriate in the context of the business; it is impossible to understand the implications of an entity's SFCF that is measured net of its CAPEX without knowing its productive capacity strategy. This includes management's ability to implement the strategy and the risks related to factors such as: production problems, technological change, equipment obsolescence, variations in raw material prices, and the effects of new information technology as well as the entity's planned responses. When different business segments have separate strategies, each should be explained. To the extent possible, the discussion should include management's outlook for the near future, not likely to exceed five years, as a set of financial projections. In businesses where major maintenance occurs only once every few years, it is appropriate to provide an explanation of the cycle and its impact on operating cash flows and capital expenditures.

Financings in Operations

In some cases, cash flows from operations are affected by financing-type activities that are included in operations; they may occur in close proximity to the transaction or not arise for several years. In addition, these undertakings are subject to various degrees of management discretion. Securitization of accounts receivable is an example of such a transaction, substantially under management's control, that can have a significant impact on a period's cash flows from operations.

Other examples may not have an impact on operating cash flows for several years; they may include asset retirement obligations, free rent arrangements, and deferred interest payments on discounted long-term obligations; those are noncash operating transactions until paid. Their trending is sometimes over the life of the contract, such as free rent at the beginning, or at termination, as for instance accrued interest on a discounted obligation.

Such operating items may have a significant effect on the entity's current or future SFCF. Accordingly, a valuator should identify them and explain the extent to which they have either consumed or provided cash in the current period or postponed to the future cash inflows and outflows, including when they are expected to be due. As well, the analyses should identify the total related obligations and the amounts expected to be paid in each of the next five years.

Example: Standardized Free Cash Flow

The next example returns to HiTech Company PLC, to demonstrate the calculation of standardized free cash flows. It starts with Net Income (4.6% of Sales) followed by: Adjustments re Non-Cash Charges (11.4%) and Changes in Working Capital Balances (–2.4%); to give Operating Cash Flow (13.6%); from this are deducted CAPEX (4.6%) and Dividends on Preferred Shares (0.7%) to arrive at SFCF (5.3%).

HiTech Co. PLC

CASH FROM OPERATIONS

Net Income	8,364	4.6%
Adjustments re: Non-Cash Charges		
Depreciation	2,488	1.4%
Depletion of PP&E	64	0.0%
Amortization of Intangibles	6,830	3.8%
Impairment of Assets	857	0.5%
Gains on Asset Sales	(145)	–0.1%
Bad Debt Provision & Recoveries	93	0.1%
Inventory Obsolescence	364	0.2%
US Tax Benefits re: Share Options	113	0.1%
Share-Based Compensation	7,398	4.1%
Deferred Income Taxes	1,052	0.6%
In-Process R&D	1,674	0.9%
Total Adjustments	20,788	11.4%
	29,152	16.0%
Changes in Working Capital Balances		
Accounts Receivable	1,142	0.6%
Inventories	(4,448)	–2.4%
Prepaids & Other	125	0.1%
Taxes Due	(270)	–0.1%
Accounts Payable	(508)	–0.3%
Accrued Expenses	(454)	–0.2%
Total Changes	(4,413)	–2.4%
Operating Cash Flow	24,739	13.6%
Capital Expenditures (CAPEX)	(8,299)	–4.6%
Dividends on Preferred Shares	(1,260)	–0.7%
Standardized Free Cash Flow	15,180	8.3%

RATIO AND TREND ANALYSES

Ratio analyses are one of the oldest methods of comparing parameters, dating back to at least the eighteenth century; however, to a valuator, trends in the ratios as well as their underlying figures are also very important.

Assets and Liabilities Structure

The structure of an entity's assets is measured by these intensity ratios:

- Capital (fixed) assets / Total assets
- Inventories / Total assets
- Current assets / Total assets
- Financial assets / Total assets

Operational gearing. Fixed costs in general are a burden on a firm's activities, since they need to be paid irrespective of production levels and revenues generated. They induce operational gearing (the ratio of fixed to total operating costs) that results in operating profit increasing or decreasing more rapidly than sales when they fluctuate; the higher the intensity of capital assets, the greater the operational gearing effect.

Financial leverage. The effect of financial leverage needs to be monitored. Working capital requirements are also a cost factor; for a growing business, solvency is vital. Increases in inventories, which may indicate a lack of control over sales, are expensive; allowing for storage space, double handling, and financing, the cost of excessive inventory is over 10% a year. Rising receivables may suggest liquidity problems at customers or some difficulties with particular orders. Common working capital ratios are:

Current Ratio = Current Assets / Current Liabilities

Quick Ratio = (Current Assets – Inventories) / Current Liabilities

Inventory Duration in Months = (Average Inventories for year) × 12 / Cost of Sales

Inventory Turnover = Annual Cost of Sales / Average Inventories

Days Receivables Outstanding = Average Receivables / Related Sales

NOTE: These ratios do not differentiate between changes in inventory quantities and prices. If averages are not available, year-end figures may be used.

Capital Structure

Equity is an important safeguard against future losses; its sufficiency is shown by the following ratios:

Equity Ratio = Total Equity / Total Assets

Tangible Ratio = Equity – Intangibles & Goodwill / Total Assets – the Intangibles & Goodwill

Debt / Equity Ratio = Total Liabilities / Total Equity

Leverage Ratio = Interest-bearing Debt / (Debt + Equity)

In applying these ratios, the fair values of debt and equity, if available, should be used in the analyses rather than the nominal values.

Financial leverage effect. If the return on total assets is higher than annual debt service, then that on the equity return is increased; unfortunately, the reverse is also true.

Interest Coverage Percentage = EBIT / Debt Interest

Fixed Charge Coverage Percentage = (Total of Debt Interest & Principal Payments + Lease Payments) / Standardized EBITDA

Debt Coverage = Total Debt Principal / SEBITDA

The first two items should be higher than 100%, the latter not more than 4.0.

Debt analyses. Capital maturity analyses separate debt into short term (less than one year), mid term (one to five years) and long term (more than five years). However, some short-term borrowers with a base amount of debt, which is being permanently rolled over may have this amount treated as mid-term debt; the closing of credit markets in 2008 and 2009 eliminated this possibility for a period.

Creditor structure analyses divide creditors into groups, such as banks, vendors, customer deposits, and others. Special risks result from excessive dependency on any one group; this risk is assessed by ratios such as bank/total debt. Depending on the situation, a detailed analysis of individual groups of creditors may be necessary.

All the ratios discussed in this section should be calculated for each year the financial statements are available and the effects of their trends considered.

Balance Sheet Analysis

The initial analysis of an entity's balance sheet is to express each element as a percentage of total assets. Trends in those figures will indicate areas where further investigation is required.

Asset cover ratios show the relation between fixed assets and their funding:

Equity Cover Percentage = Equity / Fixed Assets

Asset Cover Percentage = (Equity + Term Debts) / Fixed Assets

Capital assets should be financed only on a long-term basis.

Liquidity ratios show the entity's ability to pay short-term debts.

$$\text{Cash Ratio} = \text{Liquid Funds (Cash + Investments + Receivables) / Current Liabilities}$$
$$\text{Current Ratio} = \text{Current Assets/ Current Liabilities}$$
$$\text{Quick Ratio} = \text{(Current Assets – Inventories) / Current Liabilities}$$

Cash Flow Ratios

A standardized definition for free cash flow was discussed previously. Some other commonly used terms are:

- Net cash flow (SFCF—discontinued operations)
- Operating cash flow (Net Cash Flow – Taxes – Financial Transactions)
- Nonfinancial cash flow (Operating Cash Flow – Working Capital Changes)

Some common ratios are:

$$\text{Internal financing rate} = \text{SFCF / Turnover}$$
$$\text{CAPEX financing rate} = \text{SFCF / CAPEX}$$

Cost and Profit Ratios

In addition to analyzing the balance sheet of an entity, it is essential to display each item of the income statement as a percentage of sales. Subsequently, other profit ratios based on invested capital may be applied.

$$\text{Return on Equity} = \text{Annual Net Earnings (before/after taxes) / Average Equity}$$
$$\text{Return on Assets} = \text{EBIT / Average Total Assets}$$
$$\text{Return on Invested Capital} = \text{EBIT / Average (Total Debt + Equity)}$$
$$\text{Return on Capital Employed} = \text{(Operating Profit – Costs of Capital) / Invested Capital}$$

Some common cost ratios show the structure and influence of major cost categories:

$$\text{Personnel Ratio} = \text{Personnel Expenditures / Total Costs}$$
$$\text{Average Wage} = \text{Personnel Expenditures / Number of Employees}$$
$$\text{Material Ratio} = \text{Costs of Material / Cost of Sales}$$
$$\text{Depreciation Ratio} = \text{Depreciation / Cost of Sales}$$

Growth analysis is commonly done by combinations of ratios (tree structure) based on capital and/or turnover.

Example: Income Statement Analyses

The previous illustrations of SEBITDA and SFCF referred to HiTech Co. PLC. This example refers to its U.S. subsidiary, whose comparative income statements are set out next.

During the last five years, the U.S. operations have done poorly; their proportion of world sales dropped from 55% in 2004 to 39% in 2005 and went on down to 25% in 2008. In the current year, the United States is expected to do relatively well, as the downturn in the country started in late 2008.

	2004	2005	2006	2007	2008	2009
Parent Sales	111,226	125,198	144,663	173,263	182,056	142,000
Growth	NA	12.6%	15.5%	19.8%	5.1%	−22.0%
U.S. Sales	60,707	48,852	43,686	48,593	45,749	43,551
Growth	NA	−19.5%	−10.6%	11.2%	−5.9%	−4.8%
U.S. Proportion	54.6%	39.0%	30.2%	28.0%	25.1%	30.7%

HiTech Co. PLC.—U.S. Operations
COMPARATIVE INCOME STATEMENTS

	2004	2005	2006	2007	2008	2009 Budget
Sales	60,707	48,852	43,686	48,593	45,749	43,551
Cost of Sales	(37,894)	(31,010)	(27,299)	(31,280)	(30,154)	(27,264)
Gross Profit	22,813	17,842	16,387	17,312	15,595	16,286
Expenses						
SG&A	14,036	15,509	15,358	13,882	12,583	11,218
R&D	3,328	3,424	3,352	2,289	2,248	2,271
Foreign Exchange	(323)	642	(706)	911	(1,226)	(615)
Total Expenses	17,041	19,575	18,004	17,082	13,606	12,873
Operating Profit	5,772	(1,734)	(1,617)	230	1,990	3,413
Impairment	0	0	0	(1,564)	0	0
Interest—net	(412)	(333)	(473)	(546)	(545)	(348)
Pretax Profit	5,360	(2,067)	(2,090)	(1,880)	1,445	3,065
Income Tax	(2,090)	703	710	107	(565)	(1,200)
Net Income (Loss)	3,270	(1,364)	(1,380)	(1,773)	880	1,865

HiTech Co. PLC.—U.S. Operations
COMPARATIVE RATIO ANALYSES

	2004	2005	2006	2007	2008	2009 Budget
Sales	100.0%	100.0%	100.0%	100.0%	100.0%	100.0%
Cost of Sales	−62.4%	−63.5%	−62.5%	−64.4%	−65.9%	−62.6%
Gross Profit	37.6%	36.5%	37.5%	35.6%	34.1%	37.4%
Expenses						
SG&A	23.1%	31.7%	35.2%	28.6%	27.5%	25.8%
R&D	5.5%	7.0%	7.7%	4.7%	4.9%	5.2%
Foreign Exchange	−0.5%	1.3%	−1.6%	1.9%	−2.7%	−1.4%
Total Expenses	28.1%	40.1%	41.2%	35.2%	29.7%	29.6%
Operating Profit	9.5%	−3.5%	−3.7%	0.5%	4.3%	7.8%
Impairment	0.0%	0.0%	0.0%	−3.2%	0.0%	0.0%
Interest—net	−0.7%	−0.7%	−1.1%	−1.1%	−1.2%	−0.8%
Pretax Profit	8.8%	−4.2%	−4.8%	−3.9%	3.2%	7.0%
Income Tax	−3.4%	1.4%	1.6%	0.2%	−1.2%	−2.8%
Net Income (Loss)	5.4%	−2.8%	−3.2%	−3.6%	1.9%	4.3%

After the ratio analyses, the valuator should undertake a trend analysis. This shows that after the decline in 2005, sales were roughly steady around 75% of the 2004 level while operating profits dropped substantially.

HiTech Co. PLC.—U.S. Operations
COMPARATIVE TREND ANALYSES

	2004	2005	2006	2007	2008	2009 Budget
Sales	100.0	80.5	72.0	80.0	75.4	71.7
Cost of Sales	100.0	81.8	72.0	82.5	79.6	71.9
Gross Profit	100.0	78.2	71.8	75.9	68.4	71.4
Expenses						
SG&A	100.0	110.5	109.4	98.9	89.6	79.9
R&D	100.0	102.9	100.7	68.8	67.5	68.2
Foreign Exchange	100.0	(198.8)	218.6	(282.0)	379.4	190.4
Total Expenses	100.0	114.9	105.7	100.2	79.8	75.5
Operating Profit	100.0	(30.0)	(28.0)	4.0	34.5	59.1
Interest—net	100.0	80.8	114.8	132.5	132.3	84.5
Pretax Profit	100.0	(38.6)	(39.0)	(35.1)	27.0	57.2
Income Tax	100.0	(33.6)	(34.0)	(5.1)	27.0	57.4
Net Income (Loss)	100.0	(41.7)	(42.2)	(54.2)	26.9	57.0

Much of the parent's growth has come from acquisitions in Europe, many of which had U.S. operations. In 2005, the remaining three U.S. entities were combined. In the process, two product lines with low market shares, representing $13,300,000 (17%) of 2004 sales, were discontinued. In the next three years (2005 to 2007), there were substantial extra selling, general, and administrative (SG&A) expenses including costs of closing locations and terminating staff.

HiTech Co. PLC.—U.S. Operations
INCOME STATEMENT ADJUSTMENTS

	2004	2005	2006	2007	2008	2009 Budget
Pretax Profit	5,360	(2,067)	(2,090)	(1,880)	1,445	3,065
ADJUSTMENTS						
Cost of Sales						
Inventory Write-off		498				
SG&A						
Closing Locations		624	727	64		
Staff Termination		878	792	0		
		1,502	1,519	64		
Impairment	0	0	0	1,564	0	0
Adjusted Pretax Profit	5,360	(67)	(571)	(252)	1,445	3,065
Income Tax	(2,090)	26	223	98	(563)	(1,195)
Adjusted Earnings	3,270	(41)	(348)	(154)	881	1,870

HiTech Co. PLC.—U.S. Operations
ADJUSTMENTS RATIO ANALYSES

	2004	2005	2006	2007	2008	2009
Gross Profit	37.60%	35.50%	37.50%	35.60%	34.10%	37.40%
SG&A	23.10%	34.80%	38.60%	28.70%	27.50%	2580%
Adjusted Pretax Profit	8.80%	–0.10%	–1.30%	–0.50%	3.20%	7.00%
Income Tax	–3.40%	0.10%	0.50%	0.20%	–1.20%	–2.70%
Adjusted Earnings	5.40%	–0.10%	–0.80%	–0.30%	1.90%	4.30%

DISAGGREGATION

When undertaking a financial analysis, it is desirable to look not only at the overall business but also at the cash-generating units involved; in the United States, HiTech has four divisions. The comparative breakdowns are:

HiTech Co. PLC.—U.S. Operations
DIVISIONAL ANALYSES

$'000	2007	EAS	LIB	CSI	TVS
Sales	48,593	6,507	12,199	8,122	21,766
COS	(31,280)	(3,628)	(6,028)	(6,120)	(15,504)
Gross Proft	17,312	2,879	6,171	2,002	6,262
SG&A	13,882	1,978	5,804	803	5,297
R&D	2,289	189	1,221	408	471
Total Expense	16,171	2,167	7,025	1,211	5,768
Business Profit	1,141	712	(854)	790	493
Foreign Exchange	(911)	(112)	12	(443)	(368)
Operating Profit	231	600	(842)	348	125
Actual	**2008**	**EAS**	**LIB**	**CSI**	**TVS**
Sales	45,749	5,026	11,351	5,872	23,501
COS	(30,154)	(2,676)	(6,741)	(4,583)	(16,154)
Gross Proft	15,595	2,350	4,609	1,289	7,347
SG&A	12,583	1,367	4,675	1,053	5,489
R&D	2,248	141	1,494	260	353
Total Expense	14,831	1,508	6,169	1,313	5,842
Business Profit	764	842	(1,559)	(24)	1,505
Foreign Exchange	1,226	123	(89)	545	647
Operating Profit	1,990	964	(1,648)	521	2,152

Budget	2009	EAS	LIB	CSI	TVS
Sales	43,551	4,073	16,681	4,482	18,314
COS	(27,264)	(2,082)	(8,841)	(3,498)	(12,843)
Gross Proft	16,286	1,992	7,841	984	5,470
SG&A	11,218	1,160	5,546	938	3,573
R&D	2,271	143	1,509	263	357
Total Expense	13,488	1,302	7,055	1,201	3,930
Business Profit	2,798	689	786	(217)	1,540
Foreign Exchange	615	65	(45)	270	325
Operating Profit	3,413	754	741	53	1,865

The tables show that there are substantial differences from year to year; in 2009, a 72% increase in profits is budgeted, driven by a massive turnaround in Library. Based on this, a valuator would be justified to consider the projections to be more than normally risky.

VALUE DRIVER ANALYSES

Value driver analyses are based on ratios suitable as references; those can be growth rates of sales or costs from previous years (%), expense ratios, CAPEX and other investment requirements, inventory turnover ratio, debt to equity ratio, cash flow ratios, and so on. In general, two standard types of value drivers are used: turnover based and capital based.

OTHER ANALYSES

Looking at financial statements and cash flows is only part of the complex analyses needed for a valuation. Other so-called soft facts, set out next, are another necessary requirement.

Management and Organization

Part of any financial statement analyses is the integration of management into the organizational structure and its influence on overall performance. This interaction can be analyzed using the Porter five-factor-model (See Chapter 8.) The organizational structure has considerable influence on the effectiveness of the business's performance, whether it is centralized or decentralized, to what extent work flows are standardized, and on how well internal control and risk management systems are integrated operationally.

Personnel. Human resources are one of the most important soft facts that cannot be understood and judged from the financial statements. Efficient and motivated personnel is one of the key factors for a profitable business; productivity is normally measured by sales or value added (sales less all costs except payroll-related expenses) per employee. Important facts are salary structure, seniority, fluctuation rates, training costs, strikes, and the like.

Technologies. The basis for a valid analysis and documentation should be an inventory of existing technologies, know-how, and trade secrets. This inventory can be used for plausibility checks of R&D costs, intangible assets, and the past innovation ability of the entity.

CONCLUSION

In times of financial crisis and global economic challenges, financial statement analyses are among the most important components of the valuation process. There are many ways to perform such analyses in both theory and practice. For complete and informative results, financial statement analyses have to take into consideration other factors and influences, aside from solely financial information, which create economic value for the entity; these factors include management, human resources, and technologies. As yet, valuation theory does not put sufficient emphasis on this important subject; therefore, further studies and research are required.

12 PROJECTING FINANCIAL STATEMENTS

KLAUS HENSELMANN

GERMANY

INTRODUCTION

Value derives from future economic benefits, which will be reflected in an entity's financial statements as they occur. This chapter illustrates the task of projecting financial statements as a basis for various valuation methods.

Obviously, projected statements are needed for multiple future periods if a discounted cash flow (DCF) method is adopted. Estimated earnings can be converted into cash flows by replacing depreciation with capital expenditures and adjusting for working capital needs. Sometimes, for convenience, future earnings are discounted. In theory, earnings are not the benefit stream available to the owners, but in practice, they often serve as a good proxy as minor differences may be ignored. Finally, deducting the opportunity cost of capital from (adjusted) earnings gives residual earnings (economic value generated). The present value of residual earnings plus the capital currently invested in the firm should exactly equal the present value of the discounted cash flows.

An alternative to discounting is the capitalization of a benefit stream that is maintainable in the future, either earnings or the owners' discretionary cash flows. Those figures are based on averaging adjusted historic earnings (or cash flows) after reflecting foreseeable changes in the near future.

Even some methods under the market approach use projected financial statements. Often, the multiples applied to items such as net earnings, pretax earnings, earnings before interest and taxes (EBIT), and earnings before interest, taxes, depreciation, and amortization (EBITDA) are based on estimated numbers for the current year rather than historic data.

Specific problems to be solved in preparing projected financial statements for several years are:

- Collecting necessary information about the entity and its environment
- Analyzing and adjusting historic accounting data
- Constructing a financial model of the entity
- Determining historic value drivers
- Assessing the market and the entity's existing competitive position
- Estimating probable future changes
- Reviewing existing budgets or other management forecasts
- Making reasonable and consistent assumptions about future value drivers based on historic data
- Programming the financial model to project financial statements for the planning period
- Dealing with uncertainty in the value driver projections

This chapter focuses primarily on projections for DCF valuation methods; the examples demonstrate the major steps in financial modeling.

INFORMATION REQUIREMENTS AND DATA COLLECTION

When projecting financial statements, it is essential to look not only at the financial data but also at all factors that had a bearing on past results and are likely to affect the future. All financial statements deliver data that are directly relevant to the value of an entity. However, additional information about the entity and its environment is crucial; for a successful valuation, it is important to understand the business itself as well as changes in past profit margins, growth rates, and asset turnover.

The general information about the entity and its position within the economy should at least cover:

- *Business environment.* Economic, social, legal and political framework, industry structure and development, critical success factors, opportunities and threats
- *Business policy.* Corporate strategy (relationships between business units), business unit strategies, value-added chain, functional strategies, strengths and weaknesses, organization, business partners
- *Important activities and events.* Past and planned expenditures on updating capital assets, increasing capacity, research and development, geographic expansion, reorganization, plant closings; also, if applicable: the reasons for mergers and acquisitions, debt financings, initial public offerings, further equity issues, other unusual transactions, changes in personnel (executive management, other key personnel such as researchers, board members)

Data Sources

The next internal data provide a basis for the projected financial statements:

- *Organizational structure.* Memoranda, legal documents, shareholders' agreements, organizational chart, management team, key personnel list (local plant managers, key account managers, researchers), and related parties
- *Financial reports.* Unit and consolidated financial statements (both interim and annual), purchase price allocations, accounting policies, management reports, discussions and external presentations, segment reporting, ad hoc announcements, auditor's comments
- *Financial documents.* Listings of assets and liabilities, cost accounting and internal management reports, financing plans, budgets and projections, comparisons of budgets against actual costs, earnings tax filings and assessments, past appraisals
- *Strategic documents.* Business plans, minutes of meetings, description of strategic business units and corporate portfolio strategies; major functional strategies such as marketing (customers, products, prices, distribution channels, promotional material), production and logistics, research and development, personnel and training
- *Operational documents.* Business developments during the past year and those expected in current and future years, lists of all past and planned major activities, capital utilization and needs, operational efficiency, potential risks, performance measurement system, significant contracts (e.g., supply, purchase, rental, leasing, license, franchise, procurement, insurances), important recorded and unrecorded intangibles (e.g., patents, copyrights, trademarks)
- *Public firm information.* Web sites, press releases, brochures, catalogs

Essential external data include:

- *Economic conditions.* General situation, inflation outlook, exchange rate expectations, commodity price forecasts, anticipated interest rates, credit availability, labor market and employment changes, buyer confidence, pending tax regulations, legal developments, political trends
- *Industry analyses.* Market characteristics and size, growth or decline trends, product life cycles, market penetration, risks, current and potential competitors, barriers to entry, under- or overcapacities, economies of scale, technological innovations, possible substitutes, current and potential suppliers
- *Opinions about the entity.* Newspaper write-ups, clippings, analyst reports
- *Databases.* Available in many countries in a variety of forms, not only as printed information, such as trade publications, but also downloadable on Web sites (statistics, economic outlooks); valuators must review the material carefully, as some information may be overstated and not reliable

ADJUSTING HISTORIC DATA

To predict the future reasonably, first it is necessary to understand the past by looking at the historic financial statements and the factors that had a bearing on them. The objective is to arrive at pro forma statements that are comparable from period to period, from business to business, and that reveal the true economic position of the entity to be valued.

Adjustments can be conveniently made in a template, showing in:

>Column A: The historic information supplied (e.g., income statement)
>Column B and C: The amount of each debit or credit adjustment
>Column D: The reason for making every single adjustment
>Column E: The final adjusted balance

This chapter focuses on adjustments made to historic statements; the most frequently required normalization adjustments are discussed next.

Nonrecurring Transactions and Events

Often an entity's accounts are affected by events that are not likely to recur. Such extraordinary items should be isolated to make the analyses of past trends or industry comparisons easier. Those nonrecurring items include both random events beyond the entity's control (such as losses by fire or flood) and also transactions intentionally undertaken by management to "smooth" earnings (e.g., sales of assets). Adjusted financial statements are more reliable than those reported by accountants as a base on which to build expectations about the future.

Examples of special requirements to adjust are:

- Significant earnings and losses from asset disposals
- Exceptional depreciation of capital assets
- Significant inventory reserves
- Major allowances for bad debts
- Expenditures for litigation, uninsured claims, strikes
- Mass layoffs, extensive programs for early retirement, and other labor force restructurings
- Firm anniversary celebrations
- Costs of major product recalls (relative to their size)
- A splurge of spending on developing new markets
- Out-of-the-norm consultancy costs
- Strong fluctuations in advertising, maintenance, or training expenses

Accounting Policies and Available Statements

Accounting differences hamper the analyses of historic financial statements. There are two reasons for adjustments or amendments. First, over the years, the entity may have changed its accounting policies or may have even changed from one accounting system to another. Under International Financial Reporting Standards (IFRS), such changes are applied retrospectively and are recorded directly in equity through retained earnings (International Accounting Standards [IAS] 8:22, IFRS 1:11). However, the older historic statements remain as published; adjustments should be made to eliminate this artificial distortion. Retrospective application of changes in accounting policies need not be made if doing so is impractical (IAS 8:23) or if it is unnecessary for a country's local accounting system or tax calculations. In those cases, changes in accounting policies lead to additional book earnings or losses.

Second, an entity's accounting policies may differ from those commonly accepted in an industry, which makes comparative analyses difficult. Adjustments should facilitate a comparison between the entity and other firms in the same line of business. Differences may affect inventories, construction contracts, borrowing costs, depreciation, asset revaluations, technical development, employee benefits, and joint ventures. In some countries or businesses, financial accounting may also be distorted by tax requirements.

However, the effect of accounting policies or systems on discounted cash flow valuations is usually overstated. Certainly accounting differences lead to divergent historic financial statements and also to differing projected income statements and balance sheets. Economic theory and integrated financial models show that these differences offset each other and that cash flows remain unaffected. Accounting is merely getting a picture of reality; it does not change reality itself—at least not in a straightforward way. There are only indirect influences, such as effects on the timing of tax payments, the credit rating of the entity, and its terms of payment.

The target business may be a cash-generating unit that forms only part of an existing legal entity; therefore, no formal, individual financial statements may exist; pro forma financials must be derived from bookkeeping entries and other internal reporting records.

Compensation for Owners and Related Parties

In private companies, owners may receive remuneration higher or lower than the market compensation for executives in comparable positions. Such terms distort the true benefit stream of the business and must be adjusted. The "arm's-length" principle also applies to other contractual relationships for items such as loans, rents, leases, and use of cars; all should be checked for reasonableness. Compensation paid to family members should be scrutinized.

These adjustments assume that the future owners have the power to make any necessary changes, but that is usually not true for a minority shareholder. Management compensation (for the majority shareholder) above market levels cannot be changed; therefore, unfavorable factors should be left in place. For groups of entities, transfer prices may differ from market levels. If only part of the group is being valued, it must be done on a stand-alone basis with all non–arm's-length transactions being reviewed.

Comparability of Businesses

Often businesses contain nonoperating assets. If those assets, associated liabilities, revenues, and expenses are combined with the normal operations, comparisons and projections become confused. It is therefore advisable to identify these items in the financial statements and show them separately; they should then be valued on their own.

Comparability is also adversely affected if an entity has grown mainly because of acquisitions (external growth). Some historic trends can be analyzed more precisely if consolidated pro forma statements are compiled that include the acquired subsidiary in years preceding the acquisition date. The same principle applies to other forms of reorganizations, such as dispositions.

An entity's risks affect the discount rate and thereby its value. However, capital markets assume that all firms purchase insurance against risks that are usual in its line of business. If a firm self-insures, extra earnings will be earned in the (many) damage-free years and a large loss will accrue in the rare case when a significant setback occurs. When valuing an entity that self-insures, the risk profiles should be made more comparable by subtracting, each year, a notional insurance expense.

HISTORIC VALUE DRIVERS AND FINANCIAL MODELING

Projecting financial statements is illustrated by GoodCo AG with the simplified adjusted historic financial statements shown in Exhibits 12.1 to 12.3.

Exhibit 12.1 Adjusted Historic Income Statements

Income Statements $'000	2006	2007	2008	2009
Sales	2,141	2,235	2,321	2,396
Cost of Sales	(1,181)	(1,242)	(1,304)	(1,365)
Gross Earning	960	993	1,017	1,031
Sales/Distribution Expense	(220)	(232)	(243)	(245)
Administration Expense	(348)	(362)	(370)	(385)
Depreciation Expense	(122)	(119)	(126)	(118)
Other Income (Expense)	38	39	42	44
Earnings Before Interest and Taxes (EBIT)	308	319	320	327
Interest Expense—Net	(44)	(42)	(40)	(33)
Extraordinary Gains/Losses (–)	0	(75)	0	0
Earnings Before Taxes (EBT)	264	202	280	294
Income Tax Expense	(84)	(59)	(84)	(85)
Net Earnings	180	143	195	209

Exhibit 12.2 Adjusted Historic Balance Sheets/Assets

Balance Sheets / Assets $'000	2005	2006	2007	2008	2009
Capital					
Book Value 1 January		1,065	1,050	983	942
+ Capital Expenditure		107	52	85	71
– Depreciation		(122)	(119)	(126)	(118)
= Book Value 31 December	1,065	1,050	983	942	895
Current					
Inventories	168	179	192	210	213
Receivables	73	76	79	84	87
Total Assets	1,306	1,305	1,253	1,236	1,195

Exhibit 12.3 Adjusted Historic Balance Sheets/Funds Employed

Balance Sheets / Funds Employed $'000	2005	2006	2007	2008	2009
Equity					
Ordinary Shares	100	100	100	120	120
Share Premium	50	50	50	100	100
Change in Share Capital		0	0	70	0
Retained Earnings					
Book Value 1 January		403	420	396	402
– Dividends (Paid During the Year)		(163)	(167)	(190)	(243)
Interim Balance		240	253	207	159
+ Earning (After Taxes)		180	143	195	209
= Book Value 31 December	403	420	396	402	368

Balance Sheets / Funds Employed $'000	2005	2006	2007	2008	2009
Liabilities					
Borrowings	703	680	645	550	536
Payables	50	55	62	64	71
Total Funds Employed	**1,306**	**1,305**	**1,253**	**1,236**	**1,195**

Before a financial model of the entity can be constructed, the historic value drivers must be calculated.

Key Value Drivers

Analyzing the past and projecting the future should involve relative value drivers rather than absolute figures. Generally speaking, value drivers are specific business ratios forming part of a tree structure with the cash flows on the left (Exhibit 12.4); those calculations have to be made every year.

Exhibit 12.4 Value Drivers Explaining Cash Flow

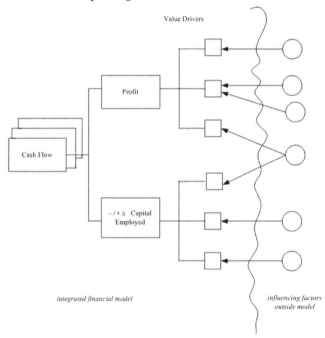

There are many ways of setting up such a system, but it should cover:

- *Growth.* Measured by turnover or assets employed
- *Profitability.* Percentage analyses of all costs in the income statement
- *Funds employed.* Different capital assets and working capital components, usually in relation to total assets
- *Capital structure.* Amount of debt or proportion of debt in relation to equity, different layers of debt, interest rates, excess cash

For example, one value driver might be the sales growth rate; this is data from the historic statements but must be estimated for the future. Factors influencing those rates include the number of potential purchasers, customer bargaining, level of competition, and barriers to entry. They all have to be analyzed for making forecasts but are outside the structure of the financial model.

For GoodCo AG, the value driver structure shown in Table 12.4 has been selected. The historic figures are already calculated; later they will be projected into the future.

Exhibit 12.5 Historic Value Drivers Explaining Cash Flows

Value Drivers	2006	2007	2008	2009
Revenues		*Year to 31 January*		
Sales—Annual Growth %	5.5%	4.4%	3.8%	3.2%
Other Income—Annual Growth %	8.6%	2.6%	7.7%	4.8%
Extraordinary Gains (Losses) $'000	0	(75)	0	0
Operating Expenses				
Cost of Sales (COS)—% of Sales	55.1%	55.6%	56.2%	57.0%
Sales/Distribution—% of Sales	10.3%	10.4%	10.5%	10.2%
Administration—% of Sales	16.3%	16.2%	15.9%	16.1%
Depreciation $'000	(122)	(119)	(126)	(118)
Income Taxation				
Effective Tax Rate—% of EBT	31.8%	29.2%	30.2%	28.8%
Funds Employed in Capital Assets				
Capital Expenditure $'000	107	52	85	71
Working Capital				
Inventories—% of Sales	8.4%	8.6%	9.1%	8.9%
Receivables—% of Sales	3.6%	3.5%	3.6%	3.6%
Payables—% of COS	4.7%	5.0%	4.9%	5.2%
Debt				
Borrowings—net	680	645	550	536
Interest Expense—% of Borrowings 1 January	6.2%	6.2%	6.3%	6.1%

The main sources of earnings are the entity's operating activities; therefore, the annual sales growth rate is the key value driver. Operating expenses that relate to sales are COS, sales/distribution, and administration. Depreciation is shown separately as an absolute number, as it depends more on past capital expenditures than sales; capacity utilization may change over time. These costs explain most of the pretax margin; additionally, there are minor gains/losses and other earnings. Extraordinary gain/loss is an absolute value driver because it has no relationship to sales and cannot be expected to follow a regular trend; for other earnings, a growth rate is used. Income tax is a special type of cost looked at as an effective rate of earnings before taxes (EBT).

The funds employed in GoodCo AG consist of capital assets (e.g., property, plant, and equipment) and working capital (e.g., inventories, receivables, payables). Inventories and receivables depend on sales; payables vary with purchases of materials but as a substitute are linked to COS. Capital expenditures are not easily explained; generally production capacity is linked to sales, but expenditures in capital assets normally are made in large amounts followed by annual maintenance costs to improve facilities. Information about gross carrying amounts and accumulated depreciation can help but is not always available; therefore, expenditure figures are assumed to be given. This plan depends on capacity usage, age of assets, and technological changes.

The example uses a very straightforward capital structure—equity plus borrowings with a single interest rate—which are not shown in detail. Although in reality the level of debt fluctuates during a year, for simplicity this is ignored in the example, and interest is determined only on the capital expenditures at the beginning of the year, which equals the closing balance at the end of the last year.

An assumption has to be made regarding the debt equity ratio given the total funds employed; a decision must be made as to how much should be borrowed and how much raised as equity. Management commonly plans for a fixed proportion of debt. If prepared based on economic rather than book values, this generally is the weighted average cost of capital (WACC); choosing an absolute debt level is simpler and more convenient when using an adjusted present value (APV) method. Finally, there is no excess cash.

VALUE DRIVERS AND PROJECTED FINANCIAL STATEMENTS

Financial statements show the results of business activities but do not reveal the causes of growth, earnings, and capital demands. Analyses of the past, present, and future outlook are an important step in projecting financial statements. To understand the business, it is therefore necessary to look at its strategy and at its strengths, weaknesses, opportunities, and threats (SWOT). Each entity operates under given external conditions. For analytical purposes, it is useful to distinguish between general economic factors (macroenvironment) and the conditions specific to the industry (microenvironment).

A macroenvironmental structure is provided by the so-called political, economic, social, and technical (PEST) analyses; its factors include:

Political
- Taxation
- Trade restrictions
- Labor situation
- Consumer law
- Antitrust regulations
- Employment level
- Environmental requirements

Economic
- Unemployment situation
- Inflation outlook
- Economic growth
- Interest rates
- Exchange rates

Social
- Population growth
- Age distribution
- Immigration and emigration
- Education
- Social conflicts
- Healthcare attitudes
- Environmental attitudes
- Lifestyles

Technical
- Technological changes
- Research and development activities

There are also several frameworks for industry analyses. One of the best known is the five forces analytical model, according to which these competitive factors determine industry profitability:

- Threat of substitute products
- Threat of established or start-up rivals
- Threat of new entrants
- Bargaining power of suppliers
- Bargaining power of customers

Many enterprises have strategic business units (entities) in multiple industries. Hence, analyses have to be conducted for each of them. To assess overall corporate strategy, all

business units should be linked and compared in a portfolio analysis. The macroenvironmental PEST factors combined with microenvironmental industry factors indicate the opportunities and threats the subject entity is facing.

However, favorable external conditions do not imply that every entity in an industry will
have the same growth rate or profitability; success also depends on the firm's internal
strengths and weaknesses. Those can be related to resources (assets, abilities, and competence), which can be compared to the resources of current and potential competitors.

There are numerous checklists for strengths and weaknesses, such as:

- **Physical resources.** Administrative and production buildings, machinery and equipment, inventories, warehouses, sales outlets, cash, research and development facilities
- **Human resources.** Operating staff, sales personnel, planners, scientists, technologists,
  designers, managers
- **Systems.** Communication, logistics, quality control, customer database, service,
  distribution channels, accounting, cash management, planning and control, compensation schedules, project assessment
- **Intangibles.** Team spirit, education and training, patents, copyrights, trademarks, contacts to business partners, image, organizational culture, licenses, know-how, innovations, qualifications, certifications, location

Comparative Analysis

Historic trend analyses of financial statements from different years display significant
tendencies and variations, such as declining growth rates, changing margins, or increasing
capital needs. All observable trends should be linked to the insights obtained in a SWOT
analysis. For example, it may be ascertained that declining growth rates are caused by increasing market saturation combined with the difficulty of finding new outlets. It is important to take into account longer market cycles, as otherwise the extrapolation of previous
years' value drivers leads to wrong projections. Useful statistical methods might be direct
and weighted arithmetic averages, geometric averages, and regression analyses with linear
and exponential trends.

Comparative analyses judge the entity against other businesses in the same industry; this
may be with the whole industry (averages) or selected competitors and help to establish
whether the entity is in line with the industry or if there are discrepancies. Discrepancies
could be permanent (market access barriers permit higher profitability) or slowly dissolve
over time (new competition). Each has to be scrutinized in light of the previous SWOT analysis. Historic trends and industry analyses are best combined. Often a graphical presentation
of key value drivers is useful. Exhibit 12.6 shows the value driver "Sales—Annual Growth in
%." A linear trend line is calculated using the firm's data from 2006 to 2009. For the following year (2010), an industrial association has presented an official forecast (+2.50%).
From those, the activity from 2010 to 2013 is estimated in both the table and graph.

Exhibit 12.6 Historic Value Drivers Explaining Cash Flows

Sales	2006	2007	2008	2009	2010	2011	2012	2013
Sales—Annual Growth	5.47%	4.39%	3.85%	3.23%	2.75%	2.50%	2.25%	2.25%
Trend line	5.32%	4.60%	3.87%	3.15%	2.42%	1.70%	0.97%	
Industry: historic/ external projection	4.43%	3.69%	3.34%	2.89%	2.50%			

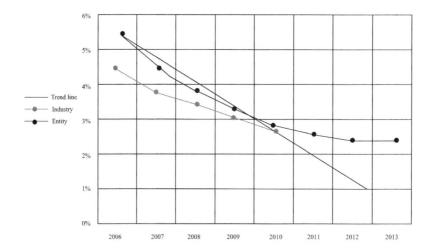

Reviewing Budgets

Usually an entity will have some forecasts or even complete budgets for the next couple of years, but often the presentation and amount of detail must be adapted to the template used for valuation. However, management projections should be treated with caution, as they require frequent adjustments. First they should be checked for adjustments that also apply to historic data: unusual transactions, accounting policies, owners' remuneration, and related-party transactions.

Also, they may be not commercially realistic as most managers anticipate steady future improvements; if the actual situation is bad, a turnaround is expected soon. Growth rates always improve, as do profit margins. Alas, economic theory and empirical evidence show that in most cases, convergence takes place. Over the years, an entity's growth will align to the industry average; above-normal returns decline to the cost of capital. If the entity expects to improve or remain superior to industry averages, there must be strong justification.

Reviewing budgets is done in four steps:

1. Check for realistic assumptions compared with adjusted historic data.
2. Compare plans with industry averages, similar firms (peer group), or the best competitors (benchmarking).
3. Determine whether the assumptions are consistent with SWOT analysis (e.g., forthcoming threats, existing weaknesses).
4. Verify internal consistency of management's assumptions (e.g., increasing sales without expanding capacity, hiring additional specialized staff without confirming their availability, increase in funds employed without confirmation of their availability).

Analyses of the planning system may also be helpful:

- How common were planning errors in the past? How far were they off? Did they always point in the same direction?
- Is the planning process more top down (budgets are often ambitious targets that can barely be achieved) or more bottom up (more often realistic forecasts of what will happen)?

Assumed Future Value Drivers

In the end, the valuator has to make assumptions about future value drivers. Statistical extrapolation of the historic factors is not recommended because external influences (environment) as well as internal circumstances (strategy) will change. New opportunities can lead to growth but may need realignment of existing operations. Altered business strategy and significant changes in functional tactics will affect projected value drivers and financial statements. For example, obsolete equipment may require high capital expenditure and reorganizations may require money for consulting. The linkage of qualitative strategic planning with monetary financial modeling represents the critical core of projecting financial statements (Exhibit 12.7).

Exhibit 12.7 Linking Qualitative and Quantitative Analyses

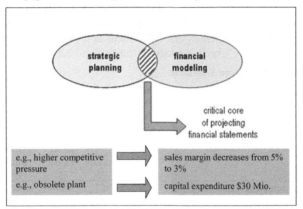

The example in Exhibit 12.7 assumes that, after careful consideration, the value drivers will result in the amounts in the years 2010 to 2013 shown in Exhibit 12.8.

Exhibit 12.8 Assumed Future Value Drivers

Value Drivers	2009	2010	2011	2012	2013
Revenues	**Actual**		**Forecast**		
Sales—Annual Growth %	3.23%	2.75%	2.50%	2.25%	2.25%
Other Income—Annual Growth %	4.76%	4.00%	4.00%	4.00%	4.00%
Extraordinary Gains (Losses) $'000	0	(200)	0	0	0
Operating Expenses					
COS—% of Sales	56.97%	57.00%	57.00%	57.00%	57.00%
Sales/Distribution Expense—% of Sales	10.23%	10.30%	10.30%	10.30%	10.30%
Administration Expense—% of Sales	16.07%	16.00%	16.00%	16.00%	16.00%
Depreciation $'000	(118)	(130)	(150)	(140)	(130)
Income Taxation					
Effective Tax Rate—in % of EBT	28.82%	30.00%	30.00%	30.00%	30.00%
Funds Employed in Capital Assets					
Capital Expenditure	71	200	300	120	120
Working Capital					
Inventories—% of Sales	8.88%	9.00%	9.00%	9.00%	9.00%
Receivables—% of Sales	3.64%	3.60%	3.60%	3.60%	3.60%
Payables—% of COGS	5.20%	5.00%	5.00%	5.00%	5.00%
Debt					
Borrowings—Net	536	650	800	690	670
Interest Expense—Borrowings 1 January	6.07%	6.20%	6.20%	6.20%	6.20%

Based on this table of actual and forecast figures, calculation of the projected income statements, balance sheets, and cash flow statements is almost a mechanical task.

Projecting the Income Statements and Balance Sheets

First, sales are projected; its value driver gives effect to the figures for each year reflecting lower growth. The COS, sales/distribution, and administrative expenses are then calculated using their value driver percentages based on those levels of sales. Depreciation is given as an absolute number as it depends on the capital assets already in place and planned capital expenditures. Those investments are scheduled according to current capacity utilization, asset age (shutdowns), and sales volume.

Other earnings increases according to the assumed growth rate; extraordinary gains or losses usually cannot be predicted; however, the example assumes that during 2010 there will be foreseeable restructuring charges. Interest expense each year is a percentage of borrowings at its start, which is the same as the closing balance at the end of the previous period. From these data, earnings before taxes are calculated; applying the effective tax rate gives the net earnings (Exhibit 12.9), which is added to the retained earnings.

Exhibit 12.10 Projected Income Statement

Income Statements $'000	2009	2010	2011	2012	2013
Sales	2,396	2,462	2,523	2,580	2,638
Cost of Sales	(1,365)	(1,403)	(1,438)	(1,471)	(1,504)
Gross Earnings	1,031	1,059	1,085	1,109	1,134
Sales/Distribution Expense	(245)	(254)	(260)	(266)	(272)
Administration Expense	(385)	(394)	(404)	(413)	(422)
Depreciation Expense	(118)	(130)	(150)	(140)	(130)
Other Income/Expense	44	46	48	49	51
Earnings Before Interest and Taxes (EBIT)	327	327	319	340	362
Interest Expense	(33)	(33)	(40)	(50)	(43)
Extraordinary Gains/Losses	0	(200)	0	0	0
Earnings Before Taxes (EBT)	294	94	279	291	319
Income Tax Expense	(85)	(28)	(84)	(87)	(96)
Net Earnings	209	66	195	204	223

On the balance sheet, the book value of capital assets in 2010 equals their value in 2009, plus capital expenditures, minus depreciation. The levels of inventories and receivables depend on sales. Combining them allows us to calculate the total assets on the balance sheet. The equity and liabilities must equal this number (see Exhibit 12.10).

Exhibit 12.10 Projected Balance Sheets/Assets

Balance Sheets / Assets $'000	2009	2010	2011	2012	2013
Capital					
Book Value 1 January	942	895	965	1,115	1,095
+ Capital Expenditure	71	200	300	120	120
− Depreciation Expense	(118)	(130)	(150)	(140)	(130)
= Book Value 31 December	895	965	1,115	1,095	1,085
Current					
Inventories	213	222	227	232	237
Receivables	87	89	91	93	95
Total Assets	1,195	1,275	1,433	1,420	1,417

Amounts for ordinary shares and share premiums remain constant. Payables are a percentage of COS. The absolute debt level is given as a value driver; planned borrowings depend on existing debt, contractual repayments, and new capital needs.

At this stage, only the year-end retained earnings is missing. It is the total funds employed, less the sum of ordinary shares, share premium, borrowings, and payables. Adding earnings gives an interim balance (see Exhibit 12.11). The difference between this and the opening retained earnings equals the dividends that must have been paid to shareholders during the year.

Exhibit 12.11 Projected Balance Sheets/Funds Employed

Balance Sheets / Funds Employed $'000	2009	2010	2011	2012	2013
Equity					
Ordinary Shares	120	120	120	120	120
Share Premium	100	100	100	100	100
Change in Share Capital	*0*	*0*	*0*	*0*	*0*
Retained Earnings					
Book Value 1 January	402	368	335	341	437
– Dividends (Paid During the Year)	(243)	(99)	(189)	(108)	(208)
Interim Balance	159	269	146	233	229
+ Net Earnings	209	66	195	204	223
= Book Value 31 December	368	335	341	437	452
Liabilities					
Borrowings	536	650	800	690	670
Payables	71	70	72	74	75
Total Funds Employed	1,195	1,275	1,433	1,420	1,417

Projected Cash Flow Statements

The format of a cash flow statement for valuation purposes differs from that used for financial reporting. In the middle of the statement, a line shows the free cash flows to the entity. Separate lines indicate the cash flows to debt holders and owners individually (see Exhibit 12.12).

Exhibit 12.12 Projected Cash Flow Statements

Cash Flow Statements $'000	2009	2010	2011	2012	2013
Self-Financing					
EBIT	327	327	319	340	362
+ Depreciation Expense	118	130	150	140	130
= Operating Cash Flow before Working Capital		457	469	480	492
Increase in Net Working Capital					
+/- De-/Increase Inventories	(3)	(9)	(6)	(5)	(5)
+/- De-/Increase Receivables	(3)	(1)	(2)	(2)	(2)
-/+ De-/Increase Payables	7	(1)	2	2	2
= Operating Cash Flow after Working Capital	446	446	463	475	486
Investment in Property, Plant, and Equipment					
– Capital Expenditure	(71)	(200)	(300)	(120)	(120)
= Regular Free Cash Flow before Taxes	375	246	163	355	366
Taxation					
– Income Tax paid in cash	(85)	(28)	(84)	(87)	(96)
= Regular Free Cash Flow after Taxes	290	218	79	268	271
Extraordinary Items					
+/- Extraordinary Gains/Losses	0	(200)	0	0	0
= **Free Cash Flow**	290	18	79	268	271
Changes in Debt and Interest					
Borrowings 1 January	550	536	650	800	690
Borrowings 31 December	536	650	800	690	670
+/- In-/Decrease of Borrowings	(14)	114	150	(110)	(20)
– Interest Expense	(33)	(33)	(40)	(50)	(43)
= **Cash Flow to Debt Holders (–)**	(47)	81	110	(160)	(63)
Changes in Share Capital and Dividends					
+/- De-/Increase in Share Capital	0	0	0	0	0
– Dividends	(243)	(99)	(189)	(108)	(208)
= **Cash Flow to Owners (–)**	(243)	(99)	(189)	(108)	(208)

Those cash flows are calculated indirectly starting with earnings before interest and taxes; depreciation is a noncash expense, so it is added back to get the operating cash flow before changes in working capital. Sales are not identical to the cash inflows they generate, which are less than the increase in receivables. Likewise, cash outflows depend on COS, but higher inventories demand additional cash while larger payables set cash free; the result is the operating cash flow after changes in net working capital. This figure is reduced by capital investment and earnings taxes currently paid in cash. After extraordinary items, the result is the free cash flows of the entity, which is needed for certain valuation methods. The cash flow to debt holders consists of interest and repayments of borrowings; debt increases are deducted. The remaining balance is the cash flow to owners, used for the equity valuation method. In the absence of changes in share capital, it is the same as the dividends paid.

Refined Financial Models

The described model is intended to demonstrate the basic concepts. However, often, it is desirable to employ a more sophisticated model. Its feasibility depends on the information available as well as the time and budget for the valuation. It is possible and desirable with certain items, including both fixed (inflation-related) and variable (volume-determined) costs, to include more balance sheet and income statement items and their value drivers. Categories such as cost of sales could be subdivided into materials, labor, and so on; this increases the scale of the model but also its complexity.

A further step is to introduce more realistic cause-and-effect relationships. Payables vary with purchases rather than total cost of sales; interest expenses depend on changing debt levels during the year, as well as its numerous sources, all with different interest rates.

Many relationships are not proportional. Some energy costs vary with production; others, such as heating of administrative buildings, are independent of it. For value drivers, it does not matter that costs are variable in the short run; it suffices that they can be built up or cut back within a year. However, some expenditures, such as rent, are effectively fixed.

Another major enhancement of the model is separating volumes and prices. An entity increases selling prices 5% in a year. If COS is calculated as a percentage of sales, projected costs will increase as well. This is not realistic; basing costs on revenues rather than on sales volume assumes that prices are constant. The same process can be applied to expenditures: labor, materials, and the like. This may result in virtually fixed labor costs, number of people, and salaries. Tax planning can be enhanced; instead of multiplying the EBT by an effective tax rate, it is possible to project the tax base separately and to determine the amounts to be paid immediately and those to be deferred. Often the entity has multiple business units that operate in different industries with unique environments (opportunities, threats) and specific resource positions (strengths, weaknesses). In this situation, separate partial financial models should be used with their respective value drivers geared toward the assets, liabilities, revenues, and expenses of each business unit. The partial projections should then be combined to present a forecast for the whole enterprise. The valuator must decide what degree of model complexity is necessary or useful.

UNCERTAINTY IN DATA

The described model and its enhancements attempt to increase the accuracy with which a financial forecast can be made. However, it is impossible to avoid all inaccuracies. The likelihood of projections becoming fact diminishes the further they run into the future. Methods for dealing with such uncertainties are sensitivity analyses, scenarios, or Monte Carlo simulations.

Sensitivity Analysis

Rather than predicting one precise number, sometimes it is useful to know the range of possible values. Sensitivity analysis is used to determine how a DCF valuation model reacts to changes in the value drivers. For example, how do changes in costs of materials affect the projected financial statements and thus the net present value of the future cash flows? In a sensitivity analysis, usually only one variable at a time is varied, with all the others being kept at their initial (quasi-secure) amounts.

This process helps to build confidence in the model by quantifying the uncertainties associated with its parameters. Also, it allows the valuator to determine the level of accuracy necessary to make the model sufficiently useful and valid. Sensitivity analysis can also indicate which parameter values are reasonable to use in the model. In any case, it is essential to ensure that the underlying economic assumptions are realistic. A disadvantage is that sensitivity analysis is valid only if the isolated change of one parameter does not imply further variations of others (e.g., a change in prices might in reality lead to altered volumes).

Scenarios

Scenario planning is a means of representing different future situations (scenarios) in a systematic way but without requiring probabilities. A particular scenario comprises assumptions about future external conditions and internal firm policies. If, for instance, the volumes decrease, cost cuts and disinvestments occur. Such assumptions, taken together, will affect the value drivers in the financial model. Scenarios are alternative pictures of the future. Only a limited number, usually three or four, are considered. The valuator concentrates on extreme scenarios (e.g., positive extreme, negative extreme, and trend) or especially relevant situations.

MONTE CARLO SIMULATIONS

In most projections, the outcome depends to a large extent on the choices of inputs. Minor changes in one of these, say gross margins, can have significant effects at the net earnings level. One well-established way of dealing with this problem is a Monte Carlo simulation, one of the most powerful tools available to analyze business decisions. Add-on computer programs (@Risk™ or Crystal Ball™) allow the valuator to apply the technique in Excel. The process is started by assigning a range and probability distribution to each value driver. Once the simulation picks a figure for each input based on its probability, the model determines the outcome. This is repeated 1,000 or more times to arrive at many different outcomes; their average (mean) is the most likely result.

Traditional financial forecasts have limitations associated with the imprecise treatment of risks due to being based on single-point estimates of the value drivers. Monte Carlo simulations, however, work well in situations containing numerous what-if scenarios and unknowns related to the future of a business. They are especially useful to reflect the impact of multiple scenarios and unknowns, which are difficult to embody properly in a standard spreadsheet or decision tree analysis.

The histogram shown in Exhibit 12.13 provides comprehensive information. For example, it estimates the probability that an entity has a DCF value greater than any particular amount.

Exhibit 12.13 Monte Carlo Simulation

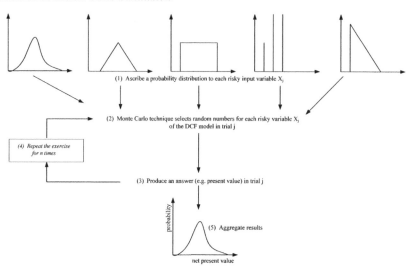

Simulation Process

Follow these seven steps to perform a Monte Carlo Simulation for the sales of one product of an entity whose inputs have a range of possible values:

1. Specify a range of possible amounts for inputs (e.g., selling price, units sold, market share) of the largest sales category.
2. Establish the most probable behavior of each (e.g., selling prices are equally likely within the range; units sold are more usually clustered at the lower end, etc.)
3. Define the outputs from each of the thousands of iterations to be performed.
4. Run the model which randomly selects a figure for each input using the likely range and assigned distribution and calculates numerous scenarios with various combinations.
5. Review the results, which are the distribution of the individual calculated outputs represented as a histogram, with the mean the most likely outcome.
6. Repeat the process for each other major sales category.
7. Undertake the same procedures for each of the principal operating expenses.

The power of Monte Carlo simulations to consider and account for potential variables of the inputs in a projection makes them very useful tools for valuators.

Example

This example is modified from Kennedy.[1] Consider a product revenue forecast with these assumptions:

Selling price $5.00 per unit but could vary from $4.00 to $5.50 per unit
Total units sold 1,000,000, but could be as low as zero; the most probable figure is 1,000,000 plus or minus 20%.

---

[1] William Kennedy, *"Rising to the Top of Your Game in Valuation and Financial Forensics,"* *Fifteenth Annual Consultants' Conference, NACVA 2008.*

A spreadsheet gives the most likely answer:

Sales = Unit price × Unit sales = $5.00 × 1,000,000 = $5,000,000

Range of forecast possibilities:

Best case	$5.50 × 1,100,000	=	$6,050,000
Minimum case	$4.00 × 900,000	=	$3,600,000
Worst case	$5.00 × 0	=	$0

The Monte Carlo simulation recalculates the spreadsheet at least 1,000 times, changing, at random, the selling price and number of units sold within their estimated ranges. It then accumulates all conclusions and calculates the mean ($4,986,000) as the most likely answer. This amount is only 0.3% below the spreadsheet's answer ($5,000,000) but it is much more supportable as the spreadsheet figure suffers from the embedded risks that actual sales could vary from $3,600,000 to $6,050,000, and possibly less.

The assumptions for each variable were:

• Price per unit followed a triangular distribution with a minimum of $4.00, a maximum of $5.50, and centering at $5.00. This was selected as there were minimum, maximum, and most likely values, and no information regarding any other distribution (i.e., normal, uniform, etc.) was available.

• Number of units sold followed a lognormal distribution with a mean of 1,000 and a standard deviation of 20%, which allows for the possibility that no units would be sold, is positively skewed (meaning more selections are made from the lower half and thus conservative), and the amount cannot be negative.

The statistics for our example are:

Statistic	Forecast Value	Statistic	Forecast Value
Trials	1,000	Skewness	0.5623
Mean	$4,986	Kurtosis	3.40
Median	$4,875	Coefficient of Variability	0.1982
Standard Deviation	$988	Minimum	$2,578
Variance	$976,591	Maximum	$8,674

Exhibit 12.14 Histogram of Simulation Results

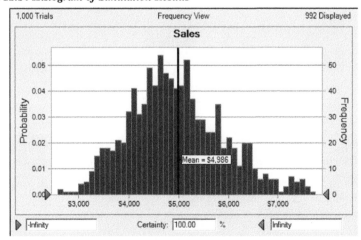

Source: William Kennedy, "Rising to the Top of Your Game in Valuation and Financial Forensics," Fifteenth Annual Consultants' Conference, NACVA 2008.

13 IMPAIRMENT TESTING[1]

FRANK BOLLMANN AND ANDREAS JOEST

GERMANY

INTRODUCTION

Impairment testing was introduced to ensure that the carrying amount of an asset recognized on the balance sheets does not exceed its recoverable amount. Therefore, basically all assets are subject to a test for impairment, under either International Accounting Standards (IAS) 36, *Impairment of Assets,* or another standard. An academically sound standard, IAS 36 sets out sets of rules covering how tangible and intangible assets, including goodwill, have to be tested for impairments. However, in applying it, due to two different value concepts, several issues lead to difficulties and ambiguity, especially with goodwill; those are clarified in this chapter.

IAS 36 applies two unrelated value concepts, fair value less cost to sell (FVLCS), and value in use (VIU) to test the integrity of the carrying amount of an asset. FVLCS is market price based, representing the value in exchange. VIU, however, represents the reporting entity's assessment of its very specific ability to exploit the asset to generate cash flows: It is the entity's present value over its economic useful life. By introducing these two concepts, considered to be of equal reliability, IAS 36 deviates significantly from the concepts applied in IAS 16, *Property, Plant and Equipment,* or IAS 39, *Financial Instruments: Recognition and Measurement,* as well as under U.S. generally accepted accounting principles (GAAP).

IMPAIRMENT TESTING

IAS 36, *Impairment of Assets,* was first issued in 1998 and has been amended several times, most recently in 2008. The standard's scope is to ensure that assets are carried at no more than their recoverable amount and to define how that is calculated. Further guidance is provided by several related interpretations: Standard Industrial Classification (SIC) codes 32, *Intangible Assets—Web Site Costs,* International Financial Reporting Interpretations Committee (IFRIC) 1, *Changes in Existing Decommissioning, Restoration and Similar Liabilities;* IFRIC 10, *Interim Financial Reporting and Impairment;* and IFRIC 12, *Service Concession Arrangements.* They apply, in principle, to all tangible and intangible assets, except for:

- Inventories (IAS 2, *Inventories*)
- Assets arising from construction contracts (IAS 11, *Construction Contracts*)
- Deferred tax assets (IAS 12, *Income Taxes*)
- Assets arising from employee benefits (IAS 19, *Employee Benefits*)
- Financial assets within the scope of IAS 39, *Financial Instruments: Recognition and Measurement*

---

[1] *This chapter was written in the spring of 2009 and reflects the current version of any standard or paper mentioned. The authors are grateful for the contribution of the task force of the Duff & Phelps International Office of Professional Practice.*

- Investment property measured at fair value (IAS 40, *Investment Property*)
- Biological assets related to agricultural activity that are measured at fair value less estimated point-of-sale costs (IAS 41, *Agriculture*)
- Deferred acquisition costs and intangible assets, arising from insurance contracts within the scope of International Financial Reporting Standards (IFRS) 4, *Insurance Contracts*
- Noncurrent assets (or disposal groups) classified as held for sale in accordance with IFRS 5, *Non-current Assets Held for Sale and Discontinued Operations*

At each reporting date, an entity assesses whether there is any indication that a covered asset (IAS 36:9) is impaired. For this, a list of internal and external indicators of a possible trigger is supplied. External indicators are:

- Market value declines
- Negative changes in technology, markets, economy, or laws
- Increases in market interest rates
- Share price below book value

Internal indicators could be:

- Obsolescence or physical damage to the asset
- The asset being part of a restructuring or held for disposal
- Worse economic performance than expected (IAS 36:12)

These lists are not exhaustive, and materiality should be considered (IAS 36:13). An indication that an asset may be impaired suggests that its useful life, depreciation method, or residual value should be reviewed and adjusted (IAS 36:17). Impairment tests are mandatory each reporting period for intangible assets with an indefinite useful life, intangible assets not yet available for use, and goodwill. Regardless of the annual mandatory test, the indicators can also trigger an additional examination (IAS 36:10).

The recoverable amount of an asset is the higher of its FVLCS and its VIU (IAS 36.10). FVLCS is determined on an individual basis. However, if the asset does not generate cash flows that are largely independent of those from other assets, the recoverable amount is determined for the cash-generating unit (CGU) to which the asset belongs. A CGU is the smallest identifiable group of assets that generates cash inflows that are largely independent of the cash inflows from other assets or groups of assets (IAS 36.6).

For the purpose of impairment testing, goodwill acquired in a business combination is allocated to each CGU, or group of CGUs, that are expected to benefit from the synergies of the combination (IAS 36.80).

Any impairment loss, the carrying amount of an asset less its recoverable amount, is recognized immediately in the income statement (IAS 36.59). If the asset has been revalued in accordance with another standard, such as IAS 16, *Property, Plant and Equipment*, the impairment loss is treated as a revaluation decrease in accordance with the appropriate standard. An impairment loss for a CGU is allocated (IAS 36.104) to reduce first the carrying amount of any goodwill allocated to it and then, the other assets pro rata, based on their carrying amounts.

A previously recognized impairment loss may be reversed if there is a change in circumstances, since the last impairment loss, such as in the estimates used to determine the asset's recoverable amount. In those situations, the carrying amount of the asset is increased to its recoverable amount but may not exceed the lower of (a) the carrying amount had no impairment loss previously been recorded, or (b) the value initially recorded (IAS 36.110–121). A goodwill impairment must not be reversed (IAS 36.124). Various countries have issued further guidance to clarify the application of IAS 36 with respect to local requirements (for Germany it is IDW RS HFA 16 (IDW - Institut der Wirtschaftsprüfer in Deutschland, Institute of Auditors in Germany, RS - Rechnungslegungsstandard, Accounting Standard, HFA - Hauptfachausschuss, Technical Committee)

VALUE CONCEPTS IN IMPAIRMENT TESTING

The fair value concepts of IAS 36 differ significantly from those of IAS 39, *Financial Instruments: Recognition and Measurement,* or IAS 16, as it defines an asset's recoverable amount as the higher of its FVLCS and its VIU. Therefore, it is not always necessary to determine both the FVLCS and the VIU; if either exceeds the asset's carrying amount, there is no impairment.

For assets held for sale, the VIU will consist mainly of the net disposal proceeds, because the future cash flows from their continuing use until disposal are likely to be negligible; therefore, the recoverable amount will be FVLCS (IAS 36.21). In some cases, estimates, averages, and computational shortcuts may provide reasonable approximations for determining FVLCS or VIU; of course, this heavily depends on materiality.

Fair Value Less Costs to Sell

Basically FVLCS is the fair value of an asset from observable prices in an active market or observable comparable transactions; in other words using Level 1 or Level 2 inputs. Level 1 inputs are "quoted prices (unadjusted) in active markets for identical assets or liabilities that the reporting entity has the ability to access as of the measurement date." Level 2 inputs are "inputs other than quoted prices included within Level 1 that are observable for the asset or liability either directly or indirectly through corroboration with observable market data. While a Level 1 input requires an observable market quote for an identical asset in an active market, a Level 2 input is characterized as an observable market quote (a) for a "comparable (similar)" asset in an active market or (b) for an identical or similar asset in a market that is not active.

The difference from fair value as discussed in other IFRS is the recognition of transactional expenses in cost to sell; these have to be carefully estimated and reflected unless they are negligible. As a result, the FVLCS concept cannot be applied to all classes of assets in a sensible manner. For example, price and transaction data should be observable for general equipment, such as machine tools that can be broadly used. However, specialized machines or, even more important, intangibles may be so unique that the Market Approach is not applicable; in such a case, only the VIU needs to be determined.

IAS 36.25 through 36.29 provides guidance on determining an asset's FVLCS and establishes the order of methods recommended:

1. If there is a binding sale agreement, use that price less costs of disposal: IAS 36.25: "the best evidence of an asset's FVLCS is a price in a binding sale agreement in an arm's-length transaction, adjusted for incremental costs that would be directly attributable to the disposal of the asset."

2. In the absence of a binding sales agreement, for an asset that is traded in an active market, FVLCS is the market price less the costs of disposal. The appropriate market price is the current bid price if available; if not available, the most recent transaction price may provide a basis from which to estimate FVLCS, provided that there has not been a significant change in economic circumstances since the transaction date (IAS 36.26). This information should be used with great care, as an impairment test is triggered by external or internal indicators, which usually reflect a change in circumstances.

3. Without a binding sale agreement or an active market, FVLCS should be estimated based on the best information available, such as the outcome of recent transactions for similar assets within the industry, diligently considering the reliability of such data. The idea is to reflect the amount that an entity could obtain, at the balance sheet date, from the disposal of the asset after deducting all related costs. Values determined in forced sales do not constitute FVLCS, unless the firm is compelled to sell immediately (IAS 36:27).

Besides applying to single assets, IAS 36 applies to CGUs. In the absence of a binding sales agreement or an active market, the best estimate for the FVLCS of an asset/CGU will most likely be the present value of the future cash flows anticipated from that asset/CGU reflecting the average market participant's capabilities to exploit it. For CGUs, the use of an appropriate multiple to estimate FVLCS can be feasible. Thus, if management projections are used, they need to be free from any specific synergies or conditions that another entity does not have; synergies available to any market participant should be considered. Therefore, the use of projections from external sources, such as broker or analyst reports, industry estimates, or the like, should be preferred, as the FVLCS is not the same as the VIU. Consequently, the discount rate needs to be derived from an appropriate peer group, not from the entity's cost of capital and leverage.

The use of replacement costs, suggested as a way to determine fair value in IAS 16.31, is explicitly prohibited in IAS 36, as the mere cost to replace an asset does not reflect the economic benefit it will deliver in the future (IAS 36:BZ28 and 36:BZ29).

The costs of disposal are the additional direct costs only, not existing expenses or overhead (IAS 36.28). They are deducted from fair value to determine FVLCS if they have not been previously recorded as liabilities in connection with the recognition of the asset. Examples of such items are:

*   Sales commissions
*   Legal fees
*   Stamp duties and similar transaction taxes
*   Dismantling and removal charges
*   Direct incremental costs to bring the asset into salable condition

For the FVLCS of CGUs used for goodwill impairments, mergers and acquisitions (M&A) advisory fees could be a cost of disposal. However, termination benefits (as defined in IAS 19, *Employee Benefits*) and expenditures associated with reorganizing a business following the disposal of an asset are not costs of disposal. Sources of information for costs of disposal include observable transactions, quoted disposal prices, consultants' databases, management estimates, and industry rules.

Value in Use

As stated by its name, VIU is not a transaction price but rather the value of the asset or CGU to the reporting entity. To calculate VIU, only the Income Approach can sensibly be applied. To determine the VIU of an asset, the entity first estimates the future net cash flows to be derived from its ultimate disposal, and then applies an appropriate discount rate to them. The cash flow calculations should take into account the entity's specific capabilities to exploit the asset or CGU, while the discount rate needs to reflect the firm's specific WACC. Thus, it is explicitly not fair value as determined in other IFRS or in the FVLCS concept. For the cash flow projections, the use of management budgets is recommended, provided that they are based on reasonable and supportable assumptions, represent the most recent forecasts, and can be sensibly extrapolated for future periods (IAS 36.33).

The discount rates used to determine VIU must be pretax rates that reflect both the time value of money and the risks, specific to the asset, for which adjustments have not been made in the projections of the future cash flows (IAS 36.55). In practice, a posttax discount rate is used which is applied to posttax cash flows (see below).

The assumptions underlying the cash flow projections should be reasonable and supportable concerning the economic conditions expected over the remaining useful life of the asset; greater weight should be given to external evidence, which should not just be a market-based view. This external evidence is used to validate the assumptions regarding total market volume, market share, market growth, price developments, and general economic environment. Sources for such external evidence would be brokers' and industry reports and competitors' reflections of the business environment, market intelligence, and banks' assessments of the respective economies.

Fair Value Less Costs to Sell versus Value in Use

The recoverable amount is defined by IAS 36 as the higher of FVLCS or VIU based on the assumption that rational business decision-making would always opt for the more economical way of exploiting the asset: that is, sale or continued use (IAS 36.BZ9). As shown earlier, the FVLCS uses the market's assessment of the general value of the asset, referred to as the market price at which it can be sold (value in exchange). The VIU actually considers the specific entity's capability to exploit the asset by assessing the cash flows expected from it (IAS 36:33).

IAS 36 explicitly considers management's assessment of the VIU of the asset to be as reliable as the general market's assessment used to estimate the FVLCS. This is evidenced by the fact that the higher of both values determines the recoverable amount. The bases for this conclusion (IAS 36:BZ17) are listed next.

- Preference should not be given to the market's expectation of the recoverable amount of an asset (basis for fair value when market values are available and for net selling price) over a reasonable estimate performed by the individual enterprise that owns the asset (basis for fair value when market values are not available and for VIU). For example, the enterprise may have information about future cash flows that is superior to that available in the market. In addition, it may plan to use the asset in a different manner from the market's view of the highest and best use.
- Market values are a way to estimate fair value but only if they reflect the fact that both parties, the buyer and the seller, are willing to enter a transaction. If an enterprise can generate greater cash flows by using an asset than by selling it, it would be misleading to base recoverable amount solely on the market price because a rational entity would not be willing to sell. Therefore, "recoverable amount" should not refer only to a transaction between two parties (which is unlikely to happen) but should also consider an asset's service potential to the enterprise.
- Recoverable amount of an asset is the amount that an enterprise can expect to recover from that asset, including the effect of synergy with other assets that are relevant.

The International Accounting Standards Board (IASB) believes that VIU would be a reasonable estimate of fair value as stated in other IFRSs in the absence of a deep and liquid market. Due to the unique nature of many assets within the scope of IAS 36, it is assumed that observable market prices are unlikely to exist for goodwill, for most intangible assets, and for many items of property, plant and equipment (IAS 36:BZ18).

Current Issues in Determining the Recoverable Amount

Regarding the use of external evidence especially with respect to goodwill impairment testing, there is disagreement as to whether the sum of the recoverable amounts of the CGUs tested for impairment, including allocated goodwill, should be reconciled to the market capitalization of a publicly listed company. If so, it is suggested that input parameters derived from the market capitalization should be used to derive input factors in determining VIU.

This discussion was originated in the United States, where the Securities and Exchange Commission (SEC) and the American Institute of Certified Public Accountants (AICPA) stated that the reconciliation of the total of the fair values of an entity's reporting units (RUs) to its market capitalization would be a good test for the appropriateness of the RUs' fair values. The SEC's chief accountant stated that reconciliation does not necessarily need to be only quantitative but also can be qualitative. For example, an entity should be able to explain why any difference between the total enterprise value (TEV) (or the sum of the values of the RUs) and the market capitalization is not indicative of an impairment issue.[2]

The argument is based on the fair value hierarchy set out in SFAS 157, *Fair Value Measurements*, which assumes that observable prices in active markets are the most reliable indicators of fair values. Although the IASB issued SFAS 157 as a discussion paper (DP), *Fair Value Measurements*, according to IAS 36, it is not appropriate to apply this GAAP practice to the impairment testing procedures as the DP is not a binding document and has no relevance for IFRS.

The argument does not consider that the determination of "fair value" to estimate recoverable amounts according to IAS 36 significantly deviates from the determination of fair value according to other standards. The hierarchy in applying IFRS is first always to consider the specific standard; as IAS 36 explicitly states how the recoverable amount is to be determined, it is inappropriate to apply a different scheme.

To close a potential gap between the total of the fair values of the CGUs and market capitalization, it has been suggested that management's existing cash flow projections and the market capitalization be used to estimate an implicit cost of capital. This implicit cost of capital would then be applied to determine the VIU of the CGU to be tested, thus incorporating an adequate risk premium in the discount rate. This technique raises five issues and should be avoided.

1. Calculating implicit discount rates by using the market cap and management projections leads to a circularity problem.
2. In theory, markets work efficiently, assuming all participants have full information. In reality, external sources, such as broker reports, have less information than management itself and hence external sources are a less reliable or at least different basis for decision making. Using an appropriate management forecast and market capitalization, which is based on external analyses, for discount rate estimation will not generate meaningful results.
3. IAS 36:BZ18 explicitly states: "Observable market prices are unlikely to exist for goodwill, most intangible assets and many items of property, plant and equipment." A "market-based" VIU is inappropriate; to determine the recoverable amount, either concept, FVLCS or VIU, needs to be applied consistently.
4. The VIU is designed by IAS 36 to be a value concept and explicitly supports the idea that management's assessment is as reliable as the market value used in

[2] Robert G. Fox III, "Remarks before the 2008 AICPA National Conference on Current SEC and PCAOB Developments," Office of the Chief Accountant, U.S. Securities and Exchange Commission, Washington, D.C., December 8, 2008.

FVLCS. Mixing market values and management assessment will significantly damage the integrity of either methodology or lead to wrong and meaningless results.

5. Risk premiums derived from implicit discount rates may assume too optimistic expectations of future cash flows. If the projections are diligently reviewed, proven to be supportable, and in line with IAS 36, there is no need to apply additional risk premiums.

As mentioned earlier, external information should be used to verify the cash flow projections. If they seem too optimistic, they need to be corrected directly. It is not advisable to use inappropriate cash flow projections and to apply an unrelated risk premium. Simply applying the implicit discount rates derived from market cap and management projections would be purely a quantitative reconciliation.

Nevertheless, a decline in market capitalization is a triggering event which should cause a critical look at the possibility of impairment. Moreover, a significant difference between the market capitalization at the reporting date and the sum of the VIUs of the CGUs should cause a thorough challenge to the underlying forecasts.

ALLOCATION OF GOODWILL TO CGUS OR GROUPS OF CGUS

Impairment testing gained particular importance after IFRS 3 was introduced in 2004 and the pooling-of-interest method for business combinations was abolished. As a result, goodwill had to be recognized in every merger and acquisition. However, it was no longer subject to amortization but classified as a special intangible asset with an indefinite useful life subject to an impairment test each year.

Goodwill results only from business combinations; the buyer needs to recognize the assets and liabilities of the target on in its balance sheet at fair values. In addition, previously unrecognized intangibles, such as brands, trade names, or customer relationships, need to be recorded individually at fair value. When they have determinable useful lives, they are subject to amortization. The difference between the purchase price and acquired book values of the target's recorded net assets cannot always be explained by these intangibles, and a residual amount called goodwill remains. This fact reflects expectations of the target's future financial performance which cannot be allocated to identified items. Goodwill accordingly bears the biggest risk of all assets; it represents historic expectations of future financial developments, which need to be reviewed annually.

For the purpose of impairment testing, according to IAS 36, goodwill, from the acquisition date, must be allocated to each of the acquirer's CGUs, or groups of CGUs, that are expected to benefit from the synergies of the business combination, irrespective of whether any other assets or liabilities of the target are assigned to those CGUs or groups of CGUs (IAS 36.65–79).

Each CGU or group of CGUs to which goodwill is allocated should represent the lowest level within the entity at which it is monitored by management and not be larger than a segment based on either the entity's primary or secondary reporting format determined in accordance with IFRS 8, *Operating Segments.*

As there are different means of allocation, the first step is to choose an appropriate allocation key. This should match as much as possible future values created (goodwill) and the corresponding assets necessary to generate them (invested capital). Moreover, considering the materiality of goodwill, it should be easily tracked over time and minimize implementation complexity. The decision should be guided by weighting theoretical approaches against practical considerations, such as the level of details available in the business plan. It is also possible to allocate goodwill according to financial aggregates such as sales, EBITDA or EBIT. The advantage is the ease of implementation; this is only advisable for a "quick and dirty" proxy analysis or if there is a lack of more detailed information and the amount is not material, the downside lack of accuracy. Such aggregates are easy to track and adjust; therefore, they are well suited for a quick allocation where goodwill is not material. However, a sales allocation does not embody cost synergies between CGUs. The advantage of earnings before interest, taxes, depreciation and amortization (EBITDA) is that it reflects them. Earnings before interest and taxes (EBIT) also includes cost synergies as well as some indication of other assets (property, plant, and equipment [PP&E], working capital, intangibles) that may be required by the business, in cases where the current assets levels are normative in creating future CGU value. However, like the previous financial aggregates, it does not provide a split between CGUs regarding capital expenditure (CAPEX) synergies, CAPEX requirements, changes in working capital; nor does it reflect potential tax rate differences.

An alternative is an allocation based on free cash flows. This method has the distinct advantage of including all synergies and integrating differences between CGUs regarding tax rates, fixed assets, and working capital. However, its practicability is heavily impaired by the fact that it may be difficult to track and may be hard to adjust. Due to the shortcomings of the allocations just discussed, it is advisable to allocate goodwill according to the business enterprise values (BEV) of the CGUs. This has two major advantages: BEV is the most accurate indicator of value creation, and the BEV of each CGU needs to be determined for impairment testing. Allocating goodwill at initial recognition according to the relative BEV is not only the most accurate technique, but it also avoids inconsistencies in future impairment tests. However, it is difficult to adjust for long-term parameter changes. Business at a CGU level may be generated by assets from several reporting units, such as supply centers in several countries.

To refine the methodology further, BEV minus invested capital, which provides the most accurate match between value creation and asset utilization, is recommended for the allocation. It may furthermore incentivize the reporting entity to anticipate the mandatory work that has to be done when the impairment test is expected to result in an actual charge. Nonetheless, it still bears the disadvantages mentioned earlier.

If synergies are determinable for the individual CGUs, the goodwill resulting from them should be allocated based on their distribution; the balance should then be allotted based on BEV minus invested capital. This ensures that the maximum level of accuracy is achieved at the cost of significant inputs and attention. If this is not possible due to a lack of information, BEV alone should be used if goodwill is material. This ensures a consistent process for future impairment tests and may indicate potential impairment risks at a very early stage.

DETERMINATION OF INPUT FACTORS

The input factors are essentially those needed for discounted cash flow (DCF) models. As already mentioned, these can be used to determine either or both of the VIU and the FVLCS. For estimating the latter, the views of general market participants need to be reflected in the cash flows and the applied discount rate.

Cash Flows

To calculate the VIU or estimate the FVLCS of an asset or CGU, it is necessary to determine their expected cash flows. IAS 36.30 requires five elements to be reflected in the calculation of an asset's VIU:

1. An estimate of the future cash flows the entity expects to derive from it
2. Expectations about possible variations in their amounts or timings
3. The time value of money, represented by the current market risk-free rate of interest
4. The price for bearing the uncertainties inherent in the asset

5. Other factors, such as illiquidity, that market participants would reflect in pricing the anticipated future cash flows from the asset

Projections of future cash flows include (IAS 36.39 and 52):

- Cash inflows from the continuing use of the asset
- Cash outflows required to generate the inflows that can be directly attributed, or allocated on a reasonable and consistent basis, to the asset
- Net cash flows, if any, to be received (or paid) for the disposal of the asset at the end of its useful life (This is the amount that an entity expects to obtain from the disposal of the asset in an arm's-length transaction between knowledgeable, willing parties, after deducting the estimated costs of disposal.)

An entity should use the most recent management budgets and forecasts, which are presumed not to go beyond five years. This rule is intended to avoid any effects from hockey sticks (rapid, unexplained increases in sales and profits). Therefore, for beyond five years, an entity should extrapolate the cost structure of the earlier budgets, using a steady or declining growth rate for sales; this should not exceed the long-term average growth for the products, industries, or countries in which the entity operates or for the market in which the asset is used (IAS 36.33–36.35). A five-year forecast is not mandatory if the entity's planning period is shorter.

Management is required by IAS 36.34 to examine the sources of differences between past cash flow projections and actual cash flows achieved, to ensure that the assumptions on which its current cash flow projections are based are consistent with past actual outcomes. This should be part of any business plan review, as it is a good indicator of too optimistic or too pessimistic planning. The cash flow projections should relate to the asset in its current condition—future restructurings to which the entity is not committed and expenditures to improve or enhance the asset's performance should not be anticipated (IAS 36.44).

It is not always easy to tell whether an investment in an asset/CGU is to maintain the asset/CGU or to enhance it. As an example, should the investments of a mobile phone network provider for the switch from 2G technology to 3G technology be classified as maintenance or enhancements? It can be argued that the switch is essential to maintain the network's market position and the 3G cash flows need to be considered in the VIU calculation; conversely, the switch can be viewed as a material enhancement of the network and the 3G cash flows omitted from the projections. The decision of which argument to follow should be based on a general economic view of the business model of an entity. Without the 3G technology, the mobile phone network would most probably be out of business in the medium term. As a result, the 3G investment is to maintain the competitiveness of the entity, and the related cash flows need to be included.

Estimates of future cash flows should not include cash inflows or outflows from financing activities or income tax receipts or payments (IAS 36.50). Tax effects are excluded to avoid double counting, as tax implications are recognized in accordance with IAS 12, *Income Taxes*, as deferred taxes. In calculating the FVLCS using an Income Approach, management forecasts are usually not appropriate. The cash flows need to be determined without any entity-specific elements; they may include only those synergies that can be obtained by any market participant. As a result, it is necessary either to set up a neutral forecast from scratch or to adjust the management forecast to eliminate company-specific synergies. For neutral forecasts, which are recommended, it can be helpful to use input from broker reports or similar sources.

Discount Rate

For impairment testing according to IAS 36, the discount rates applied to the cash flow projections must be pretax rates that reflect both the time value of money and the risks specific to the asset for which the future cash flow estimates have not been adjusted (IAS 36.55). In practice, a posttax discount rate is applied to posttax cash flows. An implicit pretax discount rate can be calculated by iteration using the fair value resulting from discounting the posttax cash flows by a posttax discount rate; this should give the same result as applying a pretax discount rate to pretax cash flows (IAS 36:BCZ85). This roundabout process is necessary as all discount rate inputs specific to comparable companies (e.g., betas in the Capital Asset Pricing Model, etc.) are derived from posttax earnings. One common choice for a discount rate applied in DCF models is the entity's weighted average cost of capital (WACC) for VIU calculations and a peer group WACC for FVLCS.[3]

In general, a WACC is determined by weighting the cost of debt and the cost of equity according to the underlying capital structure. Usually the tax shield—benefits from interest expenses from debt financing being tax deductible—is incorporated in the formula. The way the tax shield is incorporated into the WACC formula is heavily dependent on the tax regime and the mode of deductibility.[4] In Germany, for example, a cap for the tax deductibility is determined by the company's EBITDA (so-called *Zinsschranke*). In such cases, the effective, not the nominal, tax rates are used.

In determining cost of equity, usually the CAPM is applied, which provides an estimate of the cost of capital for a company based on the costs to the subject company of both debt and equity finance and the relative portions of each in its capital structure. Usually, the capital structure is estimated at a point in time (the valuation date) using debt and equity data from comparable companies identified. However, given the recent impact of depressed market conditions on most companies' market capitalization, debt tends to be overestimated. This can distort the WACC either through releveraging the beta or through the weightings applied to the costs of debt and equity respectively.

Further, where applicable, prices of traded bonds for comparable companies provide a basis by which to adjust book value of term debt to reflect more accurately the correct capital structure for the WACC calculation.

In view of current market volatility, it may be appropriate to consider some historic period in order to obtain a more accurate estimate of external pricing inputs, such as risk-free and debt rates, and capital structures. The acceptable window will vary depending on the input, but risk-free and debt rates should be as of the valuation date or within a six-month window if more appropriate (as it currently is); the optimal capital structure can be assessed over a longer period, as it will fluctuate over time.

FVLCS is calculated based on a market participant's view of the entity company and its value. As such, a WACC based on an optimized capital structure indicated by the average debt to equity ratios of the comparable companies is an appropriate discount rate; the relevant inputs may be obtained from a peer group analysis.

VIU adopts a more internal view of the firm's future. Thus, it may be suitable to select an entity-specific capital structure for the discount rate; as a result, it is likely to differ from that used for the FVLCS.

If a small-stock premium is applied to the cost of equity, the FVLCS methodology requires that each CGU be considered individually; as a result, it may be less appropriate to

---

[3] *For more information on cost of capital and the WACC, see S. Pratt and R. Grabowski,* **Cost of Capital***, 3rd ed. (Hoboken, NJ: John Wiley & Sons, 2008).*

[4] *Ibid., pp. 265–296.*

assess the small-stock premium on a group of CGUs collectively. Thus, both the small-stock premium and overall discount rate overall are higher for the FVLCS than the VIU approach.

The VIU includes consideration of synergies in the value of the entity. As a result, the small-stock premium for a group of CGUs is assessed based on its size. This technique allows for use of a lower small-stock premium in estimating the cost of equity in the discount rate as the CGUs, collectively, achieve a higher value than the total of their individual amounts.

In an impairment test, discount rates need to be determined for individual CGUs; which may differ from those for the business as a whole, provided that their specific risk profiles support the appropriate rates. Adjustments to the entity's discount rate should be applied so that the sum of the discounted cash flows derived for the individual CGUs is equal to that of the business as a whole.

Finally, the selection of "appropriate" input parameters and their subsequent processing will not always ensure that the correct discount rate is identified. Careful sense checks are required to ensure the appropriateness of the individual components of the cost of capital relative to each other but also in the context of current market conditions and historic trends; reasonable adjustments should be made to inputs where necessary.

Example: Impairment Test

An electronics company in Asia has a cash-generating unit involved in computer communications. The CGU is incorporated as a subsidiary in another country. Due to the applicable tax laws, it is mainly financed with debt from the parent and other sources.

Fair value less costs to sell. Management has decided to establish the fair value of the CGU by the Market Approach using a sample of six comparable, publicly traded entities. As the parent is publicly traded, no discount for lack of marketability was considered necessary.

		Market			
Ticker	31-December-08 Price	Shares '000	Cap. $'000	Debt $'000	TEV $'000
DXVI	$ 8.11	28,344	229,869	6,843	236,712
ASBD	$ 3.30	120,473	397,561	5,108	402,669
ANPH	$ 5.08	61,446	312,416	1,687	313,833
WINX	$ 16.55	16,573	274,288	3,500	277,788
COFZ	$ 22.64	20,268	458,879	2,353	461,232
GPTJ	$ 33.42	9,128	305,064	6,246	311,310

Value in use. To determine the value in use, the pretax cash flows were projected for 2009 to 2013 and a terminal amount calculated. The pretax WACC of 12.4% was calculated and used as the discount rate. Due to the thin capitalization, the market approach fair value of the equity is only 3.1% of the related Total Enterprise Value (TEV). Therefore a venture capital pretax rate of 75% was chosen as the cost of equity, to give the parent's investment an overall pretax return of 19.2%, equivalent to the firm's hurdle rate for new project (12.5% after tax).

Pretax WACC Calculation

Pretax WACC Calculation

		Value $'000	Pre-Tax Rate of Return	Product $'000
Parent Loan	28.1%	21,070	13.0%	2,739
Equity	3.1%	2,339	75.0%	1,754
Investment	31.2%	23,409	19.2%	4,493
Bank Obligation	31.3%	23,465	8.5%	1,995
Note Payable	37.5%	28,126	10.0%	2,813
Market Approach Fair Value	100.0%	75,000	12.4%	9,300

Value in Use

		2008	2009	2010	2011	2012	$'000 2013	Terminal Amount
Sales		85,379	75,313	79,832	87,815	94,840	100,531	104,552
Growth		na	–11.8%	6.0%	10.0%	8.0%	6.0%	4.0%
Cost of Sales		41,237	33,463	35,471	39,018	42,140	44,668	46,455
Gross Profit		44,142	41,850	44,361	48,797	52,701	55,863	58,097
Margin		51.7%	55.6%	55.6%	55.6%	55.6%	55.6%	55.6%
Expenses								
SG&A	7.6%	6,469	6,792	7,132	7,489	8,113	8,519	8,945
Marketing	9.1%	7,759	8,303	8,884	9,506	10,171	10,883	11,645
R&D	2.4%	2,080	2,163	2,250	2,340	2,433	2,531	2,632
		16,308	17,258	18,266	19,334	20,717	21,932	23,221
EBITDA		27,833	24,592	26,095	29,463	31,983	33,930	34,876
Margin		32.6%	32.7%	32.7%	33.6%	33.7%	33.8%	33.4%
Depreciation		(7,934)	(11,118)	(11,148)	(11,548)	(13,048)	(14,048)	(14,648)
Interest		(5,594)	(5,874)	(6,168)	(6,476)	(6,800)	(7,140)	(7,497)
Pretax Profit		14,305	7,600	8,780	11,439	12,136	12,743	12,731
Income Tax	35%	(5,007)	(2,660)	(3,073)	(4,004)	(4,247)	(4,460)	(4,456)
Net Earnings		9,298	4,940	5,707	7,435	7,888	8,283	8,275
Margin		10.9%	6.6%	7.1%	8.5%	8.3%	8.2%	7.9%
Income Tax		5,007	2,660	3,073	4,004	4,247	4,460	4,456
CAPEX		(15,920)	(150)	(2,000)	(7,500)	(5,000)	(3,000)	(3,000)
Working Capital		502	1,550	(696)	(1,229)	(1,082)	(876)	(619)
Pretax Cash Flow		(1,113)	9,000	6,084	2,710	6,054	8,866	9,112
Margin		–1.3%	12.0%	7.6%	3.1%	6.4%	8.8%	8.7%
Cap. Amount		Discount Rate		12.4%	Capitalization Rate			8.4%
Terminal Amount								94,952
PV Factor			0.8897	0.7915	0.7042	0.6265	0.5574	0.5574
Present Values			8,007	4,716	1,908	3,793	4,942	52,925
Total PVs	Years 1 to 5	23,466	Terminal Amount.		52,925	TEV	76,391	

Impairment decision. The two methodologies give the results shown in the next table for FVLCS and VIU.

Impairment Test

	FVLCS $'000	VIU $'000
Total Enterprise Value	71,458	76,391
Parent Loan	(21,070)	(21,070)
Bank Obligation	(23,465)	(23,465)
Note Payable	(28,126)	(28,126)
Equity	(1,203)	3,730
Carrying Amount	2,403	2,403

The IFRS impairment test requires comparing the higher of the FVLCS and VIU with the carrying amount. The FVLCS is negative at $1,203,000 while the VIU is $3,730,000. The carrying amount is $2,403,000, so there is no impairment.

CONCLUSION

IAS 36 introduces two value concepts to test the assets within its scope for impairment. FVLCS reflects the general market's assessment of the value of an asset or a CGU, representing a transaction approach. VIU is a real value concept that represents the entity's internal assessment of the value of an asset or a CGU, including its very specific capabilities to generate cash flows from them.

In general, the FVLCS is determined by observable market prices or market-based valuation methods. When sufficient reliable information is available, estimates of the FVLCS can be calculated by using DCF models. In such situations, it is necessary to use input factors that represent the general market assessment of the respective assets. Accordingly, the cash flow projections may include only those synergies that the average market participant can use and must omit any company-specific benefits; the discount rate is determined from peer group inputs.

The VIU expresses a firm's potential to generate cash flows from an asset or a CGU. As a result, the cash flow projections include all entity-specific synergies, and the discount rate is calculated using similar inputs. Considering management's assessment of the value of an asset or CGU does not mean just copying the underlying business plan. As for every valuation, all assumptions and projections need to be challenged and verified.

As the recoverable amount is defined as the higher of the FVLCS and the VIU, these concepts are equally important. As a rule of thumb, in bullish markets, the FVLCS usually produces the higher value, while in bear markets, the VIU normally exceeds it. For any impairment test, a certain level of experience in corporate valuation is required, to appropriately allocate goodwill to CGUs and to diligently assess the FVLCS or VIU of the respective CGUs. This is equally true for generating the appropriate cash flow projections and for calculating the appropriate discount rate.

14 AUDITING VALUATION REPORTS

ANDREAS BERTSCH

GERMANY

INTRODUCTION

There are many different reasons for valuing of a business or any other item, such as an intangible asset. In many cases, entrepreneurial initiatives constitute the most important reasons. For instance, it is essential to know the fair value of a business and its assets if it is to be bought or sold. Valuations for accounting purposes, such as purchase price allocations (PPA), according to International Financial Reporting Standards (IFRS) 3, *Business Combinations*, or the impairment testing of assets and goodwill under International Accounting Standards (IAS) 36, *Impairment of Assets,* have recently gained importance; in all cases, the valuation report is critical.

Auditing is the final step in the process and has a key role in communicating the results of the report. The report is a written document which aims to inform the reader about the value of the subject entity, business interest, asset, or liability; the conclusion may be a discrete amount or a range within which the "true value" will fall. Among other things, the report must reveal the basis of the valuation, setting out in detail the significant underlying assumptions and establishing comprehensible and verifiable conclusions. (See Chapter 6.)

Various groups and institutions, such as investment banks, consulting firms, and tax advisory or accounting firms, value businesses for different reasons. In many cases, especially if used to prepare financial statements, an audit of the valuation report by an independent knowledgeable party is required; the auditor's opinion must include whether the valuation is prepared in conformity with the relevant standards.

The Institut der Wirtschaftsprüfer (Institute of Public Auditors in Germany [IDW]) has published a standard "Principles for the Performance of Business Valuations."[1] Even if only Germans are legally obliged to apply it when carrying out business valuations, from an auditor's perspective, it depicts an international state-of-the-art standard of practice. Section 9.2 deals with valuation reports as part of the necessary documentation for the audit process.

This chapter sets out the conditions a valuation report has to fulfill to meet the requirements of an international auditing firm in five sections.

1. Terms referring to business valuations;
2. A short overview of the relevant international auditing standards;
3. The auditor's needs regarding the contents of a report.
4. Possible reasons for disregarding a valuation report,
5. Conclusions.

---

[1] *Institut der Wirtschaftsprüfer, "Principles for the Performance of Business Valuations" (Institute of Auditors in Germany, Standard 1 (IDW S 1), 2 April 2008).*

VALUATOR'S FUNCTION

"Value is an economic concept referring to the price most likely to be concluded by the buyers and sellers of a good or service that is available for purchase."[2] According to this view, there is currently agreement to a large extent between academic theory and practice that value is a hypothetical price; the key criterion is the estimate of utility. This idea gives rise to the problem that value cannot be measured by an absolute amount of money. Therefore, value is a relative or comparative term; there is not a single unique, "objective" value for a business.

The value of an asset or business is, under the restrictive assumption of IFRS, based on the present value of the future benefits expected to be derived from it; usually such benefits are measured by some variant of cash flows. The discount rate used to calculate the present values represents the return on the best, adequately comparable, alternative investment to the subject.

It is evident that the purpose of a valuation will have a strong influence on the conclusions. According to IDW Standard 1, section 2.2, possible reasons for valuations are:

- Entrepreneurial initiatives
- Financial reporting
- Tax preparation
- Statutory requirements
- Contractual agreements

Depending on the objective, a valuator may exercise various functions, of which two are discussed next because they may also be performed by an auditor.

Neutral Expert

In the function of a neutral expert, a valuator acts as an independent person possessing special skills, knowledge, and experience in the field as well as of the entity's business. He will, by means of comprehensible methods, determine an "objectified" business value.

Advisor

In the function of an advisor, a valuator determines a subjective value for decision-making purposes. In this activity, the valuator takes into account all existing individual opportunities and plans of a specific investor.

Between the two functions there is, or may be, a "natural" area of conflict. A valuator acting as advisor functions as an agent who has to pursue the interest of the principal (client), whereas a neutral expert is committed to objectivity; the latter must be independent and cannot pursue the interest of either of the parties involved.

Auditor

It should be noted that an individual conducting an audit of a valuation report is not allowed to act as either advisor or neutral expert; the auditor's role, among other things, is that of an independent controlling body. (See Exhibit 14.1.)

---

[2] *See International Valuation Standards, "Concepts Fundamental to Generally Accepted Valuation Principles" (GAVP), paragraph 4.5, Eighth Edition, 2007, London UK*

Exhibit 14.1 Roles of Valuator and Auditor in a Valuation

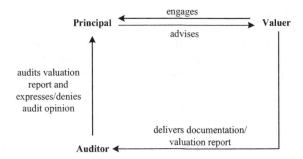

Professional rules and legislation (Sarbanes-Oxley Act) prohibit an auditor from performing, for an audit client, specific nonaudit services, including valuations. It would be incompatible with his essential independence, if an auditor supplied services which, later on, he had to audit. The management of the audited entity is responsible for financial reporting valuations. Given the complexity associated with establishing values, the firm is likely to engage an external specialist. This does not change the situation; the ultimate responsibility remains a legal obligation of the entity.

Audit Standards

The activities of an auditing firm are limited by law and by the rules of professional associations such as the American Institute of Certified Public Accountants (AICPA) or the IDW. These institutions have promulgated national standards on auditing such as the AICPA's Statements on Auditing Standards (SAS) and the German "generally accepted standards for the audit of financial statements." Not only are auditors subject to the national standards on auditing of their home country; if the country is a European Union member, auditors are subject to the International Standards of Auditing (ISAs).

The latter are prepared by the International Auditing and Assurance Standard Board (IAASB), an independent standard-setting body within the International Federation of Accountants (IFAC). Because of close collaboration between the IAASB and the American Auditing Standards Board (ASB), a technical committee of the AICPA, the ISAs also reflect the most important SAS.

There are no special standards on auditing valuation reports even though they are frequently needed within an audit of financial statements. The objective of IFRS 3 is for the acquirer to recognize the target's identifiable assets acquired and liabilities (actual and contingent) assumed at their fair values on the acquisition date as well as record any residual goodwill. The assets and goodwill subsequently have to be tested for impairment at least once a year. Thus, valuations have to be done at acquisition and subsequently on the same date each year.

Those conclusions of value form part of the financial statements, and the report should assist the auditor in understanding the processes. As an essential part of the audit working papers, the valuation report constitutes an important component of the audit documentation in general. The audit report, confirming that the financial statements are prepared in accordance with IFRS, will rely on material and statements in the valuation report.

RELEVANT ISAS

This section briefly outlines the ISAs which indirectly refer to valuation reports.

The purpose of ISA 200, *Objective and General Principles Governing an Audit of Financial Statements,* is to establish standards and to provide guidance on the objective and general principles governing audits of financial statements; it confirms the responsibility of management for their preparation and presentation, including any necessary valuation reports.

ISA 315 (Redrafted), *Identifying and Assessing the Risks of Material Misstatement Through Understanding the Entity and Its Environment,* in particular deals with gathering information as an essential part of risk assessment. Potential consequences of assessed risks are the subject of ISA 330 (Redrafted), *The Auditor's Responses to Assessed Risks.*

ISA 540, *Auditing Accounting Estimates, Including Fair Value Accounting Estimates and Related Disclosures*, discusses, in general, basic questions referring to accounting estimates without any particular details about fair value measurement.

ISA 545, *Auditing Fair Value Measurements and Disclosures,* includes, among other things, detailed advice on understanding the entity's process for determining fair value measurements and assessing risk. Because of partially overlapping contents of ISAs 540 and 545, the IFAC has recently published ISA 540 Revised and Redrafted, which summarizes and soon will replace the previous standards. It is effective for audits of financial statements for periods beginning on or after December 15, 2009. ISA 540R has a close thematic relation to ISAs 315R and 330R, which also will be effective at that time.

ISA 620, *Using the Work of an Expert,* expresses the requirements with which experts must comply so that their work is adequate for the purposes of an audit.

STRUCTURE AND CONTENT OF VALUATION REPORTS

From the auditor's point of view, and to satisfy the relevant IAS, a detailed written valuation report should include, to the extent applicable, these sections at a minimum:

Executive Summary, including at least:

> Client
> Purpose of engagement
> Valuation standards applied
> Valuation date
> Subject (entity, business interest, financial, physical or intangible asset, liability or contingency)

Description of the subject:

> Legal status
> Economic basis
> Tax matters

Details of the relied-on information: Historic financial statements (at least five years)

> Their analyses
> Forecasts,projections,budgets on the basis of underlying assumptions for at least the next fiscal year, preferably five
> Availability and quality of initial data (including opinions of other experts on particular items
> Plausibility checks of budgeted figures
> Definition of responsibility for information provided

Presentation of the valuation:

> Description of valuation methods selected
> Reasons for rejection of others
> Sources of the underlying parameters (cost of capital, growth rate, tax levels, etc.)
> Basis of all significant assumptions
> Explanation of the valuation conclusion
> Plausibility check of the conclusion

The text or appendixes should set out comprehensible and detailed explanations of all calculations involved, including determining sensitivity of the conclusion to changes in significant assumptions

Some of the points just mentioned are discussed in more detail later in the text.

Separation of Management's and Auditor's Responsibilities

Management is responsible for the valuation and the information disclosed in the valuation report; in connection with that obligation, it needs to:

* Establish organizational procedures to assure complete and adequate documentation of all the valuation activities.
* Select appropriate valuation methods and models.
* Arrange the collection of all necessary and desired data (benchmarks).
* Define and adequately support all significant assumptions.
* Prepare the valuation report.
* Ensure that the presentation and disclosure of the valuation conclusions for financial statement purposes are in accordance with IFRS.

If management engages a valuator as an expert to determine certain required values, it is responsible for assessing the expert's qualifications. Management has to ensure that the expert possesses special skills, knowledge, and experience in the field of valuation applicable to the particular subject. The professional qualification of the valuator should be documented in the report. Even when using an expert, the overall responsibility still remains with management.

In contrast, the auditor's responsibility is limited to assessing whether the significant assumptions used by management and any expert in the valuation process provide a reasonable basis for measuring the particular value in the context of an audit of the financial statements taken as a whole. The objective of the audit procedures is, therefore, to obtain sufficient and appropriate audit evidence to provide an opinion on the assumptions themselves. (See ISA 545.) The auditor may not shift responsibilities to the valuator; therefore, the auditor has to perform substantive procedures to test the entity's valuation conclusions, including those prepared by the valuator.

As part of the auditor's working papers, the valuation report must in general enable any knowledgeable reader to understand the results of the valuation processes and estimate the effects of the assumptions made on the conclusions (the so-called intersubjective audit trail). The valuator's report is the basis for the auditor assessing the risks, whether from error or fraud, of material misstatement of the value conclusions, which depend on other factors, including the reliability of management's processes.

Description of the Subject

From reading the description of the subject in the report, the auditor should obtain a sufficient level of knowledge of the entity's business to assess the significance of the conclusions. The report should enable the auditor to plan and perform the audit in accordance with professional standards. The description should supply a thorough understanding of the events, transactions, and practices in the business that, in the auditor's judgment, might have a significant effect on the valuation conclusions.

The report must also provide sufficient insight into the economic situation of the entity, such as competitive conditions; this should cover specific existing and potential competitors, regulatory requirements, and manufacturing and distribution capabilities. After reading the report, the auditor should be able to understand adequately the future prospects of the entity so as to assess the reasonableness of its financial forecasts, projections, and budgets. The report should also inform the auditor about the legal situations and tax positions of the entity and its owners since both aspects will influence future cash flows and hence the subject's value. This discussion and detailed knowledge of the entity's business has gained importance in light of the 2008–2009 financial market collapse and the ongoing general economic crisis. The information will help the auditor to design effective substantive audit procedures.

Using the Work of a Valuator

In many cases, as already mentioned, management is supported in the valuation process by a specialist, most often an outside expert engaged for the specific task. In large firms especially, sometimes management may use an in-house specialist.

The auditor should evaluate the specialist's qualifications by looking at his or her:

- Professional certification, including licensing by, or membership in, appropriate bodies.
- Experience and reputation in the appropriate field of valuation.

By reading the report, the auditor should obtain sufficient evidence that the work performed by the expert is adequate for the indicated purposes. After such reading, the auditor should:

- Understand the objective and scope of the specialist's work as well as any restrictions placed on it.
- Evaluate any restrictions on the specialist's access to necessary information.
- Comprehend the methods used and assumptions adopted.
- Have details of the specific items needed to perform the assessment and support the audit procedures.

In addition, the auditor should confirm directly with the expert the terms of the latter's engagement. For reasons of integrity and objectivity, it is essential for the auditor to understand the relationship of the valuator and management. This is due to the possibility of direct or indirect control or significant influence on the valuator's work. The expert therefore should disclose the existence of any circumstances that might give rise to a possible conflict of interest. From the disclosures of the relationship between valuator and management, the auditor is able to assess the risk that the specialist's objectivity and neutrality might be affected.

Testing Significant Assumptions, Valuation Models and Underlying Data

All valuation methods are based on assumptions. The report has to thoroughly disclose and support all the significant assumptions underlying each adopted method under one of three approaches: market, income and cost. This will allow the auditor to evaluate whether the significant assumptions, individually and together, seem reasonable and realistic. Additionally, they should be consistent with all of these points:[3]

---

[3] *See AICPA, Auditing Fair Value Measurements and Disclosures, Statement of Auditing Standards (SAS) No. 101, paragraph 59, New York 2003.*

- General economic environment
- Situation of the specific industry
- Entity's particular circumstances
- Existing market information
- Strategic plans of the entity, including what management expects will be the outcome of specific objectives and activities
- Assumptions made in previous valuation assignments, if appropriate
- Past conditions experienced by the entity to the extent they are currently applicable
- Risks associated with future cash flows, including potential variability in their amounts and timing together with any related effects on the selected discount rate

The value conclusions based on the underlying assumptions are influenced mainly by the method selected. Therefore, the valuation model, its parameters, and its input data have to be thoroughly described so that the auditor can recalculate the valuation step by step. As well, the report should include, possibly in appendixes, calculations of the sensitivity of the valuation to changes in each significant assumption.

Valuation model. The auditor will evaluate the appropriateness and the applicability of the valuation model. The latter may be limited by the relevant standard. For example, IDW S 1 requires business valuations to be determined by means of a discounted cash flow method under the Income Approach; the use of the Market Approach is allowed only to assess the plausibility of such values. In contrast, IFRS 3 and, in particular, IAS 39, *Financial Instruments: Recognition and Measurement*, express a clear preference for the Market Approach in estimating fair values of assets and liabilities. The Cost Approach, which assumes the value of an asset or entity is its replacement costs, is inappropriate in many cases, as it looks to the past, not to the future.

Significant assumptions. Irrespective of the approaches used, all significant assumptions have to be explained in detail and reviewed carefully by the auditor. The key assumption of the Market Approach is that the selected guideline is really comparable to the subject. Only in rare circumstances will there be quoted prices from active markets, which are the best audit evidence of fair value. In the context of the global financial crisis, many markets are no longer active, and information from inactive or illiquid markets is not reliable; in those cases, the valuation has to be done by using other techniques, using market data as support.

Discount rates. The crucial factor in computing present value of forecast cash flows is the discount rate, which has to reflect a suitable term and risk-adjusted yield curve. The discount rate typically consists of two components: the basic risk-free interest rate for various maturities of zero-coupon government bonds and the term-related credit spread. In illiquid markets, a third component, the liquidity premium has to be considered as well. These factors should be based on objective market information, which is more relevant and reliable than subjective management estimates.

All input data and its sources have to be disclosed in the valuation report so that the auditor may evaluate their accuracy, completeness, and relevance. He or she will review the assumptions for internal consistency, including whether the management's intent and ability to carry out specific courses of action is consistent with the entity's plans and past achievements. In addition, the auditor will verify, on a random basis, the correctness of sources of the underlying data. These activities help the auditor to assess the risks, whether due to error or fraud, of material misstatement by management.

For corroborative purposes, the auditor should prepare independent value estimates by comparing the results in the valuation report with those obtained by using an internally developed version of the valuator's model. Instead of management's assumptions, the auditor may apply his or her own in the course of the audit to test the sensitivity of the valuation.

This helps the auditor to understand better the influence of particular factors on the value. Significant differences between management's and the auditor's estimate have to be settled within the audit procedures.

DISREGARDING VALUATIONS

The auditor has the sole responsibility for the audit conclusion. ISA 620, paragraph 16, explains that when issuing an unmodified report, the auditor should not refer to the work of an expert, as such a reference might be misunderstood to be a qualification of the auditor's opinion or a division of responsibility, neither of which is intended.

In some circumstances, an auditor may have doubts concerning the evidence supporting a valuation report. Possible reasons may be unrealistic assumptions, unsuitable valuation methods, or lack of objectivity by the expert. If the information in the valuation report does not provide sufficient appropriate audit evidence or if its conclusions are not consistent with other audit evidence, the auditor should modify or, in extreme cases, refuse to issue the report.

CONCLUSION

Due to the complexity of valuation processes, this work often is performed by a specialist. The function a valuator exercises may be that of an advisor or a neutral expert. Those functions differ fundamentally and cannot be performed by one person at the same time. Only a value determined by a neutral expert fulfils the conditions of a report which is suitable to be audited.

A good valuation report should completely satisfy all professional and engagement requirements. After reading it, the auditor has to understand and assess the basic data, methodologies, underlying assumptions, fundamental considerations and conclusions; the time and effort to undertake those steps must be economically justifiable. With respect to the data on which the value is based, the auditor will review its accuracy, completeness, and relevance. It must be possible for the auditor to calculate values or modify input data used in the valuation model.

An auditable valuation report should be well written, properly organized, and characterized by these qualities:

- *Thorough.* Include all relevant data and analyses that affect the conclusion.
- *Balanced.* Discuss impartially all relevant positive and negative factors affecting the value.
- *Comprehensible.* Write in clear and concise terms, with minimal use of technical jargon so that the reader is able to follow the work done and the conclusions reached.
- *Coherent.* Flow logically from the data presented to the final conclusion with internally consistent conclusions and analyses.
- *Well supported.* Thoroughly document each step, presenting detailed calculations and identifying the data sources so that another expert can follow the process and reach a similar conclusion.

15 COPYRIGHTS

FERNANDO TORRES

Mᴇxɪᴄᴏ

INTRODUCTION

The term "copyright" is generally used to designate the bundle of exclusive rights regulating the use of specific expressions of ideas or information. The author of an original creation obtains the ability to limit, or control, its use and reproduction; this is not perpetual but, compared with other intellectual property rights (IPR), generally has a long duration. Copyright legislation, which started in Britain about 1710, was originally enacted through much of the world to protect authors' writings. Due to the continuous evolution of technology, there has been an ever-expanding understanding of the term "writings." Copyrights now cover works as diverse as architectural design, software, and digital recordings as well as industrial designs. Some jurisdictions apply separate or overlapping laws to designs or industrial designs; for example, in the United States, many commercial or industrial designs are covered by design patents.

Copyrights, in general, cover only the form or manner in which an idea or information has been manifested. They are not meant to cover the actual ideas, concepts, facts, styles, or techniques that may be embodied in or represented by the copyrighted work; however, functional or fashion designs are not usually protected.

A copyright gives the owner the exclusive right to reproduce, distribute, perform, display, or license his or her work, including parts of it. Therefore, the copyrights on the Mickey Mouse cartoons allow The Walt Disney Company to exclude others from distributing copies or creating derivative works including a similar character. However, they do not extend to the creation of artistic works reflecting the general idea of "anthropomorphic mice." Limited exceptions exist for types of "fair use," such as book reviews. Current copyright law covers works whether a copyright notice is attached or not and whether it was registered or not.

One economic consequence of copyrights is an opportunity to trade; the owner can transfer those rights (in whole or in part) if another has a more profitable use for them; therefore, copyrighted works are intangible assets. They can be applied commercially and may have significant value. From an economic, or business, perspective, the need for copyright protection is reinforced if there is demand for the work in the marketplace. Consequently, allocating the potential profit may cause difficulties as well as give rise to significant competitive consequences. When a protected work is used, or copied, without authorization, copyright laws provide for the prosecution of such infringement and the recovery of monetary damages, not only those actually suffered by the owner, but potentially the disgorgement of the infringer's profits (if any).

Finally, the financial reporting of copyrights must reflect their economic position within the framework established by the standards of the International Valuation Standards Council (IVSC), International Accounting Standards Board (IASB), and Financial Accounting Standards Board (FASB). As with other intangibles, the central concern for such financial reporting is the quality and relevance of their valuations. Copyrights present special challenges to conventional valuation methodologies and are at the forefront of practical innovations in the way IPR are created, granted, and commercialized.

COPYRIGHTS AS INTERNATIONAL ASSETS

In most countries, copyright laws are standardized through international arrangements, such as the Berne Convention, rather than through myriad bilateral agreements. In 1886, this established recognition of copyrights among sovereign nations. Under it, copyrights for creative works do not have to be asserted or declared but are automatically in force when generated. Therefore, an author need not "register" or "apply for" a copyright in countries adhering to the convention. As soon as a work is "fixed,"—that is, written or recorded on some physical medium—its author is automatically entitled to all copyrights in the work and to any derivative works, unless and until the author explicitly disclaims them or until the copyright expires.

The Berne Convention also results in foreign authors being treated equivalently to domestic authors in any participating country. The United Kingdom signed in 1887 but did not implement large parts of it until more than 100 years later, with the passage of the Copyright, Designs, and Patents Act of 1988; the United States did not sign on until 1989. Under the convention, each country's legislation is expected to determine ultimately which types of works will be protected by it.

Listed next are the most commonly recognized legal rights of copyright owners and the authors' simultaneous moral rights.

Components of Copyrights	*Moral Rights of Copyright Owner*
To reproduce the work	Paternity(to be known as the author)
To copy the work	Integrity (to prevent others from distorting the work)
To adapt (derivative works)	Disclosure (right to control publication)
To distribute the work	Withdrawal (right to withdraw, modify, or disavow the work)
To publicly perform the work	

Works protectable by copyrights include:

Every production in the literary, scientific and artistic domain, whatever may be the mode or form of its expression, such as books, pamphlets and other writings; lectures, addresses, sermons and other works of the same nature; dramatic or dramatico-musical works; choreographic works and entertainments in dumb show; musical compositions with or without words; cinematographic works to which are assimilated works expressed by a process analogous to cinematography; works of drawing, painting, architecture, sculpture, engraving and lithography; photographic works to which are assimilated works expressed by a process analogous to photography; works of applied art; illustrations, maps, plans, sketches and three-dimensional works relative to geography, topography, architecture or science.[1]

With respect to software copyrights, the World International Property Organization Copyright Treaty of 1996 (an amendment to the Berne Convention) updates protection in this field not by simply explicitly including computer programs as protected literary works but by defining protection for databases. Compilations of data for which the selection or arrangement of the contents are sufficiently original are protected as compilations, although the specific scope of database copyrights is not yet standardized around the world, not even across the Atlantic, for that matter. One current technology-oriented provision requires treaty nations to provide adequate and effective protection against the circumvention of technical

---

[1]	*Berne Convention, Paris Text 1971, Article 2(1).*

measures that restrict the ability of others to exercise the rights of a software copyright owner. Copyright and patent protection for software varies significantly from country to country. International software protection is listed, courtesy of the Silicon Valley law firm Fenwick & West LLP, at: www.softwareprotection.com/chart.htm. Software valuation is dealt with in Chapter 33.

COPYRIGHTS AS FINANCIAL ASSETS

Copyrights are a unique class of intangible assets. Although they share with trademarks and patents the characteristic of being exclusive rights to use, or exclude others from using, the underlying assets, they do not arise from specific formalities; they are the owner's property from the moment the underlying work is created. Furthermore, as mentioned earlier, copyrights are now recognized virtually around the world.

Other than for software and traditional writings or artworks, enterprises throughout the world have copyrights in many different forms:

- Policies and procedures, operating instructions, and the content of other similar manuals developed internally for an organization's own use
- Advertising copy, and the symbols, logo devices, and other creative elements embodied in marketing materials (in print, audio, and/or video formats)
- Marketing and informational content on an organization's Web site
- Images in a firm's catalog or Web site
- In the apparel industry, the artwork reproduced on garments as well as some fabric designs
- In the publishing industry, copyrights are held in the products themselves

Media entities may have a variety of copyrights; for example:

- Film has distinct copyrights in the screenplay and the motion picture itself.
- Recordings have distinct rights for the composer, lyricist, performer(s), and owner.

REPORTING STANDARDS

Copyrights are reported as assets in financial statements under the IFRS, only if certain conditions are met (International Accounting Standard [IAS] 38). At the highest level of abstraction, a copyright is an asset only if it has been either created or purchased by the entity that controls it, and if future economic benefits are expected from such control. This implies that a copyright should be valued only if future economic benefits are expected from it. In certain cases, the value may disappear before the legal copyright expires. However, a certain class of copyrights may not directly support a flow of benefits, but its control provides important advantages, perhaps even vital safeguards to the survival of the organization. Examples are: recipes of food products, such as Coca-Cola, and formulas of chemical substances. To the extent they are not protected by patents, copyrights are a strong legal substitute. Nevertheless, as it is normally not in a firm's best interest to publish recipes or formulas, it may be more advantageous to protect them as trade secrets. Copyrights and trade secrets share many characteristics; how to characterize and protect specific assets is one of the functions of intellectual property counsel.

The next requirement a copyright must meet to be recognized is for it to be "identifiable." The relevant IFRS requirement is that the item be capable of being separated or divided from the entity and sold, transferred, licensed, rented or exchanged, individually or together with a related contract, identifiable asset or liability, regardless of whether the entity intends to do so or not. Alternatively, copyrights are identifiable because they arise from contractual (e.g., a logo for a firm designed under contract) or other legal rights (e.g., the copyright of a compact disc created by a recording studio), regardless of whether those rights are transferable or separable from the entity or from other rights and obligations (e.g., the logo design may form part of a trademark). These requirements are always considered satisfied if the copyrights are acquired in a business combination, or an asset purchase.

Only for internally generated copyrights must it be shown that (a) it is probable that the expected future economic benefits attributable to the asset will flow to the entity; and (b) its cost can be measured reliably (IAS 38). Reporting internally generated copyrights, as well as other intangible assets, has specific restrictions, as such generated brands, mastheads, publishing titles, customer lists, and similar elements are not recognized as intangible assets.

MEASURING COPYRIGHT VALUE

IFRS clearly specifies that an intangible asset shall be measured initially at cost. This implies that, as more value accrues to a copyright over time (e.g., a particular design or a sound recording), this incremental value is reflected in the current profits of the entity rather than in the fair value of the copyright itself. IFRS, however, recognizes that, where active markets—defined subsequently—exist for a class of intangibles, an entity may elect to use the alternative revaluation model, with the increase in value accruing to the copyright, rather than overstating the profitability of the entity. This is an important departure from generally accepted accounting principles.

According to the IFRS, the cost of a separately acquired intangible asset comprises: (a) its purchase price, including import duties and nonrefundable purchase taxes, after deducting trade discounts and rebates; and (b) any directly attributable cost of preparing the asset for its intended use. If a copyright is acquired in a business combination, its deemed cost is its fair value on the acquisition date.

Some industries develop copyrights as an essential aspect of their operations; examples include: an image licensing entity; a design firm; or the media, arts, recording, and film industries in general. Copyrights arising from the development phase of internal projects may be recognized under IFRS provided they meet the general notion of an asset.

Such internally generated copyrights are reportable by the entity if, and only if, it can demonstrate all of these six points:

1. The technical feasibility of completing the intangible asset so that it will be available for use or sale.
2. Its intention to complete the intangible asset and use or sell it.
3. Its ability to use or sell the intangible asset.
4. How the intangible asset will generate probable future economic benefits. To do this, the entity should demonstrate the existence of a market for the output of the intangible, the intangible itself, or, if to be used internally, the usefulness of the intangible.
5. The availability of adequate technical, financial, and other resources to complete the development and to use or sell the intangible asset.
6. Its ability to measure reliably the expenditure attributable to the intangible asset during its development.

In the context of a typical business (neither a media nor entertainment company), most copyrights are neither developed nor acquired for their own sake but rather are necessary components of other items. For example, most corporate Web sites have (licensed) images and other media copyrights (internally developed, acquired, or "licensed in"). Those are not separable and seldom have identifiable revenue; consequently, they cannot be recognized on their own. However, they still may be valued indirectly as part of a brand, a Web site or for internal purposes in preparation for a sale, license, acquisition, or business combination.

For identified, recognized copyrights, an entity can choose either the cost or the revaluation model for its intangible assets accounting. In the cost model, copyrights are carried at their cost, less accumulated amortization and any accumulated impairment losses. In the revaluation model, the starting point is fair value determined in relation to an active market; the revalued amount is its fair value at that date less subsequent accumulated amortization and any later accumulated impairment losses. Revaluations must be made frequently enough so that, at the end of the reporting period, the carrying amount of the asset does not differ materially from its fair value, unless there is not an active market for those assets. If a copyright is accounted for using the revaluation model, all other assets in its class are also to be accounted for in the same way. The biggest challenge in applying the revaluation model to intangibles in general is that an active market must exist and generate objective prices that reflect the assets' fair value. Unlike conventional securities markets, markets for copyrights must meet the three IFRS conditions:

1. The items traded in the market are homogeneous.
2. Willing buyers and sellers can normally be found at any time.
3. Prices are publicly available

Increasingly, organized markets involving the licensing of copyrights can meet those requirements if the items traded are defined as "digital images" which have active licensing markets with publicly available prices. Sound recordings and the copyrights stemming from the creation and production of audiovisual entertainment may be the next segment that can meet these requirements. In practice, however, copyright owners cannot yet obtain the necessary reliable valuations to apply the revaluation mode. Practitioners must nonetheless be ready to adopt it as it becomes relevant in specific segments, since it will improve the quality of the reported information. There remains some controversy over the applicability of the IFRS definition of "active market," particularly since intangibles are inherently heterogeneous (see International Valuation Guidance Note (IVGN) 16, *Valuation of Intangible Assets for IFRS Reporting Purposes*).

A key consideration in measuring the fair values of copyrights is the period over which the asset is expected to be available for use by the entity. Based on local laws, copyrights in most countries have finite lives; their remaining useful economic lives may be shorter than the legal term, depending on the period the entity actually intends to use it or the terms of the licenses involved. If the contractual or other legal rights are conveyed for a limited term that can be renewed, the useful life of the intangible asset shall include the renewal period(s) only if there is evidence to support renewal by the entity without significant cost (IAS 38).

In general, most signatories to the Berne Convention have one basic copyright term: Works are automatically protected from the moment of their creation for the period ending 70 years after the author's death. There are nuances in this basic term when, for example, the work was created before the country signed the convention or when some countries have extended copyright terms for certain categories. In the United States, the term is longer for works of corporate authorship: 120 years after creation, or 95 years following publication, whichever is the earlier. In Britain, for corporate works, it is 70 years after the earlier of its "making" or "communication to the public." It is the appraiser's responsibility, as one of the key elements of the valuation process, to ascertain the applicable term of the subject copyright.

VALUATION PROCESS

This section sets out a simple valuation framework for copyrights and presents a number of real-world applications.

Basic Outline

Regardless of their specific nuances and characteristics, in general, all copyright valuations have a common outline:

- Statutory Identification
- Methodology Selection
- Asset Attributes
- External Parameters
- Valuation Analyses
- Appraisal Report

Statutory identification. Since a copyright is recognized only if future economic benefits from its control are expected to flow to the owner, the first step is a double one: identifying all legal copyrights and then selecting only those that will generate economic benefits to the firm. Copyrights should be described and classified according to the procedures set out in IFRS 3. Often a specific description will be necessary because copyrights are unique by nature, and fair value varies widely with each specific expression. The task of identification is not always straightforward. While the text of marketing brochures and internal communications are copyrighted, they are not sold or licensed and, therefore, no flow of economic benefits can be expected from them. A business operating an online store, however, is likely to obtain sufficient information from its customers to create a database that may be very valuable to related businesses. In most jurisdictions, this database will be protected, if not as a database (in the European Union), at least as a compilation (in the United States). In a business combination or asset acquisition, it can bring an identifiable benefit stream to the acquirer. Such a database, assembled by a high-end apparel business, might assist the marketing efforts of accessories makers, fashion magazines, and other businesses targeting the same consumer segment. Marketing and leveraging of customer information, it must be noted, is subject to privacy protections and other regulations in many jurisdictions.

Methodology selection. The specific methods chosen to value a copyright will depend on:

- The information available
- How it is used to generate a benefit flow
- The purpose
- Transactional or financial reporting
- The nature of any market for the asset

All three approaches—cost, market, and income—should be considered.

Cost approach. The Cost Approach to valuation is often appropriate in a business combination, given that the accounting system of the target will generally provide adequate information about the actual historic costs incurred in designing, developing, registering, and maintaining the copyright. However, in general, total cost is not an accurate representation of fair value. In a hypothetical negotiation, when the seller is not forced to act, the cost of its copyrights is only the minimum amount it would rationally expect in an arm's-length transaction. Some compensation would be needed for the entrepreneurial incentive concerned in creating and parting with a valuable asset. The buyer would respond to the net benefit that it expects to derive from the asset.

Market approach. The Market Approach is increasingly a viable method to value copyrights. More and more copyright licensing takes place with publicly traded companies that report the terms of licensing contracts for such activities as: artwork for apparel; images and audio for publishing and Web sites; content for information aggregators on the Internet; and music and video files. Obtaining contract terms, or the contracts themselves attached to filings with regulators, is increasingly facilitated by online database search engines. The overriding limitation is their scope of applicability, as they omit many industry segments and copyright types, particularly in traditional lines of business or segments where private firms dominate. Useful databases include www.RoyaltyStat.com (United States) and www.sedar.com (Canada), among others.

The nature of copyrights is that they are unique, almost by definition, and issues of comparability arise in applying the market approach. In addition to the specific properties in comparable transactions, many contracts specify lump-sum fees, and unit or annual rather than percentage of revenue royalties. In practice, many licenses bundle copyrights together with trademarks, rights of publicity, or other intangibles in a single-fee structure. Such cases represent a challenge to the identification of the asset, and may preclude its recognition under the IFRS.

To illustrate the variety of factors a copyright valuation using the Market Approach must consider, Exhibit 15.1 contains a sample of representative examples of copyright licenses found in public filings.

Exhibit 15.1 Representative Copyright Licenses: Media, Merchandising, New Products (Summary, year, and territory)

Exclusive copyright sublicense to use the "Land O' Lakes" trademarks and recipes to manufacture, have manufactured and distribute licensor's products in the single serve channel of distribution packaging. (1997, United States)	Copyrights license to use raw audio and video footage from initial infomercial to create additional infomercials and advertisements for an [electric product] and related accessories. (2005, Worldwide with exceptions)	Exclusive copyrights and trademark sublicense to manufacture and sell products related to telephones, such as long distance and local services, and prepaid and postpaid calling cards, imprinted with reproductions of works of art located in the Museum of Treasures of St. Peters in the Vatican, but not for sale through a fundraising program or a retail store operation. (2000, Asia; Australia; Canada; Mexico; South America; United States)
Exclusive copyrights license to use licensor's name, likeness, and logo to manufacture, sell, license, distribute, and exploit merchandise of any kind through mail order and retail sources. (2000, Worldwide)	Exclusive engagement to furnish recording services of artists and producers to record and deliver singles and to provide related musical performances services; and copyright license to use artist's name, likeness, and biographical material. (1999, UK and Canada)	Nonexclusive copyrights license to manufacture, sell, and distribute commemorative coins and merchandise embodying the name and image of musical artists, including The Beatles, The Blues Brothers, John Lennon, Grateful Dead, and Janis Joplin. (1996, Worldwide with exceptions)
Copyrights license to incorporate and distribute headlines from the Dow Jones Online News into licensee's electronic products and services which deliver information from equity and commodity exchanges as well as sports information, stock quotes, and weather information, via wireless transmission technologies to individual subscribers and authorized resellers. (1996, Canada & United States)	Exclusive copyrights license to use the "ZDNet Japan" trademark to reproduce, publicly perform, display, transmit, and distribute an online, Japanese-language edition of a service via the World Wide Web. (1997, Japan)	Exclusive copyrights license to publish the nonfiction work entitled "[Title]", in English and Spanish and in hardcover and paperback editions. (1999, Canada; Philippines; United States)

The brief sample presented in the exhibit highlights the characteristics of the publicly available information, most of which relates to exclusive deals and many to international licenses. The medium, which includes online, is the industry where license terms are most frequently disclosed; the next is merchandising. Copyrights are often licensed as a bundle with trademarks and technology transfers. Where these characteristics are relevant for the subject copyright, the Market Approach can yield reliable results.

Income approach. In the identification of a copyright, the presence of an expected income stream to the owner is necessary. This supplies the basic input for the Income Approach. The central question is how best to measure the economic contribution of the subject copyright. Is it a revenue stream that only accrues to the business if it controls the asset, such as a published book? Or is it an identifiable incremental profit stream enhanced by the copyright when used in conjunction with other intangibles (such as a trademark, a domain name, or a patent)? Can the copyright be out-licensed to generate an identified royalty stream over a period?

In enforcing copyrights through litigation, the Income Approach is commonly used to measure the economic damages generated by an infringement that causes the loss of sales and profits to the legitimate owner. Alternatively, it can also be used to measure to what extent the infringer has benefited from the illegality and often supports a claim for the disgorgement of infringer's profits. The precise treatment of copyright damages in an international setting is, however, beyond the scope of this book.

Most applicable approach. Generally, the Income Approach tends to measure the upper bound of a negotiated arm's-length price range for a copyright. No buyer would pay for the full net benefits from using the copyright, as there would be no profit incentive; the Cost Approach gives the lower bound. The Market Approach, therefore, may be seen as giving the best measure of an expected negotiated price, as long as the comparability of the asset and the market transactions selected is satisfactory.

The most applicable approach should be selected based on the specific circumstances of each class of subject copyrights. On occasion, more than one may be used, but each measures a different concept. Therefore, averaging the results of a variety of methods is likely to yield an unsatisfactory result.

Asset Attributes

Once a suitable approach has been selected, the process continues by refining the information characteristics of the subject asset. This typically entails gathering the applicable historic cost information, including directly attributable acquisition and maintenance costs (such as registration renewals). If the value will be related to identified revenues, then it is necessary to forecast those amounts over the remaining useful life of the copyright, which may be shorter than the balance of the legal term (e.g., a formula that relies on chemicals later judged hazardous), or it may outlast its statutory protection (such as some music from the first half of the twentieth century).

External Parameters

As explained elsewhere in this book, the valuation of future streams of revenue or profits must be discounted to present value. The usual discount rates reflect systemic risk as well as the additional risks of equity investing, the industry, and the specific class of assets. (Intangibles are riskier than other assets.) This last point must not be understated in the case of copyrights. As far as they are expressions of ideas, societies change, and, consequently, the markets for the expressions of ideas tend to be more volatile than those for tangible goods. Careful consideration of the specific risk level of each type of copyright asset identified is important, particularly if long remaining useful lives are used. Otherwise, discount rates will be too low and copyright values will be overstated, necessitating significant impairment charges in the future. In some cases, a revaluation model may be indicated if only to maintain a relevant assessment of the remaining useful life and appropriate risk level of an asset.

Valuation Analyses

After obtaining the proper information, selecting the methodology, and deriving the applicable internal and external parameters, valuing a typical copyright resolves into a proper application of general valuation principles. The main difference may be the length of the remaining useful life; that of the typical copyright is often much longer than most other IPR, such as patents, but it will never be as long (or indefinite) as in the case of famous trademarks and brands.

Appraisal Report

The final step in valuing a copyright is communicating the conclusions. While only aggregate values find their way into published financial information, solid documentation of the process is indispensable to preserve the quality of the information produced, support future impairments, and facilitate potential transactions. A complete report should cover these items:

- Identity of reporting entity
- Control characteristics
- Purpose and intended use of calculated value
- Valuation date
- Identification and description of the asset
- Applicable financial reporting standard
- Sources of information used
- Valuation approaches or methods considered and selected
- Valuation process
- Conclusions

CASE STUDY I: INTERNALLY CREATED ASSETS

This section illustrates a few of the wide array of copyright valuation situations, including assessing the value of an asset that is not usually recognized.

Valuing an Asset for Transfer

The first example considers the case of a copyright that has been created and used but does not qualify to be recognized in the financial statements. The question arises: Given the principles of IFRS, why value an internally created copyright? Such valuations are performed for a variety of purposes, including:

- Transactions (or potential transactions)
- Litigation
- Compliance, including financial reporting and transfer pricing
- Strategy, including corporate tax strategies, technology transfer, as well as estate and personal financial planning

One such situation was the donation of copyrights to a university for a large collection of theater works. The recipient needed the value of the gift in order to assign a commensurate naming right to the donor. This basic scenario arises, for example, when a corporation acquires an image library for its Web site or when a creative enterprise places its copyright assets in a separate entity.

Process

In this example, Mr. Broadway was a prolific writer of theater plays that were published during his life, who paid close attention to the requirements of copyright laws. As mentioned, the United States signed the Berne Convention only in 1989. Before then, a series of laws, registrations, registration renewal requirements, and copyright terms had been in force going all the way back to the United States' Constitution in 1776. Mr. Broadway's 27 major plays continue to be performed by amateur groups and professional companies. These copyrights have economic value because professional performances generate royalties and profit participations, and amateur versions are licensed on an academic-year basis to thousands of schools throughout the country. The university receiving this copyright portfolio can expect a stream of economic benefits for a long period.

Statutory Identification

The copyrights are readily identified as each play is well known and has been registered. Consequently, the copyright term of each item could be clearly determined. The next table, for example, shows a selection of works, the year of each publication, and the last year of the copyright term. As the table illustrates, these copyrights still have between 25 and 50 years of remaining statutory life.

Exhibit 15.2 Copyright Term of Selected Works, Mr. Broadway's Assets

Play Title	Year of Publication	Last Year of Copyright Term
A	1936	2031
B	1936	2031
C	1951	2046
D	1951	2046
E	1954	2049
F	1955	2050
G	1957	2052
H	1959	2054
I	1960	2055
J	1962	2057
K	1963	2058
L	1965	2060

Methodology Selection

In considering the best method to value this portfolio, two characteristics are important.

1. The copyrights have and will continue to generate a stream of income.
2. These plays are not readily comparable to more modern ones, as they have accumulated substantial recognition; thus, the fair value has little relationship with the historic costs of the original creation.

Consequently, this is a clear case where the Cost Approach is not applicable nor is the Market Approach reliable because there are few, if any, play scripts being transacted in active markets, and most licensing activity relates to broadcast media, not live performances. The Income Approach, consequently, is the best choice. The fair value of the copyright portfolio is clearly related to the present value of the expected economic income associated with its ownership. Furthermore, since the flow of income is variable and expected over a finite period, the yield capitalization method is the most suitable to calculate its value.

Asset Attributes

The subject copyright portfolio has generated, in the last few years, the royalty revenue shown in Exhibit 15.3, divided here between the best-known plays and grouping the rest under "other works," since they do not account for a material portion of the income. The historic information was compiled by the accountants for the estate of Mr. Broadway from monthly reports issued by a variety of production companies and licensing agencies.

Exhibit 15.3 Annual Royalty Income, Mr. Broadway's Copyright Portfolio ($'000)

Year	Play E	Play F	Other Works	Total
2000	$ 28	$ 53	$ 41	$ 122
2001	43	75	14	132
2002	50	39	85	175
2003	30	117	47	194
2004	39	26	110	175
2005	62	86	28	176
2006	29	58	96	183

Revenue forecasts for the valuation must be based on an analysis of the various sources of the royalties listed in Exhibit 15.3 as well as on a review of the expectations regarding "revival" versions of some of these plays. (In the past, this generated important royalty flows.) A significant portion of the royalties has considerable stability. As the exhibit shows, there has been a general upward trend in revenues. From 2007 to 2016, revenue is projected to continue growing at 8% per year; after that, growth is expected to decline over time to the long-run inflation expectation (3.0%). For the revenue forecasts, specific periods were considered during which the projected growth rate gradually adjusts to the long-term trend. In this example, a rate of 7% was selected for the decade beginning 2017, with further 1% declines every 10 years until 2060, the end of the last copyright protection term. Along the forecast term, finally, royalty for the earliest plays will stop, resulting in further episodic declines in revenues.

External Parameters

The basic external parameter to consider in the valuation is the appropriate discount rate. A comprehensive analysis of its characteristics revealed that the risk level of Mr. Broadway's portfolio is more comparable to one of fixed-income securities than equities. To determine a corporate discount rate, the elements of the weighted average cost of capital (WACC) are well established. In a case like this, it is often necessary to rely on the alternative build-up method using data from Ibbotson Associates' "Stocks, Bonds, Bills & Inflation," now published by Morningstar. This method entails constructing the appropriate discount rate by considering these four components (see Chapter 9):

1. The long horizon real return to capital in the economy (assume 2%).
2. The expected long-term inflation rate (assume 3%).
3. The additional long-term risk associated with corporate fixed income securities (assume a 2% spread).
4. The risk premium specific to the intangible asset class (assume 3%). There is empirical support for an intangible asset risk spread of between 2% and 5%. In this case, the selection corresponds to a low-risk scenario.

The discount rate is the total of those four factors, in this case, 10%. Obviously, in any specific application, the inflation and risk profile of the jurisdiction, as well as the growth in revenues, may vary greatly.

Valuation Analyses

The fair value of the copyright portfolio is the net present value, at the discount rate just determined, of the projected royalties over the various copyright terms. Given the length of the projected period, Exhibit 15.4 shows only a summary of the calculations. The discount rate is applied using the midyear convention, so that the fair value of the portfolio is estimated as of the end of 2006.

Exhibit 15.4 Expected Annual Royalty Income, Mr. Broadway's Copyright Portfolio (Thousands USD)

Year	Periods to Discount	Total Royalty Revenue	Present Value (PV) Factor	PV Royalty Revenue
2007	0.5	$ 198	0.9535	$ 188
2008	1.5	213	0.8668	185
2009	2.5	231	0.7880	182
2010	3.5	249	0.7164	178
2011	4.5	269	0.6512	175
2012	5.5	290	0.5920	172
2013	6.5	314	0.5382	169
2014	7.5	339	0.4893	166
2015	8.5	366	0.4448	163
2016	9.5	395	0.4044	160
2017	10.5	423	0.3676	155
2018	11.5	452	0.3342	151
2019	12.5	484	0.3038	147
2020	13.5	518	0.2762	143
2021	14.5	554	0.2511	139
2022	15.5	593	0.2283	135
2023	16.5	634	0.2075	132
2024	17.5	679	0.1886	128
2025	18.5	726	0.1715	125
2026	19.5	777	0.1559	121
2027	20.5	824	0.1417	117
2028	21.5	873	0.1288	113
2029	22.5	926	0.1171	108
2030	23.5	981	0.1065	104
2031	24.5	1,040	0.0968	101
2032	25.5	997	0.0880	88
2033	26.5	1,056	0.0800	85
2034	27.5	1,120	0.0727	81
2035	28.5	1,187	0.0661	78
2036	29.5	1,258	0.0601	76
2037	30.5	1,321	0.0546	72
2038	31.5	1,387	0.0497	69
2039	32.5	1,457	0.0452	66
2040	33.5	1,529	0.0411	63
2041	34.5	1,606	0.0373	60
2042	35.5	1,686	0.0339	57
2043	36.5	1,770	0.0308	55
2044	37.5	1,859	0.0280	52
2045	38.5	1,952	0.0255	50
2046	39.5	2,049	0.0232	47
2047	40.5	2,073	0.0211	44
2048	41.5	2,156	0.0192	41
2049	42.5	2,242	0.0174	39
2050	43.5	1,715	0.0158	27
2051	44.5	845	0.0144	12
2052	45.5	879	0.0131	11
2053	46.5	912	0.0119	11
2054	47.5	948	0.0108	10

Year	Periods to Discount	Total Royalty Revenue	Present Value (PV) Factor	PV Royalty Revenue
2055	48.5	963	0.0098	9
2056	49.5	1,000	0.0089	9
2057	50.5	1,030	0.0081	8
2058	51.5	1,027	0.0074	8
2059	52.5	1,058	0.0067	7
2060	53.5	1,090	0.0061	7
			NPV	**$ 4,899**

Valuation Conclusions

In this simplified example, the current fair value of Mr. Broadway's copyright portfolio is approximately $4.9 million. In practice, it is customary to consider the consequences of errors in estimating the amount of risk by varying the discount rate within a suitable range, in conjunction with various revenue growth rates. While the entire conclusion is dependent on certain assumptions, it is essential to quantify the sensitivity of the final figure to key variables. This sensitivity analysis can then inform the valuator and management about the likelihood of material impairment charges in the future as the actual performance deviates from the expected path.

In this case, because of the long remaining life of those copyrights, the valuator would likely suggest the adoption of the revaluation model to reflect the gift in the recipient's statement of financial position. During the copyrights' remaining life, materially significant changes might make the original fair value underreport the asset as rights to make movies (or remake ones previously made) based on the plays may create additional royalties. These and other considerations about uncertainties over the next 50 years would support such choice vis-à-vis the cost model.

CASE STUDY II: DIGITAL COPYRIGHTS

Copyright valuation projects frequently arise in connection with acquisitions. This example considers a broadcaster (TV-XMPL) that acquires the assets of a production firm (Content Limitada); among them is a copyright portfolio. The objective is to determine the fair value of this asset under IFRS.

Identification and Asset Attributes

The copyrights include seven different television series created by Content Limitada, with total production costs shown in Exhibit 15.4.

Exhibit 15.5 Total Production Costs, Content Limitada

TV Series	Production Year	Production Cost ($'000)	Annual Revenue ($'000)
AA	1990	120	5
BB	1995	150	100
CC	1997	225	0
DD	2000	500	50
EE	2003	400	100
FF	2004	1,000	250
GG	2006	500	10

The copyrights are initially classified into three groups: Obsolete (TV Series CC), which is no longer producing revenue and is not expected to do so in the near future; Legacy (Series AA and BB), which still generates revenue but has less than three years of foreseeable demand, and Core (Series DD through GG), which currently deliver sales and are expected to do so for more than three years.

The Obsolete series will not be recognized under IFRS since no revenue is expected and, while still under copyright protection, they do not qualify as assets. The Legacy series qualify as assets, but, due to their short remaining lives, special attention should be paid to their revenue forecasts, as their only source of sales is DVD releases, as they do not benefit from any distribution contracts. The remaining, Core assets, are subject to established contracts that allow for reliable royalty projections; management expects them to perform as average properties, declining to half their present annual revenue, as they enter DVD release once the existing broadcasting contracts expire.

Methodology Selection

Upon reviewing the characteristics of each class, the valuator recommends a value of zero for the obsolete assets, allocating 100% of their cost, if any, to goodwill. The Legacy assets should be valued under a strict cost model, as there is substantial uncertainty as to the continuity of their revenues; if they exceed the acquisition cost, that will mostly be the result of efficient management at TV-XMPL, and all incremental revenue should be attributed to the acquirer. The Core assets, for which the Income Approach is the most relevant, may be better reported under the revaluation model, as they are significant assets in a dynamic industry and may appreciate as the global demand for this type of IPR expands.

External Parameters

The applicable discount rate in this case is the WACC for the industry (assumed at 20%). The expected growth of royalties, mainly reflecting inflation and export expansion, is 10%.

Valuation Analyses

Each of the two groups of copyrights expected to generate revenues, Legacy and Core, is valued by a different approach.

Legacy group. This group is valued under the Cost Approach, with Exhibit 15.6 reflecting the various components to be taken into account. The starting point is the acquisition cost, derived from the transaction documents; other considerations are: the acquirer's additional costs to reestablish the assets' revenue generation; direct labor costs to film and reedit title sequences; direct costs of repackaging existing DVD inventory (assumed outsourced); and allocations of administrative, transportation, and supervisory costs to the rebranding process.

Exhibit 15.6 Cost Approach Valuation, Legacy Copyright Class

Category	Legacy Assets ($'000)
Acquisition Cost	1,050
Rebranding Costs	1
Editing	5
Packaging	4
Indirect Cost Allocation	5
Total Value	1,065

Exhibit 15.6 gives a value of $1,065,000 to the Legacy assets; management estimates that they will continue to generate revenues for only the next two years, giving rise to annual amortization charges of $532,500.

Core group. For the Core assets, the Income Approach valuation is based on detailed revenue projections for each TV series, as illustrated in Exhibit 15.7.

Exhibit 15.7 Income Approach Valuation, Core Copyright Class, Revenue Forecast ($'000)

Year	DD	EE	FF	GG
2009	55.00	110.00	275.00	11.00
2010	60.50	121.00	302.50	12.10
2011	66.55	133.10	332.75	13.31
2012	36.60	146.41	366.03	14.64
2013	39.53	161.05	402.63	16.11
2014	41.90	177.16	442.89	17.72
2015	43.58	97.44	487.18	19.49
2016	44.45	105.23	267.95	21.44
2017	35.56	111.54	289.38	23.58
2018	-	116.01	306.75	12.97
2019	-	118.33	319.02	14.01
Beyond (2025)		112.41	350.92	15.06

The value of those assets is the present value, at the 20% discount rate estimated for this project of each year's expected revenues. For simplicity, revenue expected after 2019 is assumed to be received during 2025. The high discount rate, reflecting the risks typical in the industry, yields a fair value of approximately $3 million, which is consistent with the allocated acquisition cost (see Exhibit 15.8).

Exhibit 15.8 Income Approach Valuation, Core Copyright Class, Revenue Forecast Valuation ($'000)

Category	Core Assets ($'000)	PV Revenue ($'000)
Acquisition Cost	3,100	
2009	451	494
2010	496	453
2011	546	415
2012	564	357
2013	619	327
2014	680	299
2015	648	238
2016	439	134
2017	460	117
2018	436	93
2019	451	80
Beyond (2025)	478	28
TOTAL		3,036

Valuation Conclusions

The values of the acquired assets in this example are shown in Exhibit 15.9.

Exhibit 15.9 Valuation Summary, TV-XMPL's Acquisition of Content Ltd. ($'000)

Asset Class	Acquisition Cost	Fair Value	Goodwill Impact
Obsolete	50	0	50
Legacy	1,050	1,065	–15
Core	3,100	3,036	64
Total	4,200	4,101	99

Each asset class will be amortized over its remaining (finite) useful life, with only approximately 2% of the acquisition cost being recorded as goodwill.

CASE STUDY III: ENFORCING COPYRIGHTS

Most cases of copyright infringement are in the recording and film industries. Nevertheless, in everyday business practice, it has been easy, if not advantageous, to ignore the copyrights of others. Eventually, enforcement actions can have serious financial consequences, and a valuation of the infringed copyrights is usually at the core of courts' determination to establish the recovery for prevailing owners. As noted at the beginning of this chapter, copyrights are internationally enforced, and remedies are localized. The next example is based on an actual case in the United States, but the underlying principles are valid in most jurisdictions.

Copyrights as Property

Lowry's Reports, Inc., a six-person business, publishes a daily newsletter titled *New York Stock Exchange Market Trend Analysis* and carefully registers every issue with the United States Copyright Office, although this formality is not strictly necessary. Lowry's newsletter is well respected among investors for its technical analyses and stock ratings, indicators, and recommendations. By choice, Lowry's limits subscriptions to individuals. Subscribers must execute agreements that strictly prohibit unauthorized copying or dissemination of the newsletter or its contents; no institutions or groups are allowed to subscribe. In 2003, Lowry's filed a copyright infringement suit against investment brokerage firm Legg Mason, Inc.

According to the evidence in the case, the copyright infringement began in 1994, when an administrative employee in Legg Mason's Baltimore research department subscribed.[2] The technical analyses numbers contained in the newsletter were communicated daily to the firm's brokers during their customary "morning call," and for years the whole daily issue was faxed to branch offices and further distributed among Legg Mason's 1,540 stockbrokers. Starting in 1999, the research department posted every daily and weekly issue of Lowry's publication on Legg Mason's intranet; additional copies circulated via e-mail.

Copyright Valuation

In this example, the copyright valuation process was applied to estimate the loss (or actual economic damage) suffered by Lowry's before considering how the actual enforcement case was resolved.

Identification. The asset in this situation is clearly identified based on the copyright registrations and in the company's financial records by the customer subscription revenues. A list of all copyright registrations for the 2,250 daily issues between 1994 and 2002 was attached to the valuation report to fully support the analyses.

Methodology selection. The goal of the valuation is to determine the present value (as of 2003) of the profits Lowry's lost as a result of the infringing reproduction of the newsletter within the Legg Mason organization. The Income Approach is the most suitable methodology in this situation, because the case is not concerned with the value of the newsletter as a whole, which would be the conclusion of the Market Approach, and the copyright owner did not lose the actual cost of producing the asset, only incremental revenue.

Asset attributes. For this example, the relevant asset attributes are summarized in the next set of facts. The infringement period runs for the full year of 1994 through the end of 2002. Each year, 250 daily issues are published and sold through a subscription service at $700 per year. Over the nine years under consideration, an increasing number of infringing copies were made by the defendant, according to the schedule shown in Exhibit 15.10. In the absence of an infringement, each broker would have had to be a subscriber to get the information; thus, Lowry lost the sales estimated in the exhibit. In the United States at least, a patent infringement case would require the additional step of proving that the plaintiff would have had the capacity to make the lost sales claimed, or only a portion of them; this is not required in copyright cases.

---

[2]   *271 F. Supp.2d 737, Civil No. WDQ-01-3898 (D. Md., July 10, 2003).*

Exhibit 15.10 Lost Subscription Revenue, Lowry's v. Legg Mason Copyright Case
(Hypothetical, in thousands of $US)

Year	Issues copied	Copies made from each issue	Subscription Revenue Lost @ $700/yr
1994	250	100	$ 70
1995	250	250	175
1996	250	500	350
1997	250	750	525
1998	250	1,000	700
1999	250	1,200	840
2000	250	1,350	945
2001	250	1,540	1,078
2002	250	1,540	1,078
Total			$ 5,761

As shown, total lost sales amounted to $5.76 million. The value to the copyright owner is not directly the lost sales but only the net profit derived from them; this valuation uses the average 20% net margin, derived from analyses of the operations during the relevant period. In U.S. civil litigation, the relevant measure is net profits before income taxes, since monies awarded for damages are taxable.

External parameters. One peculiarity of this case is that the Income Approach was applied to past revenues, while it is the Cost Approach that looks at past expenditures. Thus, to calculate present values as of 2003, past lost profits have to be adjusted for the lost opportunity that is another consequence of the infringement. For instance, the profits that should have been made in 1994 would have been reinvested in the company according to its policies. Although it is difficult to model how such additional cash flows would have been used, a simplifying assumption (in litigation and this example) is that those lost profits would have continued generating earnings at the firm's average net return on equity (ROE) of 15%. Depending on the jurisdiction, however, this rate is sometimes reduced to the prevailing risk-free rate. Thus, past lost profits would be brought to their present value by compounding earnings at this rate.

Valuation analysis. The previously estimated lost revenue is now valued by applying a net profit margin, to determine annual lost profits, and compounded at the ROE, to arrive at the net present value of the copyright infringement damages in this case (see Exhibit 15.11).

Exhibit 15.11 Present Value of Lost Profits, Lowry's v. Legg Mason Copyright Case
(Hypothetical, in thousands US$)

Year	Issues copied	Copies made from each issue	Subscription Revenue Lost @ $700/yr	Net Profit Margin @ 20%	Opportunity Lost @ 15%	Total PV Damages
1994	250	100	$ 70	$ 14	$ 35	$ 49
1995	250	250	175	35	72	107
1996	250	500	350	70	116	186
1997	250	750	525	105	138	243
1998	250	1,000	700	140	142	282
1999	250	1,200	840	168	126	294
2000	250	1,350	945	189	98	287
2001	250	1,540	1,078	216	70	285
2002	250	1,540	1,078	216	32	248
Total			$ 5,761	$1,152	$829	$1,981

The result is a total of approximately $2 million. Comparing this with the avoided subscription cost ($5.7 million) shows that this can be only a partial measure of the damages, if infringement litigation is to serve as a deterrent. Simply put, if the only remedy available to Lowry's was merely to recover lost profits, Legg Mason would have acted rationally as, by definition, the correct subscription cost would have been 2.9 times the adjusted lost profit infringement damages; this is a central issue in copyright enforcement.

Valuation Conclusions

The preceding valuation only calculated the value of the copyrights portfolio to its owner; it did not quantify the benefit the infringer derived. In this case, an accurate accounting of the infringer's profits would be very complicated. Legg Mason benefited from following, and advising clients to follow, the technical indicators and recommendations in Lowry's newsletter, from which everybody profited. If this was not the case, presumably, Legg Mason would not have persisted on the infringement.

An alternative to accurately accounting for the exact profit apportionment of huge numbers of stock trades is the award of statutory damages; because of the diligent registration of Lowry's newsletter, this remedy, which in the United States is applicable only to registered copyrights, was available.

Judge's Action

Rather than considering a lost profits calculation like the one in this example, the trial judge instructed the jury that, if it found that Legg Mason had knowingly or recklessly disregarded possible infringements of Lowry's copyrights, the law permitted it to award up to $150,000 in damages for each issue of Lowry's newsletter covered by a separate registered copyright. The jury awarded $50,000 for each infringement that occurred before Lowry's gave notice of infringement and $100,000 for each work infringed after the notice.

In those circumstances, a court has a broad discretion to award an amount that it deems "just" taking into account all the circumstances and the need to deter and punish the guilty, encourage copyright enforcement, and ensure that the infringer does not benefit from its actions. In the end, the jury trial resulted in a finding that Legg Mason had willfully infringed the copyrights of Lowry's Reports and awarded Lowry's statutory damages of just under $20 million. The prestigious investment brokerage, therefore, ended up paying $2,400 for each $700 subscription it had avoided.

16 CUSTOMER RELATIONSHIPS

BRANDI L. RUFFALO

UNITED STATES

INTRODUCTION

The customer is king in all businesses. Without buyers for products or services, the firm will fail. Although they are important to every entity, not all businesses have customer relationships; those are created through ongoing, repeated interactions between buyers and an entity. They lead to clients developing a good impression of the firm, thereby improving the chances they will continue to buy. The expectation of continuing sales to existing customers due to such relationships is a valuable intangible asset. In fact, numerous firms have been acquired for the sole purpose of gaining access to their customers. Customer relationships are among the most prevalent intangible assets, even within large, multiline organizations.

For many entities, the ability to retain long-term relationships with loyal customers remains a primary objective, as each interaction creates ongoing, lasting financial benefits. In the extreme form, customer relationships are the predominant driver of a firm's value. Here is the sum of the lifetime values of existing and future purchasers. From a purely mathematical point of view:

$$\text{Business Value} = \sum_{1}^{\text{All Customers}} \text{NPV [Expected Customer Cash Flows]}$$

$$\text{Business Value} = \sum_{1}^{\text{All Customers}} \text{NPV [(Probability of Continuing Relationship)} \times \text{(Purchase Frequency \& Duration)} \times \text{(Economic Benefit of Transaction)]}$$

The importance of identifying and quantifying customer relationships, which can be one of the most valuable soft assets, has increased substantially over the past few years due to the introduction of International Financial Reporting Standard (IFRS) 3.

Variables that Define Customer Relationships

Obtaining customers through advertising, promotions, word of mouth, and other marketing endeavors is an essential activity to a successful business. A description of the necessary techniques is beyond the scope of this chapter, but the general idea to "first get 'em, then massage 'em" has been successfully practiced for centuries. Add to this, the need to obtain as much information as possible about them and their buying habits.

When valuing customer relationships, it is important to understand the benefits that the target's customers derive by using its products or services: in other words, why they buy and for how long they can be expected to do so. The acquirer's ability to retain them and the level of available information about them is critical to the existence and value of customer relationships.

Ability to Retain the Relationships

A business's ability to retain the target's customer relationships is a significant source of value as long as those relationships continue to generate cash flows. Customers, or even customer segments, will go on doing business with an entity over a long period without changing or even reviewing their buying decisions. In such cases, the customer relationships will have significant value, since they are likely to contribute consistent, ongoing cash flows for a long time. If there are new or changing influences on customers' behavior, such as new competitors, that value may be lost.

Level of Customer Information

A firm's ability to capture and retain information about its customers increases the potential value of the relationships; for instance, having basic information—name, phone number, e-mail, address—is the minimum needed to keep up regular contact. The situation can be improved by tracking buying habits, purchasing preferences, propensities to pay, and other factors, which are much more useful in helping to maintain and expand the relationships.

Customers without a Relationship

Some customers who make one-time purchases or are strictly price shoppers do not have an established ongoing relationship with a firm; additionally, there are former customers who used to have recurring relationships but have ceased to do business with a firm. A long period of inactivity without interaction suggests that the entity can no longer expect any further economic benefit from those particular customers; for that reason, they have limited value. Finally, some enterprises, such as movie theaters and fast food outlets, mainly have "anonymous" customers about whom they have no information at all. Retail stores that rely solely on location and "transactional" purchases do not have any customer relationships; their location often has value, but this should not be confused with the importance of customer relationships.

In general, the next groups of buyers are not considered to lead to customer relationships:

- One-time buyers, without a recurring connection
- Former purchasers, who have not generated any business for a certain period (which will vary depending on the nature of the industry)
- Individuals about whom the vendor does not have basic data

Customers with a Relationship

Customer relationships exist when there is an ongoing interaction between the customer and the entity. This is validated and strengthened when both parties are able to get in touch with one another. Not only should customers know the firm that provides a particular service, but also, sellers should be able to identify customers to collect and track appropriate information in order to enhance their relationships. In a number of industries, customer relationships may be sold or transferred, which means that a buyer can take over the continued expectation of customer patronage and recurring economic benefits. This can best be seen when a bank acquires a branch of another institution; usually, most of the existing customer relationships and their deposits remain after the transaction is complete.

Other than those just mentioned, all customer relationships have value; some of the information tracked to enhance them by different types of businesses are outlined next.

Business	*Customer*	*Special Information*
Newspaper	Subscribers	Address/neighborhood
Magazine	Subscribers	Specific or general interests
Insurance agencies	Insured	Homeowners' policy and level of coverage
		Coverage of incremental items
		Driving records, claims records
Financial advisors	Investors	Level of wealth/savings
		Risk tolerances
		Preferences
		Investment goals and objectives
Mortgage lenders	Homeowners	Price of home
		Mortgage: amount, interest rate, amortization schedule
		Income and assets used to qualify for mortgage
Physicians/hospitals	Patients	Medical records and history
		Allergies and prescription patterns
		Insurance and deductible amounts

RANGE OF RELATIONSHIPS

Once the existence of customer relationships is recognized, it is important to establish where each relationship falls in the range of values, as shown in Exhibit 16.1.

Exhibit 16.1 Range of Customer Relationship Values

At the low end, customer relationships are not a significant value driver; customers view the service or product as a commodity, continually reassessing who or what they buy at every purchase. At the high end, relationships are a primary value driver. The next listings illustrate the different characteristics of businesses with limited as opposed to strong customer relationships.

Characteristics of Businesses with *Limited Customer Relationships*	*Characteristics of Businesses with* *Strong Customer Relationships*
Commodity products/services	Exclusivity of product/service
Location, convenience drives purchase	Not driven by location/convenience
Use of nonowned brand names	Brands are owned or exclusively licensed
Relationships tied to people	Limited effect of discounting
Seasons or events drive purchase	Relationships tied to business
Require constant advertising/promotion	Less need for advertising/promotion
Volatile sales	Customer may prepay or wait for delivery
Low cost of customer replacement	Long sales cycle
Discounting used to drive sales	Up-front investment in customers
Short sales cycle/spot purchase	Product/service difficult to substitute

Although the listed characteristics provide an outline for assessing customer relationships, it is important to note that they may also indicate the existence of other intangible assets, such as trade names, brands, and/or proprietary technologies that contribute to the creation of value. This may lead to lower values for customer relationships.

Contractual and Noncontractual Relationships

Customer relationships may arise from contracts, such as those for supplies or services, but they are not essential to establishing a relationship. The link created through the contract may be complemented by outside components that create value. IFRS provides guidelines for both contractual and noncontractual relationships. The next section sets out specific language for several important variables relating to customer relationships.

RELEVANT IFRS LANGUAGE

IFRS 3 (2008) lists customer relationships as one of the five identified areas for potentially recognizable intangible assets, separate from goodwill, in a business combination. Like other intangibles, they should be recognized if they meet either the separability or contractual-legal criterion identified in International Accounting Standard (IAS) 38.12.

Contractual-Legal Criterion

An intangible that arises from contractual or other legal rights is recognizable regardless of whether those rights are transferable or separable from the target or from other rights and obligations (IAS 38.12[b]). Intangible assets identified as having a contractual base may also be separable, but this is not a necessary condition to meet the criterion (IFRS 3[2008].IE17).

Separability criterion. The separability criterion means that an acquired intangible asset is capable of being separated or divided from the target and sold, transferred, licensed, rented, or exchanged, either individually or together with a related contract, identifiable asset, or liability. An acquired intangible meets this criterion if there is evidence of exchange transactions for that type of asset, or an asset of a similar type, even if those transactions are infrequent, and regardless of whether the acquirer is involved in them (IFRS 3[2008].B33). This standard presumes that when an intangible asset satisfies either of the criteria, sufficient information should exist to reliably measure its fair value. As a result, a value must be established for that intangible; originally, IFRS 3(2004) included reliability of measurement as a condition for recognition.

Examples of Customer-Related Intangibles

The examples of customer-related intangibles provided by the International Accounting Standards Board (IASB) are order backlogs, customer contracts, noncontractual customer relationships, and customer lists, as shown next. Accordingly, both contractual and noncontractual relationships should be recognized (IFRS 3[2008].IE23). The most common noncontractual relationships are customer lists; see below.

Class	*Basis*
Order or production backlog	Contractual
Customer contracts and related customer relationships	Contractual
Noncontractual customer relationships	Separable
Customer lists	Separable

Order or production backlog. An order or production backlog arises from contracts such as purchase or sales orders that have not yet been delivered in full. If acquired in a business combination, this meets the contractual-legal criterion, even if the purchase or sales orders are subsequently canceled (IFRS 3[2008].IE25).

Customer contracts and customer relationships. Customer lists and related information (buying patterns, demographics, etc.) are identifiable assets that are not based on contractual obligations. Customer relationships may be contractual or noncontractual but should be identified whether they are separable or not. If an entity establishes relationships with its customers through contracts, the relationships arise from contractual rights. Therefore, customer contracts and the accompanying relationships acquired in a business combination meet the contractual-legal criterion, even if confidentiality or other contractual terms prohibit the sale or transfer of a contract separately from the target (IFRS 3[2008].IE26). A customer contract and the associated customer relationship are not necessarily the same but may represent two distinct intangible assets. Both their useful lives and the patterns in which their economic benefits are consumed may differ (IFRS 3[2008].IE27).

A relationship exists between an entity and its customer if (a) the entity has information about and regular contact with the customer, and (b) the customer has the ability to make direct contact with the entity. Such relationships meet the contractual-legal criterion if an entity regularly enters into contracts, such as standing orders, with its customers, regardless of whether any exists at the valuation date. Also, customer relationships are created from other means than contracts, such as through regular contacts by sales or service representatives (IFRS 3[2008].IE28).

Examples

The next examples, based on IFRS 3(2008).IE.30, illustrate the recognition of the intangible assets acquired in a business combination that represent customer contracts and relationships.

Acquirer (AC) acquires Target (TC) in a business combination on 31 December 2008.

- TC has a five-year agreement to supply goods to Customer A. Both TC and AC believe that Customer A will renew the agreement, which is not separable, at the end of the current period. Whether cancelable or not, the agreement meets the contractual-legal criterion. Additionally, because TC established its relationship with Customer A through a contract, not only the agreement itself but also TC's customer relationship meets the criterion.

- TC manufactures goods in two distinct lines of business, sporting goods and electronics; Customer B purchases both. TC has a contract with Customer B to be its exclusive provider of sporting goods but has no contract for the supply of electronics. Both TC and AC believe that only one overall customer relationship exists between TC and Customer B. The contract to be Customer B's exclusive supplier of sporting goods, whether cancelable or not, meets the contractual-legal criterion. Additionally, because TC established that relationship through a contract, it also meets the criterion. Because TC has only one relationship with Customer B, its fair value incorporates estimates relating to sales of both sporting goods and electronics. However, if AC determines that the two relationships with Customer B are separate, AC would likely determine that the electronics relationship did not meet the separability criterion as an intangible asset.

- TC does business with its customers solely through purchase and sales orders. At 31 December, 2008, it had a backlog of purchase orders from 60% of its customers, all recurring buyers. So are the other 40%, but, as of that date, there were no open purchase orders or other contracts with them. Regardless of whether they are cancelable or not, the purchase orders meet the contractual-legal criterion. Additionally, because TC solely deals through contracts, not only the purchase orders but also the customer relationships meet the criterion. As TC has a practice of establishing contracts with the remaining 40% of its customers, those relationships also arise through contractual rights and meet the criterion, even though there are no current contracts in force.

• TC is an insurance company with a portfolio of one-year automobile contracts that are cancelable by the policy holders. Because TC establishes its relationships with them through contracts, the customer relationships meet the contractual-legal criterion, even though the contracts are cancelable. IAS 36, *Impairment of Assets*, and IAS 38, *Intangible Assets*, apply to those relationships.

Depositor Relationships

According to IFRS 3(2008).B34, customer relationships acquired in a business combination that do not arise from a contract may, nevertheless, be identifiable intangible assets, if the relationship is separable. Exchange transactions for similar assets which indicate that other entities have sold or otherwise transferred a particular type of noncontractual customer relationships provide evidence of separability. Even though an intangible asset may not be individually separable from the target, it meets the criterion if it is separable in combination with a related contract, identifiable asset, or liability. For instance, financial institutions, such as banks and trust companies, commonly transfer deposit liabilities and the associated depositor relationships in recorded exchange transactions through purchases and sales of established branches. Therefore, an acquirer should recognize the depositor relationship as an intangible asset separate from goodwill.

Customer Lists

Customer lists consist of information about customers, including their names and contact information; it may be solely a paper listing or a database that includes other information, as for instance order and payment histories and demographic details. Customer lists do not usually arise from contractual or other legal rights but are often leased or exchanged. Therefore, a customer or subscriber list acquired in a business combination normally meets the separability criterion (IFRS 3[2008].IE24). Even if a target believes its lists have characteristics different from others, the fact that such documents are frequently licensed generally means that an acquired list also meets the criterion (IFRS 3[2008].B33). However, that is not met if the terms of confidentiality or other agreements prohibit an entity from selling, leasing, or otherwise exchanging information about its customers.

Professional-service firms (e.g., accountants, lawyers, mortgage brokers, advertising agencies, investment advisors, insurance agents) all have customer relationships that are typically not contractual but are separable from the entity.

VALUE INDICATORS

The value of customer relationships is derived from their expected future economic benefits; acquirers are willing to pay for these future earnings if they anticipate that the relationships will remain strong after the change of ownership. To quantify their value, future cash flows from existing customers at the time of acquisition must be estimated based on certain indicators. This can be difficult, since each firm's customers have different characteristics. Additionally, there may be many different groups (or segments) of customers within an entity. Those will likely have various life expectancies, purchasing patterns, product mixes, and service requirements. Therefore, this section first discusses customer segmentation, then customer life expectancy, both of which affect revenues and profitability.

Customer Segmentation

In valuing customer relationships, it is important to understand the segmentation of customers. This is based on groupings of customers with similar characteristics; the goal is to quantify the economic differences between them over their lifetimes. The concept of loyalty affects the strength of customer relationships and provides a useful framework for segmentation. Over time, loyal customers tend not only to make more purchases but also to choose more products with higher average prices. Loyalty improves customers' purchase frequency, volume, mix of products/services, levels of profitability, and retention rates. Therefore, loyalty, which is based on many factors, determines the profitability of a group; it includes satisfaction, which is the aggregate of buyers' sentiments towards the product or service, forms the basis of retaining purchasers in competitive circumstances, and generates:

- Repeat purchases
- Higher volumes
- Greater participation in a product line
- Resistance to competitive pressures

Those variables lead to greater life expectancy, higher revenues, lower costs to serve, and ultimately higher net cash flows. As a result, they increase the value of the customer relationships.

The major work in this field is *The Loyalty Effect* by Frederick Reichheld, of Bain & Company, the international management consultants.[1] The book's theme is that although U.S. corporations lose at least half of their customers within five years, half of their employees within four years, and half of their investors in one year, loyalty is not dead; instead it remains one of the most significant factors in successfully continuing in business. One way of raising customers' lifetime values is to increase retention rates; according to Reichheld, improving them by five percentage points may result in as much as a double-digit gain in lifetime profits.

Life Expectancy/Duration

Firms can capture future economic benefits from existing customers only if they maintain their relationships. Therefore, it is essential to understand the duration of a customer relationship. It begins with the first purchase and ends when the customer no longer needs the product/service or when he or she switches to a competitor. The difficulty of assessing the appropriate life of customer relationships complicates determining such values. Duration and life expectancies may be estimated through a number of techniques including analyzing past trends in customer behavior and applying them to the acquired customers.

Customers may decide at any time to stop utilizing an entity's products or services for many reasons, which include:

- Dissatisfaction with the firm's products/service
- Competitive products that provide better benefits (quality, price, etc.)
- Relocation to different geographic areas

Over time, most customers stop doing business with the entity; several methods to estimate their life expectancy are discussed in the next section.

Life expectancy metrics. To identify the life expectancy of various customer groups, it is helpful to consider a variety of models over the relevant historic period. The statistics used will depend on the amount and quality of available data. Such a lifetime analysis assists in determining the remaining useful lives of the customer relationships, which is important in establishing both the related cash flows and the period over which the asset should be amortized.

Depending on the availability of data, one or more of these measures may be useful:

---

[1] *Frederick Reichheld, **The Loyalty Effect** (Boston: Harvard Business School, 1996).*

- *Retention rate.* The proportion of a customer group at the beginning of a period (usually a year) that is still buying at the end; for example, a cellular phone company may lose up to 5% of its customers each year due to contracts expiring and being replaced by technology and competitors. The retention rate is 95% and in future years should decline slowly.
- *Maintenance rate.* The number of customers retained divided by those lost; in our cellular phone example, this is 95% divided by 5%, or 19 times; this should rise in the future.
- *Churn rate.* The number of customers lost in any period divided by the total of (a) those at the beginning plus (b) those added; returning to the cellular phone example, if 5% of the customers at the beginning of the year are lost and 8% are added, the churn rate is 4.6%; this should decline over time.

A review of those rates over time offers a look into what can be expected looking forward; making the calculations for all relevant customer segments gives further insight into each of their expected lives. Other than survivor curves, there are no generally accepted means of estimating such periods; therefore, different firms adopt various techniques, which are often qualitative rather than quantitative.

Survivor curves. The application of survivor curves to historic attrition rates previously discussed provides a rigorous method to substantiate the analyses of customer life spans. A number of statistical techniques are available. Two categories, Iowa-type, and Weibull distributions, are the primary survivor curves employed by valuators. The Iowa-type curves were developed from empirical observation of the retirement experience for a wide variety of physical assets, originally in the U.S. railway industry, while Weibull distributions are a theoretical mathematical construct used to describe survivorship characteristics for a range of populations. Survivor-curve selection comes either from a formal statistical analysis or from the exercise of informed judgment regarding population mortality. Statistical analyses of customer populations rely on actuarial techniques to establish remaining useful lives (RULs) of customer relationships while informed judgment selects a survivor curve based on experience. Once a suitable curve has been chosen, it is relatively easy to estimate the RUL, which is an integral part of all valuation methods:

- *Income approach.* The projected period for the economic income
- *Cost approach.* The basis of the amount deducted for obsolescence
- *Market approach.* Its analysis helps select/reject/adjust comparable transaction data

Revenues

Customers' purchasing behavior reflected in their customer relationships produces a revenue stream for the entity, which reflects their frequency and volume of purchases over time. Frequency records the number of purchases that a group of customers makes over a specific period. This is only one component of the value; it does not measure the size of the benefit, only how often it occurs. Volume represents the size of the purchases by the group over time, reflecting the number of items and their price. Higher prices and quantities of items purchased mean more potential value for the customer relationship. Volume and frequency combine to determine the revenue derived from a customer group in a month, quarter, or year.

Not all customers are created equal, and the well-established 80/20 rule applies. Reichheld divides them into four categories of declining importance: "Loyalists," "Growables," "Satisfieds," and "Also Rans." In general, profits come mainly from Loyalists, who have the only customer relationships with significant value. The Growables and Satisfieds contribute to overhead and keep the business alive while the Also Rans are likely actually to reduce earnings.

The groups all differ in sales profitability; assessing this profitability is important in valuing of the relationship, but it is often difficult to determine, as it depends on hard-to-obtain information. Ideally, management should establish by customer group:

- Underlying trends in sales
- Seasonal patterns
- Products/services mix
- Effective gross margins
- Cost drivers, such as the numbers of sales calls, orders, shipments, invoices, support requests, as well as average receivable balances; these will allow reasonable allocations of the appropriate expenses

Those analyses will enable the costs required to serve a group of customers to be combined with the margins associated with their purchases in order to create an image of the value of the relationships.

Contributory Assets

In addition to the allocation of the costs to service customers, it is important to determine the additional assets required to maintain their future relationships. These include:

- Working capital
- Property, plant, and equipment
- Intangibles (in-process research and development, assembled workforce, software, patented and unpatented technologies, trade names, trademarks, etc.)

Establishing the levels of and returns on the contributory assets is a major problem in valuing customer relationships. For a bank, contributory assets are branches and staff; for a retailer, location, display space, inventory, experienced employees, and convenient financing. Every situation likely will include intangible assets, such as brand names and the core technologies necessary to obtain and run a business.

Valuators seek to separate the net cash flows generated by the relationships from those attributable to the other items. This is usually done by: (a) deducting an imputed return on each class of contributory asset; (b) using a percentage of cash flows based on industry experience; or (c) capitalizing the excess earnings obtained from the customer over a "normal" margin, which can be done in one of two ways: using the average achieved by the firm in the past or using publicly traded guidelines. In the first case, only the few customers with above-average margins qualify; in the second, if the entity has higher margins than the average of the guidelines, nearly everyone is included; in the author's view, the latter is the appropriate position.

VALUATION METHODOLOGIES

Other than for bank branches, there are few reported transactions in customer relationships; therefore, nearly all of them are valued by the income or cost approaches.

Income Approach

A discounted cash flow (DCF) method under the income approach is probably the most commonly used technique for valuing customer relationships. The objective is to obtain the present value of the anticipated future economic benefits generated by the relationships.

Before beginning the valuation, it is necessary to determine two things, whether the customer relationships generate discernible cash flows and how long the relationships are expected to continue. To use the DCF method effectively, those cash flows should be both measurable and separable. The economic benefits from relationships are based on the anticipated future revenues less expenses and investments. In the analyses, after allowing for some attrition, only revenue from existing customers is considered. Often the intangible asset consists of a group of customer relationships maintained by the entity; they are valued in aggregate based on their average characteristics. However, any relationship representing more than, say, 10% of sales could be substantial enough to warrant a separate analysis.

The balance of this chapter assumes valuing a group of relationships, starting with an estimate of future revenues. The process is a multistep one, considering only existing customers and excluding revenues from new ones. Existing customers and historic revenues should be reviewed to see if there are any abnormal, or potentially nonrecurring, items that should be removed; these might include large, one-time purchases or projects that are not expected to recur.

The next step is to determine the adjustment to be made in each year of the projected period to account for anticipated attrition. This will be based on the anticipated annual loss of current customers, as discussed earlier in the chapter. The two key variables that should be considered separately in projecting revenues are quantities and prices. Usually the quantities each customer purchases are assumed to be constant, while prices may increase, decrease, or remain level, reflecting expected inflation over the projected period.

After revenues from existing customers have been established, it is necessary to determine the associated expenses, which represent all operating and other costs required to service those recurring relationships. Ideally, the entity would provide historic gross margins by customer group. As this figure is normally unavailable, the firm's average by product is generally used. When performing those analyses, it is important to review the customer lives. Newer buyers may have higher servicing costs, while more established relationships are likely to require less maintenance. A portion of expenses is often fixed overhead, but, as attrition takes place and is reflected in the revenues, certain overheads may also decline; costs associated with acquiring and keeping new customers should not be included.

Subtracting the expenses from revenues provides a form of earnings before interest, taxes, depreciation and amortization (EBITDA), as all costs are calculated on a debt-free basis and ignore how the entity is financed. This amount is then allocated between customer relationships and contributory assets. As discussed previously, three techniques can be applied; it is preferable to establish rates of return on the fair values of all contributory assets, which are deducted after direct costs. Income tax at the entity's effective rate is then subtracted to determine the net customer cash flows, which are used in a net present value calculation with no terminal amount.

Cost Approach

The cost approach is used sometimes to value customer relationships in place of the income approach because of the inherent difficulties in segregating customer specific cash flows. The cost approach attempts to quantify the current and expected costs to replace existing customer relationships. It does this by relying on the economic principle of substitution, whereby an investor is only willing to purchase an asset for the costs of obtaining a similar asset through constructing either a duplicate or a replacement with the same functionality.

In theory, this approach seems reasonable, but in practice, there is no correlation between value and cost, especially for intangible assets. Identifying and quantifying all costs associated with replacing every existing customer can be as problematic as segregating customer-specific cash flows. The expenditures necessary to generate relationships will vary widely, as they include items such as direct mailings, sales calls, travel and living expenses, and design of marketing materials. It is essential to consider the cost of unsuccessful efforts; if it requires five mailings to establish one relationship, its cost is that of all five, not just the successful one. In addition, most relationships require ongoing maintenance, support, and sales follow-up, activities that have a major bearing on potential buyers.

This method is commonly applied to professional-service firms or retail stores, using replacement costs of all the assets—financial, physical and intangible, including the going-concern element. Valuing the financial and physical assets is usually relatively simple but time consuming. Intangible assets, including customer relationships, are not as easy to value. Some valuators capitalize excess earnings to arrive at a total for such items. To the extent that an assembled workforce is a contributory asset, its replacement cost can be developed using fees charged by placement firms, plus salaries and benefits adjusted for the learning curves of the various classes of employees.

Ultimately, when valuing customer relationships, the cost approach is less valid than the income approach, because it does not consider the economic benefits generated from the relationships. If investors were able to re-create the intangible asset (group of customer relationships sustained by the entity), they would expect economic benefits greater than the costs it would take to develop it. Therefore, the cost approach provides only the bottom of a range of values.

Reasonableness Tests

All values for intangible assets must be subjected to one or more reasonableness tests, because of the significant uncertainties in their calculation. Not only should at least two applicable methods be used, it is often desirable to look at multiple scenarios. The most important test is to compare the value obtained for an intangible to a benchmark by establishing the value of the total business, either from guidelines or by capitalizing earnings. Deducting the financial and physical assets establishes an implicit amount for all intangible assets and goodwill. This is allocated between the various components, including the going-concern element, which covers the assembled workforce and other items necessary for an operating business that IASB includes in goodwill.

A second significant test is to match the values of intangible assets expressed as multiples of revenues with those disclosed for acquisitions of similar enterprises. A third is to consider the costs and time required to recreate a comparable intangible, and a fourth is to analyze the supply of and demand for similar assets, whether they are available or not, and the costs to acquire them.

Finally, common sense, not to rule out intuition, must be applied always, by adjusting the assumptions based on the valuator's experience and industry knowledge, just as it should be always remembered that valuation is both an art and a science.

Regardless of the techniques used to arrive at the fair values of the intangible assets, many practitioners believe that, even when acquired customer relationships are "at market" and do not generate an excess return, they have a nominal fair value of at least their acquisition cost. This is because they are in place and need only minimal further costs for maintenance.

EXAMPLE

One industry where customer relationships are of great importance is retailing. To demonstrate their value, two separate types of retailers are used as examples; the first is a discount women's wear chain, the second a stand-alone pharmacy.

Women's Wear Chain

During year 1, when it was acquired, all the stores are assumed to obtain a total of 10,000 new customers, of which 40% make one or two purchases and then drift away. The remainder stay more or less loyal; thereafter, the retention rate jumps to 80% and continues to rise. Also in year 1, 4% of customers recommend the chain to a friend, who becomes a customer; subsequently, the referral rate more than doubles. In year 5, there is an average of 3,400 customers of whom 1,666 (49%) are referrals.

Initially in year 1, a customer spends $240 on five items, averaging $48 each. Those who remain loyal continue to buy more each subsequent year, reaching $1,000 for 14 items by year 6. As shown in the next table, applying the five stages at a discount rate of 16%, the entity's cost of equity, a seven-year life results in a lifetime value (LTV) of $750,000 for the group, or $75.00 each; this is 3.2 times their acquisition costs of $23.62. Changing the useful life to five years reduces the LTV by 37% to $47.42, which is still twice what it costs to obtain one.

Customer Lifetime Value – Women's Wear Chain

	Year 1	*Year 2*	*Year 3*	*Year 4*	*Year 5*	*Year 6*	*Year 7*
CUSTOMERS							
Acquired	10,000						
Retention Rate	60%	80%	82%	84%	86%	88%	88%
Retained		6,000	4,800	3,936	3,306	2,843	2,502
Referral Rate	4%	8%	9%	9%	9%	9%	9%
Referred		400	480	432	354	298	256
Opening	–	6,400	5,280	4,368	3,660	3,141	2,758
Closing	6,400	5,280	4,368	3,660	3,140	2,758	2,427
Average	8,200	5,480	4,824	4,014	3,400	2,949	2,593
REVENUES							
Items Purchased	5.0	8.5	12.0	13.0	13.5	14.0	14.5
Increase		70%	41%	8%	4%	4%	4%
Average Price	48	56	60	64	68	72	76
Increase		17%	7%	7%	6%	6%	6%
Spending Rate	240	476	720	832	918	1,008	1,102
Revenue	1,968	2,780	3,473	3,340	3,122	2,973	2,857
Increase		41%	25%	–4%	–7%	–5%	–4%
COSTS							
Acquisition	(236)						
Direct Margin	40	42	44	44	44	44	44
Direct	$ (1,181)	$ (1,612)	$ (1,945)	$ (1,870)	$ (1,748)	$ (1,665)	$ (1,600)
Service							
New	(800)	(32)	(38)	(35)	(28)	(24)	(20)
Existing		(54)	(40)	(36)	(30)	(27)	(23)
Total	$ (2,217)	$ (1,699)	$ (2,207)	$ (1,941)	$ (1,807)	$ (1,715)	$ (1,644)
EBITDA	$ (249)	$ 1,081	$ 1,446	$ 1,399	$ 1,315	$ 1,258	$ 1,213
For Supporting Assets	(441)	(654)	(856)	(823)	(769)	(773)	(704)
Contribution	(690)	427	590	576	546	525	509
Income Tax	241	(150)	(207)	(202)	(191)	(184)	(178)
Net Customer Cash Flow	(448)	278	383	374	355	341	331
Values							
Net Customer Cash Flow	$ (448)	$ 278	$ 383	$ 374	$ 355	$ 341	$ 331
PV Factor	0.926	0.798	0.688	0.593	0.511	0.441	0.380
Present Value	(415)	222	264	222	181	150	126
Total Present Values	$750						
Total Present Value Per Customer	$ 75.00						
Acquisition Cost	$ 23.62						

Pharmacy

Other acquisitions have a very different pattern; consider, for example, a stand-alone pharmacy. Based on prescriptions filled, there are 5,066 identified customers at the beginning of year 1. After analyzing past activity, management determines that, because of moves and deaths, historic retention rates have been: year 1, 85%; year 2, 75%; year 3, 50%; year 4,

25%; and year 5, 10%. This means that, even allowing for a 4% referral rate, only one of the original customers remained at the end of year 7, as shown in the next table.

Customer Lifetime Value – Pharmacy

	Year 1	Year 2	Year 3	Year 4	Year 5	Year 6	Year 7
CUSTOMERS							
Acquired	5,066						
Retention Rate	85%	75%	50%	25%	10%	10%	10%
Retained		4,306	3,230	1,615	404	40	4
Referral Rate	4%	4%	4%	4%	4%	4%	4%
Referred		203	172	129	65	16	2
Opening	-	4,509	3,402	1,744	468	57	6
Closing	4,509	3,402	1,744	468	57	6	1
Average	4,787	3,955	2,573	1,106	262	31	3
REVENUES							
Spending Rate	400	412	424	437	450	464	477
Revenue	1,915	1,630	1,091	483	118	14	1
Increase		−14.9%	−33.1%	−55.7%	−75.6%	−87.8%	−89.7%
COSTS							
Direct Margin	22%	22%	23%	23%	23%	23%	3%
Direct	$ (1,501)	$ (1,271)	$ (845)	$ (375)	$ (92)	$ (11)	$ (1)
Service							
New	-	(16)	(14)	(10)	(5)	(1)	-
Existing	(48)	(38)	(24)	(10)	(2)	-	-
Total	$ (1,549)	$ (1,325)	$ (883)	$ (395)	$ (99)	$ (13)	$ (1)
EBITDA	$ 366	$ 305	$ 208	$ 89	$ 19	$ 2	$ -
For Supporting Assets	(232)	(201)	(137)	(61)	(15)	(2)	-
Contribution	134	104	71	28	4	-	-
Income Tax	(47)	(36)	(25)	(10)	(2)	-	-
Net Customer Cash Flow	87	68	46	18	2	-	-
Values							
PV Factor	0.926	0.798	0.688	0.593	0.511	0.441	0.380
Present Value	81	54	31	11	1	-	-
Total Present Values	$ 178						
Total Present Value Per Customer	$ 35.20						
Acquisition Cost	$ 22.68						

Here due to aggressive chain competition, the pickup in the value of the customer relationships is only 55% of their acquisition costs.

CONCLUSION

This chapter began with the statement "the customer is king" and demonstrated that relationships with customers are essential to every business. Even so (except perhaps for retailers and sales executives) many managers recognize neither the importance nor the value of customers; a number of mergers and acquisitions have taken place solely to obtain the customer base or subscriber lists of firms, whether they are failing or flourishing. The effective life of a customer relationship—up to seven years—is longer than that of many other intangible assets, and their value is normally substantially higher than the direct costs of acquisition.

17 DERIVATIVES AND FINANCIAL INSTRUMENTS

SAMUEL YAT CHIU CHAN AND LISA CHENG

HONG KONG

INTRODUCTION

Convertible bonds (CBs) have become immensely popular in the last decade, both as a financing alternative and to investors. They are a type of compound financial instrument combining a fixed-coupon, fixed-maturity debt component with, as the equity element, an option that allows its holders to convert the principal into the issuer's ordinary shares at a predetermined price. Generally speaking, CBs have a lower cost of financing compared with straight bonds with the same risk profile. Their structures are customized, case-specific depending on:

- Market conditions
- Risks involved
- Targeted returns
- The bargaining power of the parties

CBs are highly sought after by investors because of the option to participate in the potential capital appreciation of the issuer's ordinary shares.

As the title of this chapter implies, it is devoted to the valuation of derivatives and financial instruments, with an emphasis on valuing a pre–initial public offering (pre-IPO) CBs, one of the many alternative ways of funding the transition of privately held entities to publicly listed companies. For a number of years, CBs have been issued at unprecedented rates in the Asian capital markets, with China being the most notable participant. It is important to understand the impact of International Financial Reporting Standards (IFRS) 7 as well as International Accounting Standard (IAS) 32 and IAS 39 on the valuation of pre-IPO CBs.

Valuation Issues

Valuing a CB was once relatively simple, as an analyst had only to put a price on the debt component and treat the equity element as a residual (the principal minus the fair value of the debt). (See Exhibit 17.1.)

Exhibit 17.1 Fair Value of the CB

With the introduction of IFRS 7, following IAS 32 and IAS 39, which respectively deal with the disclosure, presentation, recognition, and measurement of financial instruments, the valuation of CBs has become a challenge without definitive guidelines. A detailed discussion of IAS 32 and 39 appears later in this chapter.

Basics of Convertible Bonds

A CB is literally the summation of the letters C and B; with B being a low-coupon, medium-term bond similar to others available in the market, and C being the option to convert the bond's principal into a specific number of the issuer's ordinary shares. Issuing a CB often appears to be cheap financing, as usually it earns a lower coupon than a comparable regular bond; the compensation is the conversion option. Buyers are aware that there is no guarantee on how the underlying shares will perform. However, depending on the circumstances, they can have significant adverse effects on earnings.

Pre-IPO Convertible Bonds

As the name implies, pre-IPO CBs are structured to finance the activities of privately held companies leading to an IPO; they are a type of venture-capital financing which in recent years has become common for pre-IPO companies, because traditional sources, such as commercial banks, are often reluctant to approve loans with high credit and business risks.

As opposed to publicly listed firms, privately owned entities often experience constraints with regard to financing the growth of their businesses. This is critical if they plan an IPO, as the additional funding often determines if a firm will be able to achieve a successful listing.

Qualifying IPO Features

A pre-IPO CB is different from other CBs in that it usually includes a qualifying IPO feature (QIPO), which sets out certain requirements that must be met in order to compel the holder to convert the CB into ordinary shares. A QIPO requires more than just a successful listing of the shares; also, it will usually include other terms, such as the minimum IPO share price (generally twice that of the CB conversion), expected IPO date (within 18 months of the issue), and IPO market and liquidity requirements (trading on an internationally recognized stock exchange such as Hong Kong's). Those features are designed to ensure that investors are guaranteed a certain return on their investments, as their main objective is to dispose of the shares and profit from the capital appreciation. In the event that the QIPO fails to be achieved, the investors are compensated in other predetermined ways, such as a redemption premium to give a specific internal rate of return (usually around 12%). During the pre-IPO period, the investors are normally granted a certain number of directors so as to participate directly in the IPO process.

Deconstructing an IPO CB. As discussed earlier, issuing pre-IPO CBs is a relatively cost-effective alternative for financing entities planning an IPO, because of the lower coupon as well as the possibility that the firm will not have to repay the principal as a result of conversion, although the current owners would be diluted. However, valuations of pre-IPO CBs are no longer as straightforward, as IAS 39 requires the conversion option and any embedded derivatives (discussed later) to be valued separately and to charge changes in their fair values directly to the profit and loss (P&L) account.

The risks of material misstatements in the financial statements are significantly increased by the embedded derivatives (such as put options based on a share's price performance, share adjustment rights, etc.) that sophisticated investors now require to be included in pre-IPO CBs. Yet issuers often overlook their impact; for example, share adjustment rights based on a guaranteed level of profits require the issuer to compensate the investor with extra shares if its earnings fall short of a target. The total of the fair values of the embedded derivatives, conversion option, and debt components of a CB may easily exceed its principal amount. Exhibit 17.2 illustrates the basic concept of CBs with embedded derivatives, conversion option, and debt components.

Exhibit 17.2 Fair Value of Embedded Derivatives

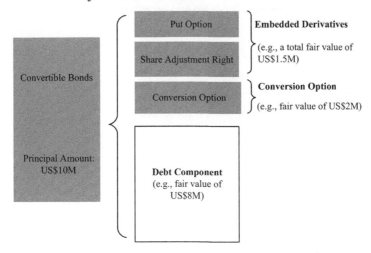

OVERVIEW OF IFRS 7, IAS 32, AND IAS 39

It is essential for valuators to keep up with current accounting standards; however, this chapter presents only a brief overview of each relevant standard, including scope, definition, interpretation, and accounting implications, before discussing their actual applications in a case study.

IFRS 7, *Financial Instruments: Disclosures*

The objective of IFRS 7 is to require entities to make disclosures that enable users of their financial statements to evaluate:

1. Significance of financial statements

    Balance sheet
    Income statement
    Statement of comprehensive income
    Statement of changes in equity
    Accounting policies
    Hedge accounting
    Fair value disclosures

2. Nature and extent of risks arising from financial instruments (i.e., qualitative and quantitative disclosures)

IAS 32, *Financial Instruments: Presentation*

The objective of IAS 32 is to enhance the understanding by financial-statement users of the significance of an entity's financial instruments by clarifying their classification as either a liability or equity. Under the current version of IAS 32, a financial instrument is classified as either a liability or an equity security according to its substance, not its legal form. Classification is made when the instrument is recognized at its inception according to the tree shown in Exhibit 17.3; even if there is an alteration in circumstances, no subsequent changes are allowed.

Exhibit 17.3 IAS 32, Classification of Financial Instruments as Either a Liability or an Equity

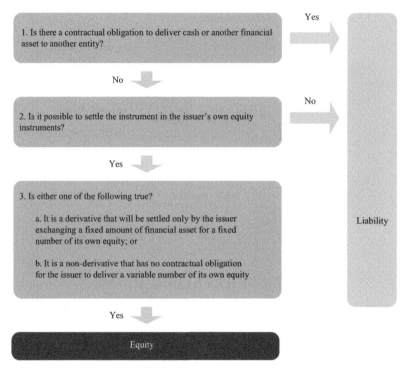

The critical features in differentiating a financial liability from an equity security are:

- The existence of a contractual obligation to deliver cash or other financial assets
- If the issuer is obligated to deliver a variable number of its own equity securities

If either is true, then the financial instrument will be classified as a liability.

IAS 39, *Financial Instruments: Recognition and Measurement*

The objective of IAS 39 is to establish principles for the recognition and measurement of various financial assets and liabilities.

Initial recognition and measurement. Once the entity becomes a party to the contractual provisions of a financial instrument, a financial asset or liability must be recognized on the balance sheet and measured at fair value, which IASB defines as "the amount for which an asset could be exchanged, or a liability settled, between knowledgeable, willing parties in an arm's-length transaction."

Classification of financial assets. IAS 39 classifies financial assets into the four categories shown in Exhibit 17.4 with different measurement requirements.

Exhibit 17.4 IAS 39, Classification of Financial Assets or Liabilities

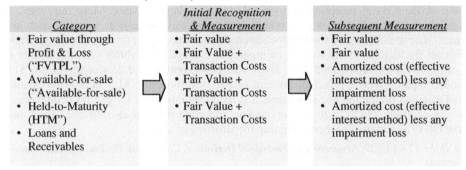

Category	Initial Recognition & Measurement	Subsequent Measurement
• Fair value through Profit & Loss ("FVTPL")	• Fair value	• Fair value
• Available-for-sale ("Available-for-sale)	• Fair Value + Transaction Costs	• Fair value
• Held-to-Maturity (HTM")	• Fair Value + Transaction Costs	• Amortized cost (effective interest method) less any impairment loss
• Loans and Receivables	• Fair Value + Transaction Costs	• Amortized cost (effective interest method) less any impairment loss

Derivatives. According to IAS 39, a derivative is a financial instrument with these characteristics:

- Its value changes in response to the change in another variable.
- The initial investment is zero or an amount that is smaller than would be required for other types of investment with similar responses to changes in market factors
- It is settled at a future date.

According to IAS 39, an embedded derivative is a component of a hybrid instrument that also includes a host contract such as a bond. Any such items must be separated from their hosts and accounted for separately when all three of the criteria shown in Exhibit 17.5 are met.

Exhibit 17.5 IAS 39: Criteria to Determine if Embedded Derivative Needs to Be Measured Separately

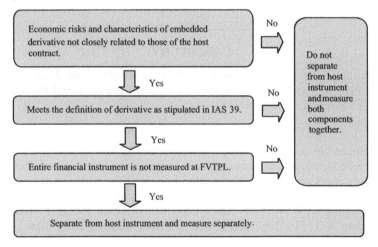

Not separable from the host. If the embedded derivatives are not separable from the host instrument, then the valuation of CBs is relatively simple; the debt component is valued using the effective interest method, and the fair value of the derivatives components is the residual.

Separated from the host. If the embedded derivatives are to be separated from the host according to IAS 39, then they have to be valued separately, usually by an option-pricing model. When all the elements are separately valued, the total of the fair value of the embedded derivatives, conversion option, and debt component will likely differ from the principal amount of the CBs at inception and on subsequent valuation dates. More important, the changes in the fair values of the embedded derivatives and conversion option at each measurement date are charged to the income statement as either a gain or loss; this may result in significant fluctuations in the issuer's earnings. For example, in Exhibit 17.6, the total of the fair values of the two embedded derivatives, conversion option, and debt component is $11.5 million compared with a principal amount of $10.0 million; the $1.5 million in excess is treated as a loss on the income statement. It is therefore important for pre-IPO companies to plan very carefully and to factor in the financial reporting risk and also the risk of not meeting the QIPO requirements when designing the structure of a CB.

Exhibit 17.6 IAS 39: Separation of Embedded Derivative, Conversion Option, and Debt Component

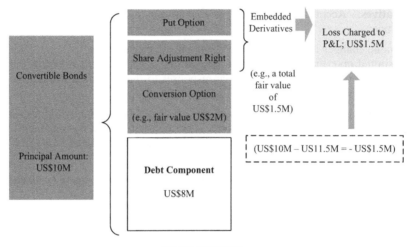

CASE STUDY

This case study relates to the issuance of CBs by a pre-IPO from Wing Hong Co. Limited ("Wing Hong" or the "Company"), their subsequent valuation, and the underlying implications of IFRS 7, IAS 32, and IAS 39.

Background

Wing Hong and its subsidiaries (together referred to as the "Group") are principally engaged in the manufacturing and marketing of electronics in China, where they have a nationwide sales network and are a market leader. In light of the booming domestic economy, the Company decided that it would be in its best interest to access the international capital market by arranging an IPO on the Stock Exchange of Hong Kong; a successful listing would necessitate Wing Hong meeting a number of requirements both financial and operational.

Exhibit 17.7 Corporate Structure upon Conversion of the pre-IPO CBs

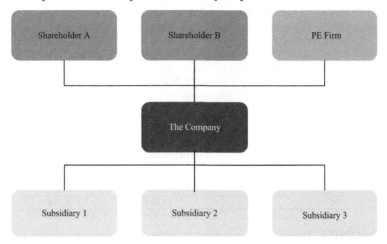

Attracted by Wing Hong's potential, a private equity (PE) firm, Song Yi Partners, expressed interest in investing in it and assisting in the IPO. Following several rounds of negotiations, the Company agreed to sell an issue of pre-IPO CBs to Song Yi. The proceeds were to be used to build a new production line and expand its sales network in an effort to further increase its market share. The effective ownership, on a diluted basis as shown in Exhibit 17.7 above would initially be:

Shareholder A	50.0% (60% undiluted)
Shareholder B	33.3% (40% undiluted)
PE Firm	16.7%

Terms of the CB

In summary, the terms of the pre-IPO CBs were:

Issue Date	2 January 2006
Maturity Date	1 January 2010
Principal Amount	US $10,000,000
Face Value of each CB	US $1,000 (10,000 bonds)
Term (years)	4
Coupon Rate (per annum)	2.5%
Interest Payments (per annum)	1
Redemption Premium (per annum)	12%
Redemption Amount	US $14,800,000
Conversion Price for each CB	US $1,000
Convertible Shares for the CBs	10,000
Exchange Rate: USD/RMB (to calculate conversion shares)	Variable
Put Option	A right for investor to put the CBs to the Company if its share price drops below US $950

Conversion shares. The pre-IPO CBs may be converted in whole or in part in to the Company's ordinary shares, upon meeting all requirements of the QIPO, at the option of the investor. The number of shares issuable on conversion is determined as:

$$A2N = A1 \times (R2/R1)$$

Where:

N	=	Number of ordinary shares issuable on conversion
A1	=	Outstanding principal amount of the debt together with the redemption premium being converted
R1	=	USD (United States Dollar) / CNY (Chinese Yuan) exchange rate of 8.0702 as at the issue date of 2 January 2006
R2	=	USD/CNY exchange rate quoted by Bloomberg for Spot Renminbis (Yaun) on the immediately preceding business day

Parameters

	Issue Date 2 January 2006	Valuation Date 30 September 2006
A1	US $10,000,000	US $10,000,000
R1	8.0702	8.0702
R2	8.0702	7.9040
A2	US $10,000,000	US $9,794,057
N	**10,000**	**9,794**
Effective price per share	US $ 1,000	US $ 1,021

Effect of QIPO. Investors always want assurances that their investments will generate a certain level of return on conversion; therefore, pre-IPO CBs are usually structured to include QIPO features. These trigger the conversion option of the CBs, once certain criteria have been met. In the case of Wing Hong, they referred to an IPO on the Stock Exchange of Hong Kong, at an offer price of not less than twice the conversion price. If the conversion is not triggered within 18 months after the issue date, a redemption premium of 12% a year applies.

The Offering

Initially, Song Yi invested US $10 million in the Company at an effective price/earnings ratio (PER) of 4.14x, based on a valuation of US $60 million and net earnings of US $14.5 million (the guaranteed profit) for the year ended 31 December 2005. Wing Hong was listed on 30 December 2006 with a market capitalization of $300 million, based on the expected net earnings of $20 million for the year ended 31 December 2006, and a market PER of 15x. On the IPO, Song Yi, the private equity firm, had earned approximately $40 million for its 16.67% converted interest (US $300 million × 16.67% = $50 million less $10 million cost) from its investment. The timeline is shown in Exhibit 17.8.

Exhibit 17.8 Timeline of Events

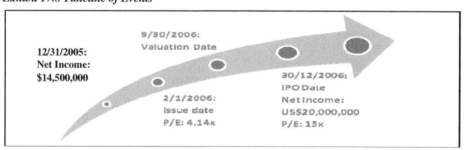

Classification of Pre-IPO CBs

Before a financial instrument is recognized and recorded on an entity's financial statements, it must be classified as a liability or equity in accordance with IAS 32. This is critical, as the related accounting treatments affect significantly the reported earnings and financial position of the issues. The classification of the pre-IPO CBs issued by the Company is as follows:

1. The debt component of the pre-IPO CBs has a contractual obligation to deliver cash (coupon payments, principal and redemption premium) to the holder, which automatically makes it a liability.

2. For the equity component, there is no contractual obligation to deliver cash or another financial asset to the holder, and on conversion it is possible to settle the instrument with the Company's own ordinary shares. However, the conversion option is classified as a liability under IAS 32 (see Exhibit 17.9) due to the fact that the number of common shares into which the pre-IPO CBs are convertible would vary according to a preset formula, which takes into account changes in the USD/CNY exchange rate.

Exhibit 17.9 IAS Classification

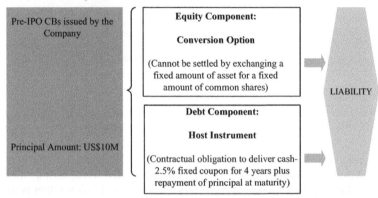

The debt component sets out Wing Hong's liability for coupon payments and the repayment of the principal and redemption premium on maturity, while the conversion option represents a liability to deliver a variable number of ordinary shares upon the holder exercising its rights.

Recognition and Measurement

As previously mentioned, IAS 39 requires the equity component—the conversion option in this case—to be measured separately from the host if it meets all of the three criteria shown in Exhibit 17.10.

Exhibit 17.10 IAS 39: Measurement of Equity Component

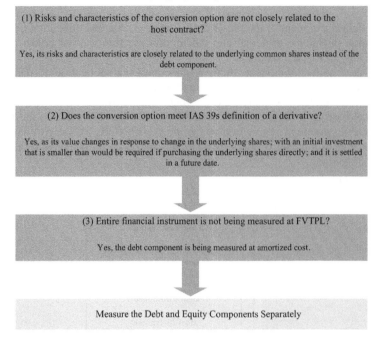

Since the risks and characteristics of the conversion option into a variable number of ordinary shares, based on a preset formula, are not closely related to the host debt component, it meets IAS 39's definition of a derivative and is classified as a liability that is measured at FVTPL; the conversion option is valued separately from the debt component.

IAS 39 also requires that all embedded derivatives be separated from their hosts (i.e., bifurcated), if they meet the criteria mentioned in Exhibit 17.5. Since the put option (a right for the investor to put the CBs to the Company if the share price drops below $950) is "embedded" in the pre-IPO CBs and it also meets the three aforementioned criteria of IAS 39, the put option also will be valued separately as an embedded derivative.

VALUATION OF THE DEBT COMPONENT

A pre-IPO CB is a compound financial instrument which is not traded on an active market; in addition, the conversion component alone cannot be detached from the host instrument for an independent transfer; consequently, its fair value can be obtained only by applying various valuation methodologies and it cannot be obtained simply from the open market. In accordance with IAS 32 and IAS 39, its value is as set out in Exhibit 17.11.

Exhibit 17.11 Fair Value of the Pre-IPO CBs Separating Conversion Option and Embedded Derivatives

Suitable Methodology

The effective interest method is one of the most common means of determining the fair value of a debt instrument and is the technique adopted. It is a means of calculating the amortized cost of a financial asset or liability and allocating the interest income or expense over the relevant period. The effective interest rate (normal cost of debt) is that which discounts all estimated future cash payments or receipts back to the principal amount at the date of issue. When estimating the effective interest rate, a valuator needs to consider cash flows from all contractual terms of the CB (coupon payments, repayment of principal, redemption premium, etc.), excluding future credit losses. The fair value of the debt component is the present value of all relevant future cash flows discounted at the current-market interest rate. This is usually obtained from instruments of comparable credit quality that provide substantially the same cash flows for an identical term but without a conversion option or embedded derivatives.

Effective Interest Method: Application

Exhibit 17.12 Effective Interest Method

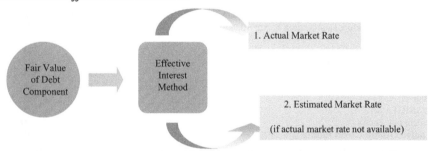

There are two main techniques to estimate an effective interest rate for an entity; see Exhibit 17.12. The first, which is also the more direct and simple, if data are obtainable, is to use the current borrowing rate of the firm itself as the market rate. Wing Hong had been borrowing at about 8.0% from local commercial banks. However, taking into consideration the size of the pre-IPO CB, the risks involved, and the redemption premium of 12.0% per year if the QIPO conditions are not satisfied, the past borrowing rate was not considered applicable.

The second, if a suitable market rate is not available, is to build up an estimate of the interest rate using credit spread and specific entity risk adjustments. This procedure has three steps:

1. Estimate the entity's credit rating.
2. Estimate the Market Rate.
3. Make specific company risk adjustments.

Estimating the entity's credit rating. The Standard & Poor's (S&P) adjusted key U.S. industrial financial ratios for long-term debt is the usual starting point for estimating an entity's market rate. These are the median financial ratios for U.S. industrial companies by rating category, which allow valuators to assess the credit quality of a firm. These mainly focus on the ability to generate future cash flows and repay the debt. The range is from the highest (AAA) to firms in default (D). The table covers seven categories from AAA to CCC, of which the first four are investment grade and the remaining three are "junk."

Adjusted Key US Industrial Financial Ratios, Long-Term Debt
Three-year (2005 to 2007) averages

	AAA	*AA*	*A*	*BBB*	*BB*	*B*	*CCC*
Oper. Income (bef. D&A)/revenues (%)	22.2	26.5	19.8	17.0	17.2	16.2	10.5
Return on capital (%)	27.0	28.4	21.8	15.2	12.4	8.7	2.7
EBIT interest coverage (x)	26.2	16.4	11.2	5.8	3.4	1.4	0.4
EBITDA interest coverage (x)	32.0	19.5	13.5	7.8	4.8	2.3	1.1
FFO/debt (%)	155.5	79.2	54.5	35.5	25.7	11.5	2.5
Free oper. Cash flow/debt (%)	129.9	40.6	31.2	16.1	7.1	2.2	(3.6)
Disc. Cash flow/debt (%)	84.4	23.3	19.9	10.3	5.5	0.7	(3.6)
Debt/EBITDA (x)	0.4	0.9	1.5	2.2	3.1	5.5	8.6
Debt/debt plus equity (%)	12.3	35.2	36.8	44.5	52.5	73.2	98.9
No. of companies	6	14	111	213	306	354	22

Source: CreditStats: Adjusted Key U.S. Industrial and Utility Financial Ratios, Standard & Poor's

Based on the ratios in this table, a letter grade can be assigned to the similar ratios of the entity; the most frequent grade is considered to be the firm's overall credit rating. Using "return on capital" as an example, the Company's ratio of 12.5% is greater than the BB median of 12.4% but less than the BBB of 15.2%; as 12.5% is close to 12.4%, BB is assigned to this item.

Case-Specific Key Financial Ratios	**Company Ratio**	**Rating**
Operating income (before Depreciation & Amortization)/revenues (%)	18.2	BBB
Return on capital (%)	12.5	BB
EBIT interest coverage (x)	1.9	B
EBITDA interest coverage (x)	3.2	B
Funds from operations/debt (%)	9.5	B
Free operating cash flow/debt (%)	2.0	B
Discounted cash flow/debt (%)	1.2	B
Debt/EBIDTA (x)	2.8	BB
Debt/debt plus equity (%)	50.2	BB
Estimated Overall Credit Rating		**B**

Based on the analyses indicated, "BBB" is represented by one ratio, "B" by five, and "BB" by three; the estimated overall credit rating of the Company is "B."

Estimating the market rate. Various sources including Bloomberg enable a valuator to estimate the average market yields at a particular date of straight debt securities with different ratings and maturities, as shown next.

Selected Four-Year Bond Yields
as at Issue Date of 2 January 2006

Rating	Yield
AAA	4.76%
AA	4.79%
A+	4.83%
A	4.89%
A–	4.99%
BBB+	5.11%
BBB	5.19%
BBB–	5.43%
BB+	5.73%
BB	6.18%
BB–	6.69%
B+	6.80%
B	**7.31%**
B–	7.74%

Source: Bloomberg: FMCI

The rate of 7.31% represents the average market yield of all available B-rated straight debt securities with a four-year term in the U.S. market selected by Bloomberg. The relationship of yield and credit rating is shown in Exhibit 17.13.

Exhibit 17.13 4-Year U.S. Industrial Bond Yields by Rating

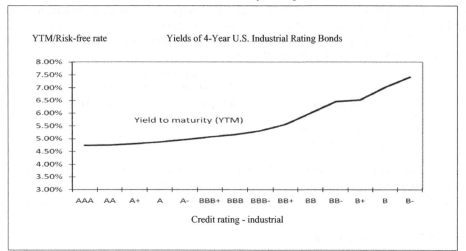

A U.S. market rate was chosen instead of one from China because the Chinese corporate bond market, still in the development stage, was far from being efficient, and market rates are difficult to obtain; in addition, the CBs are denominated in U.S. dollars.

Specific company risk adjustments. To estimate an effective market rate that closely matches an entity's risk profile and the actual situation, five entity-specific risk adjustments must be considered:

1. *Country risk premium (CRP).* Since the average market rate is from the United States, a CRP has to be added to reflect the Company's location in China. Damodaran Online, the homepage for Professor Aswath Damodaran of New York University (pages.stern.nyu.edu/~adamodar) on 10 March 2006 gave the United States a total risk premium of 5.00% compared with 7.10% for China; this spread of 2.1% is the established CRP for China
2. *Lack of management depth.* The chief executive officer is already well past retirement age but there is no successor chosen.
3. *Increased competition.* The electronic product industry in China is suffering from rising competition due to an influx of market entrants.
4. *Overreliance on a single supplier.* More than 50% of the Company's raw materials come from one firm, which poses significant operational risks should it suffer any type of stoppage.
5. *Additional return required.* The investor seeks additional compensation as a result of its advisory services in relation to the IPO.

Estimated Effective Market Rate (Build-up Method)

Average rate based on "B"	7.3%
Country risk premium—China	2.1%
Lack of management depth	3.0%
Increase in competition	3.0%
Over reliance on single supplier	3.0%
Additional return for investor	2.0%
Total	**20.4%**

Taking into account all the additional risks results in an effective market rate of 20.4%.

As this estimate of the effective market rate is subject to many entity-specific adjustments, which are difficult to quantify, it is essential to support it by empirical data on the return required by venture capitalist for pre-IPO financings. The next table summarizes the results of two studies by QED Research, Inc. (QED Report) and William Sahlman of Harvard University (Venture Capital method). Those show the return venture capitalists usually require at different stages of the business life cycle. The table indicates that returns in the 20% range are not excessive for the pre-IPO stage.

	Empirical Studies of Venture Capital Rates of Return	
Stage of Development	**QED Report**	**Venture Capital Method**
Start-up	50–70%	50–70%
First Stage "Early Development"	40–60%	40–60%
Second Stage "Expansion"	35–50%	30–50%
Bridge/IPO	25–35%	20–35%

Using the estimated effective market rate of 20.4% to discount all future contractual cash flows (interest payments, principal, and redemption premium) of the CB's debt component results in it having a fair value of US $7,682,000 as of 2 January 2006; this equates to $768.20 per $1,000 bond.

Value of the Conversion Option

Most derivatives are not traded in an active market; therefore, values have to be derived by other techniques, most commonly the Black-Scholes option pricing model.

Black-Scholes model. The Black-Scholes model has become the standard method of pricing options since it was first developed by Fischer Black and Myron Scholes in 1973. It assumes the option can be exercised only at expiration, requires both the risk-free rate and the volatility of the underlying share price to remain constant, and uses these five key determinants of an option's value:

1. Share price
2. Exercise price
3. Volatility
4. Time to expiration
5. Risk-free rate

In addition, it assumes a normal distribution of underlying asset returns and a lognormal distribution for the underlying stock prices. However, in reality, share price distributions often depart greatly from lognormal. The primary advantage of using the Black-Scholes model is its speed. However, as it only calculates a value at a single moment in time, it cannot accurately price options that are exercisable at any time.

Binomial option pricing model. The binomial option pricing model (BOPM) was developed by Cox, Ross, and Rubinstein in 1979 and has been widely adopted because of its ability to account for a variety of conditions. Most of its parameters used in the model are similar to those of Black-Scholes, but it has the ability to consider the situation of the underlying asset over time.

It breaks down the period to expiry into different intervals, using a binomial tree of share prices working forward from the present. It assumes that share prices will either move up or down at each node only by an amount calculated using volatility and the remaining time. The tree produces a binomial distribution of underlying share prices and represents all possible paths that price could take during the options life. On expiry, all terminal option values for each of the final possible share prices are known; the value at each step is then calculated by working back to the present. The main advantage of the BOPM model is its ability to price options accurately because it allows for the possibility of early exercise. The obvious weakness is that it is more technical than Black Scholes, requiring more time and modeling skills.

Value of Conversion Option

Since the BOPM can take into account the terms of the QIPO (minimum IPO share price and expected IPO date), it was applied to the conversion option of the pre-IPO CBs issued by Wing Hong.

Value of Embedded Derivative (Put Option)

The embedded put option was also valued by BOPM. The next table outlines the parameters used as well as the option's fair value at each date.

Binomial Option Pricing Model:	Issue Date 1/2/2006	Valuation Date 30/9/2006
Implied Share Price	US $980	US $1,175
Conversion Price	US $950	US $950
Time to Maturity	2 years	1.34 years
Risk-free Rate	4.0%	3.5%
Stock Volatility	40.00%	45.00%
Dividend Yield	3.50%	3.50%
Put Option Value	US $179.60	US $120.99
Convertible Shares	10,000	9,794
Fair Value of Put Option	US $1,796,000	US $1,184,976

In valuing the conversion option and embedded derivative, a key parameter is the share price. In practice, for pre-IPO firms, the business is valued using standard methodologies to arrive at an implied price per share.

Methods Considered and Rejected

This particular case study applied methods under the Income and Market Approach Market Approaches but rejected the Cost Approach as Wing Hong is an expanding business, and the Cost Approach fails to consider the benefits of the additional financing and planned IPO.

Market Approach

The Market Approach develops a value using the principle of substitution. This simply means that if one thing is similar to another and could replace the other, then they must be equal. Furthermore, the price of two alike and similar items should approximate one another. For the Market Approach to be used successfully, there must be sufficient guideline entities, or the industry composition must be such that meaningful comparisons can be made; an alternative is to use transactions in the entity's shares.

This latter method was adopted for the 30 September 2006 valuation because one shareholder had sold part of his holding to a professional investor on 15 May 2006, before the IPO.

Income Approach

The Income Approach is the most generally accepted means of determining a value indication of a business, ownership interest, or intangible asset using one or more methods that convert anticipated economic benefits into a single amount.

To deal with the situation where an entity intends to make an IPO and face the uncertainties of listing, the cash flows of two different scenarios—"with IPO" and "without IPO"—should be taken into account. Historic data from the Stock Exchange of Hong Kong indicates the success rate of IPOs after filing the relevant documents is about 50%. Consequently, the expected and weighted business value was calculated using the probabilities of

50% for each scenario; a discount for lack of marketability was then applied to reflect the minority nonmarketable value of the firm.

Discount for lack of marketability. An interest in a privately held firm has limited liquidity/marketability; accordingly, it has a higher risk and lower relative value; the difference is known as the discount for lack of marketability (DLOM). There are two types of empirical studies and a model to quantify DLOM.

1. Discounts on the sale of restricted shares of publicly traded companies (restricted stock studies).
2. Discounts on the sale of closely held company shares compared with prices of subsequent IPOs of the same company's shares (pre-IPO studies).
3. Depending on the studies or model adopted, DLOM usually falls into a range of 10% to 50%.

Implied Share Prices

	Issue Date 2/1/2006	Valuation Date 30/9/2006
Income Approach—DCF	$980	$1,175
Market Approach—Guideline Public Company	$950	$1,130
Company Transactions Method 15/5/2006	NA	$1,160
Conclusion of Value	**$980**	**$1,175**

In the case study, when the implied share price changes, the values of the conversion option and the put option also change. For example, a higher implied share price will result in a greater value for the conversion option and a lower one for the put. At the same time, the fair value of the conversion option will rise as the expected IPO date comes closer because of a lower DLOM and a reduced discount rate. This results in investors benefiting while the Company will have to charge a loss to its income statement.

Valuation Conclusions

The fair value of the pre-IPO CBs is the summation of the debt component, conversion option, and embedded derivative; the next table sets out the respective values that we have valued.

Fair Value of the Pre-IPO CBs	Notes	Issue Date 2/1/2006	Valuation Date 30/9/2006
Debt Component (US$)	A	7,681,993	8,636,575
Conversion Option (US$)	B	2,733,100	4,123,274
Embedded Derivative (Put Option) (US$)	C	1,796,000	1,184,976
Fair Value of CBs (US$)		12,211,093	13,944,825
Accrued Interest Expense (US$)		–	(954,582)
Conversion Option: Fair Value Changes as Gain/(Loss) (US$)		–	(1,390,174)
Put Option: Fair Value Changes as Gain /(Loss) (US$)		–	611,024

A. *The increase in the debt component is the accrued interest for the period.*
B. *The change in fair value of the conversion option is a result of IAS 39, which classifies it as a FVTPL to be measured separately at fair value. During the period to 30 September 2006, its fair value increased by US $1,390,174, which was charged as a loss to Wing Hong. The resulting unexpected drop in earnings could have jeopardized its chances of going public successfully, as well as meeting the other terms of the pre-IPO CBs, such as the profit guarantee.*
C. *The put option is also classified as a FVTPL and valued separately. The increase in the implied share price decreased its fair value, resulting in a gain of US $611,024 to offset part of the common options loss.*

SUMMARY

Here we summarize the valuation issues discussed in this chapter.

"C" + "B" > CB

Under IAS 32 and IAS 39, issuers of pre-IPO CBs need to classify the different components into either liabilities or equity and then measure their fair values. In most cases of pre-IPO CBs, the conversion option and embedded derivatives are measured separately; often the total of their fair values of the debt component, conversion option, and embedded derivatives will be higher than the principal amount of the CB, which results in "C" + "B" > CB; the exercise showed the difference as a loss.

Complex Valuation Process with Many Variables

The necessary valuation processes are complex as each element has to be valued separately, involving many variables that may change significantly over time. Obtaining fair values for the conversion option and embedded derivatives involves option pricing models as well as business valuation methods for the implied share price in addition to other data and assumptions. A variation in any number of parameters may lead to a significant change in the total value of the CB.

Potential Obstacles of an IPO

Potential obstacles of an IPO present major financial reporting risks for the issuer of CBs, as all changes in the fair values of the conversion option and embedded derivative are charged directly to earnings. This risk is often overlooked by managers, who may not be aware of the accounting implications of IAS 32 and IAS 39. In extreme cases, such reductions in reported earnings may be so severe as to prevent the issuer from meeting the listing requirements and possibly the terms of the QIPO.

Cheap Stock

Cheap stock is a term referring to ordinary shares issued, before an IPO, at a discount to their fair value. If the implied share price used to value the conversion option is lower than fair value, such securities will be subject to strict scrutiny by the relevant securities authorities.

Complex Capital Structure

Entities with multiple classes of securities are said to have a complex capital structure, and usually their valuations are done using one of three primary allocation methods: option pricing model, probability-weighted expected returns, and current values.

CONCLUSION

As discussed, pre-IPO CBs are compound financial instruments, which combine fixed income and equity characteristics. Accordingly, their valuation is not straightforward, as it involves considering separately a plain vanilla bond, a simple conversion option, and one or more embedded derivatives. The value of the debt component varies with changes in interest rates, while the conversion option and the embedded derivatives are sensitive to the share price and the terms of the CB.

Valuation is a range concept; since there are uncertainties as to the fair value of the entity due to changes in market conditions and the probability of a successful listing; different variables are used to value the conversion option and embedded derivatives. Therefore, an exact fair value for pre-IPO CBs cannot be ascertained, only a reasonable range.

IFRS 7, IAS 32, and IAS 39, which govern the disclosure, presentation, recognition, and measurement of financial instruments, are increasingly being adopted by firms all around the world. The scope of these standards is wide-ranging, intertwined, and sometimes confusing. They spur controversy as to their interpretations as well as applications under various scenarios. Notwithstanding the challenges, entities and their auditors are grappling with the complicated areas and uncertainties. In the meantime, it is essential that valuators be aware of recent developments in applying them, as fair value measurements of financial instruments are now subject to a high degree of scrutiny.

All stakeholders should familiarize themselves with these standards, especially would-be issuers of CBs; they must be aware that sudden charges to earnings may result from the CBs increasing in value because of successful operations. Discussions, debates, and amendments over the application of the standards are likely to persist.

18 DOMAIN NAMES

WES ANSON

UNITED STATES

INTRODUCTION

The intent of this chapter is to describe a particular class of assets, domain names, and discuss the special issues affecting their valuation. To some extent it covers the relationship of domain names to other intellectual property rights (IPRs), most notably trademarks and Web sites, but it mainly covers free-standing unattached domain names.

The focus is to explain this new, ever-expanding, and rapidly changing asset class. It looks at some of the legal and business issues that affect the values, providing a picture of specific, historic as well as current domain name values. The latter part of this chapter is an actual case study from our practice using actual facts and conclusions with no attempt to manipulate or filter the techniques or conclusions.

DOMAIN NAME SYSTEM

The Domain Name System (DNS) is designed to help online users find their way around the Internet as quickly and simply as possible. Just as each home in a community has a specific street address, every computer on the Internet has a unique identifying number, its Internet Protocol Address (IPA). Essentially, this is a unique long string of numbers that is random at best and almost impossible to remember at worst. Therefore, the DNS provides a simple way of expressing that address as a domain name rather than the string of numbers. Instead of typing 206.251.241.29, for example, one enters www.consor.com—and is immediately directed to the Web site for that particular firm.

The DNS is managed by the Internet Corporation for Assigned Names and Numbers (ICANN). It is a nonprofit corporation, headquartered in California and was created in 1998 to oversee Internet-related issues, addresses, and other tasks. Previously this work had been performed directly on behalf of the U.S. government by other organizations. ICANN's tasks now include responsibility for IPA, space allocation, protocols, generic, and country top-level domains. In those roles it is responsible for assigning all domain names and IP (Internet Protocol) addresses, so as to maintain the stability of the Internet and to ensure there is broad representation of the entire global community on it.

One important task for ICANN is the resolution of domain name ownership issues, particularly for generic top-level domains (gTLDS). This was solved by drafting a Uniform Dispute Resolution Policy (UDRP) in close cooperation with the World Intellectual Property Organization (WIPO). To register a name with ICANN, any applicant must agree to be bound by the UDRP, which is now the accepted method of resolving such disputes. As to domain names, ICANN currently distinguishes five types of top-level domains (TLDs), the last part of all Internet names (e.g. .com, .net. .org, etc.):

1. Infrastructure TLDs (such as .arpa)
2. Country TLDs (such as .us, .uk, .de, etc.)

3. Sponsored TLDs from private organizations that establish and restrict their eligibility (such as .aero for aerospace and air transport, .gov, .edu)
4. Generic TLDs (such as .com, .net, .org), open for registration to anyone in the world
5. Generic restricted TLDs (such as .biz, .name, .pro), which are supposed to be issued with more scrutiny

In addition, a group of internationalized domain names are currently being tested.

The largest type is country TLDs, as virtually every nation has its own domain, including obscure locations such as the Pitcairn Islands (.pn) and the Island of St. Helena (.sh).

In June 2008 ICANN approved a new program that will allow organizations, groups, and individuals to register Internet addresses outside the existing TLD rules. These new TLDs could be expanded to include common words such as .banks, for example. They cover TLDs in languages that do not rely on Roman characters, including Arabic, Chinese, and Cyrillic. ICANN has also proposed allowing individual corporations, for example, to develop new TLDs (e.g. .ibm, .pg, etc.). There is a swirl of controversy over these proposals, and the issues were not nearly at the point of being resolved at the time of writing.

The domain name market is enormous. At year-end 2008, there was a total global base of 177 million registrations among the TLDs. In addition, there were another 71 million registered under various country TLDs for a total of approximately 250 million domain names; growth has been between 10% and 20% in each of the last five years.

DOMAIN NAMES IN LAW AND UNDER IFRS

Domain names are classified as IPRs, a form of intangible assets.

The key difference between them is that IPRs have been granted legal protection and recognition. Their ownership has been verified and registered with one or more national or international bodies; they include:

- Trademarks and service marks
- Patents
- Trade secrets
- Copyrights
- Domain names

This is a very small group of definable assets; however, in many cases, each IPR is often supported by other physical and intangible assets. In the case of patents, technical know-how may be essential to the process. In the case of trademarks, logos, jingles, or other copyrighted materials may support the brand. Specific domain names may be, and often are, associated with Web sites and other Internet assets. Separately, they are frequently related to and duplicative of particular trademarks, which form part of a brand.

Domain names may be free-standing, as many are, without any association to other assets; however, those in active use are normally associated with a Web site. This will likely consist of a broad range of related assets, including an operating platform, data warehouse, software source code, and e-commerce marketing systems. In such a case, the valuation of the domain name on its own is a tricky proposition, as is discussed later.

Often a domain name represents the Internet version of a registered trademark. Examples are Pringles.com as a partner asset to and part of the trademark Pringles; or coca-cola.com as part of the trademark and broad bundle of assets forming the Coca-Cola brand. As with Web site–related domain names, those are difficult, if not impossible, to separate in value from the related trademark and brand.

Another consideration when dealing with a domain name as an IPR is that, even though it is registered, it does not have the same level of protection as a trademark. In terms of protection, a domain name is not as strong in many ways as a copyright and certainly does not provide the rigid protections of a patent. Also, quite importantly, a domain name can be taken away from the registrant if it is found to conflict with a registered trademark of another owner. There is no control over how many additional domains ICANN may add over time; therefore, a domain name like money.net may soon find itself surrounded by new domains such as money.bank, money.finance, and money.goldmansachs in an ever-expanding universe.

A domain name can have a value ascribed specifically to it as an individual asset. However, when it is part of a trademark/brand bundle, it should not be assigned a separate value. Naturally, for internal planning, it may be useful from time to time to prepare a stand-alone valuation to aid management in allocating resources and prioritizing decisions in IPRs. As stated, the value of an independent domain name is influenced by how it is to be used and, of course, by its business or marketing utility.

Standards in Valuing Domain Names

Domain names are treated very similarly by both Statements of Financial Accounting Standards (SFAS) and International Financial Reporting Standards (IFRS) in both definition and value methodologies. An intangible asset, which includes a domain name, is defined by International Accounting Standards (IAS) 38: "An identifiable nonmonetary asset without physical substance." Also: "An asset is a resource that is controlled by the enterprise as a result of past events (for example, purchase or self-creation) and from which future economic benefits (inflows of cash or other assets) are expected." Thus, the three critical attributes of an intangible asset are:

1. Identifiability
2. Control (power to obtain benefits from the asset)
3. Future economic benefits (such as revenues or reduced future costs)

Note that internally generated intangibles, such as brands, titles, and customer lists, are not to be recognized as intangible assets for accounting purposes.

Under IFRS 3, *Business Combinations,* intangible assets are recognized if they meet the criteria of IAS 38. However, IFRS 3 specifically lists trademarks and trade names, Internet domain names, trade dress and newspaper mastheads as marketing-related intangible assets. With respect to methodologies, the owner of a domain name can choose either the cost or the revaluation model for its accounting policy. The revaluation model may be used only if an active market exists for the assets; in fact, there is a very active market for buying and selling domain names.

RISE AND FALL OF DOMAIN NAME VALUES

In the 1980s, when Internet assets and domain names were relatively new and valuation techniques haphazard at best, prices for domain names were modest—seldom more than the cost of registration. During the enormous dot-com boom of the late 1990s, prices of domain names climbed to astronomical heights, along with the share prices of countless dot-com entities that failed to survive. Since the collapse of dot-com shares in 2000 and 2001, the value of domain names has peaked, fallen, and, stabilized. While they have risen slightly in the last five years, in general, domain name values have stabilized as the dot-com economy and related share prices have returned to reality. The recent economic pressures in 2008 and early 2009 have once again dampened enthusiasm for high values. The average price for a domain name fell by nearly 50% in 2008 as compared to 2007.

In a 1999 review of domain name prices, at least 10 were listed at starting bids of more than $1 million, going up to the low eight figures. More important, at that time, the average selling price for a domain name was in the range of $15,000.

By the late 1980s and into the early 1990s, large and small corporations, private individuals, and not-for-profit groups learned to log on to the Internet. This led to an explosion of usage; by 1993, the Internet was growing geometrically every month. The pricing frenzy was fueled by the dot-com boom of the late 1990s. The logic (if there was any) was that domain names and Internet sites would be the platforms for virtually all types of commerce. There was talk of strategic alliances eliminating competition, the death of retail stores, the demise of cable television and wire line telecommunications, and a foretold loss of privacy. More realistic voices speak today. After all, a domain name is only an address on a communications network—in concept, not terribly different from a telephone number—and the supply seems endlessly expandable.

The mean price of a domain name in 2008 was about $600 and the median $750, with the vast majority of sales at below $1,000 each. As shown in the case study later in this chapter, values continue to fall, even for those domain names that appear to have a high utility—and that would have commanded very high prices at the beginning of the millennium. For example, marketprice.com, breather.com, sleepstudies.com, fitnesscamp.com, and countrystore.com all sold for between $2,000 and $4,000. Part of the reason is increasingly sophisticated search engines that look beyond domain names for metatags, thus reducing the business or click-through value of any given name.

CYBER-SQUATTING, TYPO-SQUATTING, AND SEARCH ENGINES

Before the final two sections on the valuation process and case studies, there are a few other issues to keep in mind. Cyber-squatting is perhaps one of the most widely used, but in some ways least understood, terms related to domain name use and misuse. The correct definition is registering or using a domain name with bad-faith intent to profit from the goodwill of a trademark belonging to someone else. The U.S. federal Anticyber-squatting Consumer Protection Act speaks to this issue; it particularly addresses cyber-squatting for profit when a registrant offers to sell a domain name to the owner of a trademark with the same name at an inflated price. Often the cyber-squatter will use a related Web site to express derogatory comments about the trademark, person, or company that the domain name is meant to represent—a thinly disguised effort at blackmail to encourage the subject to purchase the domain name.

A related issue is typo-squatting, sometimes called URL (uniform resource locator) hijacking. In this, a cyber-squatter looks for mistakes and typographical errors commonly made by Internet users when seeking a particular Web site. If users accidentally type in an incorrect or misspelled address, they may be led to an alternative Web site. Generally, their targets are frequently visited Web sites, and the typo-squatter usually owns a similar Web site with a common misspelling or foreign-language version. An example would be Micrasoft.com instead of Microsoft.com. This type of illegal activity can be very dangerous, as typo-squatters sometimes uses their sites to distribute viruses, spyware, or inappropriate materials, such as pornography. A variation on cyber-squatting is name-jacking. In this process, the name-jacker purchases a well-known individual's name as a second-level domain (such as tomcruise.info). He then uses that site to attract visitors seeking the famous Tom Cruise. The name-jacked site can then be sold to Mr. Cruise or used to sell products or services related to that individual.

As a consequence of the items just mentioned, a valuator should consider cyber-squatting, typo-squatting, and other possible legal challenges. The UDRP is the relevant court and research should be undertaken to ensure that the subject domain name does not currently have any disputes pending against it or if there were any actions in the past.

Cyber-squatting issues can have an impact on not only the value of the domain name but also on any related trademark or brand name. An example of the potential effects on the value of domain names and trademarks was a 1996 case involving Hasbro, the toy manufacturer, and Internet Entertainment Group (IEG), which operated pornography sites. Hasbro owns the trademark to Candy Land, a well-known children's board game, and uses the domain name candyland.com. IEG name-jacked candyland.net, along with other variations, for an adult entertainment site. The core issues at trial were, first, infringement of the Hasbro trademark and, second, ownership of the various domain names.

In its defense, IEG stated: "There are hundreds of companies utilizing the 'Candy Land' name in the United States, including a Candy Land massage parlor and two companies that were recently producing products on the Internet." However, the court agreed with Hasbro that by using candyland.net, IEG interfered with the toy maker's trademark and enjoined IEG from using the name of the game to promote its sexually explicit material, but it refused to halt the adult programming on the Internet. Instead, users who accessed the site were referred to IEG's new domain name, adultplayground.com, where all its services would continue; after 90 days, IEG was to stop using the candyland.net name. It was left up to ICANN to transfer the domain names.

VALUATION PROCESS

In valuing domain names, unlike with other forms of IPRs or even other asset classes, special considerations occur. Interestingly, however, domain names share a single important trait with real estate: location, location, location. In other words, the location (or spelling) of a domain name gives it much of its intrinsic value. As a simple example, Microsoft.com has, quite obviously, the perfect location on the Internet; a very similar domain name, Bicrosoft.com, has little, if any, value. Simply by shifting the location, or spelling, of a domain name by one letter can substantially affect its value.

Valuation Considerations

When looking at domain names, certain questions should occur to a valuator and be thought about before commencing the project:

- Is the value of the domain name an intrinsic part of a parent trademark, and therefore embedded in its value, or does the domain name appear to be a separate asset producing incremental value?
- Does the value of the domain name depend on an underlying trademark, or is it a stand-alone situation?
- Does the particular domain name exist in a vacuum, or are there other Internet assets connected to it at the time of the valuation? If so, then they have to be assessed separately, and their value may be dependent to some extent on that of the domain name.
- Are the three traditional approaches useful for those assets? If so, what are the most effective valuation methods used for domain names in various situations: stand-alone, trademark based, and/or Web site based?

A key problem in valuing a domain name is how to separate it from other related assets. The domain name value must not be confused with overall Web site value, as other Internet assets, such as operating platform, and software databases, associated with the domain name in the Web site are, in fact, separate items. Similarly, it must not be confused with that of an underlying trademark. In the previous example, Microsoft.com, the domain name represents a tiny fraction of the overall value of the Microsoft brand—and, in fact, it should always be valued as part of the Microsoft trademark/brand. An exception to this rule, discussed in one scenario, is that a valuation may be done for internal purposes, but not for financial reporting. An immutable principle of domain name valuation is that if it is a stand-alone asset, not part of a Web site or a larger trademark/brand asset, the value is by definition going to be less than if it were associated with either a Web site or a trademark.

Another major concern in valuing domain names is the uncertainty surrounding their namesakes. ICANN is constantly experimenting with creating additional domains. Each new one means that another namesake may be registered that is identical to the domain name being valued, with the exception of the dependent suffix (such as .com, .biz, .info, .mobi). Under ICANN's latest decision, potentially hundreds, if not thousands, of new domains will be allowed. Namesakes will be registerable by anyone able to spend $185,000, the proposed price. This will mean that suffixes such as .bank, .loan, .finance, .primerate, .interest, and others will someday soon be separate domains, potentially reducing the value of those that currently serve the financial community.

As is well known, uncertainty and volatility travel together. And there is volatility in the pricing and market for domain names. Over the last decade, the average price of a domain name has dropped from $30,000 to $15,000 to less than $1,000. Yet those domain names with the greatest value 10 years ago remain among the most valuable today. It is in the middle and bottom end of the market where the greatest uncertainty regarding values continues to exist. This means that a valuator needs to exercise caution, particularly with stand-alone domain names. As a result of those concerns and considerations, methodologies have to be considered carefully for each situation. In addition, "new methodologies" have been developed and are being used more often.

Methodologies

As with all assets, the three generally accepted approaches, recognized by IFRS, apply:

1. The market approach, reflecting comparative market prices and sales data
2. The income approach, using imputed or real income to establish value
3. The cost approach, which applies the depreciated replacement cost to value the asset

Their use for intangible assets is discussed at length elsewhere in this volume. Because domain names are relatively new assets and exist in a volatile market, there is no agreement among practitioners or in literature as to which method is best in any given situation. A review of the literature finds some claiming that a cost-based method is the only reliable one; others say that market comparables are best; while a third school plumps for the income approach whenever possible. Even the Internal Revenue Service is not clear on which it believes to be most acceptable for domain names. However, judging by other rulings, the income approach is probably preferable for that particular authority. Some general guidelines, however, can be stated with certainty:

- If the domain name is newly acquired, the cost approach is the most accurate.
- If the domain name is a stand-alone asset with no attachment to a Web site or brand name, then the market approach is preferable.
- If the domain name is attached to a Web site, the income approach is recommended, although the market approach may yield a different higher value.

New Methodologies

The best known of the new methodologies is the so-called statistical approach. When a valuator has to appraise a large portfolio of domain names, a statistical model can be very appropriate. However, it is simply a technique under the market approach. The difference is that the statistical model factors in many more variables to establish a basis of value, which is then compared to the sale prices of other domain names to arrive at comparable values.

There is an active debate on which variables are important in establishing and predicting value of a domain name. Some include the obvious, such as the number of letters in the name, accuracy of spelling, and word count. Statistical models can be very useful in valuing large portfolios of domain names that are primarily stand-alone assets. A case study in this chapter considers valuing a large portfolio of domain names applying a statistical model to establish values via an assessment of market comparables.

One specialized domain-name appraisal company claims to consider all of these factors during its domain name valuation process:

- Recent domain sales
- Brand recognition
- Domain marketability
- E-commerce value
- Top-level domain value
- Industry value
- Recall value
- Zones taken
- Prefix
- Suffix
- Number of terms
- Web frequency
- Search frequency
- Letter count
- Number count
- Word count
- Hyphen count
- Search engine optimization potential
- Word popularity spoken
- Word popularity written
- Phrase popularity spoken
- Phrase popularity written
- Keyword search popularity
- Pay per click (PPC) popularity

When all is said and done, it all comes back to market comparables. Today this is not necessarily bad, because the amount of knowledge and published data on domain name sales is extensive and growing rapidly. A large body of verifiable data on market comparables is available from various sources on the Internet, including Afternic.com, Domainmart.com, Accuratedomains.com, Aboutdomains.com, and, of course, Yahoo! and Google. Critics of statistical modeling generally fall into four broad areas.

1. This group says that there are simply too many variables, and the resulting model makes it difficult to obtain a specific value.
2. Another group claims that these new so-called experts are, in fact, not experts at all. This may be a valid criticism in many cases; nonetheless, a number of trained economists in professional valuation firms use statistical modeling to great advantage.
3. Other critics say there is not enough data. While this may have been true a few years ago, there is now a rapidly growing data flow.

4.   Some are concerned that the statistical results and value conclusions are confusing. While the results may be complex, they are rarely unclear; they reach specific conclusions as to value ranges, which are certainly useful to valuators.

The income approach is useful and appropriate when valuing domain names attached to Web sites or if they are part of a larger trademark bundle. A brief hypothetical example illustrates this: XYZ Corporation has a trademark worth $50 million. Assume it has an active Web site and that the domain name is the same as the trademark (Epic.com and the Epic brand). By measuring the amount of traffic that comes in via the domain name, one can establish the value generated by the domain name. That may be based on the number of inquiries received, which may lead to new customers or new sales. Alternatively, the domain name and Web site may be generating 5% of the brand's total sales because of clicks on the domain name. In that case, one could establish a value based on estimates of the value of each inquiry, or on the sales and cash flows generated though the domain name.

This brief example shows the advantages of the income approach. In the case of domain names, the specific advantages are that value is based on actual activity or revenue and reflects the economic benefits generated by a specific domain name.

Valuation Scenarios

This section on the valuation process concludes with a discussion of three different scenarios: a stand-alone domain name, a Web site–based domain name, and one related to a trademark or brand.

Stand-alone domain names. In this case two approaches are possible, cost or market. If the domain name has been recently acquired, then cost is the most appropriate method. Taking the original cost, establishing that it has maintained its relative value, and adding any maintenance or development costs subsequently incurred can result in an accurate conclusion of value.

Under the market approach, the valuator looks to recent transactions to establish how many similar domain names applicable to analogous businesses or activities have been sold and at what prices. These comparables are then used to establish a range of values. A more complex approach to market comparables is to employ a statistical modeling technique, as discussed earlier.

Web site–based domain names. With a Web site–based domain name, normally the valuator values the entire Web site, including its operating platform, software, and so on, and then separates out the secondary assets, isolating the value of the domain name. Alternatively, the domain name is valued in isolation. In the first instance, the income, market, or cost approach could be used. In most instances, an income method will be most reflective of true value. When the domain name alone is being valued, then the income approach is recommended, reflecting the economic activity generated by it.

Brand-based domain names. If a domain name is part of a brand and duplicates the underlying trademark, then it is not a stand-alone asset. Under IFRS, such a domain name is part of the trademark and would not be valued separately. There are some situations where such a domain name might need to be valued separately (e.g., a contemplated sale); then market comparables would, in all likelihood, be the most appropriate technique.

Valuations for internal purposes. When valuing a domain name for internal purposes, two methods may be considered:

1.   Look at the economic activity generated directly by the domain name, as discussed earlier, and use that as a basis of economic value under the income approach.
2.   Assign a relative proportion of the overall trademark value to the domain name. This informal method assumes the domain represents some percentage of the over-

all brand value. For example, if the brand has a market value of $10 million, based on analyses of activity for the domain name, it could be assumed to account for 5% of that value, or $500,000.

Internal valuations are useful for asset allocations and to measure the effectiveness of the Internet component of an entity's overall activities.

CASE STUDY BACKGROUND

Within the last year or two, the owner of a portfolio of domain names retained a major valuation firm to provide an estimate of fair market value for the portfolio. That portfolio comprised more than 1,100 items, and the purpose of the valuation was to assist in selling it. To accomplish this, the names were first divided into three sections: Geographic Names, Jewels, and the Remainder. Geographic Names included these items, which represented the most valuable component.

Geographic Names (partial list)

Asia.com	Munich.com
Berlin.com	Rome.com
Dublin.com	Saopaulino.com
Europe.com	Singapoere.com
Japan.com	Tokyo.com
London.com	Usa.com
Madrid.com	

Typically, a Jewel among domain names is a short, easily remembered .com, with broad market applicability and high commercial development potential. The portfolio contains the following Jewels, to be valued individually:

Jewels (partial list)

Accountant.com	Lawyer.com
Alumni.com	Lobbyist.com
Atheist.com	Matches.com
Attractive.com	Pediatrician.com
Caress.com	Politician.com
Comic.com	Post.com
Couple.com	Seductive.com
Doctor.com & Dr.com	Teachers.org
Feelings.com	Techie.com
Gardener.com	Tempting.com
Homosexual.net	Tvstar.com

The Remainder was a diverse array of .com, .net, and .org domain names, which were valued in 13 bundles:

.com	.net	.org
One word	One word	One word
Two words	Two words	Two words
Three words	Hyphenations/Numbers	
Hyphenations/Numbers	Mail based	
Fan based		
Mail based		
Legal issues		

CASE STUDY ANALYSES

After 2000, the decline of Internet-based companies forced the reassessment of their core assets, especially domain names, whose values have declined substantially over the years. One exception is the single word, fewer than seven letters, .com domain name with a discernible meaning, which are now rarities in the market. Such short, memorable, and suggestive domain names carry instant brand recognition, credibility, and traffic, which ultimately translate into higher values. However, over the last few years, even these precious gems have declined significantly in value. The offerings of most online auction houses, such as eBay or GreatDomains.com, are littered with long-winded, confusing domain names that usually bring minimal value. Very rarely are short and simple .com domain names for sale.

Smart Search Engines

In the 1990s, searching for a specific topic on the Internet culminated with a list of mostly irrelevant Web sites. Today, advanced search engines are essential in finding pertinent information. Specialists, such as Google, utilize sophisticated technology to index entire Web pages for easy access to requested information. An integral part of their success is that metatags are now built into Web sites. Those are keywords, describing the site's contents, to be sniffed out by search engines and displayed for easy access. As a result, domain names no longer have to describe the content. A Web site owner can now count on metatags to lure potential customers, lessening the significance and value of the domain name.

Decrease in Importance and Value of Domain Names

The result of those trends has been a vast reduction in the value of domain names. Even though short descriptive domain names of seven or eight letters are found occasionally, rarely do they command prices above $100,000 due to these key factors:

- The decline in importance of .com operations and unique Internet presence
- A general decline in value of all dot-com–related assets
- The increasing intelligence of search engines, utilizing metatags as a domain name search alternative when looking for a particular topic

The next table, a number and price comparison of generic top-level domains, illustrates that the average sales price in 2008 was roughly half of what it was in 2007.

TLD	Sold Domains 2007	Sold Domains 2008	Total Sales Revenue 2007 in $	Total Sales Revenue 2008 in $	Average Sales Price 2007 in $	Average Sales Price 2008 in $
.com	12,417	17,643	62,286,440	44,078,322	5,016	2,512
.net	1,484	2,080	3,017,362	3,490,519	2,033	1,670
.org	815	1,301	1,582,586	1,610,945	1,942	1,244
.biz	469	368	528,417	289,988	1,126	790
.info	1,111	1,599	1,212,035	1,340,219	1,091	841

Source: Sedo Secondary Domain Market Study, 2008

Equally important, prices for geographic TLDs (country code Top Level Domains—ccTLDs) also continue to drop. Most notably, the average price of a .co.uk in 2008 was less than half of the average for 2007; the average sale price for all domain names in 2008 was roughly $2,000, with the median between $600 and $750. In other words, a typical domain name is now worth only around $700.

Other Considerations

In valuing the portfolio, two additional factors were considered:

1. The majority of the domain names did not include any supporting intellectual property such as Web sites, trademarks, or copyrights.
2. Based on documents from the client, these had been identified as significant revenue generators:

- London.com, England.com, and Britain.com yield $300,000 per year to redirect traffic to the lessee's designated Web sites.
- Paris.com brings in $90,000 annually in redirect fees from Paris Hotels.com.
- Doctor.com and usa.com generated $72,660 in revenue.

VALMATRIX® Methodology

All three of the accepted approaches—cost, income, and market— were considered in valuing the portfolio. In addition, VALMATRIX® was applied. This is a proprietary statistical analysis tool to measure the relative strengths of competing domain names. It analyzes four primary drivers of domain name value:

1. Top-level domain (20%)

   .com
   .net
   .org

2. Domain name structure (20%)

   Number of letters
   Number of words/syllables
   Existence of homonyms/misspellings
   Existence of abbreviations/hyphenations/numbers

3. Market awareness/recognition (30%)

   Memory retention/recall value
   Descriptive power
   Brand recognition
   International appeal/universality
   Relevance to market/applicable industry
   Search engine compatibility

4. Commercial development potential (30%)

   Focus within industry (broad or specific)
   Generic nature
   Branding potential
   Target market(s)
   Extendibility
   Advertising potential

Domain names are ranked on a 200-point system; the VALMATRIX® score is then compared with those of competing domain names to estimate its potential value.

Methods Employed

Careful consideration of the domain names listed, their related intellectual property, various appropriate methodologies, information available, and the surrounding circumstances led to the conclusion that the market-comparable method in conjunction with VALMATRIX® would provide the most accurate measure of fair market value for the domain name portfolio. Details of the valuation process are discussed next.

Geographic names. The Geographic names were valued individually based on comparable transactions. Although the number of comparables was limited, their prices served as a starting point for valuing the top domain names. Adjustments were made based on tourism, economic uncertainties, and Internet search activity. Although definitive values were difficult to project, the final figure is believed to represent a realistic sales price.

Jewels. Jewels is the second most valuable group. Jewels typically are easily remembered one-word .coms with fewer than 10 letters that do not require substantial advertising budgets to entice people to their Web sites. They rarely contain misspellings, abbreviations, hyphenations, or numbers, and attract diverse demographics due to the wide range of content on such sites. This ability will tend to generate greater traffic and encourage advertisers to pay a premium for web banners, links, and/or pop-ups. Further, the domain name should have universal appeal so it could be employed on a global scale.

The VALMATRIX® model combined with market comparables was chosen. The first step is to calculate an individual score for each Jewel as well as for all comparable transactions. The latter were plotted on a scatter diagram with VALMATRIX® score on the x-axis and sales price on the y-axis; that illustrated a direct relationship between them. The plotting of the comparable transactions data allows development of a regression equation. Once this is created, valuing the Jewels requires simply entering each domain name's VALMATRIX® score into the regression equation and solving for a sales price.

Balance of the portfolio. The balance of the portfolio was also valued based on comparable transactions. For each of the 13 bundles, the most closely related sale transactions occurring over the last 12 months were listed. The median price of comparable transactions for each bundle was calculated and applied to all domain names within the corresponding category.

Exceptions to this methodology of using market comparables to value certain domain names categories are listed next.

- Mail-based .coms were valued at $100 each.
- Fan-based .coms were valued at $150 each.
- Two-word .net, hyphenations/numbers, and mail-based categories were discounted 40% from their .com counterparts
- Two-word .orgs were discounted 90% from two-word .coms.
- Collector.org, graduate.org, and musician.org were deemed comparable to the one-word .com category and valued at $1,700 each as they are believed to have greater potential than the average .org.
- Domain names that have or could potentially have legal issues were discounted 40% for the elevated risk.

Conclusions

In this particular case, despite economic conditions, significant value was considered to exist in the portfolio, even after the fall in price of the average domain name. Analyses were performed to determine a fair market value for a sale of the portfolio. The market comparables method in conjunction with VALMATRIX® statistical analysis was determined to provide the most accurate measure of fair market value.

An exhaustive review of the documents supplied by the client and a thorough analysis of comparable domain name sales, as well as application of proprietary VALMATRIX® statistical analysis, resulted in these conclusions:

Section	Fair Market Value $
Geographic Names	1,250,000
Jewels	352,000
Remainder	165,000
Total Portfolio	1,767,000
Rounded	1,750,000

19 HEDGING

RICHARD PEDDE

CANADA

INTRODUCTION

This chapter is designed to give an overview of hedging and the hedging process and describes the evaluation of a hedging program by an entity. Many corporations and even government entities engage in hedging. Various accounting policies attempt to capture the value of a hedge. Given the significant price movements in many commodities, especially during the second half of 2008, many hedging strategies did not perform as expected or, worse, had a large negative impact on earnings.

WHAT IS HEDGING?

The term is best explained with a true-life example. In November 2007, the *New York Times* predicted that Southwest Airlines could once again dominate the domestic airline industry. It had long been known for good customer service and high labor productivity; less well known is that starting in 2000, Southwest engaged in jet fuel hedging, which helped keep it very profitable. In 2004, hedging gains generated $455 million; in 2005, $892 million, in 2006, $675 million and in the first nine months of 2007, $439 million. At that time, Southwest used a variety of contracts to lock in most of its fuel needs through 2009. The price was equivalent to $51 per barrel of crude, which in November 2007 sold for $90 per barrel; the value of the contracts was then over $2 billion.

Oil Price Changes

By the second quarter (Q2) of 2008, with crude soaring to almost $150 per barrel, the hedges had been extended to 2010 and were now worth $6 billion, as the airline expected fuel prices to remain high. While other airlines were forced to raise fares in order to cover rising fuel costs, Southwest used the hedging gains to improve efficiencies and market share. Exhibit 19.1 shows what happened to the price of crude; it sets out the daily closing prices for the latest crude oil futures contract traded on New York Mercantile Exchange.

Exhibit 19.1 NYMEX Crude Oil Futures

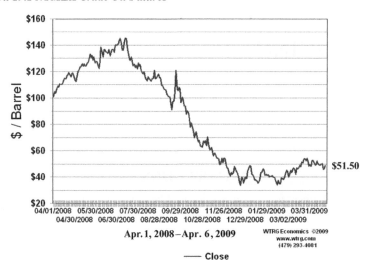

However, by the third quarter (Q3) of 2008, with crude oil plunging and fuel prices following, as shown in the exhibit, Southwest reported its first loss in 17 years, as the value of the contracts dropped to $2.5 billion; by year-end 2008, they had virtually no value at all. Southwest's growth had been postponed indefinitely, as Standard & Poor's (S&P) cut its credit rating from A– to BBB+; the firm had to raise $400 million in the bond market, in part to cover hedging losses For this loan, Southwest put up 17 jets as collateral and paid 10.5% interest, nearly double what it had been in 2004.

Southwest was not alone in this predicament: in Q3 2008, United Airlines and US Airways incurred almost $2 billion in accounting losses on their hedges; other airlines suffered similar fates. To add to the confusion, airlines account for hedging losses at different times in their reporting cycles and in different ways. Because hedges are put on months in advance, such write-downs are likely to continue. As of the beginning of 2009, American Airlines, for example, had hedged 34% of its expected 2009 fuel consumption at the equivalent of $71 to $99 per barrel of crude. United said it had hedged 28% of its expected 2009 usage at $101 to $114 per barrel, while Southwest hedged 75% of its 2009 needs at $73 per barrel. All of those hedges are at prices much higher than the average $45 per barrel of Q1 2009. The S&P airline analyst Betsy J. Snyder said, "It's like you can't win. People bother you when you don't hedge, and when you do, and prices go down, you get hit."[1]

DEFINITION OF HEDGING

The Organization for Economic Co-operation and Development (OECD) in a report entitled "Economic Outlook: Sources and Methods." defines hedging as the use of financial instruments, such as futures contracts, to offset risks in an investment portfolio as an increase in the value of the hedging instrument is supposed to offset declines in other assets.[2] Hedges can obviously involve instruments other than financial contracts and are often used outside of investment portfolios. The importance of this definition is that it introduces the concept of risk; in setting up a hedging program, the objective should be to decrease, not increase, risk.

---

[1] *Betsey J. Snyder, New York Times, 17 October 2008*

[2] *Organization for Economic Co-operation and Development, "Economic Outlook: Sources and Methods,"*

In this context, *risk* is not the commonly understood "source of danger" but a deviation from an expected outcome. For example, supposing an investor has $100 in a savings account at a bank earning 5%; after one year he expects to have $105. Bank failure would clearly lead to less than $105; hence, it is a risk to this individual. Such risks include not just unexpected losses but also unanticipated gains. Continuing with the savings account example, the investor is faced with paying tax on the interest. The tax code might be changed: if interest was exempted, most investors would rejoice. Alas, this too is a risk factor; the changes could easily have resulted in higher taxes.

As implied by the OECD definition, in finance, a hedge of a commercial activity is a position established in one market to offset the price risk of a similar position in another. When the value of the hedged position goes up, that of the hedge should go down. As such, a hedging program should reduce the volatility of both revenues and expenses and also that of the value of the commercial activity itself. In theory, a hedge should serve to smooth changes in value.

IS THE RISK HEDGEABLE?

Categories of risks that can be and commonly are hedged include changes in interest rates (a rise in these rates will increase borrowing costs), the chance a borrower will not pay the amount owing when due, and exchange rates from cash flows generated abroad. In addition, risks to changes in equity prices are frequently hedged by investors. Once a risk has been identified, the question as to whether it is hedgeable remains. Correlation analyses of price movements between the risky asset or cash flow and various hedging vehicles can provide some guidance. To the extent the price changes move in perfect unison—a correlation of 1.0—an exact neutralization can be achieved.

Unfortunately, as the cliché goes, "Perfect hedges can be found only in English gardens." That is, the correlation of price movements is normally less than 1. Whether a correlation of 0.8 or 0.9 constitutes a reasonable hedge depends entirely on the risk appetites of those involved. Some feel that even a much weaker relationship will reduce the long-term variability, while others believe that such a low figure may increase short-term volatility. The deviation from a perfect correlation is generally referred to as *basis risk* and is discussed later.

COMMON HEDGING VEHICLES

Common vehicles used to hedge are forwards, futures, and option contracts, all of which were used as early as the late seventeenth century. With these forming the base, over the last 50 years a plethora of additional vehicles has been developed and a huge global hedge market has evolved. Among the newer vehicles are swaps, collars, funded puts, put spreads, and average price options. Valuing those demands an understanding of basic financial building blocks.

Forward Contracts

A forward contract is an agreement between two parties, such as an airline and a refinery, in which one party (the refinery) agrees to deliver an agreed quantity (80,000 gallons) of a product (jet fuel) to the other (an airline) at an established price (equivalent to $80 crude) on a specified future date (May 2009) at a predetermined place (Heathrow). Since forwards are privately negotiated contracts, it is difficult to change any component or even get out of them unless the other party agrees. This inflexibility can cause problems: Suppose the airline experiences less than the forecasted demand resulting in canceled flights, and therefore, needs less fuel than contracted. As a result, the excess has to be sold on the open market—hopefully at a profit, or at a loss, which is more probable.

If any of the conditions are not met by either party, the one affected can demand compensation. Clearly, the largest risk faced by either is overall performance; at the extreme, the question is: Will the counterparty be a viable entity throughout the contract? There have been numerous incidents over the last two decades of airlines declaring bankruptcy; if the price of the fuel underlying the forward contracts has risen sharply, however, the refiner would suffer a financial loss.

To mitigate such risks, often, users of forward contracts are required to post collateral to offset unrealized losses. As a result, any participant needs to monitor its own relative market position with each counterparty. One technique to limit counterparty risk is to enforce a specific credit rating—AA, for example. However, as the recent AIG debacle has shown, credit ratings may not be sufficient either. Some forward contracts include material adverse change (MAC) clauses. Should either party suffer a MAC, the other can demand the posting of additional collateral or even unwind the contract at the prevailing market price. Though financial statements usually cover the credit status of forward contract counterparties, a recently suggested improvement is to present their market-determined default probability adjusted values.

In the case of Southwest Airlines, at year-end 2007, it held $2 billion in cash collateral against forward contracts with "nine counterparties containing early termination rights and/or bilateral collateral provisions whereby security is required if market risk exposure exceeds a specified threshold amount or credit ratings fall below certain levels."[3] As fuel prices declined substantially in the second half of 2008 and the value of these contracts declined, Southwest not only had to return the cash collateral but had to raise funds to post the required margin. In addition to the collateral requirements arising from a decline in fuel prices, further funds were required because of Southwest's credit downgrade. Forward contracts can certainly help corporations manage their input price risks, but in the process, they incur counterparty risks with suppliers and liquidity risks to fulfill their collateral obligations.

Futures Contracts

Futures contracts, while in many ways similar to forwards, have additional features that avoid the counterparty risks. Unlike customized forwards, futures contracts are traded on organized exchanges in a variety of commodities including many agricultural goods, major and minor currencies, differing forms of energy, countless financial instruments, and a range of metals. Each exchange determines the standardized terms of its contracts including delivery month(s), locations, acceptable grades/quality, and contract size.

The opportunity to make or take delivery plays a crucial role in helping to ensure that futures prices accurately reflect the actual cash market value of the relevant item. If futures prices are too high, a dealer would sell the front (most recent) contract in the futures market while simultaneously purchasing the underlying item in the cash market, which would then be delivered against the futures obligations. A mirror-image trade would be executed if the futures price was too low vis-à-vis the cash market. Even though relatively few positions, about 2%, are settled this way, the ability to deliver ensures a close correlation between the markets.

Crucial to the functioning of a futures market is the clearinghouse, which has three primary roles:

---

[3] *Southwest Airlines, Annual Report 2007*

1. Matching buy and sell transactions. Every futures contract involves both a buyer and a seller, and by matching them in a timely fashion, the clearinghouse guarantees that adequate margin is maintained by financially qualified entities based on their net long and short positions.
2. Ensuring the integrity of the contracts traded. Because the value of the contracts changes minute by minute, the clearinghouse has to ensure the payment to those who accrue gains are collected from those incurring losses.
3. Providing a delivery mechanism so that the futures prices track those of the underlying item.

Matching Trades

Every transaction must be "cleared" by, or through, a clearinghouse member firm. Exhibit 19.2 illustrates the clearing of on-floor buy/sell trades; electronic transactions eliminate some steps.

Exhibit 19.2 Clearinghouse Trade Confirmation Flow

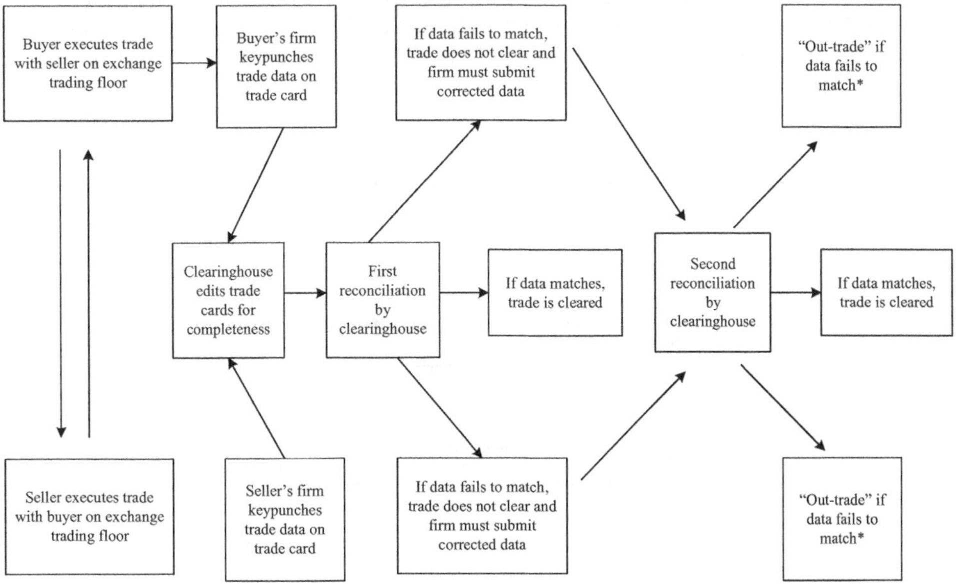

*For the trade to clear, firms must submit corrected trade data the following morning.

ASSURING INTEGRITY OF FUTURE CONTRACTS

An exchange needs to ensure that winners receive their spoils and losers pay the piper. Obviously this becomes more significant as trading leverage increases. Futures contracts typically require no down payment and only a fraction of their value as margin. The system assures buyers and sellers who realize gains that the money will be there on a daily basis. The key is that the clearinghouse becomes the obligator on each contract cleared by interposing itself into the trades as the buyer to every seller and the seller to every buyer, thus severing the linkage between the original counterparties. It is the clearinghouse that largely differentiates futures contracts from forwards.

Another benefit of a clearinghouse is improved liquidity in the "secondary" market. Due to changing perceptions of the underlying item's value, most contracts are not held to maturity and therefore not delivered. Suppose an airline wants to cash out after a substantial market rally in jet fuel. As is human nature, the seller hangs on, thinking the rally was an aberration, and wants to avoid crystallizing its losses. In a forward, the buyer must come to an agreement with the original seller. Failing that, it must enter into a second contract mirroring the first, but this time as the seller. The result is the buyer has two offsetting contracts with their associated credit risks. In a futures market, the buyer does not need to come to an agreement with anyone but must merely sell to a new buyer.

Settlement and Mark to Market

Maintaining the good-faith deposit, paid by a buyer to a seller to demonstrate its intention to complete the purchase, requires a well-functioning settlement and margining process. In this, settlement prices play a significant role; each day a settlement price for every tradable contract is published shortly after the close of trading. This is not necessarily the last traded price but is within the range of transactions at or near the close of business. If a particular contract did not trade at the close, a nominal settlement price is established based on those of other relevant contracts. When the settlement prices are published, all purchases and sales made that day are, for clearing purposes only, adjusted to them, and all open transactions are considered to have been made at that level. If Southwest had purchased a jet fuel contract at $2.00 per gallon and the market had closed and settled at $1.90, it would be required to pay $0.10 per gallon to the clearinghouse. (See Exhibits 19.3 and 19.4 for flow diagrams of initiating and liquidating trades in futures markets.)

Exhibit 19.3 Initiating Trades and Order Flow for Futures Contracts

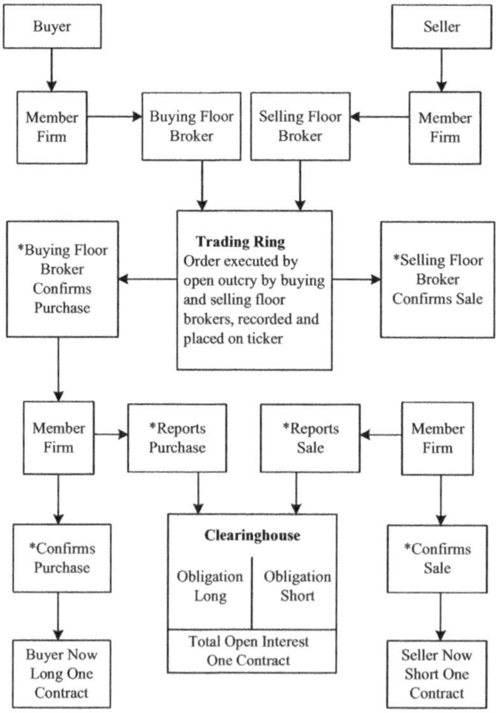

*Includes price, quantity, delivery month, and time of transaction

Exhibit 19.4 Liquidating Trades and Order Flow for Futures Contracts

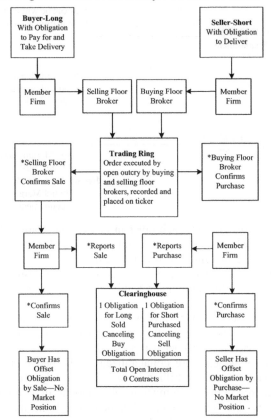

Includes price, quantity, delivery month, and time of transaction

REQUIRED MARGINS

Margins are an important function of futures contracts as they ensure that hedgers and traders with winning positions are able to realize their profits. An "initial" margin must be posted at the time of opening a trade; "maintenance" margin is the amount that must be on deposit after adverse market moves; "variation" margin must be posted to restore an amount on deposit to the maintenance level. Each exchange establishes its own margin requirements for each contract based on the expected variability in its prices.

Exhibit 19.5 Comparison of Initial, Maintenance, and Variation Margins

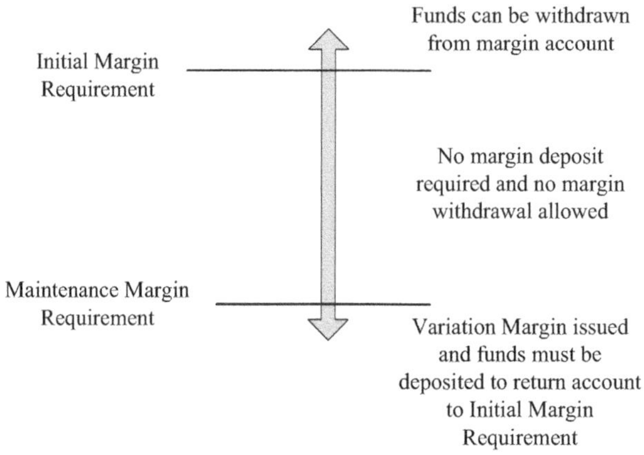

The various margins differ from each other in one crucial feature: the initial margin is simply good-faith money while maintenance margins are passed from the loser to the winner. Only when the maintenance margin is insufficient and variation margin calls are not met is the initial margin transferred. All variation margins must be in cash, as only that is transferred from loser to winner. Most exchanges require members to liquidate positions that are not properly margined.

This mark-to-market and margining process is different from that for forwards. It is applied daily to all open futures positions so that gains and losses are settled daily. In Q2 2008, when crude oil was approaching $150 per barrel, Southwest had forward fuel price contracts worth $6 billion, some of which were collateralized. If the hedges had been via futures, Southwest would have had the full $6 billion in cash. Conversely, once fuel prices declined, it would have been required to deposit a much greater amount. In addition to making margin calls after price changes, the exchanges can alter both initial and maintenance margins, if there is higher volatility in prices. The significant changes in commodity prices during 2008 tested the inherent creditworthiness of both forward and futures contracts. All major exchanges fully honored every futures contract; this was not true for all forwards.

PROBLEMS WITH FUTURES CONTRACTS

Although futures contracts are available on hundreds of different items, trading volume is concentrated in a few dozen. The result is a lack of liquidity in many contracts leading to the cockroach motel problem: "Once you get in, you can't get out." Airlines face this as trading volumes in jet fuel contracts are very low. This has forced them to use other energy contracts, such as heating oil and crude futures, in what is commonly referred to as cross hedging. Though such a hedge reduces the oil price risk, it still leaves the jet fuel–specific component. Hurricane Katrina resulted in the closing of much of the refining capacity of jet fuel, which not only caused a shortage but also caused a surplus of crude. Most often, the correlation between the two will be high, but when the traditional relationship breaks down, hedgers may be left with even more risk.

The lack of perfect correlation between the hedge vehicle and the hedged item is the *basis risk*. The most common source of basis risk is the difference between the cash market price of an item and the price of the front-month futures contract on that item. It also arises from cash and futures market differences in delivery locations, quality, and timing. The ability to deliver usually ensures that the basis for equivalent specifications becomes narrower by the time the futures contract matures; that is, the correlation is close to 1.0. However, this does not always occur; when the Chicago Board of Trade July 2008 wheat contract matured, the deviation between cash and futures prices was nearly 25%. In evaluating a hedging program using futures, the lack of liquidity, basis risk in cross hedging, and cash/futures deviations must be considered.

VALUING FUTURES CONTRACTS

Valuing a futures contract is relatively easy, as the settlement prices are published on the Internet. The data in the next table came from the New York Mercantile Exchange (NYMEX) Web site. Every transaction is marked to market using this Level 1 data. A light sweet crude contract is 1,000 barrels for delivery at Cushing, Oklahoma.

NYMEX CRUDE OIL TRADING DATA—6 APRIL 2009

Month	Settlement	Month	Settlement	Month	Settlement
May-09	$51.05	November-10	$67.35	May-12	$72.92
June-09	$53.38	December-10	$67.82	June-12	$73.11
July-09	$55.40	January-11	$68.26	July-12	$73.29
August-09	$56.76	February-11	$68.68	August-12	$73.47
September-09	$57.84	March-11	$69.07	September-12	$73.64
October-09	$58.88	April-11	$69.44	October-12	$73.81
November-09	$59.79	May-11	$69.80	November-12	$73.98
December-09	$60.67	June-11	$70.16	December-12	$74.15
January-10	$61.44	July-11	$70.50	January-13	$74.32
February-10	$62.14	August-11	$70.80	March-13	$74.66
March-10	$62.81	September-11	$71.09	June-13	$75.17
April-10	$63.46	October-11	$71.35	October-13	$75.85
May-10	$64.09	November-11	$71.60	November-13	$76.02
June-10	$64.71	December-11	$71.85	December-13	$76.19
July-10	$65.29	January-12	$72.09	June-14	$77.29
August-10	$65.83	February-12	$72.32	December-14	$78.34
September-10	$66.35	March-12	$72.53	June-15	$79.39
October-10	$66.86	April-12	$72.73		

On April 6, 2009, a contract maturing in October 2010 had a value of $66,860; if the maturity date was October 2013, it would be $75,850, or $8,990 (13.4%) higher, reflecting interest at 4.3% over the period. This is the normal situation, confusingly called a backwardation market. From time to time, the pattern inverts and futures prices for faraway deliveries (such as in 2013) are less than the spot price. This usually occurs when speculative activity is rampant and there is some benefit to owning the item at present; the situation is known as a contango market.

Valuing Forward Contracts

Valuing a forward is more complex and is theoretically done by a no-arbitrage model; this assumes a dealer (such as an investment bank) can either buy (go long) or sell (go short) and hold the item, using borrowed money at the annual rate r. The complex formula is:

$$F_{t_1 T} = (S_t + s)e^{r(T-t)}$$

Where

$F_{t_1 T}$ = forward price at time T

S_t = spot price at time t (now)

s = storage and carrying costs

e = natural logarithm

r = borrowing rate between t and T

For crude oil, the figures are

$$S_t = \$51.05 \ (3 \text{ April } 2009)$$
$$s = \$0.45 \text{ a month}$$
$$r = 1.6\% \text{ a year}$$
$$F_{t,T} = \text{in three months (July)}$$
$$= (\$51.05 + (3*0.045)) \, e^{(0.016 \times 0.25)}$$
$$= \$52.61$$
$$\text{Futures price} = \$55.40$$

Another method, suitable for long-term forwards, is to use the present value of the difference between the contract and related prices.

Example

Airline AG Future Jet Fuel Purchases

Month	Volume	Price	Crude Equivalent	Futures Price
	000 gallons			
May-09	20,000	$1.70	$62.86	$53.38
June-09	20,000	$1.70	$62.86	$55.40
July-09	30,000	$1.75	$64.71	$56.76
August-09	30,000	$1.75	$64.71	$57.84
September-09	30,000	$1.75	$64.71	$58.88
October-09	20,000	$1.75	$64.71	$59.79
November-09	15,000	$1.75	$64.71	$60.67
December-09	25,000	$1.75	$64.71	$61.44

Month	Crude Profit (Loss)	Jet Fuel Conversion	Total Profit (Loss)	PV Factor 9.0%	Present Value $'000
April-10	($9.48)	($0.26)	($5,126.37)	0.9929	(5,090)
May-10	($7.46)	($0.20)	($4,033.74)	0.9858	(3,976)
June-10	($7.95)	($0.21)	($6,447.16)	0.9787	(6,310)
July-10	($6.87)	($0.19)	($5,570.89)	0.9717	(5,413)
August-10	($5.83)	($0.16)	($4,727.07)	0.9648	(4,561)
September-10	($4.92)	($0.13)	($2,659.15)	0.9579	(2,547)
October-10	($4.04)	($0.11)	($1,637.37)	0.9510	(1,557)
January -10	($3.27)	($0.09)	($2,208.32)	0.9442	2,085)
					(31,539)

The result is a loss based on crude futures of $31.5 million on hedging jet fuel with forwards; it uses a barrel of crude oil/gallon of jet fuel price ratio of 36.9749, based on the April 6, 2009, average relationship of crude and heating oil settlement prices.

HEDGING WITH OPTIONS

Some hedging programs include options that grant the right but not the obligation to buy (a call option) a certain quantity of an item from the issuer at a stated price within a specified period. A put option grants the right but not the obligation to sell that item. In return for the rights, the holder pays the issuer a premium. In a sense, options are a form of insurance; in return for the premium, the holder is protected from adverse scenarios. Options on many items trade on exchanges and confer all the benefits and risks associated with futures contracts. Options that confer all the benefits and risks associated with forwards are also available from counterparties.

Suppose an airline wishes to protect itself against higher fuel prices but does not want to post collateral. By purchasing a call option, it will have the right but not the obligation to buy a set quantity of fuel from a refiner at a specified price within a certain timeframe. Obviously it will take advantage of this right only should the price of fuel increase above the exercise price. This illustrates an additional component of hedging. Futures or forward contracts, which have symmetrically equal but opposite payoffs to the risk, will result in hedging reducing the variation of outcomes. With options, only the negative variation is eliminated. If Southwest had hedged with call options, they would have become as valuable as the actual forwards as the price of fuel rose; this means that counterparty performance issues are identical; the financial statements will show similar gains, and all the fuel price volatility will be reflected in the income statement. If, however, the fuel price goes down, the loss is limited to the cost of the options.

VALUING OPTIONS

The value of an option is the complex function of numerous variables and the interplay between them. Among these are the relationship between the exercise and prevailing price of the item, the time until expiration, the distribution of expected daily price changes, as well as the relative return on the item versus the cost of holding it. The subject is covered in Chapters 17 and 32.

NATURAL HEDGES

Many hedges do not involve the instruments mentioned but rather are natural hedges; those reduce an undesired risk, for example, by matching revenues, expenses, and cash flows. A U.S.-based exporter faces the risk of an appreciation in the dollar; a natural hedge is to have a production facility in the market to which it is exporting. Clearly, this entails other risks, such as expropriation, which may not be hedgeable. Once an entity opens a foreign operation, it may have a further natural hedge by borrowing in the local currency to finance such operations. Natural hedges are entity specific and must be evaluated on an individual basis.

ACCOUNTING FOR HEDGES

In theory, an effective hedging strategy smoothes out changes in shareholder value. Until the late 1990s, most gains and losses on hedging instruments were deferred in the financial statements or were kept off balance sheet until it was appropriate to include them in net income. Statement of Financial Accounting Standards (SFAS) 133 released in June 1998 followed by International Accounting Standard (IAS) 39 put an end to such treatment. Current hedge accounting is a variation from what would normally be applied according to generally accepted accounting principles to enable a matching of certain offsetting gains and losses in net income. As mentioned in the last section, many types of transactions that may form a hedging strategy in economic terms do not qualify for hedge accounting, which is an attempt to treat the hedged position and the hedging instrument in a similar fashion.

In the normal course of business, some organizations base their hedging strategies on portfolios of positions with exposure to offsetting risks. Such a portfolio approach may include a combination of hedged and hedge vehicle positions, with the strategies based on net amounts. For example, the lack of a direct hedge for jet fuel, much less in specific locations, has led airlines to hedge with a basket of energy products including Brent (North Sea) crude, West Texas Intermediate crude (NYMEX), unleaded gasoline and heating oil (NYMEX). However, IFRS precludes hedge accounting based on a net portfolio basis. As with Southwest, this may increase the volatility in reported financials.

Ultimately, all financial instruments should be on the balance sheet at fair value. Hedge accounting, a special treatment to ensure that the timing of income recognition on the hedged item matches that of the hedging instrument, attempts to do this. Application of hedge accounting is optional and subjective; identical situations at two different entities may be given different accounting treatments. While hedge accounting requires that effective hedging relationships are in place, the opposite is not true: An effective hedging relationship does not require hedge accounting. The alternative is measure the hedging instruments at fair value, with gains and losses recognized in net earnings.

SFAS 133 and IAS 39 define hedge accounting and establish accounting and reporting requirements for derivatives; their focus is on the hedging instrument rather than on the hedged risk, with a broad definition of "derivative" in SFAS 133:9:

> *A derivative instrument is a financial instrument or other contract with all three of the following characteristics:*
>
> > *It has (1) one or more underlying and (2) one or more notional amounts (by any other name) or payment provisions or both. Those terms determine the amount of the settlement or settlements, and, in some cases, whether or not a settlement is required.*
> >
> > *It requires no initial net investment or an initial net investment that is smaller than would be required for other types of contracts that would be expected to have a similar response to changes in market factors.*
> >
> > *Its terms require or permit net settlement, it can readily be settled net by a means outside the contract, or it provides for delivery of an asset that puts the recipient in a position not substantially different from net settlement."*

Hedge accounting is a method under which certain gains and losses are recognized in net income simultaneously, when otherwise they would have been recorded in different periods; the conditions for this are:

1. Management must have previously identified and documented a hedging strategy. This should include: the nature of the risk or risks being hedged, in accordance with the organization's risk management strategy; amounts and other characteristics of hedged and hedging positions; and the anticipated and designated periods during which hedge accounting will be applied. Any hedging relationship must be designated and documented to set out (a) the risk management objective and strategy for the relationship, and (b) the method for assessing the effectiveness of the hedge program. This is statistically measured by the correlation of changes in fair values or cash flows of the hedged and hedging items.

2. From the start, it must be ensured that (a) the transactions to be hedged be identified as probable and (b) the hedging relationship will be reasonably effective during its expected term.

3. The effectiveness of a hedge must be reliably measurable and subject to regular checks (at least every three months) until the end of the designated hedging period.

Under SFAS 133, there are two types of hedge accounting; they produce similar long-term net effects on income but differ in short-term timing.

1. *Fair value hedges* consist of measuring both the hedged position and hedging instrument at fair value and in recognizing the offsetting changes immediately in net earnings. The hedged position can include a recognized asset or liability or an unrecognized firm commitment. The related derivatives are mark to market through earnings and will offset the changes in the values of the underlying exposures. What is important is that the changes in fair value of both the hedged position and the hedge instrument are recognized in the current period.

2. *Cash flow hedges* consist of temporarily charging unrealized gains and losses on hedging instruments to Other Comprehensive Income (OCI) until they are transferred to net earnings, as the offsetting losses/gains of the hedged positions are

realized. As with fair value hedges, the hedged position can include highly probable forecast transactions attributable to a specific risk or the variability in the cash flows of a recognized asset or liability. The "effective" portions of the hedging instruments are marked to market, carried at fair value, and recorded in OCI; the ineffective portions are recorded in current earnings. This delays the recognition in net earnings of any gains or losses, which should offset each other, from both the hedged risks and the hedging instruments, until the cash flows from the hedged position have been realized. The hedging gains/losses previously in OCI are then transferred to earnings.

Much of the controversy surrounding hedge accounting arises from the possibility that it increases financial statement volatility. Previously ineffective and imprecise hedges could be "hidden" and recognized only on maturity. In contrast to these obviously positive effects, this hedge accounting does not recognize the importance of some common practices, such as macro hedges and portfolio hedging. As is shown by Southwest, the result is a greater chance that, for technical reasons, hedge mismatches will create volatile earnings that do not necessarily reflect the economics of the hedging relationships.

SOUTHWEST AIRLINES' SITUATION

Southwest Airlines' 2007 Annual Report has an interesting discussion of the impact accounting policies have on valuation, or perceived valuation, of the entity. To summarize:

	Profit (in $mm)	Operating Income (in $mm)
2006	499	934
2007	645	791
Change	146	–143
% Year on Year	29.3%	–15.3%

The difference between profit and operating income is largely related to the ineffectiveness, as per SFAS 133, of some hedges and therefore the absence of hedge accounting for certain fuel derivatives. Following the standard, the fair values for both the hedging instruments and forward jet fuel prices are estimated before the hedges settle. Fair value of the hedge vehicles, even over-the-counter ones, often can be independently estimated, at least by the counterparty. Since there is no reliable forward market for jet fuel, to measure the effectiveness of its hedged vehicles for SFAS 133, Southwest must estimate future prices of jet fuel. According to Southwest's Annual Report, this is done through "the observation of similar commodity futures prices (such as crude oil, heating oil and unleaded gasoline) and adjusted based on variations of those like commodities to the Company's ultimate expected price to be paid for jet fuel at the specific locations in which the Company hedges."

Because of the increased volatility in energy markets, the effectiveness under SFAS 133 of some hedges, especially unleaded gasoline, has changed so much that some instruments no longer qualify for hedge accounting. Southwest states: "Ineffectiveness is inherent in hedging jet fuel with derivative positions based in other crude oil related commodities." Southwest expects to consume 1.5 billion gallons of jet fuel a year, which means that its costs change by $15 million for each $0.01 increase or decrease in the fuel price. In view of its size, management considers it important to hedge this expense. As a result: "[E]ven though these derivatives may not qualify for SFAS 133 special accounting, the Company continues to hold the instruments as it believes they continue to represent good 'economic hedges' in its goal to minimize jet fuel costs." Because of this stance, Southwest is willing to accept higher volatility in its periodic financial results. The firm has also stated that it believes operating income provides a better indication of financial performance than net earnings.

EPILOGUE: BARRICK'S EXPERIENCE

Some forms of risk are inherent to a specific business activity while others are considered to be a natural part of the commercial activity. In the same way, some hedging programs, by offsetting downside risks, will reduce future benefits. In early 2003, after approximately 15 years of a successful gold hedging program that returned an estimated $2.2 billion of additional profit, Barrick Gold Corporation, the second largest North American gold producer, changed its strategy. Previously, hedging had earned approximately $65 an ounce (between 16% and 21%) above the spot price of gold over the period. However, now that the price of gold was starting to rise, the program had become an issue with investors who feared Barrick was not in a position to take advantage of the great potential gains.

Over the years, Barrick had used numerous different hedging vehicles, from simple futures and forwards to the increasingly complex swaps, collars, and average price put options. Market participants considered that firm to be one of the most sophisticated risk managers. In comparison to Southwest's hedging a significant (~25%) portion of its expenses, Barrick was hedging a substantial portion of its revenue. During 2003, in spite of having cut back its hedge position from 26% to 20% of its approximately 87 million ounces of reserves, Barrick's share price had declined by 11% to about $22, while the price of gold had risen by 18%. This share price decline reflected investors' fears that if the price of gold continued to rise, Barrick would be selling its production for less than its nonhedged competitors would.

In Q1 2007, Barrick reported a charge of $557 million to exit the last of its hedge positions; this eliminated its hedge book for current production. Since then the price of gold has risen 40%; Barrick's shares rose by 23%, while the Dow Jones Industrial Average has dropped 40 %.

As Barrick's experience shows, perceptions of a successful hedging program change with time and circumstances. In the late 1980s, Barrick focused on being, and was valued as, a very efficient producer of gold with little gold price risk. That is, its share price reflected the discounted hedged value of its future gold production; 20 years later, investors consider the inherent and unhedged gold price risk (and opportunity) as an advantage.

20 INTELLECTUAL PROPERTY RIGHTS

BYEONGIL JEONG

KOREA

INTRODUCTION

As a class of intangible assets, protected by law, intellectual property rights (IPR) are an internationally recognized concept, encompassing copyright, related matters, and what is legally "industrial property" since the Paris Convention of 1883 for the Protection of Industrial Property. This covers patents, trade names, trademarks, service marks, designs, and unfair competition. All intellectual properties are intangible assets that either make a creation possible or that a creation makes possible.[1]

Currently, intangible assets are a broad category, which include new types of IPR such as digital contents of display features, semiconductor circuitry designs, human identity features, and trade identity symbols.

Innovation

Technology is the process by which humans modify nature to meet their needs and wants. It is closely associated with innovation, which is the transformation of ideas into new and useful products or processes. Innovation requires not only creative people and organizations but also the availability of technology as well as science and engineering talent.[2]

Innovation leads from technologies to inventions that should be useful for creating, manufacturing, or processing a product. To be patentable, an invention must be new, useful, or nonobvious in order to satisfy the requirements for a patent application.

There is no definition of the term "invention" in the U.S. Patent Act, nor in the related *Manual of Patent Examining Procedure*. The dictionary definition is: "a new, useful, and non-obvious process, machine, or product"; in common use, the term also covers: a new, useful, and nonobvious improvement of a process, machine, or product.[3] Not every invention can be patented in every country, as most have developed specific criteria. In Korea, the definition of invention in the patent act is, in essence, "the highly advanced creation of a technical idea."

A patentable invention does not mean a patented technology but a completed invention that meets local criteria. Technologies fall into two classes: one does not satisfy the conditions for a patent (e.g., it may not meet the nonobvious criterion); the other class is

---

[1] See Donald S. Chisum and Michael A. Jacobs, *Understanding Intellectual Property Law* (New York: Matthew Bender, 1998).

[2] See www.nae.edu/nae/techlithome.nsf/weblinks/KGRG-55A3ER

[3] www.lectlaw.com/def/i068.htm.

one for which a patent application may be filed. The former are normally treated as know-how" or trade secret, defined as: "Any formula, pattern, device or compilation of information which is used in one's business and gives him an opportunity to obtain competitiveness over who do not know or use it." (See Chapter 34.) A patented invention means an invention for which a patent has been granted although the invention may not yet have been commercialized.

Patentable inventions comprise three groups:

1. Those for which no patent application is to be made due to the need for disclosure
2. Filed applications
3. Granted patent

The reason for the different categories is that the value of any invention differs significantly according to the strength or weakness of its protection. Hence, a patented invention may be much more valuable than a concept or an immature invention, which is not sufficiently finished to be transferable independently.

Valuing Technologies

A major factor affecting value is the degree of usefulness or desirability of the subject, especially in comparison with other things. In the same way, part of any valuation assignment is a comparative assessment or measurement of the subject with respect to its embodiment of a certain value.[4] The basic concept of valuing a technology starts with the well-known five Ws—who, when, where, what, why—and one H—how. To have value, a technology should exist through both documentation and implementation by its owner. Therefore, the client (Who: the owner, licensee, or buyer?) primarily decides the subject (What technology is to be valued?), and establishes the purpose (Why is it being appraised?). To accomplish their purpose, valuators need additional facts: How will the asset be used? Where will it be implemented? and When will it start?

VALUATION PYRAMID

In planning a valuation of IPR, the concept of the valuation pyramid is very useful.[5] Working up from the bottom, the pyramid has four levels: foundation, profile, methodology, and solution (see Exhibit 20.1), each supported by appropriate analyses.

---

[4] *See N. Reschu,* **Introduction to Value Theory** *(Englewood Cliffs, NJ: Prentice-Hall, 1969).*

[5] *See Paul Flignor and David Orozco, "Intangible Asset & Intellectual Property Valuation: A Multidisciplinary Perspective," ipthoght.com, June 2006.*

Exhibit 20.1 Valuation Pyramid

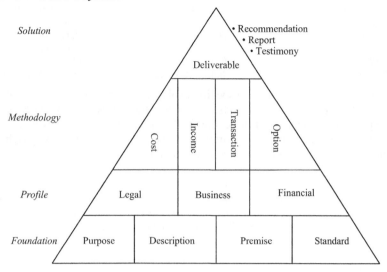

The first level, Foundation, is the underlying rationale for and key assumptions of the valuation. The second level, Profile, defines the legal business and financial attributes of the IPR. The third level, Methodology, is where the specific quantifications and analyses are performed to generate conclusions while the top level, Solution, addresses how the analyses and conclusions help solve problems or generate recommendations. This matches well with the basic concept of 5W+H.

Why (are we valuing the subject?)	Purpose
What (is the asset?)	Description
Who (is the assumed buyer?)	Standard
When, where, and how (will the asset be used?)	Premises

Foundation Level

The foundation level covers four essential characteristics of the valuation: (1) purpose, (2) description, (3) premise, and (4) standard.

Purpose. The *purpose* of the valuation defines the legal or regulatory situation, jurisdiction, and acceptable methodologies for that particular field. The six key reasons for a valuation assignment are shown in Exhibit 20.2.

Exhibit 20.2 Valuation Purposes and Standards

Transactions—Mergers and Acquisitions/Licensing	Financial Reporting	Bankruptcy/ Reorganization
Audience	*Audience*	*Audience*
Management	Investors	Bankruptcy Judge
Investor	Regulations	Creditors
Standards	*Standards*	*Standards*
Company Specific	International Financial Reporting Standards	Statute/Case Law Bank Requirements

	Tax	Legal	Financing/ Securitization
Audience	Tax Authorities	*Audience* Trial Court	*Audience* Creditors Investors
Standards	Tax Law	*Standards* Statutes/Case Law	*Standards* Statues/Case Law

Description. The *description* is a specific explanation of the characteristics of the IPR, which may include patents, trade secrets, copyrights, trademarks, and trade dress; in particular, the periods and degrees of protection in the different countries in which the owner operates must be covered. Of great importance are the terms of any monopoly rights.

The next table is an overview of U.S. intellectual property regimes.

Intellectual Property Regime	*Origin of Rights*	*Prerequisites to Protection*	*Scope of Protection*	*Life*	*Test for Infringement*
Trade secret	Investment of time and money, guarded from others	Recognition of value and utility	Confidential information	Life of confidentiality	Means of derivation
Utility patent	Granted by Federal Government on application by inventor	New, useful, and nonobvious subject matter	Useful process, machine, article of manufacture, or composition of matter	17 years from date of grant or 20 years from date of application	Manufacture, use, sale, offer for sale in U.S., or import of claimed invention
Copyright	Creation of original "works" of authorship, fixed in tangible form	Originality, registration, and copyright notice required if publicly enforced	Works of authorship	Variable on the order of 100 years or longer; life of author plus 70 years	Copying, performing, distributing
Trademark	Adoption and use in commerce	Used in commerce to identify and distinguish business, goods and services, federal registration required for federal enforcement	Words, names, symbols, and other devices	Unlimited as long as property is used in commerce	Likelihood of confusion, mistake, or deception

Source: Adapted from James G. Conley and David Orozco, "Intellectual Property—The Ground Rules," Kellogg School of Management Technical Note 7-305-501 (August 2005).

Premise. The *premise* refers to the underlying assumption on how the asset will be exploited in the future; the most common, the "highest and best use" concept, is based on real estate practice and adopted by generally accepted accounting principles (GAAP) in the United States though Statement of Financial Accounting Standards (SFAS) 157, *Fair Value Measurements*. This ascribes to the subject the highest value under foreseeable circumstances, regardless of the current application. One area where the premise is of crucial importance is in bankruptcy, where the distinction between an orderly disposition and a distressed sale can have a significant impact on value.

Standard. Valuation *standards* refer to the definition of value adopted, which ties back to the purpose. The most common are the "fair market value" and "market value" for tax purposes and "fair value" under International Financial Reporting Standards or U.S. GAAP. Another common standard in the United States is legal fair value, which is often used to compensate a party for the involuntary termination of the use of an asset, such as through expropriation or under eminent domain, where the vendor is not willing to sell.

Profile level. The profile level refers to the legal, business, strategic and financial characteristics of the IPR. It articulates the issues that dictate the opportunities and limitations of the asset and ultimately its ability to generate income and create value; much of the effort of a valuator takes place at this level.

Legal. All IPR have legal ownership aspects; as they have no physical form and the marginal cost to replicate is often close to zero, the legal protection provides an important component of value. However, because each form of intellectual property has unique characteristics, each must be examined within the larger business content.

The next table presents an example of patent legal characteristics and valuation effects.

Patents Legal Attribute	*Valuation Impact*
Scope—Number of Claim Elements	More elements means it is easier to substitute pieces of the puzzle and "design around" the invention
Time left before 20-year rights expire	Patents lose value as time elapses
Patent grants owner the right to make, use, or sell, (and import if a process)	Allows carving out different parts of value chains in one market
Continuation strategy	Presence of a continuation strategy can extend the scope and time of the parent patent ("evergreening")
Accused infringer has been sent a cease-and-desist letter	Willful (treble) damages may accrue when notice is received
Value chain position of accused infringer	More downstream may mean greater damages (value added of offering is greater)
Patenting of multiple patent forms (machines, processes, compounds, products)	Multiple forms increases licensing opportunity and defensive position

Business. Since valuation is in many ways simply the quantification of business strategy, frameworks such as Michael Porter's Five Forces Analysis are a good starting point for assessing the business dynamics of the IPR. (See Chapter 7.) Factors affecting the business profile include barriers to exploitation, market life cycle of the underlying offerings, bundled services or other items, competitors' products and services, customer and supplier dynamics, government regulation, and potential new disruptive technologies. In the economic characterization, the residual income and position in the life cycle are important elements.

Legally protected IPR, which give an exclusive monopoly on exploitation of a given asset, can be either routine or entrepreneurial. Routine IPR grant benefits that also can be obtained from a noninfringing alternative. In the pharmaceutical industry, the patents of the compound tend to be entrepreneurial, as the patented molecule is unique and is a critical factor in the success of the drug. Other elements, such as manufacturing, sales, and distribution, may be obtained from a multitude of sources. Conversely, in industry, IPR tend to be routine as the benefits of the technology are likely available from other sources and can provide an upper bound on the value of the asset. In complex manufacturing, such as the automotive industry, there can be several types of entrepreneurial IPR, including platform technology and trade names/trademarks.

Financial. The financial profile includes: price premiums, total expected revenues, costs, related savings, and capital investments necessary for the IPR directly, or indirectly, to create value. Usually, the financial profile is performed iteratively with the valuation methodology, to put figures on the financial effect of the activities involved in creating value from the IPR:

- Projected revenues, costs, and capital requirements associated with commercialization
- Estimated time to commercialization
- Estimated cost of noninfringing alternatives
- Time value of money (cost of capital) associated with the IPR
- Impact of the commercialization on working capital (receivables and inventory payables)

Typically, the financial profile should cover the entire useful life of the IPR.

Methodology Level

Typically, all valuation methodologies form part of one of the three standard approaches: Income, Market, and Cost. Over the past decade, some methods have been developed for valuing IPR by purely mathematical means; those are in the process of becoming a new Formula Approach (which covers real options, binomial models, and Monte Carlo simulations).

Income approach: Discounted cash flows. The Income Approach is normally applied by discounting expected future returns to a present value; it is very useful for many types of intellectual property. To use the Income Approach successfully, it is important to determine:

- What economic benefit can be expected?
- How long are such benefits expected to continue?
- Will the benefits increase or decrease over the years?
- What risks are involved with achieving the anticipated benefits?

Benefits are best measured by the net cash flow derived.

Example: Discounted Cash Flow Value of a Patent

Discount Rate: 15%   Annual Revenue: $200,000
Anticipate useful lifetime: 5 years   Tax Rate: 25%

Average Annual Income $	Year	Present Value Factor @ 15%	Present Value $
200,000	1	0.869565	173,913
200,000	2	0.756144	151,229
200,000	3	0.657516	131,503
200,000	4	0.571753	114,351
200,000	5	0.497177	99,435
Total			670,431
Less Income Tax			167,608
			502,823

Income approach: Capitalization of income. Another method under the Income Approach is the capitalization of net income. This works best for IPR with long or indefinite lives, such as trademarks. The capitalization relationship for any asset is expressed as Rate = Income/Value. The value is fixed, and the income is the net potential profit after expenses. The costs of equity and debt must be taken into account if financing is involved. Therefore, Net Annual Income =Asset Value × Royalty Rate less applicable income taxes.

Example: Capitalized Value of a Patent

Anticipate useful life time: 5 years   Debt Portion: 90%
Annual Revenues: $200,000   Cost of Debt: 5%
Expenses: 25%   Required Equity Return: 15%
Tax Rate: 25%

The net annual income is $112,500 ($200,000 − ($200,000 × 0.25) = $150,000 × (1 − 25%). If annual interest rate is 5% for the 90% financing and the return on the 10% equity is 15%, then the Weighted Average Cost of Capital (WACC) is 5.1% [90% × 5% (1 − 25%)+ 10% × 15% = 3.575% + 1.5% = 5.075%].

Therefore, the overall capitalization rate is 25.1%, made up of 5% return on investment and 20% return of investment over five years for a value of $448,207.[6]

Market approach. Transaction-based methods under the Market Approach are in many ways the simplest to understand. They reflect the actual prices paid for comparable IPR under similar circumstances. The price can be either for a direct acquisition, such as a private sale or auction, or for a license to use. This technique provides a theoretically accurate estimate of value because every patent covers novel technology. However, to apply it, a comparative technology that has been valued already should exist. In reality, it is of little or no utility "because no two patents (copyrights, etc.) are similar enough for the sale price of one to define the value of another."[7]

Typically, there are two stages to a transactional method valuation: screening and adjustments. *Screening* refers to the process of identifying similar third-party transactions with sufficient information on pricing, scope, terms, and conditions to be deemed comparable. *Adjustments* refer to explicit quantifiable changes in the values due to specific rationale. However, adjustments must be made with care, as too many adjustments may limit the comparability of the outside evidence and could compromise the credibility of the method.

Cost approach. The Cost Approach begins with a determination of the current duplication (reproduction) or replacement cost as if new. From this duplication cost new (DCN) or replacement cost new (RCN) deductions are made for depreciation, loss of functionality, etc. This method is almost nonexistent for IPR since "it costs as much to get a worthless patent (copyright, etc.) as it does to protect a valuable invention,"[8] and nearly every IPR is absolutely irreplaceable.

Formula approach. The Formula Approach, which is in the course of being generally accepted, refers to nontraditional mathematical formula-based valuation methods that are useful in valuing IPR. Examples are real options, binomial models, and Monte Carlo simulations. They require extreme care in building the models as they are often highly sensitive to changes in underlying assumptions and parameters. The real option method is based on the successful Black-Scholes model for pricing financial options (calls and puts). The basic premise behind this method is that investments with asymmetric payoffs (potentially large profits and only limited losses) will have a higher value as the level of uncertainty (known as volatility) increases. Consequently, real option methods are most useful where large capital investments are undertaken with highly uncertain and far-off payoffs, as in the pharmaceutical and petroleum exploration sectors.

---

[6]   *See Marc S. Friedman, and Lindsey H. Taylor, "Basis of Intellectual Property Protection for Software Under U.S. Law," Computer Forensics Online 2, No. 1 (November 1998), www.shk-dplc.com/c.*

[7]   *Rick Neifeld, "Patent Valuation from a Practical Viewpoint" and "Some Interesting Patent Value Statistics" from the Patent Value Predictor Model, www.neifeld.com.*

[8]   *Sivaramjani Thambisetty, "Patents as Credence Goods," **Oxford Journal of Legal Studies** (Winter 2007).*

Binomial (expansion) models, using decision trees, are the most intuitive of these methods, as the required events and decisions are modeled explicitly, each with its own probabilities. An important aspect of building a binomial model is to ensure that all potential alternatives and scenarios are considered. (See Chapter 29.)

Monte Carlo simulations, named for the gambling popularized at the Mediterranean resort, model low-probability payoffs over multiple iterations. They are helpful in estimating the spread of diseases, engineering tolerances, and even the probability of a country winning the World Cup of soccer.

Solution Level

The final step of the valuation process is to express the analyses in a written report that meaningfully helps to resolve a business issue. (See Chapter 6.) Deliverables generally fall into one of the three categories that derive from the issues described in "Purpose":

1. *Planning recommendation.* Support for decisions whether to enter into a sale or license transaction for the IPR; it could be for a licensing strategy, tax management issue or bankruptcy/dissolution.
2. *Compliance.* Financial reporting, tax filings or regulatory requirements.
3. *Dispute resolution.* Export reports and testimony concerns infringement claims or contractual violations of the IPR.

FACTORS AFFECTING IPR VALUATION

Some additional factors that affect the value of IPR include industry and competition, alternative solutions, contributory assets, costs of development and commercialization, and regulations.

Industry and Competition

In seeking IPR comparability, the first arena is the industry itself. Market share, barriers, and profits are derived from the industry, which decides the value of a business and determines competitors (including prospective competitors). The value of the IPR will be influenced by industry cycles and economics. Competitors may also affect the amount and duration of profitability because of newly developed items.

Alternative Solutions

An innovative technology presents a unique valuation challenge. However, the economic benefits are based on the short-term and the long-term abilities to protect the technology, at least until competitors appear. The success of a potential competitor in finding alternative solutions for the innovative technology will affect the economic remaining life and value of the IPR.

Contributory Assets

No product is created by technology alone. It also relies on the firm's reputation, trademarks and customer confidence, operating plants and working capital, as well as the assembled workforce.

Costs of Development and Commercialization

Market acceptance of the potential product should be evaluated before commercialization; the time and effort necessary to progress from the IPR to a product ready for sale (including production costs, advertising expenses, and market entry activities) must be considered. Government approval may be a barrier for making the product commercially viable. All such expenditures should be considered globally and domestically.

Regulations

Sometimes government regulations, permissions, or approvals pose significant barriers to commercializing a technology. If the target industry is heavily regulated, the costs and risks of entry will be higher. This means the value of the IPR will be relatively diminished.

APPLICATION TO PATENTS

The valuation factors for a patent application are different from those for a granted one because the invention may be rejected or treated as an unfinished technology. Typical valuation factors for granted patents are set out next.[9]

Valuation Classification	Subitem	Valuation Item
Technicalization	Patentability	Status
		Claims
		Duration
		Alternative solutions
	Innovation	Technological level
		Difficulties in development
		Excellence
		Novelty
		Completeness
		Usage range
	Environment	Technology infrastructure
		Technical support and regulation
		Execution opportunities
		Limitations
		Ripple effect
		Newer technologies
Commercialization	Industry Characteristics	Market size
		Market growth
		Market life cycle
	Competition Characteristics	Barriers to entry
		Market structure
		Market status
	Commercialized Characteristics	Time for commercialization
		Developing degree
		Facilities and processes
		Investment and wholesale value
		Profit and stability

Technicalization

Patentability

- *Status.* Of all applications, this should be reported by counsel on a step-by-step basis.
- *Claims.* Consider terms and the size of the claims.
- *Duration.* The practicable economic period may be less that the legal term.

---

[9] See Park Sun Young, *"Development of a Categorized Checklist for a Valuation of Patent Technology,"* **Intellectual Patent Review** 6 (2007): 50.

- *Alternative solutions.* Consider the possibility of the emergence of an alternative solution in short term.

Innovation

- *Technology level.* Basic technologies, equivalent to a basic technology, major, medium and slight improvement technologies.
- *Difficulties in development.* The expected and unexpected difficulties in developing a technology compared with the current scientific level of existing technologies.
- *Excellence.* Competitive advantage and improved characteristics compared with alternative and equivalent technologies.
- *Novelty.* Differences from current technologies.
- *Completeness.* Degree of development or commercialization.
- *Usage range.* How broad a range of new and existing products may be affected.

Environment

- *Technology infrastructure.* Status of specialist, accumulated knowledge, performance tests and whether or not it represents reasonable return on the expenditure.
- *Technical support and regulation.* Factors related to approval or/and permission and what effect it may have on the value.
- *Execution opportunities.* The possibility in applying the technology to another process or product.
- *Limitations.* What are the limitations in commercializing and technical implementation?
- *Ripple effect.* The depth and width of using of the technology and the effect on other technologies.
- *Newer technology.* The possibility of the existence and emergence of competitive/alternative newer technologies comparable to the subject.

Commercialization

Industry and Market Characteristics

- *Market size.* The present market size of the products feasible within two or three years.
- *Market growth.* Growth forecasts applicable for the market compared to expected economic growth and that of rapid growth products.
- *Market life cycle.* The current position based on market life cycle characteristics and steps at which the technology and the product are applied.

Competition Characteristics

- *Barriers to entry.* The social, economic, environment factors and barriers of law and regulation to market entry.
- *Market structure.* The competitive structure of the market chain.
- *Market status.* Degree of competition and the effect on the entity.

Commercialized Characteristics

- *Time to commercialization.* Value the time to commercialize the patent technology.
- *Developing degree.* Term, size and effort to commercialize the patented technology.
- *Facilities and processes.* The production equipment, capacity, and process needed.
- *Investment and wholesale value.* The scale of profit margin to capital expenditures.
- *Profit stability.* Earnings stability after commercialization in three to five years.

CONCLUSION

A number of methods exist to value technologies and their related IPR. For such situations, there is no hierarchy of methods, and all are, in principle, equally applicable. Selecting a proper method depends on a number of factors set out in the valuation pyramid; for a patented technology, the main ones are technicalization and commercialization. The former has three items: patentability, innovation, and environment; the latter has three characteristics: industry/market, competition, and commercialization. In spite of using multiple methods to value a particular IPR with robust and complete analyses, the valuation of a technology could be affected by those factors.

21 INTANGIBLE ASSETS

STAN SORIN

ROMANIA

While there is a long history of valuing tangible assets dating back to Roman and Babylonian times, the application of the three traditional approaches to intangible assets is less than two decades old. This chapter deals with the basic principles and particularities of valuing intangible assets for International Financial Reporting Standards (IFRS). It refers briefly to the numerous problems relating to identifiable intangible assets, which can be divided into two main aspects: (1) advanced knowledge of valuation principles and methods and (2) the great importance of the valuator's professional judgment. Although, as in any other new and complex problem, there are still differences of opinion in these matters; although a consensus is emerging which combines several points of view, creating a consistent and unified methodology for valuing intangible assets, including intellectual property rights (IPR).

INTANGIBLE ASSETS

An "intangible" differs from a financial or physical asset in two major ways. The first is that its value depends, at least partly, on the context in which the asset is used to generate revenue, so that its "value in use" may differ from its fair value. The other is that it can generate more than one revenue stream at a time. Revised International Valuation Guidance Note (IVGN) 4, published in draft by the International Valuation Standards Council (IVSC) in January 2009, defines an intangible asset as:

> *a nonmonetary asset that manifests itself by its economic properties. It does not have physical substance but grants rights and privileges to its owner that usually generate income.*

In addition, the definition should reflect that an intangible asset "may also reduce costs." An intangible asset is valued only if it is identifiable. This requires that it either:

- Is separable (i.e., capable of being separated or divided from the entity and sold, transferred, licensed, rented or exchanged, either individually or together with a related contract, asset or liability, regardless of whether the entity intends to do so); or
- Arise from contractual or other legal rights, regardless of whether those rights are transferable or separable from the entity or from other rights and obligations.

If an intangible asset is not identifiable, it is treated as part of goodwill. This is the residual amount remaining after the values of all physical, intangible, and financial assets, less actual and contingent liabilities, have been deducted from the total value of an entity.

IFRS 3 divides intangible assets into five categories:

1. Marketing related
2. Customer and supplier related
3. Artistic related
4. Technology related

5. Contract

A sixth category is often added to this list:

6. Governmental

Marketing-Related Assets

- Trademarks, trade names
- Service marks, collective marks, certification marks
- Trade dress (unique color, shape or package design)
- Newspaper or magazine mastheads
- Internet domain names

Customer- and Supplier-Related Assets

- Customer lists
- Order or production backlog
- Customer contracts and pertinent relationships

A "customer list" refers to known purchasers. The term "customer base" applies to a group of customers not known or identifiable to the company, for instance, patrons of a fast food franchise or a movie theatre. Therefore, as it is not separable, a customer base is not an intangible asset.

Artistic-Related Assets

- Plays, operas, ballets, and so on
- Books, magazines, newspapers, literary works
- Musical works, such as compositions, lyrics, jingles
- Pictures, photographs
- Video and audiovisual material, including motion pictures, music videos, and television programs

These artistic items are intangible assets when they are copyrighted and may be transferred, either in whole through assignments or in part through licensing agreements. In turn, copyrights give rise to subsidiary rights. For a work of fiction, these include paperback editions, translations, and dramatic, film, or television adaptations. The fair value of a copyright involves consideration of all outstanding assignments or licenses.

Technology-Related Assets

- Patents
- Computer software, display formats, mask works, and so on
- Nonpatented technologies
- Databases
- Trade secrets, such as proprietary formulas, processes, recipes, and the like

Contract Assets

- Licenses, royalties, stand-still agreements (refraining from action)
- Advertising, construction, management, service, or supply agreements
- Leases
- Construction permits
- Franchises
- Rights to broadcast programs
- Use of certain equipment

- User rights, such as drilling, water, air, mineral, route authorities, and timber cutting
- Servicing rights, as for mortgages
- Employment contracts

Governmental Assets

Many valuators find it useful to subdivide IFRS 3's contract section by separating, into a special category, licenses granted by various levels of government, most of which have characteristics that are different from commercial contracts.

SKILLS OF THE VALUATOR

Valuing intangible assets is one of the most intricate challenges facing a professional valuator. The primary difficulty arises from the complexity of the processes involved, as the values of the various assets can be determined reliably only after preparing a valuation of the entity as a whole and after determining the fair value (equivalent to market value) of every asset or liability involved.

To value intangible assets, one must possess not only basic knowledge regarding the valuation procedures but also knowledge of all appropriate valuation approaches, methods, and techniques. In most developed countries, valuators specialize in one of the four types of properties acknowledged by the IVSC: real property, businesses, personal property, and financial interests.

The 2007 edition of the International Valuation Standards (IVS) defines a business valuator as "a person who, by education, training, and experience is qualified to perform a valuation of a business, business ownership interest, security and/or intangible assets."

IVGN 4 stipulates: "Although many of the principles, methods and techniques of intangible asset valuation are similar to those used in others fields of valuation, valuations of intangible assets require special education, training, skills, and experience."

Those quotes emphasize the need for the valuator to be fully aware not only of the requirements of the valuation and financial reporting standards but also of recent developments regarding the complex methodologies for valuing identifiable intangible assets.

RECONCILIATION TO ENTITY VALUE

The fair value of an entity owning internally generated intangible assets, which are not recorded on the balance sheet, cannot be determined appropriately by the Asset Approach. Depending on circumstances, it should be valued by the Market Approach or a discounted cash flows method under the Income Approach. As the value of any asset reflects the future benefits resulting from it, the fair value of each item will be obtained by some means from estimates of the cash flows they are expected to generate.

Therefore, a valuator can prepare a balance sheet adjusted to comprise all the assets involved, including those not recorded due to accounting conventions. This document represents the structure of the entity's net worth and gives potential investors more information regarding the "hidden values" represented by intangible assets for which they are prepared to pay. Under IFRS 3, *Business Combinations*, an entity is to account for each transaction by the acquisition method; International Accounting Standard (IAS) 38 requires that all identifiable intangible assets arising from a business combination are recognized at their fair values. Goodwill, which includes all unrecognized intangibles, is recorded as the difference between the total of all financial, physical, and intangible assets less liabilities and the fair value of the underlying equity. That simplifies the reconciliation of different values because the fair values of the equity, determined by the various methods, will be close.

One problem in valuing intangible assets is that they may have a negative value. Examples are office leases taken on at the peak of the market, or patents that are no longer in use and of no interest to potential buyers. The negative values would be represented by either the rent in excess of the current levels or the annual fees necessary to maintain the legal protection of the patents. In IFRS, the concept of negative fair value does not exist for separate assets; therefore, such items must be recorded at a fair value of zero with the potential extra costs recorded as a liability or a reduction of goodwill.

The application of the identifiable intangible asset valuation methodologies should be undertaken by following these five steps:

1. Estimate the entity value using a discounted cash flow (DCF) method or using the Market Approach.
2. Estimate the fair value of all the financial and physical assets and liabilities using methodologies discussed in other chapters.
3. Calculate the implied value of all the intangibles as the difference between the entity value and the fair values of all the other components of the invested capital.
4. Separately identify the intangible assets, which can be valued reliably using appropriate techniques.
5. Calculate the goodwill as a residual amount.

These steps are necessary as IFRS 3 does not deal with the valuation of the business, only with relevant assets and liabilities. The reconciliation process requires preparation of an adjusted balance sheet of the target; that includes the internally generated intangible assets, which are eventually purchased by the acquirer, most of which will have been valued by some version of the DCF method. Their implied rates of return will increase with risk. From them, the valuator will calculate the weighted average return on assets (WARA), which should be substantially the same as the entity's weighted average cost of capital (WACC).

VALUATION OF INTANGIBLE ASSETS FOR IFRS REPORTING PURPOSES

Worldwide, there are five main standards relating to the valuation of intangible assets:

1. IVGN 4, *Valuation of Intangible Assets*
2. IVGN 16, *Valuation of Intangible Assets for IFRS Reporting Purposes*
3. American Institute of Certified Public Accountants (AICPA), *Valuation of a Business, Business Ownership Interest, Security, or Intangible Asset*
4. American Society of Appraisers: Business Valuation Standard IX, *Intangible Asset Valuation*
5. Internal Revenue Service, *Internal Revenue Manual* (IRM) Part 4, Intangible Property Valuation Guidelines

To select the appropriate valuation methodologies for intangible assets, it is essential to be thoroughly familiar with all five standards; note that the IVGN is in the process of being revised. In addition, the valuator should be familiar with:

- IAS 36, *Impairment of Assets*
- IAS 38, *Intangible Assets*
- IFRS 3, *Business Combinations*
- IFRS 5, *Noncurrent Assets Held for Sale and Discontinued Operations*

In addition, certain material in the related U.S. standards is useful, such as Uniform Standards of Professional Appraisal Practice (USPAP) issued by the Appraisal Foundation, and Statements of Financial Accounting Standards (SFAS) issued by the Financial Accounting Standards Board (FASB).

- USPAP Standard 9, *Business Appraisal, Development*
- USPAP Standard 10, *Business Appraisal, Reporting*
- IVGN 6, *Business Valuation*
- SFAS 157, *Fair Value Measurements*

VALUATION METHODS FOR INTANGIBLES

The most common methods for valuing intangible assets can be grouped under the three traditional approaches.

1. Market approach and Transactional methods
2. Income approach

    a. Relief-from-royalty (R-f-R) method
    b. Premium profit or incremental income method
    c. Multiperiod excess earnings method (MPEE)

3. Cost approach: Depreciated replacement cost (DRC) method

In recent years, since the development of personal computers, the formula approach, which involves option pricing and mathematical models, has become more important. Section 4.48.5 of the IRM indicates two additional valuation methods: The Monte Carlo or probabilistic method and the option pricing model (OPM).

In measuring the fair value of intangible assets acquired in a business combination, IAS 38: 41outlines the methods to be applied to unique intangible assets:

> *Entities that are regularly involved in the purchase and sale of unique assets may have developed techniques for estimating their fair value indirectly. These techniques may be used for initial measurement of an intangible asset acquired in a business combination. These techniques include, when appropriate:*
>
> *a. Applying multiples reflecting current transactions to indicators that drive the profitability of the asset (such as revenue, market shares and operating profit) or to the royalty stream that could be obtained from licensing the intangible asset to another party in arm's-length transaction (as in "the relief-from-royalty" approach [method]), or*
> *b. Discounting estimated future net cash flows from the assets.*

The next chart presents systematically the approaches and methods for valuation of identifiable intangible assets which can be used for all purposes, including financial reporting.

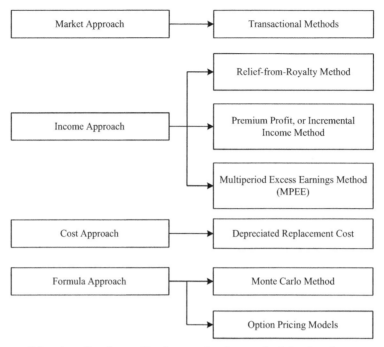

Unlike traditional applications of business valuation methodologies, there are seven particularities in the case of intangible assets:

1. No standard valuation methods exist for specific intangible assets, although there are some with more or less relevance. The use of more than one method for each item is recommended to confirm the consistency of the values. Because the degree of relevance from the three traditional approaches is different, sometimes it is appropriate to use only one, but, more frequently, several methods, depending on the available data.

The next table presents preferred approach and primary valuation method for commonly valued intangible assets.

Intangible Assets	Preferred Approach	Primary Valuation Method
Assembled workforce	Cost	DRC
Computer software	Cost Market	DRC Transactional method
Customer contracts and pertinent relationships	Income	MPEE
Trademark, trade name	Income Income	R-f-R Premium profit
Patented technology	Income Income Formula	R-f-R Premium profit OPM
Noncompetition agreement	Income	Premium profit
Unpatented technology	Income	MPEE
In-process research and development (IPR&D) projects	Income Formula	MPEE OPM

2. Due to their unique characteristics, there are few active markets for intangible assets. A number of patent auctions have been held in various cities, and there are transactions of various kinds in government licenses, such as radio stations in the United States, or taxi medallions in Canada. This means the transactional method can be used only in a few cases. Significant professional judgment is required in making adjustments to the sale prices of similar items and to the valuation multiples derived from such transactions.

For that reason, the preferred valuation methods relate to the Income Approach allocating the total net cash flows to the various types of assets, physical and intangible, and determining their appropriate rates of return.

There are four particularities in applying the three valuation methods listed under the Income Approach

a. Only the cash flows attributable to the particular intangible asset are subject to discounting, unlike in business valuation, where the net cash flows (either applicable to invested capital or equity) are discounted. This requires detailed knowledge and normally the assistance of management regarding the allocation of the net cash flows of the entity to the various assets. The discount rate will depend on the returns expected by investors with different risk tolerances. Certain intangible assets (trademarks and patents) are an exception and can be valued using the R-f-R or incremental income methods. Because the royalty cash flows are entirely generated by the intangible assets, an allocation process is not necessary.

b. The discounting of future cash flows is preferable to the capitalization of income method because the annual cash flows attributable to an intangible asset are variable, neither a constant amount nor increasing or decreasing at a specific annual rate. Usually the cash flows allotted to the intangible assets have a downward trend during their remaining useful life.

c. In applying the going-concern principle to a business, it is assumed that the net cash flows to invested capital have an indefinite life. Consequently, a terminal amount should be calculated at the end of the specific projected period. When valuing separate intangible assets, their net cash flows will be forecast only for their remaining useful life. That gives rise to an element of judgment requiring detailed knowledge of the market, technology in use, susceptibility to future change, and the like. From those, the valuator and management will make decisions about the remaining economic useful lives, which are likely to be less than the balance of the legally protected period. This is especially true for intangible assets, such as IPR, and those that arise from contractual rights.

d. IAS 38 stipulates that the residual values of intangibles are usually zero, except when there is an active market, or if there is a clear intention of another entity buying them at the end of their current useful life. Such conditions exist only in very few cases, simplifying the efforts of the valuator to present reliable assumptions regarding future residual values of an intangible asset. When a trademark is valued using the R-f-R method, a residual value is often calculated using the Gordon Growth Model, as effectively the legally protected period of a trademark is indefinite.

3. After applying the valuation methods with primary and secondary relevance, there may be substantial differences between the resulting amounts. The choice of an arithmetic average for the final amount is not appropriate, because the various valu-

ation methods are likely to differ in degrees of suitability. It is therefore recommended that the results of the method with greatest relevance be chosen and modified upward or downward, based on the results of the secondary methods.

4. In preparing a business valuation, it is common to express a conclusion as a range of values, whose mean is treated as a selected amount. However, in preparing a valuation of intangible assets for a purchase price allocation under IFRS 3, it is essential to obtain a single amount, not a range. Therefore, depending on circumstances, the previously mentioned techniques should be applied rounded to the closest appropriate multiple of thousands of dollars, to avoid the appearance of spurious accuracy.

5. Although an assembled workforce is not recognized as an identifiable intangible asset, it must be valued separately to accurately calculate contributory asset charges under the MPEE method. The reason that an assembled workforce is not an intangible asset is that an entity has limited power of control over the benefits generated by it. As a result, it is reflected as goodwill in the financial statements.

6. Some intangible assets are closely related to other physical and intangible items and will usually be sold as part of a group of assets. Examples are a brand which includes trademark, trade dress, formulas, recipes, and technological expertise, all of which may or may not be legally protected. In some cases, such as whiskeys, the appropriately aged inventories essential to maintaining the uniformity of the product, are included. In such circumstances, the fair value would be determined for the total group. IAS 38: 36 and 37 specify that the acquirer can recognize as a single item either: (a) a combination of an intangible asset together with related physical items, or (b) a number of complementary intangibles such as "technologies." This simplifies the work of the valuator because it limits the number of intangible assets involved in a particular business combination.

7. In many countries, especially in the United States, intangible assets obtained in a business combination can be deducted for tax purposes. In such jurisdictions, the fair values of most intangible assets with limited useful lives, valued under the income or cost approaches, have two elements: (a) the calculated amount and (b) the tax amortization benefit (TAB) resulting from its deductibility over time.

The concept of TAB was introduced in the United States by the AICPA Practice Aid, *Assets Acquired in a Business Combination to Be Used in Research and Development Activities: A Focus on Software, Electronic Devices and Pharmaceutical Industries,* which covers the valuation of IPR&D. Its use in establishing the fair value of intangible assets is not expressly mentioned in IFRS. Whether it should be added or not depends on the valuation method used and on the specific local tax rules.

EXAMPLES

This section sets out examples of three of the commonly used methodologies for valuing intangible assets: R-f-R for a patent, premium profit for a trademark, and depreciated replacement cost for an assembled workforce.

Relief-from-Royalty for a Patent

In this example, not only is the patent expiring in five years but, as it relates to an analogue medical device for which a new model with digital technology is already on the market, sales, which relate only to replacements, are expected to decline rapidly; in 2013 the product will be withdrawn. This method gives a value of $420,000 (rounded) for the patent.

	2009	2010	2011	2012	$'000 2013
Future Net Sales	8,000.0	6,000.0	4,000.00	2,000.0	500.0
Royalty Stream before Tax @ 5%	400.0	300.0	200.0	100.0	25.0
Maintenance R&D, 1.5% of Sales	(120.0)	(90.0)	(60.0)	(30.0)	(7.5)
Net Royalty	280.0	210.0	140.0	70.0	17.5
Income tax @ 40%	(112.0)	(84.0)	56.0	(28.0)	(7.0)
Royalty Stream after Tax @ 40%	168.0	126.0	196.0	42.0	10.5
Discount Factor @ 16%, midyear convention	0.929	0.800	0.690	0.595	0.513
Present Value	156.0	100.9	135.2	25.0	5.4
Fair Value of Patent—total of present values	422.4				
Rounded	420.0				

Premium Profit for a Trademark

The valuator was able to obtain the unit costs of a generic (nonbranded) food item from Asia that is very similar to the branded Romanian product; the extra profit was $0.12 (3%) per unit, or $480,000 in the base year 2008.

Structure of the Unit Price	*Trademarked Product*	*Generic Item*
	$	$
Price	4.00	3.00
COS	(1.00)	(0.80)
Gross profit	3.00	2.20
Selling and marketing expenses	(0.60)	(0.20)
General and administrative expenses	(0.40)	(0.20)
Operating profit	2.00	1.80
Income tax @ 40%	(0.80)	(0.72)
Net operating profit	1.20	1.08
Incremental net profit	0.12	
Sales units in base year	4,000,000	
Incremental net profit—total	$ 480,000	

It is a specialty product, and unit volume is expected to decrease by 20% a year from 2009 to 2013, when it will be withdrawn. The value of the trademark is $825,000 (rounded). More about this method is found in Chapter 35.

	Forecast Period				
	2009	2010	2011	2012	2013
Incremental net profit—total	384,000	307,200	245,760	196,608	157,286
Discount factor @ 16%, midyear convention	0.800	0.690	0.595	0.513	0.442
Present value of incremental net profit	307,358	211,971	146,187	100,819	69,530
Trademark value	835,864				
Rounded	825,000				

Depreciated Replacement Cost for Assembled Workforce

While by definition not a tangible asset, the assembled workforce of an entity has to be valued to calculate the contributory asset charges for several valuation techniques. This is done usually by the DRC method. In this example, the workforce is productive and long established, so no depreciation is applied to its replacement cost of $2,300,000 (rounded); under other circumstances, this deduction may be as high as 25%.

Employee years of service	Number of employees by category	Base compensation $'000	Benefits and additional compensation $'000	Total compensation $'000	Cost to recruit	Cost to hire	Cost to train	Total cost to recruit, hire, and train	Replacement cost of assembled workforce $'000
0-5	10	523	52	575	2.5%	3.0%	15.0%	20.5%	118
6-10	15	1,120	112	1,232	3.0%	5.0%	20.0%	28.0%	345
11-15	22	1,944	194	2,138	4.0%	5.0%	23.0%	32.0%	684
16-20	18	1,820	182	2,002	5.0%	6.0%	25.0%	36.0%	721
20+	8	898	90	988	5.0%	8.0%	30.0%	43.0%	425
Totals	73	6,305	630	6,935					2,293
								Rounded	2,300

HIERARCHY OF VALUING INTANGIBLES

The appropriate hierarchy for valuing intangible assets depends on the credibility of the available information on which the necessary assumptions are based. Generally accepted is:

- Assembled workforce
- Computer software
- Trademark, trade name
- Customer contracts and related relationships
- Noncompetition agreement
- Protected (patented) technology
- Unpatented technology
- IPR&D projects

The economic logic regarding this ranking is based on the reliability of each asset's participation in generating net cash flows. In accordance with the IFRS procedure of recognizing an asset only if it is probable to generate future economic benefits, the assembled workforce must rank first, as no cash flow can be generated without the activities of the employees. In addition, its fair value determined for contributory asset purposes is normally done by the cost–to–re-create method, which involves relatively fewer assumptions than are required for other items.

Conversely, unpatented technology and IPR&D projects occupy the last rank because the appropriate valuation approach, MPEE, is complex and based on many assumptions regarding the previous allocations of net cash flows to other assets.

VALUATION PREMISES

There are two basic valuation premises:

1. Going concern, which describes the situation where the ownership being transferred is that of an operating entity
2. Liquidation, where all assets are transferred without the operations or after the closure of the business

For intangible asset valuations, the two premises are slightly different: in use and in exchange, the latter referring to the price, which could be obtained in a well conducted sale. SFAS 157:A4 states:

> *The valuation premise used to measure fair value of an asset depends on the highest and best use of the asset by market participants. If the asset would provide maximum value to the market participants, principally through its use in combination with others assets as a group (highest and best use is "in-use"), the asset would be measured using an in-use valuation premise. If the asset would provide maximum value to the market participants principally on a stand-alone basis (highest and best use is "in-exchange"), the asset would be measured using an in-exchange valuation premise.*

Under IAS 36, *Impairment of Assets*, value-in-use is calculated from the assumptions and applications actually adopted by the present owner. Conversely, fair value (in exchange) is based on what a third party would be willing to pay. In general, under this standard, the amount adopted is the higher of the value-in-use or fair value less costs to sell, the latter reflecting the in-exchange premise. IFRS 5, *Noncurrent Assets Held for Sale and Discontinued Operations*, requires any asset, financial, physical or intangible, covered by it to be carried at fair value less costs to sell.

DEFENSIVE INTANGIBLE ASSETS

At its December 2008 meeting, the International Accounting Standards Board (IASB) discussed defensive intangible assets, which are intangible assets acquired in a business combination where the buyer does not intend to use them directly or does not intend to use them in the same way as other market participants. The decision in IFRS 3R, *Business Combinations*, that such items should be recognized and measured at fair value was confirmed. However, IASB tentatively decided not to provide or address:

- Explicit guidance on measuring their fair values
- Their subsequent accounting
- Any additional disclosures required

Irrespective of the IASB conclusions, such intangible assets have to be valued. As they are not intended to be used directly, they will not generate revenues or cash flows; therefore, they cannot be valued directly by the Income Approach. There are two alternatives:

1. Assume that they will be used in the same fashion as by other market participants and determine an exit value based on notional revenues and cash flows.
2. Recognize their nature as defensive, based on preventing somebody else doing something, and estimate the hypothetical reductions in the entity's cash flows that would occur if that somebody else actually did the something.

VALUATION ASSUMPTIONS

International Valuation Standards define "assumptions" as being

[S]uppositions taken to be true. Assumptions involve facts, conditions or situations affecting the subject of, or approach to, a valuation which may not be capable or worthy of verification. They are matters that, once declared, are to be accepted in understanding the valuation. All the assumptions underlying a valuation should be reasonable.

Those assumptions describe the conditions of the assets being valued or the circumstances under which they are assumed to be sold. The term "valuation assumption" always has the meaning of a statement considered to be true. There are two types: standard assumptions and special assumptions.

Standard assumptions refer to the inputs necessary for the application of the appropriate valuation methods. They are defined by the AICPA in *Valuation of a Business, Business Ownership, Interest, Security, or Intangible Asset*, Appendix C, as:

Statements or inputs used for the accomplishment of the mission of estimating the value that serves as a basis for the application of a particular valuation method.

"Special, unusual or extraordinary assumptions" are defined by IVS as

any additional assumptions relating to matters covered in the due diligence process, or may relate to other issues, such as the identity of the purchaser, the physical state of the property, the presence of environmental pollutants (e.g., ground water contamination), or the ability to redevelop the property.

It must be emphasized that special assumptions are normally not appropriate when determining fair value for IFRS. If they have been made, the valuation report must include a specific reference to them, and they should be agreed to by the auditor.

VALUATION PROCESS

Definition of the Assignment

- Identification of the intangible assets
- Rights and privileges attached to ownership

- Owner of the intangible assets
- Valuation date
- Purpose of valuation
- User and intended use of valuation report

- Basis of value
- Valuation premise
- Special, unusual or extraordinary assumptions (not recommended)

Collection and Analysis of Data

- Characteristics of the intangible assets (remaining life, function, market position, suitability for alternative uses)
- History of intangible assets

- Relevant financial data (inputs for all selected valuation methods)
- Benchmarking relevant data
- Economic factors that may affect the value of intangible assets

- Supply and demand

- Prior transactions with identical or similar intangible assets

Valuation Approaches

- Market
- Income
- Cost

Value Conclusion

- Synthesis of value indications
- Explanations of differences

- Effects of special, unusual, or extraordinary assumptions (if agreed to by auditor)

- Final value estimate as a definitive (single) amount

22 LEASES

ANDREA R. ISOM AND TERRY A. ISOM

UNITED STATES

INTRODUCTION

In its most basic form, a lease is an agreement between a provider (the lessor), who renders a service for a periodic fee (rental or lease payments) to a user (the lessee). Those services can consist of one or all of the standard economic factors of production: labor, capital (equipment), land (real estate), raw materials, natural resources, and so on.

By far, the most common lease is the supplying of equipment. However, there is a current and growing trend toward leases that bundle one or more other factors into the package. For example, a lease often includes not only the use of the equipment but also its maintenance and repair during the term. Thus, it is not uncommon for all three factors of production to be included:

1. Capital (equipment or real estate).
2. Labor (maintenance and repair).
3. Raw materials (required spare parts, supplies, etc.).

Such agreements are known as full-service leases.

Elements of a Lease

A lease usually is expressed through a written contract specifying the periodic remuneration; the time during which the lessee can expect exclusive, uninterrupted use of the equipment and/or services; and what action is to be taken on expiry. The remuneration or service fees may be called rent, rental payments, or lease payments, depending on the location, type, and/or duration of the contract. They can be either fixed, periodic amounts or be determined as a function of some factor other than time, such as machine usage, revenue or profit generated by the leased services, or changes in interest rates.

Actions on Expiry

In general, at the termination of a lease concerning equipment, there are four alternatives for the lessee:

1. Purchase the equipment (either at fair value or an option price).
2. Renew the lease for another defined, noncancelable period.
3. Renew the lease on a month-to-month basis.
4. Return the equipment to the lessor.

In conformance with the lease's term, returning the equipment (to the lessor) may require the lessee to (a) pay a nonrenewal penalty, (b) honor a guarantee stipulating that the returned equipment is worth at least a minimum amount, should it be sold for less, or (c) renovate the equipment so that it is worth a "guaranteed residual." Residual-guarantee leases are called TRAC (terminal rental adjustment clause) leases.

Lease Types and Classifications

The leasing industry uses, quite literally, hundreds of trade terms to describe their transactions. Understanding this jargon requires a clear comprehension of the business as well as the legal, tax, and accounting status of any particular deal. Leasing terminology is not generally interchangeable between industry disciplines. For example, a capital lease accounted for under International Accounting Standard (IAS) 17, *Leases,* does not necessarily have the same treatment or meaning to the taxing authorities in the country of either the lessee or lessor. It is important that valuators understand IAS 17 and its related interpretations:

- International Financial Reporting Interpretations Committee (IFRIC) 12, *Service Concession Arrangements*
- Standing Interpretation Committee (SIC) 15, *Operating Leases—Incentives*
- SIC 27, *Evaluating the Substance of Transaction in the Legal Form of a Lease*

IAS 17 applies to all leases, other than agreements for minerals, oil, natural gas, and similar nonregenerative resources; or licenses covering films, videos, plays, manuscripts, patents, copyrights, and related items. (IAS 17:2)

However, it does not establish the basis of measurement for these leased assets:

- Property held by lessees that is accounted for as an investment property for which the lessee uses the fair value model, set out in IAS 40
- Investment property provided by lessors under an operating lease (IAS 40)
- Biological assets held by lessees under finance leases (IAS 41)
- Biological assets provided by lessors under operating leases (IAS 41)

Finance Leases

A finance lease is defined by IAS 17:4 as one that transfers substantially all the risks and rewards incident to ownership; all other leases are operating leases. The classification is made at the inception of the contract. Whether a lease is a finance lease or an operating lease depends on the substance of the transaction rather than the form. Situations that would normally lead to a lease being classified as a finance lease include (IAS 17:10):

- Ownership of the asset is transferred to the lessee by the end of the period.
- There is an option to purchase the asset at a price that is expected to be sufficiently lower than fair value at the date it becomes exercisable, so that at inception, it is reasonably certain that the option will be exercised.
- The period covers the major part of the economic life of the asset, even if title is not transferred.
- At inception, the present value of the minimum lease payments amounts to substantially all of the asset's fair value.
- The assets are of such a specialized nature that only the lessee is able to use them without major modifications.
- If the lessee is entitled to cancel, any associated losses are borne by it.
- Gains or losses from fluctuations in the fair value of the residual are for the account of the lessee.
- The lessee has the ability to continue to lease after maturity for a secondary period at a rent that is substantially lower than market.

These rules are not always conclusive; if it is clear from other features of the transaction that substantially all the risks and rewards of ownership are not transferred, it is an operating lease. Some characteristics that would prevent it from being a finance lease include contingent rents on ownership transfer or a payment equivalent to the then fair value of the underlying asset.

Real estate leases. Normally land has an indefinite economic life; therefore, regardless of length, it is subject to an operating lease, as the eventual reversion to the lessor means that substantially all the risks and rewards of ownership are not transferred.

In classifying a lease of land and building, under normal conditions, each element would be considered separately. The minimum lease payments are allocated between them in proportion to their fair values. Normally, the land element is classified as an operating lease, unless title passes at the end of the period. The building elements are classified as operating or finance leases by applying the previous criteria (IAS 17:15). However, separate measurement of the land and building elements is not required, if the lessee's interest in both is classified as an investment property in accordance with IAS 40 and the fair value model is adopted (IAS 17:18). If it is not clear whether both elements have the same classification, allocation of the minimum lease payments between the two is required.

DEFINITIONS

IAS 17.4 sets out a number of specialized definitions.

Commencement. The commencement of the lease term is the date from which the lessee is entitled to exercise its right to use the asset; it is the date of initial recognition as appropriate, of the assets, liabilities, income or expenses resulting from the lease.

Contingent rent. Contingent rent is that portion of the lease payments that is not fixed but based on the future amount of a factor that changes other than with the passage of time (percentage of sales, amount of use, price indices, market rates of interest etc.).

Economic life. Economic life is either the period over which an asset is expected to be economically usable by one or more parties or the number of production or similar units anticipated to be obtained from the asset.

Gross investment. Gross investment in a lease is the aggregate of the minimum lease payments receivable by the lessor under a finance lease and any unguaranteed residual value accruing to it.

Inception. The inception of a lease is the earlier of the date of the lease agreement or the date of commitment by the parties to its principal provisions at this time: a lease is classified as either operating or finance; in the case of a finance lease, the amounts to be recognized are established.

Initial costs. Initial direct costs are incremental expenses that are directly attributable to negotiating and arranging a lease, except for such items incurred by manufacturer or dealer lessors.

Interest rates. The interest rate implicit in the lease terms is the discount rate which, at inception, causes the aggregate present value of (a) the minimum lease payments, and (b) the unguaranteed residual value to be equal to the sum of (i) the fair value of the leased asset and (ii) any initial direct costs to the lessor.

The lessee's incremental borrowing rate is the rate of interest it would have to pay on a similar lease or, if that is not determinable, the rate that, at inception, the lessee would incur to borrow over a similar term and with similar security, the funds necessary to purchase the asset.

Minimum payments. Minimum lease payments are those that the lessee makes, or can be required to make over the term, excluding contingent rent, costs for services and taxes to be paid by and reimbursed by the lessor together with:

- For a lessee, any amounts guaranteed by it or a party related to it.
- For a lessor, any residual value guaranteed by the lessee, a party related to it, or an unrelated third party that is financially capable of discharging the obligations under a guarantee.

In some cases, the lessee has an option to purchase the asset at a price anticipated to be sufficiently lower than fair value at the date it becomes exercisable for it to be reasonably certain, at inception, that it will be exercised. In this situation, the minimum lease payments are those due over the term to the expected date of exercise of the option, plus any payment required to exercise it. Fair value is the amount for which an asset could be exchanged, or a liability settled, between knowledgeable, willing parties in an arm's-length transaction.

Net investment. Net investment in a lease is the gross investment, discounted at the interest rate implicit in the lease terms.

Residual value. Guaranteed residual value is:

- For a lessee, that part of the residual value that is guaranteed by the lessee or a party related to it; the amount of the guarantee is the maximum amount that could, in any event, become payable.
- For a lessor, that part of the residual value that is guaranteed by the lessee or a related party that is financially capable of discharging the obligation.

That portion of the residual value of the leased asset, the realization of which by the lessor is not assured, or which is guaranteed solely by a related party, is considered unguaranteed.

Term. The lease term is the noncancelable period for which the lessee has contracted to lease the asset together with any further periods for which it has an option to continue to lease the asset, with or without further payment, when, at inception, it is reasonably certain that the option will be exercised.

Unearned income. Unearned income is the difference between the gross and the net investment.

Useful life. Useful life is the estimated remaining period, from commencement of the lease term, without limitation by the lease term, over which the economic benefits embodied in the asset are expected to be consumed by the entity.

LEVERAGED LEASES

"Single investor lease" is a jargon phrase describing all leases that are not leveraged according to specific criteria in Statement of Financial Accounting Standards (SFAS) 13, *Accounting for Leases*. The term is misleading, since more than one investor may participate in a single-investor lease. A leveraged lease, however, is one that satisfies these criteria:

- The lease must be funded with a *substantial amount* of nonrecourse debt; this is usually assumed to be more than 30% of equipment cost.
- The use of nonrecourse debt must be agreed to (although not necessarily funded) at the inception of the lease; subsequent use of nonrecourse debt (after inception) does not result in a leveraged lease but rather in an assigned lease, which is accounted for differently.
- A leveraged lease cannot be anything other than a direct finance lease, which does not contain manufacturer's or dealer's profit or loss on the transaction.
- The lessor's net investment (lease payments, less nonrecourse debt payments, plus residual value, less unearned income) declines during the early years of the transaction and rises in later years; such fluctuations in the net investment may occur more than once.

- If an investment tax credit is part of the transaction, the deferral method must be used; if the flow-through method is adopted by the lessor, the lease will not technically be deemed leveraged.

There are significant differences between the accounting and tax definitions of a leveraged lease, especially in the United States. This may result in a situation where the lessor enjoys such treatment on its tax return but not on its financial statements.

FINANCIAL REPORTING

Using leasing as a means to fund the acquisition of an asset has a direct impact on the lessee's financial statements. Compared to an installment loan to purchase it, lease financing will affect not only the balance sheet but also the income and cash flow statements of the entity. Accounting rules for capital leases, rental programs, and operating leases are different from those for installment loans. Capital lease accounting rules are generally more complicated than operating lease treatments or rental reporting; the former more closely resemble loan accounting, whereas assets obtained under operating leases and rental agreements do not usually appear on the lessee's balance sheet as either assets or liabilities. The next example contrasts an installment loan purchase with a finance lease, operating lease, and rental agreement.

Example: Equipment Financing

ABC Manufacturing Company is faced with five alternative courses of action with respect to a planned expansion on 1 January 2010.

Case

A. No transactions (comparison base).
B. Purchase equipment using an installment loan.
C. Obtain the use of equipment with a finance lease.
D. Enter into an operating lease for the equipment.
E. Rent the equipment as needed on a monthly basis.

Overall Assumptions

Capital Cost	50,000
Overhead Savings	16,000
Commencement Date	1 January 2010
Additional Revenue	8,000
Rate of Return	48.00%

Depreciation	Year	Tax	Ownership	Finance Lease
	1	20.00%	18.00%	20.00%
	2	32.00%	18.00%	20.00%
	3	19.20%	18.00%	20.00%
	4	11.52%	18.00%	20.00%
	5	11.52%	18.00%	20.00%
	6	5.76%		0.00%
	Salvage	0.00%	10.00%	0.00%
		100.00%	100.00%	100.00%

Case A: No Transactions

Case B: Installment Loan		**Case C: Finance Lease**	
Down Payment	7,500	Lease Liability	45,014
Installment Loan	42,500	Monthly Payment	985
Monthly Payment	930	Number of Payments	60
Number of Payments	60	Implicit Interest Rate	11.28%
Interest Rate – APR	11.28%	Purchase Option	11,946
		Lessor's Residual	9,557

Year	Interest	Principal		Year	Interest	Principal
1	4,454	6,706		1	4,718	7,102
2	3,658	7,502		2	3,214	7,946
3	2,617	8,543		3	2,241	8,919
4	1,728	9,432		4	1,364	9,796
5	843	10,317		5	569	11,251
	13,300	42,500			12,106	45,014

Case D: Operating Lease		**Case E: Monthly Rental**	
Monthly Payment	995	Monthly Payment	1,090
Number of Payments	60	Number of Payments	n/a

Installment Loan Terms

- Down payment $7,500.
- Loan balance of $42,500; interest rate is 11.28% annual percentage rate.
- Loan payments: 60 payments/periods at $930 per month in arrears.
- First-year amortization includes 12 loan payments.

Interest Expense	$4,454	
Principal Paid	6,706	
12 Total Payments	$11,160	(12 × $930)

- Remaining balance due $35,794 of which $7,502 principal is due within the next 12 months and $28,292 thereafter

Capital Lease Terms

- 60 lease payments/periods at $985 per month/period in arrears.
- Lessee's IAS17 present value discount rate is 11.28%, the current market borrowing rate applicable to debt of equal term; this is lower than the lease's implicit rate of 11.64%
- Present value of minimum lease payments, representing the equipment cost capitalized, is $45,014
- Lease payable liability is also $45,014, which matches the amount of capitalized equipment
- $9,003 per year book depreciation, assuming no salvage value ($45,014 ÷ 5 = $9,003)
- First-year amortization of 12 lease payments:

Interest Expense	$4,718	
Principal Paid	7,102	
12 Total Payments	$11,820	(12 × $985)

- Remaining lease payable of $37,912, of which $7,946 is due within the next 12 months (current), and $29,966 thereafter.
- $9,557 lessee's purchase option, not expected to be exercised.
- $9,557 lessor's expected residual value.

Operating Lease Terms

- 60 Lease payments of $995 in arrears.

Rental Terms

- 12 monthly rental payments of $1,200 in arrears; this is renewable annually for four years at the end of the initial noncancelable 12-month term.

Statement Presentation

The next financial statements describe the impact of the five cases. They are shown on a pro forma basis, giving effect to the first fiscal year's experience with the four different financing alternatives.

ABC Manufacturing Company
Pro Forma Income Statements Year to 31 December 2010

		No Transaction	Purchase/ Loan	Finance Lease	Operating Lease	Monthly Rental
Sales		450,000	458,000	458,000	458,000	458,000
Cost of Sales		(310,000)	(294,000)	(294,000)	(294,000)	(294,000)
Gross Profit		140,000	164,000	164,000	164,000	164,000
Gross Margin		31.1%	35.8%	35.8%	35.8%	35.8%
Expenses						
Operating		55,000	55,000	55,000	55,000	55,000
Rent		-	-	-	11,940	13,080
Depreciation–Existing		15,000	15,000	15,000	15,000	15,000
Depreciation–Control		-	9,000	9,003	-	-
		70,000	79,000	79,003	81,940	83,080
EBIT		70,000	85,000	84,997	82,060	80,920
Interest–Existing		(7,200)	(7,200)	(7,200)	(7,200)	(7,200)
Interest–Control		-	(4,454)	(4,718)		
EBT		62,800	73,346	73,079	74,860	73,720
Tax	35%	(21,980)	(25,671)	(25,578)	(26,201)	(25,802)
Net Earnings		40,820	47,675	47,501	48,659	47,918
Index		100.0	116.8	116.4	119.2	117.4

ABC Manufacturing Company
Pro Forma Cash Flow Statements Year to 31 December 2010

	No Transaction	Purchase/ Loan	Finance Lease	Operating Lease	Monthly Rental
Operating Activities					
Net Earnings	40,820	47,675	47,501	48,659	47,918
Depreciation	15,000	24,000	24,003	15,000	15,000
Deferred Taxes	8,190	8,540	7,294	8,190	8,190
	64,010	80,215	78,798	71,849	71,108
Noncash Items	(12,000)	(12,000)	(12,000)	(12,000)	(12,000)
	52,010	68,215	66,798	59,849	59,108
Investing Activities					
Equipment	-	(50,000)	-	-	-
Finance Lease	-	-	(45,014)	-	-
	-	(50,000)	(45,014)	-	-
Financing Activities					
Installment Loan	-	42,500			
Finance Lease			45,014		
Principal Repayments		(6,706)	(7,102)		
Dividends	(30,000)	(30,000)	(30,000)	(30,000)	(30,000)
	(30,000)	5,794	7,912	(30,000)	(30,000)
Net Cash Increase	22,010	24,009	29,696	29,849	29,108
Opening Balance	5,000	5,000	5,000	5,000	5,000
Closing Balance	27,010	29,009	34,696	34,849	34,108

ABC Manufacturing Company
Pro Forma Balance Sheets at 31 December 2010

	No Transaction	Purchase/ Loan	Finance Lease	Operating Lease	Monthly Rental
ASSETS					
Current					
Cash	27,010	29,009	34,696	34,849	34,108
Receivables	18,000	18,000	18,000	18,000	18,000
Inventories	15,500	15,500	15,500	15,500	15,500
Total	60,510	62,509	68,196	68,349	67,608
Fixed					
Plant & Equipment	145,000	195,000	145,000	145,000	145,000
Accumulated Depreciation	(30,000)	(39,000)	(30,000)	(30,000)	(30,000)
	115,000	156,000	115,000	115,000	115,000
Finance Lease	-	-	45,014	-	-
Accumulated Depreciation	-	-	(9,003)		
	-	-	36,011	-	-
Total	115,000	156,000	151,011	115,000	115,000
	175,510	218,509	219,207	183,349	182,608
LIABILITIES					
Current					
Bank Operating	10,000	10,000	10,000	10,000	10,000
Payables	9,000	9,000	9,000	9,000	9,000
Current Portion – Loan	-	7,502	-	-	-
Current Portion – Lease	-	-	7,946		
	19,000	26,502	26,946	19,000	19,000
Term					
Bank Term Loan	50,000	50,000	50,000	50,000	50,000
Installment Loan	-	28,292			
Finance Lease			29,966		
Deferred Taxes	8,190	8,540	7,294	8,190	8,190
	58,190	86,832	87,260	58,190	58,190
Total	77,190	113,334	114,206	77,190	77,190
EQUITY					
Ordinary	57,500	57,500	57,500	57,500	57,500
Retained Earnings					
Opening	30,000	30,000	30,000	30,000	30,000
Net Earnings	40,820	47,675	47,501	48,659	47,918
Dividends	(30,000)	(30,000)	(30,000)	(30,000)	(30,000)
Closing	40,820	47,675	47,501	48,659	47,918
	98,320	105,175	105,001	106,159	105,418
	175,510	218,509	219,207	183,349	182,608

Off–Balance Sheet Reporting and Disclosure

Consider the column "Operating Lease" on the ABC Company's pro forma balance sheet. Even though a $50,000 piece of equipment will have been used all year, under an operating lease, the firm's total assets at year-end would be about the same as if the transaction had never materialized. Compare column 1 of the balance sheet with column 4. Notice also that no new equipment appears under the operating lease, or rental columns, nor is any liability recorded for their obligations. Those financial reporting effects represent what is commonly called an off–balance sheet transaction. Neither the equipment nor its associated financing appear on the balance sheet when an operating lease is used. If a capital lease is used, an asset of $45,014 appears rather than the $50,000 retail cost of the equipment.

This difference arises because, for a finance lease, IAS 17 requires that only the present value of the minimum lease payments be capitalized. Suppose the lessee was also obligated either to (a) guarantee that the residual value of the equipment at the end of the lease would equal the lessor's expected value of $9,557, or (b) be obligated to buy the equipment at a stated "put" price of $9,557. Then $5,452, the present value of $9,557, would be added to the $45,014, giving a total capitalized amount of $50,466. This would then be reduced to $50,000, as the capitalized amount shall not exceed the fair value.

However, in our example, the lessee is not required to guarantee an expected residual value but merely has a purchase option; this provides an opportunity, but not an obligation, to acquire the equipment. Accordingly, in the example, neither the residual amount nor the lessee's option price is capitalized. The $4,986 difference between the $50,000 cost and the capitalized amount of $45,014 represents partial off–balance sheet financing.

This is often an overlooked advantage; however, operating leases and monthly rentals have greater benefits, since neither their effective debt nor related assets appear anywhere in the financial statements. Lease financing, apart from its impact on net income, also improves various financial ratios that measure liquidity and solvency; the figures set out next demonstrate the differences.

BALANCE SHEET ANALYSES

	No Transaction	Purchase/ Loan	Finance Lease	Operating Lease	Monthly Rental
Current Ratio	3.18	2.36	2.53	3.60	3.56
Quick Ratio	2.37	1.77	1.96	2.78	2.74
Debt/Equity	0.61	0.91	0.93	0.57	0.57
Working Capital	41,510	36,007	41,250	49,349	48,608

Since no debt, short or long term, appears with an operating lease or rental, the liquidity and solvency ratios are greatly enhanced. Keep in mind, however, that these are only apparent benefits, because the cash flows and real future cash obligations of operating leases and rentals are identical to those of the capital lease and close to the loan obligation. To emphasize this point, consider the Cash Flow Statement: The net cash increase during the current year is the same under both types of leases. However, the cash increase under the loan alternative is smaller because of the $7,500 required down payment. Thus, from a cash flow viewpoint, leasing is typically superior, because most leases are structured either with no or with very little deposit (typically one or two payments). A loan, however, generally is structured with a significant down payment, frequently 10% to 20%. Therefore, in addition to the cash flow advantages, leasing results in better liquidity.

Accounting by Lessee

The next principles should be applied in the financial statements of the lessee.

- At commencement, finance leases should be recorded as an asset and a liability at the lower of (a) the fair value of the asset and (b) the present value of the minimum lease payments, discounted if practicable at the interest rate implicit in the lease, otherwise at the incremental borrowing rate.
- Finance lease payments should be apportioned between the finance charge and the liability, so as to produce a constant periodic rate of interest on the remaining balance (IAS 17.25).
- Depreciation of assets held under finance leases should be consistent with that for owned assets; if there is no reasonable certainty that the lessee will obtain ownership at the end of the period, the asset should be depreciated over the shorter of the lease term or its economic life (IAS 17.27).

- For operating leases, the lease payments should be recognized as an expense over the term by a straight-line method, unless another systematic basis is more representative of the user's benefit (IAS 17.33).
- Incentives for a new or renewed operating lease should be recognized as a reduction of the rental expense over the term, irrespective of their nature, form, or timing (SIC 15).

Accounting by Lessors

These next principles should be applied in the financial statements of lessors.

- At commencement, the lessor should record a finance lease on its balance sheet as a receivable, at an amount equal to its net investment (IAS 17.36).
- The lessor should recognize income based on a pattern reflecting a constant periodic rate of return on its outstanding net investment outstanding (IAS 17.39).
- Assets held for operating leases should be presented on the balance sheet according to their nature (IAS 17.49); lease income should be recognized over the term by a straight-line method, unless another systematic basis is more representative of the time pattern in which the user's benefits from the asset are diminished (IAS 17.50).

Incentives for a new or renewed operating lease should be recognized as a reduction of the rental income over the term, irrespective of their nature, form, or timing (SIC 15).

- Manufacturer or dealer lessors should include the profit or loss on the "sale" in the same period as for a cash transaction; if artificially low rates of interest are charged, the selling profit should be restricted to that which would be earned if commercial interest was charged (IAS 17.42).
- Initial direct and incremental costs of lessors are recognized over the term; this does not apply to manufacturer or dealers, where such costs are an expense when the sales profit is recognized.

Sales and Leaseback

For a sale and leaseback, also known as a "sale-leaseback" in the U.S., resulting in a finance lease, any excess of the proceeds over the carrying amount is deferred and amortized over the lease term (IAS 17.59). For such a transaction that results in an operating lease (IAS 17.61), if:

- The sale is clearly at fair value, any profit or loss is recognized immediately.
- The sale price is below fair value, the profit or loss should be recognized immediately, except if the loss is offset by future below-market rents; in that case, it should be amortized over the term.
- The sale price is above fair value, any gain should be deferred and amortized over the term.
- The fair value is less than the carrying amount, the difference should be recognized as a loss immediately (IAS 17.63).

Impact on Net Income

An operating lease increases net income during its early years; that is not as well understood or as widely known as the balance sheet effect. However, operating leases for periods roughly equal to the asset's economic life may have a favorable impact on the income statement relative to the installment loan or capital lease alternatives.

Present Value Depreciation (sometimes known as actuarial or sinking fund depreciation) is forced on the equipment user with an operating lease. During the early years, this is considerably less than the conventional straight-line amounts; in the later years, it is higher. This accounting issue is not the same as Modified Accelerated Cost Recovery System (MACRS) tax depreciation in the United States; for the lessee, all payments on an operating lease are tax deductible.

In the periodic payments, lessors charge the lessee for both cost recovery and interest. Cost recovery is to defray the loss of equipment value over time occasioned by wear and tear as well as technological obsolescence. Since the payment is the same each month and interest expense diminishes over time, depreciation must increase commensurately; this results in a higher net income for the early years.

RETURN ENHANCEMENT

An entity's return on assets (ROA) is enhanced not only by the off–balance sheet financing available from leasing but also increased earnings; ABC Manufacturing Company's ROA is calculated on a gross and net basis in the next example, which demonstrates the different ROAs under each financing alternative.

ABC Manufacturing Company
Return on Asset Effects

	No Transaction	Purchase/ Loan	Finance Lease	Operating Lease	Monthly Rental
Conventional					
<u>Net Earnings</u>	23.3%	21.8%	21.7%	26.5%	26.2%
Total Assets					
Adjusted					
<u>Net Earnings + Interest (1–t)</u>	30.7%	30.1%	28.2%	34.2%	33.8%
Assets – C L–DT					

The ROA, under the operating lease is better than the others, because of the effect of higher earnings, while assets decrease or change very little. For similar reasons, monthly rental returns, while not as good as those for an operating lease, are higher than the others.

Obviously, this is an extremely pragmatic justification for the use of operating leases. Even if not completely acceptable theoretically, the lure of operating leases and rentals as a means to manipulate financial results is widespread in the United States and many other countries. Their popularity remains intact, because many enterprises currently judge the financial performance of divisions, subsidiaries, and cash-generating units on ROA and reported net earnings.

EFFECT OF LEASING ON VALUE

As the examples indicate, leasing often has a favorable impact on an entity's financial ratios. In comparison to financing alternatives, it can also improve cash flows and net incomes. Even if a firm intends to acquire the equipment outright, an initial lease may make sense, especially if the entity is highly leveraged or has limited credit options, provided there are the requisite cash flows and working capital to cover the payments.

The fact that a lease is properly accounted for under IFRS does not mean that its true impact on an entity's value may be determined without adjustments (often extensive) to the balance sheet and income statement. All leases, even operating leases and rentals, are quasi–debt instruments and should be treated as such for valuation purpose, especially when developing true cash flows. Lease payments represent a real contractual obligation, with implied, though not explicit, principal and interest portions, both of which affect an entity's debt level and therefore equity value as well as reported income. A relatively straightforward summary is: If they owe it, show it. It is important to remember the criteria in IAS 17.4, which is that a finance lease transfers substantially all risks and rewards of ownership to the lessee; otherwise it is an operating lease.

Values to Lessee

Any lease will have different values to the lessee and lessor, depending on their situations. The simple finance lease taken out by ABC Manufacturing has two values to each party: one, if the option is exercised, the other, if it is not.

As shown in the next examples, the 48% pretax return on the investment in the equipment is sufficient to give it a significant value at 31 December 2010. This is based on discounting the net incremental cash flow at the implicit lease rate; that, rather than the entity's Weighted Average Cost of Capital (WACC), is the appropriate rate, as the asset is totally financed. The net present value of the contribution, net of the lease obligation, is $23,706.

Finance Lease

ABC Manufacturing Company
Value of Finance Lease at 31 December 2010

		2011	2012	2013	2014	
Benefits						
Extra Revenue		8,000	8,000	8,000	8,000	
Saved Costs		16,000	16,000	16,000	16,000	
		24,000	24,000	24,000	24,000	
Costs						
Lease Payments		11,820	11,820	11,820	11,820	
Maintenance		-	500	500	500	
		11,820	12,320	12,320	12,320	
Incremental Cash Flow		12,180	11,680	11,680	11,680	
Income Tax	35%	(4,263)	(4,088)	(4,088)	(4,088)	
Net Incremental Cash Flow		7,917	7,592	7,592	7,592	
Present Value	11.28%	0.8986	0.8075	0.7257	0.6521	
Present Value Net of Lease		7,114	6,131	5,509	4,951	23,706

Purchase option. Due to the significant annual cash flows, the equipment purchase option has a value. This is also calculated based on the net incremental cash flows. In the first year after the term, 2015, it is sufficient to cover the option price and contribute to operations. The total present value, again at the lease rate, is $24,515, higher than the value of the lease; together at $48,221, they are almost equal to the cost of the equipment.

ABC Manufacturing Company
Value of Finance Lease at 31 December 2010

Option Price	11,946	Remaining Life–Years		8		
		2015	2016	2017	2018	
Benefits						
Extra Revenue		8,000	8,000	8,000	8,000	
Saved Costs		16,000	16,000	16,000	16,000	
		24,000	24,000	24,000	24,000	
Costs						
Purchase Price		11,946	-	-	-	
Maintenance		1,500	1,500	2,000	2,500	
		13,446	1,500	2,000	2,500	
Incremental Cash Flow		10,554	22,500	22,000	21,500	
Purchase Price		11,946				
Depreciation		(2,987)	(2,987)	(2,987)	(2,987)	
Taxable Income		19,513	19,513	19,013	18,513	
Income Tax	35%	(6,830)	(6,830)	(6,655)	(6,480)	
Net Incremental Cash Flow		3,724	15,670	15,345	15,020	
Present Value	11.28%	0.5860	0.5266	0.4732	0.4253	
Present Value		2,182	8,252	7,262	6,388	24,084

Operating lease. The operating lease also has a value due to the incremental cash flows, which are discounted at the implicit lease rate of 12%, based on a salvage value of $5,000. There is no option to purchase the equipment, merely to continue to lease at the same rate. This would only add $12,840 of value rather than the $24,515 of the finance lease option.

ABC Manufacturing Company
Value of Operating Lease at 31 December 2010

		2011	2012	2013	2014	
Benefits						
Extra Revenue		8,000	8,000	8,000	8,000	
Saved Costs		16,000	16,000	16,000	16,000	
		24,000	24,000	24,000	24,000	
Costs						
Rent		11,940	11,940	11,940	11,940	
Maintenance		-	500	500	500	
		11,940	12,440	12,440	12,440	
Incremental Cash Flow		12,060	11,560	11,560	11,560	
Income Tax	35%	(4,221)	(4,046)	(4,046)	(4,046)	
Net Incremental Cash Flow		7,839	7,514	7,514	7,514	
Present Value Factor	12.00%	0.8929	0.7972	0.7118	0.6355	
Present Value		6,999	5,990	5,348	4,775	23,113

		2011	2012	2013	2014	
Benefits						
Extra Revenue		8,000	8,000	8,000	8,000	
Saved Costs		16,000	16,000	16,000	16,000	
		24,000	24,000	24,000	24,000	
Costs						
Rent		11,940	11,940	11,940	11,940	
Maintenance		1,500	1,500	2,000	2,500	
		13,440	13,440	13,940	14,440	
Incremental Cash Flow		10,560	10,560	10,060	9,560	
Income Tax	35%	(3,696)	(3,696)	(3,521)	(3,346)	
Net Incremental Cash Flow		6,864	6,864	6,539	6,214	
Present Value Factor	0.00%	0.5674	0.5066	0.4523	0.4039	
Present Value		3,895	3,478	2,958	2,510	12,840

Values to Lessor

The values of the ABC Manufacturing Company lease to PQR Leasing Company are again calculated on a discounted cash flow basis using its WACC of 7.65%. Traditionally this rate is relatively low, as leasing companies have been highly leveraged major borrowers. The profit depends on whether the option is exercised or not.

PQR Leasing Company
Value of ABC Lease at 31 December 2010

		2010	2011	2012	2013	2014	2015 No Option	2015 No Option
Benefits								
Lease Payments		11,820	11,820	11,820	11,820	11,820		
Sale		-	-	-	-	-	5,000	11,946
		11,820	11,820	11,820	11,820	11,820	5,000	11,946
Costs								
Purchase Price		50,000						
Administration	1.5%	177	177	177	177	177	250	250
		50,177	177	177	177	177	250	250
Incremental Cash Flow		(38,357)	11,643	11,643	11,643	11,643	4,750	11,696
Purchase Price		50,000						
Depreciation		(10,000)	(16,000)	(9,600)	(5,760)	(5,760)	(2,880)	(2,880)
Taxable Income		1,643	(4,357)	2,043	5,883	5,883	1,870	8,816
Income Tax	35%	(575)	1,525	(715)	(2,059)	(2,059)	(655)	(3,086)
Net Cash Flow		(38,932)	13,168	10,928	9,584	9,584	4,096	8,611
Present Value Factor	7.65%	1.0000	0.9289	0.8629	0.8016	0.7446	0.6917	0.6917
Present Value		(38,932)	12,232	9,430	7,682	7,136	2,833	5,956
Total – No Option		381			Total – Option Exercise	3,504		

CONCLUSION

As shown in this chapter, both the accounting under IAS 17 and taxation of leases is complex. In general, reported profit and leverage are improved, in the short term, by an operating rather than a finance lease, although over the term, payments on both are substantially the same. In addition, there are several other types of leases that are only dealt with cursorily under IAS 17. Three common versions are sales type, such as offered by automotive manufacturers; direct financing, which are similar to ABC's finance lease; and leveraged, which, as previously mentioned, involves three parties: lessee, lessor, and nonrecourse lender. Such agreements are usually very complex, and the guidance of SFAS 13, *Accounting for Leases*, while nonauthoritarian, is often helpful.

23 LIABILITIES

KARRILYN WILCOX

CANADA

INTRODUCTION

A liability is a legal or constructive obligation resulting from past events or transactions, the settlement of which leads to a probable cash outflow and may also include future economic costs; another view is that a liability is a present obligation to transfer assets or provide services in the future. Liabilities are normally classified as either current (due within one year or a normal operating cycle, whichever is longer) or term (noncurrent). The International Financial Reporting Standards (IFRS) requires separation into current or noncurrent unless a liquidity-based presentation is more relevant, such as for banks. Well-known examples of liabilities include bank loans, accounts payable, commercial paper, pension plan obligations, and bonds. Changes in law or actions by an entity can cause the timing of the event to differ from that of the liability. For example, a change in environmental laws can result in a liability for the cleanup of a polluted site years after the related actions.

TYPES OF LIABILITIES

There are various sources of liabilities. A brief discussion of several of the more common liabilities, identified as current or term, is presented next.

Current Liabilities

- *Accounts payable or trade credits.* Occur when a firm purchases goods from another and does not pay cash immediately for them.
- *Unearned revenue.* Created when an entity collects cash in advance of providing goods or services.
- *Notes payable.* Reflect amounts owed to creditors, either on demand or a fixed date; they may also be noncurrent if the maturities are greater than one year
- *Provisions.* Estimates of liabilities that have not yet crystallized (e.g., a lawsuit that has not been settled).
- *Accruals.* Liabilities incurred that have either not been invoiced or are due at an unknown date (e.g., vacation pay).
- *Bank loans.* Includes transaction credits for deals lines of credit (entitle borrowings up to a stated maximum over a specified time) and term loans (fixed amounts payable in installments to a stated maturity). Most are reflected by a promissory note specifying the amount borrowed, interest rate, maturity repayment schedule, collateral (if any) and other applicable conditions.
- *Commercial paper.* Short-term transferable promissory notes sold by large firms in multiples of $100,000 for maturities of 30, 60, and 90 days.
- *Bankers' acceptance.* Forms of commercial paper guaranteed by a bank.
- *Taxes payable.* Occur when an entity's taxes have been recognized but not yet paid.

- *Current portion of long-term debt.* Represents the portion of the term debt due in the next year.
- *Other short-term liabilities.* Includes all items not in another category (e.g., wages earned but not yet due).

For valuation purposes, current liabilities contain items related to operations only.

Term Liabilities

- *Employee benefits.* Cover net obligations for pension and healthcare plans.
- *Lease obligations.* Both capital and operating are similar to bonds as they also require periodic payments of interest and principal (usually blended monthly payments)
- *Deferred taxes.* Timing differences between earning profits and their subsequent taxation may lead to current and term tax assets or liabilities.
- *Bonds.* Term borrowing arrangements involving specific payments on one or more specified dates; they may be secured or unsecured (debentures), issued in series, and have various priorities (e.g., senior, junior and subordinated); for valuation purposes, term bank loans are equivalent to highly rated bonds.

REPORTING LIABILITIES: BORROWERS

Current accounting standards require a mixture of measurement bases. On the borrower's balance sheet, bank loans or notes payable are shown at the face amount with any related discounts recorded as assets to be amortized against income over their terms. Bonds, however, are shown at amortized cost. Financial instruments, which are any derivative (e.g., option, forward, swap, or future) or liability hedged with a derivative, are recorded at fair value.

Since the balance sheet contains a mixture of measurement bases, the amount it shows as equity should not be interpreted as the value of the firm. A valuator must adjust the financial statements to better reflect the entity's earning potential and creditworthiness.

REPORTING LIABILITIES: LENDERS

International Accounting Standard (IAS) 39 distinguishes between three classes of securities (liabilities of others): available for sale, trading, and held to maturity. Each is reported differently on the balance sheet and income statement. Available-for-sale securities (those not expected to be held to maturity or traded in the near term) are shown at fair value, and any gain (or loss) is taken directly to stockholder equity through other comprehensive income without touching the income statement. Trading securities (intended to be sold in the near term) are held at fair value with the gains or losses taken directly to income. Held-to-maturity securities are recorded at amortized cost; hence neither a gain nor a loss is reported until it is realized. The next table summarizes the different classification.

	Available for Sale	**Trading**	**Held to Maturity**
Balance Sheet	Fair value Unrealized gain or loss reported as other comprehensive income in shareholders' equity	Fair value	Amortized cost
Income Statement	Dividends Interest Realized gains or losses	Dividends Interest Realized and unrealized gains or losses	Interest Realized gain or losses

NATURE OF BONDS

To raise funds, firms often issue bonds, which obligate the issuer to make payments of interest, and sometimes principal, to the lender on specified dates. This section summarizes the different types of bonds and how to determine their fair values.

Terminology

Unusual nomenclature is often used when referring to bonds.

- *Coupon rate.* The stated annual interest rate expressed as a percentage of face value (e.g., 8.75%).
- *Time to maturity.* Period (in years) until final repayment of principal (e.g., 6.205 years).
- *Yield to maturity.* The internal rate of return on a noncallable bond.
- *Par value.* The face value to be repaid on maturity (which is generally $1,000).
- *Offer price.* The price (expressed as a percentage of par) at which the bond could be purchased in the market (e.g., 72.65).
- *Bid price.* The price (expressed as a percentage of par) at which the bond could be sold in the market (e.g., 70.25).
- *Maturity date.* The date on which the final repayment of principal must be made.
- *Yield to call.* The internal rate of return on a callable bond. (These bonds are discussed later in the chapter.)
- *Bond indenture.* Specifies the rights and obligations (the coupon rate, maturity date and total amount issued) of the borrower to the lenders.
- *Bond covenants.* Contract provisions, both negative and affirmative, that limit the actions of the borrower (e.g., debt/earnings before interest, taxes, depreciation and amortization not to exceed 3.5 times).
- *Negative covenants.* Prohibitions on the borrower, such as restrictions on asset sales, negative pledge of collateral (i.e., not granting it to other lenders), and restrictions on additional borrowings.
- *Affirmative covenants.* Actions the borrower promises to perform, such as maintenance of certain financial ratios (e.g., interest coverage of 2.5 times) and the timely payment of principal and interest.

Special Features

To a bond, entities may attach call, conversion, retraction, or floating rate features, all of which affect its value.

Call rights. Many bonds have features allowing the issuer to redeem them at a specific call price (normally at a premium to par) before maturity. If interest rates decline in the future, the entity may decide to redeem the existing bonds at the call price and issue new ones at a lower yield. Obviously, this is valuable to the firm but detrimental to the bondholders. Therefore, as compensation for this risk, callable bonds tend to be issued with higher coupons than similar, noncallable, plain vanilla issues.

Conversion rights. Conversion rights grant the bondholder an option to exchange the bond for a specified number of equity securities, usually ordinary shares. Unlike call provisions, these benefit the bondholders. Therefore, such securities are issued with lower coupons than similar nonconvertible issues.

Retraction and extension rights. Retractable bonds give the holder an option to retire them at par on a specific date; conversely, extendable bonds allow the holder to extend the life of the bonds to a second, later maturity date. Since these additional privileges benefit the bondholder, retractable and extendable bonds are issued at slightly lower coupon rates than conventional securities.

Floating-rate bonds. In most cases, the coupon rate on a bond is fixed; on floating-rate bonds, the coupon varies every three or six months at a premium to some established measure of interest rates, such as the London Inter-Bank Offered Rate (LIBOR) or Canadian Prime rate. The foremost risk with floating-rate bonds involves the financial health of the entity; if that deteriorates, investors will demand a higher yield, and the bond prices will decline. Floating-rate bonds adjust to variations in market interest rates but not to changes in the issuer's financial health.

Bond Risks

Although bonds are considered less volatile than equity securities, significant risks associated with bonds include those listed next.

- *Interest rate.* Risk that interest rates will change negatively, affecting the value of the bond; several factors affect this: maturity, yield, coupon and any embedded call or put embedded options.
- *Call and prepayment.* Risk that the bond will be called or repaid early; an investor holding a bond that is called will not receive the remaining coupons and must reinvest the proceeds at current market rates (usually lower than the coupon).
- *Yield curve.* Risk of experiencing an adverse shift in the term structure market interest rates, short term being riskier than long term.
- *Reinvestment.* Risk that the investor will receive a lower rate on reinvestment after maturity; factors increasing this risk include high coupon and call features.
- *Liquidity.* Risk of not being able to sell the bond at its fair value; the wider the bid/ask spread, the lower the liquidity.
- *Volatility.* Likelihood of fluctuations in interest rates that affect a bond's value.
- *Inflation.* Risk that the prices of goods and services rise more than the investors expected.
- *Event.* External event causes a change in the credit rating of the borrower; examples include natural disasters, corporate restructuring, and regulatory issues.
- *Sovereign.* Risk that the government of the borrower's jurisdiction will change its laws or regulations, negatively affecting the value of the bond.
- *Credit.* Relative probability of default; this is discussed further later in the chapter.

Some of these risks affect many bonds (e.g., interest rate, yield curve, and credit), but not all risks affect every bond; investors demand higher yields for greater risks.

VALUATION OF BONDS

Bonds can be issued with or without coupons. The first example values a bond without coupon payments; the second values a bond with semiannual coupon payments.

Zero-Coupon Bonds

A zero-coupon bond requires the issuer to repay the principal on maturity; however, no interest payments are required during its life. Therefore, the bond's value is the present value of the single payment.

$$\text{Value of a zero-coupon bond} = \frac{\text{Face Amount}}{(1+r)^{\wedge}T}$$

Where

r = discount rate
T = time in years to maturity

The fair value of a five-year zero-coupon bond currently trading to yield 5% can be estimated as:

$$= \$1000/1.05^{\wedge}5 = \$783.53$$

Because the face amount is fixed, the fair value varies inversely with the discount rate.

Coupon Bonds

A coupon bond requires periodic interest payments (coupons) as well as the principal on maturity. Therefore, valuing a five-year bond ($1,000 face amount) with a coupon rate of 5% paid semiannually requires considering two separate cash flows, the coupons at regular intervals and the face amount at maturity.

Bond Value = Present value of its coupons + Present value of face amount

or, expressed another way,

$$\text{Value} = \sum_{t=1} \frac{\text{Coupon}}{(1+r)^{\wedge}t} + \frac{\text{Par Value}}{(1+r)^{\wedge}t}$$

Where

life = T periods
r = Interest rate corresponding to a t-period zero-coupon bond

The first step is to determine each coupon payment. As the coupon rate (5%) is expressed as a percentage of par ($1,000), the two figures are multiplied to get the annual interest of $50. However, coupons are semiannual payments, so the interest is divided by 2 for the semiannual cash flow. For simplicity, assume the spot rates for zero-coupon government bonds set out in the next table are appropriate for discounting this issue; in practice, a risk premium is added to the spot rates for corporate bonds. Many introductory finance textbooks use a single discount rate; however, that is not realistic as it assumes a flat yield curve, which is not often found in the real world.

The next table summarizes the related cash flows and present value (PV).

Year	Cash Flow $	Spot Rate %	PV Factor	Present Value $
0.5	25.00	5.00	0.9756	24.89
1.0	25.00	5.15	0.9510	23.78
1.5	25.00	5.45	0.9232	23.08
2.0	25.00	5.55	0.8976	22.44
2.5	25.00	5.95	0.8651	21.63
3.0	25.00	6.05	0.8384	20.96
3.5	25.00	6.11	0.8122	20.30
4.0	25.00	6.15	0.7876	19.69
4.5	25.00	6.20	0.7625	19.06
5.0	1,025.00	6.25	0.7385	756.97
				952.30

YIELD TO MATURITY

Any discount rate is a function of a real risk-free rate of return, a premium to compensate for expected inflation, and further risk premiums to reflect cash flow specific characteristics. On the same basis, yield to maturity (YTM) is a function of a real risk-free rate, an inflation premium, and risk premiums for bond specific characteristics. Generally, the market yield for zero-coupon government bonds is used as a proxy for the nominal (including inflation premium) risk-free rate. The total of the risk premiums is referred to as the yield spread and generally is measured as the difference between the yields on the particular bond and that of a government security of comparable maturity.

Floating-Rate Bonds

The procedure for valuing a floating-rate bond is similar to that of a coupon bond except that the spread over the base rate such as LIBOR is important. An investment-grade floating-rate bond with a margin of 300 basis points (100 basis points equals one percentage point) or more, as a first approximation, has a value of par.

CREDIT RISK

Corporate bonds are exposed to three types of credit risks: dangers of default, spreads, and downgrade threats.

Dangers of Default

Default danger measures an entity's ability to pay its obligations. Since the probability of bankruptcy may differ widely, default risk ratings provide essential information to creditors. Bond default risks are measured worldwide by rating agencies such as Standard & Poor's (S&P), Moody's and in Canada, Dominion Bond Rating Service (DBRS). These agencies provide financial information on entities and credit ratings for securities of large firms and municipalities. All of them assign a letter grade to a security, working downward from AAA (S&P and DBRS) or Aaa (Moody's). Rating classes are modified with a plus or minus by S&P; 'high' or 'low' by DBRS; or 1, 2, or 3 suffix by Moody's (e.g., Aaa1, Aaa2, etc.) to provide a more accurate indicator. Currently, only five U.S. corporations are rated AAA by S&P: Automatic Data Processing, Exxon Mobil, Johnson & Johnson, Pfizer, and Microsoft. Since early 2009, General Electric has not been included in the list.

Summary of Bond Ratings

S&P	Moody's	DBRS	
AAA	Aaa	AAA	Ability to pay obligations is extremely strong–high grade
AA	Aa	AA	Very strong ability to pay obligations—high grade
A	A	A	Strong ability to pay obligations—high grade
BBB	Baa	BBB	Adequate ability to pay obligations—medium grade
BB–CC	Ba	BB–CC	Speculative ability to pay obligations—low grade
CC	Ca	CC	Speculative ability to pay obligations—junk
C	C	C	Reserved for bonds that do not pay interest
D	D	D	Debt is in default and payment of obligations is in arrears

Bond rating determination. Bond ratings are based largely on analyses of five groups of financial ratios:

1. *Coverage.* Measures of earnings to fixed costs, such as times interest earned and fixed-charge coverage; low or declining figures signal possible difficulties.

2. *Liquidity.* Measure of ability to pay amounts coming due, such as current and quick ratios.
3. *Profitability.* Measures rates of return on assets and equity; higher profitability reduces risks.
4. *Leverage.* Measures of debt relative to equity; excess debt suggests difficulty in paying obligations.
5. *Cash flow to debt.* Measures cash generation to liabilities.

The next table provides the median financial ratios for Moody's ratings. When there is no rating available for an entity, the median ratios can be used to develop a proxy rating.

	Aaa–Aa	A	Baa	Ba	B	Caa–C	IG	SG
Interest Coverage	16	8.6	5.4	3.7	1.9	0.7	6.5	2.1
Asset Coverage	3.7	2.4	2.3	2	1.3	1	2.4	1.4
Leverage (%)	32.0	41.7	44.8	49.8	68.7	92.2	43.6	66.8
Cash Flow to Debt (%)	53.4	32.6	25.8	21.6	12.1	6.4	28.4	12.7
Return on Assets (%)	11.6	7.5	5.3	4.4	1.7	–2.1	6.3	1.9
Profit (%)	11.8	9.0	6.7	5.0	2.0	–2.6	7.8	2.1
Liquidity (%)	7.8	4.7	4.0	4.3	3.9	3.3	4.6	3.9
Revenue Stability	7.2	7.3	6.1	5.2	6.1	7.3	6.6	5.9

Source: Moody's ratings and financial database as of July 1, 2006

Enterprise risk management. In the third quarter of 2008, S&P introduced Enterprise Risk Management (ERM) analyses into its corporate ratings. The object is to identify deterioration or improvements in credit standings before they are observed in the financial statements. An entity's ERM is set at one of four levels: weak, adequate, strong, and excellent.

Weak

- Missing complete controls for one or more major risks
- Limited capabilities to consistently identify, measure and comprehensively manage risk exposure and limit losses
- Losses may be widespread on a set of predetermined risk/loss tolerance guidelines
- Risk and risk management may sometimes be considered in the firm's corporate judgement

Adequate

- Manages risk in separate silos
- Maintains complete control processes because the firm has capabilities to identify, measure and manage most major risk exposures and losses
- Firm risk/loss tolerance guidelines are less developed
- Unexpected losses are somewhat likely to occur
- Risk and risk management are often important considerations in the firm's corporate judgement

Strong

- Demonstrates an enterprise-wide view of risks while still focused on loss control
- Has control processes for major risks, giving them advantages due to lower expected losses in tough times
- Can consistently identify, measure and manage risk exposures and losses in predetermined tolerance guidelines
- Unlikely to experience unexpected losses outside of its tolerance levels
- Risk and risk management are usually important considerations in the firm's corporate judgement

Excellent

- Possesses all the characteristics of a 'strong' ERM program
- Demonstrates risk/reward optimization

- Very well-developed capabilities to consistently identify, measure and manage risk exposures and losses within the entity's predetermined tolerance guidelines
- Risk and risk management are always important considerations in the firm's corporate judgement
- Highly unlikely that the firm will experience losses outside of its risk tolerance

Source: StandardandPoors.com, Ratings Resources, Definitions

Credit Spreads

The term 'credit spread' refers to divergence in yields of bonds with differing credit ratings. Exhibit 23.1 plots the behavior of U.S. yields for various credit ratings since 2004.

Exhibit 23.1 US Years over Time

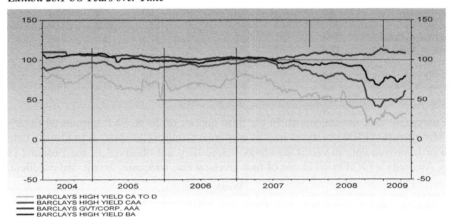

Source: Thomson Reuters Datastream

Credit spreads narrow during expansions and broaden during recessions/contractions. In a recession, investors become concerned about the perceived risk in corporate bonds as defaults become more likely. Hence, investors in nearly all countries move some money out of corporate bonds into government bonds, causing the prices of corporate bonds to fall and their yields to rise. Conversely, the price of government bonds rise and their yields fall, widening the spread; in a period of an expansion, the opposite holds true.

Interpreting credit spreads in this environment. In most countries, credit spreads have become larger; in Canada, for example, at the peak of the credit crisis (December 2008), credit spreads reached record levels.

Exhibit 23.2 A-Rated Corporate Bond Spread

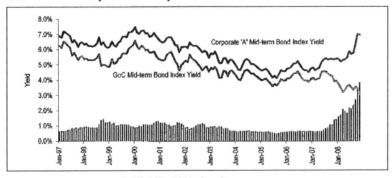

Source: Company reports and CIBC World Markets Inc.

However, care must be taken when interpreting corporate bond spreads during extreme environments (such as the present) because of:

- *Liquidity premiums.* Numerous studies have sought to explain observed credit spreads that, historically, tend to exceed those explicable by the probability of default; the latter is often reasoned as the single theoretical source of such credit spreads in an efficient market. At least part of the nondefault component of the spread is commonly attributed to liquidity premiums—required incremental returns to compensate for the comparative lack of liquidity of corporate bonds. Such lack of marketability and the related liquidity premium is likely to rise disproportionately during times characterized by flights to quality and rising default rates. Illiquidity in economic conditions may reflect more accurately the deteriorating credit quality and solvency of debt owners rather than of the borrowers themselves.
- *Asymmetric returns.* In tough economic times, when the probability of corporate default rises, the negatively skewed asymmetry in corporate bond returns (i.e., the fat left tail) relative to share returns is enhanced. Thus, it would be reasonable to expect the risk premiums of corporate debt to rise disproportionately to those of equities.
- *Difficulty in diversifying.* The negative return asymmetry inherent in corporate bonds further implies that an extraordinarily large number of bonds must be held to obtain adequate diversification of nonsystemic risk; this may result in incremental corporate credit spreads during difficult economic times.
- *Impact of taxes.* As corporate bond and share valuations decline and corresponding yields rise, the higher tax rates associated with bond interest may lead to a proportionately larger increase in their yields relative to those of dividend yields to maintain tax equivalence.

Downgrade Threats

A firm's credit rating can change; an improvement in a rating of C to BBB is referred to as an upgrade while changes from a BBB to a C is a downgrade. For investment-grade bonds, the probability of a downgrade is much higher than that of an upgrade. Investors lose money when a bond is downgraded, as its price falls to give the higher yield necessary to compensate for the greater risks.

A useful tool for gauging downgrade threats is the rating transition matrix, available for 1-year, 2-year, 5-year and 10-year bonds; those with a longer term have a lower probability of retaining their original rating.

Hypothetical One-Year Transition Matrix

Rating at the start of a year	Rating at end of the first year (%)									
	AAA	AA	A	BBB	BB	B	CCC	D	N.R.	Total
AAA	90.34	5.62	0.39	0.08	0.03	0	0		3.54	100
AA	0.64	88.78	6.72	0.47	0.06	0.09	0.02	0.01	3.21	100
A	0.07	2.16	87.94	4.97	0.47	0.19	0.01	0.04	4.16	100
BBB	0.03	0.24	4.56	84.26	4.19	0.76	0.15	0.22	5.59	100
BB	0.03	0.06	0.4	6.09	76.09	6.82	0.96	0.98	8.58	100
B	0	0.09	0.29	0.41	5.11	74.62	3.43	5.3	10.76	100
CCC	0.13	0	0.26	0.77	1.66	8.93	53.19	21.94	13.14	100

The rows of the matrix indicate the rating at the start of a year, while the columns indicate the ratings at the end of the first year. There is a 10.6% probability that an AA-rated bond will be downgraded by the end of any year and a 0.6% probability that it will be upgraded, 16.5 to 1 odds.

Bond Prices Over Time

When the YTM is greater than the coupon rate, a bond sells at a discount; when the YTM is lower, it will sell at a premium. As at maturity, the holders will receive full repayment of principal, bond prices converge over time to par, as illustrated in Exhibit 23.3.

Exhibit 23.3 Convergence of Bond Prices

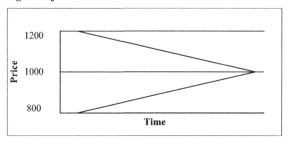

VALUATION OF SPECIAL OBLIGATIONS

The previous section dealt with valuing bonds and other similar liabilities; this section discusses the valuation of special obligations: accruals, provisions, and contingent liabilities. Provisions and contingent liabilities are obligations such as an uncertain timing or an amount, whose valuation is challenging because of great uncertainties about the related cash flows and the risks to be reflected in the discount rate. Provisions differ from accruals, although both require estimates as much more uncertainty exists with provisions.

Relevant Standard

Issued in 1998 and substantially revised in 2005, IAS 37, *Provisions, Contingent Liabilities and Contingent Assets*, and its related interpretations—International Financial Reporting Interpretations Committee (IFRIC) 1, *Changes in Existing Decommissioning, Restoration and Similar Liabilities*; IFRIC 5, *Right to Interest Arising from Decommissioning, Restoration and Environmental Funds*; IFRIC 6, *Liabilities Arising from Participating in a Specific Market—Waste Electrical and Electronic Equipment*; and IFRIC 17, *Distributions of Noncash Assets to Owners*—are designed to ensure appropriate recognition criteria and measurement bases for those subjects. IAS 37 excludes obligations and contingencies arising from:

- Financial instruments carried at fair value (applies to those at amortized cost)
- Nononerous executory contracts
- All insurance company policy liabilities and items covered by another standard, such as construction contracts; IAS 12, *Income Taxes;* IAS 17, *Leases;* and IAS 19, *Employee Benefits*

Measurement of Accruals or Provisions

According to IAS 37, an accrual or a provision must be recognized if:

- A present legal or constructive obligation exists.
- Payment is probable ('more likely than not').
- The amount can be estimated reliably.

The amount recognized is the best estimate of the payment an entity would make rationally to settle the obligation or transfer it to a third party at the close of a reporting period, even if the transaction occurs after its end. For accruals that generally have little uncertainty and a short time horizon, discounting is not normally required.

For a provision covering an individual obligation, such as a settlement of a lawsuit or cleanup of a site, the best estimate might be the single most likely outcome, adjusted for risk. When the provision is for a number of similar obligations (such as product warranties), the class must be considered as a whole because the likelihood of an outflow of resources increases as its size expands. This means that one-time situations (restructuring, environmental cleanup, settlement of a lawsuit) are measured at the most likely amount and that large populations of events (warranties, customer refunds) are measured at a probability-weighted expected value.

Both are determined pretax, at present value, using a pretax discount rate that reflects the current time value of money and the market's assessment of the risks and uncertainties surrounding the underlying events. Most discount rates, such as weighted average cost of capital (WACC), are calculated on a post-tax basis; thus, in practice, such calculations are normally prepared on a posttax basis and than grossed up accordingly to represent a pretax amount. If some or all of the expenditures are expected to be reimbursed by others, the required provision should be reduced only when it is virtually certain that the reimbursement will be received on settlement; such reduction must not exceed the provision.

Future events. Since future events can affect the amount required to settle a liability, their measurement should:

- Forecast reasonable changes in applying existing technology.
- Ignore possible gains on sale of assets.
- Consider changes in legislation only if virtually certain to be enacted.

If there is sufficient objective evidence with respect to these factors, the amount recognized should reflect any advantages (or disadvantages). However, potential costs that may need to be incurred, assuming they could be avoided by the entity's future actions, should not be included. In practice, firms are only able to recognize costs of work that has been carried out but not paid for at the end of the reporting period. For example, if an offshore oil platform is required to be removed and the seabed restored after production ceases, a provision for the eventuality should be accrued added to the cost of the asset and depreciated over the estimated life.

Example: Product Warranties

XYZ Manufacture SA provides a two-year warranty on its goods from the date of purchase. Based on past experience, it is more likely than not that there will be some claims. Historically in relation to sales, claims percentages have been: 2006, 0.75%; 2007, 1.20%; 2008, 0.95%. Management has asked a valuator to determine what provision should be recognized in 2009. The appropriate figure needs to reflect timing through a weighted average, rather than by discounting; therefore, the rate should be $(0.75 \times 1) + (1.2 \times 2) + (0.95 \times 3) / 6\% = (0.75 + 2.40 + 2.85) / 6\% = 6 / 6\% = 1.00\%$. On sales of \$325,623,000, the amount is \$3,256,230 rounded to \$3,250,000.

Example: Cleanup

ABC Oil Inc. caused contamination but cleaned up the site only after being required to do so under the laws of the relevant countries. One country has no legislation regarding cleaning up polluted land, so ABC Oil has been contaminating several sites for a number of years without setting aside funds for cleaning. At year-end 2008, the firm is virtually certain that a draft law requiring cleaning of already polluted land will be enacted shortly. ABC Oil estimates \$450 million as the cost to clean up the contaminated locations and estimates it will have completed the cleaning by the next fiscal year-end. ABC Oil has a WACC of 15%, with a cost of equity for the project of 12% and a corporate tax rate of 40%. The valuation has to indentify the obligating event and calculate the payment, timing, and discount rate.

The obligating event is the contamination of the land. Since an outflow is probable, ABC Oil needs to recognize as a provision the best estimate of the cleaning costs (IAS 37.14 and 22). The total pretax costs are $450 million to be paid in fiscal 2009; therefore, it must be discounted for one year at 12%, the equity rate for the project. Hence, the present value factor is 0.893 and the provision, calculated on a pretax basis, is $401,850,000.

Restructurings. A restructuring occurs when there is a sale or termination of a line of business, closure of a facility, change in management structure, or a fundamental reorganisation. A constructive obligation arises when a firm has undertaken both (a) and (b):

a. Development of a formal restructuring plan identifying the

    • Business or part of it affected; principal facilities concerned
    • Location, function, and approximate number of employees to be compensated for termination
    • Expenditures to be undertaken
    • Timing of the plan's implementation

b. Raising valid expectations in those affected that it will carry out the restructuring by starting to implement that plan or by announcing its main features.

The timing of restructuring provisions should be accrued in this way:

• *Sale of operation.* Only after a binding sale agreement, if it is obtained subsequent to the end of the reporting period, disclose but do not accrue.
• *Closure or reorganisation.* Only after a detailed formal plan is adopted and announced publicly; a board decision is not enough.
• *Future operating losses.* None should be recognized even in a restructuring.
• *Restructuring follows an acquisition.* Amounts for terminating employees, closing facilities, and eliminating product lines only if announced at acquisition and a detailed formal plan is adopted within three months.

Restructuring provisions include only the direct expenditures arising from the activities that are both necessary and not associated with ongoing operations. They do not include costs for retraining or relocating continuing staff, marketing, or investment in new systems. Provisions should be used only for their original purpose, reviewed at the end of each reporting period, and adjusted to reflect the current best estimate; if necessary, they may be reversed.

Contingent Liabilities

A contingent liability is: (a) a possible obligation that occurs from past activities and will be established only by the occurrence or nonoccurrence of one or more uncertain future events not wholly within the control of the firm; or (b) a present obligation that arises from past activities events but has not been recognized because it is not probable that an outflow of resources will be required to settle the obligation or the amount of the obligation cannot be determined with sufficient reliability.

All contingent liabilities are required to be disclosed and assessed continually. When it becomes probable that an outflow of economic resources will be required, a provision is recognized in the financial statements of the period.

Example: Litigation

MNO plc is being sued for product liability in the amount of $80 million; during the discovery process in 2008, actual damages of $13 million have been identified. On this basis, MNO and its insurer offered to settle for $17 million, allowing a 30% contingency fee for the plaintiff's attorney. On any judgment or settlement, the insurer is liable for 80% of the first $40 million and 50% of the balance to a maximum of $50 million; this would represent a total payout of $76 million.

The trial is scheduled for May 2009. MNO has to establish a provision at its 2008 year-end. The minimum provision is $3.4 million made up of the settlement ($17 million) less the 80% portion ($13.6 million) to be recovered from the insurer. The maximum is $30 million consisting of the claim ($80 million) less the maximum recovery from the insurer ($50 million).

The lawyers estimate that the chance of a total loss is 10%; of the plaintiff accepting a 20% improved settlement on the courthouse steps, 50%; of a total win, 15%; and somewhere between the better settlement and the claim, 25%; legal fees will be $2.2 million win, lose, or draw. This gives a provision of $8.4 million made up as indicated:

Event	Probability %	Payment $ million	Provision $ million
Total Loss	10	80.0	8.0
Settlement	50	20.4	10.2
Win	15	0	0
Draw	25	50.2 (a)	12.6
			30.8
Insurer 80%			(24.6)
			6.2
Legal Fees			2.2
Recorded Contingent Liability			8.4

(a) Midpoint of $20.4 million and $80 million

Disclosure

Unless the possibility of any outflow in settlement is remote, the entity is required to provide a brief description of the nature of each class of contingent liability and, where practicable:

- An estimate of the financial effect, using the guidance on measurement discussed earlier
- An indication of the uncertainties surrounding the amount or timing of any outflows
- The possibility of partial or full reimbursement from another party

IAS 37 recognizes that in extremely rare cases, disclosure of some or all of the required information would seriously prejudice the entity's position in a dispute. In such cases, disclosure of the information is not required but only the general nature of the dispute, the fact that certain information has not been disclosed, and the reasons.

Solvency Analyses

Solvency analyses test an entity's ability to pay its obligations as they come due. A solvency opinion, by design, aims to assure the directors of the entity and the lenders that the transaction will not subject the firm and the other creditors to undue financial distress and that the entity is not likely to become insolvent. The U.S. Federal Bankruptcy Code defines *insolvent* as the condition in which the total of an entity's debts exceeds the value of its property at a fair valuation. A solvency analysis addresses these key tests embodied in the Bankruptcy Code and fraudulent conveyance laws of the United States:

- *Balance sheet test.* Does the value of the entity's assets exceed the amount of the entity's liabilities?

    In this, all financial physical and intangible assets are adjusted to fair value (see Chapter 1) while each liability, including those containing embedded derivatives, is taken at the higher of the face amount (recorded balance) or fair value (restated amount). The balance sheet test is passed when the total fair values of the entity's assets are greater than the entity's total liabilities.

- *Cash flow test.* Will the entity generate adequate cash flow to service all of its liabilities as they come due?

  In this, the valuator analyzes the ability of the entity to service its liabilities as they come due. This includes analyses of the historic and projected earnings and cash flows. The cash flow test is passed if the entity can pay its future debt obligations in each of the projected periods from:

  - Excess cash balances available on the solvency test date
  - Available undiscounted cash flow expected to be generated during the projection period
  - Any available unused credit commitments

- *Capital adequacy test.* Does the entity have sufficient capital to run its business operations?

  In this test (also known as the reasonable capital test), the valuator analyzes if the entity will have sufficient funds to meet all its operating expense, capital expenditure requirements and debt repayment obligations. The entity passes the test if it has enough cash on hand or available unused credit commitments to do so.

CONCLUSION

The valuation of liabilities is a relatively new and surprisingly complex matter. An easy way to look at liabilities is to value them as assets to the supplier of credit; however, this is not correct. Nor is the concept that their fair value is the amount that it would take to settle them. The best way to value a liability is to consider what the entity would have to pay a third party with a similar credit standing to take it over, which is not always the face amount. For complex debt packages of convertible bonds, accompanied by share purchase warrants, it may be substantially less as the consideration received from their sale is allotted to the various assets: warrants, conversion rights, and interest being added based on the relative fair values.

24 MANUFACTURING IN CRISIS PERIODS

EMRE BURCKIN, AYSE PAMUKCU, AND ZEYNEP BURCKIN EORGLU

TURKEY

INTRODUCTION

Manufacturing throughout the world was in a state of collapse during the last half of 2008 and the first of 2009. In 2008, automobiles, the sector's most significant segment, suffered its worst year since 1980; its regional outputs for 2007 and 2008 together with projections for 2009 are presented in the next table.

	2007 million	Allocation %	2008 million	Change %	2009 million	Change %	Allocation %
North America	16.2	22.8	13.3	−17.9	11.7	−13.7	18.8
China	8.8	12.4	9.4	6.8	10.0	6.0	16.1
Europe	16.9	23.8	15.4	−8.9	13.7	−12.4	22.0
Rest of the World	29.1	41.0	28.4	−2.4	26.8	−6.0	43.1
	71.0	100.0	66.5	−6.3	62.2	−6.9	100.0

Sources: Engineering Live, China Daily, China View

Between 2007 and 2009, unit sales in North America are expected to fall by 27.8%, and two of the "Big Three" domestic firms went bankrupt in 2009. Truly, it is a period of factory-floor blues with massive oversupply everywhere in the manufacturing supply chains. This worldwide decline has had an enormous impact on values; traditional methods no longer seem to apply. Therefore, this chapter recommends a mixed methodology for valuing manufacturers in this crisis period.

VALUATION METHODOLOGIES

The definition of value greatly depends on the objective of the assignment; this chapter is concerned with fair value under International Financial Reporting Standards (IFRS). As discussed in other chapters, it must reflect economic measurable features as well as benefits to the owners. All acceptable methods can be bundled into one of the three traditional approaches; each is discussed at length in a separate chapter.

Cost Approach

The Cost Approach is based on the costs to duplicate or replace the firm's entire financial and physical assets; other methods are used for significant intangible assets.

Income Approach

The main criteria for the Income Approach are that the entity has a positive expected future economic result. There are two types of methods: capitalization and discounting. Included in the latter are methods to establish the additional value generated or destroyed by operations such as economic value generated.

Market Approach

The market approach obtains a value for an entity or an asset by looking at either stock exchange or private transactions in securities of comparable firms or sales of similar items. The two basic sets of methods are guideline public companies and transactions in comparable assets.

Values in Crises

Valuing a business is a complex and delicate task. An early step in the analyses is to select the best method for the situation; the criteria are dynamic and evolve continuously. For those reasons, it is not possible to use the same methods as in the past for entities characterized by crises in their industries. To avoid being deemed subjective, it is important that any method adopted has these characteristics:

- *Objective.* Based on real and verifiable data, free from personal considerations of the valuator and external subjective variables.
- *Neutral.* Not taking into account the interest of any particular stakeholder; it is general, independent, and universally applicable.
- *Rational.* Comes from a logical, clear, and reasonable process applicable to the subject.
- *Stable.* Not affected by temporary and mutable elements or extraordinary events.

INTERNATIONAL ORIENTATION

In the valuation profession, there are various schools of thought in different areas of the world regarding the use of some methods in preference to others. The differences tend to be due to diverse views of businesses. The main goal of the valuation process is to establish the fair value of an entity or asset by the appropriate means. In countries with no reliable financial markets, the goal is to determine the economic capital value.

Therefore, economic methods (asset based or discounting) are used in much of continental Europe, Japan, and many other Asian countries. The Anglo-Saxon world tends to be more market based, as there are thousands of quoted firms in a number of those countries.

The methods commonly used in different nations are:

- *France.* Asset based and capitalization methods are the most used.
- *Germany.* The accounting profession considers discounted cash flow methods the most suitable.
- *United Kingdom.* Capitalization methods are common as well as the market approach as the nation has an efficient, well-developed, and dynamic stock market.
- *Italy.* Asset and capitalization methods are the most used.
- *The Netherlands.* The methods most used are capitalization and market-based ones, although the market orientation is less strong than in Britain,
- *United States.* The orientation is strongly toward the market.
- *Canada.* All methods are used depending on circumstances.

EFFECTS OF THE RECENT FINANCIAL CRISIS

During the six months from the autumn of 2008 to the spring of 2009, very substantial declines—in general over 30%—were observed in the prices of traded shares throughout the world due to a worsening economic situation. In such an environment, the main problem for firms, their owners and managers, is making, and implementing without delay, appropriate operating decisions in rapidly changing macroeconomic conditions. For this reason, the true road map of the crisis in a particular industrial segment is of importance to valuators as well to owners and managers; an inappropriate road map could lead all parties wrong. The improper positioning of a firm even on an appropriate road map may also mean a waste of resources.

The financial statements of an entity should reflect its actual financial and commercial situation. This depends on rapid recording of transactions so that all decisions reflect up-to-date information. The continued evolution of business administration techniques has moved strategic decisions and business policy to higher levels, and has in many aspects improved valuation methods.

The authors suggest that under current conditions, a hybrid method is suitable for manufacturers worldwide, combining some of the generally accepted models using these fundamental components:

- Invested capital (equity and debt) of the entity
- Normal profits calculated from the industry's average return on equity
- Profits expected to be generated in the next few years
- Anticipated long-term growth in profits
- Suitable discount rates

In conventional accounting and finance texts, a number of valuation methods are described, along with their main deficiencies and inadequacies as well as advantages. Although some methods and models were developed for different situations, there is no adequate explanation of relative importance. Another difficulty is that the applicability of methods and models to different industries (e.g., manufacturing or service) is not properly identified.

This chapter deals with valuation of manufacturing entities in a crisis period, when there is constant pressure from customers to lower prices (one significant firm's target is 1% a quarter or 5% a year) in an era of great overcapacity. The authors have decided to develop a methodology that seeks to mitigate the criticized negative impacts of the generally accepted techniques in these difficult times when even well-established firms are reporting losses.

Mitigating fully the adverse effects requires combining elements of the cost and income approaches and determining suggested weights for each component. Although the method has been developed for manufacturers, it should be useful for any kind of business. It combines three generally accepted techniques: Fair Value equals Investment Equity at Fair Value obtained mainly by the Cost or Market Approach (times C weight) plus Capitalized Normal Profits (times [1 − C] weight) plus the present value of excessive or missing profits for a limited period, up to three years.

It may be mathematically expressed as equation 24.1:

$$V = C.A + \left((1-c)\,\frac{A.r}{I_1} \right)$$

$$\pm \left[\frac{(R_1 - A.r)}{(1 + I_2)^1} + \frac{(R_2 - A.r)}{(1 + I_2)^2} + \cdots + \frac{(R_n - A.r)}{(1 + I_2)^n} \right] \tag{24.1}$$

Where

V	=	fair value
c	=	weight coefficient (which varies by industry)
A	=	investment equity
$R_{1..n}$	=	profit generated by the firm in each period
Đ1	=	capitalization rate = discount rate – growth rate

APPLICATION OF THE METHOD

The proposed phases of the suggested method are determined by:

• Individual formulas for each component
• Weights, discount and capitalization rates
• General profitability of industry

Investment Equity at Fair Value

This component requires restating all tangible assets to their fair values using the cost or market approaches as appropriate. In general, there are likely to be small reductions from book values for receivables and minimal increases for inventories; the fair values for finished goods are based on the net amounts recoverable (after discounts, allowances for returns, etc.) less selling, distribution, and warranty expense, as in effect the manufacturing profit has already been earned. Normally, raw materials, however, will show a reduction due to restocking charges.

The major changes are likely to be in fixed assets, as any real estate probably will show significant increases over cost while, depending on the nature of their physical decline and functional obsolescence, the plant and equipment may be worth more or less than their cost less the financial depreciation actually deducted (i.e., net book value). Details of how the amounts may be calculated are shown in a later example.

Capitalized Normal Profits

The second component is based on capitalizing the normal profits of the firm. This is not based on the actual past results but on the average returns on equity (ROE) of the industry for the last three years. To ensure an apples-to-apples comparison, that return is applied to the book value of the equity at the valuation date.

The industry ROE may be obtained from:

• Research among current participants in the relevant industry
• Ratios published by Chambers of Commerce or similar sources
• Rates published by tax authorities
• Rates as declared by the midterm and long-term loans

For the example, we have chosen the first source: the profitability ratios of 15 businesses in the particular industry. If differences between the industry's and the entity's averages exceeds four percentage points, the selected amount should be their mean on the basis that the entity will tend to revert to the industry figure over the next five years.

Present Value of Excessive or Missing Profits for a Limited Period

The final component is the present value of excessive or missing profits for a limited time.

$$\pm \left[\frac{(R_1 - A.r)}{(1 + l_2)^1} + \frac{(R_2 - A.r)}{(1 + l_2)^2} + \cdots + \frac{(R_n - A.r)}{(1 + l_2)^n} \right]$$

For this element, the period is limited to between three and five years. The object of this limit is that excessive profits in the industry or achieved by the firm will be reduced in time through the entrance of new firms while missing profits will be ameliorated by competitors closing plants and reducing capital expenditures.

Calculation of weights. In merger pricing, one of the most important components is fixed assets. The required rates of return on the current, fixed, and intangible assets change according to the structure of the firm and nature of the industry. For example, the ratio of the fixed to the total assets in firms acting as commission agents or operating service businesses is relatively low; the ratio is actually quite high in manufacturing firms. The ratio of fixed to total assets is called the plant concentration. In our view, it, with all items restated to fair values, is a reasonable proxy for the weight of the investment equity at fair value. For a manufacturer, it puts most emphasis on the first component; for a service business, the second.

Discount rate. There are various views regarding the selection of appropriate discount rates. The most common is the entity's weighted average cost of capital (WACC). Another is to use the yield on government bonds and reflect the risks in the cash flow projections. In crisis periods, government bonds represent the country's effective interest rate structure since these securities are highly sensitive to inflationary pressures. In the reviews conducted, they varied considerably over their terms. When possible, as shown in the example, we recommend WACC.

The cost of equity should reflect the local stock market. In the example, it was based on the dividend/market value of the ordinary shares of quoted firms in the industry; this was 27% at the valuation date. However, this has to be modified, as Xanthic (the example entity used later in this chapter) is privately owned, which justified a 2.5 percentage point premium.

INVENTORIES

A significant portion of the working capital of most manufacturing entities is tied up in their inventories; this is also true for service businesses, nearly all of which have work in progress. Under IFRS, their accounting is covered with a few exceptions by International Accounting Standard (IAS) 2, which includes these key definitions:

- *Inventory.* An asset held for sale in the normal course of business; in the process of production for such sale; or in the form of materials or supplies to be consumed in the production process or rendering of services.
- *Net realizable value.* The estimated selling price in the normal course of business less estimated cost to complete and estimated costs to make a sale
- *Fair value.* The amount at which an asset could be exchanged or a liability settled, between knowledgeable, willing parties in an arm's-length transaction

This inventory asset is divided into two classes. The first, which is covered by other standards, comprises:

- Work in progress under construction and directly related service contracts (IAS 11, *Construction Contracts*)
- Financial instruments (International Accounting Standards Board [IASB] 39, *Financial Instruments*)
- Biological assets related to agricultural activity including produce at the point of harvest (IAS 41, *Agriculture*)

The second, which is excluded only from the "measurement" requirements (generally the lower of cost or net realizable value), are inventories held by:

- Producers of agriculture and forest products, agricultural produce after harvest, and minerals and mineral products, to the extent that they are measured at net realizable values in accordance with best practices within those industries; and changes in those values are recognized as income during the period
- Commodity broker-traders who measure inventories at fair value less cost to sell; again, changes in those values are recognized as profits or losses in the period

ACCOUNTING FOR INVENTORIES

The accounting for inventories is rather complex due to various classifications, high volume of activity, and various acceptable cost flow alternatives. Two types of entities must be considered, merchandisers and manufacturers. Merchandisers, generally retailers or wholesalers, have a single account for the goods held for resale, whereas manufacturers generally have four types:

1. *Raw materials.* Goods to act as inputs in the production process
2. *Work in progress.* Goods in the course of production but not yet completed
3. *Finished goods.* Completed products awaiting sale
4. *Supplies.* Consumed in the operation of a business

For either type of entity, the basic questions are the same:

- When should the items be included in inventory (ownership)?
- What costs should be included?
- What cash flow assumptions should be used?
- At what amount should they be carried (net realizable value)?

Ownership. Inventory is an asset only if it is an economic resource of the entity at the date of the financial statements. In general, purchases and sales of inventory should be recorded only when legal title passes. Although strict adherence to this rule may not appear to be important, a proper inventory cutoff at the end of an accounting period is crucial to obtain an accurate measurement of inventories and profits. The most common error is to assume that the title is synonymous with possession. This may be incorrect as (a) some goods on consignment may not be owned and (b) certain goods in transit may be owned.

Product financing arrangements. Product financing arrangements are transactions in which an entity sells inventory to a financier and agrees to repurchase it, as needed, for an amount equal to the original sales price plus carrying costs and finance charges. The purpose is to allow the seller (sponsor) to finance its original purchase. As such, it is an alternative to a secured loan where ownership does not change hands, but rather, the lender places a lien on the goods, which may be seized for nonpayment. In a variant, an entity can acquire goods from a manufacturer or dealer with the contractual understanding that they will be resold to another entity at the same price plus handling, storage, and financing costs. The purpose of either product financing arrangement is to enable the sponsor to acquire or control inventory without incurring additional reportable debt. Transactions of this type are addressed fleetingly in IAS 18.

The pertinent generally accepted accounting principle (GAAP) standard (Statement of Financial Accounting Standards [SFAS] 49, *Accounting for Product Financing Arrangements*) considers that such transactions are, in substance, no different from those where a sponsor obtains third-party financing for its inventory. As a result, Financial Accounting Standards Board ruled that when an entity sells inventory with a related repurchase arrangement, proper accounting is to record the selling price as a liability when the funds are received from the initial transfer. The sponsor then accrues carrying and financing costs in accordance with its normal accounting policies. The liability is satisfied when the inventory is repurchased; as a result, the inventory is not removed from the financial statements of the sponsor and no sale is recorded, despite legal title having passed to the financer (i.e., substance over form). For valuation purposes, in the absence of guidance in IAS 2, best practice is to follow SFAS 49 and adjust the financial statements.

Right to return. A related inventory issue that requires consideration by valuators exists when the buyer has the right to return the merchandise. This is found in newspaper, magazine, book publishing, and recording industries where "sale or return" terms are typical. IAS 18 notes that when the buyer has the right to rescind the transaction under defined conditions and the seller cannot, with reasonable confidence, estimate the likelihood of this occurrence, the retention of significant risks of ownership prevents recording a sale. Again, GAAP usefully elaborates on the situation in SFAS 48, *Revenue Recognition When Right of Return Exists*. Under both standards, the sale is recorded only if the future amount of the returns can reasonably be estimated. If this is not possible, recording the sale is suspended until further returns are unlikely. Although legal title has passed to the buyer, the seller must continue to include the goods in its inventory.

In some cases, a side agreement may grant the nominal customer greatly expanded or even unlimited return privileges, when the formal sales document (e.g., bill of sale, bill of lading, etc.) make no such reference. This is highly suggestive of an apparent attempt to overstate revenues in the current period and risk reporting higher-than-usual returns later. In such circumstances, these sales should not be recognized, and the nominally sold goods should be returned to the entity's inventory.

Costs Included

IAS 21 established the lower of cost and net realizable value as the basis for the valuation of inventories. In contrast to IAS 16, *Property, Plant and Equipment,* or IAS 40, *Investment Property*, there is no option for revaluing inventories to current replacement cost or fair value; presumably, this is due to the far shorter period they are held, thereby limiting the cumulative impact of inflation or other economic factors on the reported amounts.

The primary basis of inventories is cost; according to IAS 2, this is defined as the total of all costs of purchase, conversion, and other costs incurred in bringing the inventories to their present location and condition. This definition allows for significant interpretations of the amounts to be included.

Raw materials. For a manufacturer's raw materials and a retailer's merchandise that are purchased outright and not intended for further conversion, the identification of the costs related to the inventories is relatively straightforward. They will include all expenditures for bringing the goods to the point of sale and putting them in a suitable condition. These cover purchase price, transportation charges, annual insurance, and handling costs. Trade discounts, rebates, and other such items are deducted; failure to do so would result in inventory carrying amounts in excess of true historic costs. To the extent under IFRS 3 or other standards that they have to be restated at fair value, this will be the net realizable value taking into account restocking charges, delivery, and other costs to sell.

Conversion costs. For manufacturers' goods, conversion costs should include all operating expenditures that are directly associated with the units produced, such as labor and overhead. The allocation of overhead must be systematic and rational; in the case of fixed operating costs (rent or real estate taxes, which do not vary directly with the level of production), the process should be based on normal output levels. Accordingly, in periods of unusually low activity, a portion of the costs must be charged directly to operations.

Such costs include all expenses directly attributable to the units of production, direct labor as well as variable and fixed manufacturing overheads. *Fixed overheads* are those costs such as depreciation that remain constant irrespective of the units produced. *Variable over-heads* are those that vary directly with production, such as repairs, maintenance, utilities, indirect labor, production supervision, indirect materials and supplies, quality control and inspection, and small tools that are not capitalized.

The allocation of overhead to the cost of conversion should be based on an average percentage over a number of periods, taking into account any change in capacity. Costs not allocated reasonably to inventory are expensed as costs are incurred.

Other inventory costs. Costs (other than for materials and conversion) that may be taken into inventories are those necessary to bring the goods to their present condition and location. Examples might include certain design and preproduction expenditures intended to benefit specific classes of customers. Conversely, all research and most development costs (per IAS 38) typically do *not* become part of inventory. Also excluded are administration and selling expenses, which are deducted as incurred, wasted materials, labor, or other production expenditures, and most storage costs.

Borrowing costs. In general, borrowing costs are not included in inventories since the period required to prepare the goods for sale will not be significant. However, where a lengthy production process is required, such as for fine wines (three to five years) and spirits (five or more years), the provisions of IAS 23, *Borrowing Costs*, are applicable, and a portion of them would become part of the inventory.

EXAMPLE: XANTHIC AS

Xanthic AS was incorporated in Turkey in 1998 as a custom metal fabricator. It now produces various metal goods sold through wholesale and retail channels. It employs 44 people of whom 30 work in the plant, 11 in administration and sales, with 3 managers. The valuation date is 30 April 2009.

Invested Equity Capital

As shown in the summary balance sheets at the valuation date (Exhibit 24.1), the invested equity capital is $3,825,816 at book value and $5,417,995 at fair value. The latter amount was obtained by restating all the recorded financial and physical assets; intangible assets are excluded deliberately. Allowing for a 1% risk provision, the invested equity capital at fair value is $1,592,179, or 41.6% above its book value.

Exhibit 24.1 Summary Balance Sheet as at 30 April 2009

	Book Value $	Fair Value $	
Assets			
Current	3,144,983	3,166,298	43.1%
Fixed	2,535,673	4,180,000	56.9%
Total Assets	5,680,656	7,346,298	100.0%
Liabilities			
Current	1,854,840	1,854,840	
Risk Provision	-	73,463	
Total Liabilities	1,854,840	1,928,303	
Invested Equity Capital	3,825,816	5,417,995	

Working capital. Exhibit 24.2 presents the working capital position of the entity; adjustments have been made to arrive at fair values for the notes receivable and inventories.

Exhibit 24.2 Schedule of Working Capital as at 30 April 2009

	Book Value $	Fair Value $
Assets		
Cash	173,734	173,734
Receivables	1,279,612	1,279,612
Notes Receivable	250,067	227,543
Inventories	1,441,570	1,485,409
	3,144,983	3,166,298
Liabilities		
Bank	593,413	593,413
Payables	750,251	750,251
Taxes Due	72,253	72,253
Accruals	438,923	438,923
	1,854,840	1,854,840
Working Capital	1,290,143	1,311,458
Current Ratio	1.70	1.71

Notes receivable. The notes receivable are due by three primary customers and are payable over the next 21 months. They were issued in 2008 in Turkish lira bearing interest at 12% (200 basis points [bp] more than the usual bank loan rate of 10%). Since then Turkish bank loan rates have risen to approximately 18%, and therefore all the cash flows, both principal and interest, have to be discounted over the period at 20% (200 bp more than the bank loan rate). The reduction in value is 8.9%, or $227,500.

Inventories. Exhibit 24.3 presents details of Xanthic's inventories indicating the importance of raw materials (38%) and finished goods (55%).

Exhibit 24.3 Schedule of Inventories as at 30 April 2009

	Book Value $	Fair Value $	Change
Raw Materials	554,000	504,694	–8.9%
Work in Progress	61,300	61,300	0.0%
Finished Goods	796,107	889,252	11.7%
Supplies	30,163	30,163	0.0%
	1,441,570	1,485,409	3.0%

Under IFRS, they are stated at the lower of cost or market on a first in, first out (FIFO) basis. Analyzing fair values (based on market prices) raw materials should be decreased by 8.9%, for selling and restocking charges and, to reflect current net realizable values, finished goods rose by 11.7%. No change was made in work in progress or supplies; the overall increase is 3.0%

Fixed assets. Details of the firm's fixed assets are found in Table 4 which shows the importance of the carrying amounts of the buildings (62%) compared with the plant and equipment (38%).

Exhibit 24.4 Schedule of Fixed Assets as at 30 April 2009

	Cost	Accumulated Depreciation	Net Book Value $	Fair Value $	Change from Cost
Buildings	2,352,646	(789,057)	1,563,589	2,810,000	19.5%
Machinery	860,305	(472,864)	387,441	575,000	–33.2%
Vehicles	366,483	(27,242)	339,241	293,000	–20.0%
Equipment	184,251	(14,050)	170,201	129,000	–30.0%
Plant	932,009	(856,808)	75,201	373,000	–60.0%
	4,695,694	(2,160,021)	2,535,673	4,180,000	–11.0%

Xanthic is aggressive in its depreciation, having written off 92% of the cost of its original plant built in 1999, reflecting a 10-year operating life. The economically useful period is not restated at 15 years with a 10% salvage value. The original leased building, purchased a year later, has been written down by 34% while marketing and equipment purchased over the years as volumes increased is written down by 55%, again over a 10-year life. However, the purchases of vehicles (7.4%) and equipment, mainly computers (7.6%), in late 2008, seem to be overvalued.

As real estate prices have risen at least 2% a year in dollar terms, (19.5% over nine years), the building, including land, has been restated to $2,810,000. Based on engineering studies, the original plant has a remaining useful life of about 6 years and the additional machinery, as much of it is computer controlled, a further 10 years. However, the vehicles and computers are now secondhand and have decreased in value by at least 20% and 30% respectively; over all, there is a $164,400 write-up.

Capitalized Normal Earnings

To obtain the normal earnings of Xanthic, this method looks at the average ROE of the industry to the past three years and applies it to the valuation date book equity. Exhibit 24.5 sets out the historic income statements for the past five years and the first four months of 2009.

Exhibit 24.5 Summary Income Statements, 2004–2009

	2004	2005	2006	2007	$ 2008	2009 (4 mos)
Sales	2,368,895	3,716,441	5,604,506	7,966,072	10,335,893	3,289,830
Growth		56.9%	50.8%	42.1%	29.7%	–4.5%
Direct Costs	(1,579,264)	(2,695,949)	(4,313,545)	(6,203,683)	(8,534,642)	(2,752,285)
Gross Profit	789,631	1,020,492	1,290,961	1,762,389	1,801,251	537,545
Gross Margin	33.3%	27.5%	23.0%	22.1%	17.4%	16.3%
SG&A*	(607,303)	(725,008)	(950,065)	(1,125,037)	(1,362,501)	(476,889)
EBIT**	182,328	295,484	340,896	637,352	438,750	60,656
Interest – net	(66,609)	(94,543)	(22,792)	858	21,450	(6,364)
EBT***	115,719	200,942	318,104	638,210	460,200	54,293
Margin	4.9%	5.4%	5.7%	8.0%	4.5%	1.7%
Income Tax	(23,144)	(40,188)	(63,621)	(127,642)	(92,040)	(10,859)
Net Earnings	92,575	160,753	254,483	510,568	368,160	43,434

   * *Selling General & Administratice*
  ** *Earnings Before Interest & Taxes*
*** *Earnings Before Taxes*

Return on equity. Exhibit 24.6 sets out the firm's book after-tax ROE for the last five years as well as that of the industry for the last three (2006 to 2008). The industry average ROE is 23.5%, compared with 12.7% for the firm, giving Xanthic an average deviation of 10.8%. Therefore, as the firm would be expected to revert to the industry mean over time, initially by adding more debt, a figure of 18%, the rounded mean of Xanthic and the industry, has been selected.

Exhibit 24.6 Schedule of Return on Equity, 2004–2009

	2004	2005	2006	2007	$ 2008	2009 (4 mos)
Opening Equity	2,395,842	2,488,418	2,649,171	2,903,654	3,414,222	3,782,382
Net Earnings	92,575	160,753	254,483	510,568	368,160	43,434
ROE	3.9%	6.5%	9.6%	17.6%	10.8%	3.4%

	Average				Selected
Industry ROE	23.5%	24.0%	31.5%	15.0%	
Xanthic	12.7%	9.6%	17.6%	10.8%	18.0%
Xanthic Difference	–10.8%	–14.4%	–13.9%	–4.2%	

Growth rate. Xanthic has shown considerable growth in operating earnings before taxes (31.7% annually between 2004 and 2008). The increases in trend earnings figures for 2010 and 2011 are 15.9% and 13.7% respectively. For the long term after 2011, 10% seems plausible; this is just below one-third of the previous performance.

Discount rate. The discount rate is Xanthic's WACC developed from the average 27% cost of listed equity obtained from the dividend/market value ratios for 15 firms in the Turkish metal fabrication industry; a premium of 2.5% was added for private ownership. (See Exhibit 24.7.)

Exhibit 24.7 Calculation of WACC as at 30 April 2009

		Book Value $	Fair Value $
Invested Debt Capital – Bank		593,413	593,413
Invested Equity Capital		3,825,816	5,417,995
		4,419,229	6,011,408
Debt/Debt + Equity		13.4%	9.9%

Cost of Debt	18.0%	Cost of Listed Equity	27.0%
Tax Rate	20.0%	Lack of Liquidity Premium	2.5%
Net Cost of Debt	14.4%	Net Cost of Equity	29.5%

	Net Cost	Portion	Contribution
Debt	14.4%	13.4%	1.9%
Equity	29.5%	86.6%	25.5%
WACC			27.4%

The 27.4% discount rate less the 10% anticipated growth equals a 17.4% capitalization rate for a price earnings ratio (PER) of 5.76 times.

Normal earnings. The anticipated normal earnings of Xanthic are $680,028 based on applying the average ROE of 18.0% to the 2009 opening book equity of $3,782,382 dated 30 April 2009 less $34,109 profit for the period. Capitalization at 17.4% gives an implicit value of $3,914,419. (See Exhibit 24.8.)

Exhibit 24.8 Calculation of Capitalized Normal Earnings

Opening Equity	3,782, 382 Selected ROE	18.0%
Normal Earnings		$680,028
Discount Rate WACC		27.4%
Projected Growth		–10.0%
Capitalization Rate		17.4%
Implicit PER		5.76
Capitalized Amount		3,914,419

Present Value of Excess (Missing) Profits

The excess (missing) profits are calculated from the differences for the next three years (2009–2011) of projected profits from trend earnings based to 2008.

Trend earnings. Trend earnings were calculated by fitting trend lines to the net earnings of Xanthic from 2004 to 2008 by means of quadratic equations. The total net earnings in Exhibit 24.9 are $74,060 for 2003 (year 0). The fit is not very good, as R^2 equals only 34%. Four of the five years are below the trend and only 2007 is above the trend.

Exhibit 24.9 Calculation of Trend Earnings, 2004–2011

	2004	2005	2006	2007	$ 2008	Totals
Net Earnings	92,575	160,753	254,483	510,568	368,160	1,460,600
Weight	1	2	3	4	5	15
Product	92,575	321,506	763,449	2,042,272	1,840,800	5,060,603
Weight Squared	1	4	9	16	25	55
Equations	1,460,600	= 15A + 6B	5,060,603	= 55A +	Growth Ratio Projected	
Solutions	A =	80,502	B =	42,178	31.7%	10.0%

	2004	2005	2006	2007	2008
Net Earnings	92,575	160,753	254,483	510,568	368,160
Trend Earnings	122,680	203,182	283,684	364,186	444,688
Variation	(30,105)	(42,429)	(29,201)	146,382	(76,528)	(31,880)
	–24.5%	–20.9%	–10.3%	40.2%	–17.2%

Missing profits. Exhibit 24.10 presents the trend, projected, and normal profits for 2009 to 2011. By the latter year, trend profits are expected to reach the normal level.

Exhibit 24.10 Present Values of Extra Profits, 2009–2011

	2007	2008	2009	2010	2011
Trend Earnings	364,186	444,688	525,190	605,692	686,194
Reported Earnings	510,568	368,160	130,300	260,600	521,200
Normal Earnings		8	680,028	680,028	680,028
Over/Under Trend	146,382	(76,528)	(394,890)	(345,092)	(164,994)
Percentage	28.7%	–20.8%	–75.2%	–57.0%	–24.0%
Extra/(Missing) Profits			(394,890)	(345,092)	(164,994)
Present Value Factor	27.4%		0.7851	0.6164	0.4839
Present Values			(310,028)	(212,708)	(79,844)
Total Present Values			(602,580)		

The projected profits for the three years (2009–2011) continue to be below trend due to an anticipated slow recovery from the 2009 economic collapse, attaining the 2007 level only in 2011. The present value of the missing profits is ($602,580).

Final Value Result

The three elements making up the final results and their related benefits are set out in Exhibit 24.11.

Exhibit 24.11 Calculation of Final Value Result

	Amount	Weight	Contribution
Invested Equity Capital	5,417,995	56.9%	3,082,807
Capitalized Normal Earnings	3,914,419	43.1%	1,687,138
Present Value Extra Profits			(602,580)
Formula Fair Value			4,167,364
Rounded			4,150,000
Mean	4,666,207		

Exhibit 24.11 sets out the calculation of the fair value by the formula at $4,150,000 (23.5% below the fair values of the underlying net assets). The effective PER is 31.8, reflecting the recent decline in 2009 profits related to the worldwide crisis in manufacturing.

CONCLUSION

This chapter set out a mixed methodology developed for manufacturers that may be applied in any industry when the necessary data are available.

25 MINERAL PROPERTIES

MICHAEL J. LAWRENCE

AUSTRALIA

INTRODUCTION

All valuations are time and circumstance specific so the valuation date is critical. Also, every valuation of a mineral property is to some degree subjective; its validity depends on the capability, qualifications, experience, and reputation of the valuator who chooses the appropriate methods as well as the quality quantum and inherent riskiness of the assumptions and material parameters adopted in the process. Hence, values may change rapidly, positively or negatively, with additional exploration, fluctuations in the relevant commodity market, or modifications of the statutory, legal, or sociopolitical frameworks.

Often a technical value is derived initially, to which is applied a premium or discounts reflecting positive or negative economic factors, stock market trends, and strategic or other considerations at the valuation date, to estimate fair value. This technical value of a mineral property depends on the availability and extent of reliable information on the project and the nature of the subject property as well as the due diligence and technical skills of the valuator. Fair value should be selected as the most likely figure from within a range, after taking into account the risks involved, such as the possible variation in ore grades, metallurgical recoveries, capital expenditures, operating costs, commodity prices, and exchange rates.

METHODOLOGY DEPENDS ON DEVELOPMENT STATUS

The amount of available reliable data usually determines the appropriate valuation methodology at each stage of a mineral property's development. The overall process is to move from conceptual geological modeling, through scoping, pre-feasibility, and feasibility studies to final design, construct, and commissioning contracts, and then to production. Each has an increasing level of confidence and certainty to its conclusions due to greater accuracy and precision in the inputs.

Ignoring legal impediments, the basic principle is that a newly discovered mineral deposit is sequentially subjected over time to increasingly more detailed and rigorous examinations to determine if it should be developed and ultimately mined. This is done by taking the geological results and establishing, with more and more confidence, the amount of salable, quality mineralization present (resources/reserves) and whether it is technically feasible to exploit and economically sound to do so. The process requires examining in detail all the available mining, treatment, transport, and marketing options; doing this involves increasingly more explicit geotechnical, hydrological, environmental, archaeological, title, and social investigations. The next table sets out which approaches are generally used for properties at various stages.

Technical review approach	Exploration properties	Development properties	Production properties	Dormant properties		Defunct properties
				Economically viable	Not viable	
Cash Flow	Not generally used	Widely used	Widely used	Widely used	Not generally used	Not generally used
Sales Comparative	Widely used	Less widely used	Quite widely used	Quite widely used	Widely used	Widely used
Cost	Quite widely used	Not generally used	Not generally used		Less widely used	Quite widely used

Source: The South African Mineral Valuation Working Group (SAMVAL) Code

Types of Studies

The main types of studies of mineral properties are:

- *Scoping study.* What *could* the mineral project deposit be? Is it sensible to continue to explore it? This is a preliminary review with inputs accurate to only ±40% to ±50%.
- *Pre-feasibility study.* What *should* the mineral project be? Which is the optimum way forward? This involves examining and reviewing *all* of the available options/alternatives with inputs accurate to ±20% to ±25%.
- *Feasibility study.* What *will* the mineral project be? What are the likely risks and rewards of the chosen project configuration and parameters? Is the investment case likely to vary significantly? This is a holistic techno-economic and sociopolitical analysis that seeks to identify and propose the means of managing all the possible project killer risks and provide a reliable estimate of project value with inputs accurate to ±10% to ±15%. Often the term *bankable* is added to emphasize this purpose.

During each of the processes, it is necessary to identify the risks involved, quantify them, and develop risk management/mitigation regimes to address their likely impact on the ultimate profitability. The content of material agreements and the actual equitable interests held (or to be earned) is also relevant in allocating the estimated value amongst the participants, as is the security of tenure, title, legal standing, exploration license, and mining lease.

SOURCES OF VALUE

The value of an exploration property is based primarily on its demonstrable ability to be prospected, or its 'prospectivity' (future potential) and the success of previous exploration efforts. Exploration is intended to demonstrate the existence of mineralization capable of being mined, processed, and sold at a reasonable profit. The value of more developed projects resides in the quantity/quality of the mineral deposit that will be exploited to yield a profit over time. Integral to this process, then, is the careful transition from exploration results, through mineral resources, inferred to indicated to measured, to ore reserves, probable and then proved. This transition occurs as confidence grows in the reasonableness of the interpreted geometry tonnage of the deposit and the reliability of its estimated grade.

Exhibit 25.1 Effect of Exploration

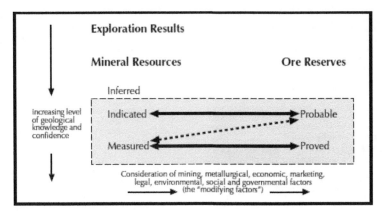

Source: Australian Joint Ore Resources Committee (JORC) Code (2004), p. 6.

Australian Requirements

The requirements of the VALMIN Code (the technical assessment and valuation of mineral and petroleum assets and securities for independent expert reports, 2005) in Australia relating to a mineral property valuation report are presented in Exhibit 25.2. The code covers the technical assessment and valuation of mineral and petroleum assets and securities for independent expert reports. It is binding on members of the Australian Institute of Mining and Metallurgy when preparing public independent expert reports required by law.

VALUATION METHODOLOGIES

It is critical that the various terms and concepts involved in a valuation report are clearly understood. They are all listed in the Glossary to this book even though various jurisdictions have slightly different meanings for many of them. The first activity in a valuation assignment is to identify the type of property involved. Mineral assets do not easily fit into the International Valuation Standards (IVS) categories; depending on if it is an exploration prospect, project or mine, Guidance Note (GN) 1, *Real Property,* or GN6, *Businesses,* may apply.

Exhibit 25.2 General Contents of a Valuation Report

The outcome of a Valuation Report[D42] will usually be the Fair Market Value[D43] of a Mineral or Petroleum Asset or Security comprising a Technical Value[D36] plus or minus, in some cases, a premium or discount to account for such factors as market, strategic considerations or special circumstances. However, it should be recognised that some Assets, such as Exploration Areas may not have a Technical Value.

45. *The Expert should state in the Report its specific purpose (and that of any subsidiary reports), its terms of reference and if there are any limitations on its use for other purposes.*

DECLARATIONS

46. The Expert or Specialists **must** declare in a Report that it has been prepared in accordance with the VALMIN Code or, if it is not fully compliant, indicate those areas where it is not and explain why this is so.

47. A Report **must** state the names, qualifications, memberships of appropriate Professional Associations, relevant experience and, where applicable, appropriate licence details of the Expert and of each Specialist and **must** identify the nature and contribution of each of them to the Report.

48. *Where a Report is prepared within a corporation or firm, the name, the registered address and, if registered in Australia, the Australian Business Number (ABN), Australian Registered Body Number (ARBN) or Australian Company Number (ACN) and, where relevant, the Australian Financial Services Licence (AFSL) Number of the corporation or firm should be stated in it.*

The name of the Expert responsible for the Report **must** be included in it and he or she **must** personally sign the Report.

COST OF A REPORT

49. The cost of a Report will normally reflect the complexity of the Technical Assessment or Valuation, the amount of data available and the specific assessment or valuation difficulties encountered.

Time and cost constraints **must not** be permitted to compromise fundamental compliance with the requirements of the Code. Any restrictions so caused to the depth of analysis or the extent of detail required **must** be recorded in the Report.

CONTENT OF A REPORT

50. A Report is likely to be used by readers having different interests and depths of technical knowledge. For the sake of clarity, but recognising that the use of technical language is sometimes essential (in which case a glossary of terms may be helpful), the Report should be written in plain

English and **must** contain all information which the Commissioning Entity and others likely to rely on the Report, including investors and their professional advisers, would reasonably require, and reasonably expect to find in the Report, for the purpose of making an informed decision about the subject of the Report. For example:

(a) information regarding the sources of data used;

(b) a description of the relevant Mineral or Petroleum Assets, including their location, plant, equipment, infrastructure and ownership;

(c) an account of the Material history of the Mineral or Petroleum Assets.

(d) sufficient information to allow experienced investment analysts to understand how the Technical Assessment and/or Valuation was prepared, including details (summarised if appropriate) of any financial model used and of sensitivities to variation

(e) sufficient information about the valuation method(s) used so that another Expert can understand the procedures used and replicate the Valuation;

(f) a review of any other matters that are Material to the Report;

(g) a balanced, objective and concise statement of the Expert's review and conclusions so that an informed layman can have a clear understanding of the Mineral or Petroleum Assets or Securities concerned, their Value (if applicable) and of the attendant Risks;

(h) a concise summary setting out the key data and important assumptions made and the conclusions drawn by the Expert and/or Specialists, qualified if necessary according to the insufficient or inadequate information provisions of Clause 54.

DATA AND INFORMATION

51. *Detailed technical information and data should be included in the Report if their understanding is important to the Technical Assessment or Valuation. Explanations of unusual or new technical processes and activities that may be Material to the understanding of the Technical Assessment or Valuation should be included, where commercial confidentiality considerations allow. The use is encouraged of tables, maps, graphical presentations and a glossary of terms and acronyms.*

52. Experts and Specialists **must** not rely uncritically on the data and other information provided, either by the Commissioning Entity or obtained otherwise. They **must** undertake suitable checks, enquiries, analyses and verification procedures to establish reasonable grounds for establishing the soundness of the contents and conclusions of the Report.

Note: Procedural and mandatory clauses and paragraphs are in normal typeface, except that the word "**must**" is in **bold**, discretionary clauses and paragraphs are in *italics* and those Definitions incorporated in the text of the Code are in **bold**.

Source: VALMIN Code (2005), p. 11

Best practice is for the valuator to adopt more than one of the three basic approaches with as many of his or her component methods as is reasonable in the particular circumstances. Because of the diversity of situations, there are no standard formulas for mineral properties, nor is there any single best method. In particular, the market is neither as efficient nor as open and unrestricted as many assume. Therefore, the competence and judgment of the valuator is the critical factor, since all valuations, especially market-based ones, are time and circumstance specific.

Equitable Interests in the Asset

The simplest case is where a party already appears to own a 100% interest in a mineral property. However, even then, the valuator should be cognizant of the impact of various government royalties (usually of the order of 4%) or of third-party interests that may be identified only if a discounted cash flow (DCF) method is used. Their effect is that less than 100% of the estimated value should be attributed to the owner, since all royalties represent an effective transfer of equity in a project. Related to this is the possible existence of nongovernmental royalty owners or parties with free-carried or limited contribution interests, which may be hidden away in material agreements and deal documents. It is critical that thorough due diligence be performed in this area.

When a property is being valued subject to an option agreement before a transaction, generally, it has only a nominal value to the option holder. However, it may have a posttransaction value, which must be smaller than that if the interest had been already acquired. Otherwise, there is the illogical situation where the owner of the actual interest is allocated the same value as that assigned to a potential purchaser or one that will earn that right in the future, with its attendant risks. Some discount must be applied to the normal value for the probability that the deal may not be finalized, no matter how small that risk is.

What Value Is Being Estimated?

Valuators in Australasia are primarily asked to determine the 'fair value' or 'market value' of a mineral asset at a certain date. The first issue is whether it is to be valued 'stand-alone' or within a corporate structure. Market Approach methods that rely on transactions involving market capitalization data for entities rather than projects must take that factor into account by adjusting any transaction values to make them comparable.

This matter is somewhat clouded because IVS separately defines both fair value and market value. It considers that fair value is the service value of an asset determined in conditions other than those prevailing in a normal market, by means other than by using market sales comparison data, such as under the Income Approach. (It is similar to the 'value in use' of International Accounting Standard 36). IVS, however, defines *market value* as the result of an objective valuation of specified identified ownership rights to a specific asset as at a given date. It is similar to the VALMIN Code's definition but properly emphasizes the need for adequate marketing time; for minimal properties, it unduly favors use of comparable market data.

In Australasia, *fair market value* is defined by VALMIN as the estimated amount of money (or the cash equivalent of some other consideration) for which a mineral asset should change hands on the valuation date. It must be between a willing buyer and a willing seller in an arm's-length transaction in which each party has acted knowledgeably, prudently, and without compulsion.

In the U.S., the Uniform Standards of Appraisal Practice (USPAP) have a definition of market value that is very much linked to its real property background. It is:

the most probable price that a property should bring in a competitive and open market under all conditions requisite to a fair sale, the buyer and seller each acting prudently and knowledgeably, and assuming the price is not affected by undue stimulus.

Implicit in this definition is the consummation of a sale at a specified date and the passing of title from seller to buyer under conditions whereby:

- *Buyer and seller are typically motivated.*
- *Both parties are well informed or well advised, and acting in what they consider are their best interests.*
- *A reasonable time is allowed for exposure in the open market.*
- *Payment is made in terms of cash in United States dollars or in terms of financial arrangements comparable thereto*
- *The price represents the normal consideration for the property sold unaffected by special or creative financing or sales concessions granted by anyone associated with the sale.*

Unfortunately, many of USPAP's strict requirements in the real world equal willingness to deal and equal negotiating power, existence of a total arm's-length relationship, equality of knowledge about the asset, equal levels of prudence, openness, and equilibrium of the market.

APPLICABLE TECHNIQUES

As many elements are undeniably subjective, there are limitations on mineral asset valuation methodologies, but the final amounts obtained are by no means guesswork. In any event, an honest, subjective experiential valuation is often more realistic than a sophisticated one out of a computer.[1]

To achieve a persuasive result, there must be a demonstrably rational basis to the selected methods. Otherwise, the valuation conclusion becomes nothing more than financial engineering of the what-number-did-you-have-in-mind? school. Whether inappropriate methodologies are used or not, too often valuation reports contain blatant abuse of logic in the choice of inputs or in the way the chosen method is interpreted.[2]

Income Approach

Discounting methods may be used for some predevelopment situations but should always be applied to development projects and operating mines, because at those stages there

---

[1] *For an overview of the methods for valuing exploration properties, see M. J. Lawrence, "The Exploration Geologist's Approach to Valuation," pp. 107–124, in **Mining and Petroleum Valuation** 1989 (MINVAL '89), ed. P. Stitt and F. Cook (Sydney: Australasian Institute of Mining and Metallurgy, 1989); M. J. Lawrence, "Valuation of Exploration Prospects—The Usefulness of Rating Methods," in **Proceedings of the 27th Annual Conference New Zealand Branch Australasian Institute of Mining and Metallurgy** (Wellington, NZ: Australasian Institute of Mining and Metallurgy, August 1993). M. J. Lawrence, "An Overview of Valuation Methods for Exploration Properties," pp. 205–223, in **Mineral Valuation Methodologies 1994** (VALMIN '94), No. 10/94, Sydney, October 1994 (Melbourne: Australasian Institute of Mining and Metallurgy); I. S. Thompson, "A Critique of Valuation Methods for Exploration Properties and Undeveloped Mineral Resources," in Proceedings PDAC Short Course 3, **Canadian Mineral Valuation Standards**, Toronto, 10–13 March 2002 (PDAC: Toronto, 2002). For specific commodity examples, see M. J. Lawrence and R. G. Hancock, "New Zealand Alluvial Mineral Property Valuation," in **Proceedings of the 26th Annual Conference, New Zealand Branch Australasian Institute of Mining and Metallurgy,** Dunedin, New Zealand, August (Wellington, NZ: Australasian Institute of Mining and Metallurgy, 1992), which reviews alluvial gold valuations, and M. J. Lawrence, "Valuation Methodology for Iron Ore Mineral Properties—Thoughts of an Old Valuator," pp. 11–18, in **Iron Ore 2007 Proceedings**, Perth, 20–22 August (Melbourne: Australasian Institute of Mining and Metallurgy-CSIRO, 2007), which examines valuation options for iron ore.*

[2] *See M. J. Lawrence and G. J. A. Dewar, "Mineral Property Valuation or 'What Number Did You Have in Mind?'" Keynote address, pp. 13–27, in **Proceedings PACRIM '99 Congress**, Bali, Indonesia, 10–13 October (Melbourne: Australasian Institute of Mining and Metallurgy, 1999), for details and examples.*

should exist sufficient, reliable information to make realistic calculations. Measured and indicated mineral resources will have been estimated (even perhaps ore reserves), and mining, processing, transport and commodity input data are known or can be reasonably assumed from scoping, pre-feasibility or feasibility studies. From such information, an estimate of value can be derived with a reasonable degree of confidence. Other chapters discuss this method; here the focus is on techniques applicable to the bulk of mineral properties where there is insufficient data available to enable its use.[3]

Cost Approach: Multiple of Exploration Expenditures Method

The Cost Approach is used where useful previous and committed future exploration expenditures are known or can be reasonably estimated. It is based on the fact that a grassroots exploration area commences with only a nominal value that reflects the cost of obtaining the legal right to explore and that the value rises proportionately with the obtaining of positive results from increasing exploration expenditures. There is also the premise that a vendor requires reimbursement of the funds spent plus some premium related to the risks taken and for the potential rewards indicated by the increased prospectivity. Conversely, where exploration results are consistently negative, exploration expenditure will decrease along with the prospect's value.

The technique relies heavily upon the admittedly subjective technical assessment of the prospect by the valuator. For most mineral property valuations, the valuator should also be a geologist. The key is the prospectivity enhancement multiplier (PEM), which determines the adjustment for enhancement/diminution to the property's overall exploration potential needed to be made to the exploration expenditure base (EEB).

Lawrence/MINVAL PEM Schema

0.0   No further exploration is justified, the property should be relinquished.

0.0–0.5 Exploration has significantly downgraded the prospectivity, the property remains at the grassroots stage in spite of considerable past and current expenditures. Further exploration is not is justified and a joint venture (JV) based on future royalties, or disposal (by sale or relinquishment) are the best options.

0.5–1.0 Past and recent exploration has maintained rather than enhanced, or slightly downgraded the prospectivity, further field exploration is not justified without geological reassessment. A noncontributory JV would be the best alternative.

1.0–1.3 Further exploration is justified, based on previous results and the potential of the deposit based on the geological model adopted. Recent exploration has maintained or slightly enhanced (but not downgraded) the prospectivity. Contributory JVs should be considered.

1.3–1.5 The available data have considerably increased the prospectivity of the property by identifying and defining geochemical or geophysical anomalies and other exploration targets. Further exploration is justified. Contributory JVs could still be considered, but it may be worth going to the next stage alone, if the results are so encouraging.

1.5–2.0 Recent exploration has enhanced the prospectivity, past results have identified several drill target(s), and reconnaissance drilling has found interesting mineralization. Further exploration is definitely justified. The PEM rises with the number of targets involved and mineralization found.

---

[3] *See M. J. Lawrence, "DCF/NPV Modeling: Valuation Practice or Financial Engineering?" paper presented to SME Annual Meeting Valuation Session, Salt Lake City, UT, 28 February–4 March 2000, for a critique of the misuse of the discounted cash flow/net present value modeling method.*

2.0–2.5 Exploration has defined a target(s) with some intersections of economic interest. Infill drilling is justified to try to define a resource. Continue exploration alone or negotiate a favorable JV.

2.5–3.0 A small resource is likely to be defined by the current drilling with potential for extension down dip or along strike. A scoping study should be undertaken. Progress does not yet justify a pre-feasibility study. Any JV should include a carried interest to the bankable feasibility study stage.

3.0–5.0 Resources of variable significance have been defined with economic features, indicated by a pre-feasibility study, that make early conversion to reserves probable. Additional resources are also likely from more drilling. Consider a feasibility study before selling any equity.

The choice of a prospect's PEM in the range of 0.0 to 5.0, usually 0.5 to 3.0, depends on the success of the exploration to date and an assessment of the future potential. The likelihood that the geologic concept, which forms the basis of the current and future exploration programs, will locate an ore body is important. However, obtaining encouraging results from the expenditure is more significant. A PEM of less than 1.0 means that further exploration is not justified. Drilling must have found mineralization to justify a PEM of greater than 2.0.

The EEB takes into account only *relevant* and *effective* past exploration and near-term proposed, and budget-approved, future expenditures adjusted for excessive administrative charges or inappropriate costs, plus the statutory minimum commitments to retain the properties. Generally, PEMs for future expenditures should not exceed those for the incurred EEB. Such valuations should be done on a property-by-property basis.

Market Approach: Comparable Sales Method

The Market Approach uses recent transaction prices of the mineral asset, or previous sales of similar assets, as a guide to the project's value. To be a reliable source, the assets involved must be truly comparable in terms of location, timing commodity, as well as arm's-length transactions.[4]

Unit values. Values are most commonly derived on the basis of tonne of the Australian Joint Ore Resources Committee (JORC) Code categories of Resources and Reserves on the property that were acquired or sold in the relevant transactions. Using gold, the metric is $/ozAu (Au=gold) derived from actual transactions. Loucks and Dempsey[5] proposed that at a then–base price of US$150/ozAu, reserves in an exploration stage were worth US$7/ozAu (5%), at prefeasibility US$15/ozAu (10%), at feasibility US$30/ozAu (20%), and in production US$100/ozAu (66.6%). For operating mines taking into account expected increases in the price of gold, they suggested $200/oz (133%) for annual production of around 50,000 oz to 100,000 oz per year and $250/oz (166%) for those with greater output. Rightly, they pointed out that the best yardstick for operating mines is the cash profit margin.

A Specialist Report on February 27, 2001, which formed part of the New Hampton Goldfields Limited's defense to a bid, claimed, based on a spot gold price of US$290/ozAu (483/ozAu at A$1.00=US$0.60), appropriate yardstick values of less than A$10/ozAu (usually A$3/ozAu to A$5/ozAu) for low-grade resources beyond the present economic limits of an open pit; A$10/ozAu to A$30/ozAu for adequately defined resources, with a reason-

[4]   See M. J. Lawrence, "An Outline of Market-Based Approaches for Mineral Asset Valuation Best Practice," pp. 115–137, in **Mineral Asset Valuation Issues for the Next Millennium** 2001 (VALMIN '01), No. 5/01, Sydney, 25–26 October (Melbourne: Australasian Institute of Mining and Metallurgy, 2001), for an extensive review of market-based methodologies.
[5]   T. A. Loucks and S. Dempsey, "Mining Finance: Some Perspectives of the Small Miner," **SEG Newsletter**, No. 28 (January 1997).

able expectation that reserves will be established; and greater than A$30/ozAu for resources for which there is a good likelihood of a high conversion rate to reserves and/or proximity to an existing plant.

MINVAL currently uses values of around A$50/ozAu for gold reserves in nonoperating mines (a range of A$40/ozAu to A$75/ozAu), and from A$5/ozAu to A$10/ozAu, up to A$20/ozAu to A$25/ozAu, for gold resources, depending on their quality and the surrounding circumstances.

Sales must be comparable. Most practitioners who support use of the comparable sales method acknowledge that the historic transactions have to be comparable, and relatively recent, to be useful. However, this precondition is ignored often in practice because on close examination, the most comparable sales are clearly not comparable to the subject progress.

A commonly held view is that 'where there are no anomalies affecting a market, the price at which property changes hands in the ordinary course of business and the market, is usually its true value.'[6] This position is generally true, and underpins the Market Approach, which is dominated by the deep and liquid real estate markets, in which details of numerous transactions are publicly available. But it tends to obscure the very important fact that nearly every mineral deposit is unique—they are not at all like houses—and the number of transactions is vastly less than for real estate. The problem is to find truly comparable sales on which to base a transactional value. Thus, it is essential to emphasize the unique characteristics of each mineral deposit, its geological characteristics, and surrounding properties. Most are purchased because of what they contain (resources of the commodity to be mined and sold) rather than for what they can be used.

A mineral property's main worth lies in the quality and quantity of its mineralization, but ore bodies are intrinsically unique in their mineral assemblage, structural setting, depth, and mode of emplacement, which makes simple comparisons difficult. Whilst resource and reserve estimates also appear to be indisputable, different valuators may have legitimately different views on their categorization quantity and quality due to diverse but reasonable choices for grade cutoffs, dilution, mining loss, and bulk densities. Again, direct comparisons are hazardous.

Mineral deposits are found in widely varying geographical situations with attendant variations in topography, access, vegetation, climate, and rainfall. Their individual geotechnical and hydrogeological characteristics, which affect mining practices, as well as things like the safety of tailings dams and structures, are also likely to be dissimilar. Even if the mineralization could be assumed to be exactly the same, in two different locations, there would be logistical difficulties to overcome when developing them as well as specific geographical constraints, particularly water supply and the impact of the weather on proposed operations. Any so-called comparable deposits will have different levels of existing infrastructure, variable quality, state of repair and appropriateness of existing equipment, and jurisdictional differences, all of which affect their respective sale prices and values.

In fact, projects always develop at different times in response to perceived supply and demand factors even though this is not normally economically efficient. Mineral properties cannot be valued as if all of them will be in production at once, as do some tax authorities. Nevertheless, those likely to be in production soon are more valuable than ones whose development lies in the future. This simply reflects the time value of money and the various risk profiles, again emphasizing the noncomparability of simple sales data.

Valuation dates and premium/discounts. Inevitably, even supposedly comparable sales of mineral properties at the same stage of development will have occurred at different

---

[6] *See C. J. Malcolm in Commissioner of State Taxation (Western Australia) v. Nischu Pty Ltd, 91 ATC 4371 (at 4376), which also listed a federal court and South Australia Supreme Court cases in support of this view.*

times, in different markets, under different jurisdictions. Those made at peaks and valleys of economic cycles (boom/bust or bull/bear markets) involve premiums or discounts, so it is important to consider what influence this factor might have had on the particular figure. For example, sometimes a premium is paid for mineral properties above their underlying technical values, because of market demand beyond the expected changes in commodity prices. This may be for a variety of reasons:

- Level of control obtained
- Perceived synergies in operating or marketing
- Management strengths
- Belief in the existence of untested resources or reserves
- New processing technology
- Diversification of risk
- The size of the entity and its credit rating
- Access to capital
- Special advantages to one party

Even when transaction values appear comparable, they will have occurred mostly in the past. In such cases, the selection of the most appropriate inflator/deflator to bring them up to date is difficult.

What was bought in the transaction? Usually, important information about commercial transactions is confidential with only sketchy details released to the public. For example, were comparable interests acquired? Free-carried interests or royalties may not be publicly disclosed; other rights and interests (e.g., timber rights, improvements and plant/equipment or sales contracts, etc.) or encumbrances/obligations (JV commitments, environmental restoration, debt, unresolved lawsuits, taxes, etc.) may be sold or retained by the purchaser. All of those have to be stripped out in order for sales data to be useful, The final price may have been influenced by commercial-in-confidence information available to the purchaser but not the market. There may be trade-offs or concessions in respect of other projects, even in different jurisdictions.

These matters exacerbate the difficulties of determining comparability, as does the fact that the transaction may be inside or outside a corporate structure. If it is inside, the value of the financial envelope (hedge book [the hedging, positives, and any related assets being hedged], working capital, other assets or investments, net of related liabilities) surrounding the project has to be determined.

Location. Climate and rainfall/water supply all have an impact on a project's technical feasibility and economic viability, particularly regarding its equipment requirements and productivity. Those parameters impact primarily capital and operating costs. Key risk factors that justify a premium or discount for relatively similar projects in various jurisdictions include prospective buyers' perceptions of:

- The location's political stability
- Corruptibility index
- Labor situation
- General level of personal and property security
- Social and environmental circumstances
- The nature of its financial/taxation regime

Similarly, the amounts and quality of the infrastructure in place will vary. Thus, it is always very difficult to ensure that sales comparisons are realistic and reasonable.

Mining method. Certain types of deposit allow particular mining methods. Historically, those that could be mined through open pits have enjoyed a preference over ore bodies that could be exploited only by more expensive and difficult selective underground methods. Hence, for the same minerals with similar deposit geometry, those at shallow depths are generally more highly valued than deeper ones, while those with the lowest overburden stripping ratios and the least mining dilution are the most favored. Shallow open pits enjoy capital and operating cost advantages, and they are also relatively easier to manage and have an inherent flexibility of operations. High-margin projects can better withstand commodity price cycles than low-margin projects, so they command a premium. Thus, one really can compare only sales of projects having similar mining methods and, even then, only those located fairly close together on the cost curve, having similar revenue projections.

Deposit size and complexity. The market seems to prefer large, high-grade, world-class deposits for reasons other than their obvious commercial advantages. Perhaps it is the comfort of having a significant resource/reserve buffer and a longer period to resolve unexpected problems. Finally, the management time and effort needed to develop a small project is often not markedly less than for a large one. Hence, for otherwise similar projects, there is a premium for larger deposits, even over smaller but higher-grade ones.

There is also a desire for deposits with mineralogical and metallurgical simplicity, whenever possible, with minimal contaminants, hence the known preference for gold over base metal deposits and free-milling ores over refractory ones. Those that are structurally complex or have geotechnical problems are penalized since they are more difficult and costly to mine and to process. Again, to be useful, apparently comparable projects must include similar metallurgical treatment, plant design, recovery, and final product quality.

Marketability. Mineral deposits whose products have stringent quality specifications and consequently specialized markets (most industrial materials), or whose buyers are very well organized (diamonds and to a lesser extent coal and iron ore) do not have the deep and free market for traded commodities, such as gold and base metals; therefore, they tend to suffer a discount. When trying to compare like with like, it is critical to ensure this is exactly what one is doing.

As noted, it is hard to adjust for the time of the transaction in market-based methods, as there are the overall bull/bear market influences to consider in both metal prices and foreign exchange rates as well as capital and operating costs. They provide part of the economic envelope around the technical characteristics of a mineral property valuation; they are not constant, further reducing the comparability of sales data. In general, when trying to standardize transactional values from different times, the change in the dollar commodity unit prices is the best way to adjust them.

Market Approach: Yardstick Methods

Where a mineral resource remains in the inferred category, or where economic viability cannot be readily demonstrated, yardstick methods may be appropriate. They ascribe heavily discounted in situ values to resources or small reserves, based on subjective estimates of future profits per tonne. They result in values of around 0.5% to 5% (more commonly 1% to 3%) of the in situ gross metal content of the delineated mineralization using the spot metal price as at the valuation date. For example, 1% (at a gold price of US$900/oz) is akin to a valuation metric of $9/oz for inferred resources at an exploration property, whereas 5% equates to $45/oz for ore reserves. The chosen percentage is based on, among other things:

- The valuator's risk assessment of the assigned JORC Code's resource/reserve category
- The commodity's likely extraction and treatment costs
- Availability/proximity of transport
- Available infrastructure, particularly a suitable processing facility

- Physiography and maturity of the mineral field

Clearly, it is a very subjective method whose results depend entirely on the expertise of the valuator.

A variant of this method is to use the average of successful explorers' discovery cost for a prospect with delineated resources. MINVAL research (based on Metals Economics Group and Newcrest Mining data) indicates that in respect of major gold finds of 1997 to 2008, discovery cost averaged US$17.22/ozAu for successful explorers and US$31.88/ozAu for all major gold producers. Both exclude Newcrest's US$12.72/ozAu; the weighted average gold discovery cost for all explorers (including Newcrest) was US$14.63/ozAu.

Yet another version is to assign a subjective $value/unit of area (hectare or square km), supposedly based upon previous sales of comparable properties, this is not recommended as a primary method except for properties with perceived prospectivity but little else. As an example, gold values/km^2, based on numerous transactions, range from A$2,000 to A$10,000 (more commonly A$3,000 to A$5,000) depending on the type of title, size, prospectivity, and proximity to successful exploration results. Yardstick methods suffer from lack of real comparability of data, since their unit amounts are derived from sales transactions whose comparability, as just described, must be regarded as suspect.

Market Approach: Joint Venture Terms Method

The joint venture terms method relies on the terms of existing arm's-length JV agreements, presumably for relevant, nearby, and/or similar properties. JV agreements typically have staged earn-in phases for expenditures made over time, with later stages at the choice of the entity farming in. The value of its equity at any stage is the sum of the value of liquid assets (cash or shares) transferred to the seller (farminee) plus the present value of future exploration expenditures; however, normally, some minimum expenditures are committed by the buyer (farminor). Such funds are committed expenditures rather than notional expenditures, and may or may not entitle that party to an earned interest if it walks away at an early stage. Nevertheless, in the case of a simple deal, the value ($V_{100\%}$) of the entire property, where the farminor agreed to spend $E to earn an interest of I%, and has done so, may be estimated in this way:

$$\$V_{100\%} = (\$E \, / \, I\%) \times 100\%$$

In a typical earn-in agreement, the values assigned to each of the various stages can be combined in this way:

$$\$V_{100\%} = \$VStage\ 1 + \$VStage\ 2 + \dots$$

Multistage agreements. The value assigned to the second and subsequent earn-in stages always involves discounted funds (at the farminor's Weighted Average Cost of Capital or an expected industry rate), and is likely to require exponentially increasing probability factors (in the range 1% to 90%) for the likelihood that any stage will be completed. In applying the JV terms method, only the first stage should be considered in estimating cash value equivalence. The total project value of the initial earn-in period can be estimated by assigning a 100% value, based on the deemed equity of the farminor:

$$V_{100} = \frac{100}{D}\left[CP + \left(CE \times \frac{1}{(1+I)^{\frac{1}{2}}} \right) + \left(EE \times \frac{1}{(1+I)^{\frac{1}{2}}} \times P \right) \right]$$

Where:

V_{100} =   value of 100% equity in the project

D   =   deemed equity of the farminor (%)

CP = cash equivalent of initial payments of cash and/or stock ($)

CE = cash equivalent of committed but future exploration expenditure and payment of cash and/or stock ($)

EE = uncommitted notional exploration expenditure proposed in the agreement and/or uncommitted future cash payments ($)

I   = discount rate (% per annum)

t   = term of the stage (years)

P   = probability factor between 0 and 1 assigned by the valuator and reflecting the likelihood that the stage will proceed to completion

JV terms are mostly specific to a particular project and so cannot be used realistically for the valuation of other mineral assets. Knowledge of them may enable the construction of relatively realistic synthetic JVs for sanity checks, but, the use of conceptual JV terms as a primary valuation tool is inappropriate since it is too open to manipulation.

Market Adjustments

The DCF and MEE (Multiple of Exploration Expenditures) methods only generate a technical value, which excludes any premium or discount for market, strategic, or other considerations. Inevitably, technical values using these methods appear low in optimistic (bull market) situations but high in a pessimistic (bear) markets. Hence, they must be converted to fair values by considering the applicable current market premium/discount, if any. However, market sentiment is already part of values derived by the JV terms and the comparable sales methods. Some valuators forget that they always must compare apples with apples, not with oranges, and miss this basic distinction between the various methods.

Previous valuations, recent broad economic metrics, and share market indicators are useful in this context. Even though current market sentiment is clearly relevant, caution must be exercised in the application of a market premium/discount because its effect can be both transient and highly subjective in a particular economic climate. The use of any such premium must be fully explained and justified on reasonable grounds. Discounts are rarely seen, except in bank-lending transactions where the 'real' value is critical or when the predator in a hostile takeover attempts to minimize the value of the target. Generally, the older the data on which such valuations are based, the more likely it is that any built-in market sentiment must be reconsidered very carefully for its continued applicability.

For retrospective valuations, intervening events must not be taken into account. For example, in the classic case of takeovers by a government, the fair value of what was taken is the only amount required; consequential damages are not included. The relevant and important valuation principle is that only events reasonably foreseeable at the valuation date may be considered. In some jurisdictions, courts have allowed hindsight to operate when establishing the reasonableness of past predictions.

Since a reliable and acceptable valuation of a mineral property largely depends on the results of previous technical reviews and assessments, only appropriately qualified professionals, with suitable experience, should undertake them. The reader is again reminded of the considerable subjectivity of the process, depending as it does on individual professional judgment. All value estimates are time dependent and are particularly influenced by the market conditions at the valuation date.

Any attempt to quantify the chances of exploration success is clearly speculative, and predicted profitable returns from mining development scenarios are not guaranteed. When reaching a conclusion as to the value of a mineral property, the valuator should rely on reasonable and considered assumptions, based on knowledge of the owner's past and present experience, reputation, and competence. Other factors include exploration success to date, the current quality and status of its technical data, the exploration and development team, management, and available financial resources. Assumptions also have to be made about future events, particularly commodity prices and the ability of the owner to produce and market product of the required quality to achieve budgeted profit levels.

General economic factors and changing societal requirements are part of the risks in a valuation. Factors affecting a proposed mining development include inflation, currency fluctuations, changes in interest rates, industrial unrest, and land access. In some countries, native-land rights, environmental standards, taxation, and royalties must be considered. They all affect the owner's ability to finance a project as well as fund exploration, development, and mining operations. Future actions of any government involved is also important.

To address all relevant risks, valuators must incorporate appropriate probability factors into their methodologies and fully explain their selection. The use of a single discount factor to address unspecified, numerous probability factors is unacceptable.[7]

Multiple methods. When valuing a mineral property, the valuator should use as many methods as are appropriate for its stage of development and the purpose of the report. In a few instances, a single technique may be considered suitable. The values generated by each approach (usually based on the average of the related methods chosen) are compared to identify whether there is any consensus of results such as grouping around a particular level. Any clustering suggests the most rational value for the mineral property and gives some comfort as to the reliability of the results.

Most commonly, a valuator accepts a specific amount generated by a particular approach as the preferred case (most likely scenario) rather than using an average; however, the range of values from a low case (pessimistic scenario) to a high case (optimistic scenario), should encompass the extremes from all methods. Only very rarely is the preferred value the arithmetic average of the low and high ends of the range, there is rarely any logical justification to accept a simple arithmetic mean as the preferred value.

Use of a DCF/net present value (NPV) method is still not favored in many jurisdictions in the United States, particularly for litigation purposes; preference is given to the Market Approach. However, most transactions involving developing and operating mines tend to have a DCF analysis as their underlying basis. Few valuators would feel comfortable claiming that the best way to value such entities would be simply to average the NPVs for a number of supposedly similar operating projects. Unfortunately, many valuators see no problem in using average transactional values/unit in a current report, even though acquisition prices are commonly based on NPVs.

The NPV method should never be applied to a mineral property that is only at an exploration stage, based on hypothetical cash flows from a postulated exploitation scenario. However, it is appropriate to calculate the conceptual NPV of the income stream that might be

---

[7] *For an outline of the risks inherent in assessing mineral ventures, see: M. J. Lawrence "Overview of Mineral Project Risk Issues and Role of Mineral Industry Professionals (especially Consultants) in Risk Reduction Strategies," pp. 45–52, in* **Proceedings PACRIM '04 Congress,** *Adelaide, 19–22 September (Melbourne: Australasian Institute of Mining and Metallurgy, 2004); M. J. Lawrence, "Minimising Mineral Project Risk: New Zealand in a Global Context," pp. 266–290, in* **Proceedings 2005 New Zealand Minerals Conference— Realising New Zealand's Mineral Potential,** *Ministry of Economic Development (Crown Minerals), Auckland, New Zealand, 13–16 November 2005; and M. J. Lawrence, "Mineral Project Due Diligence: Where Cynical Minds Meet Money," pp. 249–264, in* **2008 (41st) New Zealand AusIMM Annual Conference Proceedings,** *Finance and the Minerals Industry, Wellington, New Zealand, 31 August–3 September (Wellington, NZ: Australasian Institute of Mining and Metallurgy, 2008). For the role of due diligence in project assessments and valuations, see M. J. Lawrence, "Australian Project Valuation: Possible Lessons for Canadian Developers," pp. 69–96, in* **Mineral Property Valuation and Investor Concerns Short Course,** *Toronto, 11–15 March (Toronto: Prospectors and Developers Association of Canada/Canadian Bar Association, 1998); M. J. Lawrence, "The VALMIN Code and Guidelines (1998): An Aide Memoire to Assist in Its Interpretation,"* **AusIMM Bulletin 3** *(May 1998): 80–83; and Lawrence, "Mineral Project Due Diligence."*

generated by leasing the project, obtaining royalties from it, farming the surface, or considering a nonmineral highest-and-best use—for example, residential development.

At this point, it is worthwhile to reflect on exactly what is determined by DCF analysis. Valuators tend to consider before- or after-tax values only in this context, with a general preference for after-tax amounts. The author considers that the other valuation methods discussed implicitly derive after-tax values, although taxation issues do not arise in most of them. This means that such amounts can be averaged to obtain a fair value provided the NPV is adjusted for the market premium/discount.

Of course, some owners can use past losses and structure their affairs to minimize the impact of taxes, but others cannot. Hence, it should be clearly stated on which taxation basis fair value has been determined. This is another reason why care must be taken when using projected sales data; the 'comparable' projects likely will be in different places subject to various tax regimes.

The author suggests that whichever values are chosen on technical grounds, sovereign risk must be factored into the selection of the final figure. There is a reluctance to pay as much for a mineral property located in a region with sociopolitical problems compared with one where the fiscal and security regime is benign. Similarly, properties located near environmentally sensitive areas, or where there are as-yet-unresolved title conflicts, have less value than ones without such problems.

CONCLUSION

Each jurisdiction has its own rules and requirements that must be respected. However, the increasing globalization of the mining industry makes it essential that international standards of project assessment and valuation, as well as International Financial Reporting Standards, be as similar as possible from the viewpoints of the relevant regulatory and professional bodies. The same applies to the terms used; even though the IVS terminology is well developed (mainly for real estate), the generally accepted, historic terminology of the mining industry should not be totally disregarded.

Professionals must also be able to practice across international and interstate boundaries. Hence, the accreditation (registration) and the maintenance of continuing professional development of the authors of valuation reports as well as the ability to discipline them effectively through codes of ethics must be similar between international jurisdictions to facilitate the mobility of those professionals.

26 PASS-THROUGH ENTITIES

LAURA J. TINDALL AND JOHN L. CASALENA

UNITED STATES

INTRODUCTION

A pass-through entity is an organization that does not pay tax itself but passes through the taxable income to its owners who then pay it individually. As with all valuations, when appraising a pass-through entity, the purpose, the standard of value, and certain unique characteristics of the entity, such as owner/management control, must be considered.

There are many types of pass-through entities; some publicly traded, others privately held, that are discussed in this chapter. Reasons for selecting this format include owner/management control, liability protection, and maximization of cash flows by minimizing taxes. Usually they:

- Allow more management discretion with less ownership.
- Limit the liability of owners.
- Avoid double taxation of distributions (dividends).

Generally, nonprofit organizations, including pension funds, are not allowed to invest in pass-through entities, which in many jurisdictions have specific requirements to maintain their particular protection. Items of taxable income of a pass-through entity retain their characteristics to the taxable owners.

FORMS OF ENTITIES

This section identifies the most popular forms of pass-through entities. Although they all have the same tax effect, they have different legal requirements and restrictions; none is appropriate for every situation. The Shakespeare saying "A rose by any other name would smell as sweet" applies to most types of pass-through entities; although they may have various names in different countries, they have very similar tax results.

Income Trust

Many countries have forms of income trusts, unincorporated entities, normally established by a trust deed, that hold income-producing assets and pass on the earnings, usually through cash payments that are taxed directly to its owners. Depending on local laws, income trusts may or may not be publicly traded. For example, the United States allows both public and private offerings. With the increasing aging population often preferring stable investment income, the popularity of this format is expected to increase. However, the Canadian situation suggests that governments may intervene. The Canadian experience to be described should serve as a warning to investors who might purchase income trusts expecting a safe, continuous flow of tax-free cash.

Income trusts pass on their earnings and the related taxation to their owners. In Canada, conversion of taxable corporations became common in the early 2000s, although the first was listed on the Toronto Stock Exchange (TSX) in 1995. Demand was strong; by 2002, 79% of all money raised by Canadian initial public offerings was from income trusts; they also had been used in the early 1980s in Australia, but their beneficial tax treatment was effectively abolished. Recognizing income trusts' preferential tax treatment as an advantage over the corporate form, during 2006, the Canadian federal government provided incentives for investors in corporations and introduced a special tax regime for existing income trusts starting in 2011; new trusts would become subject to it in 2007. As a result of this announcement, the median price of trust units quoted on the TSX dropped by 13%, equivalent to a 15% premium for the structure. The Canadian Department of Finance issued a press release stating:

> *Canadian income trusts enjoy special corporate tax privileges. Canadian income trusts have been gaining popularity since the beginning of 2004 as a beneficial corporate structure alternative for firms. The benefit of becoming a Canadian income trust is that the corporation, as it is currently structured, will pay little to no corporate income tax. This is because cash distributions are paid out to unit holders before income taxes are calculated. If, once expenses have been covered, all of a firm's remaining cash is paid out to unit-holders, the firm is able to entirely avoid paying income tax.*

> *Recognizing the tax advantage of income trusts avoidance of double taxation, in 2006, the Canadian government adopted the Tax Fairness Plan for Canadians, which restored balance and fairness to the federal tax system by creating a level playing field between income trusts and corporations. Canadian Department of Finance Press Release*

The announcement introduced a gross-up and credit system for corporate dividends received by individual taxpayers resident in Canada. Under this, a gross-up of 45% of eligible dividends (those taxed at the highest rate) or 25% of other dividends (taxed at a lower rate) is added in calculating taxable income; the amount of the gross-up is then applied as a credit against taxes due.

Real Estate Investment Trust

A real estate investment trust (REIT) is a real estate entity, either a corporation or a trust, that sells shares (units) to the public. In one way, REITs are similar to any other shares in that they represent ownership in an operating business; however, a REIT, which has been introduced in a number of countries, has two unique features:

1. Its primary business must be to own and manage groups of income-producing properties.
2. It must distribute at least 90% of its taxable profits as dividends.

Normally a REIT also has to fulfill several additional but less important requirements.

Regulated Investment Company

A regulated investment company, commonly known as a mutual fund, is a corporation or trust owning publicly traded shares and is authorized to: sell and purchase its own shares to and from the public at their net asset value, and pass on, directly to its owners, the dividends, capital gains, and interest earned on its investments. This avoids any double taxing of the investment distributions. Many countries have this structure.

Joint Venture

A joint venture (JV) is a very common type of pass-through entity. It is a contractual association between two or more parties engaged in a business for profit without forming an actual partnership or corporation. It is similar to a partnership, with one key difference: A partnership generally involves an ongoing, long-term business relationship, whereas, normally, a joint venture is based on a single transaction or project.

Individuals or entities choose to enter JVs to share strengths, minimize risks, and increase competitive advantages. JVs may be distinct business units (a new entity is sometimes created to hold the assets and liabilities as a bare trustee), or collaborations between existing businesses. An example of such a deal is a high-technology firm contracting with a manufacturer to bring its ideas for a new product to market; the former providing the know-how, the latter the means.

All JVs are initiated by the parties entering into an agreement that specifies their mutual responsibilities and goals. As this contract is crucial for avoiding trouble later, the parties must be specific about their intents as well as being aware of any limitations. Every JV also involves certain rights and duties; both parties have a mutual right to control the enterprise, share in the profits, and an obligation to contribute to any losses; each has a fiduciary responsibility, owes a standard of care to the others, and must act in good faith in matters that concern the common interest. A JV may terminate at a time specified in the contract, upon the accomplishment of its purpose, on the death or bankruptcy of an active participant, or if a court decides that disagreements between the members make its continuation impractical.

In the oil and gas industry, JVs are very common, often as collaborations between local and foreign firms; about 75% of those entered into by U.S. entities are international. Often they are seen as a viable means for those involved to complement their skills and financial capabilities. However, studies show overall failure rates of up to 60%, with more than 50% either failing to get going or fading away within five years.[1]

JVs in less developed countries show even greater instability, especially those involving governments; they have higher-than-average incidences of failure, as private firms seem to be better equipped to supply the needed skills, marketing networks, and the like. Furthermore, JVs tend to fail miserably if demand for their products or services is highly volatile, or if there are rapid changes in underlying technologies. Some countries, such as the People's Republic of China and, to a lesser extent, India, require foreign entities to form JVs with domestic firms in order to enter certain segments of the market. This often forces technology transfers and assigning managerial control to the domestic participant.

Although, as noted, JVs are usually for a specific project or based on a single business transaction, there are instances where they continue because of mutual benefits; for example:

> *Sony Ericsson is yet another example of a joint venture. The Japanese company, Sony had global marketing expertise and the Swedish company Ericsson had technology that made it big in telecommunications. The two companies joined forces, each contributing its expertise, and mobile phones came to the world. This demonstrates how each partner in the venture has its own contribution that makes such a partnership work.*[2]

Limited Liability Company

A limited liability company (LLC) is a relatively new business structure allowed by statute in many parts of the United States and numerous other countries. LLCs are popular because, similar to a corporation, the personal liability for their debts and actions is limited to the capital the owners have invested. However, other features are more like those of a partnership, providing management flexibility and the benefits of pass-through taxation.

Owners of an LLC are called members; since most jurisdictions do not restrict ownership, members may include individuals, corporations, other LLCs, and foreign entities. There is no maximum or minimum number of members; single-member LLCs with only one owner are widely permitted. A few types of businesses, such as banks and insurance companies,

---

[1] *Osborn, 2003.*

[2] *"Examples of Today's Joint Ventures,"* **Joint Venture Intelligence,** *November 2008*

generally cannot be LLCs. A great appeal is that profits may be distributed as determined by the members, regardless of the ownership interests. Like many partnerships, an LLC is dissolved when a member dies or undergoes bankruptcy, irrespective of the number of survivors.

Partnership: Civil Law

A partnership is a form of business entity found the world over in which the owners share the profits and losses, as they may decide. In civil law systems, which cover most of Europe, a partnership is a contract between individuals who, in a spirit of cooperation, agree to carry on a business; contribute to it by combining property, knowledge, or activities; and share its profits or losses. A partnership agreement or declaration of partnership is essential; in some jurisdictions, this must be registered and available for public inspection. In many countries, a partnership is also considered to be a legal entity, although the various systems have reached differing conclusions on this point. Features of partnerships in selected civil law countries are presented next.

Germany. In Germany, partnerships may exist in the legal forms of civil partnership (Gesellschaft bürgerlichen Rechts, GbR), general partnership (Offene Handelsgesellschaft, OHG) or limited partnership (Kommanditgesellschaft, KG); Although an OHG can be created by a single individual, there are normally two or more partners; in it, all of them are individually liable for all debts. There are two types of partners in a KG: one or more general partners with unlimited liabilities who manage it, and numerous limited partners. The former may include a corporation, the latter are normally individuals who invest money but are not involved in day-to-day functions; their liability is restricted to their capital contributions. Although a partnership itself is not a legal entity, it may acquire rights and incur liabilities, obtain title to real estate, and sue or be sued.

China. In the People's Republic of China, a partnership may be a general partnership or a limited liability partnership. A general partnership comprises partners who bear joint and several liabilities for its debts. A limited liability partnership includes general (unlimited) partners and limited partners, who are liable only to the extent of their capital contributions.

Japan. Japanese law provides for *nin-i-komiai*, "voluntary partnerships," which are created by contract and do not exist as a legal entity; a recent statute allows for limited liability partnerships. One form of partnership unique to the country is the *tokumei kumiai* (anonymous partnership) in which all the assets and liabilities are the property or obligation of the manager, normally a corporation; the partners merely participate in profits or losses and have limited liability as long as they remain anonymous in their capacity as partners and do not participate in its operations. Japan also provides for partnership-like corporations called *mochibun kaisha*.

Partnership: Common Law

Under common law, which covers most of the English-speaking world, the basic form is a general partnership, in which all partners participate in managing the business and are personally liable for its debts. Two other forms have been developed in most countries: the limited partnership (LP), in which certain partners relinquish their rights to manage the business in exchange for limited liability for the partnership's debts, and the limited liability partnership (LLP), in which all partners have some degree of limited liability.

General partners have an obligation of strict liability to third parties injured by the partnership; depending on circumstances, they may have joint or joint and several liability, while that of limited partners is restricted to their investment. A silent partner is one who shares in the profits and losses of the business but who is uninvolved in its management and whose association with it is not publicly known. Features of partnerships in selected common law countries are presented next.

Australia. For a partnership in Australia to exist, four criteria must be satisfied:

1. Valid agreement between the parties
2. Carrying on a business—any trade, occupation, or profession
3. Acting in common—meaning there is some mutuality of rights, interests and obligations
4. Looking to profit—partners share profits and losses, thus charitable organizations cannot be partnerships

Hong Kong. A partnership is a business entity formed under the Hong Kong Partnerships Ordinance, which defines it as "the relation between persons carrying on a business in common with a view of profit" that is not considered a joint stock company or an incorporated company. If the entity registers with the Registrar of Companies, it takes the form of a limited partnership, as defined in the Limited Partnerships Ordinance; however, if it fails to register, it becomes a general partnership by default.

India and Pakistan. As both countries share the same constitutional heritage, since 1932 partnerships in India have been defined as the "relation between two or more persons who have agreed to share the profits and losses according to their ratio of business run by all or any one of them acting for all" (India Partnership Act, 1932). Since its separation from India in 1947, partnerships in Pakistan have also been conducted under the Indian Partnership Act of 1932.

United States of America. The federal government does not have any specific statutes governing partnerships; instead, they are treated as a matter for the states, which mainly follow common law principles, whether for general, limited, or limited liability partnerships. The National Conference of Commissioners on Uniform State Laws has issued nonbinding Uniform Partnership and Uniform Limited Partnership Acts. Although there are no federal laws regarding partnerships, there is an extensive statutory scheme for their taxation. Title 26, Subchapter K, of Chapter 1 of the Internal Revenue Code creates tax consequences of such scale and scope that it effectively serves as a federal statutory scheme for partnerships.

Limited Partnership

Limited partnerships are the most common form of flow-through entity. Normally, limited partners are allocated nearly all the profits, losses, capital gains, and tax benefits, while the general partner collects fees and a small percentage of both profits and capital gains but not losses. Typically, in the United States, limited partnerships are used for real estate, oil and gas, and equipment leasing businesses; recently, they have been expanded to finance movies, research and development, and special projects. In Germany, they are used for a wider range of operating businesses. They may be financed publicly or privately; typically public limited partnerships are sold through brokerage firms but do not trade actively; in the United States the number of partners in private offerings is normally restricted to 35 investors, with no limit on the individual amounts.

In some jurisdictions, limited partners may not draw out or receive back any part of their contributions to the partnership during its lifetime, except with the unanimous consent of the partners, nor take part in the management of the business or have the power to bind the firm. If they do, they become liable for all its debts and obligations up to the amount drawn out or received back, or incurred while taking part in management.

Islamic law. The *Qirad* and *Mudaraba* of Islamic law were the precursors to the modern limited partnership. These were developed in the medieval Islamic world, when its economies flourished and early trading companies, big businesses, contracts, bills of exchange, and long-distance international trade were established. In tenth-century Italy, the *Qirad* and *Mudaraba* concepts were adapted as the *commenda*, a form of limited partnership that was used generally for financing trade.

S Corporation

One of the most popular forms of business entity in the United States is a corporation that elects to be a pass-through entity under Subchapter S of the Internal Revenue Code. Created in 1958 and called an S corporation, this status has certain other requirements; it must:

- Be a domestic corporation.
- Have only one class of stock.
- Limit ownership to U.S. citizens or residents.
- Accept no more than 100 shareholders.

Subchapter S shareholders include in their personal tax returns their pro rata portion of capital gains, ordinary income, and tax preference items, whether any distributions of cash have taken place or not. If a distribution does not occur in the year the income is reported by the shareholders, it may be made in a future year as the undistributed earnings have already been taxed.

This situation is very useful for start-ups, because the usual losses in early years pass directly to the shareholders. When the firm becomes profitable, such entities frequently limit their cash distributions to the amounts necessary for the shareholders to pay their related income taxes; few other countries have such corporations.

VALUATION CONSIDERATIONS

As in any valuation, purpose, standard of value, and the unique factors of the firm are of major importance. In many pass-through entities, particularly those with a relatively small number of owners, one or more are also the managers. In this situation, the valuator should check for any apparent owner bias in the financial data. Because the pass-through entity pays little, if any, income taxes, a challenge to the valuator is identifying tax considerations that may affect its value. It is essential that the methods applied are appropriate for the type and size of the entity.

Standard of Value

A standard of value can have different meanings in different situations, depending on the purpose, as laws and/or regulations may modify the definitions set out in the glossary of this book. This chapter deals mainly with fair value under International Financial Reporting Standards. Often, in pass-through owners' agreements, written or oral, the terms "fair market value" or "market value" are used, yet the implicit understanding is that they are pro rata amounts, meaning that the normal discounts for minority positions or lack of marketability are not to be taken.

Management Control

Depending on the purpose and standard of value, special adjustments to the financial data may be necessary for a pass-through entity. Normal adjustments for regular corporations include, but are not limited to removing unusual and nonrecurring items and adjusting book depreciation to economic charges based on the useful lives of the assets. Owner bias may be found in unaudited financial statements prepared for filing tax returns. Those may include inconsistencies in financial data, nonmarket level charges (rent and compensation), and discretionary expenses (nonoperating items).

Charges and unusual expenses can best be identified by percentage analyses of the financial statements. Normalization adjustments may be necessary to remedy inconsistencies, restate nonmarket charges, and eliminate discretionary expenses. Any adjustments should take into account the size of the subject ownership. If the objective is to determine the fair value of a minority position in Fafner KG, for example, no adjustments may be appropriate, as a minority owner would have no control over the costs and activities of the entity, nor of his or her portion of the allotted earnings.

A common problem found in the accounting for pass-through entities is the payment and deduction of salaries or wages to members or partners. Many jurisdictions, such as the United States, prohibit members and partners from taking and deducting compensation as salaries and wages. Rather, if they perform a service for the entity, they may take fees (guaranteed payments in the United States), deductible to the entity and treated as self-employment income.

COMPARABLE CAPITALIZATION RATE

Because a pass-through entity is not subject to any taxes, the valuator must address tax considerations when determining a capitalization rate; the term "cap rate" is used throughout this section, but the principles apply equally to discount rates. A basic valuation concept is that the characteristics of the income stream must be matched with a relevant capitalization rate; otherwise, the value is not supportable.

Common practice in the United States is to reduce the entity's income by a notional tax; various sources recommend rates ranging from the maximum corporate level to the marginal personal rate of the owners; an after-tax cap rate is then applied. This simplistic technique avoids the common error, seen in many tax valuations, of making no adjustment for the differences in pretax versus posttax "earnings," showing no awareness that the data used to compile standard cap rates is after tax while the income stream is pretax. Such a lack of comparability may result in the valuator's conclusions being rejected.

Example

Unaware Practitioner has been retained by a litigant to estimate the value of a pass-through entity with $100,000 of normalized trailing 12 months income, which he determines is a good proxy for the next 12 months:

Normalized Income	100,000
Cap Rate—20%	1,000/0.20
Indicated Value	500,000

Experienced Expert agrees that $100,000 is a good base income and concurs with the 20% cap rate. However, she knows that the $100,000 normalized income has not been taxed and the cap rate was derived from after-tax income streams. She therefore believes the next adjustment is necessary for comparability:

Proxy Pretax Income	100,000
Tax at Maximum US Corporate Rate (35%)	35,000
Proxy After-Tax Income	65,000
After-Tax Cap Rate	20%
Indicated Value	325,000

Aware that courts sometimes have trouble grasping valuation issues, she also prepares an alternative schedule that serves as a proof of her initial calculation:

Cap Rate Compiled from After-Tax Data	20%
Tax at Maximum US Corporate Rate	35%
Convert After-Tax Cap Rate to Pretax	0.20/(1–0.35) = 30.75%
Divide Proxy Income by .3075	$ 100,000/0.3075
Indicated Value	$ 325,000

Characteristics of cap rate data. Most valuators are aware that published investment return information, used in many developed countries to establish cap rates, is derived from public company after-tax data; in general, this is calculated after corporate taxes at the entity level, but before any taxes paid by shareholders on capital gains or dividends.

Few realize that estimates of values of pass-through entities using the Income Approach—Capitalization of Earnings Method adopting cap rates from publicly traded corporations are likely distorted. This is due to the differences in some jurisdictions, such as the United States, of the tax treatments for pass-through entities and regular corporations, of ordinary income, capital gains, and dividends (earnings). The major variant is that a pass-through entity's owners pay income tax on its earnings, whether distributed in that year or not. When distributions (similar to dividends of regular corporations) are received, they are tax free, as the underlying profits had been taxed previously. A regular corporation's shareholders pay individual corporate tax in the year incurred, and subsequent personally, on capital gains and dividends received.

The earnings of a for-profit entity are taxed in these ways:

- Regular corporations are taxed at the entity level.
- Regular corporate dividends are taxed at the investor level.
- Pass-through entity earnings are taxed at the owner level.

S Corporation Valuation Models

Numerous practitioners have created S corporation valuation models that, in most cases, may also be applied to limited partnerships and income trusts. Please consult the source notes for more information on the specific methods.

- Simplified model[3]
- Grabowski model[4]
- Van Vleet model [5]
- Treharne model[6]
- Mercer model[7]

These models all accomplish substantially the same goal: recognition of the avoided dividend and capital gains taxes. The Delaware Chancery Court also accomplished this with the model it used in the Delaware Radiology case.[8]

Determining the appropriate capitalization rate is one of the most difficult steps in any valuation; it becomes even more complicated for pass-through entities. The valuator needs to select an appropriate basis and make adjustments for any differences that exist between it and the subject. It is essential, particularly in valuation reports for tax purposes, to explain in detail the processes used in reaching a:

---

[3] *Fannon's Guide to the Valuation of Subchapter S Corporations, BV Resources, 2007.*

[4] *Roger J. Grabowski, "S Corporation Valuations in a Post-Gross World,"* **Business Valuation Review** *(September 2004).*

[5] *Daniel Van Vleet, "The S Corp Economic Adjustment Model,"* **Business Valuation Review** *(September 2004).*

[6] *Chris D. Treharne, "Valuation of Minority Interests in Subchapter S Corporations."*

[7] *Z. Christopher Mercer, "Are S Corporations Worth More than C Corporations?"* **Business Valuation Review** *(September 2004).*

[8] *See Nancy Fannon, "The 'Real' S Corp Debate: Impact of Embedded Tax Rates from Public Markets," 2008. Retrieved June 16, 2009, from www.fannonval.com/sCorp/S%20Corp%20Valuation--2008%20Update.pdf.*

No matter which model the analyst uses, if any, the key is to think through the foundation for the valuation model and carefully select the valuation inputs in order to reach a logical conclusion that a buyer and seller would be likely to agree upon.[9]

SALES OF PASS-THROUGH ENTITIES

In many regions that tax capital gains, owners of pass-through entities, such as limited partnerships, have the ability to apply the taxed undistributed earnings to increase their basis for such purposes and reduce any payments on a sale.

One significant consideration in the acquisition of a business is the net cost to the acquirer. If it is a nontaxable (share exchange) transaction, studies have shown that in the United States and likely most of the rest of the world, there is no significant difference between the price paid for a regular corporation and a pass-through entity. Yet if it is a taxable transaction in the United States, studies indicate that there is a benefit to acquiring a pass-through entity, as it allows the buyer to elect to restate, at the effective acquisition costs (fair value), all the assets acquired and liabilities assumed.

Pass-Through Entity Premium

A continuing topic of debate, mainly in the United States but also elsewhere, is whether or not there is any additional value in a pass-through entity, such as a limited partnership or S corporation, over a regular corporation. Several papers have set out theories for valuing minority interests in pass-through entities. Some experts consider that there is no difference in value between a pass-through entity and a regular corporation with similar pretax profits, while others believe there is a premium due to the owners' tax savings. Most of the research has been done comparing S corporations with regular corporations.

The argument supporting a premium is that a buyer, given a choice, will opt for the pass-through entity, as its owners are: (a) subject to only one level of tax rather than two on any distributions, and (b) receive an addition, over original cost, to their tax basis if the taxable income they report exceeds the distributions received. Owners of a regular corporation have no such benefit; therefore, the taxable capital gain on a sale of their shares, at the same price, will be greater.

	Regular Corporation		Pass-Through Entity	
	Case A	Case B	Case A	Case B
	$	$	$	$
Pretax Profit	500	500	500	500
Corporate Tax–50%	(200)	(200)	0	0
Net Income	300	300	500	500
Distribution	300	200	500	200
Personal Taxes on:				
Distributions	(45)	(30)	0	0
Profit	0	0	(190)	(190)
Net Cash Received	255	170	310	10
Increase in Basis				300
Potential Capital Gains Tax Saving				45

The table illustrates, in the United States, the difference in cash to the owners of a regular corporation and a pass-through entity for two cases. Case A is a distribution of all the profits, Case B is only sufficient for the pass-through owners to pay the related taxes. Other assumptions are: 40% combined state and federal corporate tax, 15% personal tax on dividends and capital gains, and 38% state and federal personal income tax.

---

[9] *James R. Hitchner, **Financial Valuation: Applications and Models**, 2nd ed. (Hoboken, NJ: John Wiley & Sons, 2006).*

When a business is sold, the differences between pass-through entities and regular corporations become more pronounced. Merle Erickson and Shiing-wu Wang[10] show that flow-through entities may sell for a higher price. They examine the different acquisition tax structures for the two forms, comparing purchase prices across sets of taxable acquisitions for shares of S corporations and regular corporations. They estimate the tax benefits of an S corporation can total approximately 12% to 17% of the deal's value, a part of which is often captured by the target's shareholders through a higher selling price.

Nancy Fannon, author of major works on the subject, states:

Nearly all financial analysts who have seriously studied the issue now agree that the value of an S corporation or interest in it is often greater than a comparable publicly traded C [regular] corporation. This differential is typically between 5%–20%, and not anywhere near the 65% premium that has been placed on them by the I.R.S. and in tax court decisions.[11]

However, James DiGabriele[12] takes the opposite position. His study compared actual market data from private sales of S Corporations and regular corporations. He used a simple regression analysis to test the hypothesis and concluded that market data does not indicate that S corporations are more valuable than otherwise identical, regular corporations.

James Lurie states:

When an appraiser is estimating the price which a hypothetical buyer would pay to a hypothetical seller for shares of corporate stock, there is neither empirical evidence or logical progression which can lead to the conclusion that the stock of an existing S-corporation should sell at a substantial premium to the stock of a similarly situated [regular] C-corporation.[13]

James R. Hitchner also addresses this issue:

Increasingly, Subchapter S Corporations are thought to be worth more than an otherwise identical Subchapter C (regular) corporation. This additional value arises because of the Subchapter S Corporation's ability to avoid double taxation at both the corporate and shareholder levels.

Since the market does not indicate the existence of an S corporation premium and to the extent such a premium does exist it exists only to particular investors (i.e., exhibits characteristics of investment value) the majority of valuation professionals conclude that when valuing a controlling interest in an S corporation under the fair market value standard, the earnings of the S corporation must be adjusted for income taxes as if the company were a C corporation. It gets more complicated when valuing minority interests.[14]

CONCLUSION

Every valuation is unique as to the purpose, standard of value, and specifics of the subject. Valuations of pass-through entities present additional challenges beyond those of taxable bodies. Therefore, a valuator should usually follow Hitchner and adjust the reported profits of the flow-through entity for notional tax at the applicable regular corporate rate and then consider adopting a pass-through entity premium.

There are valid arguments for and against such a premise; some considerations are:

---

[10] *Merle Erickson and Shiing-wu Wang, "The Effect of Organizational Form on Acquisition Price."*

[11] *Nancy J. Fannon, S Corporations and Value: Simplifying the Debate.*

[12] *James A. DiGabriele, "A Valuation Dilemma: Are S Corporations Worth More than Otherwise Identical C Corporations?" Forensic Examiner 12, No. 11 & 12 (2003).*

[13] *James B. Lurie, "The S-Corporation, Fair Market Value, and Their Intersection with the Real World," Business Appraisal Practice (Winter 2003–2004).*

[14] *Hitchner addresses this issue in Financial Valuation.*

- Is the valuation for a minority interest or 100% of the entity?
- Is the income approach applicable?
- What is the subject's distribution policy? Is it reasonable to expect it to continue?
- How likely is a sale of the interest?
- Has there been any basis accumulation? If so, how much? Will it continue to accumulate?

Whether or not a premium for a pass-through entity over a comparable regular corporation is appropriate depends on the purpose, the standard of value, and the specifics of the situation. In general, small adjustments of the order of 10% appear justified by the data.

27 PATENTS

HEINZ GODDAR AND ULRICH MOSER

GERMANY

INTRODUCTION

According to the Massachusetts Institute of Technology (MIT) *Technology Review*, innovation in technology is estimated to account for as much as 90% of new economic growth in the United States during the last five years.[1] The reason is that better technology, often represented by patents, allows many things to be produced more cheaply and even creates new markets. Such intangible assets are playing an ever more influential role in valuation practice. The main reasons are the fundamental changes that have occurred in many accounting standards, particularly those concerning business combinations (International Financial Reporting Standard [IFRS] 3) and the impairment of assets (International Accounting Standard [IAS] 36). As set out in IFRS 3 illustrative examples A to E, and Statement of Financial Accounting Standard (SFAS) 141 A.14, intangible assets can be divided into various categories, of which patents, especially those covering technologies, are of great importance.

In the past 10 years, the number of patent applications filed in the United States (unlike copyrights, a separate patent must be sought for each country) more than tripled, rising from about 150,000 in 1998 to nearly 500,000 in 2008. In the same period, the number issued each year doubled from around 95,000 to about 195,000 in 2000; since then, it has stayed roughly flat. As a result, there is a backlog of 1.2 million applications; it takes nearly three years and a minimum of $40,000 in fees from filing to approval/disposition. Of these grants, in 2008, the 10 largest recipients obtained about 11%; only 49% went to U.S. firms, with 22% to Japanese, and 5% each to those in Germany and South Korea.

This chapter discusses both the theoretical principles involved in valuing patents as well as their implementation in illustrative examples. The first section briefly considers some basic valuation principles relevant to patents. This is followed by an analysis of patents—or, more precisely, of patented technologies—from the valuator's point of view. Then those aspects of the income approach that are applicable to patents are discussed and their practical application is explained.

VALUATION PRINCIPLES

A precondition for any valuation, in addition to a thorough understanding of the appropriate methodologies, is a clear and unambiguous delineation of the subject and an awareness of the reasons for the assignment. The value of an item, whether a patent or all the shares of an entity, is derived from the benefit that it brings its owner.[2] These can be measured in three ways:

---

[1] *MIT Technology Review*, *"Can Technology Save the Economy?,"* David Rotman, 21 April 2009.

[2] See G. V. Smith and R. L. Parr, *Valuation of Intellectual Property and Intangible Assets,* 3rd ed. (New York: John Wiley & Sons 2000), pp. 152, 163.

1. Income likely to be generated in future (income approach)
2. Existing market prices for the object concerned or for comparable objects (market approach)
3. Cost of obtaining a comparable item (cost approach)

Relating to intangible assets, hybrid methods have been developed in practice that combine elements of both the market and the income approaches.[3]

The real options method used by some practitioners is not considered in this chapter.[4]

Subject to Be Valued

The subject of a valuation may consist of an individual asset, such as an item of machinery, a patent or trademark, groups of assets (an operating plant or patent portfolio), entities, or entire enterprises (parent and numerous divisions and subsidiary entities). In this chapter, the asset to be valued is described as the subject." The major reason to define the subject is that it establishes some essential parameters of the valuation, particularly the sources of future income, the types of comparable assets, or the nature of the cost estimation program.

In the valuation process, especially of individual assets, interrelationships between the subject and other assets must be taken into consideration if the subject is part of a larger entity (a patent in a portfolio, or a machine in an operating plant). This is essential with the Income Approach, where numerous assets interact to create a cash-generating unit; typically, individual assets are not capable of generating income on their own. If, in a simple example, a patent protects the major component of a product, in most cases, its income generation will require, at least as contributory assets, manufacturing facilities, an assembled workforce, and working capital. To value the patent, its contribution to the total income of the entity must be isolated.[5]

Reasons for the Valuation

Often, valuations of patents are connected with transactions, which may involve: entire enterprises, various entities, individual assets, as well as a wide variety of bundles of different items. Transactions may be carried out in numerous ways, depending on the underlying purpose. They may, for example, take the form of selling or purchasing the item concerned, entering strategic partnerships, taking out or issuing licenses to assets, or issuing a wide range of equity or debt securities. (See Exhibit 27.1.)

---

[3] See Goddar, "Die wirtschaftliche Bewertung gewerblicher Schutzrechte beim Erwerb technologieorientierter Unternehmen," in *Mitteilungen der deutschen Patentanwalte* (1995), pp. 357–366; Khoury/Lukeman, "Valuation of BioPharm Intellectual Property: Focus on Research Tools and Platform Technology," *les nouvelles* (2002): 50; and Drews, "Patent Valuation Techniques" *les nouvelles* (2007): 365 ff.

[4] See Copeland/Antikarov, *Real Options: A Practitioner's Guide* (New York, 2001); Mum, Real Options Analysis (Hoboken, NJ: 2002); Ernst/Hacker/Moser/Auge-Dickhut (eds.), "Praxis der Unternehmehmemsbewertung und Akquisitionsfinanzierung."

[5] See Kidder/Mody (fn. 4), p. 190, and Sullivan/Edvinsson, "A Model for Managing Intellectual Capital," Parr/Sullivan (eds.), Technology Licensing.

Exhibit 27.1 Background to Patent Valuations

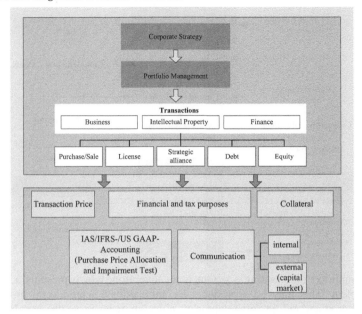

In the case of financial, physical, or intangible asset transactions, the purpose is often to calculate maximum and minimum price limits for the parties in preparation for negotiations. Also similar reports may be needed to allocate the final purchase price to the individual assets acquired and liabilities assumed, in accordance with IFRS 3.

PORTFOLIO ACTIVITIES

Often the reasons for valuing a patent or a group of patents are bound up with corporate strategy.[6] This determines an enterprise's portfolio of business units (entities) and the exploitation of potential opportunities.[7]

Strategic planning in this sense is a complex form of portfolio management; it comprises not only the business units but also corporate assets, such as facilities or patents. If the entity has adopted the concept of shareholder value, the management of its various portfolios should reflect those considerations. In some cases, patent valuations are performed for communication purposes. This may be to quantify value generation within the firm, such as through research and development (R&D) activities or for the benefit of management or the board. It may also be for disclosing the activity to outside parties, especially capital markets.

VALUING PATENTS

In valuing patents, it is first necessary to study the fundamental conditions responsible for their generating value; this requires distinguishing between the intellectual property right (IPR) on one hand and the technology that it encapsulates on the other. (See Exhibit 27.2.)

---

[6] *Ibid.*

[7] *For the connection of corporate strategy with R&D activities and patenting, see Wijk, "Measuring the Effectiveness of a Company's Patent Assets," **les nouvelles** (2001): 25–33.*

Exhibit 27.2 Factors in Patent Values

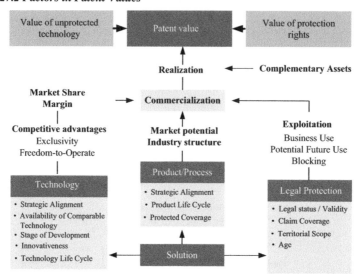

One precondition for granting a patent is an invention, which presents a solution to a technical problem. This may be a product, a component of a product, a process used to manufacture a product, and, in some countries, a design or business process. It must have a technical element, novelty, and an inventive step that is not obvious.[8] This becomes particularly important when it embodies a technology or part of a technology. Boer states: "Technology is the application of knowledge to useful objectives. It is usually built on previous technology by adding new technology input or new scientific knowledge";[9] in the illustrative examples, the solution is assumed to be a technology.

A technology may be exploited by being implemented in products or in processes which manufactured them. Its success is determined principally by the products' attractiveness and positioning in the market, especially their volume and growth as well as the structure of the industry. The technology may, for example, enable its user to differentiate products from those of the competition and obtain higher prices. Other benefits may, however, be reduced costs, enabling the user to achieve higher sales through lower prices, thus capturing market share. This shows the connection between an entity's technologies and competitive strategies.

There is no competitive advantage from a technology which is also available to competitors; such is the case when the publication of the patent application and reverse engineering of the product allow an experienced engineer to understand it. The protective effect of a patent is important here, as it grants its owner a monopoly right to prohibit others from using the invention.

Factors enhancing values. The legal monopoly created by a patent is only for a limited time period, normally 20 years from filing. This may make it possible to exploit the technology in a number of ways, such as through products in which it is used or on the basis on which they are produced. Another way to exploit the technology is to grant one or more parties a license to use it under specific conditions. Patents may, however, still benefit their owners, even if they do not affect output. Often an entity can manufacture products based on

---

[8]   *See the German Patent Act sections 1:1, 3:1-4, and their reference to the state of the art.*

[9]   *Boer in* **The Valuation of Technology, Business and Financial Issues in R & D** *(New York, 1999), pp. 4 ff.*

a patented technology. In addition, it can possess patents protecting an alternative solution, putting it in a better position to exclude potential competitors. When patents are filed and renewed, mainly to prevent a competitor from exploiting an invention, they are called blocking patents.

Legal Factors

Creating legal protection includes these parameters relevant to any valuation:

- Legal status. Existence/maintenance of the application or granted patent
- Current status. Of applications, or granted patents subject to opposition or nullity proceedings
- Validity. Legal position of the patent in comparison to the state of the art
- Scope of protection
- Exploitation of the patent dependent on third-party IPR
- Territories covered
- Ages and remaining terms of the patents
- Involvement in infringement actions? Are parties suing or being sued under the patent? Status of the litigation?
- Agreements with third parties. Licenses granted or taken out? Toleration agreements? Nonaggression agreements?

Benefits of Technologies

Protected technologies are not only important for competitive advantages. Patents can also enhance an entity's freedom to maneuver or shield it against action by others, giving it more freedom to operate. When an entity has patents of its own, they constitute an important "currency" for cross-licensing others' patents, which may be useful when implementing the firm's own technologies. Core technologies that link up with the entity's basic competencies have an importance which is fundamentally different from those of marginal or "me-too" technologies.

Product or Process

The importance of a product for an entity, and thus the significance of the components or processes used for making it, is determined by the corporate strategy, as is the importance of technologies. The key point is the product/market strategy of the enterprise, which proceeds from the question of what is to be offered (product) and to whom it is to be offered (market). Empirical studies show that the sales of goods usually follow a typical curve, known as the product life cycle. This is commonly divided into introductory, growth, maturity, and degeneration phases. The importance of this concept results from the awareness that most products have a limited useful life, which may affect the technology's life cycle; sometimes it is possible to continue exploiting a patented technology through successor or related products.With product patents, the technology may cover only a part of the product or merely a single component. The size of the patent's share is particularly important for licensing agreements, where it is frequently used as the basis for calculating the royalty payments.

Determining the Useful Life of a Patent

The useful life of a patent depends on:

1. Its remaining legal term
2. The technological life cycle
3. The product life cycles of all the items manufactured applying the underlying technology

In this context, the average period for which patents are maintained may be a good criterion for determining its likely remaining useful life. According to the German Patent and Trademark Office, the average period for which German patents are maintained is currently 14 years rather than their 20-year legal life.

Patents and Underlying Technologies

Patents are characterized by their underlying technologies and their legal protective effects. These give rise to two techniques on which a value may be based. The first is that the value of a patent lies in the difference between the profit earned through the existing protection and what might be earned if there were no protection.[10] The second links the value of a patent—as with trade secrets—to the underlying technology; in other words, that is the subject, and, accordingly, all the relevant income is attributed to it.

To clarify which view should be chosen, it is necessary to consider the reasons for the valuation. The majority of cases, even if they are only hypothetical, are concerned with transaction prices, in the sense of upper or lower limits for purchasers or vendors. One consequence of disposing of a patented technology might be that the vendor will no longer be permitted to manufacture and market the related products. When calculating the future income associated with a patented technology, all contributory assets have to be taken into consideration. Only if the selling price exceeds the present value of this lost future income is there no reduction in the entity's value. Therefore, the lower or upper price limits for the sale or purchase of a patent must be based on the underlying technology and not on the legal protective effect. The value of the legal protective effect conferred by a patent is the difference between the value of the patented technology and that of unprotected technology. That amount may be relevant in deciding whether to patent a technology or treat it as a trade secret.

PATENT PORTFOLIOS

Exhibit 27.3 Valuation of Patent Portfolio or Single Patent

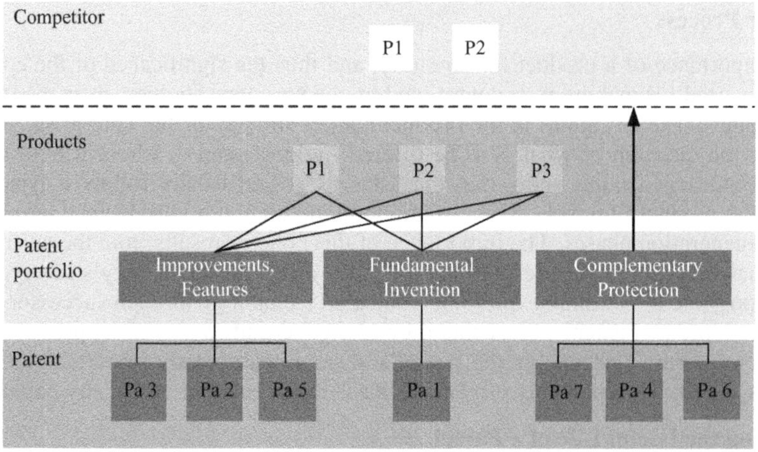

An entity obtains sales and income by manufacturing and marketing products using a technology, which is protected by a basic patent and others relating to improvements and

---

[10] See Pitkethly, *The Valuation of Patents: A Review of Patent Valuation Methods with Consideration of Option Based Methods and the Potential for Further Research* (Oxford, 1997), p. 2.

additional features. The profits may, however, also be dependent on blocking complementary protection patents, which prevent or restrict competitors from achieving sales and profits with similar items. In some cases, a single patent can protect a technology or product, particularly in the pharmaceutical industry, where most drugs have only one fundamental molecule patent, which is filed in numerous jurisdictions. When defining the subject, it is necessary to establish whether it should be the individual patent, part of a portfolio, or indeed the entire portfolio; the answer usually depends on the reasons for the assignment.

Valuing Patented Technologies: Income Approach

The Income Approach bases the value of an item on the benefits it is likely to generate in the future. If it is an individual asset, such as a patented technology, in general, the future income can be obtained only with the assistance of contributory assets. The remainder of this chapter analyzes the contributions of the patented technologies to the entity's future total income under the various appropriate valuation methods.

Contribution of Patented Technologies to Income

Investigating the contribution of a patented technology to the income of an entity presupposes a very precise definition of income; for patents, the obvious answer is free cash flow. The benefits of technologies to their users come from the competitive advantages they generate, either through differentiation advantages or costs. A well-known example of better prices is in pharmaceuticals, where patented drugs sell for significantly more than chemically identical generics; it also applies to products, such as cameras, that may possess features which appeal to users and are not yet in competitors' offerings. Technology-induced advantages which reduce costs may generate larger volumes by passing on some of the savings through lower prices. If the margin per unit remains unchanged, there will be a proportional increase in the gross profit. Cost benefits of this kind often arise when process patents lead to savings in material, manpower, or both.

Increases in free cash flow from patented technologies may also result from reductions in selling general and administrative expenses (SG&A), the working capital required, and the capital expenditure needed (CAPEX). Reductions in SG&A and working capital are frequently achieved through improved business processes, which, in certain countries, may be protected by patents. Value-enhancing effects in capital expenditures are not limited to reducing the amounts but also delay them.

Other effects may accompany such influences on free cash flow. Because of higher manufacturing costs, additional features in a product often lead to an increase in the cost of sales. Also this may be reflected in higher inventories and working capital needs. Another source of working capital increases may come from larger accounts receivable due to higher prices from the differentiation. Manufacturing a product with additional features could even require additional capital expenditure. In addition, price increases connected with the differentiation may affect marketing plans, and thus SG&A, though this could equally well be a reduction as an increase.

APPROPRIATE METHODS

Under the Income Approach, four methods are generally accepted for valuing patents: incremental income, residual value, relief from royalty, and profit split.

Incremental Income Method

The incremental income method starts with an analysis of the influence of the subject (patented technology) on the future free cash flow of the business. This is not clear in the

American Institute of Certified Public Accountants (AICPA), Practice Aid, *Assets Acquired in a Business Combination to Be Used in Research and Development Activities*, which deals extensively with in-process R&D (IPR&D), the predecessor of a patentable invention.[11] The value of the subject, taking taxes into account, is the present value of the increases in such future free cash flows. As it deals with the free cash flows, which can be directly attributed to the subject, the method is referred to as the direct technique. It is often applied to technologies, which result in identifiable cost savings.[12]

Because of the need to isolate the incremental income attributable to the subject, this technique has limited application. Even for products which, thanks to special features, can be sold for higher prices than those of competitors, the benefit may be influenced by contributory assets, such as a trademark or assembled workforce. In most cases, it is simply not possible to determine the effect of a particular technology on selling prices or volumes; therefore, patented technologies are valued usually by indirect techniques.

Residual Value Method

The residual value method estimates a figure for the subject by deducting from the entity value of the business those of all the other assets. It therefore necessitates determining not only the value of the business but also the values of the other assets; thus, this method involves all the problems of the other methods.

The usual procedure is to deduct from the income of the business the contributions from the other assets; the remaining "excess earnings" are considered attributable to the subject. For that reason, it is sometimes referred to as the multiperiod excess earnings method.[13] Although it must own as well as use the technology, the business does not need to own the other assets; they may, for example, be leased.

The two principal requirements for this method are:

1. It must be possible to set out reasons why the excess earnings are attributable solely to the subject; this is usually assumed away when the subject is the principal asset of the business.
2. All the other assets have to be identifiable and susceptible to valuation. In particular, the valuator must reasonably establish their contribution to the total income.

A detailed discussion of the first requirement is beyond the scope of this chapter. The authors would merely point out that this method tends to overvalue the subject, as any possible synergies from the interactions of the various assets are attributed totally to the subject, which, in effect, is assigned a major element of goodwill.

Relief-from-Royalty Method

Another indirect technique is the relief-from-royalty method. This is based on the concept that the owner of an asset—in this case, technology—does not need to license it from a third party, which would require paying royalties; therefore, the owner is "relieved" from them. The payments saved are attributed as income to the subject, consequently, whose value is the payments' present value, taking taxes into account, over the remaining useful life.[14]

---

[11] AICPA, Practice Aid, *Assets Acquired in a Business Combination to Be Used in Research and Development Activities: A Focus on Software, Electronic Devices, and Pharmaceutical Industries* (2001).

[12] *Ibid., n. 41, 2.2.10.*

[13] *Ibid., n. 41, 2.1.10 and 16.*

[14] See Anson/Suchy, *Intellectual Property Valuation: A Primer for Identifying and Determining Value* (Chicago, 2005), pp. 35ff.

Such relieved payments are calculated with reference to the projected financial information of the business, based on established royalty rates, which are usually obtained from license agreements for comparable assets. The two principal conditions for using this method are:

1. Comparable assets, the subject of license agreements, can be identified.
2. The valuator is able to know the detailed terms of the related agreements to assess the comparability of possible transactions and calculate the applicable royalty rates.

If the first condition is met, the scope of the method is relatively broad. To identify comparable transactions and to determine the contents of the agreements not only requires knowledge of case law and relevant publications but, to an increasing extent, access to databases, such as Royalty Source (www.royaltysource.com).

Conceptually, the relief-from-royalty method is part of the Income Approach; however, because of references to market transactions, it is also sometimes described as a hybrid method.

Profit Split Method

Practical rules of thumb are applied in a number of industries to divide the income of a business between the licensee and owner (profit split). The 25% rule, dating back to Edison's film patents, dictates that a quarter of the income should go to the owner of the intellectual property (the licensor) and 75% to the producer (the licensee); the justification is that the producer should receive the lion's share because of risks assumed.[15]

In certain industries, mainly engineering, royalty rates, especially licenses based on turnover, tend to be guided by this rule. Smith and Parr speak of "self-fulfilling prophecies" in this context.[16] Accordingly, the profit split method is suitable to calculate payments for the relief-from-royalty method. An important use is establishing the plausibility of valuation parameters, such as royalty rates.

Discount Rates

To determine the value of a subject, it is necessary to compare the future income attributed to it with alternative investments by discounting the returns from both investments; they should have a similar term and risk. The discount rate that satisfies this condition is the asset-specific rate of return.

Calculating the Term Equivalent Cost of Capital

The weighted average cost of capital of an entity (WACC) is composed of the cost of equity (r_E) and the after-tax cost of debt (r_F); they are weighted according to their shares of the entity value, the sum of the market values of the equity (E), and debt (D). One common method of calculating the cost of equity is the Capital Asset Pricing Model (CAPM); in it, the cost of equity is composed of the risk-free rate (r_f), plus a risk premium. This risk-free rate must be term equivalent to the useful life of the asset. The risk premium is determined by multiplying the market's equity risk premium $(r_M - r_f)$ by the firm's beta, which is defined as the covariance between the expected return on its ordinary shares and that of the market, divided by the variance of the return of the market. It may also be determined separately from comparable companies (peer group), where the weighting of the cost of debt and equity

---

[15] *A detailed presentation is in Goldscheider/Jarosz/Mulhern, "Use of the 25 Per Cent Rule in Valuing IP,"* **les nouvelles** *(2002): 123ff.*

[16] *See G. V. Smith and R. L. Parr,* **Valuation of Intellectual Property and Intangible Assets,** *3rd ed. (New York: John Wiley & Sons 2000), pp. 152, 163.*

is based on their aggregate capital structure. When valuing an individual asset that can generate income only in collaboration with others, the required rate of return must be reasonable and reflect the relevant risks. For intangible assets, the rate often exceeds the cost of equity.

Allowing for the Asset-Specific Risk

The risks inherent in an asset can be measured by the volatility of the income associated with them.[17] An entity may be regarded as a bundle of assets, each with its own volatility and specific risks that interact to create its income.

New technology, for example, may make an existing one totally obsolete, but the current machinery might, with modifications, be able to manufacture the products using a replacement process. In such a case, the contribution to income from the new technology is likely to exhibit higher volatility and thus involve a higher asset-specific risk than the machinery. The basic idea in calculating asset-specific adjustments is that the overall rate of return generated by all the assets should correspond to that demanded by investors in the entity. Therefore, the weighted average return on assets (WARA) should be equal to WACC.

ILLUSTRATIVE EXAMPLES

The next simple numerical examples illustrate the processes involved in applying several different methods under the Income Approach to the valuation of a patented technology.

Basic Assumptions

Special Products Ltd. (SPL) is the proprietor of a patented process technology. As part of an extensive restructuring project, it is necessary to value the technology as of 1 January 2007. SPL manufactures several models of a single product; the patented technology reduces the production costs of the entire range. From past experience, management believes that the technology, which has a remaining useful life of eight years, is covered by six European patents, one U.S. patent, and six patents in other countries, with remaining terms of 10 to 12 years.

Based on legal counsel's assessments, the protection of the technology is considered high; therefore, the entire SPL product range is effectively protected against any kind of imitation by competitors. The assessments took particular account of the patents' validity, extent of the protection, and territories covered.

The Business

Exhibit 27.4 contains the profit projections for SPL until 2011. At the valuation date, the fixed assets and working capital were appraised at $100 million and $118.2 million respectively; the tax rate is 40% and the WACC 7.08%.

Exhibit 27.4 SPL Projected Income

		2007	2008	2009	2010	$' millions 2011
Sales		360	389	404	412	421
Cost of Sales		(241)	(259)	(270)	(275)	(280)
Gross Profit		119	130	134	137	141
Gross Margin		33.1%	33.4%	33.2%	33.3%	33.5%
SG&A		(61)	(67)	(68)	(69)	(70)
EBIT		58	63	66	68	71
Tax	40%	(23)	(25)	(26)	(27)	(28)
NOPAT		35	38	40	41	43

---

[17] See Moser/Schieszl, *"Untemehmenswertanalysen, auf der Basis von Simulationsrechnungen am Beispiel eines Biotech-Untemehmens,"* in **FB** (2001): 530–541.

The WACC of 7.08% is calculated in the normal manner on the basis of 40% debt and 60% equity.

Exhibit 27.5 Calculation of WACC

				Weight	Product
Cost of Equity					
Risk-free Rate		4.00%			
Market Risk Premium	4.50%				
Beta	1.20	5.40%	9.40%	60.0%	5.64%
Cost of Debt					
Term & Risk Equivalent		6.00%			
Tax	40%	−2.40%	3.60%	40.0%	1.44%
WACC					7.08%

Incremental Income Analysis

Because of the positioning of its products compared to competitors, SPL sees no need to lower its prices or otherwise pass on the cost benefits. Management assumes that this advantageous situation will not change for the remainder of the technology's life and that it will continue to have no bearing on the products' volume and price structure. The major difference from its competitors is the margins; this means that the contribution of the technology to future income—the incremental profits—can be identified.

To calculate the value of the technology, certain parameters must be determined: the annual cost savings, the remaining useful life, the asset-specific rate of return, and the tax amortization benefit (TAB). The latter arises from the fact that in most countries a separately acquired intangible asset can be amortized for tax purposes. For simplicity, the year-end rather than midyear discounting convention was adopted.

Future cost savings. Analyses of the technology's impacts on material usage revealed that they depend on the specific version, as materials of different qualities are used in the various models; therefore, the annual cost savings are determined not only by the number of units manufactured but also by the product mix. Calculating the annual savings requires projecting sales until the end of the asset's useful life. Because of the technology life cycle and the state of development of the relevant markets, SPL assumes that, after the end of the projected period (2007–2011), revenues will grow with the market at 2% annually. After the projected period, the product mix of the last year of the plan is assumed to continue. At the end of the technology's useful life, 2014, it will be replaced by a successor process before year-end. The projected sales and corresponding cost savings are shown in Exhibit 27.6.

Exhibit 27.6 Projected Sales and Margin Improvement

$' millions

	2007	2008	2009	2010
Sales	360	389	404	412
Growth	20%	8%	4%	2%
Extra Gross Profit	16.4	19.1	18.9	19.6
Margin Improvement	4.6%	4.9%	4.7%	4.8%

	2011	2012	2013	2014 (10 mos)
Sales	421	429	438	372
Growth	2%	2%	2%	−15%
Extra Gross Profit	21.0	21.4	21.9	18.6
Margin Improvement	5.0%	5.0%	5.0%	5.0%

Asset-Specific Rate of Return

The point of departure in calculating an asset-specific rate of return is the term-equivalent WACC, which is adjusted for the asset-specific risks. Due to the time required, it is not possible to identify and value every asset, so management decided to apply a markup to the term-equivalent WACC (7.08 %); in this case, a figure of 2.02% was chosen to give an asset-specific rate of return of 9.10%, just below the 9.40% cost of equity.

Tax Amortization Benefit

The planned restructuring project at SPL requires the technology to be valued after tax. The tax amortization benefit (TAB) is calculated by applying a step-up factor to the present value of the income from the subject to obtain the fair value, which includes the TAB; the calculation of the step-up factor is shown in Exhibit 27.7.

Exhibit 27.7 Tax Amortization Benefit Calculation

Depreciation Method	Straight Line	WACC	7.08%
Period	8 Years	Patent Premium	2.02%
		Cost of Capital	9.10%

Year	P V Factor	Amortization	Am Factor
2007	0.9166	0.1250	0.1146
2008	0.8401	0.1250	0.1050
2009	0.7701	0.1250	0.0963
2010	0.7058	0.1250	0.0882
2011	0.6470	0.1250	0.0809
2012	0.5930	0.1250	0.0741
2013	0.5435	0.1250	0.0679
2014	0.4982	0.1250	0.0623
Total Present Values Amortization			0.6893
Tax Rate			40%
Tax Saving			27.57%
Step-up (1/1-tax saving)			1.3807

Value of the Technology

The value of the patented technology is arrived at by discounting the annual cost savings resulting from it; since the improvements in margins are subject to SPL's corporate taxes, the additional burdens must be deducted. The TAB is then added to the present value of the future cost savings to get fair value. The calculations are in Exhibit 27.8.

Exhibit 27.8 Valuation: Incremental Income Method

$' millions

		2007	2008	2009	2010
Sales		360	389	404	412
Extra Gross Profit		16.4	19.1	18.9	19.6
Tax	40%	(6.6)	(7.7)	(7.5)	(7.8)
Net Incremental Income		9.8	11.5	11.3	11.7
PV Factor	9.10%	0.9166	0.8401	0.7701	0.7058
Present Value		9.0	9.6	8.7	8.3

		2011	2012	2013	2014 (10 mos)
Sales		421	429	438	372
Extra Gross Profit		21.0	21.4	21.9	18.6
Tax	40%	(8.4)	(8.6)	(8.7)	(7.4)
Net Incremental Income		12.6	12.8	13.1	11.1
PV Factor	9.10%	0.6470	0.5930	0.5435	0.4982
Present Value		8.2	7.6	7.1	5.6

Total Present Values	64.1 TAB	24.4 Fair Value	88.5

RELIEF-FROM-ROYALTY METHOD

Another value of the patented technology is the present value of the notional royalty payments which the entity saves because of its ownership. To do this, it is first necessary to determine the future royalties either from comparable transactions or from a profit split. The asset-specific rate of return and the TAB step-up factor remain unchanged.

Royalty Payments Saved

Usually royalties are determined by applying a fixed rate to an agreed base, normally revenues. Often further payments are made, either up front for training and other services or at milestones with annual minimums. The first step is to identify licensing transactions for comparable technologies. Then the consensus terms of such licenses are applied to the subject for its remaining useful life. A search of databases revealed that the royalties for licenses of patented technologies comparable to the subject are typically applied to sales. Based on six agreements, the median royalty is approximately 4%; no importance was given to any other relevant terms. The notional royalty payments saved are obtained by applying a rate of 4% to the projected sales up to the end of the useful life of the technology; the details are shown in Exhibit 27.9.

Exhibit 27.9 Valuation: Relief-from-Royalty Method

$' millions

		2007	2008	2009	2010
Sales		360	389	404	412
Royalty Payments					
On Sales	4.0%	14.4	15.6	16.2	16.5
Training		1.0	-	-	-
Royalty Savings		15.4	15.6	16.2	16.5
Tax	40%	(6.2)	(6.2)	(6.5)	(6.6)
Net Royalty Savings		9.2	9.3	9.7	9.9
PV Factor	9.10%	0.9166	0.8401	0.7701	0.7058
Present Value		8.5	7.8	7.5	7.0

		2011	2012	2013	2014 (10 mos)
Sales		421	429	438	372
Royalty Payments					
On Sales	4.0%	16.8	17.2	17.5	14.9
Tax	40%	(6.7)	(6.9)	(7.0)	(6.0)
Net Royalty Savings		10.1	10.3	10.5	8.9
PV Factor	9.10%	0.6470	0.5930	0.5435	0.4982
Present Value		6.5	6.1	5.7	4.4
Total Present Value		53.6 TAB		20.4 Fair Value	74.0

Value by a Profit Split

Sometimes royalty payments are determined by applying rules of thumb specific to an industry to split the profit to which the patented technology contributes between the parties. Before adopting this method, it is necessary to establish if such a rule of thumb is applicable. Analyses of licensing agreements reveal that it is indeed customary in the industry to apply the 25% rule to earnings before interest and taxes (EBIT).

To forecast the relevant EBIT, the first step is to analyze in detail the income statements and balance sheets for the last three fiscal years as well as management's previous projections. Upon doing this, it was discovered that, based on its past record, management's EBIT projections for the period could be used without modification. The figures beyond the projected period to the end of the technologies' life were determined by applying the EBIT margins at the end of the projected period (16.9% in 2011) to the anticipated sales for the remaining years. The future saved royalty payments are 25% of such EBIT, as shown in Exhibit 27.10.

Exhibit 27.10 Value by a Profit Split Method

$' millions

		2007	2008	2009	2010
Sales		360	389	404	412
EBIT		57.6	63.2	65.6	67.9
Owner Spilt	25%	14.4	15.8	16.4	17.0
Tax	40%	(5.8)	(6.3)	(6.6)	(6.8)
Net Cash Flow		8.6	9.5	9.8	10.2
PV Factor	9.10%	0.9166	0.8401	0.7701	0.7058
Present Value		7.9	8.0	7.6	7.2

		2011	2012	2013	2014 (10 mos)
Sales		421	429	438	372
EBIT		71.2	72.6	74.1	62.9
Owner Spilt	25%	17.8	18.1	18.5	15.7
Tax	40%	(7.1)	(7.3)	(7.4)	(6.3)
Net Royalty Savings		10.7	10.9	11.1	9.4
PV Factor	9.10%	0.6470	0.5930	0.5435	0.4982
Present Value		6.9	6.5	6.0	4.7

| Total Present Values | | 54.8 TAB | | 20.8 Fair Value | 75.6 |

Value of the Patented Technology

The value of the patented technology by those methods is obtained by discounting the future saved royalty payments after tax; in line with the previous techniques, it is also necessary to add the TAB. Two royalty based values of the patented technology were set out in Exhibits 27.9 and 10. With a royalty calculated on the basis of licensing transactions, the value is $74.0 million, while, under the profit split, the comparable figure is $75.6 million, or 2.2% higher, a reasonable match. The more accurate value under the Incremental Income method is $88.8 million, or 17% higher, as it also includes the value of the improvements to the technology made by SPL.

RESIDUAL VALUE METHOD

The last set of examples looks at the value of the patented technology as the major asset of SPL, with all the other items being contributing assets. There are two ways to calculate the residual value: either as the difference between that of the entity and those of all the other assets, or as the present value of the excess earnings; they are likely to lead to different results; it is therefore necessary to analyze and interpret the reasons.

Direct Calculation

In view of the simplified assumptions of SPL, whose only assets are working capital, fixed assets, and technology, there is no difficulty in directly calculating the residual value. First, the value of SPL on its own has to be determined (see Exhibit 27.11); then all contributing assets are identified and valued. The process for the fixed assets, which gives an amount of $100 million, is set out in Exhibit 27.13. Since the working capital is already known, it is not necessary to show how it would be calculated in practice. Finally, the values of the fixed assets and working capital are deducted from the value of the entity.

Exhibit 27.11 Valuation: SPL

$' millions

		2007	2008	2009	2010
Sales		360	389	404	412
EBIT		57.6	63.2	65.6	67.9
Tax	40%	(23.0)	(25.3)	(26.2)	(27.2)
NOPAT		34.6	37.9	39.4	40.7
Changes WC		(43.2)	(3.5)	(1.8)	(1.0)
Net CAPEX		(11.0)	(1.0)	(13.0)	(1.0)
Free Cash Flow		(19.6)	33.4	24.6	38.8
PV Factor	7.08%	0.9339	0.8721	0.8145	0.7606
Present Value		(18.3)	29.2	20.0	29.5

		2011	2012	2013	2014 (10 mos)	
Sales		421	429	438	372	
EBIT		71.2	72.6	74.1	62.9	
Tax	40%	(28.5)	(29.0)	(29.6)	(25.2)	
NOPAT		42.7	43.5	44.4	37.7	
Changes WC		(1.1)	(1.0)	(1.1)	127.6	Liquidation
Net CAPEX		(15.0)	(1.5)	(18.0)	62.0	Liquidation
Free Cash Flow		26.6	41.1	25.4	227.3	
PV Factor	7.08%	0.7103	0.6634	0.6195	0.5785	
Present Value		18.9	27.2	15.7	131.5	

Total Present Values	253.7				
Working Capital	(90.0)				
Fixed Assets	(100.4)				
Patented Technology	63.3	+ TAB	24.1	Fair Value	87.4

The value of SPL, the point of departure for calculating the residual value, includes all associated assets; accordingly, it must be the entity, not the equity, value. The free cash flows of the firm for the useful life of the technology are forecast and discounted by its WACC; they are obtained by deducting from the already calculated EBIT:

- Corporate taxes
- Changes in working capital
- Net capital expenditures in excess of depreciation and amortization (the latter were projected separately)

In determining the value of SPL, amortization of the technology was not taken into consideration. Exhibit 27.12 determines its value, including straight-line, amortization of the subject over its remaining useful life.

Exhibit 27.12 Valuation: SPL Amortizing Technology

$' millions

		2007	2008	2009	2010
Sales		360	389	404	412
EBIT		57.6	63.2	65.6	67.9
Amortization	92.5	(11.6)	(11.6)	(11.6)	(11.6)
EBIT–Amortization		46.0	51.6	54.0	56.3
Tax	40%	(18.4)	(20.7)	(21.6)	(22.5)
NOPAT–Amortization		27.6	31.0	32.4	33.8
Amortization		11.6	11.6	11.6	11.6
Changes WC		(43.2)	(3.5)	(1.8)	(1.0)
Net CAPEX		(11.0)	(1.0)	(13.0)	(1.0)
Free Cash Flow		(15.0)	38.1	29.2	43.4
PV Factor	7.08%	0.9339	0.8721	0.8145	0.7606
Present Value		(14.0)	33.2	23.8	33.0

		2011	2012	2013	2014 (10 mos)	
Sales		421	429	438	372	
EBIT		71.2	72.6	74.1	62.9	
Amortization	92.5	(11.6)	(11.6)	(11.6)	(11.6)	
EBIT–Amortization		59.6	61.0	62.5	51.4	
Tax	40%	(23.9)	(24.4)	(25.0)	(20.5)	
NOPAT		47.3	48.2	49.1	42.4	
Amortization		11.6	11.6	11.6	11.6	
Changes WC		(1.1)	(1.0)	(1.1)	127.6	Liquidation
Net CAPEX		(15.0)	(1.5)	(18.0)	62.0	Liquidation
Free Cash Flow		42.8	57.3	41.6	243.5	
PV Factor	7.08%	0.7103	0.6634	0.6195	0.5785	
Present Value		30.4	38.0	25.7	140.9	

	Present Values	Rates of Return	2007 Returns
Total Present Values	311.0	11.1%	34.6
Working Capital	(118.2)	3.0%	(3.5)
Fixed Assets	(100.4)	7.0%	(7.0)
Patented Technology–TAB	92.4	26.0%	24.0

Excess Earnings Method

Calculating the residual value by means of the excess earnings method begins by determining the returns on the contributory assets, which are deducted to establishing the excess earnings. Discounting them by their asset-specific rates of return gives the value of the technology. Applying this method involves a number of areas which are the subject of disagreement between practitioners. The procedure is therefore merely sketched briefly.

Contributory asset charges consist of two components: a return on the related invested capital plus the return of it over time. The values of a contributory asset start with its fair value at the valuation date. In subsequent periods, it is reduced by depreciation and increased by any further expenditure; the annual return of capital is the balance of these changes. The return on capital is calculated from its level at the beginning of each period and the asset-specific rate of return. Calculations of the returns of, as well as on, capital for SPL's fixed assets are summed up in Exhibit 27.13, based on detailed projections.

Exhibit 27.13 Valuation: SPL Fixed Assets

		2007	2008	2009	2010
Return on Capital	7.00%	7.0	6.9	6.1	6.1
Return of Capital net of CAPEX		1.5	11.5	(0.5)	11.5
Year-end Balance	100.0	98.5	87.0	87.5	76.0
Cash Flow		8.5	18.4	5.6	17.6
PV Factor	7.00%	0.9346	0.8734	0.8163	0.7629
Present Value		7.9	16.1	4.6	13.4

		2011	2012	2013	2014 (10 mos)
Return on Capital	7.00%	5.3	5.5	4.7	4.3
Return of Capital net of CAPEX		(2.5)	11.0	(5.5)	74.5
Year-end Balance		78.5	67.5	73.0	(1.5)
Cash Flow		2.8	16.5	(0.8)	78.8
PV Factor	40%	0.7130	0.6663	0.6227	0.5820
Present Value	7.00%	2.0	11.0	(0.5)	45.8
Total Present Values		100.4			

Calculating the Excess Earnings

It has already been explained that SPL's income should be understood to be its free cash flow. This means that to calculate the excess earnings, it is necessary to deduct the contributory assets charges. In the example, this calculation is simplified, because: the free cash flow is arrived at by deducting (a) the changes in working capital and (b) the net capital expenditure (CAPEX less depreciation) from the net operating profit less adjusted taxes (NOPLAT). Therefore, the excess earnings are obtained by deducting the returns on the funds invested in working capital and fixed assets from NOPLAT, as shown in Exhibit 27.14.

Exhibit 27.14 Valuation: Technology Using Excess Earnings

		2007	2008	2009	$ millions 2010
Sales		360	389	404	412
EBIT		57.6	63.2	65.6	67.9
Tax	40%	(23.0)	(25.3)	(26.2)	(27.2)
NOPAT		34.6	37.9	39.4	40.7
Return on Investment					
Working Capital	3.0%	(3.5)	(3.7)	(3.8)	(3.9)
Fixed Assets	7.0%	(7.0)	(6.9)	(6.1)	(6.1)
Excess Earnings		24.0	27.4	29.5	30.8
PV Factor	26.0%	0.7939	0.6303	0.5004	0.3972
Present Value		19.1	17.3	14.8	12.2
		2011	**2012**	**2013**	**2014** (10 mos)
Sales		421	429	438	372
EBIT		71.2	72.6	74.1	62.9
Tax	40%	(28.5)	(29.0)	(29.6)	(25.2)
NOPAT		42.7	43.5	44.4	37.7
Return on Investment					
Working Capital	3.0%	(4.0)	(4.1)	(4.2)	(4.3)
Fixed Assets	7.0%	(5.3)	(5.5)	(4.7)	(4.3)
Excess Earnings		33.4	34.0	35.6	29.2
PV Factor	26.0%	0.2504	0.1988	0.1578	0.1253
Present Value		8.4	6.8	5.6	3.7
Total Present Values + TAB		87.7		Fair Value	87.7

In practice, the benefits of the contributory assets to income are often modeled on the basis of notional leases with monthly blended payments to avoid recording income contributions twice; the starting parameter chosen, from which the notional lease payments have to be deducted, is typically EBITDA. Since EBIT is obtained by deducting depreciation and amortization from EBITDA, the notional lease payments are established as annuities; the payment for working capital only needs to include a return on the invested funds, whereas depreciation also has to be considered in the case of fixed assets.

ASSET-SPECIFIC RATES OF RETURN

Asset-specific rates of return are calculated on a term- and risk-equivalent basis. The first aspect requires taking the useful life of the subject into account; the second, in practice, is normally implemented through an asset-specific risk markup/markdown. The basis for it is that WARA, which is calculated from the asset-specific rates of return, weighted by their fair values, should be identical to WACC. With that method, a difficulty nevertheless arises that the asset-specific risk markups on the term-equivalent cost of capital are not known; therefore, they first have to be obtained by other means; the excess earnings are then discounted at that rate (see Exhibit 27.12).

SUMMARY OF THE RESULTS

Exhibit 27.15 summarizes the values of the patented technology by the six different methods. Since each involves specific application requirements, they differ, including the

TAB where relevant, from $48.5 million (value of SPL) to $88.5 million (incremental income) and are comparable to only a limited extent; obviously, the choice of method may have a significant influence on the result. Accordingly, the valuator must ensure that the basic assumptions of the method selected are fully supported by the underlying facts.

Exhibit 27.15 Summary of Technology Values

	Exhibit	Present Values	Tax Amortization Benefit	Fair Value	Variance
Incremental Income	27.8	64.1	24.4	88.5	5.0%
Relief from Royalty	27.9	53.6	20.4	74.0	−12.2%
Profit Spilt	27.1	84.8	20.8	75.6	−10.3%
Value SPL	27.11	63.3	24.1	87.4	370.0%
Amortizing Technology	27.12	66.9	25.5	92.4	9.7%
Excess Earnings	27.14	63.5	24.2	87.7	4.1%
				84.3	0.0%

CONCLUSION

This chapter considers patents as assets to be valued; the key factor is the competitive advantage associated with them, specifically the legal protection provided to the underlying technologies and related products. In this context, the value of a patent is composed of the value of the unprotected technology plus that of the legal protection; it must be borne in mind that, normally, a technology is protected not just by a single patent but a portfolio.

The basic valuation approaches—income, market, and cost, and the need to delineate in detail the subject and possible methods of determining fair values—were briefly outlined. All of those rely on the contribution of a patented technology to the total income generated by all the assets involved with the business. On this basis, six methods were illustrated:

- Incremental income has a limited scope since, in many cases, the basic requirement of isolating the relevant amounts cannot be met
- Relief from royalty has a considerably broader range; it is applicable if comparable assets are the subject of license agreements and the data needed to calculate royalties are available; alternatively, the 25% rule may be applied.
- Residual value presupposes that the subject is the leading asset for the entity's income generation, plus all contributory assets have to be identified and valued; the problematic aspect is that all the synergies resulting from the interaction of the assets involved are allocated to the subject.

Those illustrative examples demonstrate the practical application of the different methods. With residual value methods in the form of the excess earnings technique, particular importance should be attached to determining the contributory asset charges and to calculating the asset-specific rates of return.

28 PETROLEUM RESOURCES

J. RICHARD CLAYWELL

UNITED STATES

INTRODUCTION

During 2008, the price of crude oil ranged from a high of about $147 a barrel (July) to a low of around $38 (December), while that of natural gas in the United States varied between $13.40 per million British thermal units (MMbtus) to approximately $5.00. Such enormous changes (–74% for oil, –63% for gas) had a significant impact on many industries (see Chapter 19). To preserve supplies, many multinational enterprises (MNEs) have acquired interests in petroleum resources as a natural hedge; this chapter deals with their valuation.

Exhibits 28.1 and 28.2 show the changes in crude oil and natural gas futures prices for the year to 22 April 2009.

Exhibit 28.1 NYMEX Crude Oil Futures

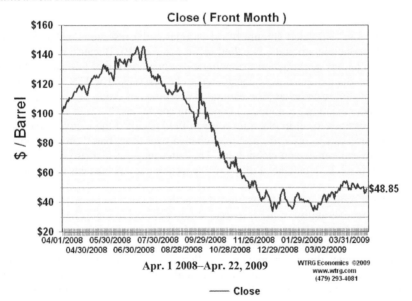

Apr. 1 2008–Apr. 22, 2009

WTRG Economics ©2009
www.wtrg.com
(479) 293-4081

—— Close

Exhibit 28.2 NYMEX Natural Gas Futures

OIL RESERVES

Before discussing valuation methodologies, it is essential to understand the industry's terminology. The total estimated amount of oil in a particular reservoir, including both producible and nonproducible amounts, is called oil in place (OiP). Because of reservoir characteristics and limitations in extraction technologies, only a fraction of OiP can be brought to the surface; this producible portion is considered to be reserves. The U.S. Energy Information Agency defines oil reserves as "the estimated quantities of crude oil that are claimed to be recoverable under existing economic and operating conditions."[1]

The ratio of reserves to oil in place for a given field is called the recovery factor; it varies greatly from reservoir to reservoir and may change over time, based on operating history and in response to economics and technology. The latter may cause a rise over time if additional investment is made in enhanced oil recovery techniques, such as gas injection or water flooding.

As subsurface geology cannot be examined directly, indirect techniques are used to estimate the size and recoverability of the resource. While new technologies have increased their accuracy, significant uncertainties remain. In general, due to pressure from the Securities and Exchange Commission (SEC), early estimates of an oil field's reserves are conservative and tend to grow with time; this phenomenon is called reserves growth.[2] Many oil-producing nations do not reveal their reservoir engineering field data; instead, they provide unaudited claims for their oil reserves. Numbers disclosed by national governments are also sometimes manipulated for political reasons.

---

[1]   *Glossary of the U.S. Energy Information Agency (Washington, DC, 2007).*

[2]   *David F. Morehouse, **The Intricate Puzzle of Oil and Gas Reserves Growth** (Washington, DC U.S. Energy Information Administration, 1997).*

According to Moneyterms.co.uk, reserves are those quantities of petroleum claimed to be commercially recoverable by application of development projects to known accumulations under defined conditions; they must satisfy four criteria by being:

1. Discovered through one or more exploratory wells
2. Recoverable using existing technology
3. Commercially viable
4. In the ground

All reserve estimates involve uncertainty, depending on the amount of reliable geologic and engineering data available and their interpretation. Their relative degree of uncertainty is expressed by dividing them into two principal classifications, proved and unproved. The latter are further subdivided into "probable" and "possible" to indicate their situation. The most commonly accepted definitions of types of reserves are based on those approved by the Society of Petroleum Engineers and the World Petroleum Council in 1997.

Proved Reserves

Proved reserves are defined as those claiming to have a *reasonable certainty* (normally at least 90% confidence) of being recoverable under existing economic and political conditions, and using existing technology.[3] Industry specialists refer to this as P90 (i.e., having a 90% certainty of being produced); reserves are either proved developed (PD) or proved undeveloped (PUD). PD reserves are those that can be produced with existing wells and perforations or from additional reservoirs with minimal additional investment or operating expenses. PUD reserves require further capital investment (drilling new wells, installing gas compression, etc.) to bring the oil or gas to the surface.

The SEC allows only proved reserved to be reported by oil companies to investors. Therefore, entities listed on U.S. stock exchanges must substantiate their claims, but many governments and national oil companies do not disclose verifying data.

Unproved Reserves

Probable reserves are based on median estimates, with a 50% confidence level of recovery referred to as P50 or 2P (proved plus probable); possible reserves are even less likely to be recovered. The term "possible reserves" is used often for reserves with at least a 10% certainty of being recovered (P10). Reserves may be classified as possible based on: varying interpretations of geology, reserves not producible at commercial rates, uncertainty due to reserve infill, and projected reserves based on future recovery methods. Unproved reserves are used internally by oil companies and government agencies for planning purposes. Total reserves sometimes are referred to as 3P (proved plus probable plus possible).

Techniques for Estimating Reserves

The oil in a subsurface reservoir is called OiP. The portion that can be recovered is considered to be a reserve. The amount that is not recoverable is ignored unless (or until) methods are developed to extract it.

The different methods of calculating oil reserves can be grouped into three general categories: volumetric, material balance, and production performance; each method has its advantages and drawbacks.[4]

---

[3] *Society of Petroleum Engineers, Petroleum Reserves Definitions, Petroleum Resources Management System (Richardson, TX, 1997).*

[4] *William C. Lyons, **Standard Handbook of Petroleum & Natural Gas Engineering:** Gulf Professional Publishing, Woburn, MA, 2005).*

Volumetric method. Volumetric methods attempt to determine the amount of OiP from the size of the reservoir as well as the physical properties of its rocks and fluids. This is then multiplied by recovery factor based on those from other fields with similar characteristics to arrive at a reserve number. Current recovery factors for oil fields around the world typically range between 10% and 60%, although some are over 80%. The wide variance is due largely to the diversity of fluid and reservoir characteristics for different deposits.[5] The method is most useful early in the life of the reservoir, before significant production has begun.

Materials balance method. The materials balance method for an oil field uses an equation that relates the volume of oil, water, and gas that has been extracted from a reservoir and the change in reservoir pressure to calculate the remaining OiP. It assumes that, as fluids are produced, there will be a change in the reservoir pressure caused by the remaining volume of oil and gas. Extensive pressure-volume-temperature analyses and an accurate pressure history of the field are required by this method. Some production (typically 5% to 10% of ultimate recovery) is needed, unless reliable pressure history can be used from a field with similar rock and fluid characteristics.[6]

Production decline curve method. The decline curve method mathematically fits past production data to a decline curve so as to estimate future oil output. The three most common decline curves are exponential, hyperbolic, and harmonic. It is assumed that the production will decline on a reasonably smooth curve, and therefore allowances must be made for shut-in wells and production restrictions. The curve can be expressed mathematically or plotted on a graph; this method has the advantage of (implicitly) including all reservoir characteristics but requires a sufficient history to establish a statistically significant trend, ideally when production is not curtailed by regulatory or other artificial conditions.

Reserves growth. In recent experience, initial estimates of the size of newly discovered oil fields are usually too low but tend to increase with the years. The term "reserve growth" refers to the typical increases in estimated ultimate recovery that occur as oil fields are developed and produced.[7]

RESERVE STUDIES

A reserve study has no set form; the information provided will depend on the reporting style of the engineering firm. It is typically divided into three sections:

1. The total interest in the well
2. The particular ownership interests in the well
3. A summary and analysis of the first two sections

The first section reflects the total values for various aspects of the well based on estimates of the oil and gas production in future years; it represents 100% of the well's operations but is described as an 8/8ths interest.

The second section concentrates on the specific ownership interest being valued, reflecting the individual ownership's amounts for: total revenues, severance taxes, operating expenses, and net cash flows in each projected year. Also, the reserve report will include a present value calculation so that the discounted cash flows can be verified.

---

[5] See E. Tzimas, "Enhanced Oil Recovery Using Carbon Dioxide in the European Energy System," *European Commission Joint Energy Research Center* (2005); D. W. Green, "Enhanced Oil Recovery," *Society of Petroleum Engineers* (2003), and U.S. Department of Energy, Washington, DC, "Defining the Limits of Oil Production," *International Energy Outlook* (2008).

[6] See Lyons, **Standard Handbook of Petroleum & Natural Gas Engineering.**

[7] Ibid.

The third section summarizes all information related to the well's production. Depending on the engineering firm, material may be presented concerning how many years it will take to recover the investment. Exhibits 28.3 to 28.7 present tables that are typical of those to be found in a reserve study.

The far right of Exhibit 28.5 shows a column titled Present Value (PV) setting out, at a 10% discount rate, what the engineers have estimated to be the present values of the cash flows.

Exhibit 28.3

End Month-Year	Working Interest $000's	Revenue Interest $000's	Gross Oil MBO	Gross Gas MMF	Net Oil MBO	Net Gas MMF
6-09	12.787	10.750	47.966	1,792.559	5.478	191.466
6-10	13.334	11.199	32.198	1,184.536	3.869	131.833
6-11	13.576	11.375	23.726	858.401	2.925	97.010
6-12	13.679	11.428	18.505	658.486	2.315	74.707
6-13	13.705	11.418	15.043	526.970	1.900	56.679
6-14	13.702	11.384	12.629	436.103	1.606	49.160
6-15	13.683	11.342	10.874	370.782	1.389	41.551
6-16	13.634	11.268	9.444	317.230	1.211	35.230
6-17	12.404	10.138	8.152	258.461	1.018	25.225
6-18	12.381	10.111	7.439	233.885	0.934	22.684
6-19	12.469	10.183	6.854	214.820	0.867	20.971
6-20	12.546	10.246	6.356	198.629	0.809	19.500
6-21	12.614	10.302	5.925	184.705	0.758	18.223
6-22	12.675	10.352	5.548	172.601	0.713	17.103
6-23	12.730	10.398	5.217	161.983	0.674	16.114

Exhibit 28.4

End Month-Year	Oil $/Barrel	Gas $/MMCF	Gross Wells	Net Oil Revenue $000's	Net Gas Revenue $000's	Net Total Revenue $000's
6-09	24.00	2.24	4	131.480	429.310	560.790
6-10	22.48	2.32	4	86.986	305.303	392.289
6-11	21.47	2.39	4	62.801	232.076	294.877
6-12	20.96	2.47	4	48.526	184.669	233.195
6-13	20.45	2.55	4	38.853	152.479	191.332
6-14	20.73	2.64	4	33.287	129.869	163.156
6-15	21.40	2.73	4	29.725	113.531	143.256
6-16	22.08	2.82	2	26.734	99.349	126.083
6-17	22.79	2.92	2	23.198	73.616	96.814
6-18	23.52	3.02	2	21.965	68.554	90.519
6-19	24.27	3.13	2	21.040	65.604	86.644
6-20	25.05	3.24	2	20.258	63.138	83.396
6-21	25.84	3.35	2	19.594	61.061	80.655
6-22	26.67	3.47	2	19.025	59.301	78.326
6-23	27.51	3.59	2	18.536	57.803	76.339

Exhibit 28.5

End Month-Year	Net Total Revenue $000's	Severance Ad Valorem Tax $000's	Operating Expenses $000's	Net Cash Flow $000's	Present Value Factor 10%	Present Value $000's
6-09	560.790	24.518	42.083	494.189	1.000	494.189
6-10	392.289	16.594	42.789	332.906	0.909	302.642
6-11	294.877	12.130	43.644	239.103	0.826	197.595
6-12	233.195	9.378	44.517	179.300	0.751	134.708
6-13	191.332	7.519	45.408	138.405	0.683	94.531
6-14	163.156	6.320	46.316	110.520	0.621	68.622
6-15	143.256	5.494	47.242	90.520	0.565	51.099
6-16	126.220	4.802	45.775	75.643	0.513	38.820
6-17	96.814	3.848	26.063	66.903	0.467	31.210
6-18	90.519	3.565	24.991	61.963	0.424	26.279
6-19	86.644	3.362	25.491	57.791	0.386	22.278
6-20	83.396	3.188	26.001	54.207	0.351	19.000
6-21	80.655	3.039	26.521	51.095	0.319	16.279
6-22	78.326	2.909	27.051	48.366	0.290	14.012
6-23	76.339	2.796	27.593	45.950	0.263	12.099
					Present Value	1,523.361

Exhibit 28.6

	Oil	Gas
Gross Wells	4	1
Gross ULT, MB, & MMP	591.774	16,149.160
Gross Cumulative, MB & MMP	316.650	6,593.221
Gross Res, MB & MMF	275.124	9,555.934
Net Res, MB & MMF	32.778	989.049
Net Revenue, MS	803.990	2,815.804
Initial Price	$24.092	$2.234
Initial Net Income Percent	11.084%	10.370%

Exhibit 28.7

		PW Percent	PW (Individual)
Life years	40	8.00%	1,631.090
Discount Percent		10.00%	1,516.250
Undiscounted Payout, Years		12.00%	1,421.755
Discounted Payout, Years		15.00%	1,307.167
Undiscounted Net/Investment		20.00%	2,046.861
Discounted Net/ Investment		25.00%	1,057.377
Rate of Return Percent		40.00%	852.100
Initial Working Interest Percent	12.425%	60.00%	698.100
		80.00%	602.142
		100.00%	535.575

WORKING INTEREST

A *working interest* means a participation in an oil and gas lease that gives the owner the right to drill for and produce oil and gas on the acreage; it also requires the owner to pay a share of the drilling and production costs. The share of production to which a working interest owner is entitled will always be smaller than the share of costs that it is required to bear, with the balance of the production accruing to the owners of various royalties. The owner of a 100% working interest in a lease burdened by a landowner's royalty of 12.5% is required to pay 100% of the costs of a well but to receive only 87.5% of the production.[8] The owner of a

---

[8]   *Statistics are from http://oilgasjobs.co.cc/glossary.*

working interest is entitled to a copy of the reserve study; based on this, it should be able to prepare a cash flow analysis of its investment.

NET PROFITS INTEREST

Net profits interest is a contractual arrangement under which the beneficiary, in exchange for consideration, receives a stated percentage of the net profits; it is not required to bear any part of the net losses. As distinguished from a working interest, this is considered a nonoperating interest, because it does not involve any rights or obligations of operating the property (costs of exploration, development, and operation). The net profits interest typically takes into account the total recoverable reserves of the field, which is normally obtained from reserve studies by geologists. The data should include the barrels of production per day (BOPD), the operating expenses, override royalty payments, and others.

The value of a net profits interest will be guided by the contract between the parties; in undertaking such an assignment, the desired information may not be available. In this situation, the valuator may be forced to use the independent information from the reserve studies. One resource for estimating the price of a barrel of oil, depending on the well's location, is either the European (North Sea) Brent or the West Texas Intermediate (WTI) spot prices; both are available in historic records dating back a number of years and as future settlement prices monthly until the end of 2012. Based on such estimates, projections can be made as to the appropriate estimated oil prices; a better source of information is projections by the operator.

Exhibit 28.8 is a valuation of a net profits interest in Equatorial Guinea. It is not in the form of a normal discounted cash flow, as the producers have some specific rights that are calculated first. In this net profits interest valuation, the government of Equatorial Guinea received 16% of the barrels produced while the operator got 2%. Since those items are contractual, they must be subtracted from the total barrels produced to arrive at the barrels of production available to the net profit holders' interests. The barrels of production after royalty shares is multiplied by the estimated price of oil to project revenues. The model then becomes a straightforward discounted cash flow projection, taking into consideration any additional contractual agreements. In this specific contract, the operator is entitled to a 20% cost recovery bypass and a cost recovery of 80% of the revenues.

Exhibit 28.8

		Discounted Cash Flow Projections				
		2008	2009	2010	2011	2012
Barrels of Production Per Year		74,118,240	66,706,416	60,035,774	54,032,197	48,628,977
Percentage Due to Equatorial Guinea/Nigeria	16.0%	11,858,918	10,673,027	9,605,724	8,645,152	7,780,636
Overriding Royalty Interest (Operator 1 share)	2.0%	305,071	274,564	247,107	222,397	200,157
Barrel of Production After Royalty Shares		61,954,251	55,758,826	50,182,943	45,164,649	40,648,184
Estimated Revenues		4,794,639,479	2,787,941,292	2,509,147,162	2,258,232,446	2,032,409,202
Percentage Due to Exxon Corporation	73.5%	(3,524,060,017)	(2,049,136,850)	(1,844,223,164)	(1,659,800,848)	(1,493,820,763)
Operator 1 Revenues		1,270,579,462	738,804,442	664,923,998	598,431,598	538,588,439
Operator 1 20% Cost Recovery Bypass		254,115,892	147,760,888	132,984,800	119,686,320	107,717,688
Estimated Costs for Recovery—CAPEX		197,372,000	197,372,000	197,372,000	197,372,000	197,372,000
Operator 1 Share of Estimated Cost Recovery at 80%		409,545,785	196,835,777	167,283,599	140,686,639	116,749,376
Total Revenues after Cost Recovery before CAPEX		861,033,677	541,968,665	497,640,399	457,744,959	421,839,063
Estimated Net Cash Flow	43.8%	377,132,751	237,382,275	217,966,495	200,492,292	184,765,510
Equatorial Guinea Income Tax	25.0%	(94,283,188)	(59,345,569)	(54,491,624)	(50,123,073)	(46,191,377)
Estimated Cash Flow After Taxes		282,849,563	178,036,707	163,474,871	150,369,219	138,574,132
Number of Years of Project (9) PV Factor at 18%		0.847	0.718	0.609	0.516	0.437
Net Present Value of Cash Flows		239,703,125	127,863,114	99,495,874	77,558,789	60,572,000

		2013	2014	2015	2016	Total
Barrels of Production Per Year		43,766,080	39,389,472	35,450,524	84,210	422,211,890
Percentage Due to Equatorial Guinea/Nigeria	16.0%	7,002,573	6,302,315	5,672,084	13,474	67,553,902
Overriding Royalty Interest (Operator 1 share)	2.0%	180,141	162,127	145,914	347	1,737,824
Barrel of Production After Royalty Shares		36,583,366	32,925,029	29,632,526	70,390	352,920,164
Estimated Revenues		1,829,168,281	1,646,251,453	1,481,626,308	3,519,490	19,342,935,113
Percentage Due to Exxon Corporation	73.5%	(1,344,438,687)	(1,209,994,818)	(1,088,995,336)	(2,586,825)	(14,217,057,308)
Operator 1 Revenues		484,729,594	436,256,635	392,630,972	932,665	5,125,877,805
Operator 1 20% Cost Recovery Bypass		96,945,919	87,251,327	78,526,194	186,533	1,025,175,561
Estimated Costs for Recovery—CAPEX		197,372,000	197,372,000	197,372,000	197,372,000	1,776,348,000
Operator 1 Share of Estimated Cost Recovery at 80%		95,205,838	75,816,654	58,366,389	(98,312,934)	1,162,177,122
Total Revenues after Cost Recovery before CAPEX		389,523,756	360,439,981	334,264,583	99,245,599	3,963,700,683

Estimated Net Cash Flow	43.8%	170,611,405	157,872,712	146,407,887	43,469,572	1,736,100,899
Equatorial Guinea Income Tax	25.0%	(42,652,851)	(39,468,178)	(36,601,972)	(10,867,393)	(434,025,225)
Estimated Cash Flow After Taxes		127,958,554	118,404,534	109,805,916	32,602,179	1,302,075,674
Number of Years of Project (9) PV Factor at 18%		0.370	0.314	0.266	0.225	4.303
Net Present Value of Cash Flows		47,399,943	37,170,143	29,212,546	7,350,357	726,325,891

Present Value of Estimated Future Cash Flows		726,325,891	
Final Year Cash Flow		7,350,357	(Will cease production, no long-term sustainable growth)
Net Cash Flow Capitalization Rate		18.0%	(The well is expected to be shut down in 2016)
Terminal Value		40,835,317	
Discount Rate and PV Factor	18%	0.226	
Present Value of Terminal Value		9,208,364	
Projected Present Value of Estimated Cash Flows		735,534,000	
John Smith Net Profits at .536%		0.6%	
Estimated Value of Net Profits		4,413,000	
Marketability Discount	20%	(882,600)	
Estimated Fair Market Value		3,530,000	

ROYALTY INTEREST

Royalties are payments, in value (money) or in kind, of a stated proportionate interest in production from mineral deposits by the lessees to the owner. The royalty rate may be an established minimum, a step scale, or a sliding scale. The step scale's royalty rate rises by steps as the production of the lease increases; the sliding scale's royalty rate is based on the average production for a period, usually a year, and applies to all output from the lease.[9]

Valuing royalty interests is substantially different from valuing working interests, mainly because of lack of information relating to most royalty interests; it is not uncommon that the only data supplied by the client are the amount received as royalties. Inquiries should be made as to the annual output for each well during the past five years and each well's estimated remaining life. If enough data are available, a calculation ought to be made of the estimated decline rate of production. In 2008, that was approximately 4% on average but varied considerably between fields.[10] The rate for the well is then compared with that of the industry, which may assist in determining the remaining life of the well.

Assume the table below represents a history of the royalties received for the well to be valued. The historic income from the well is set out in the table following.

Discuss with the client the probability of the well, in the short run, producing more or less than the historic trend indicates. Future years' expected production should be based on the most reliable information relating to past output. It can be seen from the revenues in the example that there is a steady decline of approximately 5%, which would indicate that this well's decline rate is in line with that of the industry. If available, try to obtain information on the original reserve studies that would indicate the remaining life of the well and the production levels by year, anticipated at the beginning.

Based on the information available, there are at least two ways to estimate the future production. One is to use the historical decline rate, another to plot a trend line from past

---

[9] *See http://oilgasinformation.com/oil-gas-dictionary.*

[10] *See "The 2008 IEA (International Energy Agency) WEO (World Energy Outlook)—Production Decline Rates," Euan Mearns, **Oil Drum: Europe**, 17 November 2008, Fort Collings, CO.*

figures and carry it forward. Either technique will continuously reduce the royalty income until the end of production. Exhibit 28.9 shows the historic royalty income from 1997 to 2008 and the future levels (2009 to 2014), based on both the past decline rate and a simple regression.

Exhibit 28.9 Historic and Future Royalty Income

		Historic Income		
Period	Year	Royalties $	Regression $	Decline Rate $
1	1997	20,000		
2	1998	19,000		
3	1999	18,050		
4	2000	17,148		
5	2001	16,290		
6	2002	15,476		
7	2003	14,702		
8	2004	13,967		
9	2005	13,268		
10	2006	12,605		
11	2007	11,975		
12	2008	11,376	11,376	11,376
13	2009		10,245	10,807
14	2010		9,464	10,267
15	2011		8,683	9,754
16	2012		7,903	9,266
17	2013		7,122	8,803
18	2014		6,341	8,363

As can be seen in this example, using the decline rate results in a slower decrease; if the reduction is expected to be steady, the decline rate is the best method. However, if the production changes are erratic, a regression line may be preferable. Whether the annual royalties are discounted or capitalized to determine the fair value of the royalty interest is a matter of the valuator's judgment.

Exhibit 28.10 shows the total net present value of the royalties based on a discount rate of 25%.

Exhibit 28.10 Total Net Present Value of the Royalties

			Historic Income			
Future Period	Year	Discount Rate Factor	Regression	Net Present Value $	Decline Rate	Net Present Value $
1	2009	0.800	10,245	8,196	10,807	8,646
2	2010	0.640	9,464	6,057	10,267	6,571
3	2011	0.512	8,683	4,446	9,754	4,994
4	2012	0.410	7,903	3,237	9,266	3,795
5	2013	0.328	7,122	2,334	8,803	2,885
6	2014	0.262	6,341	1,662	8,363	2,192
Total Net Present Value				25,932		29,083

The simple regression analysis is one of many ways that can be used to predict the value of an entity that holds investments in oil and gas. Other techniques that may produce a better predictor of value could be a moving average, exponential smoothing, or using transformations. The analyst should consider which method provides the best result.

DISCOUNTING CASH FLOWS

In determining the value of a royalty interest, investors ultimately look to the return on their investment as well as its recovery through the royalty payments. The quantification of the value, in today's dollars, of these expected future returns is the essence of the income approach. A capitalization method is not appropriate when two operational characteristics exist:

1. The entity's current and historic benefits are not representative of anticipated future operations.
2. The prospective rate of growth is expected to be erratic or, for some years, greater than is sustainable in the long-term.

Discount and Capitalization Rates

Discount and capitalization rates are the risk-adjusted returns used to convert future monetary receipts into capital sums. There are a number of ways to determine a discount or capitalization rate. The most common discount rate is the weighted average cost of capital; this is converted into a capitalization rate by deducting the forecast growth rate. (See Chapters 9–10.

SUMMARY

Valuing oil and gas interests is challenging but also rewarding. The key to the process is the same as valuing any other type of business activity: the ability to obtain sufficient reliable information.

29 PHARMACEUTICALS AND BIOTECHNOLOGY

SUNG-SOO SEOL

SOUTH KOREA

INTRODUCTION

There is a general saying in the valuation profession, "It is more important to understand the industry and markets than the techniques involved." It is clear that the pharmaceutical and biotechnology industries are in many ways different from others; they are based on technologies whose underlying concepts and processes that most laypeople cannot easily understand. They also differ in nature from other technology-based areas in that (a) the ratio of research and development (R&D) to sales is among the highest, at around 25% of revenue, and (b) the development process requires up to 15 years with inherent high risks during the period.

Pharmaceuticals have been developed for hundreds of years from natural sources ranging from plants, minerals, and forms of living organisms to modern synthetic chemicals. Biotechnology, whose origin came about with the discovery of the structure of DNA in 1953, can simply be defined as a group of concepts and processes that use and imitate living organisms as well as technologies involving microorganisms and biological substances, such as enzymes. The focus, however, has moved on to the engineering of cells, genes, and proteins.

INDUSTRY

Pharmaceutical firms are based on chemical manufacturing while biotechnology entities are distinguished by their underlying technologies. However, there is no clear difference between the two in the quest for drug discoveries, since many pharmaceutical companies are now adopting biotechnology. Rather, they are two major segments of the drug industry because their purposes are, in essence, the same. In commercial terms, more than 70% of biotechnology is now used for pharmaceuticals with U.S. firms being more oriented toward pharmaceutical than those in Europe.

Regulation

The drug industry is based on regulation, both from positive and negative perspectives. Patents provide protection for 20 years and sometimes can be extended. Commercialization of drugs in the United States, the world's biggest market, is tightly controlled by the Food and Drug Administration (FDA) to ensure drug safety. In certain cases, if the disease is rare or the market small, the FDA may grant, separate from any patent protection, exclusive marketing rights of three years for new treatments, five years for new chemical entities, and seven years for remedies to rare diseases; similar allowances exist in many other countries.

Approval Process

The approval process for every drug candidate starts with an Investigational New Drug Application to the FDA. After the success of Clinical Phase III trials, the candidate is submitted as a New Drug Application. There are several exceptions; if there are no alternative drugs or the candidate can be used in emergencies, a New Drug Application can be made at the end of Clinical Phase II trials.

Differences between Pharmaceutical and Biotechnology Firms

The important points for valuators are:

- Biotechnology firms are more R&D intensive and greater risk takers.
- Most biotechnology firms operate on R&D funding rather than sales revenue. A large number, including several publicly traded entities, have no sales at all. Among the approximately 380 listed companies, less than 10% are profitable.
- In capital markets, pharmaceutical firms show no significant differences from other industries; however, there are marked variances in their manufacturing and marketing.
- Returns on biotech R&D are very similar to those of venture capital investments. Of the total value, 48% to 62% is generated by the highest deciles.[1]
- Values of technology-based entities such as biotechnology firms from time to time show fantasy effects; when a new technology is expected to have a big impact appears, the implicit value of the related listed companies may go sky high, far exceeding their fair values. The biotechnology and Internet bubbles of 1999–2000 are such examples.

Current Industry Trends

Current trends in the drug industry are listed next.

- There is a lack of new products, although more than 2,000 drug candidates are in clinical trials.
- Since 2000, only between 24 and 39 new drugs have been approved each year; in that period, the contribution of biotech rose from less than 10% to nearly 30%.
- More than 200 biotech drugs have been approved by the FDA since the mid-1980s; more than 150 are on sale, and at least 50 report net earnings.[2]
- The FDA has become increasingly conservative regarding safety due to increasing failures of later-stage projects.
- Licensing and merger and acquisition (M&A) deals are being driven by big pharmaceuticals' need to extend their technologies and pipelines. Between 2000 and 2007, there were 1,234 acquisitions and 162 initial public offerings (IPOs).[3]
- There are concerns about the increased competition from generic manufacturers. Patents issued in the 1980s, the early period of biotechnology, have mostly expired. Without protection, sales declines of up to 80% can occur within a year of a generic product being launched.

---

[1] See H. G. Grabowski and J. Vernon, "The Distribution of Sales Revenues from Pharmaceutical Innovation," *Pharmacoeconomics* 18 Supple. 1 (2000): 21–32.

[2] See Ernst & Young, "Global Biotechnology Report 2006."

[3] See Karl Keegan, *Biotechnology Valuation—An Introductory Guide* (Chichester, UK: John Wiley & Sons, 2008).

DRUG DEVELOPMENT PROCESS

The drug development process is generally classified into seven stages:

1. *Discovery.* Finding and screening compounds in the R&D process
2. *Preclinical.* Test on animals for safety
3. *Clinical Phase I.* Safety test on 10 to 100 patients
4. *Clinical Phase II.* Safety and efficacy tests on 50 to 500 patients
5. *Clinical Phase III.* Safety and efficacy tests on 100 to 5,000 patients at several sites, should be at least 1,500
6. *Approval.* Review of tests by FDA
7. *Post Marketing–Clinical Phase IV.* Marketing surveillance and monitoring safety and efficacy

Times, Costs, and Success Rates

Time frames, costs, and success rates are important parameters in calculating values of drug firms. Exhibit 29.1 1 shows the famous data from the Center for the Study of Drug Development at Tufts University in Boston. As the numbers are averages and are differentiated by targeting diseases, they need to be modified for valuations. Key influences are:

- Reflecting time effects, inflation rates, and cost of capital, development costs (in 2000 dollars) of an average drug increased from $318 million in 1991 to $802 million in 2003; by 2005, it was $1.241 billion in current dollars.
- A biopharmaceutical requires an 8% longer development time and 14% greater costs than a regular pharmaceutical.
- In the 1990s, the duration of the preclinical, clinical, and approval stages was approximately 6 years, 6.3 years, and 1.8 years, respectively.[4]
- Development costs are roughly:

  - Discovery stages, 23%
    - Clinical phases, 35%
    - Manufacturing and scale-up, 15%
    - Miscellaneous, 17%
    - Nonclinical safety, 6%
    - Regulatory, 4%[5]

---

[4] *See J. DiMasi, "Drug Development in the United States from 1963 to 1999," **Clinical Pharmacology & Therapeutics 69**, No. 5 (2001): 286–296.*

[5] *See CMR International, "2006/2007 Pharmaceutical R&D Factbook."*

Exhibit 29.1 Times, Costs, and Success Rates of Drug Development

	Time (mos)		Success Rate (%)		Costs ($, MM)*	
					Pharma**	Bio
	Pharma	**Bio**	**Pharma**	**Bio**	**(2000 $)**	**(2005 $)**
Preclinical					1.6	59.9
Clinical phase						
I	12.3	19.5	71.0 (21)	83.7 (30)	15.2	32.3
II	26.0	29.3	44.2 (30)	56.3 (36)	16.7	31.6
III	33.8	32.9	68.5 (69)	64.2 (64)	27.1	45.3
Approval***	<u>18.2</u>	<u>16.0</u>		100	<u>1.8</u>	<u>1.6</u>
Total	<u>90.3</u>	<u>97.7</u>			<u>62.4</u>	<u>170.7</u>

   * *Out-of-pocket cost.*
  ** *From J. DiMasi, R. W. Hansen, and H. G. Grabowski, "The Price of Innovation: New Estimates of Drug Development Costs," **Journal of Health Economics** 22 (2003): 151–185.*
 *** *Current minimums.*

   *Source: All data except note 2 from J. DiMasi and H. G. Grabowski, "The Cost of Biopharmaceutical R&D: Is Biotechnology Different?" **Managerial and Decision Economics** 28 (2007): 469–479.*

Technologies, Projects, and Pipelines

Once a compound or new molecular item enters clinical trials, it is generally called a project. Usually a single compound does not go into trials but several based on the same technology platform do. Pharma companies want to have a large pipeline made up of many projects for different diseases. Although each project has a low chance of commercial success, pipelines reduce this weakness at the firm level; the more pipelines, the fewer the risks and the greater the value.

Licensing Practices

Licensing in the pharmaceutical industry is a little different from that in other technology-based areas because of the long development times and associated risks. Such contracts generally contain sequential compensation:

- Up-front payments at the start
- Milestone fees for achieving particular goals
- R&D funding
- Royalties after commercialization

In many cases licenses have sublicensing provisions. Of course, fees in later stages are higher than those in earlier stages. The objective of licensing deal terms is to share appropriately future costs and revenues. If the up-front payment is comparatively small, then the milestone fees are bigger; if both are relatively low, then they are usually compensated for in higher royalties after commercialization.

Alliances between big pharmaceuticals and biopharmaceuticals may cover several fields, developing technology, clinical trials, approvals, manufacturing, marketing, or sales, although most start with the development of technology. Between 1997 and 2002, the 20 biggest pharmaceutical firms formed nearly 1,500 alliances with biotech companies.[6] Since then the number has been increasing. Big pharmaceutical, which wants to add new pipelines by in-licenses, has money, manufacturing, and marketing abilities as well as experience with regulatory agencies; in contrast, biopharmaceutical lacks sufficient funds and experience. Alliances, if successful, create higher success rates and revenues than biopharmaceutical could by itself.

---

[6] *See Michael D. Lam, "Dangerous Liaisons," **Pharmaceutical Executive** 24, No. 5 (May 2004): 72.*

VALUATION STANDARDS AND METHODS

Valuations in this industry are related, in many aspects, to required standards, such as fair value; appropriate approaches; some specific methods; and supportable conclusions.

Technology Information

As in all sophisticated technology industries, much of the information required for valuations comes from understanding the technology, including its impact, probable applications, likely R&D time frames, success rates, and possible market sizes. Some valuators consider such information to be too complete to require further investigation. If they rely heavily on management, their conclusions may be distorted. Practitioners should open their eyes and ears to various viewpoints on the technologies and markets involved.

Fair Value

The valuation standards differentiate fair value from the other bases and recommend the Market Approach when practical. In this industry, the major purposes of valuations are fundraising, licensing, portfolio management, M&A, and IPOs. The objects of acquisitions and IPOs are mostly small biotechnology firms primarily based on technology and projects. Hence, valuations often reflect investment value rather than fair value; the valuation report should clearly state if such non-market-oriented amounts are used.

Conclusions of Value

Every valuator should present conclusions in the valuation report together with the supporting material. (See Chapter 6.) There are three kinds of conclusions: opinions, estimates, and indications. The latter are used at times when there are insufficient data. It is relatively easy to present an opinion if the subject is an established business and audited financial statements are available. If an early-stage technology, before the preclinical phase, is being valued, a more hypothetical probabilistic success rate is needed than for more normal projects. Furthermore, some breakthrough technologies have no reference points from which to estimate a success rate for the R&D costs, much less the essential clinical phases. Therefore, an estimate rather than an opinion is recommended by the standards of certain countries; the reasons for this decision should be clearly mentioned.[7]

Valuation Approaches

Sometimes all three traditional valuation approaches—income, cost or asset based, and market—may be applied to pharmaceutical firms. If any of these approaches is not used, the valuator should clarify the reasons why. It is difficult to use the cost approach in this industry until Phase I trials because the value generated by a technology or R&D project typically bears no relationship to its costs; likewise, it is also difficult to apply replacement cost or reproduction cost. The Market Approach is useful in limited cases, although it may be difficult to find comparables because subjects are often technologies or R&D projects; for an established pharmaceutical firm, any reasonable method can be selected.

Many methods within the Income Approach are very popular, such as discounted cash flow (DCF) techniques, real options analyses, and simulation analyses. Although numerous specialized models have been developed by academics, most are too complicated for practitioners and do not conform to the standards of valuation or lack transparency.

---

[7] *See Korea Valuation Association "Valuation Standards for Technology and Its Business" (2001).*

Some Acceptable Methods

Under the Income Approach, there are many methods of quantifying uncertainties, such as through sensitivity or scenario analyses. According to International Valuation Standard GN9, *Discounted Cash Flow*: "DCF may also be used to test the validity of conventional views by analysis of varying assumptions. The result of this type of sensitivity analysis is Investment value ÷ Worth. If DCF is used in this way the result should be identified as a value other than market value." Any sensitivity analyses should be treated with care and fully discussed in the valuation report.

A survey showing the valuation methods used in this industry was undertaken by Hartmann and Hassan.[8] They separated R&D and company levels, pharmaceutical and capital market service sectors. In the pharmaceutical or capital market service sectors, DCF methods are used more than 60% of the time. Multiples along with cash flows are widely used in the capital market service sector at the company but not the R&D level.

It is not clear from the survey whether the multiples are of revenues or adjustments to a market method, as this paper is focused on the use of real options analysis. Simple multiples, such as rules of thumb, are strictly restricted by valuation standards. Yet real options analyses are applied less than 30% of the time in every sector. The order of the frequency of real options use is: binomial tree, the Black-Sholes Option Pricing Model, and Geske models; the latter, sometimes called option tree, is a decision tree model reflecting options at each node.

Is it enough to use only DCF? Real options methods are likely to be used more frequently in the future. In 1959, even though the concept had been well developed for nearly a century, DCF was used by only 19% of firms surveyed, but by 1978, this figure had risen to 60%.[9] Currently, real options seem to be in the same situation as DCF was 50 years ago.

Real Options in the Industry

An option is a right but not an obligation to do something. In financial markets, it is generally a right to sell or buy something at a fixed price in the future, so it has a value. It is important to note that the option value is not for the object itself but for the right to sell or buy it. Thanks to Black and Sholes in the early 1970s, the value of this right can be calculated relatively easily. Since the mid-1980s, the concepts of financial options have been extended to operating activities as "real" options; these spread broadly in late 1990s and have become popular in academia.

An option to *buy* is called a call while one to *sell* is a put. Based on the way it may be exercised, there are two main types of each: European, which are exercisable only at maturity, and American, which may be exercised at any time up to maturity. When these concepts are applied to the pharmaceutical industry, R&D is looked on as a call option; if the project succeeds, there is a right but not a requirement to proceed to the next step. As this right requires finishing the previous R&D step, it is a European option.

VALUATION METHODS

The balance of this chapter briefly discusses well-known DCF methods and three real options techniques: binomial tree, option tree, and Black-Sholes. In early 2000, the Korea

---

[8] *Hartmann and Hassan, "Application of Real Options Analysis for Pharmaceutical R&D Project Valuation—Empirical Results from a Survey," **Research Policy** 35 (2006): 343–354*

[9] *See T. E. Copeland and A. Vladimir, "Real Options: A Practitioner's Guide," Texere LLC, 2000.*

Valuation Association recommended real options methods.[10] Scenario methods for estimating sales are also dealt with briefly.

DCF with Probabilities

Normal discounted cash flows or net present value methods need to be adjusted in this industry, as the cash flow for each stage cannot be projected directly but only through an anticipated success rate (p). Reflecting this, present values (PV) should be calculated as shown in equation 29.1.

$$PV = \sum p_i \, K_i \, / \, (1+r)^i \qquad (29.1)$$

Where

p	=	probability of success
K	=	revenue of each year
r	=	discount rate

Decision trees. A six-stage decision tree reflecting the typical drug development process until sales are achieved is shown in Exhibit 29.2. Any particular stage can go forward only if the previous one is successful; the discounted present value is calculated using equation 29.1.

Exhibit 29.2 Six-Stage Decision Tree

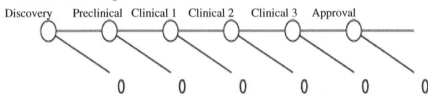

Real Options

Several methods are used to apply real option analyses to drug development. The difference between them and DCF, from the mathematical point of view, lies in two aspects: discount rate and probabilities. Traditional DCF frequently uses WACC (weighted average cost of capital) for the discount rate and empirical probabilities; real options analyses use the risk-free rate and risk-neutral probabilities.

Binomial lattice. A four-stage binomial lattice model is shown in Exhibit 29.3; at each step, there is movement either up or down. The figure at node A_0 may move either up to A_{11} or down to A_{12}. At A_{11} and A_{12}, each node proceeds with up or down, while down from node A_{11}, A_{22}, is the same as up from node A_{12}; this process proceeds to further stages at a rate of u and d, as shown in equation 29.2.

$$u = e \sqrt[3]{t} \qquad d = 1/u \qquad (29.2)$$

Where

e	=	2.718 $\sigma^2 t$	=	log variance of the price during period of time t

---

[10] *See S. Seol and C. Yoo, "Professional Real Option Models for the Valuation of Technology and Investments," **Korea Technology Innovation Society Journal** 5, No. 1 44–58.*

Exhibit 29.3 Four-Stage Binomial Lattice Model

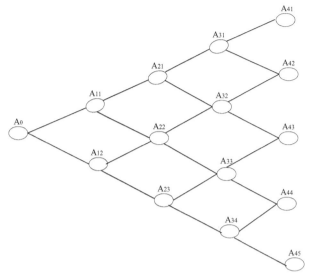

The option value at a particular node (NOV) is calculated using equation 29.1 and the risk-neutral probability by equation 29.2.

$$e - r \times t$$

$$OV = \{P \times C^+ + (1 - P) \times C\} / e^{-r \times t} \quad (29.3)$$

$$P = \{e^{r \times t} - d\} / (u - d) \quad (29.4)$$

Where

OV	=	option value at node i
C^+	=	up at time t
C^-	=	down at time t
P	=	risk-neutral probability
r	=	risk free rate

In Exhibit 29.3, assume A_{41} is 1,000, A_{42} is 600, A_{43} is 300, A_{44} is 120, is A_{45} 80, as different scenarios for sales revenues, the risk-free rate is 6%, the period of each stage is 1 year, and volatility 30%. The results are shown in Exhibit 29.4. This value can be compared to the needed investments at each stage to become net positive or negative amount.

Exhibit 29.4 Calculation of Option Value of Exhibit 29.3

t =0	t =1	t =2	t =3	Sales (t =4)
				1000
			764	
		606		600
	472		431	
363		323		300
	242		202	
		152		120
			95	
				80

NOTE: u = 1.35, d = 0.51, p = 0.527, OV = (0.527*C⁺ +0.473*C⁻)/1.06

Exhibit 29.4 is an example of the calculations for a four-stage binomial model that may be applied to four-stage development process from Clinical Phase I to sales, if the expected R&D costs at each stage are considered.

Option Tree

Although the binomial lattice model is very useful in option analyses, the structure is somewhat strange for valuators because the down price from one node may be different from the up price from another. Therefore, practitioners have changed the lattice structure to a decision tree to create the option tree model; this exists in several versions with slightly different names. Whatever the name, the meaning and calculations are the same.

Consider a simple two-stage option tree as Exhibit 29.5, using these data:

R&D expense	$6 million	Commercialization cost	$15 million
WACC	12%	Risk-free rate	6%
R&D success rate	30%	Good market probability	80%
Time: 1 year each			

The process is to calculate: (1) the option value (OV) for each node in the tree, (2) the risk-neutral probability based on the values at each tree, and (3) the option value. The OVs are calculated using equation 29.3. Risk-neutral probability is calculated by equation 29.4. Finally, an option value is obtained from equation 29.5, deducting related costs or investments.

$$OV_0 = \{P \times C^+ + (1 - P) \times C^-\} \times e^{-r_e \Delta^t} - I_0 \qquad (29.5)$$

Exhibit 29.5 Two-Stage Option Tree Model

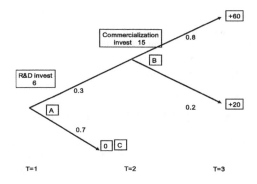

The calculations are shown next. In this model, the option value at each node represents the value of the R&D inputs assuming success.

Value at Each Node

B:	$\{(0.8 \times 60) + (0.2 \times 20)\} / 1.12$	=	46.4
Net B:	$46.4 - 15$	=	31.4
A:	$\{(0.3 \times 31.4) + (0.7 \times 0)\} / 1.12$	=	8.4

Risk-Neutral Probability

B to good sales:	$(1.06 \times 46.4 - 20) / (60 - 20)$	=	0.73
A to B:	$(1.06 \times 8.4 - 0) / (31.4 - 0)$	=	0.28

Option Value

OV_B	=	$(0.73 \times 60 + 0.27 \times 20) / (1.06)$	=	36.2
OV_A	=	$(0.28 \times 31.4 + 0.72 \times 0) / (1.06)$	=	8.3

Black-Sholes

The Black-Sholes option pricing model, which is widely used for established companies (especially by capital market participants), is not frequently applied to projects in the drug industry. It is most suitable for financial markets in which the price of underlying assets is assumed to be determined by a stochastic process reflecting the growth rate and volatility; a call option price is determined by equation 29.6.

$$OV = S \times N\,(d_1) - K \times e^{-rt} \times N(d_2) \qquad (29.6)$$

$$d_1 = \frac{\ln\left(\dfrac{S}{K}\right) + \left(r + \dfrac{\sigma^2}{2}\right)t}{\sqrt[\sigma]{t}}$$

$$d_2 = d_1 - \sqrt[\sigma]{t}$$

Where

OV	=	option value
S	=	asset price
K	=	strike price
T	=	time
r	=	risk-free rate
σ^2	=	volatility
N (·)	=	accumulated normal distribution

This model is popular as it needs only six items of data, all of which are easy to obtain in financial markets. N (·) is an accumulated normal distribution, which is easily found in most finance or statistics textbooks or through the NORMSDIST (d) function in Microsoft Excel. Assume the asset price is $100.00, exercise price after 1 year is $103.00, risk-free rate is 5%, $N(d_1)$ is 0.6, and $N(d_2)$ is 0.4. The option value is then calculated as:

$$OV = 100 \times 0.6 - 103 \times 0.4 / 2.718^{0.05} = \$20.80$$

KEY VARIABLES FOR VALUATION

Understanding the business, rather than valuation methods, is the primary difficulty in valuing drug firms. The valuator's knowledge of the industry should reflect the specific data shown in Exhibit 29.6. The information falls into three segments: input data (discussed earlier), output, and valuation. As the discount and risk-free rates have been discussed, the balance of this chapter concentrates on outputs.

Exhibit 29.6 Variables for Valuation in Drug Industry

Input	Output	Valuation
R&D costs, each stage	Revenue of each year	Discount rate
Duration time, each stage	Possible sales/years	Risk-free rate
Success rate, each stage	Exclusivity period of sales	
General costs	Sharing rate of license	

Information Sources

Although a valuator may be very familiar with the drug industry, it is likely he or she will not know the details of each market. Fortunately, there are many reference sources; good industry overviews are Ernst & Young's *"Annual Biotechnology Report"* and CMR International's *"Pharmaceutical R&D Factbook."* Detailed material can also be found in patent and licensing databases at various national patent and trademark offices and numerous pharmaceutical licensing databases. In addition a number of market reviews cover either diseases or countries.

Exclusivity of Drug Sales

Patents provide legal exclusivity for 20 years, but the effective protection period is less since most patents are registered at early R&D stages. A famous study indicates that market exclusivity averaged 13.8 years from 1995 to 2001 but fell to 11.2 years for 2002 to 2005.[11] After a patent expires, generic drugs are sold at lower prices, sometimes with discounts of up to 80%. In a few cases, sales exclusivity is lengthened by the extension of a patent or FDA action based on the specificity of a drug; it is essential for the valuator to verify this situation country by country.

Sales Estimates

In recent years, Lipitor has been the best-selling drug in the world, with 2007 revenues of US $6.15 billion; in that year, there were 37 blockbusters (drugs with revenues of over $1 billion each). However, at that time, the average revenue of the top 200 best-selling drugs was only $144 million.[12] These numbers give a valuator some insight as to possible sales revenues; all biotech researchers think their candidates are potential blockbusters, but the reality is that they are not.

Just as in other industries, sales revenues are estimated in two ways: top down and bottom up.[13] A top-down estimate is relatively simple if the market size for the drug is known; it simply requires multiplying that figure by the anticipated market share; this must not be mechanical but involves careful identification of different geographical markets and the possible need of several versions, as delivery patterns vary by country. Although good products can be sold in many countries with different market shares, each situation must be considered separately.

Bottom-up techniques are somewhat more complicated. The valuator has to

1. Identify the size of the symptomatic population in each potential market.
2. Determine the number diagnosed annually.
3. Identify the patients who might be helped.
4. Determine the number of potential users for the drug.
5. Establish potential prices depending on country patterns in drug pricing.
6. Determine the number of versions needed, and ascertain their anticipated total revenues.

Sales patterns. On average, 80% of peak sales happen five years after the launch date, and 90% after 10 years.[14] Thus, a valuator needs to know the anticipated sales curve during the exclusive period. There are three general patterns:

1. Quick increase in the early years followed by stable use until peak sales.
2. Slow increases at the beginning followed by quicker gains until peak sales.
3. Steady increases to peak sales.

---

[11] H. G. Grabowski and M. Kyle, "Generic Competition and Market Exclusivity Periods in Pharmaceuticals," *Managerial and Decision Economics* 28 (2007): 491–502.

[12] See www.drugs.com/top200.htm.

[13] See A. G. Cook, *Forecasting for the Pharmaceutical Industry, Models for New Product and In-Market Forecasting and How to Use Them* (Burlington, VT: Gower Publishing Co., 2006).

[14] Grabowski and Vernon, "The Distribution of Sales Revenues from Pharmaceutical Innovation."

The correct patterns are determined by the marketing and distribution abilities of the firms involved; better drugs do not always mean higher sales.

It is difficult for the valuator and the firm's marketing staff to estimate expected revenues. It is desirable to use three (best, average, and worst case) sales scenarios and calculate values for each; they are then combined using probabilities. In this situation, the valuator must clarify the facts and rationale for each scenario.

Sharing Earnings

In this industry, there are many reasons to license technology. In earlier stages, the lower share goes to the licensor; this increases in later stages. Examples of sharing rates are shown in Exhibit 29.7.

Exhibit 29.7 Typical Sharing Rates in Licenses

	Licensor	Licensee
Preclinical	10-20%	80-90%
IND (Investigational New Drug Application)	20-40%	60-80%
Phase I to III	40-60%	40-60%
Approval	60-80%	20-40%

*Source: B. Bogdan and R. Villiger, **Valuation in Life Science**, 2nd ed. (Berlin: Springer, 2008), p. 153.*

Licensing fees are comprised of several kinds of compensation. Generally they include up-front payments, milestone fees, and royalties, which may make it difficult to determine the total in each period. As valuators need to cover both technologies and projects, they should consider the composition of each element at every stage. The spirit of fair value is that no party should get more benefits than any other.

Example

Biotech, with only a single drug candidate entering Phase II, has been offered an alliance by Pharmaceutical with these terms:

- $10 million up front on the start of Phase II
- $15 million on the start of Phase III trial
- $20 million on approval
- $20 million on launch
- A 20% royalty on net sales

The sales exclusivity is 12 years and annual revenues of $400 million are expected at the launch. The discount rate for Biotech is estimated at 15%, and 12% for Pharmaceutical. The other key numbers are:

	Phase I	Phase II	Phase III	Approval	Sales Exclusivity
Time	1 yr	2 yrs	3 yrs	1 yr	12 yrs
Probability	0.84	0.56	0.64	0.90	-
Costs ($M)	32	31	45	2	-

	t=0	t=1	t=2	t=3	t=4	t=5	t=6	t=7–18
Costs/Revenues	(32)	(15)	(16)	(15)	(15)	(15)	(2)	400.0

The valuator has been asked to answer these questions:

1. What is the NPV of the candidate for Biotech at Phase I without considering an alliance?
2. What is the NPV to Biotech at the start of alliance after success in Phase I?
3. What is the NPV to Pharmaceutical at the start of alliance with the assumption of no more sales by Pharmaceutical?
4. Why are there different calculations for Biotech and Pharmaceutical?
5. If the sharing rate is 40% to 60%, are the terms fair?

Answer 1: US $0.1 million

	t0	t1	t2	t3	t4	t5	t6	t7–18
Status	Phase I	PII–1	PII–2	PIII–1	PIII–2	PIII–3	Approval	Launch
Probability	0.84		0.56			0.64	0.9	
Costs/Revenues	(32.0)	(15.0)	(16.0)	(15.0)	(15.0)	(15.0)	(2.0)	
PV costs r=15	(27.8)	(11.3)	(10.5)	(8.6)	(7.5)	(6.5)	(0.8)	400.0
NPV	0.1		27.9			71.8	134.7	150.4

Answer 2: –20.1 million
Answer 3: 25.2 million

	t1	t2	t3	t4	t5	t6	t7	t8–19
Biotech								
Probability	1.00		0.56			0.64	0.9	
Costs/Revenues	(32.0)	(15.0)	(16.0)	(15.0)	(15.0)	(15.0)	(2.0)	
PV cost r=15	(27.8)	(11.3)	(10.5)	(8.6)	(7.5)	(6.5)	(0.8)	400.0
NPV royalty 20% – costs	(28.8)		(10.4)			3.3	26.4	30.1
Fees	10.0		15.0			20.0	20.0	
PV fees r=15	8.7		9.9			8.6	7.5	
NPV after deal	(20.1)		(1.0)			11.1	33.9	
Pharmaceutical								
Probability	1.00		0.56			0.64	0.9	
Fees	(10.0)		(15.0)			(20.0)	(20.0)	400.0
PV fees r=12	(8.9)		(10.7)			(10.1)	(9.0)	
NPV 80%	25.2		34.2			71.7	122.1	144.8

Answer 4: Values with different perspectives are necessary to achieve fair shares.
Answer 5: Not fair as Pharmaceutical has a positive NPV and Biotech has a negative one.

30 PLANT AND EQUIPMENT

EVŽEN KÖRNER

GERMANY

INTRODUCTION

This chapter provides guidance concerning the valuation process specific to plant and equipment, often a significant portion of assets of many entities. It is a category of personal property and is referred to in various standards as plant and machinery or machinery and equipment.

What Is Plant and Equipment?

International Valuation Guidance Note (IVGN) 3, *Valuation of Plant and Equipment*, paragraph 3.2, states that plant and equipment are fixed tangible assets, other than real estate, that are: (a) held by an entity for use in the production or supply of goods or services, for rental to others, or for administrative purposes, and (b) expected to be used during more than one accounting period.

The classes of plant and equipment are:

- *Plant.* Production assets that are inextricably combined with others. They may include specialized buildings, machinery, and equipment.
- *Machinery.* Individual machines or collections of machines; a machine is an apparatus used for a specific process in connection with the operations of the entity.
- *Equipment.* Other assets, such as computers, that are used to assist the operations of the entity.

APPLICABLE STANDARDS

Under International Accounting Standard (IAS) 16, *Property, Plant and Equipment*, these assets may be included in an entity's balance sheet at either depreciated replacement cost less impairment (cost model) or at fair value at the date of revaluation less subsequent depreciation less impairment (fair value model) (IAS 16.29, 30, 31). *Fair value* is defined by IAS 16.4 as "the amount for which an asset could be exchanged or liability settled between knowledgeable willing parties in an arm's-length transaction."

Types of Value

The *fair value* of items of plant and equipment is usually their market value determined by an appraisal. Under International Financial Reporting Standards (IFRS), fair value is normally, but not always, equated to market value, defined by International Valuation Standard (IVS) 1:3.3) as "the estimated amount for which a property should exchange on the date of valuation between a willing buyer and willing seller in an arm's-length transaction after proper marketing wherein the parties had each acted knowledgeably, prudently, and without any compulsion." Plant and equipment, together with other fixed assets, may be subject to other standards, including IAS 2, *Inventories*; IAS 17, *Leases*; IAS 36 *Impairment of Assets*; IFRS 3, *Business Combinations*; and IFRS 5, *Noncurrent Assets Held for Sale and Discontinued Operations*.

Market value stipulates that an exchange is assumed to take place on an arm's-length basis, between knowledgeable and willing parties; it does not imply any particular sale method such as through a dealer or by auction; however, it requires that the sale is made after proper marketing in the most appropriate manner. It is implicit in the definition that the method should be the one that will achieve the highest price for the asset in the given set of circumstances. The definition is, however, silent as to any specific situations that might have a fundamental effect on the valuation.

When undertaking a valuation of plant and equipment, the valuator must establish and explain any additional assumptions that are appropriate, taking into consideration the nature of the asset and the purpose of the valuation. (See IVGN 3.5.2.)

While market value, as defined by IVS, implies using all valuation approaches for plant and equipment, the assumption of "market-based evidence" gives preferences to a sales comparison method under the Market Approach or a capitalization method under the Income Approach, on the basis that they rely on market-derived data. Adherence to market-based definitions, objectivity, and full disclosure of relevant matters are fundamental to all valuations for financial reporting.

Financial statements are produced on the assumption that the entity is a going concern unless management intends to liquidate it, cease trading, or has no realistic alternative but to do so (see IAS 1, para. 23). This assumption underlies the application of fair value to plant and equipment, except when there is either an intention to dispose of a particular asset or the option of disposal has to be considered, such as in an impairment test.

Valuations under IAS 16, *Property, Plant and Equipment*

The depreciated replacement cost (DRC) method is considered acceptable under IAS 16.33, when there is insufficient direct market evidence to arrive at fair value from market-based observations. DRC is defined by IVS 1.3.1 as "the current cost of replacing an asset with its modern equivalent asset less deduction for physical deterioration and all relevant forms of obsolescence and optimization."

International Public Sector Accounting Standard (IPSAS) 17, *Property, Plant and Equipment*, paragraph 43, prescribes the use of depreciated replacement cost for valuing items of plant and equipment of a specialized nature, such as "a property that is rarely if ever sold in the market, except by the way of sale of the business or entity of which it is part, due to uniqueness arising from its specialized nature and design, its configuration, size, location, or otherwise" (see also International Valuation Standards [IVS] 1.3.4). However, the classification of an asset as such does not automatically lead to the conclusion that DRC has to be adopted. Even though an asset is specialized, still, it may be possible to gather sufficient market evidence to use a sales comparison or an income capitalization method.

Values are to be reported in accordance with IVS 3, *Valuation Reporting*. To meet the requirements of IAS 16.77, the report must include:

- The effective date of the valuation
- Whether an independent (external under IVS) valuator was involved
- The methods and significant assumptions applied
- The extent to which the values were determined directly by reference to observable prices in an active market or recent market transactions on arm's-length terms, or were estimated by another technique

Valuations under IAS 17, *Leasing*

If a lease is classified as a finance lease under IAS 17, *Leases,* the fair value of the related asset is required to be determined in order to establish the amounts of both the asset and liability to be recorded by the entity on its balance sheet (IAS 17.7).

Valuations under IAS 36, IFRS 3, and IFRS 5

Impairment testing (IAS 36), business combinations (IFRS 3) and discontinued operations (IFRS 5) are discussed elsewhere in this book; none of these standards has special requirements related to the valuation of plant and equipment.

Valuations under IAS 40, *Investment Property*

Under IAS 40, *Investment Property*, an entity may opt to account for its property using the fair value model; if so it is assumed that the requirements are met by a valuator determining market value. Similar to a valuation under IAS 16, one under IAS 40 requires disclosing in the report the methods and significant assumptions adopted, including a statement whether the fair value is supported by market-based evidence or is based on other factors due to the nature of the property and lack of comparable transactions. The report must also state if the valuation was performed by an independent individual who holds recognized and relevant professional qualifications and who has recent experience in the location and category of the subject. As plant and equipment is not typically investment property, this standard may not be fully applicable.

VALUATION OF PLANT AND EQUIPMENT

There are three internationally recognized approaches to value: market, income, and cost. Each has certain strengths and weaknesses, and their application depends on the purpose, type of property involved, nature of the market, and availability of specific data that a valuator must consider in every project. It should be noted that all of these approaches should reflect, when possible, market data. When a variety of information sources are relied on, such as cost new of a property, exchanges in used markets, or rates of return required by investors, each should reflect the circumstances prevailing in a particular market at the valuation date.

In comparing the results of the various methods selected, the valuator has to analyze the strengths and weaknesses of each and must weigh the relevant factors to reach a supportable conclusion. Theoretically, all methods should yield the same result, but in reality, this is often not the case. The appraiser must reconcile the facts and circumstances applicable and consider the data, the premise of value, and the assumptions employed. Although all these approaches are discussed in other chapters, there are some specifics when applied to valuing plant and equipment.

MARKET APPROACH

The direct sales comparison method is the most common under the Market Approach. This is based on the assumption that an informed purchaser would not pay more for an item than the cost of acquiring an existing one with the same utility. This method is preferred when valuing plant and equipment for which there is a known and active secondary market. In applying it under the "in-use" premise, consideration should be given to the cost to acquire similar items of used equipment; an allowance then is made to reflect the costs of delivery, installation, taxes, fees, and duties.

A variant of the method is the use of market relationships. Recent market prices for items of plant, machinery, and equipment in a particular asset class that has an active secondary market are reviewed with respect to age and condition. Then they are compared with a benchmark price, such as the duplication (reproduction) cost new (DCN). The ratios of the market prices to benchmark amounts are applied to similar assets in the class if the specific secondary market is too thin to exhibit sufficient, appropriate, direct comparables.

Application of Sales Comparison Method

The sales comparison method is preferred under all valuation and accounting standards; it is particularly applicable when there are active markets with sufficient reliable information. In inactive markets, it is relatively unsatisfactory as the available data may not truly be representative. In addition, the valuator should carefully examine the reliability of transaction prices and ensure they are truly comparable assets. A critical factor in this method is the identification of the relevant market, which can range in scope from being highly localized to global. Supply and demand, indicated by the availability and desirability of comparable items, is the major determinant of transaction prices.

The market analysis can be made on either a direct or a statistical basis:

- Direct by comparing subject with identical or very similar items that have been sold
- Statistical by examining a significant sample of market transactions to establish similarities and dissimilarities of various attributes

While direct matching provides the best indication of market value, the process of finding identical or very similar items may be somewhat lengthy and require consideration of the different items of equipment involved, distinguishing them by model, size, capacity, and the like. There is no guarantee that the valuator will find any direct comparables.

Therefore, in practice, statistical comparisons are generally used because they have the advantage that data can be collected and analyzed in advance, providing immediate information when needed for a specific assignment. Moreover, such information can be also used, where appropriate, for direct matching. An additional benefit is that market data collected over long periods and on a global (rather than a local) basis can supply information regarding:

- Past changes and general trends in specific markets
- Variations in geographically different but economically similar markets (e.g., between Germany and France)
- Identification of a lack of demand for a specific brand, thus resulting in discounted or lower prices (e.g., Atlas Copco or Kaeser air compressors, assuming the same capacity, vintage, etc.)

Although not necessarily important for a particular engagement, such input is vital in understanding the entire market and providing the valuator with expert knowledge.

Market Data

The most common sources of market data are published auction results and transactions reported by dealers in similar items. When comparing an item with its counterpart in the secondhand market, the valuator has to consider, among other factors:

- Characteristics: physical condition, capacity, utility, functionality
- Time of sale
- Location and economic differences in the locality
- Conditions of sale
- Financing, if any
- Reliability of the data
- If it was an arm's-length transaction

Prices used as the basis of comparison may be:

- Dealer's asking
- Dealer's selling
- Auction
- Direct offer of surplus equipment
- Direct exchange between parties
- Unspecified sources

Actual sales prices, such as by a dealer or a direct exchange between parties, provide reasonably reliable information about completed transactions; however, even they may need adjustments, depending on the specific purpose of the valuation or the nature of the transactions.

Typically auctions are considered the last resort before scrapping if the assets could not be disposed of through an orderly or forced liquidation process. As such, they typically represent the lower end of an item's value. Auctions provide reasonable information for liquidation values, but their applicability for any other purpose must be carefully considered.

The Internet represents a huge source of data on equipment sales, but there is great difficulty in establishing the nature of the transactions or offerings. Therefore, even the most experienced valuator needs to exercise caution. Reported prices for unspecific types of sale should be considered somewhat unreliable because of the impossibility of making appropriate adjustment. However, they are a useful cross check to other methods, especially for rarely exchanged assets.

Example: Market Approach, Sales Comparison Method

The fair value is to be estimated for a rotary vane air compressor, made by CompAir, model 68 PUAS, capacity 1.75 m^3/min, 8bars, 11 kW, 14 years old. An analysis of current transaction data did not reveal any sales of similar items; thus a review of the broader market was conducted.

Through an independent market research firm, sales were identified of 14 compressors with similar capacity from 1.15m^3/min to 4.6m^3/min, 3 to 26 years old and from a variety of manufacturers, including CompAir. Their transaction prices were measured against that of a new model to determine a relative price ("percent-good" factor) for each comparable. Exhibit 30.1 shows the distribution.

Exhibit 30.1 Relative Prices (Percent Good) in Sales of Air Compressors Compounded with Age

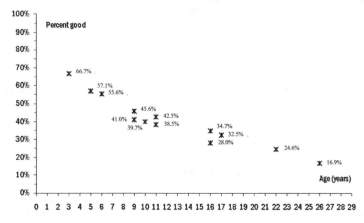

The data were further processed by regression analysis to identify any pattern in the market which could be applied to the subject. This returned an R^2 of 0.9641 and a standard error of

0.0763, which means that over 96% of the comparable data is represented by the regression. The data and the regression curve are shown in Exhibit 30.2.

Exhibit 30.2 Regression Curve of Relative Prices of Air Compressors against Age

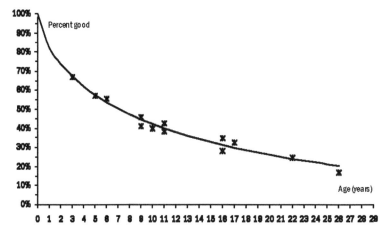

Although there were no transactions at the subject's age, the regression curve indicates that a 14-year-old compressor sells for around 35% of the new price of a similar item, as shown in Exhibit 30.3.

Exhibit 30.3 Indication of Price of Subject (14-year old) Compressor from Regression Curve

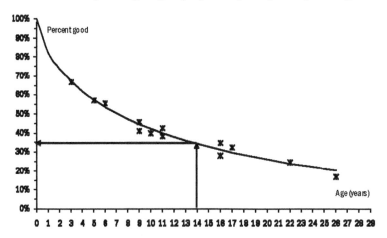

The subject equipment was in average condition, adequately maintained for its age and past use. As such, no further adjustment was necessary. Based on quotes from three dealers, the new price for this model is $9,763; the concluded fair value by the sales comparison method under the Market Approach is $3,400 ($9,763 × 35% = $3,417) rounded.

INCOME APPROACH

The Income Approach is based on the principle that an informed buyer would pay no more for a property than an amount equal to the present worth of anticipated future benefits (income) from the same or equivalent property with similar risks. The most convenient method, discounting future cash flows, is mostly applicable to investment and general-use properties where there is an established and identifiable rental market or where a specific measurable stream of benefits may be attributed to the subject. In applying this method to plant and equipment, consideration is given to either the income-generating or the cost-savings potential of the item and the associated risks and uncertainties.

Benefits Capitalization

The benefits capitalization method presents a number of obstacles. First, for most plant and equipment, the potential earnings (benefits) cannot be reasonably separated from those of the overall business; similarly; often, information regarding their respective operating costs is unavailable. Additionally, it is difficult to develop one of the most critical factors: the discount rate. When valuing an entity, there is an enormous amount of comparable market-based data; for items of plant and equipment, the valuator must seek out alternatives. The category is not as liquid as current assets, although, as discussed, many items have some marketability. The risks of specialized items or those involving unique technologies are typically higher than for units with alternative uses. Therefore, the risks and returns associated with plant and equipment are higher than those for current assets.

Ideally, the best source of required returns comes from investors who directly participate in various markets; however, this information is usually confidential; therefore, indirect methods have to be applied to determine supportable rates of return.

Suitable Techniques

The best technique for such a purpose is the *market method*. With this, the selling prices of comparable investments are compared to anticipated future benefits to derive an indication of the implicit rates of return. This method suffers from the same problem, a general lack of market-based data, as the direct approach. A second technique sometimes employed is the *comparison of quality attributes method* in which the desirability of the subject is compared to that of alternatives having known rates of return. A third, the *build-up method,* starts from a known risk-free rate to which factors are added for additional risks, the burdens of management, and the lack of liquidity to derive a suitable rate of return.

Finally, the weighted average return on assets (WARA) method may be used. This is based on the assumption that a business is a portfolio of financial, physical, and intangible assets. In other words, the fair value of the long-term debt plus that of the equity is equal to the sum of the fair values of net working capital and fixed and intangible assets. WARA is the rate of return of each category weighted by its fair value; the advantage is that the overall rate of return can be tested against that of the business using market-based information. The disadvantages, however, include the necessity of identifying and quantifying every asset owned by the entity including implicit goodwill.

Restrictions on the Income Approach

When an income method is applied to plant and equipment using an earnings stream based on a proportion of the overall entity (not on market rentals), the valuator must subtract returns on contributory assets. Those include net working capital, real property, operational know-how, trademarks and trade names, customer relationships, an assembled workforce, and other inherent intangible assets. However, a value derived by this method inevitably includes elements of goodwill and, as such, is overstated.

Taking into account all those factors, it is clear that the Income Approach is limited to plant and equipment (which may be leased out at a specific market rent) or to assets that are by nature cash generating, such as power or process plants being valued as a whole.

Example: Income Approach, Discounted Cash Flows Method

The subject in this example is a 4-axle SHIMMNS specialized rail car, designed to transport coils of steel plate in a horizontal position. To protect them from the weather, it has a folding tarpaulin, with an anticondensation layer to prevent dripping on the coils, whose supports move on little wheels along the sides of the rail car; when closed the tarpaulin can be locked at the car's ends.

Assumptions

The rail car is assumed to have eight years of remaining life (until the end of 2016), after which it will be scrapped for its estimated current metal content of $8,000. The basic technical parameters are listed next.

Number of axles	4
Wheelbase of rail car	7,000 mm
Length over buffers	12,040 mm
Loading width	2,400 mm
Floor height above top of rails	4,277 mm
Bogie type	Y 25 Lsd
Automatic brake	KE-GP
Loading capacity	68.0 tonnes
Maximum load per axle	22.5 tonnes

At present, the rail car is rented to a nonaffiliated company at $20 per day, until the end of 2010. From then on, the rent will be adjusted for estimated long-term inflation of 2%. From 2011 to 2016, utilization is assumed to drop to 95%, with the remaining 5% (i.e., 18 days) being the estimated time to find a user.

The current costs adjusted for expected future inflation for periodic refurbishments, wheel set replacements, reprofiling, maintenance, and operating expenses, which include its management, are shown next.

	2009	2010	2011	2012	2013	2014	2015	2016
Refurbishment	4,000	4,080	4,162	4,245	4,330	4,416	4,505	4,595
Wheelsets	10,000	10,200	10,404	10,612	10,824	11,041	11,262	11,487
Reprofiling	1,500	1,530	1,561	1,592	1,624	1,656	1,689	1,723
General maintenance	500	510	520	531	541	552	563	574
Salvage value	8,000	8,160	8,323	8,490	8,659	8,833	9,009	9,189
Operating expenses	2,000	2,040	2,081	2,122	2,165	2,208	2,252	2,297

Based on discussions with the client's engineering staff as well as a review of past practice, it was established that refurbishment and reprofiling will take place in 2011 and 2015, while a wheel set replacement will occur only in 2015; general maintenance is undertaken each year.

Rates of Return

The discount rate was developed based on a WARA model, using Bloomberg data; weighted average cost of capital (WACC) for the entity was estimated at 8.6%:

	Cost	Capital Structure	Weighted Cost
Equity	14.0%	40.0%	5.6%
Debt after tax	5.0%	60.0%	3.0%

The return on current assets was estimated at 4.5% using, after tax, a short-term debt rate of London Inter-Bank Offered Rate plus 1%, while the return on the associated intangible assets and goodwill is equal to the cost of equity (14.0%).

Assuming the fixed assets, which include the rail car, are typically financed with 65% long-term debt, their return is 8.2%:

	Cost	Capital Structure	Weighted Cost
Equity	14.0%	35.0%	4.9%
Debt after tax	5.0%	65.0%	3.3%
Return on tangible assets			8.2%

In this example, for simplicity, WARA is based on net book value, but, in reality, it may be necessary to value all assets. The calculated WARA is equal to WACC, which means that the return on Net Book Value (NBV) of the assets supports the overall return on the business, and thus the return on tangible assets of 8.2% is appropriate.

	Cost	Returns	Weighted Cost
Current Assets	3,000	4.5%	135
Tangible Assets	10,000	8.2%	820
Intangible Assets (+ Goodwill)	3,000	14.0%	420
WARA	16,000	8.6%	1,375

Present Value Calculations

Based on expected revenues and costs, operating cash flows were calculated and discounted at 8.2% using the midyear convention, to give $12,811 as the present value of the future income. To this must be added $5,081, the present value of the expected scrap receipt, to arrive at $18,000 rounded as the fair value of the rail car under the Income Approach. The next table shows calculation of Discounted Cash Flows.

	2009	2010	2011	2012	2013	2014	2015	2016
Rent per day	20.0	20.0	20.4	20.8	21.2	21.6	22.1	22.5
Utilization/tenant change & loss of rent	100%	100%	95%	95%	95%	95%	95%	95%
Rentable days	365	365	347	347	347	347	347	347
Net revenues	7,300	7,300	7,079	7,220	7,365	7,512	7,662	7,816
Cost of revisions	0	0	(4,162)	0	0	0	(4,505)	0
Cost of wheelsets	0	0	0	0	0	0	(11,262)	0
Cost of reprofiling	0	0	(1,561)	0	0	0	(1,689)	0
General maintenance cost	(500)	(510)	(520)	(531)	(541)	(552)	(563)	(574)
Other operating expenses	(2,000)	(2,040)	(2,081)	(2,122)	(2,165)	(2,208)	(2,252)	(2,297)
Operating expenses	(2,500)	(2,550)	(8,323)	(2,653)	(2,706)	(2,760)	(20,271)	(2,872)
Operating income	4,800	4,750	(1,244)	4,567	4,659	4,752	(12,609)	4,944
Discount periods	0.500	1.500	2.500	3.500	4.500	5.500	6.500	7.500
Present value factor @ 8.2% discount rate	0.9614	0.8885	0.8212	0.7589	0.7014	0.6483	0.5991	0.5537
Present value of income	4,615	4,220	(1,022)	3,466	3,268	3,080	(7,554)	2,738
Salvage value								9,189
Present value of salvage value								5,088
Sum of present values	12,811							
Plus: present value of salvage value	5,088							
Indicated fair value	17,899							
Indicated fair value (rounded)	**18,000**							

COST APPROACH

The Cost Approach is based on the principle that assets decrease in value (or depreciate) through aging, changes in functional utility, as well as from negative external influences. The underlying assumption is that an informed purchaser would not pay more for an item than the cost of a substitute with the same utility and functionality. Methods under this approach generally provide a meaningful indication of value for specialized items associated with a viable business or justified by economic demand.

The Cost Approach offers the only applicable methods under any of these conditions:

- When valuing property that is not traded.
- Market transactions of comparable items are not available.
- Data cannot be extrapolated from larger transactions.
- Transactions are nonexistent.
- There is lack of financial data concerning the subject property.

It should be noted that application of the Cost Approach is not without problems. The major difficulties are measuring economic obsolescence and avoiding dependence on the valuator's subjective judgments.

Application of Cost Approach

The starting point of the Cost Approach is the determination of the duplication (reproduction) cost new (DCN) or the replacement cost new (RCN). The cost to reproduce or replace the subject with a new asset, either identical (reproduction) or having the same utility (replacement), establishes the highest amount a prudent investor is likely to pay for new and unused property. Included in the DCN and RCN are both direct and indirect costs, including fees; full details of each method are set out in Chapter 2.

To determine either the DCN or RCN for plant and equipment, these methods can be used:

- Trending method
- Direct pricing
- Benchmarking techniques

Trending method. The application of the trending method presumes that the current value of plant and equipment may be obtained from the original (historic) acquisition cost, which typically is recorded in the entity's records, through adjusting (multiplying) it by an appropriate price index.

Appropriate price indices are available from statistical organizations in many countries. Other sources include manufacturers, the engineering community, professional bodies, or insurance companies, especially when estimating cost new for their policies. If the item was purchased in another country, it is necessary to adjust the indices for differences not only in the relative prices but also in exchange rates. For example, a German manufacturer sells equipment to a customer in Morocco. In such a case, the valuator has to convert the original cost in Moroccan dinars to the supplier's currency (euros) at the current exchange rate. This amount is then adjusted by a suitable German index and, finally, converted back into dinars at the current rate. Under this method, at times the DCN or RCN may be lower than original acquisition price due to price and currency changes.

The trending method is applicable generally and provides a reliable result when the subject is:

- *Relatively new.* The trending method takes into account average price change. It would be rather naive to believe that this can be reliably accurate over, say, more than 10 years; also, it generates a DCN with no reflection of technological progress. For these reasons, it is not suitable for long-life assets or those subject to rapid technological change.
- *Located in a stable economy.* Current or past hyperinflation precludes its use on the basis that such conditions make any statistical data unreliable.
- *Sold at stable prices.* This does not mean that inflation should be the same each year but rather that the price changes over time show low volatility.
- *Historic data are available.* The actual cost of property to the present owner may not necessarily be the historic cost, which is that from the time it was first constructed or installed. The trending of costs other than true historic amounts should be avoided under nearly every circumstance, as such figures may represent expenses to which the price index is not applicable

- *Purchased new.* As stated earlier, the price indices represent changes in prices of new products from original manufacturers and, as such, cannot properly be applied to secondhand items.

Providing these conditions exist, the trending method is especially suitable for large amounts of assets in a valuation engagement, where direct pricing is not practical.

Direct pricing. Although the trending method provides a quick indication of cost new, direct pricing is definitely preferable. It is the process of applying current new unit prices to the subject. Typically they are obtained from current manufacturers' price lists, quotations, and catalogs that provide the recent prices for a subject. In valuations under the "in-use" premise, they have to be increased by transportation and installation cost.

The major and possibly only significant disadvantage is the availability of data. For some items, prices may not be available at all (the item is no longer being manufactured, or the supplier is out of business); for others, the manufacturer may not be willing to disclose them. A somewhat related alternative is direct cost estimating; in this, the valuator totals the costs of material, labor, engineering, and other expenses needed to reproduce the item. This is practical for individual specialized units; however, since it requires specific knowledge and expertise of the particular industry, it is rarely used.

Benchmarking techniques. In benchmarking, the cost of an item is estimated from known prices of equipment with similar physical characteristics, functionality, and utility. Sometimes when prices are available for units with the same functionality but different capacity, a cost-to-capacity formula can be used; the relationship is given by this equation:[1]

$$\frac{\text{Cost 2}}{\text{Cost 1}} = \left(\frac{\text{Capacity 2}}{\text{Capacity 1}} \right)^{\text{Exp}}$$

The exponent factor is typically 0.6 (consequently, this method is sometimes called the 6/10s rule), but it may vary, depending on the type of property.

Other practical benchmarking techniques include battery limits and rules of thumb. In the battery limits technique, the subject is benchmarked against the total investment needed to construct a production plant producing specific products at a given capacity. This is especially useful for chemical plants, refineries, and other process plants. The *Process Economics Program (PEP) Yearbook International*, published by SRI Consulting, is an example of such investment data.

Cost new estimates derived from rules of thumb should not be given much weight, as they are approximations, not estimates. This technique is, however, useful when ballpark figures are needed in a hurry, for a quick verification of a cost new, derived by another method, or when preparing a sensitivity analysis where a high degree of accuracy is not required.

Depreciation

Once the cost new is determined, it has to be adjusted to reflect any form of depreciation. This is defined by IFRS as "the systematic allocation of depreciable amount of an asset over its useful life" (IAS 16.6 and IAS 36.6); in valuation practice, depreciation is "actual loss in value or worth of a property from all causes including those resulting from physical deterioration, functional obsolescence, and economic obsolescence."[2]

---

[1] *See Frederic C. Jelen and James H. Black,* **Cost and Optimization Engineering** *(New York: McGraw-Hill, 1983).*

[2] *See Eugene L. Grant and Paul T. Norton,* **Depreciation** *(New York: Ronald Press Company, 1955).*

Depreciation is either *curable*, "that part of physical deterioration and functional obso-lescence which is economically feasible to rectify" or *incurable*, "that part of which it is not economically feasible to deal with."[3]

Physical Deterioration

Physical deterioration is the loss in value caused by wear and tear from operation and exposure to the elements, including any lack of maintenance. (See IVGN 8, *The Cost Approach for Financial Reporting*, para. 5.4.1.) Unfortunately, the term "physical deterioration" is treated as synonymous with "depreciation," especially when there is no functional obso-lescence.

Friction, impact, vibration, fatigue, deformation, or distortion due to stress or force may cause physical deterioration, and so can decrepitude arising from the passage of time, expo-sure to natural elements, or the impact of the operating environment. Excessive physical deterioration often leads to inability to meet production standards or tolerances resulting in higher product rejections and waste of materials. Other indications of deterioration are exces-sive maintenance needs, repair costs running far above the average for similar properties. A below-average figure may indicate deferred maintenance and additional long-term decrepi-tude.

In theory, physical deterioration can be measured objectively. A machine can produce X number of parts in its lifetime, a pump will lift Y cubic meters, an offset press will print Z square meters. Assuming that: adequate records are kept of these X, Y, and Z statistics, the equipment was never rebuilt or abused, and all assets of a particular type were the same, it would be simple to calculate physical deterioration. Unfortunately, such conditions do not exist in the real world; a valuator must rely on how similar assets have performed in the past to make a judgment of the physical condition of the subject. Therefore, determination of physical deterioration may be rather subjective.

The best indicators available should be used to estimate the impact. A machine that runs 15 shifts per week will deteriorate at least three times faster than an identical unit that oper-ates only five shifts. Machinery employed in dusty, dirty, abrasive, and/or corrosive envi-ronments will suffer more than similar machinery in clean surroundings. Equipment that has recently been rebuilt is obviously in better physical condition than equipment that has not been so treated.

The physical condition observed during an inspection can be verified or adjusted by: discussions with operating, maintenance, and engineering staff; reviewing past and present replacement, maintenance, and rebuilding practices; analyzing maintenance, engineering, and production records; and consulting industry experts. Normal preventive maintenance does not affect physical deterioration; but its lack accelerates the damage at a geometric rather than straight-line rate.

Some items of plant and equipment have major components with dramatically differing characteristics; furnaces in the metal and glass industries are an example. The shell has little wear, while the refractory linings are consumed at rates directly proportional to production. Again, analyses of past maintenance practices and relining costs in comparison with past and present production helps the valuator to determine the extent of physical deterioration.

An important fact to be taken into account is that two machines of the same type, per-forming the same function but from different suppliers may differ not only in price and qual-

---

[3] See American Society of Appraisers, ***Valuing Machinery and Equipment, The Fundamentals of Appraising Machinery and Technical Assets*** *(Herndon, VA: Author, 2000).*

ity of output but also in their ability to withstand use. To depreciate them at the same rates, based on age or units produced, may lead to an incorrect conclusion of value.

In practice, physical deterioration is most commonly estimated by the economic or actual age/life methods; both are based on an accounting-like straight-line depreciation model developed by dividing the actual or effective age by an estimate of the normal useful life. In addition to the fact that this depreciation is not derived from market evidence, the other problem is that it assumes that all elements, parts, components or subsystems within the piece of equipment depreciate at the same, constant, average rate.

Age/Life Method

The basic equation of the age/life method is:

$$DEP = EA / NUL$$

Where

DEP	=	total depreciation rate
EA	=	effective age of property
NUL	=	normal useful life

The modified age/life method takes into consideration salvage value (i.e., as if the property is sold for the materials it contains or for an alternative use), at the end of its useful life. (See IVS No. 2, *Bases Other Than Market Value*, para 6.9.3.) The modified equation is:

$$DEP = EA \times (1 - SV) / NUL$$

Where

DEP	=	total depreciation rate
EA	=	effective age of property
SV	=	net salvage value at the end of normal useful life
NUL	=	normal useful life

Useful life. In determining the normal useful life of a property, the inherent relationship between maintenance and depreciation must be considered. By increasing maintenance, often the useful life may be prolonged, thereby reducing annual depreciation. Whilst no exact measure of this relationship is possible, it is advisable to consider the general level of maintenance when reviewing a property's depreciation. In valuation, the term "useful life" has many interpretations regarding definition and usage. Some practitioners consider it to be the physical life, whereas others regard it as the economic or normal useful life.

The Royal Institution of Chartered Surveyors (RICS, London, UK), Valuation Information Paper No. 10, *The Cost Approach for Financial Reporting*, paragraph 9.18, defines physical life as "how long the asset, ignoring any potential for refurbishment or reconstruction, could be used for any purpose." It is the period during which a property can be operated using normal preventive maintenance, as recommended by the manufacturer. Although the physical life often can reasonably indicate an item's useful life, a number of other issues should be considered:

- Overhauling or rebuilding can renew a property's life; this may be undertaken several times until no longer economical.
- Functional obsolescence factors, such as technological substitution, deregulation, increased competition, and rising market demands, may have a profound impact on the life of a property.

International Valuation Application No. 1, *Valuation for Financial Reporting*, paragraph 3.9, defines economic life as the "period in which an asset is expected to be economically usable by one or more users." Stated another way, it is the estimated number of years that a new property can be used before it would pay for the owners to replace it with the most economical replacement that could perform an equivalent service. It considers the time from when operations begin to the point at which the subject becomes uneconomical.

The obvious advantage of this life concept is that it considers, in addition to external economic factors, the benefits of utilization from the owner's perspective. At any point, governmental regulations may be imposed and market conditions or industry economics may change. Today, economic obsolescence factors change so quickly that many assets can suddenly become uneconomical. The drawback is that it requires the valuator to analyze the utilization of the asset from an economic point of view; this task is not always possible due to the complexity of such analyses and general lack of appropriate data.

The American Society of Appraisers defines *normal useful life* as

> *the physical life, usually in terms of years, that a new property will actually be used before it is retired from service. A property's normal useful life relates to how long similar properties actually tend to be used, as opposed to the more theoretical economic life calculation of how long a property can profitably be used.*[4]

Typically, this definition is used for valuations as it takes into account market-based experience in the industry, allows for normal wear and tear, anticipates functional and economic obsolescence, as well as other factors that might result in an early retirement.

It is ultimately the valuator's decision whether the remaining useful life is derived from normal useful life, economic life or physical life concept is selected. He must, however, provide a credible justification of the method chosen that can be explained, quantified, and defended.

Functional obsolescence. According to IVGN 8, paragraph 5.4.2, *functional obsolescence* is "a form of depreciation resulting in a loss in value caused by conditions within the property, such as changes in design, materials or process, and resulting in inadequacy, overcapacity, excess construction, lack of utility, or excess operating costs." It is described in detail in Chapter 2.

Example: Cost Approach, DCN Method

The subject is a nine-year-old film roll perforating machine, which consists of: an unrolling unit, punching unit, film guide, light marking unit, dust evacuation unit, sling regulator, and a pre-piercing and transport unit. The machine works with an intermittent feed; for each punching stroke, the film is adjusted by catching needles. The basic technical parameters are listed next.

Size	1,500 mm broad, 1,500 mm high, 600 mm deep
Weight	325 kg
Capacity	1,250 strokes/min
Maximum film coils diameter	460 mm
Original cost	$115,000
Originally acquired	01/2000

The Cost Approach was used to value the subject as there is no secondary market for this type of equipment and no income stream could be reasonably attributed to it. The starting point is determining the DCN. The original manufacturer no longer offers equipment with the same capacity, but units with 1,500 strokes per minute are available for $150,000; other than the greater capacity, these are practically identical to the subject.

The cost-to-capacity equation was used to estimate the DCN for the subject:

$$\begin{aligned} \text{DCN new} \ &= \ \text{Known cost new} \times (\text{Subject capacity} / \text{Comparable capacity})^{0.6} \\ &= \ \$150,000 \times (1,250 / 1,500)^{0.6} \\ &= \ \$134,000 \text{ (rounded)} \end{aligned}$$

---

[4] *Ibid.*

To confirm this figure, the original cost was trended using these factors from the U.S. Bureau of Labor Statistics:

Year	Index
2000	113
.	.
.	.
.	.
2009	133

The indicated increase of 18% is determined through current-year index (133), by that for the original year (113); this factor of 1.18, applied to the original purchase price of $114,400, indicates a DCN of $135,000, which supports the benchmarking number and is considered appropriate.

Physical deterioration was estimated by the modified age/life method. The useful life after discussions with the client's engineering staff and the manufacturer was concluded to be 18 years. The salvage value at that time is estimated at $2,500 (about 1.9% of cost new). Due to poor maintenance in recent years, the subject's effective age was increased from 9 to 11 years; the physical deterioration was then calculated:

$$\text{Physical deterioration} = \text{Effective age} \times (1 - \text{Salvage value}) / \text{Useful life}$$
$$= 11 \times (1 - 1.9\%) / 18 = 60.0\%$$

An inspection found that the gear box did not function properly; the repair cost is estimated at $7,000 (about 5.2% of cost new). Over the last few years, the equipment was utilized only about 75% of the time due to changes in the industry as digital-based technology has replaced classical film rolls. This lack of demand was translated into economic obsolescence through utilization analysis:

$$\text{Economic obsolescence} = 1 - (\text{Demand} / \text{Capacity})^{0.6}$$
$$= 1 - (75\% / 100\%)^{0.6} = 15.9\%$$

The fair value based on those assumptions was determined to be $43,000 (31.9% of cost new), calculated:

$$\text{Fair value} = \text{DCN} \times (1 - \text{Physical deterioration}) \times (1 - \text{Functional obsolescence})$$
$$\times (1 - \text{Economic obsolescence})$$
$$= \$135,000 \times (1 - 60.0\%) \times (1 - 5.2\%) \times (1 - 15.9\%)$$
$$= \$43,000 \text{ (rounded)}$$

CONCLUSION

Valuing plant and equipment is a complex task that requires numerous skills, including:

- Understanding the asset accounting and capitalization procedures.
- Understanding the financial aspects of business management.
- Relevant knowledge about specific industries.
- Intelligence about secondhand markets in a variety of economies.
- Technical and engineering comprehension of technology and production processes.
- Communication with management, accountants, engineers, maintenance personnel as well as machine operators.
- Ultimately, an understanding of the relationship and interaction of all the points noted earlier to a property value.

These skills are a prerequisite to a supportable valuation report as they are needed to understand properly the various valuation methods. The examples should help valuators gain confidence in applying each approach to specific items of plant and equipment.

The logic underlying the use of multiple methods is that different types of information are available for the variety of factors that influence fair value. Since valuing plant and equipment depends frequently on subjective measures and interpretation of both qualitative and quantitative data, the valuator and his or her skills are a key factor.

31 RETAIL LOCATIONS

LIM LAN YUAN

SINGAPORE

INTRODUCTION

The term "retail" is very broad, as it encompasses everything from individual outlets through freestanding stores, to large conglomerates of store chains, supermarkets, or discounters. When valuing a retail location, it is necessary first and foremost to determine the type of development in which it is situated. Generally developments may be classified into five categories:

1. Convenience (in an office or apartment building)
2. Neighborhood (high street)
3. Community strip malls
4. Regional shopping centers
5. Superregional centers

They vary as to traffic, tenants, size, and trading area. This chapter outlines the factors that contribute to retail performance and that affect the locations and values of retail developments.

RETAIL TRENDS

Despite strong growth potential and growing consumer markets, the retail industry faces a challenging environment because of the effect on purchasing preferences of shifts in demographics, lifestyles, and cultural influences as well as the aging of the population.[1] Three global trends are common in industrialized nations:

1. Retail chains are getting bigger and better financed.
2. The Internet is creating opportunities for:

    Parallel marketing
    Enhancing traditional advertising
    Diverting sales to cheaper warehouse space

3. Entertainment, through themed developments or environmental experiences, is becoming more important for attracting shoppers.

In today's economic context, globalization is an important strategy applicable to virtually all businesses. In the current deteriorating economic environment, competition is keener and maintaining market share requires new strategic thrusts. For instance, Japanese department stores (Seibu and Isetan) as well as retailers and chains from Western Europe (H&M) and the United States (Wal-Mart) are making inroads into Asia's growing consumer market. Many foreign retailers are either forming joint ventures with local companies or sell-

---

[1] L. Y. Lim, "Successful Retail Management in Asia," *Real Estate Finance* 12, No. 4 (Winter 1996): 59–64.

ing franchises. 7-Eleven convenience stores, originally from the United States, are now in Japan, South Korea, Hong Kong, China, Malaysia, the Philippines, Singapore and Taiwan; Carrefour from France is in China, Taiwan, Malaysia, Thailand, and Singapore.

DETERMINANTS OF RETAIL VALUE

As in other forms of real estate, the value of a retail development is very much affected by its location. However, establishing a reasonable figure may be very complex; besides location, its value is influenced by factors such as image and product mix. The relative importance and strength of those factors vary for different types of stores.

Location

A retail location must be considered in the context of the neighborhood it serves. Location is a major factor affecting the value of real estate with easy accessibility to public transportation being a definite advantage. In its absence, mall management should provide as much parking as possible and consider providing shuttle bus services to the nearest subway or bus stop. A shopping mall usually has a significant catchment area, and a large, well-tenanted mall can have a strong impact despite a relatively poor location. In addition to geographical location, the siting of a particular retail outlet is also important as this will affect traffic, patronage, and profitability. A location at a major intersection or facing a main road, even on a second story, is more valuable than a store on the ground floor that faces a secondary thoroughfare or is at the rear of a building. Generally, a ground-floor shop is more valuable than one on an upper floor.

Image and Profile

Typically, shopping center developers identify a likely location, secure commitments from prospective anchor tenants, begin building a facility of the scale and size they consider appropriate, and then seek out additional chain and individual tenants consistent with the proposed strategy. Once the center is open, shoppers learn about its physical and tenant characteristics through marketing efforts, promotions, and, ultimately, by a personal visit. Generally, both these elements create the consumers' image of a shopping area, whether building lobby, retail street, stand-alone store, or some form of shopping center; consumers distinguish one from another by the images projected. The significance that shoppers place on the various image dimensions of competitive areas form the basis of their relative evaluations in the market and so determine their patronage levels. These comparative overall impressions determine which areas shoppers will visit and, ultimately, in which outlets they will purchase a particular product or service. Determining the value of a retail location requires a good understanding of how an area's patronage varies as a function of changes in its image.

Trade Mix

The value of a specific retail outlet is also affected by the type of trade or merchandise being offered. *Trade mix* refers to the range of retail trades operating in any particular street or shopping mall; an interesting variety provides patrons with a wide choice. An important element for a good mix is the one or two anchor tenants which draw the crowds. In a mall, the trade mix also includes entertainment and food outlets. A location that provides a complete "one-stop" destination will likely be more attractive than a site with fewer varieties of outlets.

PERFORMANCE OF RETAIL DEVELOPMENTS

Much research has been undertaken to determine the factors that affect the performance of a retail development, focusing on the factors that affect customer's behavior patterns. Over the years, several patronage models for shopping centers have been introduced;[2] their underlying basis is that shoppers' behavior is a function of consumer, situational characteristics, and retail attractiveness.

Early patronage research focused mainly on the physical attributes of the stores; they included merchandise sold, service provided, posttransaction satisfaction, promotion, location, facilities, and atmosphere.[3] More recently, research has looked at other aspects of shopping patterns including consumer behavior.[4]

Turley and Milliman[5] conducted a comprehensive review of some 60 empirical studies of the marketing atmosphere influence on consumers; they classified them into five categories—Location, General Interior, Layout and Design, Point of Purchase and Decoration, and Human and Service.

The "General Interior" category includes lighting, scents and sounds, temperature, cleanliness, and color. Studies by the author show that atmosphere, tenant variety, promotion, facilities, and location all have a positive effect on mall patronage. A valuator should consider the following seven factors.

Location

Often consumers are motivated to choose a retail store because of its location; it is not unusual for the location to either attract or repel customers. In many countries, growth in regional shopping centers has done much to attract consumers to certain retail chains. Location is important not only for its own sake but because it contributes to overall retail strategy, especially by generating traffic. Therefore, retail sites are chosen often based on the volume of passersby, on the assumption that a certain percentage of them will become shoppers. Traffic is often the basis of retail research at the interurban and intraurban levels.[6] Estimates of population growth and trading area are used to determine the expected demand, although the important criterion is not population per se but rather store visitors.

Although sites can be, and are, evaluated based on expected retail traffic, the second important objective of location is its ability to enhance the overall image of the retailer. In general, chains such as Tiffany & Co. with a high, up-market status look for locations that match this image.

A third objective of location is that it contributes to the convenience of shoppers. Although critical for certain categories, including convenience stores, gasoline stations, and fast food outlets, convenience is generally important to most types of retail stores and will be

2   D. Bellenger and G. Moschis (eds.), *A Socialisation Model of Retail Patronage* (Ann Arbor, MI: Association for Consumer Research, 1982); K. L. Wakefield and J. Baker, "Excitement at the Mall: Determinants and Effects on Shopping Response," *Journal of Retailing* 74, No. 4 (1998): 515–539.

3   G. Fisk, "The Conceptual Model for Studying Customer Image," *Journal of Retailing.* 37 (1961–62): 1–8. J. D. Lindquist, "Meaning of Image," *Journal of Retailing* 50, No. 4 (Winter 1974–75): 29–38.

4   M. K. Hui and E. G. Bateson, "Perceived Control and the Effects of Crowding and Consumer Choice on the Service Experience," *Journal of Consumer Research* 18 (1991): 174–184. J. Baker, A. Parasuraman, D. Grewal, and G. B. Voss, "The Influence of Multiple Store Environment Cues on Perceived Merchandise Value and Patronage Intentions," *Journal of Marketing* 66 (2002): 120–141.

5   Turley, L.W., and Ronald E. Milliman, (2000) "Atmospheric Effects on Shopping Behavior. A Review of the Experimental Evidence," *Journal of Business Research.* Vol. 49, No. 2, (August, 2000) 193-211.

6   W. J. Reilly *The Law of Retail Gravitation* (New York: Author, 1931); P. D. Converse, "New Laws of Retail Gravitation," *Journal of Marketing* 14, No. 31 (October 1949): 379–384.

influenced by the specific configuration of the site. Location also requires consideration of the appropriateness, not merely the nearness of a site. Therefore, accessibility, such as the availability of public transport, is also important. The shopper should be able to reach the store easily, park without fuss, and have refreshments and services available when desired.[7]

The combination of these three objectives lead to the concept of drawing power—that is, the strength of a site to draw suitable traffic to an area.[8] Drawing power varies by area, but there is scope for quality retailers, particularly anchor stores such as major supermarkets, department stores, and discount outlets, to enhance an area's existing drawing power.

Layout and Design

Individual stores, malls, and shopping centers also are being designed, constructed, and redeveloped to keep up with changing times and tastes. Over the years, shopping centers have expanded to also become service outlets and entertainment providers. Even relatively small malls today offer fast food courts, entertainment arcades, and sometimes movie theatres. Interiors have evolved from comfortable spaces to become artistically designed, with well-furnished elements, such as multilevel atriums, curved escalators, a skating rink, and even surfing pools. A recent trend is toward megamalls; examples include Golden Resources and Zhengjia Plaza in Beijing; Vivocity and Suntec City in Singapore; Mid Valley and Pavilion in Kuala Lumpur; Siam Paragon and Seacon Square in Bangkok; West Edmonton Mall in Alberta, Canada; and Mall of America in Minneapolis. In addition, there is also a trend to focus a portion of the mall on the youth market, grouping specialized retail outlets, typically very small cubicles, in a pattern, allowing retailers to display their unique and specialty, trendy items.

Ambience

Many consumers do not visit a mall just for the functional purpose of buying a product or service; they can and do derive satisfaction from the environment itself, so their visit and activities become as important as the actual purchases. Shopping can be undertaken for both utilitarian (functional or tangible) or hedonic (pleasurable or intangible) reasons. Hence, managements and marketers focus on creating pleasure and excitement for visitors to a store or mall. Experiential shopping has become a norm in recent years; nowadays, it is often difficult to distinguish retail from nonretail activities as today's shopping centers are enlivened by children's entertainers, fashion shows, and multiplex cinemas, turning them into venues for public performances and entertainment as much as for conventional purchases. Bookshops no longer just sell books but are a place in which to relax, drink coffee, listen to stories, and meet writers. Nordstrom in the United States, for example, positions itself as an up-market retailer by creating a gracious atmosphere, including employing a piano player to serenade customers.

Tenant Variety

Another factor that can affect patronage is the tenant mix in a shopping street, mall, or center, which is the equivalent of product assortment and variety in store patronage research.[9]

---

[7] C. Guy, **Retail Development Process—Location, Property and Planning** (London: Routledge, 1994).

[8] N. Merrilees and D. Miller, **Retailing Management—A Best Practice Approach** (Victoria, NSW: RMIT Press, 1996).

[9] S. J. Arnold, T. H. Oum, and D. J. Tigert, "Determinant Attributes in Retail Patronage: Seasonal, Temporal, Regional and International Comparisons," **Journal of Marketing Research** 20, No. 2 (May 1983): 149–157.

It is often said that no shopping center can exist without an anchor outlet.[10] The presence of key tenants not only sets the tone and image but also ensures the success of the development. In addition to anchor tenants, a good supporting mix is important. Themed developments provide synergistic tenants that can draw potential customers from substantial distances— what urban economists call agglomerative market drawing power.[11]

A center that offers a wide variety of products and services is likely to attract more shoppers because it allows consumers the advantage of comparing offerings conveniently. Retail management will deliberately group shops in clusters to take advantage of consumers' multi-purpose shopping habits.[12] Product variety, both within individual outlets and across competing ones, is likely to attract consumers looking for specific items. Studies have shown that the variety of a shopping center's tenants influences customers' selection, frequency of visits, the center's image, and size of average purchase.[13] Such studies have also shown that tenant mix and location within a mall influence the time consumers spend there and their patterns of movement.[14]

Bloch et al.[15] discovered that exploring new products or stores was a perceived benefit of the mall experience; they suggested it tapped into consumers' desires for variety and choices. Customers who are motivated to explore a number of stores due to variety-seeking tendencies or shopping tasks, are likely to stay longer and have the tendency to visit again. Malls that contain a relatively wide assortment of stores, restaurants, and entertainment outlets tend to generate greater opportunities for consumers to shop, eat, and enjoy themselves, thereby encouraging them to return.[16]

Promotion

Another factor that has an impact on shopping behavior is promotion. However, much recent research focused on the individual store rather than shopping center promotion.[17] Many of today's high-performance retailers use aggressive promotion tactics to bring traffic into their stores and move consumers to the appropriate selling areas, enticing them to purchase. Seeking longer-term benefits, center managements engage in institutional advertising to create a positive image in consumers' minds. Their objective is to establish long-term relationships with shoppers and get them to perceive the retailers as good citizens in the community.

In the short term, retailers engage, often aggressively, in advertising and sales promotions. Their most common objectives are to increase the purchases of existing customers and to attract new customers. By advertising a shopping center, management hopes to attract new

---

[10] M. J. Ross, **Shopping Centre Development Handbook** *(Washington, DC: Urban Land Institute, 1997)*.

[11] *Lim, "Successful Retail Management in Asia."*

[12] A. Ghosh, *"The Value of a Mall and Other Insights from a Revised Central Place Model,"* **Journal of Retailing** *62, No. 1 (Spring 1986): 79–97.*

[13] J. Hopper, A. Stilley, and T. J. Lipscomb, *"An Investigation of Differences between Male and Female Outshoppers: Strategic Implications,"* **Akron Business and Economic Review** *22, No. 4 (Winter 1991): 109–120.*

[14] S. Brown, *"Shopper Circulation in a Planned Shopping Centre,"* **International Journal of Retail and Distribution Management** *19, No. 1 (January/February1991): 17–24.*

[15] P. H. Bloch, N. M. Ridgway, and S. A. Dawson, *"The Shopping Mall as Consumer Habitat,"* **Journal of Retailing** *70, No. 1 (1994): 23–42.*

[16] *Wakefield and Baker, "Excitement at the Mall."*

[17] D. M. Hardesty and W. O. Bearden, *"Consumer Evaluations of Different Promotion Types and Price Presentations: The Moderating Role of Promotional Benefit Level,"* **Journal of Retailing** *79, No. 1 (2003): 17–25.*

faces from the retailers' primary or secondary catchment areas as well as those who have just moved into the area.

Retailers also use sales promotions, which provide short-term incentives, and publicity to increase the effectiveness of their advertising. Sales promotions can significantly help a particular center distinguish itself from competitors. Retailers have long known that consumers change their shopping habits and brand preferences to take advantage of promotions, especially those that offer something new, special, or exciting. Because similar stores are able to attract the same shoppers, merchandise alone does not make an outlet exciting. In-store happenings can generate excitement while in-store displays seek to increase traffic and encourage impulse buying.

Well-managed publicity should be integrated with other elements of promotion to reinforce the store's image. Retailers can expand their trading area by offering entertainment, promoting unique merchandise offerings, or creating an image that it is an "in" place to shop.[18] Activities such as sales promotions, special events, and functions tend to generate excitement and increase patronage. Store activities, such as entertainment events, product demonstrations, participation in community affairs, promotional programs, and public service proceedings, are special occasions staged by management to attract potential consumers to the center in the hope of encouraging continued patronage.[19]

Scale and Facilities

The size of the development is particularly important for a shopping center, as it affects patronage. Those of considerable size and great variety will provide a convenient shopping environment for patrons with different needs. Without a strong theme, a mall may have difficulty attracting enough crowds.

Facilities will have an impact on the effectiveness of operations. For instance, adequate parking is more important to a shopping center than to an office building. This is particularly so when the center is not on public transportation. Vertical transportation is essential for both offices and shops; the most important and common means, and the one which gives maximum exposure to stores, is the escalator. The number, positioning, and layout of escalators are a major factor and especially important for upper-floor retail units.

The availability and adequacy of loading and unloading facilities is also very important, as they facilitate movement of both incoming supplies and outgoing goods. Inefficient facilities are costly as they lower productivity and delay transfer times.

Property Management

In many cities, competition between and within shopping centers is intense. Those in one country may also compete with those in neighboring states. Hence, center managements need to identify ways to accentuate their image to attract shoppers. Part of their activities include proactive maintenance to keep the mall in a good state of repair as well as timely upgrading and refurbishment.

With each passing year, shopping centers built in the 1970s that were, at the time, considered ultramodern suffer from the effects of physical deterioration and functional obsolescence. While aggressive maintenance may help reduce the physical wear and tear, usually, major refurbishment is required to upgrade existing space and look to compete with newer ones. In 2008 and 2009, a number of retailers took the opportunity to remodel their stores using new designs and images to keep up with changing trends. The Robinson group in

---

[18] *J. B. Mason, M. L. Mayer, and H. F. Ezell,* **Retailing***, 5th ed. (Chicago: Richard D. Irwin, 1994).*

[19] *D. Lewison,* **Retailing** *(Englewood Cliffs, NJ: Prentice-Hall, 1997).*

Bangkok renovated its Silom branch to stay competitive, due to the imminent opening of the new Central Department Store nearby. As part of an upgrade program, Funan Center in Singapore installed a giant high-definition television screen mounted in a hall specifically built to hold promotional events.

Retailer Strategies

To meet increased competition, retailers have used several strategies to boost sales and attract consumers, such as customer service, niche marketing, and new formats and innovative concepts.

Customer service. Purchasing decisions are no longer based solely on price, quality, or product range. To distinguish themselves, retailers must train their staff to provide excellent service. Some retailers offer a wide selection of products, others concentrate on value including superior service, high quality, and reasonable value.

Niche marketing. Specialization by product, or niche marketing, has been adopted to cater to the different groups of customers with extreme selection. The interests of an aging population are different from the demands of a growing group of 15- to 25-year-olds. Shoppers today are generally much younger than 30 years, and teenagers may spend up to several hundred dollars on clothes and accessories on each visit. Specialty stores, such as Takashimaya's Fashion Lab, have been introduced to cater to youth; similarly Nike Town in the United States and the Body Shop in the United Kingdom and Canada aim at aging baby boomers.

New formats and innovative concepts. Many retailers are coming up with new retail formats and concepts to survive stiff competition. Takashimaya in Singapore, for example, has generated new customer niches with lifestyle-related facilities. Its flagship store in Ngee Ann City is equipped with a fitness club, an art gallery, and a culture center that offers classes in flower arrangement and languages; the purpose is to integrate retailing with changing lifestyles.

EXAMPLE: COMMUNITY SHOPPING CENTERS

This example relates to valuing three community shopping centers (Cinnamon Ridge, Jessemin Forest, and Sunrise Avenue) owned by the same firm in a major urban area. Three methods have been selected: capitalized cash flows under the Income Approach and, separately, rent and size valuation multiples under the Market Approach.

Income Approach

In this area, the normal financing for community shopping centers is through long-term (up to 30 years) institutional mortgages for 80% of the cost; the remaining 20% is equity. The current interest rate for such loans is 6.85%, allowing for a 30-year amortization. The cash payments are 7.89% annually. On this basis, an overall appraisal rate (OAR) is developed for the capitalization of effective cash flows, revenues less operating expenses, and the very important maintenance capital expenditure (CAPEX).

In mid-2009, before the valuation date, the owner sold two similar properties. The data from those transactions were used to develop the necessary market-based valuation multiples. Exhibit 31.1 shows the actual transaction OAR for each of the two sold properties and their implicit equity cash returns. Those for the retained properties have been developed based on their grades by interpolation. The cash equity returns for the sold units were: Bishop's Park (grade A) 9.15% and Moon Gate (grade B) 10.25%; the difference is 110 basis points for the three grade interval: B, B+, A−, A; this is equivalent to 37 basis points each.

Exhibit 31.1 Calculation of Overall Appraisal Rates

Community Center	Grade	Mortgage Interest Rate (80%)	Mortgage Cash Payments	Equity Cash Return (20%)	Overall Appraisal Rate
Moon Gate	B	6.85%	7.89%	10.25%	8.36% Sold
Bishop's Park	A	6.85%	7.89%	9.15%	8.14% Sold
Cinnamon Ridge	B-	6.85%	7.89%	10.62%	8.44%
Jessemin Forrest	B	6.85%	7.89%	9.15%	8.14%
Sunrise Avenue	B+	6.85%	7.89%	8.78%	8.07%

Cash Flow Values

Exhibit 31.2 calculates the effective cash flows for each property, including the substantial maintenance CAPEX needed to ensure the properties remain absolutely current.

Exhibit 31.2 Calculation of Effective Cash Flow

Community Center	Grade	Revenue ($'000)	Operating Expenses ($'000)	Maint CAPEX ($'000)	Effective Cash Flow ($'000)	Cash Margin
Moon Gate	B	3,189	1,394	679	1,116	35.0%
Bishop's Park	A	3,704	1,818	753	1,133	30.6%
Cinnamon Ridge	B-	2,662	1,147	585	930	34.9%
Jessemin Forrest	B	3,631	1,768	790	1,073	29.6%
Sunrise Avenue	B+	3,227	1,619	993	615	19.1%

Exhibit 31.3 calculates cash flow values for all five properties using the OARs established in Exhibit 31.1; the figures for Moon Gate and Bishop's Park are the selling prices.

Exhibit 31.3 Calculation of Cash Flow Values

Community Center	Effective Cash Flow ($'000)	Vacancy Rate %	Adjusted Cash Flow ($'000)	Overall Appraisal Rate	Cash Flow Value ($'000)
Moon Gate	1,116	5.5	1,020	8.36%	12,200 Sold
Bishop's Park	1,133	7.4	1,103	8.14%	13,550 Sold
Cinnamon Ridge	930	8.5	902	8.44%	10,690
Jessemin Forrest	1,073	8.8	1,123	8.14%	13,795
Sunrise Avenue	615	9.3	979	8.07%	12,135

Rent-Based Values

Exhibit 31.4 calculates rent-based values for each property assuming a 10% vacancy rate compared with the actual levels of between 5.5% and 9.3% for the properties. The figures for Moon Gates and Bishop's Park are the sales prices. The annual factors for the retained properties are again interpolated.

Exhibit 31.4 Calculation of Rent-Based Values

Community Center	Actual Monthly Rent ($'000)	Vacancy Rate	Effective Annual Rent ($'000)	Annual Factor	Rent-Based Value ($'000)
Moon Gate	179.61	5.5%	2,053	5.94	12,200 Sold
Bishop's Park	190.61	7.4%	2,223	6.09	13,550 Sold
Cinnamon Ridge	140.77	8.5%	1,662	5.89	9,790
Jessemin Forrest	194.00	8.8%	2,297	5.94	13,655
Sunrise Avenue	174.03	9.3%	2,072	5.99	12,420

Size-Based Values

Exhibit 31.5 calculates the average rent per square foot for the different properties based on the net rentable areas and the full annual rentals (zero vacancies). The price per square foot for the three retained units has been interpolated from the market-driven figures for the two sold properties.

Exhibit 31.5 Calculation of Size-Based Values

Community Center	Net Rentable Area ('000 SF)	Full Annual Rent ($'000)	Rent per SF ($)	Price per SF ($)	Sized Based Value ($'000)
Moon Gate	115.25	2,281	19.79	105.86	12,200 Sold
Bishop's Park	111.40	2,470	22.17	121.63	13,550 Sold
Cinnamon Ridge	94.76	1,846	19.48	100.61	9,535
Jessemin Forrest	121.98	2,553	20.93	105.86	12,915
Sunrise Avenue	120.26	2,303	19.15	111.11	13,360

Reconciliation of Values

Exhibit 31.6 sets out the values for each of the retained properties by all three methods, each of which use market driven valuation multiples. The reconciled amounts are the average of the three rather than the mean or median of the ranges.

Exhibit 31.6 Reconciliation of Values

Community Center	Cash Flow Value ($'000)	Rent-Based Value ($'000)	Size-Based Value ($'000)	Value Range Low ($'000)	Value Range High ($'000)	Reconciled Value ($'000)
Cinnamon Ridge	10,690	9,790	9,535	9,535	10,690	10,000
Jessemin Forrest	13,795	13,655	12,915	12,915	13,795	13,450
Sunrise Avenue	12,135	12,420	13,360	12,135	13,360	12,630

CONCLUSION

This chapter summarizes the main features of retail development and location. It highlights, in particular, the determinants of the value of a retail outlet or shopping mall. The factors that can contribute to the successful performance of a retail development have also been discussed. Important attributes besides location include image, ambience, tenant variety, promotion, and management. These elements are important considerations when undertaking a business valuation of a retail establishment or development.

32 SHARE-BASED PAYMENTS

SHARI L. OVERSTREET, ANDREW C. SMITH

UNITED STATES

INTRODUCTION

International Financial Reporting Standard (IFRS) 2, *Share-Based Payments*, has been in effect since January 2005; in the United States, a similar pronouncement, Statement of Financial Accounting Standards (SFAS) 123R, *Share-Based Payment*, was released in 2004, as accounting for stock options was an early priority in converging generally accepted accounting principles (GAAP) and IFRS. Both boards agreed that the granting of stock options and related securities issued for goods or services should result in an expense.

This chapter is divided into three sections: the first is an overview of IFRS 2, the second deals with the valuation of employee share options, and the third covers the valuation of the ordinary shares of privately owned entities underlying those options or used for other share-based payments.

OVERVIEW OF IFRS 2

As IFRS 2 is voluminous, covering many detailed scenarios, this section summarizes only its major elements related to valuation. Further detail is found in the standard, the available guidance, and its detailed provisions. Before IFRS 2, international companies typically measured share-based transactions at their intrinsic values, similar to the practice in the United States before SFAS 123R. Under that method, compensation cost is the excess of the market price of a share at the grant or other measurement date over the amount an employee must pay to acquire it. Most share options have no intrinsic value, because, typically, the exercise price is the same as the market price; therefore, no compensation costs are recorded.

The issuance of SFAS 123R and IFRS 2 for the most part disallowed the intrinsic value method and led to most share-based payments being measured at fair value, which results in a charge to earnings. For employee stock options, fair value is measured generally as of the grant date by an option pricing model, unless observable market prices for the same or similar instruments are available. Since such options are normally not traded, their fair value must be calculated by models able to reflect the unique characteristics of the grant. Then, the resulting cost is recognized over the time for which the employee is required to provide services, usually the vesting period.

Share-Based Payments

IFRS 2 defines a share-based payment as a transaction in which the entity receives or acquires goods or services as consideration for its equity instruments, or by incurring liabilities for amounts determined by the price of the entity's equity instruments. Although the standard does not include a formal definition of either goods or services, it specifies that goods include inventories, consumables, property, plant and equipment, intangible assets, and other nonfinancial items.

The notion behind share-based payments is broader than just employee share options; IFRS 2 encompasses all issuance of shares, or rights to shares, in return for goods and services for both employees and nonemployees. It covers: share appreciation rights, employee share purchase plans, employee share ownership plans, share option plans, and plans where the issuance of shares (or rights to shares) may depend on contingencies, either market or non–market related.

The standard applies to all entities, whether publicly traded or privately held, as *IFRS for Private Entities* defers to IFRS 2 on share-based payments with no exemption for private or smaller entities. Additionally, because employees of a subsidiary may receive part of their compensation in shares of the parent, entities using a related firm's equity as consideration also fall within its scope.

Share-based payments other than for goods and services are not covered by IFRS 2, so the issuance of shares in a merger or acquisition is accounted for under IFRS 3, *Business Combinations*. Share dividends, the purchase of treasury shares, and the issuance of additional shares are also beyond its scope. Modifications (such as repricings) of the terms on which equity instruments were granted may have an effect on the expense recorded. The standard gives guidance on such modifications as well as canceled, repurchased, or replaced shares.

In addition, IFRS 2 requires the disclosure of: the nature and extent of the share-based payment arrangements that existed during the period, how the fair value of either goods or services received or equity instruments granted was determined, and the effect of the share-based payment on the entity's related financial statements. Since 2005, two interpretations of IFRS 2 have been issued: International Financial Reporting Interpretations Committee (*IFRIC*) 8, *Scope of IFRS 2*, issued January 2006, and IFRIC 11, *IFRS 2—Group and Treasury Share Transactions*, issued November 2006. IASB has also amended the standard regarding vesting conditions and cancellations.

MAJOR SHARE-BASED TRANSACTIONS

Share-based transactions involving goods or services received or acquired are recognized when the goods are obtained or as the services are received or consumed. The standard identifies three ways in which share-based transactions can be settled and the recognition requirements of the associated expenses.

Equity-Settled Share-Based Payments

In these transactions, an entity receives goods or services as consideration for equity instruments, either shares or share options. For these, the goods or services are measured at their fair value on the grant date only, and a corresponding increase in equity is recognized. If a vesting period is involved, as is generally the case with employee share options, the expense will be recognized over that period. IFRS 2 defines "vest" in this way:

> *To become an entitlement, under a share-based payment arrangement, a counterparty's right to receive cash, other assets, or equity instruments of the entity vests upon satisfaction of any specified vesting conditions.*

Cash-Settled Share-Based Payments

IFRS 2 applies to transactions in which the entity acquires goods or services by incurring a liability to transfer cash or other assets for amounts based on the price of the entity's shares or other equity instruments. The goods or services acquired are measured at the fair value of the liability. Services received and the liabilities for them are recognized as rendered. Until it is fully settled, the liability is remeasured at fair value on each reporting date as well as on the final settlement date. Changes in fair values are recognized in the income statement.

The most common example is share appreciation rights (SARs), sometimes referred to as phantom options. SARs are similar to employee options but result in a cash payment equal to the gain that would have been made by exercising the hypothetical options and immediately selling the shares. Because a cash payment is involved, IFRS 2 states they should be recognized as a liability as opposed to equity.

Cash Alternative Share-Based Payments, One Party Can Choose Cash or Equity

In some situations, an entity receives or acquires goods or services on terms that give either it or the supplier a choice of whether the transaction is settled in cash (or other assets) or by issuing equity. IFRS 2 includes separate measurement requirements for each element; however, such transactions are rare and, therefore, are not discussed in this chapter.

VALUATION OF EMPLOYEE SHARE OPTIONS

Employee share options are by far the most common share-based payments. Normally issued at market price, they have no intrinsic, only an option, value, as they are a long-term right, but not an obligation, to purchase shares that may increase in value before expiry. For accounting purposes, their fair value, when granted, is charged to earnings over the period during which they are earned (vested) by the employee.

Example: Intrinsic Value

An entity granted 100,000 share options to eight managers (to purchase 12,500 shares at $10 each) on 2 January 2004 to vest over the next three years. As the shares had a fair value of $28,000, each option is determined to have an intrinsic value of $18.00 at the date of grant. Because all 100,000 options are expected to vest, their total cost is $1.8 million, to be charged to income at $50,000 (1/36) a month over the vesting period. However, during the second quarter of 2005, a manager leaves, forfeiting his entire 12,500 options; as a result, the subsequent monthly charges are reduced pro rata.

Determining Fair Value

IFRS 2 defines "fair value" as:

The amount for which an asset could be exchanged, a liability settled, or an equity instrument granted could be exchanged, between knowledgeable, willing parties in an arm's-length transaction.

Depending on the type of share-based payment, fair value may be determined by: (a) the value of the shares, or rights to shares, given up or (b) the value of the goods or services received. IFRS 2 has a rebuttable presumption that if the share-based payment is for goods or services other than from employees, it should be measured by reference to their fair value. If, however, the payment is to employees, the transaction should be measured by the fair value of the equity granted.

When share-based payments are measured by the fair value of the equity granted, ideally that should be determined by an equivalent instrument traded in an active market. As market prices do not exist for employee share options, their fair value is determined by applying a suitable valuation technique, usually an option pricing model.

IFRS 2 permits intrinsic value in rare cases in which the fair value of the equity cannot be determined reliably. However, as opposed to valuing them only at the date of grant, the entity would be required to recalculate intrinsic value at each reporting date until exercise or final maturity.

Fair Value Models

There is no specific model for estimating the fair value of share-based payments or for quantifying an instrument's unique features. In selecting an acceptable valuation technique, IFRS 2 requires an entity to apply those factors that knowledgeable, willing market participants would consider.

It may be appropriate to use separate models for different share-based payments to reflect their particular features. Changing models from time to time may be necessary to deal with issues that require complex consideration. In any case, other than a material error, a fair value at a grant date should not be changed once it has been determined, even if that particular model is no longer suitable.

The three most common option pricing models are the Black-Scholes, binomial, and Monte Carlo simulation; each is briefly explained next and discussed elsewhere in this book; certain input variables are common to all.

Basic Input Factors

As there are no equivalents traded in active markets, IFRS 2 requires determining the fair values of employee share-based payments by a suitable technique. For this purpose, it recommends an option pricing model that, at a minimum, considers exercise price of the option, price of underlying shares, and anticipated life of the option.

Exercise price of the option. There is no guidance on determining the exercise price, merely a statement that it should be culled from the option agreement.

Price of underlying shares. Limited guidance is provided on establishing the current share price; this should be in accordance with the entity's accounting policy, which, for publicly traded entities, is usually the closing or average trading price on the grant date. Public company share prices should be analyzed to ensure they represent fair value; unusual trading volume or other activity may indicate that the public share price is not indicative of fair value. For privately held companies, the standard states that the entity should estimate the fair value of its shares based on those of similar quoted entities, net assets, or earnings. Whichever method is chosen, it should be used consistently between periods and plans.

Anticipated life of the option. Several factors affect the expected life of a typical non-traded share option given to employees, such as vesting features and behavioral considerations:

- The length of the vesting period; share options typically cannot be exercised before they vest.
- Historic experience related to previous exercise of share options.
- The price of underlying shares; employees may tend to exercise options when the share price reaches a specified level above the exercise price.
- The expected volatility of the underlying shares; employees are likely to exercise options earlier on highly volatile shares.
- The employee's level within the organization.

If a Black-Scholes model is used to determine fair value, IFRS 2 requires using the expected life of the option, which should not be less than the vesting period. An expected exercise pattern can be factored into a binomial or similar model using contractual life. Often valuators separates options into pools of employees expected to exhibit similar exercise behavior.

As the standards are similar, the guidance of SFAS 123R, which provides three methods to estimate the expected term, is applicable:

1. Simplified method under Securities and Exchange Commission Staff Accounting Bulletin (SAB 107) for plain vanilla options
2. Implied expected term obtained from the Black-Scholes model using assumptions for estimated time outstanding
3. Weighted-average outstanding time using assumptions for estimated time outstanding

Example: Expected Term

SAB 107 defines "expected term" as the average of the vesting term plus the original contractual period. Assuming a 10-year original contractual term and graded vesting over four years (25% vest annually), the expected term is 6.25 years, as indicated:

({[1-year vesting term (for the first 25% vested) plus 2-year vesting term (for the second 25%) plus 3-year vesting term (for the third 25%) plus 4-year vesting term (for the last 25%)] divided by the 4 years of vesting} plus 10-year contractual life) divided by 2

This simplifies to {[(1+2+3+4)/4] + 10} /2 = 6.25 years.

Expected volatility of share price. Volatility is a measure of the amount by which a share price is expected to fluctuate during a period. It is the annualized standard deviation of the continuously compounded rates of return on the share during that time. The expected annualized volatility of a share is the range within which the continuously compounded rate of return is expected to fall approximately two-thirds of the time (IFRS 2:B22). Historic volatility is often used for longer-term options because there is evidence that, over time, volatilities revert to an average. It may also be measured by reference to the implied volatility of traded options; however, their activity is usually thin and their terms tend to be much shorter than those of most employee options.

Establishing historic volatility is problematic for newly listed and unquoted entities. A newly listed entity should calculate historic volatility for the longest period for which trading data is available. It may also consider the historic volatility of similar listed entities following a comparable period in their lives (such as after an initial public offering [IPO]) (IFRS 2:B26). An unquoted entity has no historic information but should rely on other factors, including the historic or implied volatilities mentioned earlier (IFRS 2:B27 and 28). The next parameters are suggested by IFRS 2:B25 to be considered in establishing expected volatility:

- The time the shares have been publicly traded
- Appropriate and regular intervals for price observations
- Factors suggesting future volatility might differ from the past volatility
- Actual historic volatility of the shares
- Historic volatility of a peer group of public companies
- Other implied volatility measures
- Adjustments to reflect unique events from historic periods
- Adjustments to reflect differences in capital structure

Weighting various measures is often desirable to provide the best estimate of expected volatility for the appropriate term.

Example: Expected Volatility

In 2008, a Taiwanese privately owned solar cell manufacturer issued employee share purchase options vesting at various dates over the next three years. To establish volatility, management decided to rely on a group of competitors. As more solar firms are publicly traded in the United States than anywhere else, groups of 12 candidates, traded in that country, were reviewed; from those, three were selected: Energy Conversion Devices, Inc. (ticker ENER); Evergreen Solar, Inc. (ESLR); and MEMC Electronic Materials, Inc. (WFR). The expected volatilities for each period until a vesting date (7.6 months, 12 months, 19.6 months, 24 months, 31.6 months, 36 months) are based on the average of their weekly volatilities for periods of similar lengths in the immediate past.

Vesting Date	01-Feb-09	12-Jun-09	01-Feb-10	12-Jun-10	01-Feb-11	12-Jun-11
ENER	77.84%	70.36%	60.81%	58.83%	57.80%	58.14%
ESLR	73.92%	65.10%	58.80%	58.42%	58.95%	59.13%
WFR	53.55%	51.90%	48.71%	49.30%	51.34%	50.83%
Average	68.44%	62.46%	56.12%	55.52%	56.03%	56.03%

Predicted dividends. IFRS 2:B33 states that if the holder is entitled to dividends between the grant and exercise dates, predicted dividends should not be included in the fair value measurement. If the holder is not entitled to dividends, the fair value is reduced by the present value of the predicted dividends during the vesting period (IFRS 2:B34). It notes that assumptions about dividends should be based on publicly available information. An entity that does not pay dividends and has no plans to do so has predicted dividends of zero. However, an entity that plans to pay dividends in the future could use, for example, the average yield of a comparable peer group. Option pricing models usually require a predicted dividend yield. However, some can be modified to use an amount rather than a yield. Such an amount should take into account any historic patterns of dividend increases.

Risk-free interest rate. According to IFRS 2, the risk-free interest rate is the implied yield, available at the date of grant on zero-coupon government bonds in the currency of the exercise price, with a term equal to expected life of the option being valued. When such bonds do not exist, it may be necessary to estimate an appropriate yield from those on outstanding issues.

COMMONLY USED OPTION PRICING MODELS

There are three commonly used option pricing models, Black-Scholes, binomial, and Monte Carlo simulation.

Black-Scholes Option Pricing Model

The fundamental insight of the Black-Scholes Option Pricing Model is that it is a mathematical model of the market for an equity, in which the trading price is a stochastic (random) process. It uses a partial differential equation that must be satisfied by the price of a derivative on the equity. The Black-Scholes formula is the result obtained by solving the equation for a European call option, which typically has no right of early exercise.

This model is often described as closed form, because inputs and assumptions are uniform for the entire period of the option. It tends to be a straightforward calculation, requiring only the six previously discussed inputs:

1. Share price at grant date
2. Exercise price
3. Anticipated life
4. Expected volatility
5. Predicted dividend yield
6. Risk-free interest rate

Its strengths:

- A straightforward, extremely fast formula easily included in spreadsheets.
- Wide acceptance in the market for traded options.
- Consistent use enhances comparability between entities

Its weaknesses:

- The assumption that exercise can take place only at one moment rather than at variable dates; IFRS 2 places a special emphasis on this, and encourages use of other models if certain conditions are present.
- Volatility of the underlying shares, which may be expected to change over time, is fixed.
- Most market-based performance conditions typically cannot be taken into account.

Example: Value by Black-Scholes Model

Estimated Equity Value	$3.61
Strike Price	$4.25
Annual Dividend Rate	$0.00
Risk-free Rate	4.82%
Volatility	87.39%
Expected Term	2.50
Fair Value of Option	**$1.80**
Total number of Options Granted	2,647,059
Total Expense	**$4,776,756**

According to IFRS 2:B5, early exercise

might preclude the use of the Black-Scholes formula, which does not allow for the possibility of exercise before the end of the option's life and may not adequately reflect the effects of expected early exercise. It also does not allow for the possibility that expected volatility and other model inputs might vary over the option's life.

Binomial (Lattice) Model

The binomial model, first proposed by Cox, Ross, and Rubinstein in an article "Option Pricing: a Simplified Approach," Journal of Financial Economics, 1979, 229-263, applies a "discrete-time framework" to trace the evolution of the option's key underlying variables via a binomial lattice (tree) for a given number of intervals (time steps) between the valuation date and expiry. This model is often described as open form, because it may incorporate different values for variables (such as volatility) over the term. It can also take into account variable exercise dates. Many valuators believe the ability to vary inputs over time is more realistic for longer-term options.

A binomial model breaks down the time to expiry into a potentially large number of steps. At each it is assumed that the share price will move up or down by an amount calculated from the expected volatility and the length of the step. The likelihood of upward and downward movements is estimated using probabilities derived from the size of the upward and downward steps and the risk-free rate of return.

A tree of share prices is initially constructed working forward from the present to expiry. This generates a binomial distribution of share prices, which represents all possible paths that the price could take during the life of the option; dividends are reflected as they are paid. The process is iterative, starting at each final node and working backward to the valuation date. If the inputs and assumptions are the same, the Black-Scholes and binomial models give broadly similar results.

Its strengths are:

- Although slower than Black-Scholes, it is considered academically more accurate, particularly for options with longer vesting periods and for securities with variable dividends.
- More flexible than Black-Scholes.
- Able to take account of changing market conditions if included in inputs.

Its weaknesses are:

- Requires a considerably more complex spreadsheet to calculate the value.
- Necessitates judgmental decisions as to how various factors (e.g., employee exercise behavior) are taken into account.
- Lattice methods face several difficulties and are not practical for options with numerous sources of uncertainty (real options) or those with complicated features.

Monte Carlo Simulation Model

For option pricing, a Monte Carlo model works by simulating a large number of projected random outcomes of how the share price may move in the future. Based on each forecast share price and the proportion of options that would be exercisable, a payoff is determined. This is then discounted back to the valuation date at the risk-free rate to give a possible fair value. The procedure is repeated many times to determine the expected (average) value of the award at the valuation date.

Its strengths are:

- The most flexible procedure that can take into account complex market-based vesting conditions, exercise behaviors, and factors.
- It is easier to explain and/understand the results.
- It can be used to look at the distribution of payoffs.

Its weaknesses are:

- It requires a special program or complex spreadsheet to calculate the option's value, making it more difficult for auditors to verify.
- It may need 10,000 or more simulations to obtain an accurate answer and generally is used only where it is not possible or appropriate to use other methods.

Example: Monte Carlo Simulation

Exhibit 32.1 Flow Chart for Monte Carlo Simulations of Business Value

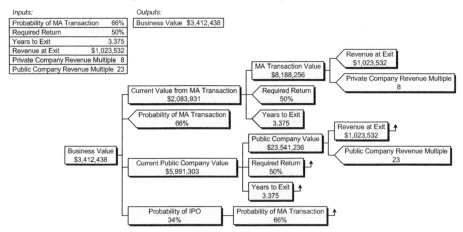

This Monte Carlo simulation involved 1 million iterations across the range of assumptions. The frequency distribution of the values is set out in Exhibit 32.2.

Exhibit 32.2 Frequency Distribution of Business Value

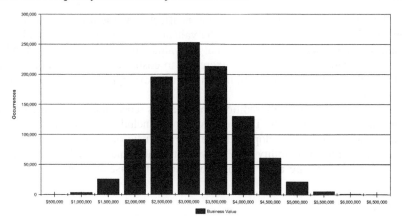

VALUATION OF UNDERLYING SHARES

As discussed, the most common share-based payments are options issued to employees; typically, because there is no open market for them, they are valued using an option pricing model. This section focuses on determining the fair value of a privately owned company's share price. Much of the text is influenced by SFAS 123R and IFRS 2; the two documents are very similar. The application and interpretation of the standard, and practices related to it, may vary by country, especially as some elements are not specifically defined.

Both IFRS 2 and SFAS 123R require that the fair value of the share price at the date of grant be estimated, but neither provides any significant guidance on the process. For publicly traded shares, it is relatively easy to estimate the fair value, as prices are published. For privately held entities, valuators often need valuations at the end of every reporting period as well as on grant dates.

To assist in determining suitable values for shares underlying the options, the American Institute of Certified Public Accountants (AICPA) Practice Aid, *Valuation of Privately-Held-Company Equity Securities Issued as Compensation,* was published in 2004. This publication offers best practices for valuations and disclosures related to privately held company equities issued as compensation; it includes options within the scope of SFAS 123(R) and IFRS 2. Most auditors consider this publication as best practice in estimating the fair values of options and their underlying shares.

Overview of the Practice Aid

The Practice Aid, intended to benefit all parties involved in the valuation of privately issued securities, was developed by staff of the AICPA and a task force of representatives from the appraisal, preparer, public accounting, venture capital, and academic communities. It is not intended to determine the value of an entity as a whole, nor is it a detailed how-to guide. Rather its objective is to give an understanding of the valuation process, the roles and responsibilities of the parties involved, and recommend best practices regarding individual minority ordinary shares. Key components include:

- Valuation methods
- Value allocation

Valuation Methods

The reliability of a fair value determination is affected by the timing (contemporaneous versus retrospective) and the objectivity of the valuator. A contemporaneous valuation considers conditions and expectations that exist at the valuation date not biased by hindsight. In a retrospective valuation, care should be exercised to ensure that the assumptions and estimates reflect only the business conditions, enterprise developments, and expectations that existed at the valuation date.

A valuator should consider all traditional approaches (cost, market, and income) and select the most appropriate methods. This process should include consideration of the entity's history, nature, and stage of development; the characteristic of its assets and liabilities; its capital structure; and the availability of reliable, comparable and verifiable data. Commonly, the results of one method are used to corroborate or otherwise support one or more other methods.

Value Allocation

Once a valuator estimates the fair value of the equity in a business, the next challenge is to allocate it among the various classes of securities. Such an equity allocation, the second phase of a valuation, requires an understanding of preferred stock rights, which comprise both economic and control privileges.

Often, multiple classes of equities are found in early-stage enterprises funded by venture capital or other private equity; each of those provides its holders with unique rights, privileges, and preferences. The Practice Aid acknowledges that value creation in such entities is frequently a high-risk process. In view of this, investors typically seek disproportionate returns and significant control or influence over the firm's activities. In those situations, there are often several series of preferred shares resulting from successive rounds of financing, each of which has specific rights. If an entity has more than one class of securities outstanding, the Practice Aid recommends three primary techniques to distribute the entity value among the various classes:

1. Current value method (CVM)
2. Option pricing method (OPM)
3. Probability weighted expected return method (PWERM)

The Practice Aid states that those are commonly used methods, some of them having roots in venture capital investment analyses. It lays out criteria to be considered when selecting a technique.

Current value method. The current value method of allocation is based on first determining the enterprise value of the business, reconciling to 100% of the equity value (which represents the amount available to both common and preferred shareholders), and then allocating the value to the various classes of equity based on their liquidation preferences or conversion rights. Depending on the equity value and the nature and amounts of the various preferences, preferred shareholders participate in the allocation, either at their liquidation amount or, if conversion would provide better economic results, as ordinary shareholders. Ordinary shares are assigned their pro rata proportion of the residual remaining after all liquidation preferences and conversion rights.

This technique is not forward looking; absent an imminent liquidity event within months of the valuation date, it fails to consider that the value of the entity may increase or decrease by the date when common shareholders receive their return on investment. The Practice Aid states that its use is limited primarily to two types of circumstances:

1. When a liquidity event is imminent and expectations about the future of the entity as a going concern are virtually irrelevant
2. When an entity is at such an early stage of its development that:
   a. No material progress has been made on the enterprise's business plan.
   b. No significant common equity value has been created in the business above the liquidation preference on the preferred shares.
   c. There is no reasonable basis for estimating the amount and timing of any such common equity value that might be created in the future.

The principal advantage of CVM is that it is easy to implement and does not require the use of complex tools. It assumes that the value of the convertible preferred shares is represented by the most favorable claim its holders have on the entity's value. As discussed, this technique is employed only in limited circumstances.

Example: Current Value Method

Estimated Value Summary	
Estimated Enterprise Value	$10,000,000
Plus Cash and Cash Equivalents	1,000,000
Less Interest-Bearing Debt	(500,000)
Estimated Equity Value (Preferred and Ordinary)	**$10,500,000**
Less Preferred Priorities	(1,815,000)
Estimated Equity Value (100% Equity Value)	**$8,685,000**
Number of Ordinary Share Equivalents	5,000,000
Estimated per Share Value	**$1.74**

Option pricing method. Although the CVM has in practice been applied for many years, its primary flaw is displayed when the preferences of the various classes of preferred shares are greater than the underlying equity value. In this situation, the implied value of the ordinary shares is zero. However, they are typically not worthless; firms would not give the shares away for free, and employees value the opportunity to buy them. In this light, the ordinary shares can be seen as call options on the future of the business.

An OPM treats both ordinary and preferred shares as call options on the equity, with exercise prices based on the rights of each class. Normally, the Black-Scholes model is used to perform the analyses. Under this technique, the ordinary shares have value only if the funds available for distribution exceed the various preferences at the time of a liquidity event—for example, a merger or sale.

Various terms of the shareholder agreements, including the seniority among the securities, dividend policy, conversion ratios, and cash allocations upon liquidation, are inputs for the OPM. It implicitly considers the effect of these terms and preferences as of a future liquidation and not as of the valuation date. When performing those analyses, a valuator must first determine the enterprise value of the business. The Black-Scholes model is then used to calculate call option values based on the various shareholder agreements; those are then used to allocate the equity value to the different groups.

The variables used for this type of analyses are:

- *Value of the underlying asset.* Most often, this value will be the implied equity value of the entity derived from the valuation analyses.
- *Breakpoints.* These replace the exercise values used to determine the fair value of an employee option. The breakpoints represent amounts used to separate the incremental returns to each class of equity according to the agreements. A separate breakpoint is built for each time when the equity allocation ratio might change. There can be as few as two breakpoints in an analysis or as many as 20, depending on the capital structure and the shareholders' agreements. This is the most time-consuming element of the

analyses and requires a thorough understanding of the funding history of the business. The technique implicitly considers the effect of the breakpoints as of a future liquidity event, not the valuation date.

- *Term.* As opposed to relating to a vesting or expected exercise time, in this analysis the term is an estimated period based on an assessment of when a merger, acquisition, IPO, or other liquidity event might occur; it is normally derived from discussions with management, directors, and investors. The expected term should incorporate entity and investor expectations, market and industry observations, product development milestones, and funding requirements.
- *Volatility of the underlying asset.* The volatility used should be an estimate of the entity's expected future volatility over a period equal to the term. Because privately held firms do not have historic volatility data, that of comparable publicly traded entities is often selected.
- *Projected dividends.* This represents the expected dividends to be paid on the various classes of equities.
- *Risk-free rate of return.* A risk-free rate that matches the term is used.

After call option values are calculated for each breakpoint, their incremental amounts are distributed to the different classes of shares based on their agreements. Those amounts are then divided by the related number of shares to get a per share figure for each class. Discounts for lack of marketability or absence of control, if applicable, should be applied to estimate the value of each ordinary share.

The OPM using the Black-Scholes technique is appropriate for situations where the entity has a number of choices available and the range of possible future outcomes is difficult to predict. The major drawback is that it is rather complex and the results are difficult to explain.

Both the PWERM and OPM consider the likelihood of future outcomes but handle them in different ways. PWERM allows for the discrete forecasts of individual scenarios (perhaps four or five), while the OPM starts with a beginning value and forecasts, with the Black-Scholes model, hundreds of future outcome scenarios along a lognormal distribution curve. There are debates among practitioners as to whether the outcome scenarios in a lognormal distribution pick up an adequate or realistic number of failure scenarios for early-stage companies.

Example: Allocation of Equity under OPM

First, the capitalization of the entity is summarized:

ABC Company–Summary Capitalization Table

Class	Shares Outstanding	Ordinary Share Equivalents	% of Outstanding
Series A Preferred	3,630,000	3,630,000	42.1%
Ordinary Shares	5,000,000	5,000,000	57.9%
Total	**8,630,000**	**8,630,000**	**100.0%**

Next, the details of the preferred shares are reviewed:

Class	Preferred	Features
Series A Preferred	$1,815,000	Participating
		Liquidation preference in the event of any liquidation, dissolution, or winding up of the entity is equal to original purchase price plus accrued and unpaid dividends. Thereafter, the remaining assets shall be paid out on a pro rata basis to the holders of ordinary shares and Series A preferred on an as-converted basis.
		8% cumulative dividend

Once the attributes of the various classes are understood, their breakpoints can be determined:

Equity Structure

Features	Preferred A	Ordinary
Interest/Dividend Rate	8.00%	NA
Cumulative	Yes	NA
Compounding	No	NA
Participating (preferences and participation)	Yes	NA
Convertible (preferences or participation)	No	NA
Redemption	No	NA
Shares Outstanding	3,630,000	5,000,000
Conversion Rate	1.00x	1.00x
Ordinary Share Equivalents	3,630,000	5,000,000
Liability/Preference at liquidity event		
Shares Outstanding	3,630,000	NA
Original Issue Price	$0.5000	NA
Capital Raised	$1,815,000	NA
Liquidation Preferences Multiple	1.00x	NA
Total Preferences	$1,815,000	
Accrued Interest as of 13 January 2009*	$0	NA
Time from 13 January 2008 to estimated liquidity event (years)	5.00	5.00
Interest/Dividend Accrued at estimated liquidity event*	$0	NA
Total Liability/Preference (estimated liquidity event)	$1,815,000	NA
Per Ordinary Share Equivalent	**$0.5000**	**NA**

* *Based on information provided by management, dividends are not expected to be declared; therefore, the analysis excludes dividends.*

The final assumptions for the OPM are then established:

Equity Value Summary

Estimated Enterprise Value	$10,000,000
Plus Cash	1,000,000
Less Interest-Bearing Debt	(500,000)
Estimated Equity Value	$10,500,000

Summary of Equity

	Preference at Liquidity	Strike Price for Preferred	Strike Price for Ordinary Participation	Shares Outstanding	Ordinary Share Equivalents	Percent
Preferred A	$1,815,000	NA	NA	3,630,000	3,630,000	42.1%
Common	NA	NA	$1,815,000	5,000,000	5,000,000	57.9%
Total				8,630,000	8,630,000	100.0%

Option Pricing Assumptions

Dividend Rate	0.00%
5y Risk-Free Rate, continuously compounded equivalent	1.60%
Volatility, 5-year average (rounded)	50%
Time to Liquidity Event	5.00

The value for each option or breakpoint is then calculated by applying the Black-Scholes model:

Call options—Black Scholes Model

Call Option	1	2
Strike Price	$0	$1,815,000
Call Option Price	**$10,500,000**	**$8,912,508**
Tranche Value	$1,587,492	$8,912,508

The equity values allocated to the various classes of shares are:

Allocating Equity value

Threshold Underlying Value			Call Option Tranche	Tranche Value	Applicable Classes	Applicable Shares	Preferred A	Ordinary Shares	Total
$0	to	$1,815,000	1-2	$1,587,492	Preferred A (A)	3,630,000	100.0%	-	100.0%
$1,815,000	to	<	2	8,912,508	Ordinary, A	8,630,000	42.1%	57.9%	100.0%
				$10,500,000		Value	$5,336,332	$5,163,678	$10,500,000
						Shares	3,630,000	5,000,000	8,630,000
						Per Share	$1.4701	$1.0327	

Probability Weighted Expected Return Method (PWERM)

Under the PWERM, the value of the ordinary shares is based on analyses of future values for the entity assuming various alternative outcomes. Those amounts are based on the probability weighted present values of expected future investment returns, considering each of the alternative outcomes as well as the rights of every class of shares. Although the outcomes in any given situation will depend on the facts and circumstances, they commonly include an IPO, merger or sale, dissolution, or continued operation as a private entity.

This technique involves forward-looking analyses of the possible future outcomes, estimating ranges of future cash flows from expected outcomes, present values for each, and the application of probability factors. A simple situation might involve a single value and date for each outcome, while more complex conditions could use a range of values and dates. Unlike the other methods, this method determines and allocates the entity's value at the same time. As outcomes can be estimated and tailored for each specific situation, PWERM is considered more accurate and easier to understand and explain than OPM.

However, as it is difficult to predict the value of a business in an IPO, merger, or acquisition three to five years in the future, PWERM requires significant judgment. In addition, it can be very time consuming, as estimating potential outcomes is often complex. This method is applied most often when there is an indication of the potential value under various scenarios, such as a sale price from its investment bankers.

Example: PWERM

Probability Weighted Expected Return Method (PWERM)

Scenario	Projected Value
1. Initial Public Offering–High Range	$30,000,000
(Average high range from Morgan Stanley and Credit Suisse)	
Est. Fully-Diluted Shares	8,630,000
IPO Dilution	25%
Common stock equivalents for the scenario	10,787,500
Total Post-Money Equity	$30,000,000
Preferred Priorities	($1,815,000)
Value to Ordinary Shares	$28,185,000
Shares	10,787,500
Per Share Value	$2.61
Number of periods	5.00
Discount Rate (WACC)	14.5%
Present Value of Share Price	**$1.33**

2. Initial Public Offering–Low Range $20,000,000

(Average low range from Morgan Stanley and Credit Suisse)

Total Post-Money Equity	$20,000,000
Preferred Priorities	($1,815,000)
Value to Ordinary Shares	$18,185,000
Ordinary Shares	10,787,500
Per Share Value	$1.69
Number of Periods	5.00
Discount Rate (WACC)	14.5%
Present Value of Share Price	**$0.86**

3. Advantageous Strategic Sale or Recapitalization

	Forecast Results in Year 5	Trailing Multiple	Implied Value
Based on Revenue Multiples	$15,000,000	1.50x	$22,500,000
Based on EBITDA Multiples	$2,000,000	10.00x	$20,000,000
Average			$21,250,000
		Preferred Priorities	($1,815,000)
		Value to Ordinary Shares	$19,435,000
		Shares	10,787,500
		Per Share Value	$1.80
		Number of Periods	5.00
		Discount Rate (WACC)	14.5%
		Present Value of Share Price	**$0.92**

4. Remain Private and Recapitalize Private Equity Interest

Based on DCF analysis assuming recap of preferred shares	$0.50

Weighted Average Per Share Value of Scenarios

	Implied Value per Ordinary Share	Probability	Weighted- Average Event Risk Adjusted Per Share Value
Initial Public Offering–High Range	$1.33	25%	$0.33
Initial Public Offering–Low Range	$0.86	35%	$0.30
Advantageous Sale or Recapitalization	$0.92	35%	$0.32
Remain Private	$0.50	5%	$0.03
Totals		100%	**$0.98**

VALUATOR AND SHARE-BASED PAYMENTS

Privately held entities in many countries engage valuators to help determine the value of their ordinary shares so that they can issue employee options in amounts that do not create tax issues and satisfy the fair value requirements of IFRS 2. In the United States, entities that are contemplating or are anywhere near a filing for an IPO should engage a valuator to determine the fair value of their shares when granting options, as the Securities and Exchange Commission typically will look back 18 to 24 months to verify if any options were granted at less than fair value, which it refers to as cheap stock. Such engagements are usually full business valuations with a focus on an equity allocation based on the Practice Aid. A 2008 survey shows the professional time spent on such assignments ranges from 60 to over 100 hours. They often turn into recurring activities, as many entities update their values more than once a year.

Additionally, valuators are engaged to calculate the fair values of share-based payments and the related expenses to be recorded on an entity's financial statements; others perform this calculation internally, using one of the many available share-based compensation programs. Typically, such engagements take less time since detailed analyses of the business, industry and financial statements are generally not necessary. They typically only require the selection and application of an appropriate methodology and range anywhere from 15 to 50 hours.

33 SOFTWARE AND SYSTEMS

SUSAN M. SAIDENS

UNITED STATES

INTRODUCTION

This chapter addresses the valuation of computer software and related data according to International Financial Reporting Standards (IFRS) with cross-references to International Valuation Guidance Notes (IVGN). Pronouncements regarding fair value for financial reporting in the United States are referred to as generally accepted accounting principles (GAAP) rather than to individual standards. These authoritative documents should be considered in valuing software:

- IFRS 3R, *Business Combinations,* issued in January 2008, to be applied to business combinations occurring on or after July 1, 2009. In certain circumstances, it can be applied sooner, but only in an accounting period beginning after June 30, 2007.
- IFRS 5, *Noncurrent Assets Held for Sale and Discontinued Operations,* applies to intangible assets whose carrying amount is anticipated to be recovered through a sale rather than by continued use.
- IAS 38R, *Intangible Assets,* prescribes the accounting treatment for intangible assets that are not specifically dealt with elsewhere, using principles-based approaches.
- IAS 36, *Impairment of Assets,* provides guidance with respect to measuring the impairment of an intangible asset, if its carrying amount exceeds the greater of fair value less costs to sell, or value in use.
- IVGN 4, *Intangible Assets,* provides assistance in rendering or using valuations of intangible assets.
- IVGN 16, *Valuation of Intangible Assets for IFRS Reporting Purpose,* still in an exposure draft, expands on IVGN 4.

IFRS defines fair value as:

The amount for which an asset could be exchanged between knowledgeable, willing parties in an arm's-length transaction.

Although both IFRS and GAAP use the same term as their standard of value for financial reporting, they have different definitions. IFRS assumes a hypothetical buyer and a hypothetical seller in a market transaction involving an *entrance* price. By contrast, GAAP looks at the hypothetical transaction from the perspective of a market participant, therefore as an *exit* price:

Fair value is the price that would be received to sell an asset or paid to transfer a liability in an orderly transaction between market participants at the measurement date.

This distinction represents the primary difference between IFRS and GAAP concerning the valuation of software; it is discussed in detail in Chapter 1. Another difference is that International Accounting Standard (IAS) 38R distinguishes between the research and the development phases with regard to internally developed software. Research costs are expensed as they occur; development costs are capitalized only when the entity can meet certain specified criteria. Under GAAP, research and development costs are capitalized only for acquired software.

COMPUTER SOFTWARE

Computer software is a written program, procedure, or set of rules and the associated documentation pertaining to the operation of a computer system; they are stored in read/write memory (www.thefreedictionary.com/computer+software). This definition includes operating systems, utilities, business applications, word processing and spreadsheets as well as computer games and electronic databases.

Approaches to Valuation

The generally accepted approaches to valuation are:

- Market Approach
- Income Approach
- Cost (Asset-based) Approach

While all three approaches are used for software, one of the methods under the Income Approach is the most common, although depreciated replacement cost (DRC) is used often for internally generated items. It is important to remember that under IFRS, whichever approach is chosen, the valuation inputs should reflect those that would be made by knowledgeable and willing parties in a hypothetical sale transaction.

What Is Being Valued?

The success of Microsoft is a prime example to understand how critical software design and development is to businesses as well as being potentially lucrative to its creators. Consequently, to obtain better protection, software is often copyrighted and/or patented. When software is to be valued, the first question is whether to value the software, the copyright, or the patent; that decision will determine the most appropriate methodology.

Intangible assets are identifiable, nonmonetary items without physical substance (IAS 38R:8). Acquired computer software is a recognized intangible asset as it meets all of these criteria (IAS 38R:10):

- It is identifiable.
- The entity has control over the asset.
- It is probable that economic benefits will flow to the entity.
- The cost of the asset can be measured reliably.

Expenditures undertaken to generate future revenues do not by themselves create an intangible asset; when recognition criteria are not met, all costs that have been incurred should be expensed (IAS 38R:10). There is a rebuttable presumption that the fair value of an intangible asset acquired in a business combination can be measured reliably (IAS 38:35).

IAS 38 offers guidance on acquired software. If it is included in the amount paid for an acquisition, it may be individually recognized. If the software is an operating system for hardware, it should be part of the cost of the hardware. Amortization of the software (an accounting, not a valuation, issue) is based on its useful life or pattern of benefits; straight-line depreciation is the default.

Data Collection

The valuator should follow the same due diligence for software as with any valuation assignment: a prudent understanding of what is being valued, how the item is to be used, who has ownership of what (the source code). All relevant data should be collected, including interviews with the acquirer's and the target's managements regarding the economic benefits, measurability, substance, life cycle position, obsolescence, and alternative future uses of the software.

MARKET APPROACH

Quoted prices in an active market are the most reliable measure of fair value (IAS 38R:39); however, there are not many trades in software and there are no active markets for it. Even if arm's-length transaction data is available, it is difficult to know the actual comparability between the item sold (guideline) and that being valued (subject), so as to determine what adjustments may be needed. Market-based valuations must establish the highest and best, or the most probable use of the asset (IVS 1, 4.1); those "are developed from data specific to the appropriate market[s] and through methods and procedures that try to reflect the deductive processes of participants in those markets."

Completed-Transaction Method

The completed transaction method used to value software is similar to that for valuing an entity; however, software transactions are significantly less frequent than sales of businesses. If such transactions can be found, valuation multiples indicated by them may provide meaningful input. Comparability of software, in terms of lines of code, costing conventions, functionality, and ease of use, make it very difficult to use this method; therefore, when it can be applied, it is generally used only as a reasonableness check.

Existing Licenses

In many cases, either the acquirer or the target has licensing agreements for software applications. If comparable to the subject software, often these can be used as a guideline. An alternative is information in public filings on sales or licenses of software; the challenge is to find the appropriate information on truly comparable products.

Relief-from-Royalty

A common technique to value software is the relief-from-royalty method; a hybrid of the market and income approaches, it is based on the principle that if the entity did not own the asset, it would have to license it to obtain the same benefits. Put another way, the value of the software is the present value of the royalty payments that the entity saves by being the owner; this method utilizes a market-derived royalty rate.

Example: Relief-from-Royalty

Target owns internally developed proprietary Web-based software called eKnowledge that is not yet commercially available. It provides for multiway trading replacing the normal two-way interaction; no one else in the market currently has this capability. Based on those unique characteristics, the relief-from-royalty method has been selected for the valuation. Under this, the economic value of the software is the present value of the expected royalty savings.

Selecting a fair royalty rate for the rights to Target's software requires analyses of market evidence and a consideration of its specific characteristics as compared to the returns being realized by existing comparable software products. This process is assisted by searching DEXA, a New York database service, for royalty rates on market transactions licensing software in the relevant Standard Industrial Classification (SIC) or the North American Industry Classification System (NAICS) codes; in this case, SIC 7372 was used. The valuation report must state the source and full details of any market royalty data used. The search produced 24 transactions. A review of the descriptions of the entities involved, the types of software licensed, and the reported dates reduced the list to the six summarized in the next table; they are all believed to be reasonably comparable with the subject software.

Exhibit 33.1 Market Royalty Rates: Software, eCommerce

Date	Licensee	Licensor	Property	Royal Rate High	Low	Fee $
2004	EZ Technology	Undisclosed	Licensed to support its software Tm platform for buyers and suppliers to transfer documents via the Internet to their small and medium trading partners	10.0%	7.5%	
2005	Interactive Publishing	Various	An online travel reservation program linking to more than 500 airlines and 30,000 hotels	14.0%	10.0%	
2006	Technologies	Worldwide Euroware	Gives merchants easy access to comparative and competitive shopping and product interactions to consumers	15.0%	15.0%	50,000
2006	Important Software	ibought You	The system designs, deploys and manages promotions, tracking individual responses to offers	10.0%	10.0%	
2007	Global PC	Investor Paradigm	Helps online investors to make faster and better decisions by thumbs-up/thumbs-down signs for shares immediately after earnings releases	15.0%	15.0%	
2008	What If	EZ Use	Licensee plans to become the market for worldwide barter by bringing together multiple groups to trade interactively online	9.0%	9.0%	
			Median	12.0%	10.0%	
			Mean	12.2%	11.1%	

Major Assumptions

- A pretax royalty rate of 9.0% was chosen, based on discussions with management and an analysis of the royalty rates for Software, eCommerce from the third-party database, which supplied the information listed. Royalties ranged from a low of 7.5% to a high of 15.0%. The median high and low rates were 12.0% and 10.0%, respectively, while the means were 12.2% and 11.1%. The 9.0% chosen is less than the low median (10.0%) but the same as that paid in the latest transaction; this product is also the most similar to the multiway trading capabilities of the subject. A valuator should not just arbitrarily rely on the median, mean, or their average; consideration of other factors is an integral part of choosing an appropriate royalty rate.
- Management's internal forecasts of sales and earnings for the software for the next four years (2009–2012) were analyzed, considered reasonable, and relied on. After discussions with the programming staff regarding the software's capabilities and reviewing the competitive situation, it was established that the firm had a three- to four-year lead; after that, a major enhancement will become necessary, and there would be much greater opposition; therefore, its remaining useful economic life is considered to be four years.
- Due to the risks involved with a unique but as yet non-revenue-producing software, a discount rate of 30% was adopted using the midyear convention; that assumes that cash flows are received, or at least available, evenly throughout the year.
- Since in the particular country acquired software can be deducted for tax purposes as an intangible asset, a tax amortization benefit (TAB) is added to the calculated value, based on a 15-year tax life, a 35% effective tax rate, and the 30% discount rate.

The fair value of the Target's software using the relief-from-royalty method is $2,250,000, as shown in the next calculations.

Exhibit 33.2 Value of eKnowledge Software

		2009	2010	2011	$'000 2012
Sales		1,500.0	4,500.0	18,000.0	54,000.0
Royalty	9.0%	135.0	405.0	1,620.0	4,860.0
Income Tax	35.0%	(47.3)	(141.8)	(567.0)	(1,701.0)
Net Royalty		87.8	263.3	1,053.0	3,159.0
PV Factor	30.0%	0.870	0.669	0.515	0.396
PV Royalties		76.3	176.1	541.8	1,250.3
Total of Present Values				2,044.5	
TAB	9.5%			194.2	
Fair Value of Software				2,238.7	
Fair Value of Software–Rounded				2,250	

INCOME APPROACH

In valuing business enterprises, the Income Approach can provide a viable way of estimating the future benefits to be received. Properly applied, it can also offer an indication of value for software. The challenge and difficulty in using this approach for software is in segregating the cash flows relating only to the software from those of the business.

Profit Split Method

In theory, similar to relief from royalty, this method assumes the subject software is owned by a third party and licensed to target under an agreement to split the profits. The percentage for each participant reflects the facts and circumstances unique to the transaction. For a valuator, establishing the appropriate percentages is daunting. Starting with the 25% rule that dates back to Edison (see Chapter 35), one should analyze all possibly relevant factors, such as what each party brings to the transaction and the potential for substitute software.

Useful Economic Life

A fundamental factor in applying the Income Approach is an estimate of the remaining useful economic life of the subject software; in other words, how long will it continue to generate positive cash flows? The term "economic life" can be defined as the period of time over which property may generate economic benefits. Determining this requires consideration of a number of metrics, such as: the software's age; expected time until a major enhancement or "rewrite" is needed; how the operating system is used; and how well it satisfies the needs of buyers, especially in terms of speed and efficiency.

Multiperiod Excess Earnings Method

A commonly accepted methodology for estimating the fair value of software is the multiperiod excess earnings method. This method projects the cash flows arising solely from the software in three steps:

1. Forecasting by year the operating, debt-free, cash flows available from the software for a period, normally five years.
2. Deducting from the debt-free cash flows after-tax returns on contributory assets, such as: working capital, property, plant and equipment, other relevant intangibles and the assembled workforce; the results are the debt-free cash flows from the software.

3. Discounting them back to present values at an appropriate risk-adjusted discount rate, which should consider the time value of money, inflation, and the risks inherent in ownership of the subject software.

The fair value of the subject software is the total of the present values of such cash flows over its remaining useful economic life plus any applicable TAB.

Example: Multiperiod Excess Earnings Method

As well as its eKnowledge software, Target owns Web-based educational software (eGAin) that is considered to be the primary intangible asset acquired. Consequently, the best technique, due to the software's significance, is the income approach using the multiperiod excess earnings method (MPEEM).

Major Assumptions

- Management's internal forecasts of sales and earnings from eGAin for the next five years (2009–2013) were analyzed, considered reasonable and relied on. After discussions with management regarding eGAin's capabilities and reviewing the market situation, it was established that the software had a significant competitive advantage in the online educational forum.
- Due to the lesser risks associated with revenue producing software, a discount rate of 20% was adopted using the midyear convention.
- Since in the subsidiary's country, acquired software cannot be deducted for tax purposes as an intangible asset, no TAB is added to the calculated value.

The fair value of Target's eGAin software using the MPEEM is $3,600,000, as shown in the next table.

Exhibit 33.3 Value of eGain Software

		2008 actual	2009	2010	2011	2012	2013 $
Sales		884,141	3,739,427	5,662,487	6,794,985	6,183,436	5,379,590
Growth		na	323%	51%	20%	–9%	–13%
EBITDA		396,979	1,682,742	2,548,119	3,057,743	2,720,712	2,313,224
EBITDA Margin		44.9%	45.0%	45.0%	45.0%	44.0%	43.0%
Depreciation		(17,683)	(74,789)	(113,250)	(135,900)	(156,932)	(181,219)
Earnings before Taxes		379,296	1,607,953	2,434,869	2,921,843	2,563,780	2,132,005
Income Taxes	38.0%	(144,132)	(611,022)	(925,250)	(1,110,300)	(974,236)	(810,162)
Net Earnings		235,164	996,931	1,509,619	1,811,543	1,589,544	1,321,843
Depreciation		17,683	74,789	113,250	135,900	156,932	181,219
Operating Cash Flow		252,847	1,071,720	1,622,869	1,947,443	1,746,476	1,503,062
Less returns on:							
Working Capital		(2,169)	(52,637)	(72,590)	(83,027)	(73,336)	(63,802)
PP&E		(181)	(4,295)	(6,597)	(8,301)	(8,301)	(8,301)
Customer Relationships		(821)	(18,771)	(18,178)	(16,264)	(11,439)	(9,952)
Noncompete Agreements		(13,972)	(19,763)	(18,138)	(12,334)	(6,530)	(6,530)
Copyrights & Trademarks		(143,726)	(237,187)	(287,331)	(287,331)	(287,331)	(287,331)
Assembled Workforce		(21,982)	(36,276)	(43,945)	(43,945)	(43,945)	(43,945)
		(182,851)	(368,929)	(446,779)	(451,202)	(430,882)	(419,861)
Debt-free Cash Flow		69,996	702,791	1,176,090	1,496,241	1,315,594	1,083,201
PV Factor	20.0%	1.000	0.909	0.758	0.631	0.526	0.438
PV Royalties		69,996	638,901	890,977	944,596	692,126	474,888
Total of Present Values				3,641,489			
Fair Value of Software				3,641,489			
Fair Value of Software–Rounded				3,600,000			

Subsequent Expenses

The nature of intangible assets is such that there will seldom be additions to or replacements of any part of them; this means software should be valued without modifications to enhance its performance. Expenditures to enable continued functioning as originally planned are expensed as maintenance when incurred. Subsequent costs to enhance software are only rarely capitalized (IAS 38R:20).

COST APPROACH

The Cost Approach establishes value based on the cost of replacing the property, less depreciation from physical deterioration and obsolescence, if present and measurable. The valuator has the choice of replacement cost new: "the current cost of a similar new property having the nearest equivalent utility to the property being valued," or reproduction cost new: "the current cost of an identical new property." The primary difference is that replacement cost relates to an asset with similar functionality and utility taking advantage of the latest technologies, while reproduction cost typically re-creates an identical item. IFRS believes that the Market Approach, if the data are available, is the best way to estimate fair value. Replacement cost, if a similar asset can be identified, is an excellent means of valuing software under the Cost Approach.

There are two primary techniques used in the Cost Approach to value software: trended historic cost and engineering build-up. For software, the trended historic cost method adjusts the actual monthly or yearly software development expenditures by an appropriate inflation-based factor to convert them to current levels. However, a business rarely knows the actual period development costs for a particular software program in sufficient detail for a valuator to use this method. Consequently, replacement costs usually are estimated using a software engineering model with actual and/or estimated development times. Those are designed to assist software managers and developers to estimate the time, human resources, and other efforts expected to be needed for a software project. Commonly, metrics such as lines of code, function points, and the like and fully loaded per hour costs of each of the various grades of staff are used.

The valuator must make sure that all relevant expenses are counted in the software's development costs, such as: employee remuneration including options, payroll taxes, employee benefits, allocated overhead costs, installing for beta testing as well as the entity's customary profit margin on such a project.

Example: Reproduction Cost, New Methodology

Another of Target's software assets is an internally developed enterprise resource planning (ERP) system that also serves its subsidiaries. Acquirer intends to transfer its records to Target's ERP during 2009. This system handles the costing of customer projects to their custom specifications and integrates all departments and functions across the firm involved with processing customer orders. Quoting has been distilled into an Excel/Visual Basic spreadsheet that provides a detailed analysis of each job, incorporating real-time raw material pricing. The ERP system then allows the finance, manufacturing, and warehousing departments to manage all their activities on a single database, so that they may easily share information and communicate with each other.

Based on research and analysis of the market for this type of ERP, it has been determined that the best method to value the system is the Cost Approach, using reproduction cost new less obsolescence. The basis for the Cost Approach is that the ERP has no directly attributable revenue/income stream due to its functioning as a supporting asset. For simplicity's sake, the example includes only one module of the ERP, called Alia, the quotation system.

Major Assumptions

- The chief information officer who created and updates the ERP system provided management with details of the current estimate of person-hours to reproduce the software using the latest technology. For the Alia module, the estimated loaded cost of $75.96/hour becomes $158,000 a person-year. This is based on: four weeks' vacation, 12 statutory holidays, and five sick days, for a total of 320 working days a year; at 6.5 effective working hours a day, this gives 2,080 working hours at $75.96 each, for a total of $157,997.
- Conversion costs for specialty technical personnel, such as an outlook parser and a notes parser, are also needed for Alia.
- Other technical manpower needs include:

Experts	Person-Years
Intro Part	0.250
Info Trax	0.167
Virtual Power	0.083
URLs	0.083
Splitter	0.083
E-Produce Tools	0.083
Imaging	0.333

- License costs for Music License, Visual Studio, and SQL were $300,000, $30,000, and $10,000, respectively.

Costs for development workstations totaled $20,000.

Exhibit 33.4 Alia Module

Staff/Contractor Requirements

Activity	Duration	Cost
	(person-years)	$
Basic Code	1.583	250,161
Outlook Parser	0.917	144,839
Notes Parser	0.500	79,000
Tester	0.500	79,000
Experts		0
IntroSpect	0.250	39,500
DocuMatrix	0.167	26,386
VirtualPartner	0.083	13,114
URLaw	0.083	13,114
Splitter	0.083	13,114
E-ProcBates	0.083	13,114
Imaging Correction	0.333	52,614
	4.582	723,956
Contingency	5.0%	36,198

Additional Licenses Needed

Verity for Music		300,000
Development Tools (Visual Studio, SDKs)		30,000
SQL Server		10,000
		340,000

Extra Hardware Required

Development Workstations (10 @ 2,000)		20,000
		360,000
Sales Tax	6.0%	21,600
		381,600
Total Estimated Reproduction Cost New		1,141,600

This table sets out the estimated reproduction cost new for Alia. If the program had been new as of the valuation date, the value would be correct. However, an obsolescence factor has to be applied in order to recognize the fact that the ERP is not brand new. Rather, it was originally installed in 2006 and may have redundant or extraneous code as a result of continuous maintenance patches over the years, or it may contain certain inefficiencies that a brand-new ERP system would not have. The expected obsolescence of 40% is based on discussions with management regarding program inefficiencies and market analysis of the economic life of similar ERP. Income taxes at 38% were deducted from the replacement cost to recognize the original deductibility of such amounts. As Target's country allows tax amortization for acquired software, a TAB was added, based on a 15-year tax life, a 38.0% tax rate and a risk-adjusted discount rate of 23.5%.

Exhibit 33.5 Conversion of RCN to Fair Value

		Cost
		$
Reproduction Cost New (RCN)		1,141,600
Obsolescence Provision	40.0%	(456,640)
Replacement Cost		684,960
Related Income Taxes	38.0%	(260,285)

		Cost $
		424,675
TAB	13.0%	55,208
Fair Value of Alia		479,883
Fair Value of Alia Rounded		475,000

The fair value for financial reporting purposes of all the acquired ERP modules using the Cost Approach is $2,200,000:

Target's ERP system

Module	Depreciate Replacement Cost $
Alia Quotes	475,000
Order Entry	345,000
Finance	810,000
Manufacturing	575,000
Warehousing	285,000
Total	2,205,000
Rounded	2,200,000

Obsolescence or Remaining Useful Life

As demonstrated in this chapter, all three traditional approaches may be used to value software. Each should include an estimate of the software's remaining useful economic life. A valuator ought to include this and any situations/conditions that might affect the future benefits in an estimate of the software's fair value. Also he or she should provide a sound analysis of any obsolescence factors; however, in most instances, there is insufficient information available about any software program from which to calculate survivor or probable life curves.

These types of obsolescence should be considered for software:

- *Functional* represents the loss in value due to a reduction in the utility of the asset over time, such as increased downtime due to maintenance as the asset ages, and redundant or extraneous code.
- *Technological* includes its "life cycle," as new products and upgrades are introduced quickly in the twenty-first century. The value of a program may decline rapidly if a development in the industry or by another vendor renders it obsolete. Other influences on declining values are: lack of major enhancements, a failure to satisfy users' current and future needs, and the feasibility of similar software being introduced.
- *Economic* represents a loss of value from factors that may not have anything to do with the software itself but be merely external economic trends. The 2008 global crisis has shown that companies and their products are perceived to have less value than before it began. Supply and demand should also be considered; for example, does the subject software have many competitive substitutes?

CONCLUSION

A fair value estimate for software must be considered in the context of the fair value in a hypothetical transaction. Does the software value make sense based on "the amount for which an asset (the software) could be exchanged between knowledgeable, willing parties in an arm's-length transaction"? In addition, if more than one method is selected, it is important for the valuator to reconcile the values in reaching a conclusion. In any engagement, the quantity and quality of the available data, the facts and circumstances unique to the situation, as well as the informed judgment of the valuator will determine ultimately the appropriate methods to estimate the fair value of software for financial reporting.

34 UNPATENTED TECHNOLOGIES

ANKE NESTLER

GERMANY

INTRODUCTION

Know-how and trade secrets are intangible assets owned by almost every organization. While they may be documented in files, drawings, concepts, and archives, such material is usually only a small part of the whole asset. Often described as something "in the head of the workforce," know-how is an integral component of the people working in an organization.

Joint Ventures

One strategy to benefit from know-how in the technology sector which is undertaken quite often is to establish partnerships or to found joint ventures, which allow the resources from several entities to be combined in a new alliance likely to create additional value.

In December 2008, Daimler AG and Evonik [Industries AG, a multinational specialty chemical manufacturer] announced that they established a strategic alliance for the development and production of Lithium-Ion Batteries. Based on lithium-ion technology from Evonik and with Daimler's expertise, both groups plan to drive forward the research, development and production of battery cells and battery systems in Germany. This strategic alliance is considered to represent an important milestone in the production of electric vehicles.

What Is Know-How?

European Commission (EC) Regulation No. 772/2004, relating to technology transfer agreements, defines "know-how" as:

a package of non-patented practical information resulting from experience and testing, which is:

- *Secret, that is, not generally known or easily accessible*
- *Substantial, that is, significant and useful for the production [...], and*
- *Identified, that is, described in a sufficiently comprehensive manner so as to make it possible to verify that it fulfills the criteria of secrecy and substantiality*

Thus, know-how is accessible only to a specific, well-known group within an organization and should be subject to protective measures to prevent disclosure. The EC definition is a good description of this type of intangible asset but should be extended, because, in general, economic (trade) secrets are different from technology-based know-how. Typical examples of know-how are: formulas, patent operating parameters, drawings, and other nonpatented technologies. Representative trade secrets are: pricing and terms from suppliers, customer lists, contracts, names of key personnel, control systems, process descriptions, and financial information (i.e., margins, acquisition costs, sales).

Importance of Know-How

Know-how can have a major impact on the economic success of a firm. Two examples from the USA and Germany demonstrate this.

> The recipe of Coca-Cola is probably one of the most famous formulas in the world. As it is not protected by a patent, this information is not public. While the ingredients have to be documented on the bottle, the formula itself is still a very well protected secret.

Not only technical know-how but also economic trade secrets may often be important for successful businesses.

> Aldi is a privately owned German discount supermarket chain operating over 8,200 stores through 66 regional companies in 18 countries. This group is a significant example of a successful entity with minimum transparency about its management strategy, financial situations and key numbers. The latter have been one of the best-kept secrets of German industry; only recent legal obligations to disclose certain financial data provided some insight into the sales of this group (about $50 billion in 2008).

PROTECTION

The main characteristic of this intangible asset class is that it is not protected by specific laws. In some cases, know-how and trade secrets are covered by copyright or fair trade laws and, in those regimes, also by common law. As a result, the extent of the protection differs from jurisdiction to jurisdiction.

Comparison with Patents

A trade secret is principally addressed in most countries if:

- It is definitely a secret and not known to the public.
- Observable measures are taken to prevent disclosure (e.g., only a small number of people have knowledge of it, employees have signed confidentiality agreements etc.).

The advantage of protecting technology by patents is that the owner of the intellectual property rights (IPR) is shielded not only against imitation and infringement but also against accidental, independent development. Additionally, as the asset is described in detail in public documents, third parties have no excuse to claim ignorance and are therefore able to avoid infringements. Know-how, in the sense of unpatented technology, though legally protected in many jurisdictions, is subject to more risks than that which has been patented. Nevertheless, there are four reasons why an owner of IPR might decide against patenting its know-how:

1. The know-how might be part of an ongoing development process. In that case, as a work in progress, the technology may not fulfill the criteria for a patent. Alternatively, research could show that other registered patents apparently exist that might affect the development process.[1] This suggests that projects in the research or development stages (early-stage technology) are know-how (or a trade secret) that could carry significant value but may be difficult to fully protect.
2. Especially with trade secrets, the owner would like to prevent the technology from becoming public. As the patenting process includes a detailed description and publication of the know-how, the owner of a "business process" patent, issuable in the United States and some other countries, may fear the copying and work-around uses

---

[1] *For a description of steps in the technological invention and valuation issues, see Mirjam Leloux and Aard Groen, "Business Valuation of Technology: An Experimental Model," les Nouvelles: Journal of the Licensing Executives Society. Vol. 42 No. 3, September 2007, 478-486. .*

by others. Even if the know-how is protected by law and an infringer can be sued, there is a possibility at that point that the patent is declared invalid; even if it is upheld and damages obtained, it is likely to become part of the industry's general knowledge.

3. A patent, if granted, only protects the know-how during a maximum period, usually 20 years. After that, others can freely use the technology as it has become part of the public domain.

4. The patent application process is time consuming and quite expensive. Thus, many small start-up entities shy away from the effort. As the criteria for patent protection varies significantly between countries, the know-how may not be able to be protected everywhere, as it does not fulfill the requirements in a particular country; this may also be the case for trade secrets.

Trends in Patents

The trend in patent applications differs widely from country to country (see Exhibit 34.1); for many years, Japan and the United States have led in the number of patents. The figures do not differentiate triadic patents, filed simultaneously in the United States, Japan, and Europe by entities that want to protect big ideas in a global market.

Exhibit 34.1 Filings for Patent Applications

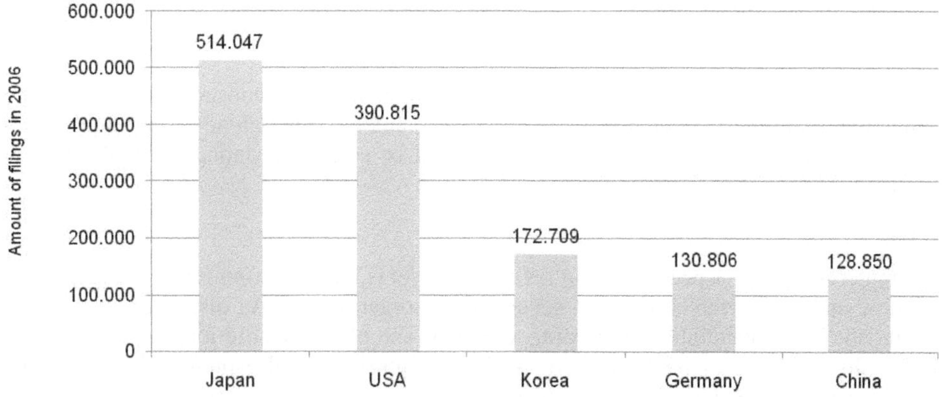

Source: World Intellectual Property Organization, World Patent Report 2008

In summary, know-how and trade secrets are unique to the owner but not available to the public, especially not to other industry participants. They are important to an organization as they give it a competitive advantage; if such know-how or trade secrets leave the organization and become known by others, they lose their confidentiality and thereby value. Once this happens, unless the discloser is legally admonished, the know-how and trade secrets are in danger of turning into general knowledge, by becoming public in the market or in relevant parts of it.

KNOW-HOW AND TRADE SECRETS ARE VALUABLE ASSETS

Know-how and trade secrets, as defined, comprise a competitive advantage that has a positive impact on an organization's profits. The loss of such information could cause substantial damage to an entity. The value of the information represents an opportunity cost, which is the loss of profits because the information has become public.

Legal Ownership

The premise of a valuable IPR is that there is no doubt about its legal ownership; to clarify that is the first step in valuing an intangible asset. Other than for registered IPR, this cannot be proven by documents. In valuing know-how, legal ownership is hard to confirm. Inquiries must be made if there are any ongoing litigation issues (outstanding or settled in the past). If a third party can claim or currently claims some ownership rights or is being attacked for breaching the entity's ownership rights of know-how, trade secrets, or other intangibles, a possible discount of the value might be indicated. In specific cases, the value to the entity might be questionable or even nothing, until these uncertainties are clarified.

Actual Asset

The next step is to identify the actual asset to be valued; a major problem in the valuation of an IPR is the separation of the subject asset from other related items, as they usually work together as part of a complete organization. In the case of Coca-Cola, it might be difficult to separate the total value between the formula (in the United States, there are at least four versions) and the brand and maybe the shape of the bottle. In other cases, the question "What is the know-how?" is more easily answered; for a new state-of-the-art plant, details of construction schedule, long-term project management techniques, engineering innovations, process know-how, drawings, and customer base are readily available. Thus, it is very difficult to separate various assets.

Value in Use and Value in Exchange

In this respect, it is essential to differentiate between the going-concern premise of using the intangible asset in the same context (value in use) and the stand-alone assumption, which means the price at which the intangible asset could be sold to an independent third party (value in exchange). (See Chapter 1.)

Security

Another important aspect of facing a valuable asset is the question of how the respective know-how and trade secrets are kept secure in the organization. As discussed, their main characteristic is confidentiality. According to experts and official institutions, entities have to face a realistic danger of losing important information. Industrial espionage is one of the gravest threats to technology-based companies.

According to one article,[2] 35% of respondents had a strong suspicion of espionage and 19% had discovered a case in their own organization. A significant problem seems to be that, in many instances (39%), the loss of know-how and trade secrets is caused by the employees themselves (see Exhibit 34.2). This is especially true for employees who leave to start up their own businesses or to work for competitors.

---

[2] *Corporate Trust, "Industrial Espionage—Damages Caused by Espionage in German Industry," 2007. www.corporate-trust.de/End.htm*

Exhibit 34.2 Reasons for Industrial Espionage

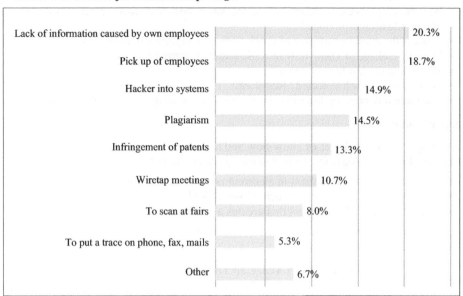

Source: Corporate Trust, "Industrial Espionage—Damages Caused by Espionage in German Industry," 2007

Information about breaches of intellectual property protection seldom becomes public, unless it leads to litigation. Organizations do not appreciate such information becoming public as it might be regarded as management carelessness because the crimes are often instigated by employees and other insiders. One researcher reports:

3Com revealed some examples of security incidents, as e.g., a caller posing to be a 3Com employee requested a faxed copy of 3Com's Research and Development organization chart from an unsuspecting human resource administrative assistant. This caller appeared to be a predatory headhunter.[3]

Security Checklist

The next questions should be considered to understand how well the know-how and trade secrets to be valued are secure or easy to copy:

- By what means are the entity's know-how and trade secrets recorded?
- Are they in one central database or numerous departmental ones?
- Is there a distinction between technical know-how and commercial trade secrets?
- How accessible are they?
- Does the organization have a security system to protect its know-how and trade secrets?
- Is this security system updated regularly?
- Is it always in force?
- Who has access to the research and development department where the know-how is generated?
- Is it restricted to certain employees?
- Does the organization work with protection codes for certain files and departments?

---

[3] *Dana St. James/Jeffrey L. Hartmann, "Developing And Implementing A Trade Secret Protection Program," **les Nouvelles** (March 2002): 23-26.*

- How current are the protection procedures of the computer systems?
- Are the employees, as "carriers" of the know-how and trade secrets, well informed about industrial espionage?
- What is the average turnover of employees with significant know-how?
- Has any leakage of know-how or trade secrets occurred recently?
- When was the last hacker attack?
- How quickly was it detected? Repulsed?
- Are there any ongoing lawsuits about know-how damages or loss of trade secrets?

Degree of Innovation

An important value driver of know-how and trade secrets might be: How extensive is the innovation? For technology, the answer to this question might be:

- An incremental improvement in a current process (technology)
- A breakthrough in an existing technological field
- A revolutionary advancement that creates a new technology.

It is assumed that regarding commercial acceptance and time to market effects, revolutionary technology creates the highest value.[4]

WHEN TO VALUE INTANGIBLE ASSETS

The valuation of intangible assets has numerous purposes. One typical use is the calculation of intellectual property damages. In certain countries, particularly the United States, the enforcement of IPR through the courts, including jury awards for economic damages, is increasing. While such litigation typically comprises patents, copyrights, and trademarks, there is the awareness that damages for less protected IPR (know-how and trade secrets) are also relevant.

Unlike fully protected IPR, the legal entitlement is more difficult in case of an infringement. Nevertheless, know-how and trade secrets usually also belong to an entity which owns protected IPR and thus can claim for additional damages. The legal framework for claiming and calculating economic damages will differ between various legal jurisdictions. Nevertheless, the underlying methodologies and calculations for know-how and trade secrets are quite similar to those for patents.[5] A typical case for claiming damages is economic espionage; the entity may try to sue the offender who breached its rights.

Reasons for Importance

Know-how and trade secrets may become relevant in many transactions, especially in asset deals. A 2008 article analyzed the importance of certain IPR in merger and acquisition (M&A) transactions.[6]

While patents are considered to be the most significant form of protection, 16% of respondents also ranked trade secrets as important. Nonetheless, performing due diligence on them is generally considered more difficult than for other IPR (see Exhibit 34.4). This may reflect the difficulty in identifying the specific economic benefits that arise from know-how or trade secrets and also the fact that such confidential information always runs the risk of being exposed.

---

[4] Terry C. Bradford, *"Assessing the Value of Technology Innovation,"* **les Nouvelles** *(June 2004): 95-97.*

[5] *For the principles of calculating IPR damages in the United States, see Brent Bersin and Lance Morman,* **les Nouvelles** *(December 2008): 248-255.*

[6] *"M&A Insights: Spotlight on Intellectual Property Rights," A Mergermarket Study in Association with CRA International and K&L Gates (December 2008).*

Exhibit 34.4 Difficulty of Performing Due Diligence for Certain Intangible Assets in an M&A Transaction

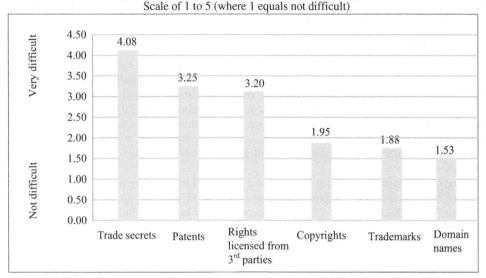

Scale of 1 to 5 (where 1 equals not difficult)

Source: *"M&A Insights: Spotlight on Intellectual Property Rights—A Mergermarket Study in Association with CRA International and K&L Gates," December 2008*

Financial Reporting

The valuation of know-how and trade secrets is also relevant for purchase price allocations according to International Financial Reporting Standard (IFRS) 3, *Business Combinations*. In a business combination, the acquirer has to recognize and measure the identifiable assets of the target obtained. Identifiable intangible assets have to fulfill the criterion of either being separable or based on contractual or other legal rights; additionally, the entity must control the specific asset and the future economic benefits flowing from it; see International Accounting Standard (IAS) 38, *Intangible Assets*.

Know-how and trade secrets cannot always be considered to be an intangible asset as defined by IAS 38.9. In those specific cases, they become part of goodwill and do not have to be valued separately. When the trade secrets or know-how are considered an asset, they are valued separately, or if appropriate in groups. The American Institute of Certified Public Accountants (AICPA) Practice Aid *"Assets Acquired in a Business Combination to Be Used in Research and Development Activities: A Focus on Software, Electronic Devices and Pharmaceutical Industries,"* New York, 2001, deals with in-process research and development (IPR&D), in detail. The Practice Aid recommends techniques for: defining, accounting for, disclosing, valuing and auditing assets acquired to be used in research and development (R&D) activities and including specific in-process R&D projects.

Finally, a valuation may be required at least indirectly if the know-how or trade secrets are violated by third parties. In such a case, it is not the value of the asset itself that is important, only the damages caused to the IPR owner by the infringement.

VALUATION METHODS

For valuing nonpatented know-how and trade secrets, the overall techniques for intangible assets apply: the Cost Approach, Market Approach, and Income Approach; see Chapter

21.[7] The application of a specific method will differ depending on the valuation purpose, the item to be assessed, and the availability of data. An important question is: Are the know-how or trade secrets being valued in commercial use? That will be true in most cases but not in some others, such as early-stage technology.

Cost Approach

The Cost Approach is based on the concept that the minimum value of an asset are the costs required to "rebuild" a similar item at the valuation date. Normally, replacement cost is used, which is the total amount needed to create (at current prices) know-how or a trade secret with equal utility. In calculations, historic costs, adjusted for inflation, may be used as approximation. Nevertheless, they should take into account sunk costs in regard to functional, technological, and economic obsolescence. In certain cases, it may be appropriate to add a margin to the value, because financial investors usually expect an appropriate rate of return.

The Cost Approach is useful in terms of a make-or-buy decision from a purchaser's perspective. At the same time, in considering its return on investment, an owner needs to know how much was already spent to reach the level of know-how or to build up the secret information.[8] A significant advantage is that normally, data are available and that replacement costs comply with realistic considerations of financial investors.

Nevertheless, even though the Cost Approach gives a first indication of possible values for know-how, there are limitations. The main weakness is that the approach does not reflect future commercial opportunities. The costs of creating know-how might understate the potential value or have been totally wasted. Additionally, a make-or-buy decision ignores time to market. Any asset available for purchase has already passed critical stages of development and has achieved a certain success; thus, a buyer saves time and takes on fewer risks.

Market Approach

The concept of the Market Approach is that similar assets should sell at similar prices. Therefore, usually an active market is considered to be the best indicator of the value of any asset. However, the approach's application requires finding and identifying transactions between third parties involving comparable intangibles. The criteria comprise, among others: the type of know-how, industry, stage of development, inherent risk or protection level, and type and date of transaction. If several market prices exist, they have to be reconciled into at least a reasonable range of values; this is a very important step, in which the valuator has to confirm the reliability of the underlying data and that the subjects are comparable to the know-how or trade secret being appraised.

Market-based intangible valuation methods are hardly ever applicable, as transactions in those types of intangible assets rarely take place, or their terms are not published. Know-how and trade secrets are often part of a merger or acquisition, perhaps even a key value driver, but they are transferred usually as either part of a business unit (legal entity) or at least as a bundle of several related IPR. Another difficulty in practice is that the actual know-how and that covered by a public transaction are usually not comparable.

The relief-from-royalty method, commonly used to value intangibles, is partially covered by the Market Approach, as royalties are derived normally from reported market transactions, which reflect prices paid by market participants to use the IPR. As the revenues and

---

[7]   *Details of the major methods are in Reilly and Schweihs,* **Valuing Intangible Assets** *(1999), 95.*

[8]   *Pierre Breese, "Valuation of Technological Intangible Assets,"* **les Nouvelles** *(June 2002): 54-57.*

cash flows on which the royalties are based come from financial projections, this method is also part of the income approach. See Chapters 21, 33, and 35.

Income Approach

In theory and practice, the Income Approach is usually considered to be the best for valuing intangibles, as it is based on expected future cash flows from the item. In the case of know-how and trade secrets, if the expected development and related cash flows are reliably predictable, other methods are preferable. For an early-stage technology entity, it is necessary to prepare a full business plan with cash flow projections reflecting: up-front development costs, the timing of expenditures, and adequate returns on other (contributory) assets required. Because of the uncertainties, usually several scenarios are required.[9]

In discounting future cash flows, only the cost of equity should be used to reflect the high risks of IPR&D. One appropriate procedure is to look to venture capital funds, which expect certain rates of return, depending on the investment's stage of development; they start at 25% and go up to 50% for technology start-ups. (See IPR&D Practice Aid, section 5.3.87.)

As mentioned, the relief-from-royalty method is appropriate in certain cases, especially for technologies that are comparable to one that has been licensed.[10] One difficult issue is to find suitable royalty rates for the subject asset; they differ significantly from industry to industry, depending on the reference figures (sales, gross profits, etc.) and are influenced by the split of obligations and costs as set out in the individual license agreements.

A current study of royalty rates collected data between September 1990 and December 2007.

> *In this study, several different industries as e.g., computer/software, semiconductors, medical and food & beverages are covered. In the result of this analysis, the most frequently negotiated royalty rate is 5% of net sales, and this across a diverse number of industries. Royalty rates range between 0.5% up to 40.0% of sales, while royalty rates above 15.0% are classified as rare and are only associated with extraordinarily profitable technologies such as those in the gaming and entertainment industry.[11]*

This method is quite difficult for trade secrets, such as customer lists, because, in general, a specific cash flow arising from the asset cannot be separated from that of the entity; likewise with R&D in projects: The IPR&D Practice Aid, section 2.1.12, states: "The task force believes that the Relief-from-Royalty method rarely would be appropriate in the valuation of specific IPR&D projects due to a lack of observable comparable royalty rates."

In some cases, a loss of income method might be appropriate to value the importance and relevance of an entity's trade secrets. In this, the entity is valued separately with and without the trade secret. The difference between the amounts is a measure of the importance of this asset to the value of the entity.

TECHNOLOGY JOINT VENTURES

Know-how is often important to joint ventures (JVs) developing new products and technologies. Valuation becomes important at different phases of this type of cooperation, as shown in Exhibit 34.3.

---

[9] *G. V. Smith and R. L. Parr, **Valuation of Intellectual Property and Intangible Assets**, 3rd ed. (2000), 501.*

[10] *See Pierre Breese, "Valuation of Technological Intangible Assets," **les Nouvelles** (June 2002): 54-57.*

[11] *Russell L. Parr, "Royalty Rates & License Fees for Technology," **les Nouvelles** (March 2009): 15-17*

Exhibit 34.3 Typical Phases of a Technological Joint Venture

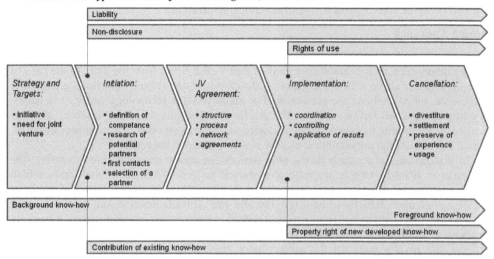

Source: German Department of Research and Education, "How to Handle Know-how in International Technology Cooperations" (Umgang mit Knowhow in Internationalen FuE-Kooperationen), 2009

Valuation Requirements

Basically, the valuations needed for the five typical phases of a joint venture are:

1. *Strategy phase.* Analyses are needed of what know-how already exists and how much additional knowledge may be needed for the planned program. At this stage, assessments are undertaken of risks and chances of a joint venture success, compared with independently creating the product.
2. *Initiation phase.* Each party's existing know-how is valued with other assets and cash; those form the basis for each participant's contribution.
3. *Agreement phase.* How the contributed know-how is protected and who will benefit from newly developed products are defined. Ownership and usage rights are established so each party is aware of all benefits and obligations.
4. *Implementation phase.* Value is created in this phase.
5. *Cancellation phase.* In this phase, settlement payments are made, which require a detailed valuation whose parameters are determined by the JV agreement. If the parties do not agree, an arbitration value may become relevant.

Example: Initiation Phase

In early January 2008, effective at the beginning of the month, two Chinese solar power companies agreed to form a 50-50 joint venture to produce photovoltaic (PV) solar wafers and cells. One participant, Wing Chow Enterprises Limited of Hong Kong, transfers to the JV its X'ide division, which produces monocrystalline polysilicon ingots and wafers; the other, Yi Solar Co. Ltd. of Shanghai, transfers its cell and module manufacturing operations. The joint venture will operate under the X'ide name.

Assets Transferred

At the valuation date, 31 December 2007, the participants contributed the financial physical and intangible assets shown on the table.

	X'ide Processing Division $'000	Yi Solar Cell/Module Operations $'000	X'ide Joint Venture $'000	Note
ASSETS				
Current				
Cash	4,209	35,122	39,331	
Receivables	2,276	7,186	9,462	
Inventories	9,546	5,510	15,055	
Prepaids	7,300	1,498	8,798	
	23,331	49,315	72,646	
Fixed (Capital)—net of depreciation				
Land	2,408	--	2,408	
Building	4,624	--	4,624	
Furnaces	2,649	--	2,649	
Equipment	756	3,639	4,395	
Construction in Progress		9,363	9,363	
Suppler Deposits	23,079	--	23,079	
	33,516	13,002	46,518	
	56,847	62,317	119,164	
LIABILITIES				
Bank Operating	5,175	--	5,175	
Bank Term	22,366	--	22,366	
Payables & Accruals	3,822	2,625	6,446	
Unearned Income	7,055	4,525	11,580	
	38,418	7,150	45,568	
REPORTED EQUITY	18,429	55,167	73,596	
INTANGIBLES				
Furnace Write-Up	4,851	--	4,851	A
Equipment Write-Up	2,844	--	2,844	B
Developed Know-How	20,700	--	20,700	C
Customer Relationships	--	26,000	26,000	D
Trade Name	24,300	--	24,300	E
Assembled Work Force	1,250	3,500	4,750	F
Supply Contracts	12,000	--	12,000	G
	65,945	29,500	95,445	
Aggregate Contributions	84,374	84,667	169,041	

Bases of Valuations of Intangibles

Note A Replacement Cost New less Physical Deterioration

Note B Replacement Cost New less Functional Obsolescence

Note C X'ide has developed know-how that enables it to build a furnace for about 25% of the commercial cost. The present value of those savings through lower depreciation during the 10-year projection period is $20,700,000, at a discount rate of 20%.

Note D The majority of Yi's sales are made in Europe, where at the end of 2007, the price of photovoltaic modules was €4.77 a watt, compared to $4.85 in Asia, which represented a 36% exchange premium. The amount ascribed to the customer relationships is the present after-tax value of this benefit, assumed to be amortized over 10 years, at a 25% discount rate.

Note E The X'ide trade name was valued by the relief-from-royalties method using a market derived royalty of 3% and a discount rate of 15%.

Note F As the formation of a joint venture is not a business combination, no goodwill is recorded, except for the assembled workforces. These are at duplication cost, based on headhunting and recruitment fees and all training and learning curve expenses.

Note G X'ide has long-term contracts with a German polysilicon supplier for about 80% of current usage at a fixed price, which is about 85% below the recent spot level. The spot price is expected to decline from 2008 to 2016, the period of the contract. The allocated amount is the present value at a 30% discount rate of the expected after-tax savings.

Example: Cancellation Phase

During 2008, the joint venture was modestly profitable, reporting a $12.5 million operating profit on sales of $395 million, compared with pro forma figures for 2007, which were $11.4 million on revenues of $142 million. In the fourth quarter, however, profits were only $1.4 million before an inventory write-down of $11.4 million.

There were three reasons for the disappointing results:

1. Cultural and language differences between Hong Kong and Shanghai
2. A rapid global decline in the prices of polysilicon and PV cells
3. Delays and start-up costs for the equipment and construction in progress at the initiation

As a loss was incurred in the first quarter of 2009, Yi Solar offered to purchase, at fair value, Wing Chow's interest in all the assets and liabilities net of cash; this was $50.5 million.

	X'ide Joint Venture $'000 31-Dec-07	X'ide Joint Venture $'000 31-Mar-09
ASSETS		
Current		
Cash	39,331	--
Receivables	9,462	17,978
Inventories	15,055	12,642
Prepaids	8,798	6,591
	72,646	37,211
Fixed (Capital)—net of depreciation		
Land	2,408	2,239
Building	4,624	4,261
Furnaces	2,649	6,250
Equipment	4,395	17,670
Construction in Progress	9,363	--
Suppler Deposits	23,079	19,473
	46,518	49,893
	119,164	87,104
LIABILITIES		
Bank Operating	5,175	--
Bank Term	22,366	--
Payables & Accruals	6,446	12,247
Unearned Income	11,580	9,148
	45,568	21,395
REPORTED EQUITY	73,596	65,709
INTANGIBLES		
Furnace Write-Up	4,851	--
Equipment Write-Up	2,844	--
Developed Know-How	20,700	9,000
Customer Relationships	26,000	12,900
Trade Name	24,300	9,200
Assembled Work Force	4,750	--
Supply Contracts	12,000	4,300
	95,445	35,400
Aggregate Contributions	169,041	101,109

The major changes in the assets outside normal operations are:

• Land and building decreased by 7%
• Developed know-how decreased by 57%
• Customer relationships decreased by 50%
• Trade name value decreased by 62%
• No payment was made for the assembled workforce
• Supply contracts declined by 64%

Each of the intangibles was valued in the same manner as for the initiation phase; comments on certain items are set out next.

During 2008, the United States and Asian price per watt, according to Solarbuzz, a consultancy, became $4.78 (–1.4%), while that in Europe decreased to €4.55 (–4.5%) and the strengthening dollar lowered the exchange premium from 36% to 25%; that reduced the value of the customer relationships by 30% to $12.9 million.

Sales in the fourth quarter of 2008 were 54% below those of the third; in the first quarter of 2009, they were down a further 8%, with a gross margin of only 1%; this reduced the value of the trade name to $9.2 million.

In the second half of 2008, polysilicon prices fell swiftly, dropping to $200 per kilogram in November, from $450 to $500 earlier in the year. An analyst predicted they would sink below $100/kg by the end of 2009 and to the $50 to $80 range in 2010; this is roughly the same level as prices in the long-term contracts.

CONCLUSION

Know-how and trade secrets are types of intangible assets that represent unpatented rather than patented technology. Thus, similar valuation principles apply. At the same time, these assets might comprise early-stage technology with unprotectable secret know-how that is difficult to assess. Trade secrets have a value to an organization, as they are unique to it, but they are usually not a marketable product or do not directly generate cash flows, except to the extent they reduce costs. The critical factor for valuing these intangibles is to determine whether they are well protected by the entity and do not become public knowledge.

35 TRADEMARKS AND BRANDS

ROGER SINCLAIR

SOUTH AFRICA

INTRODUCTION

A detailed illustration of how a brand is described for valuation purposes is provided in Chapter 21. The American Marketing Association has its own definition: a " name, term, sign, symbol or design, or a combination of them, intended to identify the goods and services of one seller or group of sellers and to differentiate them from those of the competition." It is the latter part of the definition that expresses the essential commercial purpose of branding.

In Illustrative Example 21, International Financial Reporting Standard (IFRS) 3, *Business Combinations,* states that brands are synonymous with trademarks:

> *The terms brand and brand names, often used as synonyms for trademarks and other marks, are general marketing terms.*

This serves the accounting standards well, but it is not completely correct from the marketing point of view. Marketers have long viewed brands as assets and follow a three-stage process to create a brand that has benefits for its owner.

1. Following new product research and development, names are generated and a short list created. The final choice is largely dependent on the availability of the favored name to be legally registered as a trademark and that the all-important Uniform Resource Locator (URL, a legal form of Internet address) can be universally acquired to provide the brand with an Internet presence.
2. The brand elements are created by brand specialists and graphic designers. These are the name style, colors, packaging, music, slogan, and all the elements that are geared to making the brand easily recognizable to its user group.
3. A marketing campaign will be designed and implemented to make the brand known and available to the public. Once the first dollar is exchanged by a consumer for the product or service, the brand is said to have equity, which is the value it adds to a nonbranded version and which leads to a flow of future economic benefits.

In this hierarchy, the trademark is the contractual and protective base on which the brand is built. Being legally protected means that the brand owner can defend the brand against attacks of all sorts. It also means that the brand is transferable in that the trademark on which it is based can be sold and registered in the name of the new owner.

Not all new brands succeed. Gourville[1] has found that at least half of all new product introductions fail. Brands that do succeed are very likely to have long and indefinite lives. In

---

[1] J. T. Gourville, *"The Curse of Innovation: Why Innovative New Products Fail,"* Marketing Science Institute (MSI) Working Papers 05-117, Boston, 2005.

an analysis of leading brands, Keller[2] identifies 25 current brands in major consumer categories and finds that only five had not been leaders in 1923, 85 years earlier. Because the long-term rewards are so good, marketers are willing to make considerable investments in research, development, and the introduction of new brands, even taking into account a high rate of failure, as a brand that succeeds will generate profitable cash flows far into the future.

This leads to two important considerations in valuing brands:

1. Brands have indefinite economic lives.
2. Most brands will grow rather than diminish in value over time.

ACCOUNTING SITUATION

Currently (March 2009), trademarks are only recorded in financial statements when acquired in a business combination or asset purchase. If brands (trademarks) are internally generated, they fall under International Accounting Standard (IAS) 38, which is in the process of being reviewed; it is anticipated that when it is reissued, all trademarks and brands will qualify for recognition as intangible assets whether they are internally created or acquired in a business combination.

This chapter covers the contractual-legal basis of a brand, brands as assets, the need to recognize the end user as the source of future economic benefits, and key principles applicable in the measurement of brands for IFRS 3, *Business Combinations*.

PROTECTING TRADEMARKS

Brand equity is defined as the brand's ability to add value to a nonbranded version. There are many makes of computers available on the market, but the leading brands, such as Apple, Dell, HP, IBM, and a few others, dominate. Similarly, names such as Cadbury, Lindt, Mars, Nestlé and Suchard describe different forms of the commodity called chocolate. Considerable value has been built up by the owners of those brands over many years because the brand names signify reliability, innovation, quality, taste, and related benefits such as energy, enjoyment, and fun.

However, this value can be destroyed if competitors are able to offer an identical product to, for instance, the Apple Macintosh, at a much lower price, or make available their own versions of chocolate with similar taste, look, packaging, colors, and name. Today the problem of copying is very real. Digital technology enables counterfeiters to reinvent virtually any product known to man. An extreme but factual case is a fake Ferrari 1967 P4 of which only three were ever built. A knock-off in a Thai garage, using modified Japanese parts and in 2008 about to be shipped to a European client in a $1 million sale, was seized by police before leaving the country. The key factor that prevents competitors from taking unfair advantage of the value built up in brands, and the only defense available to brand owners against those who steal their brand identity, is the registered trademark.

There is no single definition for a trademark. The wording varies from jurisdiction to jurisdiction. The definition in the United Kingdom Trade Marks Act 1994, however, captures the spirit:

> *Any sign capable of being represented graphically which is capable of distinguishing goods or services of one undertaking from those of another undertaking. A trademark may, in par-*

---

[2] *K. L. Keller, Strategic Brand Management: Building, Measuring, and Managing Brand Equity, 3rd ed. (Upper Saddle River, NJ: Pearson Prentice-Hall, 2008 edition).*

ticular, consist of words (including personal names), designs, letters, numerals or the shape of goods or their packing.[3]

In many countries, there is common law protection for trademarks that have been and continue to be in use. However, this is difficult because the plaintiff has to prove to the court that the mark has developed a reputation and goodwill and that the defendant's brand is sufficiently similar to cause confusion among the public. Rights granted through trademark registration are much more straightforward and relatively inexpensive and easy to enforce.

The Swiss-based World Intellectual Property Organization (WIPO) was founded in 1891 and set up to allow a single point of contact for international trademark registration. Various failings brought about the establishment of a parallel system called the Madrid Protocol, which commenced in 1989. More recently the European Union created the Community Trademark System, based in Alicante, Spain, which started in 1996. A number of countries, for example, the United States and Japan, have not signed any of those agreements.

To offer protection, a trademark must be registered in the countries where the product is to be made available. The flow of trademark applications is very large: WIPO alone received over 35,000 applications during 2005. In the United States, trademark applications in 1996 exceeded 200,000. So great is this demand that the pool of potential names has shrunk dramatically; therefore, it is unlikely that a trademark based on a common word or a generic product description would be available for registration. Either the word has already been registered or the authorities would not accept it because it is in public use.

This complication has led to courts creating a hierarchy of determining eligibility for registration:[4]

- *Fanciful.* Made-up words with no inherent meaning (e.g., OXO)
- *Arbitrary.* Actual words but not associated with the product (e.g., Camel)
- *Suggestive.* Real words that are suggestive of the product feature (e.g., Head 'n Shoulders)
- *Descriptive.* Common words protected only with a secondary meaning (e.g., Ivory [soap])
- *Generic.* Words synonymous with the product category (e.g., Aspirin)

A relatively recent example of successful registration occurred in 2000, when the global firm Andersen Consulting was forced to change its name to separate itself from the eponymous accounting firm, subject to a court-determined deadline. The new name, Accenture, was completely fabricated, and registration was, therefore, achieved very quickly. With heavy marketing support, the switch was made in a record 147 days.

A significant lesson learned from this example was that through well-formulated marketing communications, the value that resided in the previous name could be transferred into the new trademark quickly and effectively.

TRADEMARK INFRINGEMENT

Many countries have specific laws that apply to trademark infringement. In the United States, for example, the relevant law is the Federal Trademark Dilution Act. It deals with what it describes as "famous trademarks." This, more precisely, applies to any brand that has developed a public demand based on its reputation and goodwill. When a case is brought before a court in terms of this act, the test is if the reputation of the brand has been "blurred" or "tarnished" by competitive actions.

---

[3] *J. Fogg, "Brands as Intellectual Property," in **Brands: The New Wealth Creators**, ed. Susannah Hart and John Murphy (New York: New York University Press and Interbrand, 1998), p. 72.*

[4] *Based on Keller, **Strategic Brand Management**, pp. 179–181.*

Blurring happens when the use of an existing mark by a different company in a different category alters the unique and distinctive significance of that mark. Tarnishing occurs when a different company employs the mark in order to degrade its quality, such as in the context of a parody or satire.

An article proposes two additional concepts, "typicality" and "dominance," which would become preferred measures in court.[5]

Typicality is the "ability of a trademark to elicit recall of its own product category." In other words, the brand is typical of the category. Coca-Cola would be the most typical brand in the carbonated beverages category because, when its name is mentioned, most people would immediately associate it with its category.

Domination is "the trademark's ability to be recalled when the product category is mentioned." Or, if the carbonated beverage category is the prompt, probably, Coca-Cola would be the first name that is recalled. Leading brands are those with the highest levels of typicality and dominance; they are already in consumer memory from which buyers make their final selection.

Market research is needed to demonstrate the extent to which either of these circumstances applies; domination is considered the more valuable of the two. The court's decision would be based on the extent to which the actions of the defendant had caused, or were likely to cause, damage to the plaintiff's competitive position.

Knudson[6] provides broader guidance as to what the courts see as trademark infringement. He suggests that the courts will consider the likelihood of confusion being caused between two brands resulting in trademark infringement when one or more of these occur:

- The marks are similar.
- There is relatedness between the goods produced.
- The plaintiff is able to demonstrate a strong level of distinctiveness.
- Similar market channels are used (both trademarks are made available via the same method of distribution).
- The degree of care used by consumers in insisting on the plaintiff's brand (buyers will seek out this brand because of the perceived satisfaction it provides).
- The intent of the defendant when selecting or designing its mark. How, to whom, and for what purpose the brand will be (or is being) be marketed.
- Evidence of actual confusion.
- The likelihood of product line extension. It is the intention of the plaintiff to introduce variations of the original product or service to extend the range.

Clearly there is a preventive and financial remedy attached to the court finding, and valuation is increasingly being called on to assist in establishing the amount of the remedy.

Some trademark disputes are long lasting. Since at least 1907, Anheuser-Busch of the United States, founded in 1858, has disputed the European rights to the names "Bud" and "Budweiser" with two Czech firms "Budweiser Beer Burgerbrau" (1795) and "Budweiser Budvar" (1865). In March 2009, the European Court of First Instance refused Anheuser-Busch's latest request to register "Budweiser" as its trademark. This left unchanged the situation where Anheuser-Busch has the rights in 22 of the European Union's 27 countries, Budvar in four and both can use it in the United Kingdom.

[5]   R.A. Peterson, K. H. Smith, and P. C. Zerillo, "Trademark Dilution and the Practice of Marketing," *Journal of the Academy of Marketing Science* 22, No. 2 (Spring 1999): 255–268.

[6]   W. A. Knudson, "An Introduction to Patents, Brands, Trade Secrets, Trademarks, and Intellectual Property Rights Issues," Strategic Marketing Institute Working Paper1-0806. Product Center for Agriculture and Natural Resources, Michigan State University, 2006.

IMPORTANCE OF BRANDS AS ASSETS

Goodwill has been examined by the legal and accounting professions in a number of countries since the early part of the nineteenth century. The search has been to determine its nature and how it should be valued. Only recently was goodwill recognized as an asset and given a variety of treatments on the balance sheet. A popular convention until the mid-1980s was for acquired goodwill to be written off against the equity account immediately after acquisition.

That was fine until companies started buying others for sums of money that created goodwill sometimes as large as the shareholders' equity. These prices were being paid to acquire famous brands considered to be highly valuable. The scale of merger and acquisition activity in North America and Europe in the 1980s was unprecedented, as were the premiums being paid. This focused the minds of the accounting standard setters on finding answers to two key questions:

1. Why were companies paying large premiums over the net asset value for the firms they were buying?
2. What accounting method would allow equity depletion caused by current accounting rules and conventions to be avoided?

British companies that included Rank Hovis McDougall and Diageo put forward, as a solution, capitalizing the value of brands and placing them on the balance sheet. By treating them as assets as opposed to acquired goodwill, the need to deduct the goodwill component of the purchase price from the shareholders' equity was ameliorated.

The immediate response by the accounting profession to the treatment of brands as assets was to issue a cease-and-desist instruction. This ignited the so-called brand debate, an intense argument for and against brands as assets. Essentially, the compromise taken was to ban the practice of treating brands as assets, but that goodwill should be recognized as an asset to be amortized for no more than 20 years in the United Kingdom and 40 in the United States. That view was in line with the findings of the Barwise Commission, established in 1989 by the Institute of Chartered Accountants of England and Wales, and implemented by the London Business School.

The report that emerged from the commission's deliberations confirmed the leanings of the British accounting profession that brand valuation was contradictory to the then accounting framework. Brands did not meet the definition of an asset and could not reliably be measured, and it would not be possible to separate their future economic benefits from those flowing from other parts of the business. In 1998, the predecessor to the International Accounting Standard Board produced IAS 38, which embodied most of those considerations. This standard is still in force today but, as stated earlier, is under review. In 2001, Statement of Financial Accounting Standard (SFAS) 141, followed by IFRS 3, *Business Combinations,* and SFAS 142, *Goodwill and Other Intangible Assets,* turned this attitude toward brands on its head.

BRANDS AND CUSTOMER EQUITY

The Marketing Science Institute (MSI) of Boston aims to bridge the gap between the theory and practice of marketing. It is funded by the marketing industry and takes the lead in promoting topics that its members believe are marketing's leading edge. Every two years, the MSI announces its research priorities, areas it feels would benefit the industry and where it directs its funding. The result of the work it stimulates often appears in its list of research articles and working papers; many of them are ultimately refereed and accepted in academic journals.

In the late 1980s, the MSI responded to the brand debate and the astonishing brand-based merger and acquisition activity by holding a conference on the newly coined term, "brand equity." The objective was to define the phrase and encourage academics to invest research effort in giving it form and substance. The first of three such conferences (1988, 1991, and 1993) led to a number of papers and books. Those by current vice chairman David Aaker of Prophet, an international brand and marketing consultancy, and leading brand equity and marketing academic Kevin Lane Keller were the most influential.[7] By the mid-1990s, brand equity was established as a regular component of the MSI list of research priorities.

While at that time brands were not considered to be assets, business managers recognized their worth. Brand equity is the extent to which a brand adds value to a nonbranded product or service. Even if it was not identified as an asset, the brand was one of a known small number of intangibles that created and sustained market premiums, goodwill, and economic profit. During this period, several approaches to measuring brand equity were developed, most based on versions of the income approach.

Customers or Brands?

In July 1996, an article appeared that muddied the waters. Blattberg and Deighton[8] proclaimed: "Brands don't create wealth; customers do." According to them, the focus should not be on the brand but on the customer: True value lies in acquiring new customers and retaining those you have. They called this *customer equity,* and its coining sparked a body of literature proposing how this new idea should be measured and managed. The concept that views the customer as the asset as opposed to the brand flowed from this work, as did customer lifetime value (CLV).

Essentially, customer equity examines the worth each customer can contribute to the entity over time. This is based on knowledge of average expenditure per person and a measure of whether a person will remain as a customer or defect to a competitor. The probability of gaining new customers who will spend at a predictable rate must be added to this. CLV is the present value of these expected income flows.

This research has made an important contribution to our understanding of customers as the source of future economic benefits, the basis of any calculation of asset value under the income approach. However, customer equity suffers from two limitations:

1. It can be applied only when a database is available that records all expenditure on the brand by all its customers. Many brands have no such record of its end users.
2. Customers do not buy in a vacuum; they buy the brand. Their preferences and disappointments bring about retention and defection based on knowledge and experience of the brand. Hence it probably is reasonable to suggest a modification to the Blattberg and Deighton slogan: "Brands don't create wealth; customers do it for them."

Marketing Metrics

Another topic that has featured regularly in MSI research is marketing metrics. The recent leading item is accountability and return on investment of marketing expenditure. Mar-

---

[7] D. A. Aaker, *Managing Brand Equity: Capitalizing on the Value of a Brand Name,* (New York: Free Press, 1991); K. L. Keller, *Strategic Brand Management: Building, Measuring, and Managing Brand Equity* (Englewood Cliffs, NJ: Prentice-Hall, 1998).

[8] C. Blattberg and J. Deighton, "Managing Marketing by the Customer Equity Test," *Harvard Business Review* (July–August 1996): 136–141.

keting has suffered from a paradox for decades; while it often represents an entity's largest expenditure after human resources, there is no accepted way of reporting its effectiveness to management. One implication is that marketing people are rarely appointed as directors: Evidence suggests that only one firm in four does so.

It is not that marketing cannot be measured. The problem is to measure it in a way that is of interest to the board. Research conducted by Ambler and Riley[9] has established that the predominant measurements of marketing effectiveness are financial, such as profitability, sales, gross margin, marketing expenditure, and shareholder value. They vary in popularity, with the first two being recognized by boards in more than 90% of cases, gross margin in 80%, and the other two in between 50% and 60%.

Those are numbers critical to the performance of the entity, but they cannot be linked directly to marketing. Marketers use different measurements. For example, consumer awareness of the brand, market share, pricing relative to the competition, numbers of complaints, and consumer satisfaction are used by over 70% of firms. However, unlike the financial numbers, they are rarely viewed by boards, only by marketers. At best, the directors will discuss market share, pricing, and satisfaction, but surveys indicate that this occurs in as little as 40% of firms.

It is not hard to understand this. Directors have the task of managing the business for its owners to build shareholder wealth. The metrics they examine are those concerned with financial health. However, marketing is essential; if the firm does not win new customers and keep those it has, there will be no income to consider, but marketers have so far been incapable of showing boards how their efforts and expenditures have contributed to the objective. Recording brands as assets, now under IFRS 3 only when they are acquired in a business combination, is a partial solution. This will be helped if IAS 38 is amended to include brands internally generated. Brand valuation methodologies that conform to the guidelines of the International Valuation Standards Council (IVSC) are likely to have key marketing metrics as inputs.

BRAND VALUATION

The introduction of SFAS 141 (2001) and IFRS 3 (2005) represented an about-face by standard setters in acknowledging that trademarks are synonyms for brands and that, under certain conditions, they qualify for recognition as assets. Brands are a special class in that they almost invariably have indefinite useful lives and they appreciate rather than depreciate in value over time. In addition, they offer a definable source of future economic benefits. Marketing consultants have responded by devising numerous proprietary valuation methodologies, while valuators tend to favor the relief-from-royalty method.

The balance of this chapter sketches the emergence of brand valuation, identifies the uses to which it is put, examines the methodologies currently available, and, finally, extracts from the guidance issued by the Financial Accounting Standards Board (FASB), IASB, and IVSC some principles to determine the suitability of any valuation methodology.

Historical Background

Early experimentation in brand valuation arose during the merger and acquisition activity of the 1980s. One early exponent was Australian media mogul Rupert Murdoch, who had his publishing titles valued in 1984. Interestingly, this had the effect of strengthening the

---

[9] *T. Ambler and D. Riley, "Marketing Metrics: A Review of Performance Measures in use in the United Kingdom and Spain," draft paper, 2000; downloaded from the LBS Web site, www.lbs.lon.ac.uk/marketing.*

balance sheet of his flagship company News Corporation, which furthered the achievement of his global ambitions.

The methodology used was based on circulation and in some respects similar to the CLV. The calculation was supported by the relief-from-royalty method, still popular today. It was only in 1988 that the first proprietary methodology was created by Interbrand, a London branding consultant. In that year, its British bakery client RHM wished to value its entire portfolio of brands and record them as assets. Although several other companies followed suit in Europe and the United States, it was RHM that put the cat among the accounting pigeons and brought about the brand debate.

Over the past 20 years, Interbrand has changed its brand valuation methodology. The original exemplifies an earnings multiple system (i.e., an appropriate multiple was applied to the true earnings of the brand). The multiple was derived from an assessment of the brand strength by evaluating seven factors that Interbrand had determined and was applied to the brand earnings, the posttax, three-year weighted average of historic profits.

SELECTED APPLICATIONS

The original motivation for devising a brand valuation methodology was for financial reporting. Subsequently, this fell away as the relevant accounting standards evolved. Other uses for brand valuation arose, and the growing demand for such measurements attracted many new players. Some additional uses are set out next.

Management Controls

The marketing community has real concern about reporting its stewardship of brands. A debate revolves around the possibility of using a single brand value or a table listing a variety of metrics. Some commercially available methodologies provide management with opportunities for net present value (NPV) calculations to test the viability of accelerating brand growth with extended marketing budgets. They also allow for scenario planning, allowing managers to change inputs to see their effect on the final value. Many marketers believe that a single measure, or "silver metric," is inadequate by itself for either performance assessment or future planning.

Litigation and Trademark Protection

Brand values are used in court cases to demonstrate that brands are valuable assets. In cases of infringement or counterfeiting, those values are used by the courts to determine damages.

Franchising and Licensing

On what basis should a license fee or royalty for the use of a brand name be based? And how should this rate be adjusted if the brand increases in value? Brand value acts as a basis for calculating the rate and how it should be adjusted over time.

Finance

The use of brand valuation for IFRS is the topic of this chapter, but before any merger or acquisition transactions, both sides will want to appraise the assets involved. They will also want to look at synergies and the effect of incorporating new brands into existing portfolios. Brand valuation methodologies are used for these purposes.

Taxation

The application of brand valuation for taxation uses depends on local practices. Some countries permit the sale of a trademark to a third party, from which the original owner then leases it back with tax deductible payments. When the South African government introduced capital gains tax (CGT) on October 1, 2001, entities were given a two-year period (extended to three) to establish the base value of every tangible and intangible asset they owned at the commencement date. Brand valuation methodologies were employed to arrive at those base values.

Investor Relations

Investors place great store in anything an entity can show that enhances future earnings. Established, well-known brands are able to provide some of this comfort. Under the income approach, brand values are based on discounted future cash flows, which means that they incorporate the future economic benefits that are the bedrock of both physical and intangible assets. Strong brands contribute to the underlying value of a business.

VALUATION METHODOLOGIES

The 1988 MSI conference on brand equity stimulated a great deal of interest among marketing academics. Three years later, at the 1991 conference, three well-reasoned methods were presented for valuing brands. Each has contributed to commercial models in use today. A fourth was published two years later.

1. Srivastava and Shocker[10] submitted a framework based on brand equity strength. They pose three questions valuators need to answer:

    a. How profitable is the brand?
    b. How vulnerable are these profits?
    c. What is the brand's growth potential and how vulnerable is that growth to competitors' actions?

2. Farqhuar, Han, and Ijiri[11] set out six principles for effective brand valuation:

    a. Define that which is to be examined.
    b. Establish the value premise.
    c. Separate the brand from other sources of value.
    d. Forecast the brand's future use and value.
    e. Assure reliability of the brand valuation.
    f. Check for validity and auditability.

3. Kamakura and Russell[12] do not propose a brand valuation model but demonstrate how scanner data can be used to measure consumer behavior and to isolate the "components of brand evaluation that cannot be accounted for by the physical characteristics of the product."

---

[10] *Rajendra K. Srivastava and Allan D. Shocker, "Brand Equity: A Perspective on Its Meaning and Measurement," Marketing Science Institute (MSI) Report 91-24, 1991*

[11] *P. Farquar, J. Y. Han, and Y. Ijiri, "Recognizing and Measuring Brand Assets," MSI Report 91-119 (July 1991), Report number 91-119.*

[12] *Kamakura and Russell (MSI Report number 91-122)*

4.   Simon and Sullivan[13] submitted their proposal to a 1990 MSI conference on brand equity. Their measure is based on stock market prices and entities which have a market premium over their net asset value. They break down those premiums to isolate the portion attributable to the brand. The most important aspect of their work is: "The significance of the coefficients in the macro analysis and the response of brand equity in the micro analysis show that marketing factors are reflected in stock prices."

Brand Valuation Survey

Since then, there has been a rash of brand valuation techniques. A 2008 survey by Gabriela Salinas and Tim Ambler[14] claims to have found more than 50 specialist valuation providers. The study draws from previous research from Salinas, which identifies 18 methods that appear to be distinct.

Theirs is the first and, to the author's knowledge, the only analysis of the market for brand valuation; their main findings are useful in judging various methodologies and how they might be employed:

1.   There are eight classes of brand valuation users:

    a.   Intellectual property rights (IPR) lawyers
    b.   Valuators of intangible assets (e.g., IACVA members)
    c.   Economic value generated specialists
    d.   Market research agencies
    e.   Branding companies
    f.   Intellectual property consultants
    g.   Academics with or without proprietary methods
    h.   Accounting and auditing firms

2.   There appear to be 18 distinct methods reflecting the three basic approaches: cost, market, or income. The table is complicated because there are duplications caused by some methods covering more than one approach.

3.   Relief-from-royalty and demand driver/brand strength are the most frequently used techniques. Demand driver recognizes the source of future economic benefits as the end user and takes the strength of this demand into account in the discounted cash flow projections.

4.   Five firms utilize a method based on the price premium the brand is able to achieve.

5.   A popular technique with eight users is described as "comparison with the theoretical earnings from the equivalent unbranded product."

6.   Other methods each have fewer than five users.

7.   An important finding is how each method deals with risk. Twenty include a risk component; 11 apply their own approach to derive the risk premium. Typically it is based on some measure of demand, such as brand strength: A strong brand has a low risk premium; a weak brand, a high one. Thus the brand strength that determines the risk premium is not a financial measure. Nine methods estimate the risk premium according to finance principles, although only two use the weighted aver-

---

[13] C. J. Simon and M. W. Sullivan, "The Measurement and Determinants of Brand Equity: A Financial Approach," *Marketing Science* 12, No. 1 (1993): 2852.

[14] G. Salinas and T. Ambler, "A Taxonomy of Brand Valuation Methodologies: How Different Types of Methodology Can Help to Answer Different Types of Questions," MSI Special Report 08–204 (2008).

age cost of capital (WACC) and the Capital Asset Pricing Model (CAPM) without adjustments.

8. An essential aspect of most income based approaches is the need to determine the portion of income attributable to the brand.[15] While there are at least 13 different methods for this, the majority are brand strength analyses.

Interbrand originally established a definition of brand equity, commonly used today as the value added by a brand to a nonbranded product. Interbrand chose to "eliminate product related profit...by charging the capital tied up in the production of the brand with a return one might expect to achieve if one was simply selling a generic."[16]

This technique, usually called economic profit, is sustainable in the long term when competitive advantages "such as patents, proprietary technology, and reputation are embedded in brand names"[17] Some valuators explicitly use economic profit as a proxy for the nonbranded product or service. The technique of comparing theoretical earnings with an equivalent nonbranded product is then used to isolate the economic profit directly attributable to the brand.

FAIR VALUE FOR IFRS

As a result of the global financial crisis in the latter part of 2008 and through 2009, IASB and FASB have formed a Financial Crisis Advisory Group to examine implications for accounting standards and potential changes to the global regulatory environment. Their recommendations and governmental responses are likely to have a substantial impact on the measurement of fair value. In this section, guidance relevant to trademarks and brands has been extracted from the appropriate standards, but it is likely to change during the life of this book. It is unlikely that brands will be measured using either the cost or market approach.

Cost Approach

Some brands have existed for more than 100 years and are entrenched as consumer icons (e.g., Coca-Cola, Kellogg's, Gillette). Others are more recent but equally well established (e.g., Nike, Nestlé, Harley-Davidson). It is impossible to estimate what it would cost to replace them, if indeed any expenditure could build up the distribution, reputation, and consumer preference they have created.

Market Approach

Brands rarely change hands. When they do, they are often bought in a portfolio as part of a merger or acquisition. The market in brands is thin at the very best and in many categories nonexistent.

Income Approach

Therefore, some method under the income approach must be employed. Any entity needing to value brands for IFRS is best advised to use a method understood and approved by the standard-setting bodies. That would be present value technique.

---

[15] *Farqhuar, Han, and Ijiri, "Recognizing and Measuring Brand Assets."*

[16] *M. Birkin, "Brand Valuation." In **Understanding Brands: By 10 People Who Do**, ed. D. Cowley (London: Kogan Page, 1996), p. 191.*

[17] *R. A. Brealey, S. C. Myers, and F. Allen, **Principles of Corporate Finance**, 9th ed. (New York: McGraw-Hill, 2008), p. 308.*

FASB provides guidance on using the present value technique in its Concept Statement 7, *Using Cash Flow Information and Present Value in Accounting Measurement*. The statement suggests that these five elements should be captured in a present value calculation:

1. An estimate of future cash flows for the assets being measured.
2. Expectations about possible variations in the amount and/or timing of the cash flows representing the uncertainty inherent in them.
3. The time value of money, represented by the rate on risk-free monetary assets, which have maturity dates of durations that coincide with the period covered by the cash flows (risk-free interest rate). Generally government bonds are used because they pose neither risk of default nor uncertainty in timing to the holder.
4. The price for bearing the uncertainty inherent in the cash flows (risk premium).
5. Other case-specific factors that would be considered by market participants.

Numbers 3 and 4 are combined to create the discount rate, frequently the WACC. Its advantages are that it combines the cost of debt, which is known, with the cost of equity, often estimated by use of the CAPM or a build-up model, as discussed in Chapter 9.

In a diversified portfolio, market or systematic risk is the most important.[18] Brands often are held within a portfolio with limited diversification (Unilever has over 400 such brands spread over three industries: food; home care; and health and beauty) and therefore have unsystematic risks, which require special treatment. The "traditional" discounted cash flows method deals with risk by loading the WACC for specific factors, such as those associated with changing technologies, the availability of raw materials, and the threat of innovative competitive new products or services. Valuators have worked out subjective, specific risk premiums to deal with these; when loaded onto a WACC of 12%, it easily rises to a discount rate of 20%.

As an alternative to the single discount rate, it may be more realistic to identify the probable specific risks and account for them by: adjusting cash flows for a particular year or set of years, shifting growth bursts further forward, eliminating them altogether, or extending or shortening the number of years in the projected period. The Concept Statement makes a point which has special significance to brand valuation. FASB found the expected cash flows method to be a more effective measurement tool than the traditional method in many situations.

Economic Useful Life

IAS 38, *Intangible Assets,* is the standard for intangible assets that is currently under review. At present, it states explicitly that internally generated brands, among other intangibles, do not conform to the definition of an asset and therefore are not recognized. Once IAS 38 is revised, this will in all probability change. IFRS 3 refers to IAS 38 when it talks about identification and measurement of trademarks (brands) if they are part of a business combination or asset acquisition.

The section of IAS 38 titled "Useful Life" explains that intangible assets have either finite or indefinite useful economic lives. Note the opposite of finite in this case is indefinite, not infinite, which implies the asset would live forever; *indefinite* means that the end is not known. If an asset has a finite life, it will be amortized over that envisaged period. This would occur if there was a license, or copyright, or if the item is being used for a specific purpose with a final date. If the useful life is indefinite, the asset is carried on the balance sheet and tested annually for impairment.

---

[18] *Ibid., p. 194.*

Brands tend to have long lives and rarely lose value. Most leading brands continue to add value for their owners over their lives. (See, e.g., the annual *Business Week* survey of the world's leading brands.) If a brand displayed characteristics that required a charge to the income statement, the entity would either increase investment in the brand to reverse the downward trend or withdraw it from the market.

Fair Value Hierarchy

The principle of a hierarchy of inputs to valuations for fair value has been established by FASB in SFAS 157. IASB has indicated that its guidance will follow suit. This, too, is subject to the deliberations of the Financial Crisis Advisory Group, and in early 2009, it is difficult to know if the hierarchy as currently constituted will be changed. Assuming it will be retained, it will have considerable impact because it contains the guidance that permits the use of hybrid approaches in the valuation of brands. The hierarchy does not prioritize valuation techniques but merely the inputs that are used in the measurement. The three levels are summarized next.

Level 1. This level refers to quoted prices in active markets for identical assets that are available to the valuators on the measurement date.

Level 2. If quoted prices for identical assets are unavailable, the next level calls for quoted prices of similar assets in active markets that are observable. The guidance also permits the use of quoted prices in markets that are thinly traded as well as other financial indicators, such as interest rates and yield curves.

Level 3. This is where the valuation of trademarks and brands will almost certainly be placed because brands are rarely traded; when they are, they are invariably part of a portfolio. Level 3 inputs are unobservable; the standard permits this when no observable inputs (levels 1 and 2) are available. However, they must be inputs that market participants would use in determining a price for the asset. The standard does not state what those might be, but for brands, they might include market share, average pricing, and consumer attitudes as demonstrated by reliable market research.

EXAMPLES

The purpose of the hierarchy is not to assess valuation models but to rank their inputs and to provide consistency and comparability of the conclusions reached. The next sections set out four techniques for valuing brands, all using level 3 inputs: capitalized economic profit; relief from royalties; BrandMetrics, the author's proprietary method; and premium income.

Capitalized Economic Profits

Brands add value to a nonbranded product or service. This definition of brand equity is easy to state but hard to put into operation. There are no nonbranded banks or insurance companies. It is doubtful that any manufacturer would introduce a generic motor car, and, while there are dealer-owned brands, they are not unbranded, as they are branded by the dealer. Several of the valuation approaches included in the survey mentioned earlier attempt to model brand activity; capitalized economic profit serves the purpose as well.

Capitalized economic profits are obtained by the calculations shown in Exhibit 35.1.

1. Net Operating Profit after related Income Tax (NOPAT). This is the profit derived from the entity's operations before interest and finance charges and any income from sources other than those being valued less the related income tax.

2. Capital Employed; this is the total funds tied up in the operating business less payables. Payables are deducted because they are the main non-interest-bearing debt.
3. The rate of return expected by shareholders is usually the WACC, which includes interest-bearing debt as well as equity.
4. Economic Profit equals NOPAT less cost of capital employed (Capital Employed × WACC).
5. The value of the brand is the Economic Profit capitalized at the WACC.

Exhibit 35.1 Calculation of Capitalized Economic Profits

		$'000
Brand Operating Profit		16,000
Related Income Tax	37.5%	(6,000)
NOPAT		10,000
Capital Employed		
Property, Plant & Equipment	15,000	
Inventory	1,000	
Receivables	7,500	
Payables	(8,200)	
	15,300	
WACC	12%	
Required Return		(1,836)
Economic Profit		8,164
Capitalized Amount	12%	68,033
Rounded		68,000

This method clearly does not apply in all cases and special treatment is required for financial services and property.

a. Financial services have very few physical assets. Their capital is tied up in investments. In many markets, they are not permitted to have debt and are required to maintain statutory reserves to cover their liabilities to depositors, investors and policy holders. What happened to equity markets in 2008 illustrates just how volatile investments can be. The best method is to deduct the investments from capital employed and the related interest from NOPAT.
b. Property generates two separate profit streams, one from leases and another from the investment itself. The NOPAT therefore is the sum of those two, obtained from the entity's accounts and periodic valuations. The capital employed is the fair value of the property, plus accounting items, such as receivables.

Relief-from-Royalty

Relief from royalty is the most commonly used trademark valuation method as it is freely available, and not proprietary. The underlying assumption is that a firm would have to pay a royalty to a third party to use a trademark if it was not the owner. The value of the brand is the present value (PV) of the consequent savings as shown in the next table.

Exhibit 35.2 Calculation of Relief-from-Royalty Brand Value

		2009	2010	2011	2012	2013	Terminal Amount
Revenue		100,000	112,000	125,440	136,730	144,933	150,731
Growth		10%	12%	12%	9%	6%	4%
Royalty	5%	5,000	5,600	6,272	6,836	7,247	7,537
Tax	40%	(2,000)	(2,240)	(2,509)	(2,735)	(2,899)	(3,015)
Royalty Stream		3,000	3,360	3,763	4,102	4,348	4,522
PV Factor	12%	0.9434	0.8423	0.7521	0.6715	0.5995	0.5353
Present Value		2,830	2,830	2,830	2,754	2,607	2,421
Total Years 1 to 5		13,852		Capitalized Amount		12%	20,172

	2009	2010	$'000 2011	2012	2013	Terminal Amount
Brand Value						
Total Years 1 to 5	13,852					
Terminal Amount	20,172					
	34,024					
Rounded	34,000					

There are five underlying assumptions:

1. Growth Rates are based on management forecasts and budgets. Care must be taken not to use a constant growth figure, as this may result in unrealistic expected revenues. A prudent technique is to establish a consensus view from banks as to the population growth and inflation for the relevant market. Management's plans after the next year are then revised downward to this level.
2. Establishing the Royalty Rate is one of the problems associated with the relief-from-royalty method. Some U.S. services offer information based on published rates for different product groups. If there is a lot of activity in a group, the rate might be apparent from the reports; others offer little guidance.

    Research indicates a split of 25% of profits to the owner and 75% to the licensee (the 25% rule) is usually fair. For example, a firm has revenues of $10 million and a pretax operating profit of $ 2 million for a 20% margin. If a royalty is payable, the 25% rule establishes a rate of 5% (25% of 20%), subject to adjustment according to observed rates in the industry. However, the final figure should not be too far from this amount.
3. Often WACC for the firm is used as the Discount Rate but modified if there are special risks involved. In this case, the WACC is 12% applied on the midyear convention.
4. A Terminal Amount is added to the total of the present values of the forecast royalty stream to reflect the indefinite lives of most brands. This is calculated on a sixth year, discounted at 12%, for a present value of $ 2,421,000 a year in perpetuity. Capitalized at the WACC, this adds $20,172,000 to the $13,852,000 sum of the years one to five, giving a total value for the trademark of $34,024,000, rounded to $34,000,000.

If the jurisdiction permits tax amortization of intangible assets, a Tax Amortization Benefit (TAB) is applicable. This cannot be known until the TAB is added to the calculated amount, and the TAB cannot be worked out until the total is known. This circularity is overcome as shown next.

Exhibit 35.3 Calculation of TAB

Year	Calculated Value $'000	Tax 40.0% $'000	PV Factor	TAB $'000
2009	6,805	2,722	0.9434	2,568
2010	6,805	2,722	0.8423	2,293
2011	6,805	2,722	0.7521	2,047
2012	6,805	2,722	0.6715	1,828
2013	6,804	2,721	0.5995	1,632
	34,024			10,367

Calculated Amount	34,024
TAB	10,367
	44,391
Rounded	44,000

The TAB of $10,367,000 is added to the calculated brand value of $34,024,000 to give a final total of $44,319,000, rounded to $44,000,000.

A difficulty inherent in this method is whether to use both the annuity to depict the long life of the brand and the TAB, which seems related to brands with finite lives; one should use one or the other. A brand with an indefinite life calls for an annuity; a brand with a finite life, where the tax regime permits it, requires the TAB.

BrandMetrics, a Proprietary Method

The author has developed a proprietary income-based valuation methodology, Brand-Metrics, based on the notions that:

- Brands normally have indefinite lives.
- Brand value lies in customer-based future economic benefits.
- While the long-term future is beyond the control of the owner, short-term cash flows are influenced by both the product or service category and by the attitude of consumers to the particular brand relative to its competitors.

The model is Web based (www.brandmetrics.net), with inputs collected in Excel spreadsheets and uploaded. Its algorithms combine the data, calculate a discounted cash flow, and present a valuation report. Four categories of data are needed: financial, dilution, expected life, and brand knowledge structure (BKS).

Financial. Economic profit is used to isolate intangible from physical assets, assuming profits exceeding the cost of capital are due to intangibles built up and sustained over time. Budgets and forecasts are examined in light of typical management optimism against what has actually happened in recent years. Consensus opinions on the economic outlook of the countries in which the brand is offered are used to set conservative growth rates. The WACC is always employed to work out the economic profit and as the discount rate.

Dilution. Brand equity is what a brand adds to a nonbranded product or service. BrandMetrics uses a sophisticated and systematic method, drawn from actuarial science, to isolate the brand portion of economic profits. It does this through a resource recognition procedure which first identifies the drivers of economic profit of the business that owns the brand. It then quantifies those drivers to estimate the influence of brand equity on each. Once such amounts have been calculated, they are summed to produce the dilution percentage. This is then applied to the economic profit to generate the brand premium profit (BPP), which is the brand profit for the base year. The model uses growth rates derived from forecasts, budgets, and the bank consensus opinions as described.

Expected life. Brands compete in defined market categories, such as telecoms, energy, carbonated beverages, financial services, and chewing gum. Each is characterized by the behavior of its participants in stability or volatility of market share, brand or price loyalty, and external forces, such as availability of raw materials, distribution, local laws, and regulatory limitations. BrandMetrics examines each category to establish if participants are able to earn—or are constrained from earning—economic profits. It uses a maximum of 40 years in the evaluation based on the period the American accounting standards used to allow for amortization of goodwill. The result is the number of years of expected economic life for a category's dominant brand (DB) and a marginal brand (MB). In a category where economic profits are difficult to earn, the number of years for both DB and MB will be few; the opposite is the case if the category supports good economic profits.

Brand knowledge structure. Reliable market research is used to measure customers' perceptions not only of the specific brand but also those of competitors. The scores for several measurements are combined to provide percentages for all the brands reviewed; this is the BKS figure.

Operation of Brand Metrics

The highest BKS score is allocated to the DB and the lowest to the MB. These are then transformed into the years of expected economic life using linear interpolation. Given this, the number of years for the specific brand is a simple calculation. The model works out the number of years in the franchise run (the upward slope) and then the decay period according to a set pattern covering the balance of the life. In this example, the franchise run is seven years and the decay period a further 11. The brand value is the capitalized present value of all the cash flows captured in both periods, in this instance 17 years.

Exhibit 35.4 Pattern of Annual Brand Cash Flows

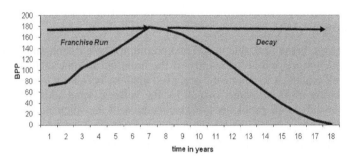

The BrandMetrics method ensures that the bulk of value is captured within the franchise run, in this example, 87%; while the decay period is longer, it accounts for only 13% of the total value. BrandMetrics does not add unsystematic risk to the WACC but reflects special risks in the consumer-based BKS.

Example

$ millions	2008 (a)	2009 (a)	2010 (c)
Operating Profit	904.00	1,042.50	1,162.70
Taxation	(247.20)	(255.30)	(238.50)
NOPAT	656.80	787.20	924.20
PP&E	2,637.00	2,754.20	3,010.00
Inventory	173.30	177.80	199.00
Receivables	662.40	789.60	736.60
Payables	(954.70)	(945.70)	(936.60)
Capital Employed	2,518.00	2,775.90	3,009.00

Notes

1. Operating Profit and other financial information is from:

    a. 2008 statements
    b. 2009 management budget
    c. 2010 forecast

2. Growth for 2011 and after is based on the consensus view of a country's growth in real gross domestic product plus inflation; its assumed rate is 8% a year.
3. Economic profit is NOPAT – Capital Employed × WACC. In 2008, this is: $656,800,000– ($2,518,000 × 9%) = $656,800,000 – $226,600 = $430,200,000.

Sometimes it is appropriate to average the capital employed over two years; if justified, a different WACC may be chosen for each year.

4. Dilution Percentage = 51%
5. BPP = $430,200,000 × 51% = $219,400,000

Expected life The detailed analyses of the brand's category produces lives for the dominant and marginal brands of 21.3 years (DB) and 4.0 years (MB) respectively. The level for each is derived from market surveys. Attitudinal measures are combined with awareness ratings to produce levels for the DB, MB, and the specific brand: DB = 71%; MB = 50%; specific brand = 63%. When the BKS is transformed mathematically by the model into expected life, the specific brand becomes 20.0 years, franchise run = 7.0, decay period = 13.0.

Brand value. The aggregate brand value is $3.0 billion (rounded), being the present value over 20 years at the WACC (9%) of the brand's economic profits ($219.4 million in 2008).

Premium Income

In most cases, brands are able to sell at a premium to their nonbranded competitors, due to consumer preference and brand loyalty. If the premium income method could be applied accurately to all brands, it would be the preferred method, because it complies most precisely with the definition of *brand equity,* which is "the value a brand adds to a nonbranded version." Unfortunately, four problems are associated with it, which make the method applicable only rarely.

1. In many categories, there are no nonbranded versions for comparison. Even store brands are, by definition, branded by the retailer.
2. Because the nonbranded version is likely owned by a competitor, it is most unlikely that the financial information required will be available.
3. Not all brands sell at a premium. They might be priced marginally higher than the category average and earn profits not through a price premium but through volume sales and by sustained market share.
4. Brand leaders, due to their high consumer awareness and preference, are able to increase revenues through product extensions. Nonbranded versions are not able to achieve this security of demand.

		$	
Unit operating profit branded product		77.25	100.0%
Unit operating profit nonbranded comparable product		(46.75)	(0.61)
Marketing costs for brand support		(15.45)	(0.20)
Extra profit from brand		15.05	0.19
Attributable to contributory assets	30%	(4.52)	(0.06)
Per unit premium profit		10.54	0.14
		$'000	
Multiply by units sold	1,646	17,341	
Income Tax	40%	(6,936)	
		10,404	
Discount Rate	12%		
Growth Rate	4%		
Capitalization Rate	8%		
Value of Brand		130,055	
Rounded		130,000	

In the example, from recognized sources, it has been possible to establish the costs of the branded and unbranded versions. Marketing costs are shown separately to indicate the investment being made in promoting the brand; in this case, the brand accounts for 70% of profits. The unit premium profit is then multiplied by the number of units sold to get a figure for the firm; after deducting tax, this is the value attributable to the brand in the initial year. To take account of future economic benefits, this is divided by a capitalization rate to produce the ultimate value. The capitalization rate is the discount rate (which could be the WACC) reduced by an amount to represent future growth.

Given sufficient information, it is possible to work out the nonbranded profit in two ways:

1. Apply the economic profit approach illustrated in this chapter to the balance sheet and income statement of the nonbranded product or service.
2. Use the financial statements of the brand owner to work out what margin a non-branded version would fetch. This could be added to the known cost of taking the brand to market.

36 TRANSFER PRICING

LIONEL W. NEWTON AND CHRISTOPHER J. STEEVES

CANADA

INTRODUCTION

Many enterprises have operations around the world and often manage subsidiaries on a geographical basis. In general, transactions within a multinational enterprise (MNE) may involve the buying and selling of internally generated products and services between wholly or partially owned entities. Taxation authorities in many countries, particularly the United States, are concerned that the prices at which those goods and services are internally transferred may be manipulated so that excessive portions of the earnings are taxed in jurisdictions with low effective tax rates or that some contributing countries do not receive their fair share of taxes on MNE earnings.

To deter this, the Organization for Economic Co-operation and Development (OECD) has prepared guidelines with respect to such transfer pricing. Valuators should be aware of them as they may affect the earnings and cash flows of corporate units. According to Canada Revenue Agency publication 1C87-2R (the Circular), paragraph 2, "Transfer prices are the prices at which services, tangible property and intangible property are traded across international borders between related parties."

One of the largest flows of goods and services in the world is between the United States and Canada. Both authors are Canadians and refer to Canadian law and publications from the Canada Revenue Agency on the Web site: www.cra-arc.gc.ca.

ARM'S-LENGTH PRINCIPLE

For a number of years, the OECD has had guidelines on transfer pricing; they follow the arm's-length principle based the concept that contractual terms agreed to by non-arm's-length parties should be consistent with those expected to arise as if the parties had no relationship. To assess non-arm's-length arrangements, parties related by ownership, control, and the like are notionally divided into separate entities, rather than following their legal position, as parts of a single enterprise.

OECD Transfer Pricing

These principles apply to both MNEs and tax administrations. All MNEs need to take the issue of arm's-length pricing seriously, as tax adjustments may arise which do not affect underlying contractual obligations. Even if the various entities within an MNE are relatively autonomous and bargain with each other to establish profitability, this may not be enough to create and satisfy the arm's-length principle.

Quite often, related companies within an MNE deal with each other in a way that arm's-length enterprises would not. An example is the use of an intangible asset, such as a trademark owned by one non-arm's-length entity and licensed to a number of others. A real problem for both tax administrations and taxpayers is the difficulty of obtaining information to support transactions on an arm's-length basis, as it may not be publicly available, and, if it is, it could be incomplete or difficult to apply.

Notwithstanding these issues, the OECD believes the arm's-length principles should apply and be the basis for assessing the pricing relationship between associated entities. According to the Circular: "A controlled transaction refers to a transaction between parties not dealing at arm's-length" and "[a]n uncontrolled transaction will either be a transaction between two arm's-length parties outside the group or between a non-arm's-length party of a group and an arm's-length party outside the group."

The object, at least in theory, is that levels of earnings recognized for tax purposes in various jurisdictions should be acceptable to a local tax administration. Whether the arm's-length principle has been applied is generally determined by a comparison of terms and conditions for a controlled transaction with those of similar transactions between arm's-length entities.

NECESSARY ANALYSES

To evaluate the comparability of transactions and check for differences, analyses should follow the three-step format set out next. If there are differences, adjustments should be made to quantify them.

1. *Identify functions* performed by the parties. This covers assets used and risks assumed; terms; and characteristics of the property or service involved such as quality, reliability, availability, volume of supply, and anticipated benefits. Adjustments are made for identified significant differences between arm's-length and non-arm's-length transactions, and these differences are quantified to arrive at an arm's-length price.

2. *Establish risks* on the basis that they will be balanced out by an increase in expected returns. The risk analyses are critical as they influence the basic financial aspects of any transaction. Functions performed are important because they will affect pricing. Who has the responsibility for marketing? Is the distributor merely an agent being reimbursed for costs and receiving an earning appropriate to risk assumed, or does it assume the full risk, such as excess inventory, accounts receivable, bad debts, and foreign exchange fluctuations? Are the contractual terms those that one would expect to see between parties dealing at arm's length? Is there a written agreement?

3. *Determine business strategies.* A firm trying to enter a market or increase its market share may temporarily charge a price that is lower than what would be expected in a true arm's-length situation. This policy could affect the non-arm's-length price, and the business strategy might, in fact, justify the situation. The problem for a tax authority is evaluating the accuracy of the claim, especially if the anticipated significant future earnings do not materialize. Does documentation exist to satisfy a tax audit and justify the fact that increased up-front costs, generating a greater market penetration, are expected to lead to a higher return at a later date? Would arm's-length parties be prepared to sacrifice initial profitability for expected returns at a later date? A written agreement may or may not be supportive of such a claim. For instance, would arm's-length parties to a short-term contract suffer initial reduced profitability or actual loss?

The OECD believes that tax audits ought to be based on the transactions actually entered into by the non-arm's-length parties. A recasting of a transaction should not take place unless there are exceptional circumstances, such as: (a) the economic substance differs from its form, and (b) the arrangements, if viewed in their totality, would not be entered into by non-arm's-length enterprises acting on a commercially reasonable basis. This is especially true if the structure would hinder a tax administration from evaluating what an appropriate arm's-length transfer price should be.

Transfer pricing does not always lend itself to simple analysis on a transaction-by-transaction basis. Sometimes separate deals are so intertwined that it is not possible to assess and evaluate them on an individual basis. Examples are long-term contracts, rights to use intangible property, and pricing of closely linked products. Quite often, an MNE may package many elements into a single transaction, such as licensing for use of patents, know-how, trademarks, and technical and administrative support. The entity's analyses should show how the various elements within the package deal are supportive of arm's-length transfer pricing.

An arm's-length pricing review often results in a range of prices. This is logical and acceptable, as independent entities, engaging in comparable transactions under similar circumstances, would not necessarily adopt the same price for analogous transactions.

INTANGIBLE ASSETS

In establishing transfer prices, it is essential to determine whether the non-arm's-length transactions involve some consideration for the use of the group's intangible assets, which may not be obvious. As set out in Chapter 21, those are not only intellectual property rights (IPR), such as patents, trademarks, copyrights, and trade secrets, but also industrial items including designs, models, formulas, recipes, tools, jigs, dies, molds, production systems, and know-how. Finally, literary and artistic rights relating to promoting and marketing a brand are included in this category. All such commercial intangibles may have considerable value, even if they are not represented on the entity's financial statements. Important marketing intangibles include customer lists, distribution channels, trade names, and symbols or pictures of products.

Patents and Trademarks

Commonly, patents are connected either to the nature of a good or to how it is produced, while trademarks are used in promoting and selling goods or services. Patents may create a monopoly in the sense that other products must not be generated in the same manner. Trademarks as such do not, as competitors can have a similar product in the marketplace using a different design. Irrespective of their source, all IPR can be sold in whole, by being assigned or, more commonly, in part, by being licensed or otherwise transferred from one entity to another.

Applying the arm's-length principle to intangible assets is usually quite a difficult process, as comparables, quite simply, may not exist or may be difficult to find. When an MNE attempts to apply arm's-length pricing to intangible property, the perspective of both the transferor of the property and the licensee must be taken into account. The transferor aims to receive an acceptable price in a transaction, whose form is likely to be different from one that would normally be adopted by an independent arm's-length entity.

Generally, the licensee, however, is not willing to pay more than the useful value of the intangible asset. Consideration has to be given to whether the licensee is required to take further steps, such as investment in facilities, perhaps on advertising, to utilize the related intangible. Factors to be considered are expected benefits, geographic limitations, import/export restrictions, degree of exclusivity, investment required, start-up expenses, opportunity to sublicense, establish distribution network, and any possibility or obligation to become involved in future developments.

If the intangible asset is a patent, the comparability analysis should look in detail at the nature of the patent, degree and duration of protection, and potential for new patents coming into existence.

When intangible assets are licensed, it is desirable to consider anticipated benefits. If these cannot be predicted with some accuracy, price adjustment clauses in the transfer agreements may be necessary. An example is a royalty rate which could be increased as sales increase. To assist with setting the initial internal rate, existing industry levels may be helpful.

PRICING METHODS

The OECD recognizes five acceptable pricing methods divided into two groups, traditional transaction methods and transactional profit methods.

Traditional Transaction Methods

1. Comparable uncontrolled price (CUP)
2. Resale price method (RPM)
3. Cost plus method (CPM)

Transactional Profit Methods

1. Profit split method (PSM)
2. Transactional net margin method (TNMM)

The choice of the method and its reliability is affected by the data available from public sources. When comparing controlled and uncontrolled transactions, the taxpayer must be able to establish that either there are no differences or, if there are differences, how they can be quantified and adjusted. At present, the focus of the OECD is on the selection of an appropriate method to equate with arm's-length prices. The OECD recognizes the lack of available and/or reliable comparable data. If more than one method is applied, several ranges of prices may be obtained; any overlap may give an indication of an arm's-length price. Ranges that are far apart are likely to indicate the unreliability of the data and further analyses and verification will be required.

Valuations for customs' clearances are normally necessary at the same time as the transfer pricing determination; firms do not have the same motivation for both sets of values. Importers generally like to have low prices, while an affiliate may wish to record a higher one to maximize deductible costs. It is foolhardy to try to claim two sets of prices, as information is shared generally between government departments.

COMPARABLE UNCONTROLLED PRICE

The CUP method compares the price charged for property or services in a controlled transaction (non-arm's-length) to that for property or services in a comparable uncontrolled transaction (arm's-length). If there are differences, they should be identifiable and quantified. In other words, accurate adjustments should be made to eliminate the impact of any differences. This is the most direct and reliable method to apply the arm's-length principle. It is particularly reliable if a company sells the same product both to affiliated entities as well as to arm's-length parties.

CUP Example: Based on Paragraph 69 of the Circular

Canco, a Canadian company, sells commodity X directly to its German subsidiary, Germanco, for internal use. Commodity X is actively traded in Germany, and an average daily German transaction price, which represents a delivered cost and includes any freight and duties, is readily available. Under the agreement between the entities, Germanco takes possession of the product at Canco's plant.

Calculation of transfer price per ton:

	$
Average daily German transaction price per ton	576
Deduct:	
Adjustment for freight	32
Adjustment for duties	28
Total adjustments	60
Transfer price per ton	516

RESALE PRICE METHOD

The Resale Price Method (RPM) begins with the price for which a product has been purchased from an affiliate, which is then sold at a higher price. That resale price is reduced by an appropriate margin representing the amount that a reseller, in arm's-length circumstances, would need to earn and cover its operating expenses. The amount of the resale price margin would be to some extent determined by the functions performed, assets used, and risks assumed. This method is particularly suitable to marketing/distribution operations. A comparable reference point may be the resale price margin the seller earns in arm's-length situations. When available, normal margins in the marketplace for similar enterprises may be a guide.

In a market economy, the return (compensation) for performing similar functions tends to be the same across various activities. Product differences are not as significant as the functions performed, risks undertaken, and assets employed. The OECD, as an example, uses companies selling toasters and blenders. In a market economy, there should be a similar level of compensation for those two. Consumers do not consider the toasters and blenders to be substitutes, but there is no reason to expect the pricing structure to be dramatically different. The appropriate resale price margin is fairly easy to determine if the reseller does not add significantly to the value of the product. It is more difficult to use the RPM to arrive at arm's-length pricing if the goods are further processed or incorporated into a more complicated product, especially in circumstances where their identity is transformed. Additionally, the OECD feels that the RPM is more accurate when the resale of the goods happens quickly. Time delays have a tendency to distort and/or introduce other factors.

Activities performed by the reseller will affect price and margin. Margins will be higher if the reseller has special expertise or brings something unusual to the transaction. If the reseller is carrying on other substantial commercial activities in addition to the resale activities with the non-arm's-length entity, then substantial margin differences are be expected. A reseller employing highly skilled staff or valuable and possibly unique assets—goodwill, for instance—may more appropriately be compared to uncontrolled transactions. Quite often, in non-arm's-length situations, there is a distribution chain, and the group has to demonstrate that the use of intermediate companies is necessary. In arm's-length situations, noncontributory organizations would not be allowed to share in the earnings.

Exclusivity could alter resale prices and margins, and should be taken into account when comparisons are made. This relationship may have the effect of stimulating greater efforts to sell a particular line of goods in order not to lose that advantage. The OECD provides the example of a distributor offering a warranty and a competitor offering no warranty; an adjustment to margins is required to take the difference into account.

RPM Example: Based on Paragraph 75 of the Circular

Britco, a U.K. firm, distributes widgets in England for its U.S. parent, Usco. Salesco, an arm's-length U.K. outfit, distributes gadgets, something that is similar to widgets, in England for Usco. The key functional differences, other than minor perceived variances, between the controlled and the uncontrolled transactions are:

- Usco bears the warranty risk in the uncontrolled transaction and Britco bears it in the case of the controlled transaction.
- Usco provides samples and promotional materials to Salesco free of cost while Britco produces, at its own expense, both samples and promotional materials.
- The English widget and gadget markets are similar. Salesco earns a commission of 15% of revenues net of discounts and allowances.

Calculation of sales commission:

	$000's
Britco's net sales of widgets to arm's-length parties	4,000
Arm's-length sales commission rate based on Usco agreement	15%
Arm's-length sales commission based on Usco agreement	600
Adjustments for functional and risk differences	
Promotional costs	10
Warranty costs	22
Total adjustments	32
Adjusted sales commissions	632

Calculation of transfer price:

	$000's
Britco's net sales of widgets to arm's-length parties	4,000
Less adjusted sales commissions	632
Transfer price	3,368

COST PLUS METHOD

CPM begins with costs incurred by a supplier of property or services to a non-arm's-length purchaser. An appropriate markup is applied to the cost to allow the vendor to make a suitable profit based on the functions performed and market conditions. This method is most useful where semifinished goods are sold between related parties or where joint facility situations exist and/or long-term buy and supply arrangements are in place. In a perfect world, the cost plus markup chosen would be the same as that earned by a supplier in comparable uncontrolled transactions.

It is often difficult to arrive at proper allocations, even for something as basic as the calculation of cost. It is important to consider differences in levels of expenses. Operating, non-operating, financing, and associated functions will affect the price being charged. The application of IFRS accounting principles can be particularly challenging. Care must be taken that the same costs and accounting applications are used.

In general, costs and expenses of an entity are divisible into three broad categories:

1. Direct costs of providing products or services, including materials, labor and direct overhead
2. Indirect costs, which may be closely related to the manufacturing process but could be common to many different products and services being handled in a factory
3. Operating expenses, which generally would relate to the entity as a whole, including management, supervisory, and general administrative functions

CPM Example: Based on Paragraph 84 of the Circular

Franco, a French company, manufactures specialized stamping equipment for arm's-length parties using designs supplied by those customers. Franco realizes its costs plus a markup of 10% on this custom manufacturing. Under the purchase orders, costs are defined as 150% of direct expenses (i.e., labor and materials). The additional 50% is intended to approximate all indirect expenses, including overhead. Franco also manufactures machines for its Italian subsidiary, Itco, using its own designs. Under the intercompany agreement, costs are the total direct and actual indirect expenses.

This example illustrates that both cost bases must be expressed in equivalent terms. Therefore, it is assumed that the transactions between Franco and the arm's-length parties are functionally comparable to those between Franco and Itco. Normal differences, such as in marketing, should be given consideration in the determination of an arm's-length markup.

Franco calculates its indirect costs and allocates them to projects according to the direct labor hours. Based on those calculations, actual indirect expenses, including overhead, for each project is 45% of direct expenses. The cost base of the comparable transactions must be restated to determine the appropriate markup.

Markup under the purchase orders:

	$000's
Direct costs	1,000
Indirect costs (50% × $1,000)	500
Total costs	1,500
Markup 10%	150
Price	1,650

Restated markup:

	$000's
Direct costs	1,000
Indirect costs (45% × $1,000)	450
Total costs	1,450
Price established above	1,650
Markup based on restated costs ($1,650–$1,450)	200
Gross markup based on restated costs ($200/$1,450)	13.8%

Calculation of the transfer price:

	$000's
Franco's direct costs related to Itco	900
Add:	
Indirect costs (45% × $900)	405
Markup [13.8% × ($900 + 405)]	180
Transfer price	1,485

PROFIT SPLIT METHOD

Often, transaction-based methods are adopted because it is difficult to obtain data for other techniques. Many independent entities form partnerships and agree to split profit. This is the basis of the PSM; it attempts to eliminate the effect of special conditions agreed on or imposed among a controlled group. The reference point is what independent enterprises would expect to realize from engaging in similar transactions in an arm's-length set of circumstances. Quite often, the amount divided may not be the total transactional profit. Appropriate allocations of profit may be readily determinable, and residual or extra profit may not easily assignable.

The PSM does not rely on comparable transactions and therefore may be easier to use, as profits are allocated based on functions performed. The method's strength is that it is unlikely for any parties to a transaction to be left in an extreme and improbable situation. However, there are several weaknesses when applying the PSM; one is that the contribution of the associated entities to the profit split will be less closely connected to the transaction. Another is the difficulty in its basic application: Associated enterprises in different jurisdictions may not have information readily available for tax administrations to assess the contribution from foreign entities. Also, if the enterprises were dealing at arm's length, the utilization of the PSM would be unusual unless it was a partnership and/or joint venture of some type. The measurement of true revenues and expenses may be difficult, as it may require making adjustments between various accounting practices in different jurisdictions. In a real-life, uncontrolled transaction, a firm would not know the actual profit or business activities of its partner.

The amounts to be divided in general terms are the operating profit. In theory, this should allow a group of associated entities to calculate their allocation based on the consistent application of profit and expenses. If the PSM is utilized on the gross profit, the expenses incurred by each enterprise should be deducted against that allocation. This system will work in circumstances where it is possible to determine, on a consistent basis and through numerous entities, the activities and risks undertaken so that the allocation of profit is fair.

PSM Example: Based on Paragraph 102 of the Circular

Taico, a Taiwanese firm, has developed and manufactures a unique computer chip, an innovative technological advance. Its Japanese subsidiary, Japanco, assembles a video game computer which incorporates the new chip together with technology developed by Japanco itself. The success of the computer is attributable to both entities, as it depends jointly on the design of the computer and the unique chip. Japanco manufactures the computers using chips from Taico and sells them to an arm's-length distributor.

In light of the innovative nature of the chip and computer, the group was unable to find comparables with similar intangible assets. Because the group could not establish a reliable degree of comparability, it could not apply a traditional transaction method or TNMM. However, reliable data are available separately on chip and computer manufacturers without innovative intangible property; they each earn a return of 10% on their manufacturing costs (excluding purchases).

The total profits are calculated in this way:

	$000's
Sales to arm's-length distributor	1,000
Deduct:	
Taico manufacturing costs	200
Japanco manufacturing costs	300
Total manufacturing costs for the group	500
Gross margin	500
Deduct:	
Taico development costs	100
Japanco development costs	50
Taico operating costs	50
Japanco operating costs	100
Subtotal	300
Net Profit	200
Taico return on manufacturing (200 × 10%)	20
Japanco return on manufacturing (300 × 10%)	30
Subtotal	50
Residual profit attributable to development	150

To simplify this example, it is assumed that the current chip and computer development costs accurately reflect each of the participants' relative contribution to the computer's technological advantage. The split of residual profit should consider the benefits over the entire expected life of the technology, which would go usually beyond the current year. However, given the foregoing assumption, the residual profit in this example would be split in this way:

Based on proportionate development costs:

	$000's
Taico share of residual profit [100/(100 + 50)] × $150	100
Japanco share of residual profit [50/(100 + 50)] × $150	50

The unit transfer price:

	$000's
Manufacturing costs	200
Development costs	100
Operating costs	50
Routine 10% return on manufacturing costs	20
Share of residual profit	100
Transfer price	470

TRANSACTIONAL NET MARGIN METHOD

The TNMM compares the net profit margin to an appropriate base (cost, sales, assets utilized) that a company uses in a controlled transaction. It operates similarly to the cost plus and resale price methods. Consequently, if those are being used or compared, they should be applied consistently. The result should be that an entity in a controlled transaction is earning an amount similar to that in an uncontrolled transaction. A functional analysis is necessary to establish whether or not the transactions are comparable; this may indicate the adjustments that are required.

A strength of the TNMM is that the margins (return on assets, operating profit, and other measures of net profit) are not severely affected by transactional differences. Another is that the functional analysis is limited to the entity being reviewed; it does not have to be compared to all the other enterprises in the group. This is particularly helpful when one party is a complex organization with many interrelated activities, or when it is difficult to obtain information.

A substantial weakness is that the net margin of a participant may be affected by factors that do not have a bearing on the price or gross margins. Additionally, it may not be possible to obtain accurate revenue and expense information related to transactions. If the TNMM is used, the particular entity may be at a disadvantage, because the local administrations may have confidential information not available to it.

Another issue when using the TNMM is that it is one-sided, being applied to only a single party to the transaction. This analysis may not consider either the overall profit of the group or that of the transaction. Comparing the profit of one entity to that of the transaction to some extent ensures that the tax administrations do not assess the individual entities for amounts greater than actually earned.

TNMM Example: Based on Paragraph 106 of the Circular

Spainco, a Spanish firm, produces a liquid product for its own use and for three foreign subsidiaries of its Swiss parent. All those entities own the rights to the product in their respective countries. Although Spainco has no internal comparable transactions, it has been able to locate data relating to a contract manufacturer using purchaser-supplied formulas. In the absences of unique intangibles, after the appropriate functional analysis, Spainco has verified that the contract manufacturer is comparable. However, it cannot obtain the relevant information at the gross margin level and is therefore unable to apply the cost plus method. The contract manufacturer realizes a net markup of 10%.

Transfer price is calculated in this way:

	$000's
Spainco cost of goods sold	1,000
Spainco operating expenses	300
Total costs	1,300
Add:	
Net markup (10% × $1,300)	130
Transfer price	1,430

GLOBAL APPORTIONMENT

As an alternative to the arm's-length principle, global apportionment sometimes is suggested. Under this system, the total profits of an MNE on a consolidated basis are allocated according to a predetermined procedure, which may be based on costs, assets, payroll, and/or sales. This should not be compared to the development of specialized formulas agreed to between tax administrations and various entities of an MNE. Those are derived from the particular facts and circumstances of the enterprise rather than being globally predetermined and mechanical.

GLOSSARY

INTRODUCTION

The terminology used in different valuation and financial standards varies slightly and needs to be regularized. The first step in its unification was the creation of the "International Glossary of Business Valuation Terms" by North American organizations: American Institute of Certified Public Accountants (AICPA), American Society of Appraisers (ASA), Canadian Institute of Chartered Business Valuators (CICBV), Institute of Business Appraisers (IBA), and National Association of Certified Valuation Analysts (NACVA), International Association of Consultants, Valuators and Analysts (IACVA) United States Charter.

However, several differences remain:

- International Valuation Standards (IVS) uses three terms—valuation approaches, methods, and procedures—but also "techniques," as in the presentation of six methods used for valuing land (International Valuation Guidance Note [IVGN] 1:5.25).
- International Financial Reporting Standards (IFRS) uses only "approaches"; see International Accounting Standards (IAS) 38:41
- Royal Institute of Chartered Surveyors (RICS) Valuation Standards (March 2009) defines "method of valuation" as being "A procedure or technique used to arrive at the value described by a basis of value."
- IVGN 4, *Valuation of Intangible Assets,* uses the expression "Income capitalisation approach to intangible asset valuation" (paragraph 5.8.2). The concept of "capitalisation" included in the name of this "approach" may lead to misunderstanding, because, in theory, the capitalization of a sustainable level of earnings or earnings growing at a consistent rate represents a shortcut for a discounted cash flow (DCF) calculation.

The editor is of the opinion that the terminology relating to the concepts and names of valuation approaches/methods/procedures/techniques should be consistent, for the benefit of a clear expression in valuation reports, regardless of the subject of the valuation and its intended purpose. Therefore, this book adopts the hierarchy presented next.

Approach

One of three traditional (market, income, cost) categories of valuation methods; each has its own chapter. A fourth (formula) approach covering statistical methods, option pricing models, and Monte Carlo Simulation, is in the course of development but is not yet codified; the related methods are described where most commonly used.

Methods

A means of achieving a valuation conclusion under one of the approaches. For example, the mergers and acquisition (M&A) method under the market approach values a business by reference to completed transactions. The guidelines method uses market multiples obtained from publicly traded comparable entities.

Techniques

Used synonymously with "processes" to define the various steps required to apply a valuation method. For example, in the traditional DCF method, the various techniques involved include: defining the appropriate cash flow, projecting it for a reasonable period (say, five years), estimating the terminal amount, establishing the long-term growth rate, and determining an appropriate discount rate.

SOURCES

This glossary of business valuation terms has been compiled, with minor editing changes, from the "International Glossary of Business Valuation Terms," 2001 edition, jointly approved by AICPA, ASA, CICBV, IBA, and NACVA, whose definitions are in bold. Definitions in plain type have been garnered from these sources:

AICPA—*Statement on Standards for Valuation Services* 1, American Institute of Certified Public Accountants, New York, New York, USA.

ASA—American Society of Appraisers Business Valuation Standards, Herndon, Virginia, USA.

CFA Institute—*Company Performances and Measures of Value Added*, CFA Institute, Charlottesville, Virginia, USA.

FASB—Standards and other documents published by the Financial Accounting Standards Board, Norwalk, Connecticut, USA.

IASB—Standards and other documents published by the International Accounting Standards Board, London, UK.

IVSC—International Valuation Standards Council, London, UK.

Pratt—*Valuing a Business: The Analysis and Appraisal of Closely Held Companies*, 2000 edition, Shannon P. Pratt, Robert F. Reilly, and Robert P. Schweihs, The McGraw-Hill Companies, Columbus, Ohio, USA.

REA—*The Dictionary of Real Estate Appraisal,* 2000 edition, Appraisal Institute, USA.

SEAT—*Glossary of Software Enterprise Applications Terminology*, P.J. Jakovljevic, TechnologyEvaluation.Com, USA.

Shirley—Glossary prepared by Mark W. Shirley, CPA, CVA, CFFA, CFE, APH, Cypress, Texas, USA.

USPAP—*Uniform Standards of Professional Appraisal Practice*, 2000 edition, The Appraisal Foundation, Washington, DC, USA.

VALMIN—The VALMIN Code establishes standards of best practice for the technical assessment and valuation of mineral and petroleum assets and securities by geologists involved in the preparation of independent experts' reports. The Australian Institute of Geoscientists, Perth, WA 6000 Australia

DEFINITIONS

Absolute Advantage. The ability of a country area or entity to produce a good using fewer resources than another would require. —Shirley

Accrued Depreciation. Any loss in value from the estimate of total cost new. At a given time, the accumulated amount of depreciation which has been entered in the account for a particular asset. Accrued depreciation is calculated as the difference between the value of a new asset and the current appraised value of the subject asset. —IVSC

Acquisition Premium. That amount, over and above the standard control premium, associated with an exclusive buyer and a specific seller that would relate to a unique set of beneficial synergies or circumstances between that buyer and seller.

Active Market. A market where all the following conditions exist: (a) the items traded within the market are homogeneous; (b) willing buyers and sellers can normally be found at any time; and (c) prices are available to the public. —IASB

Adequate Compensation. The amount of benefits of servicing that would fairly compensate a substitute servicer should one be required, which includes the profit that would be demanded in the marketplace. —FASB

Adjusted Book Value. The book value that results after asset or liability amounts are added, deleted, or changed from their respective book [recorded] amounts.

Adjusted Book Value Method. A method within the asset (cost) approach whereby all assets and liabilities (including off–balance-sheet, intangible, and contingent [items]) are adjusted to their fair market values. (Note: In Canada, the term used is "on a going concern basis.")

Advanced Exploration Areas. Mineral properties where considerable exploration has been undertaken and specific targets have been identified that warrant further detailed evaluation, usually by drill testing, trenching, or some other form of detailed geological sampling. A mineral resource estimate may or may not have been made, but sufficient work will have been undertaken on at least one prospect to provide both a good understanding of the type of mineralization present and encouragement that further work will elevate one or more of the prospects to the mineral resource category. —VALMIN.

Advanced Planning and Scheduling (APS). Techniques that deal with the analysis and planning of logistics and manufacturing over the short, intermediate, and long term. APS describes any program that uses mathematical algorithms to perform optimization or simulation of finite capacity scheduling, sourcing, capital planning, resource planning, forecasting, demand management, and others. These techniques simultaneously consider a range of constraints and business rules to provide real-time planning and scheduling, decision support, available-to-promise, and capable-to-promise capabilities. APS often generates and evaluates multiple scenarios. Management then selects one as the official plan. The five main components of an APS system are demand planning, production planning, production scheduling, distribution planning, and transportation planning. —SEAT

Age-Life Method. A method of estimating accrued depreciation by applying to the cost new of the property the ratio of the asset's effective age to its economic useful life. —IVSC

Agent. A party that acts for and on behalf of another party; for example, a third-party intermediary is an agent of a transferor if it acts on their behalf . —FASB

Aggregate Demand Curve. A graph of the level of real (inflation-adjusted) gross domestic product (GDP) purchased by households, businesses, government, and foreigners ("net exports") at different possible price levels during a period, ceteris paribus. —Shirley

Aggregate Supply Curve. A graph of the level of real GDP produced at different possible price levels during a period, ceteris paribus. —Shirley

Allocation Period. The period that is required to identify and measure the fair value of the assets acquired and the liabilities assumed in a business combination; the allocation period ends when the acquiring entity is no longer waiting for information that it has arranged to obtain and that is known to be available or obtainable. —FASB

Amortization. The systematic allocation of the depreciable [original carrying] amount of an intangible asset over its useful life. —IASB

Annuity. A series of payments made or received at intervals either for life or for a fixed number of periods. —IVSC

Application Software. A program that performs a task or process specific to a particular end-user's needs, or solves a particular problem. —SEAT

Application Programming Interface (API). A set of routines, protocols, and tools for building software applications or for communicating with programs or other systems. —SEAT

Application Service Provider (ASP). A third-party entity that manages and distributes software-based leased services and solutions to customers across a wide area network from a central data center. —SEAT

Appreciation. A rise in the price of one item such as a currency relative to another. —Shirley

Arbitrage. The activity of earning a profit by buying an item in one market and selling it at a higher price in another. —Shirley

Arbitrage Pricing Theory. A multivariate model for estimating the cost of equity capital, which incorporates several systematic risk factors.

Asset.

(1) Refers to an owned or controlled resource [as a result of past events] from which some future economic benefit can be reasonably anticipated. [also IASB]

(2) A resource controlled by an enterprise as a result of past events and from which future economic benefits are expected to flow to the enterprise.

(3) An item of property, plant, and equipment should be recognized as an asset when: (a) it is probable that future economic benefits associated with the asset will flow to the enterprise; and (b) the cost of the asset to the enterprise can be measured reliably. The term is used to denote real and personal property, both tangible and intangible. Ownership of an asset is itself an intangible. —IVSC

Asset (Asset-Based) Approach. A general way of determining a value indication of a business, business ownership interest, or security using one or more methods based on the value of the [underlying] assets net of liabilities.

Asset Valuation. In the real estate market, this expression is applied to the valuation of land, buildings, and/or plant and machinery generally for incorporation into company accounts. In other markets, besides the real estate market, this term generally refers to the valuation of an asset for sale, purchase or other purposes. —IVSC

Assumptions and Limiting Conditions. Parameters and boundaries under which a valuation is performed, as agreed upon by the valuation analyst and the client or as acknowledged or understood by the valuation analyst and the client as being due to existing circumstances. An example is the acceptance, without further verification, by the valuation analyst from the client of the client's financial statements and related information. —AICPA

Attached Call. A call option held by the transferor of a financial asset that becomes part of and is traded with the underlying instrument. Rather than being an obligation of the transferee, an attached call is traded with and diminishes the value of the underlying instrument transferred subject to that call. —FASB

Auction. A sale usually in public in which property is sold to the highest bidder, provided the amount offered equals to or exceeds any reserve price. —IVSC

Auction Realizable Value. The estimated amount that one would expect to achieve at an auction. It normally assumes that the sale is held on-site and substantially all of the assets in the inventory listing are offered for sale at one time. —IVSC

Balance of Payments. The net results of all current rather than long-term international transactions between one country and all others during a given period. —Shirley

Barter. The direct exchange of one good or service for another rather than for money. —Shirley

Base Period. The period (usually a year) chosen as a reference point for comparison with those earlier or later. —Shirley

Basic Earning Power Ratio. The ratio of the earnings from operations (earnings before interest and taxes) to total assets; a measure of the effectiveness of operations. —CFA

Beneficial Interests. Rights to receive all or portions of specified cash inflows to a trust or other entity, including senior and subordinated shares of interest, principal, or other cash inflows to be "passed through" or "paid through," premiums due to guarantors, commercial paper obligations, and residual interests, whether in the form of debt or equity. —FASB

Benefit Stream. Any level of income, cash flow, or earnings generated by an asset, group of assets, or business enterprise. When the term is used, it should be supplemented by a definition of exactly what it means in the given valuation context.

Benefits of Servicing. Revenues from contractually specified servicing fees, late charges, and other ancillary sources, including "float." —FASB

Beta (Beta Coefficient). A measure of systematic risk of a stock; the tendency of a stock's returns to correlate with changes in a specific market.

Bill of Material (BOM). A listing of all the subassemblies, parts, and raw materials that go into an assembly showing the quantity of each required. —SEAT

Blockage Discount. An amount or percentage deducted from the current market price of a publicly traded stock to reflect the decrease in the per share value of a block of stock that is of a size that could not be sold in a reasonable period of time given normal trading volume.

Business Cycle. Alternating periods of economic growth and contraction, measured by changes in real GDP. —Shirley

Business Enterprise. A commercial, industrial, service, or investment entity (or a combination thereof), pursuing an economic activity.

Business Equity. The interests, benefits, and rights inherent in the ownership of a business enterprise or a part thereof in any form (including but not necessarily limited to [shares] capital stock, partnership interests, cooperatives, sole proprietorships, options, warrants). —USPAP

Business Intelligence (BI). Sets of tools that provide graphical analysis of business information in multidimensional views enabling better decisions and improved business processes. —SEAT

Business Risk. The degree of uncertainty of realizing expected future returns of the business resulting from factors other than financial leverage. See *Financial Risk*.

Business-to-Business e-Commerce (B2B). Business conducted over the Internet with other firms. The implication is that this will cause businesses to transform themselves via supply chain management to reduce costs, improve quality, lower delivery times, and improve performance. —SEAT

Business-to-Consumer Sales (B2C). Business conducted with final consumers largely over the Internet. It includes both traditional brick and mortar businesses that offer products online and firms that only trade electronically. —SEAT

Business Valuation. The act or process of determining the value of a business enterprise or ownership interest therein.

Call Option. The right to purchase an asset at a fixed price at any time until a stated expiry date. Many call and put options on listed shares are traded either on an exchange or by dealers. See *Put Options*.

Capacity Requirements Planning (CRP). The function of establishing, measuring, and adjusting levels of capacity. The term refers to the process of determining the amount of labor and machine resources required to accomplish all the necessary tasks. —SEAT

Capital. The net investment in a firm by the suppliers of [debt and equity] capital; the net assets of the firm calculated as the difference between the total assets of the firm and the current, non–interest-bearing liabilities. —CFA

Capital Asset. See *Fixed Asset*.

Capital Asset Pricing Model (CAPM). A model in which the cost of capital for any share or portfolio of share equals a risk-free rate plus a risk premium that is proportionate to the systematic risk of the share or portfolio.

Capital Goods. The physical plants, machinery, and equipment used to produce other goods. Capital goods are human-made items that do not directly satisfy human wants. — Shirley

Capital Market Theory. A body of economic theory that divides risks into two components: systematic and unsystematic. This theory assumes that investors hold, or have the ability to hold, ordinary shares in large, well-diversified portfolios that effectively eliminates the unsystematic risk attached to an individual entity's shares. Therefore, the only risk pertinent to a study of CAPM is systematic risk.

Capital Structure. The composition of the invested capital of a business enterprise, the mix of debt and equity financing.

Capitalization.

(1) At a given date, the conversion into the equivalent capital worth of a series of net receipts, actual or estimated, over a period.
(2) In business valuation, the term refers to the capital structure of a business enterprise.
(3) In business valuation, this term also refers to the recognition of an expenditure as a capital asset rather than a period expense. Method of arriving at the value of a property by reference to net returns and an expected percentage yield or return. In some states, capitalization refers to the conversion of a stream of income into capital value using a single conversion factor. —IVSC

Capitalization Factor. Any multiple or divisor used to convert anticipated economic benefits of a single period into value.

Capitalization of Earnings Method. A method within the income approach whereby economic benefits for a representative single period are converted to value through division by a capitalization rate.

Capitalization Rate. Any divisor (usually expressed as a percentage) used to convert anticipated economic benefits of a single period into value.

Carrying Amount. The amount at which an asset is recognized in the balance sheet after deducting any accumulated amortization and accumulated impairment losses thereon. —IASB

Cash Flow. Cash that is generated over a period of time by an asset, group of assets, or business enterprise. It may be used in a general sense to encompass various levels of specifically defined cash flows. When the term is used, it should be supplemented by a qualifier (e.g., discretionary or operating) and a specific definition in the given valuation context.

Cash Flow Analysis. A study of the anticipated movement of cash into or out of an investment. —USPAP

Cash Flow Return on Investment (CFROI). The return on a firm's investment calculated using estimated inflation-adjusted gross investment, inflation-adjusted gross cash flow, and inflation-adjusted nondepreciable assets. —CFA

Ceteris Paribus. A Latin phrase that means that while certain variables are altered, "all other things remain unchanged." —Shirley

Civilian Labor Force. The number of people 16 years of age and older who are employed, or who are actively seeking a job, excluding armed forces, homemakers, discouraged workers, and those [opting out]. —Shirley

Client. The party or parties who engage an appraiser (by employment or contract) in a specific assignment. —USPAP

Client [in information systems]. A software program that is used to contact and obtain data from a server program on another computer; each client is designed to work with one or more specific servers; a Web browser is a type of client. —SEAT

Client/Server System. Distributed computing systems in which work is assigned to the computer best able to perform it from among those on a network. —SEAT

Coefficient of Variation. The standard deviation divided by the mean. —Pratt

Coincident Indicators. Variables that change at the same time as real GDP. —Shirley

Collateral. Personal or real property in which a security interest has been given. —FASB

Common-Size Statements. Financial statements in which each line is expressed as a percentage of the total. On the balance sheet, each line item is shown as a percentage of total assets, and on the income statement, each item is expressed as a percentage of sales.

Comparable Profits Method. A method of determining the value of intangible assets by comparing the profits of the subject entity with those of similar uncontrolled companies that have the same or similar complement of intangible assets as the subject company.

Comparable Sales Method (Market or Direct Market Comparison Method). A valuation procedure using sales prices or rentals of assets similar to the subject asset as a basis for estimating its market value for sale or rent. The underlying assumption is that an investor will pay no more for a property than he or she would have to pay for a similar property of comparable utility. —IVSC

Comparative Advantage. The ability of a country or area to produce a good at a lower opportunity cost than another country. —Shirley

Competence. Having relevant education, qualifications and experience, professional expertise, and holding appropriate licenses so as to have a reputation that gives authority to statements made in relation to a particular matter. —VALMIN

Complementary Good. A good that is jointly consumed with another. As a result, there is an inverse relationship between the price change for one item and the demand for its "go together" good. —Shirley

Computer-Assisted Software Engineering (CASE). The use of computerized tools to assist in the process of designing, developing, and maintaining software products and systems. —SEAT

Contributory Asset Charge. A fair return on an entity's *contributory assets*, which are tangible and intangible assets used in the production of income or cash flow associated with an intangible asset being valued. In this context, *income or cash flow* refers to an applicable measure of income or cash flow, such as net income, or operating cash flow before taxes and capital expenditures. A capital charge may be expressed as a percentage return on an economic rent associated with, or a profit split related to, the contributory assets. —AICPA

Control. The power to direct the management and policies of a business enterprise.

Control Premium. An amount or a percentage by which the pro rata value of a controlling interest exceeds the pro rata value of a noncontrolling interest in a business enterprise, to reflect the power of control.

Corporate Performance Management (CPM). A term that describes the methodologies, metrics, processes and systems used to monitor and manage the business performance of an enterprise. CPM applications translate strategically focused information into operational plans and compare them with aggregated results. —SEAT

Cost. The amount of cash or cash equivalent paid or the fair value of the other consideration given to acquire an asset at the time of its acquisition or production. —IASB

Cost Approach. A general way of determining a value indication of an individual asset by quantifying the amount of money required to replace the future service capability of that asset.

Cost Benefit Analysis. The comparison of the additional rewards and costs of an economic alternative. —Shirley

Cost of Capital. The expected rate of return that the market requires in order to attract funds to a particular investment.

Cost of Sale (COS). An accounting classification useful for determining the amount of direct materials, direct labor, and allocated overhead associated with the products sold during a given period of time. —SEAT

Curable Depreciation. Those items of physical deterioration and functional obsolescence which are economically feasible to cure. —IVSC

Current Assets.

(1) Assets not intended for use on a continuing basis in the activities of the enterprise [or realized within 12 months], such as stocks, debtors [inventories, receivables], and cash in bank and in hand. In certain circumstances, real estate, normally treated as a fixed asset, may be treated as a current asset. Examples include improved real estate held in inventory for sale.

(2) An asset that: (a) is expected to be realized in, or is held for sale or consumption in, the normal course of the enterprise's operating cycle; or (b) is held primarily for trading purposes or for the short term and expected to be realized within 12 months of the balance sheet date; or (c) is cash or a cash equivalent asset which is not restricted in its use. —IVSC

Current Cost Accounting (Approach).

(1) A method of preparing a company's accounts in which the fixed assets are stated at their value to the business based on current rather than historic costs. This refers to the present cost of acquiring a replacement asset that will provide the same service.

(2) In general, methods which use replacement cost as the primary measurement basis. If however, replacement cost is higher than both net realizable value and present value, the higher of net realizable value and present value is usually used as the measurement basis. —IVSC

Customer Relationship. A customer relationship exists between an entity and its customer if: (a) the entity has information about the customer and has regular contact with the customer and (b) the customer has the ability to make direct contact with the entity. Relationships may arise from contracts (such as supplier contracts and service contracts). However, customer relationships may arise through means other than contracts, such as through regular contact by sales or service representatives. —FASB

Database. A data processing file management system designed to establish the independence of computer programs from data files. Redundancy is minimized, and data elements can be added to, or deleted from, the file structure without necessitating changes to existing computer programs. [The term is also used for repositories of data that have been specifically selected or prepared to support making decisions.] —SEAT

Debenture. Written acknowledgment or evidence of a debt, especially stock issued [representing a floating charge on assets] as security by a company for borrowed money. —IVSC

Deflation. A decrease in the general (average) price level of goods and services in the economy. —Shirley

Depreciable Amount. The cost of an asset, or other amount substituted for cost in the financial statements, less its residual value. —IASB

Depreciated Replacement Cost (DRC). A method of valuation which is based on an estimate of the current market value of land for its existing use plus the current gross replacement (reproduction) costs of improvements less allowances for physical deterioration and all relevant forms of obsolescence and optimization. The result which is nonmarket value, is referred to as the depreciated replacement cost estimate. This result is subject to the adequate potential profitability or service potential of the enterprise. The DRC is sometimes simply referred to as the cost method of valuation. —IVSC

Depreciation.

(1) Decrease in value caused by physical deterioration, functional obsolescence, and/or economic (external) obsolescence.

(2) The systematic allocation of the depreciable amount of an asset over its useful life. In accounting, depreciation refers to one or more deductions made for accounting (taxation) purposes to allow for the actual or assumed reduction in the capital value (cost) of an asset over an assumed or prescribed period. —IVSC

Derivative. A financial instrument that is derived from some other asset, index, event, value or condition (known as the underlying).

Develop. To carry out any building, engineering, mining, or other operations in, on, over or under the land or the making of any material change in the use of any building or land. —IVSC

Development. The application of research findings or other knowledge to a plan or design for the production of new or substantially improved materials, devices, products, processes, systems, or services prior to the commencement of commercial production or use. —IASB

Development Projects. Mineral properties for which a decision has been made to proceed with construction and/or production but which are not yet commissioned or are not yet operating at design levels. —VALMIN

Direct Costs. Costs associated directly with the physical production of an asset, such as material and labor. —IVSC

Direct Relationship. A positive association between two variables. When one increases, so does the other, and when one decreases, the other follows suit. —Shirley

Discount for Lack of Control. An amount or percentage deducted from the pro rata share of the value of 100% of an equity interest in a business to reflect the absence of some or all of the powers of control.

Discount for Lack of Liquidity. An amount or percentage deducted from the value of an ownership interest to reflect the relative inability to quickly convert property to cash.

Discount for Lack of Marketability. An amount or percentage deducted from the value of an ownership interest to reflect the relative absence of marketability.

Discount for Lack of Voting Rights. An amount or percentage deducted from the per share value of a minority interest voting share to reflect the absence of voting rights.

Discount Rate. A rate of return used to convert a future monetary sum into present value.

Discounted Cash Flow (DCF). Present worth of future cash flow benefits. The most widely used form of DCF analyses are the internal rate of return (IRR) and the net present value (NPV). The techniques may be used for the valuation of land and investments and the ranking of projects. —IVSC

Discounted Cash Flow Method. A method within the income approach whereby the present value of future expected net cash flows is calculated using a discount rate.

Discrete Manufacturing. Production of distinct items such as automobiles, appliances, or computers. —SEAT

Diseconomies of Scale. A situation in which the long-run average cost curve rises as the firm increases output. —Shirley

Disposable Personal Income (DPI). The amount that households actually have to spend or save after payment of personal taxes. —Shirley

Duplication (Reproduction) Cost New. The current cost of constructing a replica of the existing asset, employing the same design and similar materials. —IVSC

EBIT. Earnings before interest and taxes. —Pratt

EBITDA. Earnings before interest, taxes, depreciation, and amortization (including other noncash charges).

EBITRAD. Earnings before interest, taxes, R&D, amortization and depreciation; this is applicable to software firms as it treats research and development as a capital, rather than an operating, cost.

E-Business. The generic name given to any type of business conducted using the Internet from online trading to self-service. —SEAT

Economic Income. Any measure of income inflow into the subject being valued which can be converted into value through either discounting or capitalization at appropriate rates. This could include net revenues, net operating income, net cash flow, and the like. —Pratt

Economic Life.

(1) The number of years over which assets are expected to render services of economic value (i.e., the time remaining for the asset to earn profits).

(2) The period over which an asset is expected to be economically usable by one or more users or the number of production or similar units expected to be obtained from the asset by one or more users. —IVSC

Economic Obsolescence. A loss in value due to factors outside the subject asset. Economic obsolescence is also called external, environmental, or locational obsolescence. Examples of economic obsolescence are changes in competition or surrounding land uses like an industrial plant near a residential area. It is deemed incurable as the expense to cure the problem is impractical. —IVSC

Economic Profit. The difference between revenues and costs over a period of time, where costs comprise expenditures, opportunity costs, and normal profits. —CFA

Economic Value Added. The dollar amount of value added over a specified period of time. Also known as economic profit. —CFA

Economies of Scale. A situation in which the long-run average cost curve declines as the firm increases output. —Shirley

Effective Age. The age of an item, such as a building, as indicated by its physical condition and utility compared to its useful life, in contrast to its chronological age. The amount of maintenance and care given to the building will help determine its effective age. A 5-year-old building may have an effective age of 10 years due to poor maintenance of the building. —IVSC

Elastic Demand. A condition in which the percentage change in quantity demanded is greater than the percentage change in price. —Shirley

Embedded Call. A call option held by the issuer of a financial instrument that is part of and trades with the underlying instrument. —FASB

Enterprise Resources Planning (ERP) System.

(1) An accounting-oriented system for identifying and planning the resources needed to take, make, ship, and account for customer orders. An ERP system differs from the typical MRP II [Materials Requirements Planning] system in technical requirements such as graphical user interface, relational database, use of fourth-generation language, and CASE tools.

(2) More generally, a method for the effective planning and control of all resources needed to take, make, ship, and account for customer orders in a manufacturing, distribution, or service business. —SEAT

Environmental Factors. Influences external to the property being valued which may have positive effect, negative effect, or no effect at all on the property's value. Hazardous or toxic substances may be found either on or off the site of the property valued. —IVSC

Equilibrium. A market condition that occurs at a particular "clearing" price and quantity when the volume demanded and that supplied are equal. —Shirley

Equipment. Ancillary assets that are used to assist the function of the enterprise. —IVSC

Equity. The owner's interest in property after deduction of all liabilities.

Equity Net Cash Flows. Those cash flows available to pay out to equity holders (in the form of dividends) after funding operations of the business enterprise, making necessary capital investments, and increasing or decreasing debt financing.

Equity Risk Premium. Rate in excess of a risk-free rate, to compensate and otherwise persuade an investor to purchase equity in instruments with a higher degree of probable incurred risk.

Excess [Redundant] Assets. Operating assets in excess of those needed for the normal operation of a business. —AICPA

Excess Earnings. That amount of anticipated economic benefits that exceeds an appropriate rate of return on the value of a selected asset base (often net tangible assets) used to generate those anticipated economic benefits.

Excess Earnings Method. A specific way of determining a value indication of a business, business ownership interest, or security determined as the sum of: (a) the value of the assets obtained by capitalizing excess earnings and (b) the value of the selected asset base. Also frequently used to value intangible assets. See *Excess Earnings*.

Exploration Areas. Mineral properties where mineralization may or may not have been identified, but where a mineral resource has not been identified. —VALMIN

eXtensible Markup Language (XML). A language facilitating direct communication among computers on the Internet. XML tags give instructions to a Web browser about the category of information. —SEAT

External Obsolescence. A reduction in the value of the subject property due to the effects, events, or conditions that are external to, and not controlled by, the current use or condition of the property. The impact of external obsolescence is typically beyond the control of the property owner. For that reason, external obsolescence is usually considered incurable. There are two types of external obsolescence: locational and economic. —Pratt

Externality. A cost or benefit imposed on people other than the consumers and producers of a good or service. —Shirley

Fair Market Value. The price, expressed in terms of cash equivalents, at which property would change hands between a hypothetical willing and able buyer and a hypothetical willing and able seller, acting at arm's length in an open and unrestricted market, when neither is under compulsion to buy or sell and when both have reason-

able knowledge of the relevant facts. (Note: In Canada, the term "price" should be replaced with "highest price.")

Fair Value.

(1) The amount for which an asset could be exchanged, or a liability settled, between knowledgeable willing parties in an arm's-length sale. In accounting, fair value anticipates a sale which may occur in differing circumstances and in conditions other than those prevailing in the open market for the normal, orderly disposition of assets. These include the possibility of a sale under short-term distress situations or other circumstances not contemplated in the market value definition. The term "fair value" is also used in legal actions to derive a settlement figure in disputes between parties, the circumstances of which may not meet the definition of market value. Hence fair value is not synonymous with market value.

(2) The amount for which an asset could be exchanged, or a liability settled, between knowledgeable, willing parties in an arm's-length transaction. —IVSC

Fair Value (GAAP). The amount at which an asset (or liability) could be bought (or incurred) or sold (or settled) in a current transaction between willing parties, that is, other than in a forced or liquidation sale. —FASB

Fair Value (IFRS). The amount for which an asset could be exchanged between knowledgeable, willing parties in an arm's-length transaction. —IASB

Fair Value (Legal). A judicial concept, defined differently in different states and countries. It refers to an equitable, just, and reasonable value for property determined without reference to a simulated or real market transaction since the property holder has no interest in entering the market at all. —Pratt

Fairness Opinion. An opinion as to whether or not the consideration in a transaction is fair from a financial point of view.

Financial Acquisition. A purchase by a buyer who expects to benefit by running the business on a stand-alone basis. Such buyers could include: a leverage buy-out firm, a venture capital company, or a management group. —Pratt

Financial Asset. Cash, evidence of an ownership interest in an entity, or a contract that conveys to a second entity a contractual right (a) to receive cash or another financial instrument from a first entity or (b) to exchange other financial instruments on potentially favorable terms with the first entity. —FASB

Financial Liability. A contract that imposes on one entity a contractual obligation (a) to deliver cash or another financial instrument to a second entity or (b) to exchange other financial instruments on potentially unfavorable terms with the second entity. —FASB

Financial Risk. The degree of uncertainty of realizing expected future returns of the business resulting from financial leverage. See *Business Risk*.

Financial Statements.

(1) In accounting, these comprise the balance sheet and income and expenditure statement (profit and loss account). They are written statements of the financial position of a person or company.

(2) A complete set of financial statements includes the following components: (a) balance sheet; (b) income statement; (c) statement showing either (1) all changes in equity; or (2) changes in equity other than those arising from capital transactions with owners and distributions to owners. (d) cash flow statement; and (e) accounting policies and explanatory costs. —IVSC

Five Ss. Sort, stabilize, shine, standardize, and sustain, representing the use of controls that enables immediate recognition of any deviation from standards.

Fixed Assets. Tangible and intangible assets which fall into two broad categories, namely, property, plant, and equipment and other long-term assets. —IVSC

Fixed Cost. Costs that do not vary as output varies and that must be paid regardless of the level of output. —Shirley

Flow Manufacturing. A form of organization, in which machines and operators handle a standard, usually uninterrupted, material flow. The operators generally perform the same tasks for each production run. A flow manufacturing shop is often referred to as a mass producer or said to be a continuous manufacturer. Each product, though variable in material specifications, follows the same pattern through the shop. —SEAT

Flow-Through Entities. Businesses that pass taxable liabilities through to their owners.

Forced Liquidation Value. Liquidation value at which the asset or assets are sold as quickly as possible, such as at an auction.

Fourth-Generation Language (4GL). A general term for a series of high-level nonprocedural [computer programming] languages that enable users or programmers to prototype and to code new systems. Nonprocedural languages use menus, question-and-answer combinations, and simpler, English-like wording to design and implement systems, update databases, generate reports, create graphs, and answer inquiries. —SEAT

Franchise Value. The value of a firm attributed to future investment opportunities that are expected to produce a return in excess of the market return. —CFA

Freehold. Real estate held in perpetuity (fee simple). —IVSC

Freestanding Call. A call that is neither embedded in nor attached to an asset subject to that call. —FASB

Functional Obsolescence. A loss in value within a structure due to changes in tastes, preferences, technical innovations, or market standards. Functional obsolescence includes excess capital costs and excess operating costs. It may be curable or incurable. —IVSC

Going Concern. An ongoing operating business enterprise.

Going Concern Value. A business valuation concept rather than one relating to individual property valuation. It is the value of an operating business/enterprise (i.e., one that is expected to continue operating) *as a whole,* and it includes goodwill, special rights, unique patents or licenses, special reserves, etc. Apportionment of this total value may be made to constituent parts, but none of these components constitutes a basis for "market value."

The value of a business enterprise that is expected to continue to operate in the future. The intangible elements of Going Concern Value result from factors such as having a trained workforce; an operational plant; and the necessary licenses, systems, and procedures in place.

Goodwill. That intangible asset arising as a result of name, reputation, customer loyalty, location, products, and similar factors not separately identified.

Guideline Public Company Method. A method within the market approach whereby market multiples are derived from market prices of stocks of companies that are engaged in the same or similar lines of business and that are actively traded on a free and open market.

Hazardous Substance. In the context of valuation, this is defined as any material within, around, or near the property being valued that has sufficient form, quantity, and bioavailability to create a negative impact on the property's market value. —IVSC.

Highest and Best Use. The most probable use of an asset which is physically possible, appropriately justified, legally permissible, financially feasible, and which results in the highest value of the asset being valued. —IVSC

Historic (Historic Cost Convention Accounting).

(1) The traditional accounting convention for the compilation of financial statements on the basis of costs actually incurred by the current owner. The use of such accounting convention may not reflect the underlying value of the assets at the date of the annual accounts.

(2) Assets are recorded at the amount of cash or cash equivalents paid or the fair value of the consideration given to acquire them at the time of their acquisition. Liabilities are recorded at the amount of proceeds received in exchange for the obligation, or in some circumstances (e.g., income taxes), at the amounts of cash or cash equivalents, expected to be paid to satisfy the liability in the normal course of business. —IVSC

Human Capital. The accumulation of education, training, experience, and health that enables a worker to enter an occupation and be productive. —Shirley

Hyperinflation. An extremely rapid—more than 50% a year—rise in the general price level. —Shirley

Hypothetical Condition. That which is or may be contrary to what exists, but is supposed for the purpose of analysis. —AICPA

Impairment Loss. The amount by which the carrying amount of an asset exceeds its recoverable amount. —IASB

Implicit Costs. The opportunity costs of using resources owned by a firm. —Shirley

Income (Income-Based) Approach. A general way of determining a value indication of a business, business ownership interest, security, or intangible asset using one or more methods that convert anticipated benefits into a present single amount.

Incurable Depreciation. Those items of physical deterioration and functional obsolescence which are not economically feasible to cure. —IVSC

Indemnity Value. The cost necessary to replace, repair, or rebuild the property insured to a condition substantially the same as, but not better or more extensive than, its condition at the time that the damage occurred taking into consideration age, condition, and remaining useful life. —IVSC

Indirect Costs. Costs associated with construction or manufacture that cannot be actually identified in the asset. Examples include insurance, financing cost and taxes during construction, architect's fees, management costs and legal expenses. —IVSC

Inflation. An increase in the general (average) price level of goods and services in an economy. —Shirley

Initial Yield. The initial net income at the date of transaction or valuation expressed as a percentage of the sale price or valuation. It is commonly known as the overall capitalization rate in the United States. —IVSC.

Intangible Assets. Nonphysical assets (such as franchises, trademarks, patents, copyrights, goodwill, equities, mineral rights, securities, and contracts, as distinguished from physical assets) that grant rights, privileges, and have economic benefits for the owner.

Internal Rate of Return. A discount rate at which the present value of the future cash flows of the investment equals the cost of the investment.

Internet. A worldwide network of computers belonging to [individuals,] businesses, governments, and universities that enables users to share information, send electronic messages, and access stored information. Also referred to as [the] (World Wide) Web, it is a mass of individual Web pages connected together. —SEAT

Intrinsic Value. The value that an investor considers, on the basis of an evaluation or available facts, to be the true or real value that will become the market value when

other investors reach the same conclusion. When the term applies to options, it is the difference between the exercise price or strike price of an option and the market value of the underlying security.

Inverse Relationship. A negative association between two variables. When one increases, the other decreases and vice versa. —Shirley

Invested Capital. The sum of equity and debt in a business enterprise. Debt is typically (a) all interest-bearing debt or (b) long-term interest-bearing debt. When the term is used, it should be supplemented by a specific definition in the given valuation context.

Invested Capital Net Cash Flows. Those cash flows available to pay out to equity holders (in the form of dividends) and debt investors (in the form of principal and interest) after funding operations of the business enterprise and making necessary capital investments.

Investment.

(1) Using a capital sum to acquire an asset which is expected to produce an acceptable flow of income and/or appreciate in capital value.
(2) The term is also used to refer to an asset acquired for the purpose of investment.
(3) An asset held by an enterprise for the accretion of wealth through distribution (such as interest, royalties, dividends and rentals), for capital appreciation or for other benefits to the investing enterprise such as those obtained through trading relationships. —IVSC

Investment Property.

(1) In real estate, this refers to property owned for the purpose of leasing to a third party, for possible future occupation by the owner, or for future development to earn rental income or profit on resale.
(2) In accounting, this refers to an investment in land or buildings that are not occupied substantially for use by, or in the operations of, the investing enterprise or another enterprise in the same group as the investing enterprise. —IVSC

Investment Risk. The degree of uncertainty as to the realization of expected returns.

Investment Value. The value to a particular owner based on individual investment requirements, as distinguished from the concept of market value which is impersonal and detached.

Just-in-Time (JIT). An approach to manufacturing based on planned elimination of all waste and continuous improvements in productivity. It encompasses the successful execution, when required, of every manufacturing activity needed to produce a final product, from design engineering to delivery and including all stages of conversion from raw material to the finished goods. —SEAT

Kaizen. Derived from the Japanese words *Kai* (change) and *Zen* (better), it is a continuous improvement philosophy based on achieving small, incremental steps in making processes better. —SEAT

Kanban. A "pull" system for the production of exactly what is ordered, when, in the correct quantities needed and requires the integration of people, process, and technology to secure the benefits of inventory and safety stock reductions while building to schedule and customer requirements. —SEAT

Key Person Discount. An amount or percentage deducted from the value of an ownership interest to reflect the reduction in value resulting from the actual or potential loss of a key person in a business enterprise.

Labor. The mental and physical capacity of workers to produce goods and services. —Shirley

Lagging Indicators. Variables that change after real GDP changes. —Shirley

Law of Diminishing Returns. The principle that beyond some point the marginal product decrease as additional units of variable factor are added to a fixed factor. —Shirley

Lead Time.

(1) The time required to perform a process or series of operations.

(2) In a logistics context, the time between recognition of the need to place an order and the receipt of the items. Individual components include order preparation, queue time, processing, transportation, and receiving and inspection. —SEAT

Leading Indicators. Variables that change before real GDP changes. —Shirley

Lean Production. An approach to production that emphasizes the minimization of all the resources (including time) used in the various activities. It involves identifying and eliminating non–value-adding activities in design, production, supply chain management, and dealing with the customers. Lean producers employ teams of multiskilled workers at all levels of the organization and use highly flexible, increasingly automated machines to produce volumes of products in potentially enormous variety. It comprises a set of principles and practices to reduce cost through the relentless reduction of waste and the simplification of all manufacturing and support processes. —SEAT

Lease.

(1) An agreement giving possession and use of land or realty or other types of assets for a fixed term in return for a specified rental payment.

(2) An agreement whereby the lessor conveys to the lessee in return for a payment or series of payments the right to use an asset for an agreed period of time. —IVSC

Leasehold. The interest of a lessee or tenant in a leased asset including rights of use and possession for a specified period of time in return for the payment of a premium and/or rent. Leaseholds may be of various duration, such as 25 years, 60 years, and 99 years. —IVSC

Lessee. A person to whom a property is rented under a lease. The lessee is commonly called a tenant. —IVSC

Lessor. One who owns the rights to use an asset, which is transferred to another (lessee) under a lease agreement. The lessor is usually referred to as the landlord. —IVSC

Letter Stock. Stock identical to a freely traded stock of a public company except for the fact that a letter stock is restricted from trading on the open market for a certain period of time, other than under SEC Rule 144. —Pratt

Levered Beta. The beta reflecting a capital structure that includes debt.

Limited Market Property. Property which, because of market conditions, unique features, or other factors, attracts relatively few potential buyers at a particular time. The central distinguishing characteristic of limited market properties is not that they are incapable of being sold in the open market but that the sale of such properties commonly require a longer marketing period than is common for more readily marketable properties. —IVSC

Liquidation Value. The net amount that would be realized if the business is terminated and the assets are sold piecemeal. Liquidation can be either *orderly* or *forced*.

Liquidator. A person appointed by the court, or by the creditors of a company, or by the members of the company for the purpose of effecting the liquidation. —IVSC

Liquidity. The ability to quickly convert property to cash or pay a liability.

Loan Security. An asset which is legally nominated to be available to a lender for realization and recovery of money owing following default by the borrower. —IVSC

Locational Obsolescence. A type of external obsolescence related to the physical environment or neighborhood in which the property is located. —Pratt

Long Run. A period sufficiently long that all inputs are variable, usually 5 to 10 years. —Shirley

Long-Run Average Cost Curve. The curve that traces the lowest cost per unit at which a firm can produce any level of output when a firm can build a plant of any desired size. —Shirley

Machine. An apparatus using or applying mechanical power, having several parts each with a definite function, and together performing certain kinds of work. For valuation purpose, this includes individual machines or collection of machines. —IVSC

Majority Control. The degree of control provided by a majority position [interest].

Majority Interest. An ownership interest greater than 50% of the voting interest in a business enterprise.

Marginal Cost. The change in total costs when one additional unit is produced. —Shirley

Marginal Tax Rate. The fraction of additional income paid in taxes. —Shirley

Market. It is the system (and on occasion, the location) in which goods and services trade between buyers and sellers through the price mechanism. The concept of a market implies an ability of goods and/or services to trade among buyers and sellers without under restriction on their activities. A market can be local, national, or international. —IVSC

Market (Market-Based) Approach. A general way of determining a value indication of a business, business ownership interest, security, or intangible asset by using one or more methods that compare the subject to similar, businesses, business ownership interests, securities, or intangible assets that have been sold.

Market Capitalization of Equity. The share price of a publicly traded stock multiplied by the number of shares outstanding.

Market Multiple. The market value of a company's stock or invested capital divided by a company measure (such as economic benefits, number of customers).

Market Structure. A classification system for the key traits of a market, including the number of firms, similarity of the products they sell, and the ease of entry into and exit from it. —Shirley

Market Value. The estimated amount for which an asset should exchange on the date of valuation between a willing buyer and a willing seller in an arm's-length transaction after proper marketing wherein the parties had each acted knowledgeably, prudently, and without compulsion. The concept of market value reflects the collective perceptions and actions of a marketplace and is the basis for valuing most resources in market-based economies. The professionally derived market value is an objective valuation of identified ownership rights to specific property as of a given date. —IVSC

Marketability. The ability to quickly convert property to cash at minimal cost.

Mass Customization. The creation of a high-volume product with a large variety of models so that a customer may specify his desired unit out of a great number of possible items while keeping manufacturing costs low because of the volume. An example is a PC in which the customer specifies processor speed, memory, hard disk size, and other low-cost assembly on a single line. —SEAT

Mass Production. High-volume output characterized by specialization of equipment and labor. —SEAT

Materiality. The contents and conclusions of a report, any contributing assessment, calculation, or the like and data and information that are of such importance that their inclusion or omission from a technical assessment or valuation may result in a reader of the report reaching a different conclusion than would otherwise be the case. The determination of what is material depends on both qualitative and quantitative factors. Something may be material in the qualitative sense because of its very nature, such as, for example, country risk. In the case of quantitative issues, the materiality of data can be assessed in terms of the extent to which the omission or inclusion of an item could lead to changes in total value according to the guidelines of the Australian Society of Accountants' Standard AAS5, that is, "material" data (or information) is such that the omission or inclusion of it could lead to changes in total value of greater than 10%; between 5% and 10%, it is discretionary. — VALMIN

Merger and Acquisition Method. A method within the market approach whereby pricing multiples are derived from transactions of significant interests in companies engaged in the same or similar lines of business.

Midyear Discounting. A convention used in the discounted future earnings method that reflects economic benefits being generated at midyear, approximating the effect of economic benefits being generated evenly throughout the year.

Mineral(s). Any naturally occurring material found in or on the Earth's crust that is useful to and/or has a value placed on it by humankind, excluding crude oil, natural gas, coal-based methane, tar sands, and oil shale, which are [all] classified as petroleum. The term specifically includes coal, shale, materials used in building and construction, uranium, and gemstones (opals, diamonds, etc.).

Mineral Asset(s) (Resource Assets or Mineral Properties). All property including, but not limited to, "real property," intellectual property, mining and exploration rights held or acquired in connection with the exploration, development, or production; together with all plant, equipment and infrastructure owned or acquired. Most can be classified as "exploration areas," "advanced exploration areas," "predevelopment projects," "development projects," or "operating mines." —VALMIN

Mining Industry (also Minerals Industry and Extractive Industry). The business of exploring for, extracting, processing, and marketing "minerals." —VALMIN

Minority Discount. A discount for lack of control applicable to a minority interest.

Minority Interest. An ownership interest less than 50% of the voting interest in a business enterprise.

Model. A simplified description of reality used to understand and predict the relationship between variables. —Shirley

Mutual Interdependence. A condition in which an action by one firm may cause a reaction from others. —Shirley

Natural Monopoly. An industry in which the long-run average cost of production declines throughout the entire market. As a result, a single firm can supply the entire market demand at a lower cost than two or more smaller firms. —Shirley

Net Assets. Total assets less total liabilities.

Net Book Value. With respect to a business enterprise, the difference between total assets (net of accumulated depreciation, depletion, and amortization) and total liabilities of a business enterprise as they appear on the balance sheet (synonymous with "shareholder's equity"). With respect to a specific asset, the capitalized cost less accumulated amortization or depreciation as it appears on the books of account of the business enterprise.

Net Current Replacement Cost.

(1) Cost that would be incurred in the marketplace in acquiring an equally satisfactory substitute asset.
(2) The cost of purchasing, at the least cost, the remaining service potential of the asset at the balance sheet date; an entry value.
(3) Put simply, the replacement cost less depreciation. —IVSC

Net Income. Revenue less expenses and taxes.

Net Present Value. The value, as of a specified date, of future cash inflows less all cash outflows (including the cost of investment) calculated using an appropriate discount rate.

Net Realizable Value.

(1) The estimated selling price of an asset in the ordinary course of business, less selling costs and costs of completion.
(2) The estimated proceeds of sale of an asset, less the selling costs; an exit value.
(3) The estimated selling price in the ordinary course of business less the estimated costs of completion and the estimated costs necessary to make the sale. Net realizable value is akin to market value less disposal costs only where all requirements of the market value definition are met. In particular, this includes sufficient time for the market value transaction to occur. Market value is ordinarily a gross figure or, more appropriately, a "face value" prior to deduction of disposition costs. —IVSC [also IASB]

Net Selling Price. The amount obtainable from the sale of an asset in an arm's-length transaction between knowledgeable, willing parties, less the costs of disposal. —IVSC

Net Tangible Asset Value. The value of the business enterprise's tangible assets (excluding excess assets and nonoperating assets) minus the value of its liabilities.

Nonoperating Assets. Assets not necessary to ongoing operations of the business enterprise. (Note: In Canada, the term used is "redundant assets.")

Nonprice Competition. The situation in which a firm competes using advertising, packaging, product development, quality, and service rather than prices. —Shirley

Normal Profit. The minimum return of a firm necessary for the suppliers of capital to retain their investment in the firm. —CFA

Normalized Earnings. Economic benefits adjusted for nonrecurring, noneconomic, or other unusual items to eliminate anomalies and/or facilitate comparisons.

Normalized Financial Statements. Financial statements adjusted for nonoperating assets and liabilities and/or for nonrecurring, noneconomic, or other unusual items to eliminate anomalies and/or facilitate comparisons.

Obsolescence. A loss in value due to a decrease in the usefulness of property caused by decay, changes in technology, people's behaviorial patterns and tastes, or environmental changes. —IVSC

Oligopoly. A market structure characterized by:

(1) Few sellers;
(2) Either a homogeneous or a differentiated product; or
(3) Difficult market entry. —Shirley

Operating Capital. Capital less goodwill and any excess cash and marketable securities. —CFA

Operating Company. A business that conducts an economic activity by generating and selling, or trading in a product or service.

Operating Mines. Mineral properties, particularly mines and processing plants, that have been commissioned and are in production. —VALMIN

Opportunity Cost. The best alternative sacrificed for a chosen action. —Shirley

Orderly Liquidation Value [of an Entity]. Liquidation value at which the asset or assets are sold over a reasonable period of time to maximize proceeds received.

PER. The ratio of the price per share of stock to the earnings per share of stock; often used as a proxy for future growth potential. —CFA

Physical Deterioration. A loss in value due to impairment of physical condition. —IVSC

Physical Life. The period during which an asset is capable of use taking into account factors such as its condition and whether it meets or is capable of meeting accepted standards and statutory requirements. —IVSC

Plant. An assemblage of assets that may include specialized nonpermanent buildings, machinery, and equipment. —IVSC

Portfolio Discount. An amount or percentage deducted from the value of a business enterprise to reflect the fact that it owns dissimilar operations or assets that may not fit well together.

Preacquisition Contingency. A contingency of an entity that is acquired in a business combination that is in existence before the consummation of the combination. A preacquisition contingency can be a contingent asset, a contingent liability, or a contingent impairment of an asset. —FASB

Predevelopment Projects. Mineral properties where mineral resources have been identified and their extent estimated (possibly incompletely) but where a decision to proceed with the development has not been made. Mineral properties at the early assessment stage, properties for which a decision has been made not to proceed with development, properties on care and maintenance, and properties held on retention titles are included in this category if mineral or petroleum resources have been identified, even if no further valuation, technical assessment, delineation, or advanced exploration is being undertaken. —VALMIN

Premise of Value. An assumption regarding the most likely set of transactional circumstances that may be applicable to the subject valuation: for example, going concern, liquidation.

Premium (Lease Premium). The price paid by an actual or prospective lessee to a lessor, usually in consideration of the rent or for the rent being reduced to below what would otherwise by payable. —IVSC

Present Value. The value, as of a specified date, of future economic benefits and/or proceeds from sale, calculated using an appropriate discount rate.

Price. An amount asked, offered, or paid for a good or service. —IVSC

Price. The amount paid for a good or service; it is a historic fact having no real relationship with "value," because of the financial motives, capabilities, or special interests of the purchaser and the state of the market at the time.

Price Discrimination. The practice of a seller charging different prices for the same product not justified by cost differences. —Shirley

Price Leadership. A pricing strategy in which a dominant firm sets the price for an industry and the other firms follow. —Shirley

Price Taker. A seller that has no control over the price of product it sells. —Shirley

Process Manufacturing. Production that adds value by mixing, separating, forming, and/or performing chemical reactions. It may be done in either batch or continuous mode. —SEAT

Product Configurator. A system, generally rule based, to be used in design-to-order, engineer-to-order, or make-to-order environments where numerous product variations exist. Product configurators perform intelligent modeling of the part or product attributes and often create solid models, drawings, bills of material, and cost estimates that can be integrated into CAD/CAM and MRP II [Materials Requirements Planning] systems as well as sales order entry systems. —SEAT

Product Differentiation. The process of creating real or apparent differences between goods and services. —Shirley

Product Life Cycle.

(1) The stages a new product goes through from introduction through growth, maturity, and decline;
(2) The time from initial research and development to the termination of sales and withdrawal of customer support; and
(3) The period during which a product can be produced and marketed profitably. — SEAT

Product Life Cycle Management (PLM). A process for guiding products from idea through retirement so as to deliver the most business value to an enterprise and its trading partners. Applications affected by PLM include product ideation, design, engineering, manufacturing processes, product data management, and product portfolio management. — SEAT

Property. A legal concept, commonly used in general reference to real estate and/or personalty. The term may be considered applicable to both the rights of ownership and to the physical item owned. —IVSC

Property, Plant, and Equipment.

(1) Assets intended for use on a continuing basis in the activities of an enterprise including land and buildings, plant and equipment, accumulated depreciation, and other categories of assets, suitably identified.
(2) Tangible assets that: (a) are held by an enterprise for use in the production or supply of goods or services, for rental to others, or for administrative purposes; and (b) are expected to be used during more than one period. —IVSC

Put Option. An option which gives the holder the right to sell an asset, normally shares, by a certain date at a fixed price .(See *Call Option*.)

Quota. A limit on the quantity of a good that may be imported in a given period. — Shirley

Range. A measure of dispersion which is defined as the spread between the highest and lowest observations. —Pratt.

Rate of Return. An amount of income (loss) and/or change in value realized or anticipated on an investment, expressed as a percentage of that investment.

Real Estate. Physical land and those human-made items that attach to the land. —IVSC

Real Interest Rate. The nominal rate of interest minus the inflation rate. —Shirley

Real Property. A nonphysical concept that refers to all rights, interest, and benefits related to the ownership of real estate. —IVSC

Real Time.

(1) The technique of coordinating data processing with related events as they occur, thereby permitting prompt reporting of conditions; and
(2) The immediate availability of data to information system uses as a transaction or event occurs. —SEAT

Recession. A downturn in the business cycle during which real GDP [gross domestic product] declines. —Shirley

Recourse. The right of a transferee of receivables to receive payment from the transferor of those receivables for (a) failure of debtors to pay when due, (b) the effects of prepayments, or (c) adjustments resulting from defects in the eligibility of the transferred receivables. —FASB

Recoverable Amount.

(1) The higher of value in use and net realizable value.
(2) The higher of an asset's net selling price and its value in use. —IVSC

Recovery. An upturn in the business cycle during which real GDP [gross domestic product] rises; also called an expansion. —Shirley

Relief-from-Royalty Method. A valuation method used to value certain intangible assets (e.g., trademarks and trade names) based on the premise that the only value that a purchaser of the assets receives is the exemption from paying a royalty for its use. Application of this method usually involves estimating the fair market value of an intangible asset by quantifying the present value of the stream of market-derived royalty payments that the owner of the intangible asset is exempted from or "relieved" from paying. —AICPA

Reproduction Cost New. See *Duplication Cost New.*

Required Rate of Return. The minimum rate of return acceptable by investors before they will commit money to an investment at a given level of risk.

Research. Original and planned investigation undertaken with the prospect of gaining new scientific or technical knowledge and understanding. —IASB

Residual Value. The net amount which an enterprise expects to obtain for an asset at the end of its useful life after deducting the expected costs of disposal. —IASB

Return on Assets [ROA]. The ratio of net income to total assets; ROA provides a measure of how profitably and efficiently a firm is using its assets. —CFA

Return on Capital. The ratio of net operating profit after taxes to capital. —CFA

Return on Equity. The amount, expressed as a percentage, earned on a company's common [ordinary] equity for a given period.

Return on Invested Capital. The amount, expressed as a percentage, earned on a company's total capital for a given period.

Return on Investment (ROI). A financial measure of the relative return from an investment, usually expressed as a percentage of earnings produced by an asset to the amount invested in the asset. —SEAT

Return. The total yield to the investor, reflecting all dividends, interest, or other cash and cash equivalents received, plus or minus any realized or unrealized appreciation or depreciation in the investment's value. —Pratt

Risk. The degree of uncertainty as to the realization of expected future returns. —Pratt

Risk-Free Rate. The rate of return available in the market on an investment free of default risk.

Risk Premium. A rate of return added to a risk-free rate to reflect risk.

Rule of Thumb. A mathematical formula developed from the relationship between price and certain variables based on experience, observation, hearsay, or a combination of these; usually industry specific.

Sales Comparison Approach. A set of procedures in which a value indication is derived by comparing the property being appraised to similar properties that have been sold recently, applying appropriate units of comparison, and making adjustments to the sale prices of the comparables based on the elements of comparison. See *Market Approach.* —Dictionary

Scrap Value. The value a wasting asset will have at the end of its predictable life, as known or ascertainable at the time when the asset was acquired or provided by the person making the disposal. —IVSC

Security. A certificate evidencing ownership or the rights to ownership in a business enterprise that (1) is represented by an instrument or by a book record or contractual agreement, (2) is of a type commonly dealt in on securities exchanges or markets or, when represented by an instrument, is commonly recognized in any area in which it is issued or dealt in as a medium for investment, and (3) either one of a class or series or, by its terms, is divisible into a class or series of shares, participations, interests, rights, or interest-bearing obligations. —AICPA

Securitization. The process by which financial assets [loans or mortgages] are transformed into securities. —FASB

Security Interest. A form of interest in property that provides that upon default of the obligation for which the security interest is given, the property may be sold in order to satisfy that obligation. —FASB

Short Run. A period of time so short that at least one input is fixed. —Shirley

Shortage. A market condition existing at any price where the quantity supplied is less than that demanded. —Shirley

Special (Interest) Purchasers. Acquirers who believe they can enjoy postacquisition economics of scale, synergies, or strategic advantages by combining the acquired business interest with their own.

Specialized Trading Property. Properties such as hotels, gas stations, restaurants, or the like may be valued at market value, recognizing that assets other than land and buildings alone are included. These properties are commonly sold in the market as an operating package that may make separate identification of land, building, and other values difficult or impossible. —IVSC

Special Value. A term relating to an extraordinary element of value over and above market value. Special value could arise, for example, by the physical, functional, or economic association of a property with some other property, such as the adjoining property. It is an increment of value that could be applicable to a particular owner or user, or prospective owner or user of the property, rather than to the market at large; that is, to a purchaser with a special interest. Special value could be associated with elements of going concern value. The valuator must ensure that such criteria are distinguished from market value, making clear any special assumptions made. —IVSC

Specialist. A "competent" (and "independent," where relevant) natural person who is retained by the "expert" to provide subsidiary reports (or sections of the valuation report) on matters on which the "expert" is not personally expert. He/she must have at least five years of suitable and preferably recent "minerals industry" experience relevant to the subject matter on which he/she contributes. A "specialist" must be a member of an appropriate, recognized professional association having an enforceable code of ethics, or explain why not. (For the full definition see *VALMIN Code*, Definition D10 and its Clause 17.)

Stagflation. The condition that occurs when an economy experiences the twin maladies of high unemployment and rapid inflation simultaneously. —Shirley

Standard of Value. The identification of the type of value being utilized in a specific engagement: for example, fair market value, fair value, investment value.

Strategic Acquisition. A purchase by a buyer who expects to benefit from synergies with the purchased company, such as horizontal and vertical integration, elimination of redundant overhead, or better prices through reduced competition. —Pratt

Strategic Sourcing. The development and management of supplier relationships to acquire goods and services in a way that aids in achieving the immediate needs of a business. It is entirely aligned with the sourcing portion of managing the procurement process. —SEAT

Subject. The security, asset or liability being valued.

Subsequent Event. An event that occurs after the valuation date. —AICPA

Substitute Good. A good that competes with another good for consumer purchases. As a result, there is a direct relationship between a price change for one good and the demand for its "competitor" items. —Shirley

Supply Chain Management (SCM). The design, planning, execution, control, and monitoring of supply chain activities with the objective of creating net value, building a competitive infrastructure, leveraging worldwide logistics, synchronizing supply with demand, and measuring performance globally. —SEAT

Surplus. A market condition existing at any price where the quantity supplied is greater than the quantity demanded. —Shirley

Sustaining Capital Reinvestment. The periodic capital outlay required to maintain operations at existing levels, net of the tax shield available from such outlays.

Systematic Risk. The uncertainty of future returns due to the sensitivity of the return on the subject investment to the movements in the return for the investment market as a whole. This kind of risk is macroeconomic and can include changes in tax law, interest rates, inflation rates, and so on. —Pratt

Tangible Asset. An asset with a physical manifestation. Examples include land and buildings, plant and machinery, fixtures and fittings, tools and equipment, and assets in the course of construction and development. —IVSC

Tariff. A tax on an import. —Shirley

Technical Assessment Reports. Involve a review of those project elements such as mining engineering, metallurgy, environmental impacts, capital and operating costs, and actual and/or projected production that may contribute to the actual and/or potential economic output from "mineral assets" as may be required to assess the economic benefit of those assets and then to determine their "technical value." —VALMIN

Technical Value. An assessment of a mineral asset's future net economic benefit at the valuation date under a set of assumptions deemed most appropriate by an expert or specialist (the valuator) excluding any premium or discount to account for such factors as market or strategic considerations. —VALMIN

Technological Obsolescence. A decrease in the value of an asset due to improvements in technology that make an asset less than an ideal replacement for itself. —Pratt

Technology. The body of knowledge and skills applied to how goods are produced. —Shirley

Terminal Value (Amount). The value at the end of the projection period in a discounted cash flows model.

Tobin's Q. The ratio of the market value of a firm's assets to the replacement cost of the firm's [tangible] assets; it is interpreted as a measure of performance because it captures the value of the firm's intangibles. —CFA

Total Cost. The sum of all fixed and variable cost at each level of output.

Transaction Method. See *Merger and Acquisition Method.*

Transparency. Literally means "easily seen through, through, clear and unmistakable, free from affectation and disguise." For the purposes of the VALMIN Code, these qualities *must* apply to the data and information used as the basis of a valuation or a technical assessment, including the assessment of resources/reserves, mining, processing and marketing issues, the valuation approach adopted, and the methodology or methodologies used, all of which must be clearly set out in the report. —VALMIN

Trough. The phase or the business cycle in which real gross domestic product (GDP) reaches its minimum after falling during a recession. —Shirley

Undivided Interest. Partial legal or beneficial ownership of an asset as a tenant in common with others. The proportion owned may be pro rata, for example, the right to receive 50% of all cash flows from a security, or non–pro rata, for example, the right to receive the interest [income] from a security while another has the right to the principal. —FASB

Unemployment Rate. The percentage of people in the labor force who are without jobs and are actively seeking one. —Shirley

Unlevered Beta. The beta reflecting a capital structure without debt.

Unsystematic Risk. The risk specific to an individual security that can be avoided through diversification.

Unsystematic Risk. The degree of uncertainty as to the realization of the expected future returns that is a function of characteristics of the individual firm, or the industry to which it belongs. This is not globally determined risk. It is firm specific, industry specific, or medium specific and can include financing, operational, management, product, litigation, and other risks. —Pratt

Useful Life. Either: (a) the period of time over which an asset is expected to be used by the enterprise; or (b) the number of production or similar units expected to be obtained from the asset by the enterprise. (See *Economic Life.*) —IASB

Utility. Refers to the usefulness or satisfaction one receives from a good or service. In valuation, land value is established by evaluating its utility in terms of the legal, physical, functional, economic, and environmental factors which govern its productive capacity. —IVSC

Vacant Possession. In real estate, refers to a right to possession of land or built-up property in respect of which there is no current occupant. —IVSC.

Valuation. The act or process of determining the value of a business, business ownership interest, security, or intangible asset.

Valuation Date. The specific point in time as of which the valuator's opinion of value applies (also referred to as "effective date" or "appraisal date").

Valuation Method. Within approaches, a specific way to determine value.

Valuation Procedure. The act, manner, and technique of performing the steps of an appraisal method [sometimes referred to as "valuation techniques"].

Valuation Report. A report that describes the results of an analysis leading to an opinion of value. There are codes of practice which a valuator must follow when preparing a valuation report. —IVSC

Valuator. One who possesses the necessary qualifications, ability, and experience to execute a valuation. In some states, licensing is required before one can act as a valuator. —IVSC

[Valuator] Business Appraiser. A person who, by education, training, and experience, is qualified to develop an appraisal of a business, business ownership interest, security, or intangible assets.

Value. An estimate of the worth of goods and services at a given time and in accordance with a particular definition of value. —IVSC

Value in Exchange.

(1) The value as recognized by a marketplace in which exchange of asset ownership notionally takes place. The IVSC definition of "market value" for appropriate financial reporting is based on the principle of value in exchange.

(2) The value, in terms of cash, of a property which is bartered for another asset or assets, with cash being the yardstick by which the comparative value of each can be assessed. —IVSC

Value in Use.

(1) The value a specific property has for a specific use to a specific user and is therefore nonmarket related.

(2) Focuses on the value that specific property contributes to the enterprise of which it is a part, without regard to the property's highest and best use or the monetary amount that might be realized upon its sale.

(3) The present value of estimated future cash flows expected to arise from the continuing use of an asset and from its disposal at the end of its useful life. —IVSC

Value Stream Map. A flow diagram that follows a product's production path, a useful way to show process problems as the "current state" map details what is occurring today, while "future state" map is the perfected product and process flow with waste and non–value-added activities removed.

Variable Cost. Costs that vary in relation to output. —Shirley

Variable Input. Any resource for which the quantity can change during the period under consideration. —Shirley

Velocity of Money. The average number of times per year a unit of the money supply is spent on final goods and services. —Shirley

Voting Control. *De jure* **[legal] control of a business enterprise.**

Wasting Asset. An asset which in real terms will generally depreciate in value over time. Examples include leasehold and extractive interests. —IVSC

Weighted Average Cost of Capital (WACC). The cost of capital (discount rate) determined by the weighted average, at market value, of the cost of all financing sources in the business enterprise's capital structure.

Work in Process (WIP). A good or goods in various stages of completion throughout the plant, including all material from raw material that has been released for initial processing up to completely processed material awaiting final inspection and acceptance as finished goods inventory. Many accounting systems also include the value of semifinished stock and components in this category. —SEAT

Working Capital. The amount by which current assets exceed current liabilities.

REFERENCES AND BIBLIOGRAPHY

TRADEMARKS AND BRANDS

Aaker D. A. 1991. *Managing Brand Equity: Capitalizing on the Value of a Brand Name.* New York: The Free Press

Ambler, T., and D. Riley. 2000. "Marketing Metrics: A Review of Performance Measures in Use in the United Kingdom and Spain." Draft paper sponsored by the Marketing Society, the Marketing Council, the Institute of Practitioners in Advertising, the Sales Promotion Consultants Association, the London Business School (LBS), and the Marketing Science Institute. Downloaded from the LBS Web site. www.lbs.lon.ac.uk/marketing.

Ambler, T., and J. Roberts. 2005. *Choosing Marketing Dashboard Metrics.* London Business School, Centre for Marketing. No. 05-709.

Barwise, P., C. Higson, A. Likierman, and P. Marsh. 1989. *Accounting for Brands.* London: London Business School and the Institute of Chartered Accountants in England and Wales.

Birkin, M. 1996. "Brand Valuation". In *Understanding Brands: By 10 People Who Do,* ed. D. Cowley. London: Kogan Page.

Blattberg, C., and J. Deighton. 1996. "Managing Marketing by the Customer Equity Test." *Harvard Business Review* (July–August): 136–141.

Brealey, R. A., S. C. Myers, and F. Allen. 2008. *Principles of Corporate Finance,* 9th ed. New York: McGraw-Hill.

Cohen, D. 1991 "Trademark Strategy Revisited." *Journal of Marketing* (July): 46–59. In Keller 2008 under *Legal Branding Considerations.* Pp. 179–181

Farquar P., J. Y. Han, and Y. Ijiri Y. 1991. "Recognizing and Measuring Brand Assets." *Marketing and Science Institute* (July), Report 91-119.

Fogg, J. 1998. "Brands as Intellectual Property." In *Brands: The New Wealth Creators,* ed. Susannah Hart and John Murphy. New York: New York University Press and Interbrand.

Gourville, J. T. 2005. "The Curse of Innovation: Why Innovative New Products Fail." Marketing Science Institute Working Paper 05-117.

Keller, K. L. 1998. *Strategic Brand Management: Building, Measuring, and Managing Brand Equity.* Englewood Cliffs, NJ: Prentice-Hall.

Keller K. L. 2008. *Strategic Brand Management: Building, Measuring, and Managing Brand Equity,* 3rd ed. Upper Saddle River, NJ: Pearson Prentice-Hall.

Knudson W. A. 2006 "An Introduction to Patents, Brands, Trade Secrets, Trademarks, and Intellectual Property Rights Issues." Strategic Marketing Institute Working Paper 1-0806. Product Center for Agriculture and Natural Resources, Michigan State University.

Peterson R. A., K. H. Smith, and P. C. Zerillo. 1999. "Trademark Dilution and the Practice of Marketing." *Journal of the Academy of Marketing Science* 22, No. 2 (Spring): 255–268.

Power, M. 1990. *Brand and Goodwill Accounting Strategies.* London: Woodhead-Faulkner Ltd., Special Report.

Rust, R. T., V. A. Zeithaml, and K. N. Lemon. 2000. *Driving Customer Equity: How Customer Lifetime Value Is Reshaping Corporate Strategy.* New York: Free Press.

Salinas, G., and T. Ambler. 2008. *A Taxonomy of Brand Valuation Methodologies: How Different Types of Methodology Can Help to Answer Different Types of Question.* Marketing Science Institute Special Report 08–204.

Simon, C. J., and M. W. Sullivan. 1993. "The Measurement and Determinants of Brand Equity: A Financial Approach." *Marketing Science* 12, No. 1: 2852.

Sinclair, R. N. 2002. *Recognizing and Evaluating Brand Equity in South African Business to Gain Financial and Operational Benefits.* PhD diss., University of the Witwatersrand, Johannesburg, pp. 76–81.

Smith, G. V., and R. L. Parr. 2007. *Intellectual Property: Valuation, Exploitation and Infringement Damages. 2007 Cumulative Supplement.* Hoboken, NJ: John Wiley & Sons.

PROJECTING FINANCIAL STATEMENTS

Carlberg, Conrad George. 2007. *Business Analysis with Microsoft Excel,* 3rd ed. Indianapolis: Que Publishing.

Charnes, John. 2007. *Financial Modeling with Crystal Ball and Excel.* Hoboken, NJ: John Wiley & Sons.

Damodaran, Aswath. 2006. *Damodaran on Valuation. Security Analysis for Investment and Corporate Finance,* 2nd ed. Hoboken, NJ: John Wiley & Sons.

Hitchner, James R. 2006. *Financial Valuation. Applications and Models,* 2nd ed. Hoboken, NJ: John Wiley & Sons.

Penman, Stephen H. 2008. *Financial Statement Analysis and Security Valuation,* 3rd ed. New York: McGraw-Hill.

Porter, Michael E. 2004. *Competitive Strategy. Techniques for Analyzing Industries and Competitors.* New York: Free Press.

Pratt, Shannon P. 2007. *Valuing a Business,* 5th ed. New York: McGraw-Hill.

Pratt, Shannon P., and Alina V. Niculita. 2008. *Valuing a Business. The Analysis and Appraisal of Closely Held Companies,* 5th ed. New York: McGraw-Hill.

Tjia, John S. 2004. *Building Financial Models. A Guide to Creating and Interpreting Financial Statements.* New York: McGraw-Hill.

INTANGIBLE ASSETS

IVSC. 2007. *International Valuation Standards,* 8th ed.

IASB. 2008. *International Financial Reporting Standards.*

FASB. SFAS 157, *Fair Value Measurements.*

RICS. 2009. *RICS Valuation Standards,* March.

AICPA. *Valuation of a Business, Business Ownership Interest, Security, or Intangible Asset.*

PROJECTING FINANCIAL STATEMENTS

Kennedy, William. 2008. "Rising to the Top of Your Game in Valuation and Financial Forensics." Presented at the NACVA 2008, Fifteenth Annual Consultants' Conference.

RETAIL LOCATIONS

Arnold, S. J., T. H. Oum, and D. J. Tigert. 1983. "Determinant Attributes in Retail Patronage: Seasonal, Temporal, Regional and International Comparisons. *Journal of Marketing Research* 20, No. 2 (May): 149–157.

Baker, J., A. Parasuraman, D. Grewal, D. and G. B. Voss. 2002. "The Influence of Multiple Store Environment Cues on Perceived Merchandise Value and Patronage Intentions." *Journal of Marketing* 66: 120–141.

Bellenger, D., and G. Moschis, eds. 1982. *A Socialisation Model of Retail Patronage*. Ann Arbor, MI: Association for Consumer Research.

Bloch, P. H., N. M. Ridgway, and S. A. Dawson. 1994. "The Shopping Mall as Consumer Habitat." *Journal of Retailing* 70, No. 1: 23–42.

Brown, S. 1991. "Shopper Circulation in a Planned Shopping Centre." *International Journal of Retail and Distribution Management* 19, No. 1 (January/February): 17–24.

Converse, P. D. 1949. "New Laws of Retail Gravitation." *Journal of Marketing* 14, No. 31 (October): 379–384.

Fisk, G. 1961–62. "The Conceptual Model for Studying Customer Image." *Journal of Retailing* 37: 1–8.

Ghosh, A. 1986. "The Value of a Mall and Other Insights from a Revised Central Place Model." *Journal of Retailing* 62, No. 1 (Spring): 79–97.

Guy, C. 1994. *The Retail Development Process—Location, Property and Planning*. London: Routledge.

Hardesty, D. M., and W. O. Bearden. 2003. "Consumer Evaluations of Different Promotion Types and Price Presentations: The Moderating Role of Promotional Benefit Level." *Journal of Retailing* 79, No. 1: 17–25.

Hopper, J., A. Stilley, and T. J. Lipscomb. 1991. "An Investigation of Differences between Male and Female Outshoppers: Strategic Implications." *Akron Business and Economic Review* 22, No. 4 (Winter): 109–120.

Hui, M. K., and E. G. Bateson. 1991. "Perceived Control and the Effects of Crowding and Consumer Choice on the Service Experience." *Journal of Consumer Research* 18: 174–184.

Lewison, D. 1997. *Retailing*. Englewood Cliffs, NJ: Prentice-Hall.

Lim, L. Y. 1996. "Successful Retail Management in Asia." *Real Estate Finance* 12, No. 4 (Winter): 59–64.

Lindquist, J. D. 1974–75. "Meaning of Image." *Journal of Retailing* 50, No. 4 (Winter): 29–38.

Mason, J. B., M. L. Mayer, and H. F. Ezell, 1994. *Retailing*, 5th ed. Burr Ridge, IL: Richard D. Irwin.

Merrilees, N., and D. Miller. 1996. *Retailing Management—A Best Practice Approach*. Collingwood, Victoria, Australia: RMIT Press.

Reilly, W. J. 1931. *The Law of Retail Gravitation*. New York: Author.

Ross, M. J. 1997. *Shopping Centre Development Handbook*. Washington, DC: Urban Land Institute.

Turley, L. W., and R. E. Milliman. 2000. "Atmospheric Effects on Shopping Behaviour: A Review of the Experimental Evidence." *Journal of Business Research* 49: 193–211.

Wakefield, K. L., and J. Baker, J. 1998. "Excitement at the Mall: Determinants and Effects on Shopping Response." *Journal of Retailing* 74, No. 4: 515–539.

COST OF CAPITAL

Banz, Rolf W. 1981. "The Relationship between Return and Market Value of Common Stocks." *Journal of Financial Economics* 9: 3–18.

Blume, Marshall E. 1974. "Unbiased Estimators of Long-Run Expected Rates of Return." *Journal of Business Finance and Accounting* 69: 634–638.

Brealey, Richard A., Stewart C. Myers, and Franklin Allen. 2006. *Principles of Corporate Finance,* 8th ed. New York: McGraw-Hill.

Buckland, Roger, and Patricia Fraser. 2001. "Political and Regulatory Risk: Beta Sensitivity in U.K. Electricity Distribution." *Journal of Regulatory Economics* 19: 5–25.

Claus, James, and Jacob Thomas. 2001. "Equity Premia as Low as Three Percent? Evidence from Analysts' Earnings Forecasts for Domestic and International Stock Markets." *Journal of Finance* 56: 1629–1666.

Cooper, Ian. 1996. "Arithmetic versus Geometric Mean Estimators: Setting Discount Rates for Capital Budgeting." *European Financial Management* 2: 157–167.

Damodaran, Aswath 2002. *Investment Valuation*, 2nd ed. Hoboken, NJ: John Wiley & Sons.

Dimson, Elroy, Paul Marsh, and Mike Staunton. 2006. "The Worldwide Equity Premium: A Smaller Puzzle." Working Paper, London Business School, 7 April.

Fama, Eugene F. 1996. "Discounting Under Uncertainty." *Journal of Business* 69: 415–428.

Fama, Eugene F., and Kenneth R. French. 1988. "Permanent and Temporary Components of Stock Prices." *Journal of Political Economy* 81: 246–273.

Fama, Eugene F., and Kenneth R. French. 1992. "The Cross-Section of Expected Stock Returns." *Journal of Finance* 47: 472–465.

Fama, Eugene F., and Kenneth R. French. 1993. "Common Risk Factors in the Returns on Stocks and Bonds." *Journal of Financial Economics* 33: 3–56.

Fama, Eugene F., and Kenneth R. French. 1996. "Multifactor Explanations of Asset Pricing Anomalies," *Journal of Finance* 51: 55–84.

Gebhardt, William R., Charles M. C. Lee, and Bhaskaran Swaminathan. 2001. "Toward an Implied Cost of Capital." *Journal of Accounting Research* 39: 135–176.

Gordon, Myron J., and Eli Shapiro. 1956. "Capital Equipment Analysis: The Required Rate of Profit." *Management Science* 3: 102–110.

Hamada, Robert S. 1972. "The Effect of the Firm's Capital Structure on the Systematic Risk of Common Stocks." *Journal of Finance* 27: 435–452.

Inselbag, Isik, and Howard Kaufold. 1997. "Two DCF Approaches for Valuing Companies under Alternative Financing Strategies (And How to Choose between Them)." *Journal of Applied Corporate Finance* 10: 114–122.

Institut der Wirtschaftsprüfer, ed. *WP Handbuch 2008—Wirtschaftsprüfung, Rechnungslegung, Beratung,* vol. 2, 13th ed. (Düsseldorf: IDW Verlag).

Jonas, Martin, Heike Wieland-Blöse, and Stefanie Schiffarth. 2005. "Basiszinssatz in der Unternehmensbewertung." *Finanz Betrieb* 7: 647–653.

Levy, Haim, and Thierry Post. 2005. *Investments.* Englewood Cliffs, NJ: Prentice-Hall.

Modigliani, Franco, and Merton H. Miller. 1963. "Corporate Income Taxes and the Cost of Capital: A Correction." *American Economic Review* 53: 433–443.

Ohlson, James A., and Beate Jüttner-Nauroth. 2005. "Expected EPS and EPS Growth as Determinants of Value." *Review of Accounting Studies* 10: 349–365.

Pellens, Bernhard, and Nils Crasselt. 2005. "Funding Strategies for Defined Benefit Plans and the Measurement of Leverage Risk," in Wolfgang Ballwieser, ed., *Current Issues in Financial Reporting and Financial Statement Analysis*, pp. 3–33. Special Issue 2/05 of *Schmalenbach Business Review* (Düsseldorf, Frankfurt am Main: Handelsblatt).

Pratt, Shannon P., and Roger J. Grabowski. 2008. *Cost of Capital—Applications and Examples.* Hoboken, NJ: John Wiley & Sons.

Reese, Raimo. 2007. *Schätzung von Eigenkapitalkosten für die Unternehmensbewertung.* Frankfurt am Main: Peter Lang.

Ross, Stephen A. 1976. "The Arbitrage Theory of Capital Asset Pricing." *Journal of Economic Theory* 13: 341–360.

Ross, Stephen A. 1977. "Risk, Return, and Arbitrage," in Irwin Friend and James L. Bicksler, eds., *Risk and Return in Finance,* pp. 189–218. Cambridge, MA: Ballenger.

Stehle, Richard. 1997. "Der Size-Effekt am deutschen Aktienmarkt." *Zeitschrift für Bankrecht und Bankwirtschaft* 9: 237–260.

Stehle, Richard. 2004. "Die Festlegung der Risikoprämie von Aktien im Rahmen der Schätzung des Wertes von börsennotierten Kapitalgesellschaften." *Die Wirtschaftsprüfung* 57: 906–927.

Svensson, Lars E. O. 1994. "Estimating and Interpreting Forward Interest Rates: Sweden 1992–1994." NBER Working Paper No. 4871. September.

Van Dijk, Mathijs A. 2007. "Is Size Dead? A Review of the Size Effect in Equity Returns." Working Paper, RSM Erasmus University. February.

Vasicek, Oldrich A. 1973. "A Note on Using Cross-Sectional Information in Bayesian Estimation of Security Betas." *Journal of Finance* 28: 1233–1239.

Wenger, Ekkehard. 2005. "Verzinsungsparameter in der Unternehmensbewertung—Betrachtungen aus theoretischer und empirischer Sicht." *Die Aktiengesellschaft, Sonderheft* 9–22.

Zimmermann, Peter. 1997. *Schätzung und Prognose von Betawerten, Eine Untersuchung am deutschen Aktienmarkt* (Bad Soden/Ts.: Uhlenb ruch).

MINERAL PROPERTIES

Lawrence, M. J. 1989. "The Exploration Geologist's Approach to Valuation," in P. Stitt and F. Cook, eds., *Mining and Petroleum Valuation 1989 (MINVAL '89),* pp. 107–124 (Sydney: Australasian Institute of Mining and Metallurgy).

Lawrence, M. J. 1992. "Mineral Valuation Bibliography." *AusIMM Bulletin* 2 (April): 1–2.

Lawrence, M. J. 1993. "Valuation of Exploration Prospects—The Usefulness of Rating Methods." *Proceedings of the 27th Annual Conference New Zealand Branch Australasian Institute of Mining and Metallurgy,* Wellington, New Zealand (Wellington: Australasian Institute of Mining and Metallurgy).

Lawrence, M. J. 1994. "An Overview of Valuation Methods for Exploration Properties," in *Mineral Valuation Methodologies 1994 (VALMIN '94),* No. 10/94, pp. 205–223, Sydney (Melbourne: Australasian Institute of Mining and Metallurgy).

Lawrence, M. J. 1995. "The AusIMM's VALMIN Code—An Objective Due Diligence Tool," in *Proceedings Mining Indonesia '95,* Jakarta, Indonesia, 23 November (Jakarta: IMA).

Lawrence, M. J. 1997a. "Project Evaluation Due Diligence—Lessons from the Busang Saga," in *Proceedings of World Gold '97,* pp. 249–264, Singapore, 1–3 September (Melbourne: Australasian Institute of Mining and Metallurgy).

Lawrence, M. J. 1997b. "An Australian Perspective on the Bre-X Scandal," in V. Danielson and J. Whyte, eds., *Bre-X, Gold Today, Gone Tomorrow—Anatomy of the Busang Swindle,* pp. 273–275 (Ontario: Northern Miner).

Lawrence, M. J. 1998a. "Australian Project Valuation: Possible Lessons for Canadian Developers," in *Mineral Property Valuation and Investor Concerns Short Course,* pp. 69–96 (Toronto: Prospectors and Developers Association of Canada/Canadian Bar Association).

Lawrence, M. J. 1998b. "The VALMIN Code and Guidelines 1998: An Aide Memoire to Assist in Its Interpretation." *AusIMM Bulletin* 3 (May): 80–83.

Lawrence, M. J. 1998c. "The Revised VALMIN and Guidelines 1998: A Code for the Technical Assessment and/or Valuation of Mineral Assets and Petroleum Assets and Mineral and Petroleum Securities for Independent Expert Reports," in *The Australasian Institute of Mining and Metallurgy Yearbook 1998–1999*, pp. 76–79 (Melbourne: Australasian Institute of Mining and Metallurgy/Executive Media).

Lawrence, M. J. 1999a. "Project Valuation Due Diligence: Advantages of the Australian System Using AusIMM's VALMIN Code 1998," presented at the Prospectors and Developers Association of Canada/Canadian Bar Association 1999, Session: Australia—Validating the Valuation, Toronto, Canada, 14–17 March (Toronto: PDAC/CIM).

Lawrence, M. J. 1999b. "Comment on Final Report of TSE/OSC Mining Standards Task Force." *AusIMM Bulletin*, No. 4 (June): 40–42.

Lawrence, M. J. 1999c. "Ethics, Liability and the AusIMM's Best Practice Codes," presented at Proceedings Students and Young Professional Conference, "Challenging Our Industry for Change," Perth, 7–11 July (Melbourne: Australasian Institute of Mining and Metallurgy).

Lawrence, M. J. 1999d. "The Globalisation of AusIMM's VALMIN Code," in *The Australasian Institute of Mining and Metallurgy Yearbook 1999–2000*, pp. 30–34 (Melbourne: Australasian Institute of Mining and Metallurgy/Executive Media).

Lawrence, M. J. 2000a. "DCF/NPV Modelling: Valuation Practice or Financial Engineering?" presented at the SME Annual Meeting Valuation Session, Salt Lake City, Utah, February 28–March 4.

Lawrence, M. J. 2000b. "The VALMIN Code 1998—The Australian Experience," presented at Mining Millennium 2000, Valuation 1—Prospectors and Developers Association of Canada/Canadian Bar Association, Session: Validating the Valuation, Toronto, Canada, 5–10 March (Toronto: PDAC/CIM).

Lawrence, M. J. 2000c. "The AusIMM's VALMIN Code 1998—Now an International Guide to Project Assessment and Valuation Best Practice, presented at Proceedings of the Codes Forum: The VALMIN and JORC Codes, After 2000: What Future for Mining, MICA Seminar, Sydney, 12 April (Sydney: MICA).

Lawrence, M. J. 2000d. "Overview of Valuation Papers Presented to SME (USA) and CIM/PDAC (Canada) Conventions in 2000," presented at Proceedings the Codes Forum: The VALMIN and JORC Codes, After 2000: What Future for Mining? MICA Seminar, Sydney, 12 April (Sydney: MICA).

Lawrence, M. J. 2000e. "History and Relevance of AusIMM's VALMIN Code 1981–2001," in *Mineral Asset Valuation Issues for the Next Millennium 2001 (VALMIN '01)*, No. 5/01, pp. 201–205, Sydney, 25–26 October (Melbourne: Australasian Institute of Mining and Metallurgy).

Lawrence, M. J. 2001a. "An Australian Perspective on Valuation Best Practice," Preprint 01-203, SME Annual Meeting, Valuation Issues II, Standards and Regulation, Denver, Colorado, 27 February.

Lawrence, M. J. 2001b. "International Accounting and Valuation Standards: A Threat or an Opportunity for AusIMM's VALMIN Code?" *AusIMM Annual Review 2001–2002* (August): 49–55.

Lawrence, M. J. 2001c. "An Outline of Market-Based Approaches for Mineral Asset Valuation Best Practice," in *Mineral Asset Valuation Issues for the Next Millennium 2001 (VALMIN '01)*, No. 5/01, pp. 115–137, 25–26 October, Sydney (Melbourne: Australasian Institute of Mining and Metallurgy).

Lawrence, M. J. 2002a. "An Update on the Australasian VALMIN Code and Its International Usefulness," in Proceedings PDAC Short Course 3, Canadian Mineral Valuation Standards, Toronto, Canada, 10–13 March (PDAC: Toronto).

Lawrence, M. J., 2002b. "The Australasian VALMIN Code 1998): Its Relevance to South African Valuation Code Initiatives," in Proceedings of the colloquium: Valuation of Mineral Projects and Properties: An African Perspective, Randburg, South Africa, 19–20 March (Johannesburg: South African Institute of Mining and Metallurgy).

Lawrence, M. J. 2002c. "Valuation Methodology for Mineral Properties: An International Perspective on What Is 'Market Value'," presented at AusIMM 2002 Annual Conference, 105 Years of Mining, Auckland, New Zealand, 2–4 September (Auckland: Australasian Institute of Mining and Metallurgy).

Lawrence, M. J., 2004. "Overview of Mineral Project Risk Issues and Role of Mineral Industry Professionals (especially Consultants) in Risk Reduction Strategies," Keynote Address, in *Proceedings PACRIM '04 Congress*, No. 5/04, pp. 45–52, Adelaide, 19–22 September (Melbourne: Australasian Institute of Mining and Metallurgy).

Lawrence, M. J. 2005. "Minimising Mineral Project Risk: New Zealand in a Global Context," in *Proceedings 2005 New Zealand Minerals Conference—Realising New Zealand's Mineral Potential*, pp. 266–290, Ministry of Economic Development (Crown Minerals), Auckland, New Zealand, 13–16 November.

Lawrence, M. J. 2007. "Valuation Methodology for Iron Ore Mineral Properties—Thoughts of an Old Valuator," Plenary Paper, in *Iron Ore 2007 Proceedings*, pp. 11–18, 20–22 August, (Melbourne: Australasian Institute of Mining and Metallurgy-CSIRO).

Lawrence, M. J. 2008. "Mineral Project Due Diligence: Where Cynical Minds Meet Money," in 2008 (41st) *New Zealand AusIMM Annual Conference Proceedings*, Finance and the Minerals Industry, pp. 249-264 August 31–September 3 (Wellington, NZ: Australasian Institute of Mining and Metallurgy).

Lawrence, M. J., and R. G. Hancock. 1992. "New Zealand Alluvial Mineral Property Valuation," in *Proceedings of the 26th Annual Conference, New Zealand Branch Australasian Institute of Mining and Metallurgy*, Dunedin, New Zealand, August 1 (Wellington, NZ: Australasian Institute of Mining and Metallurgy).

Lawrence, M. J., and C. M. Sorentino. 1994. "A Bibliography of the Valuation of Resource Assets," in *Mineral Valuation Methodologies 1994 (VALMIN '94)*, No. 10/94, pp. B147–B165, Sydney, October (Melbourne: Australasian Institute of Mining and Metallurgy).

Lawrence, M. J., and G. J. A. Dewar. 1999. "Mineral Property Valuation or 'What number did you have in mind?'" Keynote Address, in *Proceedings PACRIM '99 Congress*, pp. 13–27, Bali, Indonesia, 10–13 October (Melbourne: Australasian Institute of Mining and Metallurgy).

Loucks, T. A., and S. Dempsey. 1997. "Mining Finance: Some Perspectives of the Small Miner." *SEG Newsletter*, No. 28 (January).

Thompson, I. S. 2002. "A Critique of Valuation Methods for Exploration Properties and Undeveloped Mineral Resources," in *Proceedings PDAC Short Course 3*, *Canadian Mineral Valuation Standards,* 10–13 March (Toronto: PDAC).

PASS-THROUGH ENTITIES

Bernier v. Bernier, May 7, 2007. 2007 Mass. LEXIS 598.

Delaware Open MRI Radiology Assoc. v. Kessler. 2006. Del. Ch. 2006: 898 A.2d 290, 314.

Dallas, Robert v. Commissioner of Internal Revenue, September 28, 2006. T.C. Memo 2006-212.

Department of Finance Canada, Ministere des Finances. *Income Trusts.* Accessed May 10, 2009, www.fin.gc.ca/n06/06-061-eng.asp.

DiGabriele, James A. 2003. "A Valuation Dilemma: Are S Corporations Worth More than Otherwise Identical C Corporations?" *Forensic Examiner* 12, Nos. 11–12. Accessed June 26, 2009, http://papers.ssrn.com/sol3/papers.cfm?abstract_id=900627.

Erickson, Merle. 2002. "Tax Benefits in Acquisitions of Privately Held Corporations: The Way Companies Are Organized for Tax Purposes Affects Their Selling Price in an Acquisition," in *Capital Ideas*, a publication of the University of Chicago Graduate School of Business. Accessed June 24, 2009, www.business.ml.com/BCPublic/Specialty Services/Resources/ArticlesAndTips/Article20050811TaxBenefits+in+AcquisitionsofPri vatelyHeldCorporations.htm?printable=true.

Estate of Adams v. Commissioner of Internal Revenue. 1999. T.C. Memo 1999-254.

Estate of Heck v. Commissioner of Internal Revenue. February 5, 2002. T.C. Memo 2002-34.

Estate of Wall v. Commissioner of Internal Revenue. March 28, 2001. T.C. Memo 2001-75.

Examples of Today's Joint Ventures. Accessed June 22, 2009, www.harvard.li/examples. html.

Fannon, Nancy J. 2008. "The 'Real' S Corp Debate: Impact of Embedded Tax Rates from Public Markets." Accessed June 16, 2009. www.fannonval.com/sCorp/S%20Corp% 20Valuation--2008%20Update.pdf.

Fannon, Nancy J. "S Corporations and Value: Simplifying the Debate."

Finnerty, John D. 2002. "Adjusting the Comparable-Company Method for Tax Differences When Valuing Privately Held 'S' Corporations and LLCs." *Journal of Applied Finance* 12, No. 2 (Fall/Winter): 15–30.

Gross, Walter L. et al. v. Commissioner of Internal Revenue. 2001. T.C. Memo. 1999-254 (July 29, 1999), *aff'd.* 272 F.3d 333 (6th Cir. 2001).

Hitchner, James R. 2006. *Financial Valuation: Applications and Models,* 2nd ed. Hoboken, NJ: John Wiley & Sons. Accessed June 25, 2009, http://books.google.com/books?id= 0n8TA7c39oIC&pg=PA65&lpg=PA65&dq=hitchner+subchapter+s+premium&source= bl&ots=PE6-ZSFbeA&sig=qirvW-HQsbYwCfVPpFD_2svuVJk&hl=en&ei= bCxISvTLCoLENqClkIoB&sa=X&oi=book_result&ct=result&resnum=1.

Ibbotson, as quoted by *Court in Estate of Adams v. Commissioner of Internal Revenue.* 1999. T.C. Memo 1999-254.

"Income Trust." (n.d.). Accessed May 20, 2009, from Wikipedia, The Free Encyclopedia, http://en.wikipedia.org/wiki/Income_trust.

Internal Revenue Service, Department of the Treasury. "Limited Liability Company." (n.d.). Accessed May 28, 2009, www.irs.gov/businesses/small/article/0,,id=98277,00.html.

"Joint Venture." (n.d.). Accessed June 1, 2009, from The Free Dictionary: http://legal-dictionary.thefreedictionary.com/Joint+Venture.

"Joint Venture." (n.d.). Accessed June 14, 2009, from The Free Encyclopedia: http://en.wikipedia.org/wiki/Joint_ventures.

"Limited Parnership." (n.d.). Accessed June 12, 2009, from All Business, a D&B company: www.allbusiness.com/glossaries/limited-partnership/4943043-1.html.

Lurie, James B. (2003–2004). "The S-Corporation, Fair Market Value, and Their Intersection with the Real World." *Business Appraisal Practice* (Winter). Accessed June 27, 2009, www.capval-llc.com/_Media/scorporation.pdf.

NACVA. *International Glossary of Business Valuation Terms.* www.nacva.com/PDF/Glossary.pdf.

"Partnership." (n.d.). Accessed June 23, 2009, from Wikipedia, the Free Encyclopedia: http://en.wikipedia.org/wiki/Partnership#cite_ref-0.

"Real Estate Investment Trusts." (n.d.). Accessed May 25, 2009, from Investopedia.com: www.investopedia.com/terms/r/reit.asp.

"Regulated Investment Company." (n.d.). Accessed May 13, 2009, from Finance, Maps of World.com: http://finance.mapsofworld.com/company/investment/regulated.html.

INDEX

Printed and bound by CPI Group (UK) Ltd, Croydon, CR0 4YY

23/04/2025

14660934-0001